Communications in Computer and Information Science   **1078**

Commenced Publication in 2007
Founding and Former Series Editors:
Phoebe Chen, Alfredo Cuzzocrea, Xiaoyong Du, Orhun Kara, Ting Liu,
Krishna M. Sivalingam, Dominik Ślęzak, Takashi Washio, and Xiaokang Yang

More information about this series at http://www.springer.com/series/7899

Robertas Damaševičius · Giedrė Vasiljevienė (Eds.)

Information and Software Technologies

25th International Conference, ICIST 2019
Vilnius, Lithuania, October 10–12, 2019
Proceedings

 Springer

Editors
Robertas Damaševičius
Kaunas University of Technology
Kaunas, Lithuania

Giedrė Vasiljevienė
Kaunas University of Technology
Kaunas, Lithuania

ISSN 1865-0929   ISSN 1865-0937   (electronic)
Communications in Computer and Information Science
ISBN 978-3-030-30274-0   ISBN 978-3-030-30275-7   (eBook)
https://doi.org/10.1007/978-3-030-30275-7

This Springer imprint is published by the registered company Springer Nature Switzerland AG
The registered company address is: Gewerbestrasse 11, 6330 Cham, Switzerland

Preface

We are delighted to present you this book, *Information and Software Technologies*, which is a collection of papers that were presented at the 25th International Conference on Information and Software Technologies, ICIST 2019. The annual conference took place during October 10–12, 2019, in Vilnius, Lithuania.

The book consists of four chapters, which correspond to the four major areas that were covered during the conference, namely, "Information Systems," "Business Intelligence for Information and Software Systems," "Software Engineering," and "Information Technology Applications." These chapters are further subdivided according to the nine special sessions that were held at the conference. They are the following: (a) Innovative Applications for Knowledge Transfer Support, (b) e-Health Information Systems, (c) Intelligent Methods for Data Analysis and Computer Aided Software Engineering, (d) Intelligent Systems and Software Engineering Advances, (e) Smart e-Learning Technologies and Applications, (f) Language Technologies, (g) Digital Transformations, (h) Information Technology Security, and (i) Software and Model Metrics and Measurements.

Every year ICIST attracts researchers from all over the world, and this year was not an exception – we received 121 submissions from 32 countries. More importantly, there were participants from many more countries, which indicates that the conference is truly gaining more and more international recognition as it brings together a vast number of brilliant specialists who represent the aforementioned fields and share information about their newest scientific research investigations and the results achieved. Since we always strive to make the conference presentations and proceedings of the highest quality possible, we only accept papers that present the results of various investigations directed to the discovery of new scientific knowledge in the area of information and software technologies. Hence, only 46 papers were accepted for publication (i.e., a 38% acceptance rate). All the papers were reviewed and selected by the Program Committee, which comprised 65 reviewers (together with 64 additional reviewers) from over 80 academic institutions. As usual, each submission was reviewed following the double-blind process by at least two reviewers. When necessary, some of the papers were reviewed by three or four reviewers. Our deepest thanks and appreciation go to all the reviewers for devoting their precious time to produce thorough reviews and feedback to the authors.

We would also like to express our gratitude to the session chairs and co-chairs, Prof. Marcin Woźniak (Silesian University of Technology), Prof. Christian Napoli (University of Catania), Prof. Carsten Wolff and Prof. Christian Reimann (Dortmund University of Applied Sciences and Arts), Prof. Justyna Patalas-Maliszewska (University of Zielona Góra), Prof. Nadine Schlüter (University of Wuppertal), Prof. Rolf Engelbrecht (ProRec), Prof. Audrius Lopata (Vilnius University), Prof. Jurgita Kapočiūtė-Dzikienė (Vytautas Magnus University), Peter Dirix (University of Leuven), Prof. Jakub Swacha (University of Szcecin), Prof. Ricardo

Queiros (Polytechnic Institute of Porto), Assoc. Prof. Danguolė Rutkauskienė (Kaunas University of Technology), Prof. Radu Adrian Vasiu (Politechnica University of Timisoara), and Prof. dr. Sanjay Misra (Covenant University, Nigeria) for their expertise, assistance, and invaluable contribution in making the conference a top-quality scientific event.

In addition, we would like to thank the local Organizing Committee and the Faculty of Informatics, Kaunas University of Technology, for the conference would not have been a great success without their tremendous support. We are also grateful to the Research Council of Lithuania for financial support.

The proceedings of the ICIST 2019 conference are published as a volume of *Communications in Computer and Information Science* series for the eighth time. This would not be possible without the kind assistance provided by Leonie Kunz, Aliaksandr Birukou, and Ingrid Beyer, Springer, for which we are utmost grateful. We are very proud of this collaboration and believe that this fruitful partnership will continue for many more years to come.

July 2019

Robertas Damaševičius
Giedrė Vasiljevienė

Organization

General Chair

Rita Butkienė   Kaunas University of Technology, Lithuania

Local Organizing Committee

Giedrė Vasiljevienė (Chair)   Kaunas University of Technology, Lithuania
Romas Šleževičius   Kaunas University of Technology, Lithuania
Lina Repšienė   Kaunas University of Technology, Lithuania
Vilma Sukackė   Kaunas University of Technology, Lithuania
Gintarė Lukoševičiūtė   Kaunas University of Technology, Lithuania

Special Section Chairs

Marcin Woźniak   Silesian University of Technology, Poland
Jakub Swacha   University of Szczecin, Poland
Ricardo Queirós   School of Media, Arts and Design, Portugal
Danguolė Rutkauskienė   Kaunas University of Technology, Lithuania
Audrius Lopata   Vilnius University, Lithuania
Maria Dolores Afonso   SIANI University Institute, Spain
  Suárez
Rolf Engelbrecht   ProRec Germany, Germany
Nadine Schlüter   University of Wuppertal, Germany
Justyna   University of Zielona Gora, Poland
  Patalas-Maliszewska
Christian Napoli   University of Catania, Italy
Carsten Wolff   Dortmund University of Applied Sciences and Arts,
                                Germany
Christian Reimann   Dortmund University of Applied Sciences and Arts,
                                Germany
Michael Reiner   IMC Krems University of Applied Science, Austria
Jurgita Kapočiūtė-Dzikienė   Vytautas Magnus University, Lithuania
Peter Dirix   University of Leuven, Belgium
Sanjay Misra   Covenant University, Nigeria, and Atilim University,
                                Turkey
Robertas Damaševičius   Kaunas University of Technology, Lithuania
Radu Adrian Vasiu   Politehnica University of Timisoara, Romania
Vytenis Punys   Kaunas University of Technology, Lithuania
Giedrius Vanagas   Lithuanian University of Health Sciences, Lithuania

Program Committee

Marcin Woźniak	Silesian University of Technology, Poland
Danguolė Rutkauskienė	Kaunas University of Technology, Lithuania
Rolf Engelbrecht	ProRec Germany, Germany
Emiliano Tramontana	University of Catania, Italy
Radu Adrian Vasiu	Politechnica University of Timisoara, Romania
Vytenis Punys	Kaunas University of Technology, Lithuania
Giedrius Vanagas	Lithuanian University of Health Sciences, Lithuania
Olga Kurasova	Vilnius University, Lithuania
Jurgita Kapočiūtė-Dzikienė	Vytautas Magnus University, Lithuania
Yuh-Min Tseng	National Changhua University of Education, Taiwan
Constantine Filote	Stefan cel Mare University of Suceava, Romania
Marisa Gil	Polytechnic University of Catalonia, Spain
Saulius Gudas	Vilnius University, Lithuania
Sanda Martinčić-Ipšić	University of Rijeka, Croatia
Milena Krumova	Technical University of Sofia, Bulgaria
Mirjana Ivanovic	University of Novi Sad, Serbia
Damjan Vavpotič	University of Ljubljana, Slovenia
Sandro Leuchter	Hochschule Mannheim University of Applied Sciences, Germany
Martin Gaedke	Technical University of Chemnitz, Germany
Paulo Rupino da Cunha	University of Coimbra, Portugal
Algirdas Pakštas	Vilnius University, Lithuania
Marcin Paprzycki	Systems Research Institute, Polish Academy of Science, Poland
Janis Grabis	Riga Technical University, Latvia
Tor-Morten Grønli	Oslo School of Arts, Communication and Technology, Norway
Christophoros Nikou	University of Ioannina, Greece
Vira Shendryk	Sumy State University, Ukraine
André Schekelmann	Niederrhein University of Applied Science, Germany
Virgilijus Sakalauskas	Vilnius University, Lithuania
Dalia Krikščiūnienė	Vilnius University, Lithuania
Audrius Lopata	Vilnius University, Lithuania
Aleksandras Targamadzė	Kaunas University of Technology, Lithuania
Lovro Šubelj	University of Ljubljana, Slovenia
Karin Harbusch	University of Koblenz-Landau, Germany
Juan Manuel Vara Mesa	University of Rey Juan Carlos, Spain
Alexander Maedche	University of Mannheim, Germany
Tomas Krilavičius	Vytautas Magnus University, Lithuania
Eduard Babkin	National Research University, Russia
Tommi Mikkonen	Tampere University of Technology, Finland
Linas Laibinis	Abo Akademi University, Finland
Kuldar Taveter	Tallinn University of Technology, Estonia
Kristina Sutiene	Kaunas University of Technology, Lithuania

Janis Stirna	Stockholm University, Sweden
Justyna Patalas-Maliszewska	University of Zelona Gora, Poland
Prima Gustienė	Karlstad University, Sweden
Wojciech Mitkowski	AGH University of Science and Technology, Poland
Jorge Esparteiro Garcia	University of Porto, Portugal
Kęstutis Kapočius	Kaunas University of Technology, Lithuania
Tomas Skersys	Kaunas University of Technology, Lithuania
Martynas Patašius	Kaunas University of Technology, Lithuania
Rytis Maskeliūnas	Kaunas University of Technology, Lithuania
Rita Butkienė	Kaunas University of Technology, Lithuania
Ana Meštrović	University of Rijeka, Croatia
Andrzej Jardzioch	West Pomeranian University of Technology Szczecin, Poland
Beata Gavurova	Technical University of Košice, Slovakia
Armantas Ostreika	Kaunas University of Technology, Lithuania
Dominykas Barisas	Kaunas University of Technology, Lithuania
Eva Rakovska	University of Economics Bratislava, Slovakia
Natalia Loukachevitch	Moscow State University, Russia
Christian Napoli	University of Catania, Italy
Carsten Wolff	Dortmund University of Applied Sciences and Arts, Germany
Christian Reimann	Dortmund University of Applied Sciences and Arts, Germany
Rimvydas Simutis	Kaunas University of Technology, Lithuania
Peter Dirix	University of Leuven, Belgium
Liesbeth Augustinus	University of Leuven, Belgium
Nadine Schlüter	University Wuppertal, Germany
Jakub Swacha	University of Szczecin, Poland
Ricardo Queirós	School of Media, Arts and Design, Portugal
Michael Reiner	IMC Krems University of Applied Science, Austria
Maria Dolores Afonso Suárez	SIANI University Institute, Spain
Sanjay Misra	Covenant University, Nigeria, and Atilim University, Turkey
Zbigniew Banaszak	Warsaw University of Technology, Poland
Andrei Voronkov	University of Manchester, UK
Evgeniy Krastev	Sofia University St. Kliment Ohridsky, Bulgaria
Mariya Zlatkova Stankova	South-West University Neofit Rilski, Bulgaria
Daina Gudonienė	Kaunas University of Technology, Lithuania

Additional Reviewers

Ilhan Tarimer	Muğla Sıtkı Koçman University, Turkey
Vacius Jusas	Kaunas University of Technology, Lithuania
Zbigniew Marszałek	Silesian University of Technology, Poland

Co-editors

Robertas Damaševičius   Kaunas University of Technology, Lithuania
Giedrė Vasiljevienė   Kaunas University of Technology, Lithuania

Contents

Information Technology Applications: Special Session on Information Technology Security

Software Engineering: Special Session on Software and Model Metrics and Measurements

**Information Technology Applications: Special Session
on Language Technologies**

**Information Technology Applications: Special Session
on Smart e-Learning Technologies and Applications**

**Software Engineering: Special Session on Intelligent Systems
and Software Engineering Advances**

Information Systems: Special Session on e-Health Information Systems

Information Systems: Special Session on Digital Transformation

Information Systems: Special Session on Innovative Applications for Knowledge Transfer Support

Forecasting the Level of Expert Knowledge Using the GMDH Method

Justyna Patalas-Maliszewska[(✉)] [iD], Małgorzata Śliwa,
and Sławomir Kłos

Institute of Computer Science and Production Management,
University of Zielona Góra, Zielona Góra, Poland
{J.Patalas, M.Sliwa, S.Klos}@iizp.uz.zgora.pl

Abstract. The expert knowledge is a very important resource for the development of an enterprise, but due to its unpredictable nature, it also very difficult to manage. Due to the growing phenomenon of frequent employee turnover in companies, it is necessary to keep such knowledge in the company and then to forecast its level in order to determine the type of missing knowledge in the company for the implementation of further projects/orders. In this paper a model for forecasting the level of expert knowledge, which assumes the use of the GMDH (Group Method of Data Handling) has been proposed. The model consists of the following elements: (1) formalised, expert knowledge acquired which is stored in the knowledge base, (2) level of knowledge in the enterprise, as the result of the clustering of acquired expert knowledge using the Bayesian network, (3) the GMDH method. Finally this model is implemented in a real case study from the Research and development department of a manufacturing company.

Keywords: Expert knowledge · Forecasting the level of expert knowledge · Bayesian network · GMDH method

1 Introduction

Nowadays, expert knowledge in a production company is a resource, the appropriate development of which may determine the further development of that company. In order for acquired, expert knowledge to be of use to an enterprise, it needs to be formalised, correctly classified and finally, forecast. It is then necessary to design a solution which enables any expert knowledge so extracted. For this purpose, a review of the subject literature on the algorithms used to forecast knowledge was made, that is, genetic algorithms, the GMDH method and artificial neural networks. Their characteristics and methods of use have been briefly described.

The issue of estimating the value of knowledge within an enterprise, refers to research conducted on data and information process exploration and transformation, especially in the context of using artificial neural networks or genetic algorithm to predictive decision variants, e.g. to evaluate the effectiveness of cleaner production [1], or to understand the causes of failure of electronic products [2], to understand the distortion from the desired design [3].

© Springer Nature Switzerland AG 2019
R. Damaševičius and G. Vasiljevienė (Eds.): ICIST 2019, CCIS 1078, pp. 3–11, 2019.
https://doi.org/10.1007/978-3-030-30275-7_1

The present authors have attempted to develop an approach to forecasting the level of expert knowledge on the basis of an R&D department in a production enterprise, in order to determine the most important elements of the expert knowledge within that department. It also means to define the type of expert knowledge, which is missing in the company, in order to process further projects/orders.

In the second chapter of the present article, the subject literature has been reviewed with a view to forecasting knowledge and also a model for forecasting the level of expert knowledge, which assumes the use of the Bayesian network and the GMDH (Group Method of Data Handling) has been proposed. The third chapter presents an example of the implementation of the model in the R&D department of a production enterprise.

2   Research Model

Due to the growing phenomenon of frequent employee turnover in companies, it is necessary to keep expert knowledge in the company binding upon its employees and then to forecast its level, in order to determine the type of missing knowledge in the company so that further projects/orders can be processed. The forecasting of knowledge can be treated as an approach that not only allows knowledge to be analysed but also to be inference-based on accumulated knowledge, along with the simulation of phenomena in the future.

Collected and formalized expert knowledge can be modelled using the intelligence algorithm with a prediction model being created as an end product. Its aim is precise forecasting [4] and support for the decision-making processes. According to [5], the value of knowledge decreases by consequences related to limitations in the process of acquiring knowledge and the losses occurring therein. The forecasting of knowledge is key in today's applications where the main role is to learn and then conduct pattern recognition in images, video and sound [6].

The approach proposed by the present authors assumes that the expert knowledge acquired and collected will then be formalised and categorised using the Bayesian network; a prediction model of the level of expert knowledge, using the GMDH method, will then be built for the production enterprise. Selection of the Bayesian network was made on the basis of [7] to indicate the relationship between the identified elements of expert knowledge.

Intelligent algorithms are classified according to the understanding of knowledge that is capable of being estimated; this includes not only static systems, but also automated control systems, optimisation systems for developing new solutions, such as a replication process and an independent development process and then adapting and customising complex mathematical models based on the data analysed.

In recent publications, researchers have used intelligence optimization, meta-heuristics methods which also include genetic algorithms (GAs) [8, 9]. The goal of the use of the genetic algorithm is to find the best-value of the objective function, obtained from the available choices [10]. The evaluation-selection-reproduction stages can undergo many iterations so that the number of generations can be minimised. Genetic algorithms allow a solution to be searched for in many points of a given object. In the process of evolutionary processing, the parameters of the optimisation task have an encoded form and evolutionary-probabilistic rules are used to choose and create new solutions. Genetic algorithms are a class of procedures used for solving the task of self-organisation within systems. The search for the model of the object tested starts with an approximate, partial solution. Its evolution, which consists of a gradual increase in complexity and the selection of the best solutions, is the essence of the genetic algorithm. In the case of the knowledge estimation processes, the genetic algorithm provides the possibility of optimising the components of knowledge modules, for example, efficient selection and assignment [11] for which one can define attributes that are alternatives - by searching for appropriate solutions indicating, for example, the highest level of knowledge. Genetic algorithms results, however, seek to indicate the optimum while not necessarily verifying the state of knowledge.

The GMDH algorithm is a solution with which the models organize themselves by creating polynomials and selecting the ones with best of prediction criterion. The population chromosomes (a chromosome is a single polynomial) are exchanged in one iteration. The GMDH algorithm presents the relation of a dependent variable Y to some independent variables X_1, X_2, ..., X_m and is used to construct a higher order regression type model. The basic model of GMDH is a quadratic polynomial of two variables, usually consists of many layers [12]. The examples of using GMDH in forecasting knowledge are applying it for customer classification feature selection [13] or for detecting spam messages and email feature analysis [14]. The result of the algorithm's operation is a polynomial which is the model of the object.

Models for the prediction of activities within a company play an important role in the development of intelligent systems [15]. One of the basic issues concerning the practical use of artificial neural networks, in forecasting knowledge, is the adoption of an appropriate method for the coding of data for the input layer. In cases where the input data is quantitative in character, the problem generally comes down to its normalisation; in the case of the forecasting of expert knowledge, however, this issue becomes much more complex. We state, that the use of an artificial neural network may refer to the forecasting of the level of expert knowledge based on the examples: the parallel processing of data in real-time control systems [16]; [17] forecasting the course of the abrasiveness of the blades of the cutting tools [18], the grouping of machine construction elements [19], the monitoring of the operation of ship machinery [20].

Based on the literature review above, our model of expert knowledge is formulated thus:

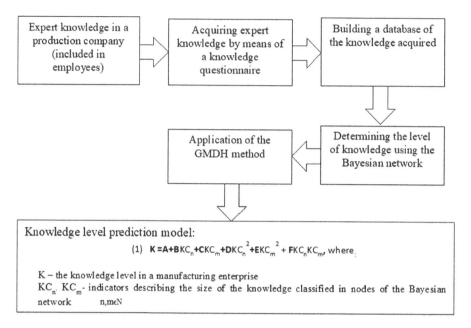

Fig. 1. Research model

The proposed research model was used in the example of an R&D department in a production company. The formalised approach to the acquisition and formalisation of expert knowledge has been described, in detail, in the works of previous authors [21, 22].

3   Description of the Research Model

The proposed model (see Fig. 1) has been implemented in the R&D department of this company. The manufacturing company studied produces small elements of car pneumatics for several key clients; it has a series of repetitive tasks for which fixed elements of expert knowledge are used in developing a project.

Expert knowledge includes the knowledge of an individual employee in a specific area [23]. The most common method of acquiring expert knowledge, namely a knowledge questionnaire, was created and used. The questionnaire with unequivocal, selectable responses from a closed list, was developed with the help of R&D staff using the direct interview method. This included questions about completed R&D projects related to the product "valve". Based on the responses collected from the employees, an ordered base of acquired knowledge was built up according to the following areas: (1) structure: construction, geometry, thread, (2) sub-structure: e.g. construction: prototype, 3D model, pattern, 3D printing, geometry: wall thickness (..), (3) completed activities: client feedback, additional studies, external consultation, internal consultation, (4) materials used: technical documentation, literature, website, customer feedback, report, (5) documents created: technical documentation, procedure, audio-video recordings, report, model, patent, (6) connected departments: technology, maintenance, purchasing, sales, production.

The knowledge base, according to the workers answers, was then created. For each answer, the value was determined according to the rule: number of responses/number of responses x maximum possibilities of responses. Bayesian networks, based on statistics, or, in our case, based on a study of the respondents' answers, allows probability to be estimated, taking into account the total possibility of an event occurring in a changing environment. The classification of events requires the selection of variables, or events, modelling of the network, that is, establishing the apexes and the relations between

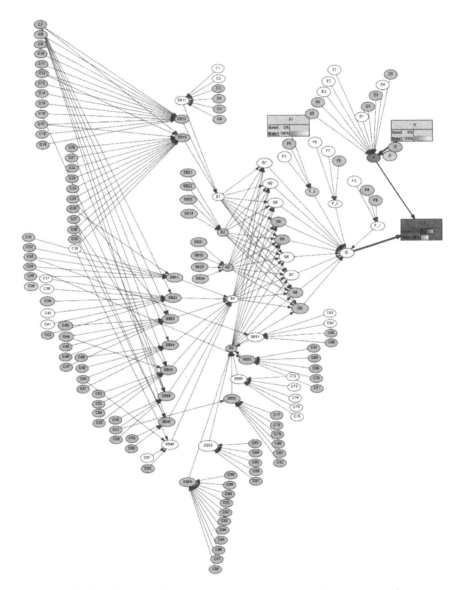

Fig. 2. The level of expert knowledge by using the Bayesian network

them, building probability tables for events [24] and updating them with expert knowledge. This creates a learning network from the training set, which facilitates the total probability of the event being investigated, to be determined.

By using the Bayesian network to define the level of expert knowledge, the nodes, so-called, were selected from among all elements included in the knowledge acquisition form: (B) structure: number of choices:{b1–b5}, (SB) sub-structure: number of choices:{b11–b13}, {b41–48}, {b51–56}, (C) keywords: number of choices:{c1–c97}, (D) connected departments: number of choices:{d1–d5}, (E) completed activities: number of choices:{e1–de}, (F) used materials: number of choices:{f1–f9}, (G) created documents: number of choices:{g1–g9}, (I) workers, who answered: number of choices:{i1–i3}, also the nodes: (N) competent team, (O) ready-made templates and finally (Z) level of knowledge were defined (see Fig. 2), by assuming that there is always a nodes: (F) and (I).

In the studied manufacturing, further research was carried out, as a result of which the knowledge base about the responses from the following knowledge questionnaires was expanded accordingly: (study 1) by one questionnaire, (2) by two more (3) by the next two. As a result of the use of the Bayesian network, the following levels of knowledge were obtained in the R&D department (Table 1).

Table 1. The levels of expert knowledge by using the Bayesian network.

Research	The level of expert knowledge (K)
Study 0	0.62
Study 1	0.64
Study 2	0.66
Study 3	0.66

The level of knowledge of a realised project is the result of the combined presence of a codified knowledge base, a competent team and ready-made templates. The higher the occurrence of component elements and the higher the level of knowledge estimated, the better reflected is the increase in knowledge within the enterprise. However, it has been noticed (see Table 1) that the level of knowledge does not change, despite further development of the knowledge base. Further research in the studied company will allow us to determinate the maximum value for the level of knowledge.

Based on the research results (see Table 1) using the GMDH method, the type of missing knowledge in the company for the implementation of further projects/orders is determined. The outcome, in the form of the estimated level of knowledge, is organised as: $K^T = [0.62;0.64;0.66;0.66]$. Each K_i is associated with indicators that describe the frequency of the response data from the knowledge questionnaire, stored in the individual nodes of the Bayesian network. A KCO (Knowledge Classification Output) map is provided to present the relationship between the formalised knowledge (based on the responses in the knowledge questionnaires) and the outcome of the estimated level of knowledge (see Table 1).

$$KCO = \begin{bmatrix} b1_1 & b4_1 & b5_1 & ..._1 & c30_1 & ..._1 & d1_1 & d4_1 & ..._1 & i3_1 \\ b1_2 & b4_2 & b5_2 & ..._2 & c30_2 & ..._2 & d1_2 & d4_2 & ..._2 & i3_2 \\ ... & ... & ... & ... & ... & ... & ... & ... & ... & ... \\ b1_n & b4_n & b5_n & ..._n & c30_n & ..._m & c1_m & d4_m & ..._m & i3_m \end{bmatrix} \qquad (1)$$

where n, m ϵ N and

B_1, ..., I_m – elements of the nodes within the Bayesian network, that is, the formalised knowledge, based on the knowledge questionnaires.

The model proposed by the present authors makes it possible to estimate the most important elements of expert knowledge, in order to complete further projects/orders successfully. The data from Bayesian network (see Fig. 2) regarding the product "valve", where designated, in all the variations of the GMDH algorithms, were investigated, using the Consulting IT computer system [25]. As a result, the best possible polynomial was obtained, with the algorithm evolution process being completed on the second iteration: model K:

$$K = 0.28 + 0.21 \times b_{47} + 0.06 \times b_{48} + 0.38 \times b_{47}^2 - 0.09 \times b_{48}^2 - 0.42 \times b_{47} \times b_{48}$$
$$(2)$$

where,

K   - the level of knowledge, forecast in the enterprise

b_{47}, b_{48} - the most important elements of expert knowledge, namely: functionalities of the product "valve": "screw plug" and "thread sealing"

As a result of the research it was found that the critical expert knowledge for the implementation of the new project for the product "valve" is knowledge about its functionality. Therefore, the decision was made to expand the knowledge questionnaire for this part, so in the case of employees', who have such expert knowledge, leave or other absences from work, do not lose this knowledge in the company.

Due to the proposed approach, it is possible to receive expert knowledge using a knowledge questionnaire, and then, using the established rules in the form of the frequency of responses, formulate a knowledge base for the needs of building the Bayesian network. As a result of the operation of the Bayesian network, a formalised knowledge base is obtained, based on which, and using the GMDH method, new knowledge about the most important elements influencing the success of the new project/order can be obtained.

4 Conclusions

The proposed approach allows the most important elements of expert knowledge to be defined in an enterprise, for the purposes of implementing new projects and orders. The prediction model of the level of knowledge, shown on the basis of an R&D department in a manufacturing enterprise, was built using the Group Method of Data Handling. Expert knowledge, acquired by means of a knowledge questionnaire, has been codified by its introduction into the knowledge base. The application of the Bayesian network, a given state in the node, was assigned through an analysis of features, that is, through the probabilities of the elements of knowledge which build this node up. The Bayesian network allowed a priori classification to the states or alternatives assigned to this node, according to the size of the knowledge element selected.

However, this is a complex procedure that requires the company's specifications, to be matched to any project/order. In the first step, it is necessary to formulate a knowledge questionnaire, where for each answer, a defined list of key words is needed. The values determined for each Bayesian network node and the level of expert knowledge can then be determined. Due to the formalised and classified knowledge obtained, it is possible to obtain the most important components of such knowledge. In our further work we are planning to apply Business Process Management Systems (BPMS) [26] for conceptualising our approach.

Acknowledgments. This work is supported by program of the Polish Minister of Science and Higher Education under the name "Regional Initiative of Excellence" in 2019–2022, project no. 003/RID/2018/19, funding amount 11 936 596.10 PLN.

References

1. Li, J., Zhang, Y., Du, D., Liu, Z.: Improvements in the decision making for Cleaner Production by data mining: case study of vanadium extraction industry using weak acid leaching process. J. Cleaner Prod. **143**, 582–597 (2017)
2. Kang, S., Kim, E., Shim, J., Cho, S., Chang, W., Kim, J.: Mining the relationship between production and customer service data for failure analysis of industrial products. Comput. Ind. Eng. **106**, 17–146 (2017)
3. Baykasoglu, A., Özbakir, L., Kulluk, S.: Classifying defect factors in fabric production via DIFACONN-miner: a case study. Expert Syst. Appl. **38**, 11321–11328 (2011)
4. Kuhn, M., Johnson, K.: Applied Predictive Modelling. Springer, New York (2013). https://doi.org/10.1007/978-1-4614-6849-3
5. Gajzler, M.: The idea of knowledge supplementation and explanation using neural networks to support decisions in construction engineering. In: Editor, F., Editor, S. (eds.) 11th International Conference on Modern Building Materials, Structures and Techniques MBMST 2013, Procedia Engineering, vol. 57, pp. 302–309 (2013)
6. Hall, P., Phan, W., Whitson, K.: The Evolution of Analytics. Opportunities and Challenges for Machine Learning in Business. O'Reilly Media, Sebastopol (2016)
7. Serrano, B.M., González-Cancelas, N., Soler-Flores, F., Camarero-Orive, A.: Classification and prediction of port variables using Bayesian Networks. Transp. Pol. **67**, 57–66 (2018)
8. Prakash, A., Chan, F.T.S., Deshmukh, S.G.: FMS scheduling with knowledge based genetic algorithm approach. Expert Syst. Appl. **38**, 3161–3171 (2011)
9. Kuah, C.T., Wong, K.Y., Wong, W.P.: Monte Carlo data envelopment analysis with genetic algorithm for knowledge management performance measurement. Expert Syst. Appl. **39**(10), 9348–9358 (2012)

10. Chakraborty, S., Chattopadhyay, P.P., Ghosh, S.K., Datta, S.: Incorporation of prior knowledge in a neural network model for continuous cooling of steel using genetic algorithm. Appl. Soft Comput. **58**, 297–306 (2017)
11. Mirhosseyni, S.H.L., Webb, P.: A hybrid fuzzy knowledge-based expert system and genetic algorithm for efficient selection and assignment of material handling equipment. Expert Syst. Appl. **36**(9), 11875–11887 (2009)
12. Farlow, S.J.: Self-organizing Methods in Modelling: GMDH-type Algorithms. Marcel Dekker Inc, New York (1984)
13. Xiao, J., Cao, H., Jiang, X., Gu, X., Xie, L.: GMDH-based semi-supervised feature selection for customer classification. Knowl. Based Syst. **12**, 236–248 (2017)
14. El-Alfy, E.M., Abdel-Aal, R.E.: Using GMDH-based networks for improved spam detection and email feature analysis. Appl. Soft Comput. **11**(1), 477–488 (2011)
15. Sobaszek, Ł., Gola, A., Kozłowski, E.: Module for prediction of technological operation times in an intelligent job scheduling system. Adv. Intell. Syst. Comput. **835**, 234–243 (2019)
16. Wu, B., Tian, Z., Chen, M.: Condition-based maintenance optimization using neural network-based health condition prediction. Qual. Reliab. Eng. Int. **29**(8), 1151–1163 (2013)
17. Li, Z., Wang, Y., Wang, K.S.: Intelligent predictive maintenance for fault diagnosis and prognosis in machine centers: Industry 4.0 scenario. Adv. Manuf. **5**(4), 377–387 (2017)
18. Gawlik, J., Kiełbus, A.: Applications of artificial intelligence methods in supervision of technological devices and product quality. In: Sikora, T., Giemza, M. (eds.) Quality Management Practice in the 21st Century. Cracow, Poland (2012)
19. Lipski, J., Pizoń, J.: Artificial intelligence in production engineering. In: Lipski, J., Świć, A., Bojanowska, A. (eds.) Innovative Methods in Production Engineering. Lublin, Poland (2014)
20. Raptodimos, Y., Lazakis, I.: An artificial neural network approach for predicting the performance of ship machinery equipment. In: International Conference on Maritime Safety and Operations, Glasgow, UK (2016)
21. Patalas-Maliszewska, J., Krebs, I.: an information system supporting the eliciting of expert knowledge for successful IT projects. In: Damaševičius, R., Vasiljevienė, G. (eds.) ICIST 2018. CCIS, vol. 920, pp. 3–13. Springer, Cham (2018). https://doi.org/10.1007/978-3-319-99972-2_1
22. Patalas-Maliszewska, J., Kłos, S.: Knowledge network for the development of software projects (KnowNetSoft). IFAC PapersOnLine **51**(11), 776–781 (2018)
23. Szwarc, E., Bach-Dąbrowska, I., Bocewicz, G.: Competence management in teacher assignment planning. In: Damaševičius, R., Vasiljevienė, G. (eds.) ICIST 2018. CCIS, vol. 920, pp. 449–460. Springer, Cham (2018). https://doi.org/10.1007/978-3-319-99972-2_37
24. Tsutsui, Y., Kubota, Y., Shimomura, Y.: A Bayesian network model for supporting the formation of PSS design knowledge. Procedia CIRP **73**, 56–60 (2018)
25. Patalas-Maliszewska, J.: Knowledge Worker Management: Value Assessment, Methods, and Application Tools. Springer, Heidelberg (2013). https://doi.org/10.1007/978-3-642-36600-0
26. Bork, D., Fil, H.G.: Formal aspects of enterprise modeling methods: a comparison framework. In: Proceedings of the 47th International Conference on System Sciences. IEEE (2014)

Declarative Model of Competences Assessment Robust to Personnel Absence

Eryk Szwarc[1]([⊠]) , Grzegorz Bocewicz[1] ,
Irena Bach-Dąbrowska[2] , and Zbigniew Banaszak[1]

[1] Faculty of Electronics and Computer Science,
Koszalin University of Technology, Sniadeckich 2, 75-453 Koszalin, Poland
eryk.szwarc@tu.koszalin.pl
[2] Finance and Management Faculty,
WSB University of Gdansk, al. Grunwaldzka 238A, 80-266 Gdansk, Poland
ibach@wsb.gda.pl

Abstract. Workers' absences are a common disruption to the provision of tasks. They make it necessary to modify task assignment, which amounts to finding suitable substitutions. Sometimes it happens that the competences of the available workers, with given constraints, e.g. hour limits, are not sufficient to find an admissible assignment modification. Therefore, it is desirable to develop a so-called robust personnel competence structure. In the case of workers' absences, a robust competence structure is a structure that allows one to find a modification of the assignment under every possible scenario of disruption. In other words, the following question is considered: does there exist, and if so, what is the competence structure robust to the disruption caused by an unexpected personnel absence? The number of potential solution variants is related to the number of competences that can be improved. For each variant, there could exist many cases of worker absence (absence of one worker, two workers, etc.). Moreover, for these, there could also exist many assignment modification variants. This an NP-hard problem. In the context of the scale of problems encountered in practice, searching for solutions using well-known algorithms (based on an exhaustive search) is a time-consuming process which does not guarantee that an admissible solution will be found. In the present study, a sufficient conditions are proposed, the fulfilment of which guarantees the existence of a non-empty set of admissible solutions. Declarative modelling and computer implementation in the form of constraint logic programming (CLP) have been applied. The potential of the proposed solution is illustrated with examples.

Keywords: Competence assessment · Declarative model · Robustness · Personnel absence · Worker assignment

1 Introduction

Task assignment is an important component of the complex scheduling problem. In a general case, the Task Assignment Problem (TAP) involves assigning resources (workers) to tasks so as to satisfy the constraints related to the personnel hour limits,

© Springer Nature Switzerland AG 2019
R. Damaševičius and G. Vasiljevienė (Eds.): ICIST 2019, CCIS 1078, pp. 12–23, 2019.
https://doi.org/10.1007/978-3-030-30275-7_2

workload, etc. [7, 8, 14]. An obvious criterion in assigning workers to tasks due to their competences, understood as a set of knowledge, experience and skills – elements that allow particular workers to realize particular tasks [4, 9, 11, 19]. The individual competences of specific employees make up the competence structure of the available personnel. This structure determines, in a natural manner, the possibility of providing a specific group of tasks. In the literature, there exist models and algorithms which allow one to answer typical questions connected with the assessment of the personnel's potential and estimation of the costs of assignment, i.e. issues in the area of analysis of competence structures [1, 5, 6, 10, 13, 15], for example: Does the given personnel with the given competence structure make it possible to provide tasks under the assumed constraints?

There are also models and algorithms which allow to answer questions connected with the possibility of strengthening the potential of the existing personnel, i.e. issues in the area of synthesis of competence structures (the few studies in this area include [17, 18]), for example: Does there exist (an improved) competence structure of the given personnel such that the worker assignment satisfies the constraints assumed?

In practice, every worker assignment plan is exposed to a defined set of disruptions, such as worker absences, changes in task numbers, etc. In this present article, we focus only on worker absences which may require modifications to the worker assignment, i.e finding suitable substitutions for absent employees. An answer to the following question is sought: Does the given competence structure of the available personnel allow to modify the assignment in the case of worker absence?

Sometimes, it happens that the given competence structure is not sufficient to find an admissible assignment modification. This type of structure is said to be non-robust to a given disruption. Cases like that lead to the formulation of a new generation of human resources management problems (omitted in the literature), which focus on the possibility of searching for a data structure (a competence structure in this case) which allows to assign resources so that specific expectations (e.g. robustness of the assignment plan to worker absence) are met [16]. In other words, an answer to the following question is sought: Does there exist (an improved) competence structure of the available personnel such that an admissible assignment modification can be made in the case of worker absence?

The number of alternative competence structures which guarantee an admissible assignment modification is related to the number of competences that can be improved. For each variant of an improved competence structure, there could exist many cases of disruption. Moreover, for each such case, there could also exist many assignment modification variants. The process of searching for a solution to this problem is illustrated using a simplified example (see Sect. 2). It shows that in the problem under consideration, the number of solutions increases exponentially. In the context of the scale of problems encountered in practice, searching for solutions using well-known algorithms (based on exhaustive search) is a time-consuming process that does not at all guarantee that an admissible solution will be found. The purpose of the present work is to propose the sufficient conditions the fulfilment of which will guarantee a non-empty set of admissible solutions.

The remainder of this paper is organized as follows: Sect. 2 provides an illustrative example of the problem of planning competence robust to unexpected personnel absence. Section 3 presents a declarative model of the problem considered. Section 4 shows the constraint satisfaction problem as an effective solving method. The last part (Sect. 5) contains conclusions and indicates the main directions of future research.

2 Motivation Example

Let us consider the following simplified example of robustness assessment of a competence structure and planning a competence structure that will be robust to unexpected worker absence. The example shows that in general the space of solutions is large, which makes the problem considered non-trivial.

Enterprise realize project, whose success is conditioned by the performing 10 tasks $o_{i,j}$ (Fig. 1a). Tasks are grouped in terms of the competences required for their realization: $O_1 = \{o_{1,1}\}, O_2 = \{o_{2,1}, o_{2,2}, o_{2,3}\}, O_3 = \{o_{3,1}, o_{3,2}\}, O_4 = \{o_{4,1}, o_{4,2}, o_{4,3}, o_{4,4}\}$. For example this means that tasks $o_{2,1}, o_{2,2}, o_{2,3}$ require the same competence hereinafter referred as O_2, ($o_{i,j}$ – means j-th task requiring i-th competence). It is assumed that each task takes 30 units of time (u.t.) and the technological order of performing tasks is known (Fig. 1a). For example, the beginning of the task $o_{2,1}$ is conditioned by the completion of $o_{4,1}$, beginning of the task $o_{2,2}$ is conditioned by the completion of $o_{4,2}$ i $o_{4,3}$, etc.

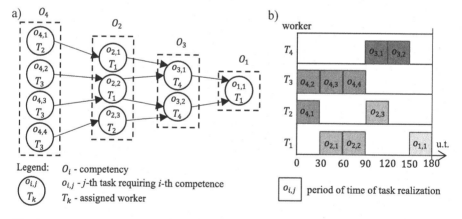

Fig. 1. Structure of considered project (a), schedule determined by assumed assignment (b)

Given are M workers $T_k (k = 1 \ldots M)$. Each worker T_k is characterised by a binary set of indicators $g_k = (g_{k,1}, \ldots, g_{k,i}, \ldots, g_{k,N})$:

- $g_{k,i} = 1$ indicates that the worker T_k has the competency O_i,
- $g_{k,i} = 0$ indicates that the worker T_k has no competency O_i.

For example, the notation $g_1 = (1, 1, 0, 0)$ means that worker T_1 has competences O_1 and O_2, and has no competences O_3 and O_4. Together, the indicators for all worker make up the competence structure of the worker team: $G = (g_{k,i}|k = 1...M;$ $i = 1...N)$, where $g_{k,i} \in \{0, 1\}$. In the example, let us consider the following competence structure G:

$$G = \begin{bmatrix} 1 & 1 & 0 & 0 \\ 0 & 1 & 0 & 1 \\ 0 & 1 & 1 & 1 \\ 1 & 0 & 1 & 1 \end{bmatrix} \begin{array}{l} \text{Competences } O_i \\ \text{Workers } T_k \end{array}$$

Each worker T_k has a limited number of hours to realize (minimum s_k and maximum z_k). An example of limitations are shown in Table 1.

Table 1. Minimum and maximum workers hour limits

	s_k	z_k
T_1	90	120
T_2	60	120
T_3	90	120
T_4	60	90

It is known that there exists a task assignment (number of tasks of given competence group O_i assigned to the k-th worker): $X = (x_{k,i}|k = 1...M; i = 1...N)$, where $x_{k,i} \in \mathbb{N}$, which satisfies the assumed limits s_k and z_k. An example of a variant of the assignment is given below:

$$X = \begin{bmatrix} 1 & 2 & 0 & 0 \\ 0 & 1 & 0 & 1 \\ 0 & 0 & 0 & 3 \\ 0 & 0 & 2 & 0 \end{bmatrix} \begin{array}{l} \text{Competences } O_i \\ \text{Workers } T_k \end{array}$$

Moreover, given is variant of project diagram with assigned employees (Fig. 1a). It shows which task $(o_{i,j})$ is assigned to which employee. For example, task $o_{4,1}$ is assigned to worker T_2, tasks $o_{4,2}$, $o_{4,3}$, $o_{4,4}$ are assigned to worker T_3, etc.

Project schedule assumes the possibility of its completion in 180 u.t. (units of time) (Fig. 1b).

As announced in the Introduction, an unexpected worker absence will be considered. An unexpected absence means that any worker and any number of workers could be absent during the of assignment X. Of course, we do not know which workers will be absent. All cases (the absence of one worker, two workers, etc.) must be considered. In general, the number of all disruption cases is $PC = \sum_{a=1}^{M} C_M^a$, where M – the number of workers. In the example considered, $M = 4$, and so $PC = 15$:

(a) 4 scenarios of one worker's absence,
(b) 6 scenarios of two workers' absence,
(c) 4 scenarios of three workers' absence,
(d) 1 scenario of four workers' absence.

To assess the robustness of the competence structure to worker absence, one has to answer the following question: does the given competence structure G allow to make an admissible modification to worker assignment X under each absence scenario? An admissible modification should be understood as a worker substitution for tasks which are assigned to the absent worker. For example, the absence of one worker requires the following modifications to assignment X:

- if the absent worker is T_1, then substitute workers are needed for tasks: $o_{1,1}$, $o_{2,1}$, $o_{2,2}$.
- if the absent worker is T_2, then substitute workers are needed for tasks: $o_{2,3}$, $o_{4,1}$.
- etc.

First, let us consider case (a) and all the scenarios of one worker's absence – see Fig. 2. It can be seen that for two out of the four possible scenarios (the absence of T_3 and T_4), no admissible modification of worker assignment X can be made.

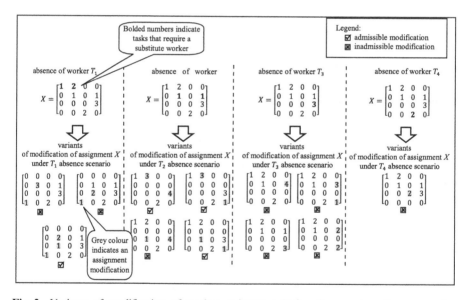

Fig. 2. Variants of modification of worker assignment X for all scenarios of a one worker absence

An important observation for each scenario of cases (b) and (c) is that the total number of working hours (300) is greater than the sum of the maximum number of hours z_k for each worker $\left(\sum_{k=1}^{M} z_k\right)$. Thus, again, no admissible modifications can be made to these cases.

Lastly, it is obvious that case (d) is a special situation when it is not possible to make any admissible modifications.

In conclusion, the answer is: the given competence structure G guarantees an admissible modification of worker assignment X under two out of the 15 worker absence scenarios. In other words, competence structure G is not robust to unexpected worker absence. Therefore, a reverse question must be asked: Does there exists a competence structure G such that an admissible modification can be made to worker assignment X under every possible absence scenario? Or, put differently, which competency $g_{k,i}$ of which worker T_k should be improved to ensure an admissible modification of assignment X? Competency improvement is understood as changing the value of competency in structure G from "0" to "1". Thus, all the possible variants of competence structures can be represented by the general formula $2^{(M \cdot N) - CP} - 1$, where CP is the number of competences with value "1" in structure G (i.e. competences which cannot be improved). In our example, $M = 4$, $N = 4$, $CP = 10$, which gives $2^{(4 \cdot 4) - 10} - 1 = 63$ variants.

It is obvious that in the example considered whatever the structure is, it would not be robust in cases (b), (c) and (d). It is only possible to find a competence structure robust to the scenarios of case (a).

It is necessary to use an exhaustive search to find an admissible solution. A tree of competence structure variants is shown in Fig. 3. Some of these variants are marked as allowing an admissible modification of X under all the scenarios of one worker's absence. The answer to the question above, then, is that there exists a competence structure G such that an admissible modification of worker assignment X can be made under every possible scenario of one worker's absence. To prove it, let us choose competence structure indicated by blue color on Fig. 3. Different schedules under every possible scenario are illustrated on Fig. 4.

However, in special cases, none of the competence structure variants guarantee an admissible modification of worker assignment X. This is especially important in real-world-sized problems, for example: $M = 10$, $N = 30$ and CP around 200, where there are $2^{(10 \cdot 30) - 200} - 1 = 2^{100} - 1$ possible competence structure variants. Because in such cases calculations are highly time consuming, and still do not guarantee that an admissible solution will be found, the following question seems worth considering: does there exist a sufficient condition such that an admissible solution is guaranteed to exist? To find an answer to this question, a competence structure with values "1" only should be considered. Let us call this structure a full-competence structure. Thus, the sufficient condition can be formulated as follows: IF for the full competence structure it is possible to make a modification to worker assignment X under each absence scenario, THEN at least one admissible solution exists. Thus, only this one variant of the competence structure should be checked for admissible solutions.

In general, the problem considered can be formulated using:

- sets of tasks and workers and the parameters that define their quantitative measures,
- decision variables that determine worker assignments and their competence structure,
- and constraints which link the sets and the decision variables.

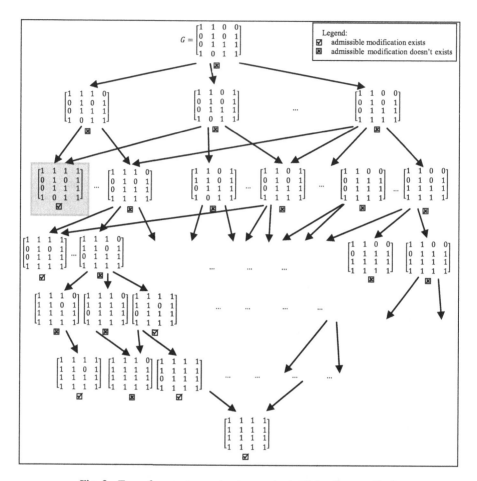

Fig. 3. Tree of competence structure variants (Color figure online)

Computing environments that are well adapted to solving this type of problems are declarative programming environments [2, 3]. They reflect the structure of the constraints of a task in a natural way by modelling the task as a so-called constraint satisfaction problem (CSP) [12].

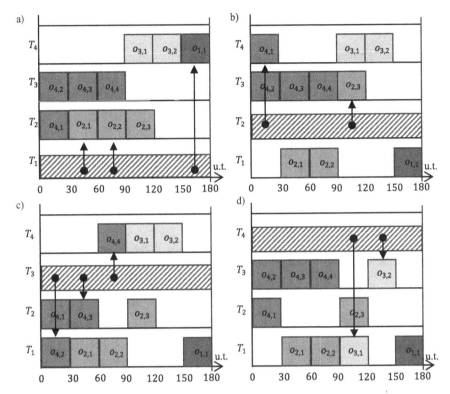

Fig. 4. Schedule under T_1 absence (a); T_2 absence (b); T_3 absence (c); T_4 absence (d)

3 Declarative Model

The following declarative model is proposed:

Sets:
O_i: competences, indexed by $i = 1, \ldots, N$,
T_k: workers, indexed by $k = 1, \ldots, M$.

Parameters:
s_k: minimum number of hours of the k-th worker $(s_k \in \mathbb{N})$,
z_k: maximum number of hours of the k-th worker $(z_k \in \mathbb{N})$.

Decision variables:
G: competence structure, defined as $G = (g_{k,i} | k = 1 \ldots M; i = 1 \ldots N)$, where $g_{k,i}$ stands for a worker's competences to realize a given task; $g_{k,i} \in \{0, 1\}$, $g_{k,i} = 0$ indicates the k-th worker has no competence O_i, $g_{k,i} = 1$ indicates the k-th worker has competence O_i.

G^j: competence structure obtained as a result of the absence of the j-th worker,
$G^j = (g_{k,i}^j | k = 1 \ldots (M-1); i = 1 \ldots N)$

X^j: task assignment for structure G^j (in the situation of the j-th worker's absence),
defined as $X^j = (x_{k,i}^j | k = 1 \ldots (M-1); i = 1 \ldots N)$, where $x_{k,i}^j \in \mathbb{N}$ means the
number of tasks $o_{i,j}$ assigned to the k-th worker in structure G^j.

Constraint related to competences:

(a) tasks can be assigned to the workers with appropriate competences:

$$x_{k,i}^j = 0, \text{ where } g_{k,i}^j = 0 \tag{1}$$

Constraints related to the number of working hours:

(b) The number of hours assigned to T_k should be greater than or equal to the
minimum number of hours given to the k-th worker:

$$\sum_{i=1}^{N} x_{k,i}^j \cdot l_i \geq s_k, \text{ where } k = 1, \ldots, M \tag{2}$$

(c) The number of hours assigned to T_k should be less than or equal to the maximum
number of hours given to the k-th worker:

$$\sum_{i=1}^{N} x_{k,i}^j \cdot l_i \leq z_k, \text{ where } k = 1, \ldots, M \tag{3}$$

Constraint related to absence:

(d) Construction of competency structures corresponding to the situation of the j-th
workers' absence:

$$g_{k,i}^j = \begin{cases} g_{k,i} & \text{when } k < j \\ g_{(k+1),i} & \text{when } k \geq j \end{cases} \tag{4}$$

Task assignment X^j which satisfies all the constraints (1)–(4) is known as the
admissible worker assignment in situation of the j-th workers' absence.

In this model, the following questions can be formulated:

(a) Does the given competence structure G guarantee an admissible worker
assignment?
(b) Does there exist, and if so, what is the competence structure G that guarantees the
existence of an admissible worker assignment?
(c) For the given competence structure G, does there exist a modification to the given
worker assignment that can be made in the case of worker absence?
(d) Does there exist, and if so, what is the competence structure G which guarantees
that a modification can be made to the worker assignment in the case of worker
absence?

We are looking for a solution where the values of all the variables satisfy all the constraints (the first solution found, or all of them). This is the well-known constraint satisfaction problem (CSP) [3].

4 Method

The solution to a CSP is obtained as a result of a systematic search of all the possible assignments of values to decision variables. The search methods can be classified according to whether the entire space of all the possible assignments is searched (an exhaustive search) or whether we search only a part of this space (a combinatorial search). The exponential complexity of an exhaustive search, even assuming that 90% of potential solutions are rejected because they do not satisfy the constraints, make them impractical to use in most everyday situations. Thus, combinatorial search methods remain the only alternative. These approaches use various heuristics to reduce the number of necessary searches in a substitution tree (heuristics that constitute a generalization of the sequence of experiments carried out earlier). Both exhaustive and combinatorial search methods use the same iterative scheme: constraint propagation and variable distribution. In other words, the variables declared in the script of a program, along with their domains and the constraints that link decision variables (relations, Boolean and algebraic expressions, etc.) are processed by the same combination of mechanisms of propagation and distribution [3, 12].

The values of the variables that do not satisfy the constraints are removed from their domains during constraint propagation. In most cases, however, the final result cannot be reached by the propagation of constraints alone. It is necessary to introduce a distribution of variables together with searching. The distribution of variables consists in introducing an additional constraint (this is often accomplished by assigning a value to one of the decision variables) and checking its compatibility (consistency) by propagating the constraints. This may result in one of the three possible outcomes:

- a solution is found (each variable has one value from its domain),
- the domains of some of the variables are narrowed down, however, no solution is found yet. This means the distribution of another variable is necessary,
- the additional constraint is incompatible with the remaining constraints; backtracking is performed and the current value of the variable is removed from the domain.

In this iterative search process, a search tree is generated in which each node corresponds to a certain state of a variable. These mechanisms were implemented in the Matlab programming environment. The tool developed in this way was used in computational experiments to assess the time of the determination of a competence structure robust to workers' absences, for a variable number of workers (5–15) and a variable number of tasks (16–32). The results are shown in Table 2. As it can be easily observed, for those assignments that involve fewer than 10 workers and 32 tasks, the time needed to determine a robust competence structure does not exceed 1000 s. Moreover, the competence structures obtained require a minimum number of changes.

Our future work will focus on the implementation of the model proposed in commercial optimization solvers, such as IBM ILOG CPLEX Optimizer, Gurobi Optimizer, Oz/Mozart etc.

Table 2. Results of computational experiments*

	1	2	3	4	5
Workers × Tasks	5 × 16	5× 24	5 × 28	5 × 32	5 × 36
Number of variables	320	480	560	640	720
Competences changed	12	17	19	21	23
Robust structure determination time [sec.]	1.14	4.18	6.62	10.46	14.75
	6	7	8	9	10
Workers × Tasks	10 × 16	10 × 24	10 × 28	10 × 32	10 × 36
Number of variables	1440	2160	2550	2880	3240
Competences changed	8	11	15	17	19
Robust structure determination time [sec.]	129	436	711	1046	>1000
	11	12	13	14	15
Workers × Tasks	15 × 16	15 × 24	15 × 28	15 × 32	15 × 36
Number of variables	3360	5040	5880	6720	7560
Competences changed	6	5	no data	no data	no data
Robust structure determination time [sec.]	>1000	>1000	>1000	>1000	>1000

*computer parameters: Intel i7-4770, 8 GB RAM

5 Concluding Remarks

The problem of improving workers' competences to make personnel robust to disruptions caused by unexpected personnel absences is rarely discussed in the literature. The declarative model proposed in this study and the constraint programming method used to solve the problem lend themselves well to implementation in commercial DSS software.

One limitation of the model proposed is the assumption that every worker can improve their competences with regard to each task. In practice, it may be that a specific worker is not able (or willing) to acquire the competences needed to realize specific tasks, e.g. because the subject matter of these tasks is out of their scope of interest. Another observation is that different workers might acquire a given competence at a different pace. Then, the problem can be formulated as an optimization problem: which of the alternative variants of the competence structure allow the fastest worker adjustment to guarantee robustness to worker absences? This type of problem should be considered in future research.

Furthermore, it should be noted that the robustness of a competence structure can be obtained by other ways than improving that structure, e.g. by increasing/decreasing employee's hour limits.

In our future work, we plan to focus on robustness of competence structures to other disruptions, such as the loss of employee qualifications (competences), changes in number of tasks, simultaneous (and/or consequent) absence of several employees.

References

1. Antosz, K.: Maintenance–identification and analysis of the competency gap. Eksploatacja i Niezawodnosc–Maintenance and Reliability **20**(3), 484–494 (2018)
2. Banaszak, Z., Bocewicz, G.: Declarative modeling for production order portfolio scheduling. Found. Manage. **6**(3), 7–24 (2014)
3. Bocewicz, G., Banaszak, Z.: Decision Support Driven Models and Algorithms of Artificial Intelligence. Warsaw University of Technology, Warsaw (2011)
4. Coolahan, J.: Key Competencies: A Developing Concept in General Compulsory Education. European Commission, Eurydice, Brussels (2002)
5. Domenech, B., Lusa, A.: A MILP model for the teacher assignment problem considering teacher's preferenes. Eur. J. Oper. Res. **249**(3), 1153–1160 (2016)
6. Gunawan, A., Ng, K.M., Poh, K.L.: A mathematical programming model for a timetabling problem. In: Proceedings of the 2008 International Conference on Scientific Computing, pp. 42–47 (2006)
7. Güler, M.G., Keskin, M.E., Döyen, A., Akyer, H.: On teaching assistant-task assignment problem: a case study. Comput. Ind. Eng. **79**, 18–26 (2015)
8. Lai, C.-M., Yeh, W.-C., Huang, Y.-C.: Entropic simplified swarm optimization for the task assignment problem. Appl. Soft Comput. **58**, 115–127 (2017)
9. Levy-Leboyer, C.: La gestion des compétences (Competence management). Les Editions d'Organisation, Paris (1996)
10. Moreira, J.J., Reis, L.P.: Multi-agent system for teaching service distribution with coalition formation. In: Rocha, Á., Correia, A.M., Wilson, T., Stroetmann, K.A. (eds.) Advances in Information Systems and Technologies. AISC, vol. 206, pp. 599–609. Springer, Heidelberg (2013). https://doi.org/10.1007/978-3-642-36981-0_55
11. Patalas-Maliszewska, J., Kłos, S.: An intelligent system for core-competence identification for industry 4.0 based on research results from German and Polish manufacturing companies. In: Burduk, A., Mazurkiewicz, D. (eds.) ISPEM 2017. AISC, vol. 637, pp. 131–139. Springer, Cham (2018). https://doi.org/10.1007/978-3-319-64465-3_13
12. Schutle, H., Smolka, G., Wurtz, J.: Finite Domain Constraint Programming in Oz. German Research Center for Artificial Intelligence, Saarbrucken (1998)
13. Serpell, A., Ferrada, X.: A competency-based model for constriction supervisor in developing countries. Pers. Rev. **36**(4), 585–602 (2007)
14. Spliet, R., Dekker, R.: The driver assignment vehicle routing problem. Networks **68**(3), 212–223 (2016)
15. Szwarc, E.: Ocena odporności planu obsady zajęć dydaktycznych na zakłócenie zmiany liczby grup zajęciowych (in Polish). Res. Enterp. Mod. Econ. Theor. Pract. **3/2018**(25), 135–145 (2018)
16. Szwarc, E., Bach-Dąbrowska, I., Bocewicz, G.: Competence management in teacher assignment planning. In: Damaševičius, R., Vasiljevienė, G. (eds.) ICIST 2018. CCIS, vol. 920, pp. 449–460. Springer, Cham (2018). https://doi.org/10.1007/978-3-319-99972-2_37
17. Wikarek, J.: Lecturers' competences configuration model for the timetabling problem. In: Ganzha, M., Maciaszek, L., Paprzycki, M. (eds.) Proceedings of the 2018 Federated Conference on Computer Science and Information Systems, vol. 15, pp. 441–444 (2018)
18. Wikarek, J., Sitek, P.: A data-driven approach to modeling and solving academic teachers' competences configuration problem. In: Nguyen, N.T., Gaol, F.L., Hong, T.-P., Trawiński, B. (eds.) ACIIDS 2019. LNCS (LNAI), vol. 11431, pp. 408–419. Springer, Cham (2019). https://doi.org/10.1007/978-3-030-14799-0_35
19. Woodruffe, C.: What is meant by competency? In: Designing and Achieving Competency. McGraw-Hill, New York (1992)

Fuzzy Delphi Method with Z-Numbers

Marcin Lawnik[1][ID], Joanna Krakowczyk[2], and Arkadiusz Banasik[1(✉)][ID]

[1] Silesian University of Technology, Kaszubska 23, 44-100 Gliwice, Poland
{marcin.lawnik,arkadiusz.banasik}@polsl.pl
[2] COIG S.A., Mikołowska 100, 40-065 Katowice, Poland
asiakrakowczyk@gmail.com

Abstract. Delphi method is one of the basic heuristic methods used in forecasting and decision making. It is based on several stages of experts' evaluation with feedback. One of the variants is the fuzzy Delphi method, which assumes that expert's opinion is expressed in fuzzy numbers. This article presents fuzzy Delphi method modification based on Z-numbers for expert's opinions. It's advantage is the fact that Z-numbers are supposed to be used to description of phenomena and processes in which we do not possess full knowledge better than fuzzy numbers. The presented version of Delphi method is used for prediction of prices of oil barrels in US Dollars.

Keywords: Delphi method · Z-numbers · Fuzzy sets

1 Introduction

The most incredible feature of human is the fact, that he or she can interpret or forecast events even if we do not have full knowledge about a phenomenon or a process. The type of such phenomenon is defined, for example, by forecasting of decision making of driver in case of overtaking the car in order to speed, distance between the car and approaching one. To make the right (safe) decision it is not needed to know the exact speed and distance, it is necessary to qualify it to the set made of linguistic variables such as *fast* or *far*.

In order to mathematical point of view, the solution of that approach can be presented, among others, by fuzzy sets [1]. The mechanism of decision making in incomplete knowledge environment was presented in [2]. There are many other application areas for fuzzy sets, i.e. [3,4], but there are some limitations according to the mathematical point of view, for example, the exact definition of membership function. This could lead to improper model definition and improper value prediction based on that model. To avoid that problems and to make a better way in modelling knowledge in conditions of uncertainty the generalization of fuzzy set was proposed - Z-number [5]. Z-number is a pair of fuzzy numbers, which first part is a variable limitation, and second part is degree of reliability. The short history of Z-numbers shows many applications in decision making situations [6–10].

R. Damaševičius and G. Vasiljevienė (Eds.): ICIST 2019, CCIS 1078, pp. 24–32, 2019.
https://doi.org/10.1007/978-3-030-30275-7_3

Another way of forecasting values of phenomenon is the so called Delphi method [11]. This forecasting method use knowledge, experience and opinions of experts from specified field. It is based on several stages evaluation by experts (for example questionnaire) of specified process with controlled feedback. The feedback is based on consideration of aggregated ratings from previous round by experts', for instance by the arithmetic mean or other descriptive statistical measures. In that way they can modify their rating to be closer to the aggregated value.

The Delphi method is widely used, for example in innovation adoption process [12], energy market forecasting [13], forecasting mobile broadband traffic [14], in health research [15] and many others.

One of the variants of Delphi method is fuzzy Delphi method, where the experts in further rounds provide evaluations which contains 3 component values a_1, a_2 i a_3, which can be described as minimal value, the most probable value and the maximal value. Those three components can be defined as fuzzy triangle number. For each string of values the arithmetic average is counted, which is sent back to the experts. In the last stage the defuzzyfication process is involved by which the forecasted value is obtained.

The fuzzy Delphi method was widely used in fields such as forecasting of fashion styles [16], evaluation of hydrogen production [17], lubricant regenerative technology selection [18], teaching methods [19], creating of teaching applications [20] or even determining socio-ecological factors that influence adherence to mammography screening in rural areas of Mexico [21].

The disadvantage of presented methods (both classical and fuzzy) is the reliability of experts' opinions. The expert may not be sure of his or her opinion in order to quantitative aspect of the opinion. That problem may be solved by additional reliability value of expert's opinion. That is the reason of using Z-number in order to credibility of expert's opinion.

This article presents Delphi method based on Z-numbers. The article contains parts as: Introduction, Preliminaries, Delphi method using Z-numbers, Example and Conclusions.

2 Preliminaries

The fuzzy set A in universe X is a set of pairs [1]

$$A = \{(x, \mu_A(x)) : x \in X\}. \tag{1}$$

The function $\mu_A : X \rightarrow [0,1]$ is called a membership function of fuzzy set A. The membership value $\mu_A(x)$ describes the degree of belonging of x in A.

One of the simplest membership function's representation is triangular membership function presented by formula

$$(a, b, c) = \begin{cases} 0, & x \leqslant a \\ \frac{x-a}{b-a}, & a < x \leqslant b \\ \frac{c-x}{c-b}, & b < x \leqslant c \\ 0, & x > c \end{cases}. \tag{2}$$

Fuzzy average $\overline{A}$ of triangular fuzzy sets $A_i = (a_i, b_i, c_i)$ can be defined by the formula [22]:

$$\overline{A} = \left(\frac{1}{n} \sum_{i=1}^{n} a_i, \frac{1}{n} \sum_{i=1}^{n} b_i, \frac{1}{n} \sum_{i=1}^{n} c_i \right). \tag{3}$$

Fuzzy number is a fuzzy Fuzzy set A (where $A \subseteq \mathbb{R}$), which membership function fulfill listed conditions [23]:

1. $\sup_{x \in \mathbb{R}} \mu_A(x) = 1$ (fuzzy set A is normal)
2. $\mu_A(\lambda x_1 + (1 - \lambda)x_2) \geq \min\{\mu_A(x_1), \mu_A(x_2)\}$ (set A is convex)
3. $\mu_A(x)$ is intervally continuous function

Z-number [5] is an ordered pair of fuzzy numbers (A, R), where number A is a fuzzy bound of real variable x, and R is a measure of reliability of the first component.

Z-number can be brought to fuzzy number by using the idea of fuzzy expected value [24]:

$$E_A(x) = \int_X x \mu_A(x) dx \tag{4}$$

Using (4) it is possible to convert Z-number into fuzzy number. The procedure is shown below [24]:

1. Mapping of second component of Z-number (R) into numerical value, for instance using center of gravity method [25]:

$$\alpha = \frac{\int x \mu_R(x) dx}{\int \mu_R(x) dx}. \tag{5}$$

2. Adding computed weight α to first component (A):

$$Z^\alpha = \{(x, \mu_{A^\alpha}(x)), \quad \mu_{A^\alpha}(x) = \alpha \mu_A(x), \quad x \in \sqrt{\alpha}X\}. \tag{6}$$

3. Conversion of fuzzy set into fuzzy number:

$$Z' = \{(x, \mu_{Z'}(x)), \quad \mu_{Z'}(x) = \mu_A \left(\frac{x}{\sqrt{\alpha}} \right), \quad x \in \sqrt{\alpha}X\}. \tag{7}$$

Set (7) in case, that the fuzzy number A is triangular (2), can be expressed by formula

$$Z' = \left(\sqrt{\alpha}a, \sqrt{\alpha}b, \sqrt{\alpha}c \right). \tag{8}$$

3 Delphi Method Using Z-Numbers

The expert's ratings can be presented in Z-numbers, where the expert shows not only the value of boundary for the requested topic but also the certainty of the boundary. This is a better use of experts' knowledge, because we may manage not only the numerical values, like in classical or fuzzy Delphi method, but also reliability of the assessment. The levels of reliability belong to defined set and the expert can only choose one element. The expert do not have further influence on his or her assessment and how it be converted into fuzzy number because he or she only gains linguistic variables without formulas of membership functions of those linguistic variables.

Delphi method with Z-numbers can be described by steps expressed below:

1. Experts E_i $(i = 1, 2, \ldots, n)$ declare their opinions giving triangular Z-numbers

$$A_i = (a_i, b_i, c_i; \text{reliability}), \tag{9}$$

   where the component *reliability* is an element of defined set of reliability values.
2. Z-numbers are transformed into triangular fuzzy numbers in order to (5)–(7). The obtained fuzzy numbers are in the form

$$A_i' = (a_i', b_i', c_i'). \tag{10}$$

3. The fuzzy average (3) is counted

$$\overline{A} = \left(\frac{1}{n} \sum_{i=1}^{n} a_i', \frac{1}{n} \sum_{i=1}^{n} b_i', \frac{1}{n} \sum_{i=1}^{n} c_i' \right). \tag{11}$$

4. Experts once again give their opinions taking into account the value (11) calculated in step 3.
5. The whole process of experts opinions repeats till stabilization of (11) in the next rounds.
6. Using the defuzzyfication process the crisp value is calculated $\overline{x}$, for instance by the center of gravity method (5)

$$\overline{x} = \frac{\int x \mu_{\overline{A}}(x) dx}{\int \mu_{\overline{A}}(x) dx}, \tag{12}$$

   which is the final predicted value.

This algorithm can be modified using below mentioned changes:

Step 2., in which Z-number is transformed into fuzzy number using (5)–(7) is very simple. Its disadvantage is the loosing of some pieces of primal information and this causes some limitation to effective use of Z-numbers [26]. It can be seen in formula (8), where the obtained value α causes shift of the triangular fuzzy number (2) to the left side of the axis of real numbers. Therefore another method of transforming the Z-number to fuzzy number can be used.

The other possibility of evaluation of reliability of assessment, which is included in first step of the algorithm, is fixing of reliability of the expert. It can be done by the person who had experience in working with the expert and has the knowledge of his or her evaluations and their consequences for the real value of estimated opinions. In that case the expert provides only the fuzzy number and the reliability is made by the manager of the process.

4 Example

The price of oil barrel has influence on many branches of economy. That is the main reason of its price forecasting [27–29]. Therefore Delphi methods could be applied to solving this issue. The example is strictly numerical one. In our example fuel market experts' were asked to prepare their opinions on price of oil barrel in one week's time. The opinions should be declared in Z-numbers having reliability's given from set:

$$\{uncertain, \ possible, \ sure, \ very \ sure\}. \tag{13}$$

The number of rounds is 2.

4.1 Round 1

Assuming that the actual price of oil barrel is equal to 54 USD, forecasts of experts' are shown in Table 1.

Table 1. Experts' opinions on price of oil barrel.

Expert	Z-number
Expert 1	(49, 58, 63; very sure)
Expert 2	(50, 57, 65; very sure)
Expert 3	(50, 59, 69; sure)
Expert 4	(53, 61, 70; sure)
Expert 5	(48, 55, 64; sure)
Expert 6	(51, 59, 70; very sure)

Membership functions for linguistic variables showing reliability of Z-numbers are defined in Table 2.

Table 2. Reliability of Z-numbers declared in Table 1.

Reliability	Fuzzy number
Very sure	(0.95, 0.97, 1)
Sure	(0.9, 0.95, 1)

Table 3. Fuzzy numbers obtained from Table 1 using the dependence (5)–(7).

Expert	Fuzzy number
Expert 1	(48.341, 57.220, 62.153)
Expert 2	(49.328, 56.233, 64.126)
Expert 3	(48.733, 57.505, 67.251)
Expert 4	(51.657, 59.454, 68.226)
Expert 5	(46.783, 53.606, 62.378)
Expert 6	(50.314, 58.207, 69.059)

After exchange of Z-numbers into fuzzy numbers in order to (5)–(7) (Table 3) and using the formula (11) we obtain following fuzzy number:

$$\overline{A} = (49.193, 57.037, 65.532). \tag{14}$$

The value (14) is send to experts, who verify their opinions in Round 2.

4.2 Round 2

The updated prices from experts' are shown in Table 4.

Table 4. 2nd Round of experts' opinions. Their opinions on price of oil barrel are declared taking into account (14).

Expert	Z-number
Expert 1	(49, 58, 63; very sure)
Expert 2	(50, 57, 65; very sure)
Expert 3	(50, 59, 67; very sure)
Expert 4	(53, 59, 69; sure)
Expert 5	(48, 56, 64; very sure)
Expert 6	(51, 59, 69; very sure)

After transformation from Z-numbers into fuzzy numbers in order to (5)–(7) (Table 5) and use of formula (11) we obtain updated fuzzy number:

$$\overline{A} = (49.387, 57.103, 65.140). \tag{15}$$

Defuzzyficating (15) using method (12), we obtain the value

$$\overline{x} = 57.210, \tag{16}$$

which is the forecasted price of oil barrel in one week's time in USD.

Graphic interpretation of both rounds of experts' ratings show Figs. 1 and 2.

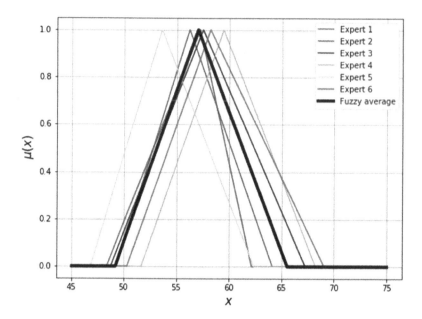

Fig. 1. First round of experts opinions on price of oil barrel in US Dollars.

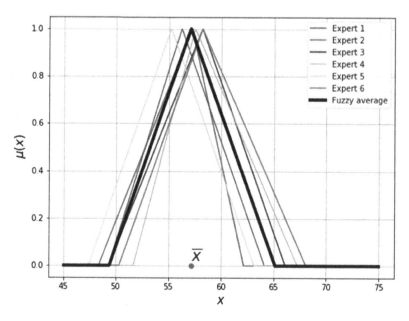

Fig. 2. Second round of opinions. The final value of forecasted price of oil barrel $\overline{x} =$ 57.210.

Table 5. Fuzzy numbers obtained from Table 4 using dependence (5)–(7).

Expert	Fuzzy number
Expert 1	(48.341, 57.220, 62.153)
Expert 2	(49.328, 56.233, 64.126)
Expert 3	(49.328, 58.207, 66.099)
Expert 4	(51.657, 57.505, 67.251)
Expert 5	(47.354, 55.247, 63.139)
Expert 6	(50.314, 58.207, 68.072)

5   Conclusions

This article presents fuzzy Delphi method based on Z-numbers. The expert's opinions presented in Z-numbers are converted into fuzzy numbers and than the fuzzy Delphi method is used. This approach gives the possibility to declare reliability of each expert in order to their ratings. The presented algorithm was used on example for forecasting price of oil barrel. The presented method can be used in industry in order to find solutions with experts' knowledge in which the decision making is needed in analyzed situation.

References

1. Zadeh, L.A.: Fuzzy sets. Inf. Control **8**(3), 338–353 (1965)
2. Bellman, R.E., Zadeh, L.A.: Decision-making in a fuzzy environment. Manage. Sci. **17**(4), 141–164 (1970)
3. Banasik, A., Kapczyński, A.: Fuzzy logic applied in databases for investors. In: Proceedings of the 5th IEEE International Workshop on Intelligent Data Acquisition Advanced Computing Systems: Technology and Applications. IDAACS 2009, pp. 612–613 (2009)
4. Banasik, A., Kapczyński, A.: Fuzzy evaluation of biometric authentication systems. In: Proceedings of the 6th IEEE International Conference on Intelligent Data Acquisition and Advanced Computing Systems: Technology and Applications, IDAACS 2011, pp. 803–806 (2011)
5. Zadeh, L.A.: A note on Z-numbers. Inf. Sci. **181**(14), 2923–2932 (2011)
6. Gardashova, L.: Application of operational approaches to solving decision making problem using Z-Numbers. Appl. Math. **5**, 1323–1334 (2014)
7. Xiao, Z.Q.: Application of Z-numbers in multi-criteria decision making. In: 2014 International Conference on Informative and Cybernetics for Computational Social Systems (ICCSS), pp. 91–95 (2014)
8. Jabbarova, A.I.: Application of Z-number concept to supplier selection problem. Procedia Comput. Sci. **120**, 473–477 (2017)
9. Krakowczyk, J., Lawnik M.: Applications of Z-numbers in decision making. Zesz. Nauk. PŚl., Org. Zarz. **113**, 195–205 (2017). (in polish)
10. Krohling, R.A., André, G.C., Pacheco, A.G.C., Dos Santos, A.S.: TODIM and TOPSIS with Z-numbers. Front. Inf. Technol. Electron. Eng. 1–9. https://doi.org/10.1631/FITEE.1700434
11. Dalkey, N., Helmer, O.: An experimental application of the DELPHI method to the use of experts. Manage. Sci. **9**(3), 458–467 (1963)

12. Pichlak, M.: The innovation adoption process: a multidimensional approach. J. Manage. Org. **22**(4), 476–494 (2016)
13. Czaplicka-Kolarz, K., Stańczyk, K., Kapusta, K.: Technology foresight for a vision of energy sector development in Poland till 2030 Delphi survey as an element of technology foresighting. Tech. Forecast. Soc. Change **76**(3), 327–338 (2009)
14. Lee, S., Cho, C., Hong, E., Yoon, B.: Forecasting mobile broadband traffic: application of scenario analysis and Delphi method. Expert Syst. Appl. **44**, 126–137 (2016)
15. de Meyrick, J.: The Delphi method and health research. Health Educ. **103**(1), 7–16 (2002)
16. Lin, C.: Application of fuzzy Delphi method (FDM) and fuzzy analytic hierarchy process (FAHP) to criteria weights for fashion design scheme evaluation. Int. J. Clothing Sci. Technol. **25**(3), 171–183 (2013)
17. Chang, P.-L., Hsu, C.-W., Chang, P.-C.: Fuzzy Delphi method for evaluating hydrogen production technologies. Int. J. Hydrogen Energy **36**(21), 14172–14179 (2011)
18. Hsu, Y.-L., Lee, C.-H., Kreng, V.B.: The application of fuzzy Delphi method and fuzzy AHP in lubricant regenerative technology selection. Expert Syst. Appl. **37**, 419–425 (2010)
19. Zhang, Z., Huang, Y., Gao E.: A fuzzy and comprehensive evaluation model for developing teaching evaluation. In: 2012 2nd International Conference on Consumer Electronics, Communications and Networks (CECNet), Yichang, pp. 774–777 (2012)
20. Kamarulzaman, N., Jomhari, N., Raus, N., Yusof, M.Z.M.: Applying the fuzzy Delphi method to analyze the user requirement for user centred design process in order to create learning applications. Indian J. Sci. Technol. **8**(32), 1–7 (2015)
21. Sánchez-Lezama, A.P., Cavazos-Arroyo, J., Albavera-Hernández, C.: Applying the fuzzy Delphi method for determining socio-ecological factors that influence adherence to mammography screening in rural areas of Mexico. Cad Saude Publica. **30**(2), 245–258 (2014)
22. Bojadziev, G., Bojadziev, M.: Fuzzy Logic for Business, Finance, and Management. Advances in Fuzzy Systems–Applications and Theory, 2nd edn. vol. 23. World Scientific Publishing Co., Pte. Ltd, Singapore (2007)
23. Hanss, M.: Applied Fuzzy Arithmetic an Introduction with Engineering Applications. Springer, Heidelberg (2005)
24. Kang, B., Wei, D., Li, Y., Deng, Y.: A method of converting Z-number to classical fuzzy number. J. Inf. Comput. Sci. **9**(3), 703–709 (2012)
25. Patel, A.V., Mohan, B.M.: Some numerical aspects of center of area defuzzification method. Fuzzy Sets Syst. **132**(3), 401–409 (2002)
26. Aliev, R.A., Huseynov, O.H., Zeinalov, L.M.: The arithmetic of continuous Z-numbers. Inf. Sci. **373**, 441–460 (2016)
27. Nelson, Y., Gerry Gemis, G., Nix, H.D.: Results of the Delphi Ix Survey of Oil Price Forecasts. California Energy Commission (1998). https://www.energy.ca.gov/reports/DELPHI-9.PDF. Accessed 25 Dec 2018
28. Chuaykoblap, S., Chutima, P., Chandrachai, A., Nupairoj, N.: Expert-based text mining with Delphi method for crude oil price prediction. Int. J. Ind. Syst. Eng. **25**(4), 545–563 (2017)
29. Xie, W., Yu, L., Xu, S., Wang, S.: A new method for crude oil price forecasting based on support vector machines. In: Alexandrov, V.N., van Albada, G.D., Sloot, P.M.A., Dongarra, J. (eds.) ICCS 2006. LNCS, vol. 3994, pp. 444–451. Springer, Heidelberg (2006). https://doi.org/10.1007/11758549_63

Use of Chatbots in Project Management

Dace Cīrule and Solvita Bērziša[(✉)]

Information Technology Institute, Riga Technical University, Kalku 1,
Riga, Latvia
dace.strelniece@gmail.com, solvita.berzisa@rtu.lv

Abstract. Over the last decade, a number of studies and forecasts have been made on the impact of AI, and one of the last Gartner research predicts that by 2020, customers will manage 85% of their relationship with the enterprise without interacting with a human. It is possible to see the growing tendency to use chatbots in the customer service field on a worldwide scale. AI chatbots that are designed for employees support is a prospective niche that will grow rapidly over the next decade and one of the areas that could benefit from AI chatbots is project management. Main work categories where chatbots could be useful is the automation of routine project management tasks, data processing and analysis.

The paper aims to demonstrate the potential of using chatbots in project management and to prove the authors' hypothesis - AI chatbots use in project management can save time for project managers (and project team) and reduce factors of project failure. The hypothesis has been tested with AI chatbot prototypes. The paper contains results of the chatbots existing and potential possibilities for project management support, proof of concept (PoC) for implementing chatbot and a brief insight into developed chatbot prototypes.

Keywords: Chatbot · Artificial intelligence (AI) · Project management · Proof of concept (PoC)

1 Introduction

Nearly 1,800 project managers globally reported that 54% of their time is spent on "administrative coordination and control tasks, such as scheduling, resource allocation and reporting" leaving behind no less important work categories like people development, strategy and innovation [1]. From a business perspective, project managers would need to focus more on those activities that contribute to business growth, leaving routine project management (PM) tasks to AI. With the development of AI solutions, like AI chatbots, the proportion of work categories may change in the closest decade where PMs could spend less time on daily routine administrative tasks [1] and more on, for example, people development and engagement. This change will change the role of project manager in the future.

Chatbot is a computer program that can imitate a human conversation using text chat, voice commands, or both [2]. Because of AI, chatbots can be 'intelligent' enough to perform tasks, solve problems and manage information without human intervention. If the chatbot uses AI methods (e.g. machine learning, natural language processing), then it can be defined as AI chatbot.

© Springer Nature Switzerland AG 2019
R. Damaševičius and G. Vasiljevienė (Eds.): ICIST 2019, CCIS 1078, pp. 33–43, 2019.
https://doi.org/10.1007/978-3-030-30275-7_4

The paper aims to demonstrate the potential of using chatbots in PM and evaluate authors' hypothesis - AI chatbots use PM can save time for project managers (and project team) and reduce factors of project failure. The paper contains results of the chatbots existing and potential possibilities for PM support, proof of concept (PoC) for implementing chatbot and a brief insight into the developed chatbot prototypes. The analysis of potential and existing capabilities of chatbots can be useful as a theoretical basis for developers and start-ups, who are planning to create a new chatbot for PM support. Capabilities of existing AI chatbots can be useful for any project manager who wants to use his/her time more efficient and is searching for the most appropriate solution. The PoC may be useful for any company that wants to understand the practical potential of a chatbot without investing a lot of resources and is searching for the right approach to start the initiative. The developed chatbot prototypes can be useful for any project managers and teams that are using tools - Slack, Jira, Skype, Google Calendar and Google Drive.

The paper is organised to cover all main results as follows: Sect. 2 describes theoretical foundation of a chatbot, theoretical use cases and analysis of the chatbots practical usage potential in PM. Section 3 describes the PoC realisation process and a brief insight into developed chatbot prototypes. Section 4 describes summary and conclusion of the developed chatbot and results.

2 PM Chatbots Feasibility Study

The future of PM is closely related to technological development, and AI is changing the way how project tasks are executed and controlled. AI solutions for PM are evolving from simple project tasks automation to forecast-based project analysis with generated advice and actions [3]. Based on Marc Lahmann research [3], the evolution of AI in PM can be divided into 4 phases (Table 1), where solutions for phases 1–3 can be found in the market, and phase 4 is a forward-looking forecast. This paper focuses on chatbots combined from Phase 2 and 3.

It is not surprising that the greatest variety of solutions are provided for Phase 1-Integration & automation – with the main focus of making PM processes more efficient. Chatbot assistants from phase 2 are taking over the basic PM tasks and relieve project teams of repetitive work that is creating little value. Phase 3 solutions - Machine learning-based PM – have a potential to be the biggest innovation in PM over the next ten years, it can give project managers more transparency about the future of the project and improve the quality of decision making. Phase 4 - Autonomous PM –in the future could act as an extension for Phase 3, especially in small, simple projects. After 10 to 20 years, it is unlikely that there will be completely autonomous AI project managers, mainly because the project budget and portfolios are controlled and will most likely be controlled by a person [3].

The authors of various studies [3, 4] see several theoretical use cases for AI chatbots in each of the competencies and knowledge areas of project manager. AI chatbots can provide the biggest support for the Technical PM competency [5] of the PMI Talent Triangle. AI chatbots have a potential of covering all knowledge areas of PM. By summarising all theoretical use cases, it was found that in order to be able to provide full support to the project managers, AI chatbots should be able to assist or replace the project manager with the following key tasks:

- Administrative tasks (e.g. generating project reports);
- Create recommendations and forecasts based on past project data (e.g. costs, resource usage, quality indicators, project schedules and risks);
- Specific work assignments (e.g. scanning, correcting contract documents, train project team)

Table 1. AI evolution in project management [3]

Phase	Executive summary	Use case example
Phase 1 Integration & automation	Streamlining and automating tasks through integration and process automation	Interaction between MS Project Online and Wunderlist for task creation and scheduling
Phase 2 Chatbot assistants	Integration and automation with additional human-computer interaction, primarily based on speech or text recognition	Stratejos.ai sends team members reminders, tracks their performance and enables the project manager to recognise top contributors based on a measurable
Phase 3 Machine learning- based PM	Enabling predictive analytics and advising the project manager based on what worked in past projects	Machine-learning-based project analytics tool predicting the expected net promoter score
Phase 4 Autonomous PM	Combining the previous phases, autonomous PM leads to little-to no human interaction in project management	Purely autonomous project managers seem unlikely within the next 10 to 20 years

As of today, there are no chatbots available that can cover all PM competencies and knowledge areas. There are specialised AI chatbots available in the market for PM and team support that can cover some of the PM competencies and knowledge areas and 4 of them are picked to be analysed in more details - Fireflies.ai, Stratejos.ai, Lili.ai and PMOtto.ai [6–10]. Table 2 summarises key functionalities that were found in specialised chatbots. Based on data in Table 2, AI chatbots functionality is more focused on automating routine PM tasks, three of them can offer functionality to identify risks (Stratejos.ai, Lili.ai and PMOtto.ai) and two chatbots (Lili.ai and PMOtto.ai) can also recommend mitigation actions. Risk identification and mitigation actions functionalities are possible under the condition of existing past project data that could be used by machine learning algorithms.

Figure 1 maps all found AI chatbots' functionalities and use cases to PM competencies in Talent Triangle [5] and knowledge areas (defined by PMI, [11]). Based on Fig. 1, all chatbots are capable of providing the biggest support to the PMs Technical competence and cover some portion of tasks in six knowledge areas: integration, scope, time, risk, communication and human resource management. Analysed AI chatbots are not covering all PM competencies and knowledge areas.

Table 2. PM Chatbots functionality

Functionality	Fireflies.ai	Stratejos.ai	Lili.ai	PMOtto.ai
Create tasks and activities in integrated project management systems	X	X	X	X
Assign tasks and activities to responsible resource	X	X	X	X
Recommend tasks and activities for project team	X	X	X	X
Create project reports		X	X	X
Recommend work estimates		X	X	X
Create and send reminders to project team		X	X	X
Identify risks		X	X	X
Identify risks and recommend mitigation actions			X	X
Recommend priorities for tasks and activities			X	X

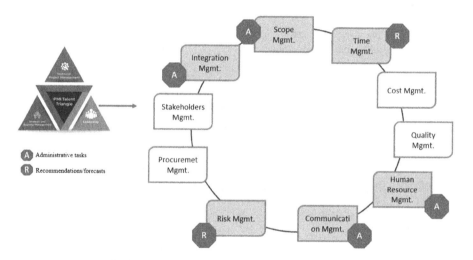

Fig. 1. Practical possibilities of analysed AI chatbots

3 PM Chatbot Prototype

In order to prove the hypothesis of the paper 'AI chatbots use in PM can save time for project managers (and project team) and reduce factors of project failure', PoC is used with the steps and realization process that can be easily re-used by any company that is interested in chatbots implementation by using one of available Conversational AI platforms. Data used in PoC are based on project manager knowledge and experience in a project used for PoC case study. Figure 2 illustrates the realization process of PoC with all key elements described in the next paragraphs.

In high level, PoC consists of three user stories that are identified in Employee Journey Mapping (EJM), two limitations and classification of a Chatbot.

One of the latest approaches for analysing and improving customer experience is a method called Customer Journey Mapping (CJM) and, respectively, if the subject is an employee, then it is defined as EJM. The main purpose of this method is to display an

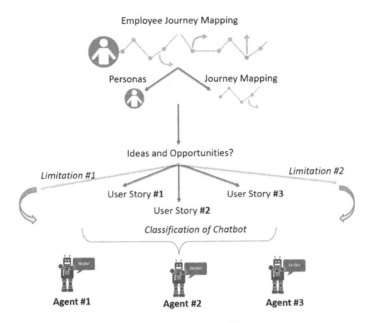

Fig. 2. The summary of PoC realisation process

employee's experience storywise by breaking it down in stages and by looking into the experience from a different point of views, which thus helps to see the problems better and make possible improvements. EJM method has two main deliverables – Persona and Journey mapping of this persona. A persona is a collective image for a specific group of employees that reflects the behaviour patterns of that group; for this paper purposes, we use selected project manager's daily experience while implementing PoC case project. The project manager's experience data is covering development phase of the project with six stages – Concept/Design, Development and Unit Tests, Ready for SIT and UAT, UAT Testing, Deploy and Closing. The duration of PoC case project development phase with six stages took about 100.17 workdays. There are tools in place that are used by the project manager and team and which will take part in further user stories – Jira is used for project planning, tracking and management, Google Drive is used for project data storage, and Google Calendar is used to schedule meetings with project stakeholders. Slack and Skype are used as main messaging platforms.

In EJM section 'Ideas and Opportunities', project manager together with the researcher, defined all improvement ideas and opportunities that he found for each stage and problem. All found ideas and opportunities are copied from EJM into Table 3 with the additional column 'Chatbot' that identifies if the idea can be potentially implemented using a Chatbot. Stage column displays for what project stage the idea or opportunity were identified.

Table 3. Description of Ideas and Opportunities and Chatbot feasibility

#	Idea or opportunity	Stage	Chatbot?
1	Use a tool that can help to find the best appointment time slot with all project stakeholders	• Concept and Design • Development and Unit Tests	Y
2	Discuss priorities for projects with concept owners and managers	• Concept and Design	N
3	Simplify and reduce the number of tools needed in the project	• Concept and Design	Y
4	Make it easier to define new change requests when requirements come from 2 different communication channels - Skype and Slack	• Development and Unit Tests	Y
5	Automate developers work with Jira where possible	• Development and Unit Tests • Ready for SIT and UAT • UAT Testing	Y
6	Involve stakeholders (where possible) in early testing phases	• UAT Testing	N
7	Automate developers work with the Deployment tool	• Deployment	Y

Table 4. The mapping of ideas and user stories

#	User story	Description	Idea #
1	Slack and Jira	As a developer, I should have the possibility by using Slack messaging platform to view, comment and make changes to assigned issues and user stories in Jira project management tool	#3 and #5
2	Skype and Calendar	As a project manager, I should have the possibility by using Skype messaging platform to plan appointments in my calendar	#1 and #3
3	Skype and Google Drive	As a project manager, I should have the possibility by using Skype messaging platform to automatically enter new change requests that come from chat conversation with project stakeholders	#3 and #4

The description of ideas and opportunities is insufficient to develop the Chatbot. Therefore, the ideas and opportunities found in the previous table are expanded by using user stories. Table 4 illustrates the mapping between ideas and user stories to be implemented.

To make PoC more suitable for real-life scenarios, two limitations have been defined:

1. The AI Chatbot should demonstrate that it uses AI methods. The purpose of this limitation is to reduce time for Chatbot configuration without entering countless test data.

2. Solutions should be tailored to business needs and free/open source where possible. The purpose of this limitation is to make sure that chosen solutions are customizable after the PoC realisation and cost-effective.

The next step is to classify chatbots using classification that is suggested by authors - Ketakee Nimavat, Tushar Champaneria [13] where Chatbots have been classified using four categories. Figure 3 illustrates that the designed PM Chatbot should match to highlighted categories: closed domain, inter-personal, information base and hybrid system.

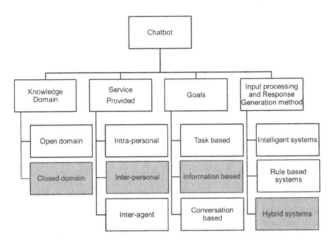

Fig. 3. Classification of a Chatbot

Designed PM Chatbot prototype implementation has done using the Dialogflow Conversational platform where for each user story a separate test agent has been created. To ensure integration with the Jira PM tool, BenTen's open-source conversational platform is used, which is integrated with the Dialogflow agent for natural

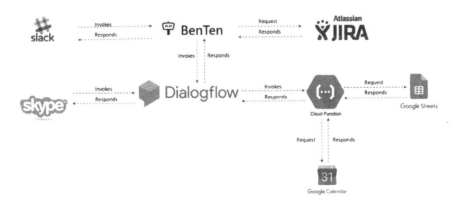

Fig. 4. High level technical solution for PoC

language processing. The relevant Google Application Interfaces (APIs) and Dialog-flow Cloud features are used to integrate with Google Drive and Google Calendar. Dialogflow is integrated with two messaging software – Skype and Slack. Figure 4 illustrates the high-level technical solution for PoC with the more detailed implementation has been described in Table 5.

Table 5. User stories implementation

User story	Implementation	Print screen example
#1	Data are being viewed and updated in Jira system, and users' communication happens through Slack messaging platform. The core of the solution is BenTen open source Conversational Platform with built-in integration with Jira. BenTen uses agent created in Dialogflow platform for input data processing and generates responses in BenTen platform.	
#2	Calendar data are viewed and updated in Google Calendar, and users' communication happens through Skype. The core of the solution is Dialogflow's Cloud Functions – index.js un package.json (Dialogflow Fulfillment section).	
#3	GoogleDrive data are viewed and updated in Google Drive, and users' communication happens through Skype. The core of the solution is Dialogflow's Cloud Functions – index.js un package.json (Dialogflow Fulfillment section).	

4 Summary and Conclusion

The PoC was successfully completed, and hypothesis validated with AI chatbot prototypes. According to the hypothesis, AI chatbot should:

- Save time for project managers and team.

The use of AI chatbots in PM can save project manager (and project team) time, which is proved not only with the benefits of implemented user stories (Fig. 5) but also by making calculations using the project data of the PoC case project used in EJM. The duration of development phase with six stages took about 100.17 workdays, PoC implementation took about 30 h, and the merging would take 30 h more, which in total would be 60 h. All used solutions and platforms in PoC were cost free. If we assume that all three implemented user stories could save at least 10 min per day for the project manager, then that would be about $\sim$ 17 h saved per project. If we assume that #1 user story could save at least 5 min per day for a development team, that is, three people for the whole development phase, then that would be about $\sim$ 25 h saved per project. In total, it would be 42 h saved per project for the whole team. After two projects of this size, the investment for implementing the Chatbot would be paid off.

- Reduce factors of project failure.

The main three goals and benefits of developed user stories were (1) to save time for a project team and project manager (2) to reduce project risks (3) to improve project transparency. The mapping of the project failure factors [12] and the benefits of developed user stories are displayed in Fig. 5. Figure 5 illustrates what benefits of implemented user stories can directly or indirectly affect and reduce project failure factors. Project failure factors that can be affected with the Chatbot are marked and split in red and blue. The benefits of created user stories are marked with blue and red identifying whether the impact to the project failure is direct or indirect. For example, the benefit of user story 'improve project transparency' can directly affect such project failure factor like - 'Lack of clearly defined and/or achievable milestones and objectives to measure progress', 'Poor communication' and 'Lack of communication by senior management'. The benefits of developed user stories and mapping to failure factors were selected by the project manager of PoC case project.

AI chatbots can provide the greatest benefit to the Technical PM competence that can be explained by the fact that the algorithms of the necessary skills (such as modelling of earned value, lifecycle management and requirements traceability) do not differ significantly among different projects or industries. Strategic and business management competence is subject to a field where the project manager operates. To be able to automate Strategic and Business Management competency, vertical chatbots solutions would be needed. Currently, none of the analysed AI chatbots are able to provide value for skills under Leadership competency (coaching, brainstorming, emotional intelligence, etc.), but that does not mean that there are no ready-made solutions for individual skills. For example, there are chatbots built specifically for training purposes (e.g. Leena.ai).

Comparing chatbots with various project management systems and tools (such as MS Project, Knightspear, Teodesk, Clarizen, Forecast), the deployment of a chatbot in ongoing projects does not require much resources and most importantly, project managers can continue to use existing PM tools as they have done so far by adjusting chatbot to their needs. The purposefully created chatbot can be an intuitive, simple and cost-effective project manager tool as has been shown with PoC in this paper.

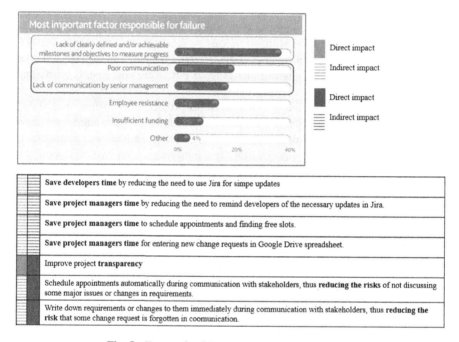

Fig. 5. Factors for failure and user stories mapping

The value of AI chatbot is the biggest when it is ready to create project recommendations and identify risks using project experience data. This can be explained by the fact that project managers often make intuitive recommendations and risk identification and initialisation of each new project is unlikely to summarise the experiences of past projects. If the project data are not centralised, mutually checked or missing, then it is not possible to use them to make any predictions or recommendations. For example, if a company does not define project portfolio management processes and project managers do not follow common processes, then it is very difficult or even impossible to apply algorithms since there are many unknown and missing data. There are AI chatbots (for example, Lili.ai) that offers AI services to solve this problem, according to the Lili.ai product offer's description, the company offers a service that can transform project experience data (such as Excel spreadsheets, PowerPoint slides) into raw data and then apply the AI methods for data analysis. Unfortunately, it is currently only a theory and the product and service are still under development, and no technical explanation of the solution is available.

Chatbots can be an excellent project manager assistant and automate a large part of routine project management tasks. However, if there is need to automate just one user story (for example # 1 - Jira integration), then the chatbot is not the most successful solution as there are several applications that can better implement Slack and Jira integration, for example, 'Jira Cloud' app.

The further planned research will focus more on predictive PM Chatbots that based on project past experience are capable to generate recommendations.

References

1. Kolbjørnsrud, V., Amico, R., Thomas, R.J.: How Artificial Intelligence Will Redefine Management. https://hbr.org/2016/11/how-artificial-intelligence-will-redefine-management
2. Smartsheet Homepage: Artificial Intelligence Chatbots Are Changing the Way You Do Business and May Impact Your Bottom Line. https://www.smartsheet.com/artificial-intelligence-chatbots
3. Lahmann, M.: AI will transform project management. Are you ready?. https://www.pwc.ch/en/insights/risk/transformation-assurance-ai-will-transform-project-management-are-you-ready.html
4. Mendieta, C: Project management & AI: a vision for the next decade. https://christianmendieta.ca/project-management-and-artificial-intelligence
5. Project Management Institute: The PMI Talent Triangle. https://www.pmi.org/-/media/pmi/documents/public/pdf/certifications/talent-triangle-flyer.pdf
6. Riter Development team: Artificial Intelligence in today's project management. https://riter.co/blog/artificial-intelligence-in-today-s-project-management
7. Fireflies Homepage. https://blogs.fireflies.ai/fireflies-customers/
8. Stratejos Homepage. https://stratejos.ai/
9. Lili Homepage. http://lili.ai/lili
10. PMOtto Homepage. https://www.pmotto.ai/
11. Project Management Institute: PMBOK® Guide – Sixth Edition. Project management Body of Knowledge (2017)
12. McCay, A. https://uxpressia.com/blog/employee-experience-journey-example
13. Nimavat, K., Champaneria, T.: Chatbots: an overview. Types, architecture, tools and future possibilities. IJSRD - Int. J. Sci. Res. Dev. 5(07), 1019–1026 (2017)

Decision-Making Algorithms for ERP Systems in Road Maintenance Work

Jānis Pekša$^{(\boxtimes)}$ (iD)

Institute of Information Technology, Riga Technical University,
Kalku Street 1, Riga, Latvia
Janis.Peksa@rtu.lv

Abstract. The article reviews the studies carried out so far for road mainte-nance work. Exploring approaches in which raw data can be processed from road weather-stations to actual forecasting and forecasting model creation. The goal is to be able to make forecasting and build the best forecasting models that will be implemented into the BaSeCaaS platform in the future. Forecasting is designed to improve the current situation during the winter months for road maintenders for better decision-making. Initially, the missing data is filled to be able to make forecasting possible. Several methods are applied and identified, which is the best from an accuracy perspective. An experiment is conducted with ARIMA the best forecasting model for the particular dataset. As well as looking for the best approach to updating the forecasting model parameter to improve accuracy and better results. The concept is created under this article, and the BPMN of Road Maintainers Case process is reflected. Uptake of the current research is depicted in forecasting UML class diagram that is created and represented within the UML sequence diagram of the forecasting process.

Keywords: Forecasting · Decision-making · ERP systems · Road maintenance

1 Introduction

Enterprise resource planning (ERP) systems are large modular enterprise applications intended for execution of the majority of enterprise business processes. They are pri-marily geared towards transaction processing. However, many modules contain com-plex decision-making logic [1]. Data processing logic is deemed as complex decision-making logic if it relies on analytical or managerial models for determining a course of action in business process execution and often requires domain-specific knowledge. Examples of decision-making logics are inventory replenishment, road-network maintenance, and production planning decisions. The demand for accurate decisions has grown forcing ERP to improve the decision-making process, at both strategic and operational levels, by providing the necessary information, tools, and capabilities necessary to enhance the decision-making process [2]. However, many modules con-tain complex forecasting methods and are part of decision-making logic [1]. Fore-casting is a process for predicting the future based on past data, and most often through a trend analysis [3]. Prediction is one of the cases that business needs in high demand to gain higher profit and continue successfully business processes [4]. ERP systems have

© Springer Nature Switzerland AG 2019
R. Damaševičius and G. Vasiljevienė (Eds.): ICIST 2019, CCIS 1078, pp. 44–55, 2019.
https://doi.org/10.1007/978-3-030-30275-7_5

limited forecasting capabilities that are implemented into a hard-coded code [5]. Enterprises spend much money to modify existing methods to satisfy their requirements [6]. Some of ERP systems do not have enough forecasting functionality. Forecasting functionality is used as an opportunity that can be enhanced by predictive capabilities in ERP systems.

Firstly, the concept between BaSeCaaS platform and the Road Maintenders with Open Data using API is represented and explained with the BPMN of Road Maintainers Case with three involved parties Road Managers, ERP systems, BaSeCaaS. Secondly, the forecasting UML class diagram is created and represented within the UML sequence diagram of forecasting. Finally, the results are represented by forecasting model with ARIMA(4,1,5), the accuracy of ARIMA(4,1,5), accuracy for each method used for missing data filling and accuracy for each algorithm that can update forecasting models parameter.

The objective of this paper is to represent architecture approach and its design on implementation of decision-making in the ERP system for the road maintenance work. As well as reflect the studies carried out so far in order to facilitate the perception of research.

The rest of the paper is structured as follows: Sect. 2 represents the background and related work; Sect. 3 concept and architecture are shown; Sect. 4 design of the forecasting is extended; Sect. 5 represents the results of researches that are made so far and Sect. 6 concludes and directs future work.

2 Background and Related Work

2.1 Decision-Making Algorithms

As already known, there are three significant categories of forecasts: economic forecasts [7, 8] defines technological forecasts and demand forecasts provided in [9] representing forecast evolution. There are many types of forecasting methods in these three categories. The research takes only quantitative forecasting methods though there are also qualitative forecasting methods like:

- Executive Opinion – use a composite forecast prepared by several individual experts [10];
- Market Survey – forecast method when speaking to members of the target audience [11];
- Delphi Method – use in policymaking and organizational decision making [12];
- Salesforce – to view the best estimate of revenue generating in a specified time frame [13].

Quantitative forecasting methods are based on mathematical models, and they are objective [14]. These methods only can be applied when the following conditions are met. The first condition is that statistical information is available about the past and the other condition and it can be assumed that some of the aspects of previous patterns will continue in the future [15]. There are many quantitative forecasting methods to reduce the number of methods to be considered the time-series forecasting is selected.

A time-series model in forecasting uses historical data as the basis for estimating future outcomes. There are two types of time-series – continuous and discrete [16]. For discrete time-series, it is the time axis that is discrete while continuous time-series the observed variable is typically a continuous variable recorded continuously on a trace. Several forecasting procedures are based on a time-series model [17]. Some of them are listed below:

- Autoregressive integrated moving average – also known as ARIMA, is fitted to time-series data to understand the data better or to predict future points in the series [18];
- Automatic model selection – the system analyzes the historical data and then selects the most eligible model [19];
- Box–Jenkins method – to find the best fit of a time-series model to past values of a time-series [20] applies autoregressive moving average (ARMA) and use ARIMA as a set;
- Linear regression – a statistical method that allows to summarize and study relationships between two continuous quantitative variables [21] and it is the best-known demand forecasting method for a trendy demand [22];
- Moving average – an analysis tool that smooths out price data by creating a regularly updated average price [23];
- Holt-Winters method – one of the time-series with the trend but with seasonality [24] and to forecast for "what-if" analysis [25] and one of popular is an additive method [26];
- Weighted moving average – puts more weight on recent data and less on past data [27].

2.2 Road Maintenance

Road maintenances works are very diverse and specific ranging from laying of the road surface to daily maintenance activities. Many stakeholders including managers, dispatchers, and maintenance teams are involved, and maintenance decisions need to be made in a timely manner [28]. Proactive maintenance activities are enabled by forecasting. Forecasting provides advance information about the required maintenance activities. The anti-slip maintenance is performed only in winter to provide anti-slip materials at a specific time and place on the road surface. The anti-slip maintenance nowadays uses live contextual data from many different sources [29] including open data sources [30] and decision-making results significantly depend on data availability [31]. A pastime may affect the essential operations of the road-network in total. One of them is driving conditions when traffic speed is rapid. The higher the speed rate, the greater the probability that accidents are possible [32]. As know, the road conditions are subject to rapid changes in surface temperature and precipitation sum. The road conditions most fluctuations are observed during the winter period; however, the road condition is also affected by the snow and icing. The road maintenance is performed for specific Road Sections belonging to a Region.

The region in research is the Republic of Latvia road network, and the dataset is taken from VAS "Latvijas valsts celi". The region consists of 52 road monitoring weather-stations that are relatively distant from each other. To be able to respond to changes in the environment on road sections near the road surface are located road monitoring weather-stations and cameras operated by different entities. The road monitoring weather-stations collects raw observations which are processed to be able to make the necessary forecasting for future decisions. For road maintainers, those predictions are crucial to making decisions daily. The road monitoring weather-stations and cameras operated by different entities can help for the decision-making. The road maintainers controlling smart road signs are available to give warning messages to drivers on a specific stage of the road network [33]. The missing information in the time-series of meteorological stations is unavoidable, owing to the full observation of all the continuous processes is almost impossible [34].

3 Concept and Architecture Between BaSeCaaS Platform and ERP Systems

Big Data Stream Processing Capabilities as a Service (BaSeCaaS) is the platform to turn real-time big data publishing and processing into a consumer product by developing real-time big data processing platform, market and associated standardized, high abstraction technological solutions. The purpose of the platform is to provide consumers with the necessary data and information for business process execution. The provided benefits are [35, 36]:

- For data owners – simplified data publishing and selling to consumers;
- For data consumers – the ability to receive on-demand data and information for executing business systems and processes, the discovery of the best data providers, access to data use best practices and lightweight data subscription process;
- For analytics – the ability to publish and sell data use best practices and patterns which are shared with all interested parties through the platform.

Big data processing can be performed as batch processing or as (real-time) stream processing. The project is concerned with processing big data streams since this approach is not as widespread as the batch processing and it has great potential. The main advantage of the stream processing is getting the instantaneous result from the data and sufficiently minimized latency between the data source and decision making. As a result of this project, it is planned to build a cloud-based platform (BaSeCaaS platform) providing big data stream processing capabilities as a service [36].

Open data is data that anyone can access, use and share. Governments, businesses, and individuals can use open data to bring about social, economic and environmental benefits [30]. The dataset of the Republic of Latvia road network is taken from VAS "Latvijas valsts celi". This dataset is open data and can be used at any time. Several tasks can be defined for the BaSeCaaS platform; if the data is too much, then they are processed horizontally, taking advantage of the platform. As real-time data is known, there is always plenty of resources and a platform to handle them effectively. As is known today, the vast majority use the Application programming interface (API) capabilities to carry out cross-platform relationships between platforms. API is a set of subroutine definitions, communication protocols, and tools for building software. A group method of communication among various components the concept is shown in Fig. 1.

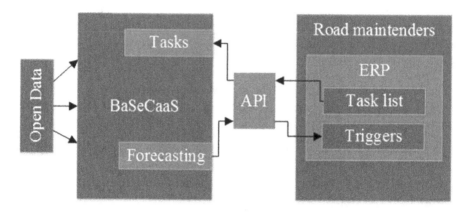

Fig. 1. The concept between BaSeCaaS platform and the Road Maintenders with Open Data using API.

The road maintenders can define a specific list of tasks sent to the BaSeCaaS platform. Tasks are needed in everyday work and can be modified or at any time can send a new task. The definition of the task depends on the situation at the specified stage of the road. During the winter months, the road maintenders are already able to predict the conditions under which the relevant road maintenance activities are required. When drawing up a list of tasks on the road maintenance work, it defines more precise events that need to be handled and in which cases there must be a feedback link or even a warning so-called trigger.

Road maintenders use ERP systems to build and record ongoing business processes. Task lists are created in ERP systems that allow road maintenders not only to see historical events but also with the BaSeCaaS forecasting models to predict future events going on even more accurately. BaSeCaaS as an additional tool allows road maintenders to make the right decisions in different situations and automatically release a trigger notification in a crisis. Forecasting is based on the corresponding definition from road maintenders, which has defined specific parameters and attributes to be able to work correctly on forecasting models and their results using BaSeCaaS platform. In Fig. 2 is represented proposal business process through Business Process Model and Notation (BPMN) showing the activity of representing processes of an enterprise with road maintenance work.

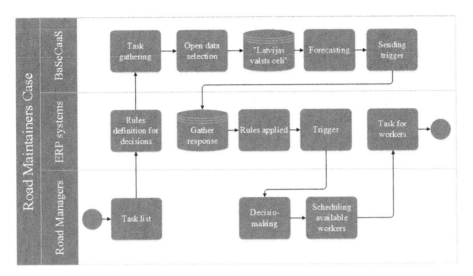

Fig. 2. The BPMN of Road Maintainers Case with three involved parties Road Managers, ERP systems, BaSeCaaS.

BPMN makes it easier to discern the business process of Road Maintainers Case from Road managers using API capabilities through the ERP system and to execute forecasting models on the BaSeCaaS platform. The Task list is transferred initially from the idea to the ERP system to create rules definition for decisions. These definitions are transferred to BaSeCaaS, which compiles the corresponding tasks. BaSeCaaS selects the relevant Open data, which in this case is the "Latvijas valsts cels" dataset. Forecasting starts according to the criteria and their tasks, data processing, selection of the forecasting model, and only then forecasting. One of the data processing is that appropriate approaches replace missing data to more accurate forecasting. The selection of the forecasting model depends at the moment on the whole of the most accurate model, which shows the best result, respectively, or is the most accurate at the moment. The BaSeCaaS platform is designed in the future to be able to choose an autonomous forecasting model for a particular dataset. After forecasting is done to ERP system is send trigger that represents response that was configured when creating task list rules definition. ERP system gathers response from BaSeCaaS and if rules apply to Road Managers definitions than trigger is sent to the Road Managers as quick as possible. Decision-making starts when Road Managers places scheduling available workers based on forecasting results. To available workers are send to specific road-network part and instructions are sent within minutes. The goal is to respond to crises that are changing dramatically.

4 Design of the Forecasting

Forecasting is widely demanded in the business environment; however, each forecasting starts with its design. For this chapter, forecasting design may include ModelSelection, Algorithms, Regions, ModelValidation and ParameterUpdate, represented in Fig. 3 with UML class diagram.

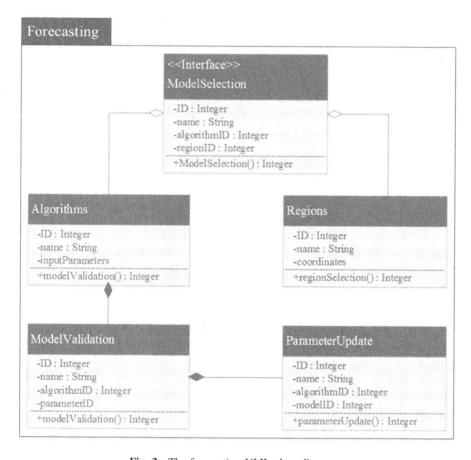

Fig. 3. The forecasting UML class diagram.

Each consists of the functionality like model selection for the best forecasting model. The most common one using algorithms are defined as the best one. On each region is used a different algorithm and is created, new model. For validation is used accuracy to tell which the best one model fits in. After running forecasting and comparing results the forecasting models parameter is updated to increase the accuracy of the forecasting model and the forecasting result. Looping through those result accuracies slightly goes up.

Any information is originally raw data, which means that the data has not been processed and has come from a primary source. In this case, raw data comes from weather-stations located in different regions. To prepare raw data, it is needed to perform data preprocessing to continue for the next step. The forecasting model is selected in the next step; however, the forecasting model is validated multiple times, and the last best model is taken. After the model is selected, forecasting can be done. As new to the forecasting, it is necessary to update the best parameter that is found to be able to improve forecasting results. The results of forecasting corresponding to specific criteria shall be sent to the trigger with the results concerned. The relevant event sequence is displayed in Fig. 4 the UML sequence diagram of the forecasting process.

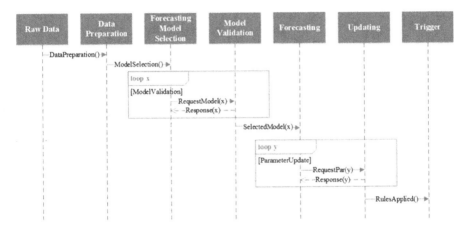

Fig. 4. The UML sequence diagram of the forecasting process.

The loops are used for finding the best forecasting model for the relevant raw data as well as the best forecasting parameter for the desired algorithm. The results of the research are carried out in the next chapter.

5 Results

In previous researches are gathered results with R programming forecasting for 416 data points in future are done with forecasting model ARIMA(4,1,5). However, the blue line representing in Fig. 5 forecasting it goes close to a straight line soon, which seems unlikely given past behavior of the time-series.

Once the model is created, the models' accuracy is checked by the precision with the accuracy function that returns ME, RMSE, MAE, MASE and ACF1 values which can be used to measure the accuracy of the model results shown in Table 1.

Forecast from ARIMA(4,1,5)

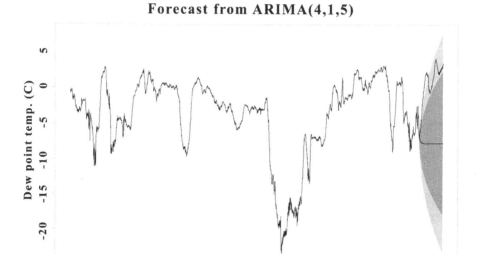

Fig. 5. The portion of data set from 6000 to 6416 data points.

Table 1. Accuracy of ARIMA(4,1,5).

Type	Accuracy
ME	0.0003
RMSE	0.205
MAE	0.124
MASE	1.006
ACF1	0.0003

The obtained results make it possible to compare them with future forecasting models in the future, which will be designed to apply the one with the least error of accuracy. Next step in the research was to deal with the missing data that is calculated using the following methods: Normal ratio method using a spreadsheet for calculation. On the other hand, k-nearest neighbors algorithm is made up of examples of the nearest training in the function space using Orange Visual Programming tool for prediction and RMSE estimation and next method MLP neural network is used with parameters neurons in hidden layers. RMSE for each method is calculated; the results are represented in Table 2.

Table 2. Accuracy for each method.

Method	RMSE
Normal ratio method	0.35
k-nearest neighbors algorithm	0.23
MLP neural network	0.21

Table 3. Accuracy for each algorithm.

Algorithm	Region RMSE							
	R1	R2	R3	R4	R5	R6	R7	R8
Simple moving average	0.02	0.36	0.38	0.36	0.54	0.83	0.62	0.48
Arithmetic mean	0.05	0.10	0.35	0.43	0.55	0.79	0.70	0.50
Bayesian average	0.10	0.27	0.37	0.39	0.53	0.73	0.65	0.47
k-Means Clustering	0.03	0.16	0.37	0.36	0.52	0.77	0.64	0.51
Expectation–Maximization	0.02	0.09	0.31	0.30	0.49	0.69	0.58	0.44

The corresponding algorithms are used for each region, and their results are reflected in Table 3.

The Expectation–maximization algorithm has proven that it is one of the most accurate compared to other algorithms. Each time a new portion of raw data comes in from the road monitoring weather-stations, the corresponding algorithm will be called to calculate an already new parameter required by algorithms to increase the accuracy of forecasting results.

6 Conclusions and Future Work

The road maintainers can analyze many sources to make decisions during the winter season to be able to serve and maintain the current road surface state more effectively. The road monitoring weather-stations allows collecting raw observations close to the road surface; allowing raw observations to be processed. To be able to predict these observations is needed. After processing the raw observations concerned, they may be used for forecasting purposes. Forecasting techniques are different types of algorithms and approaches. The researches with experiments that demonstrate the accuracy of the approach is necessary to assess the best results.

The research paper identifies further research direction on the generalized hybrid method on real-time forecasting for time-series. Compared to actual results and using a repeating method that can process real-time data and be able to adapt to the current situation, using modern solutions with programming language capabilities. One of the crucial elements is to produce so-called hybrid forecasting model for the road maintenance case. In the future, creating modular forecasting models implementation into BaSeCaaS platform using it as autonomous decision-making support service for road maintenance managers.

References

1. Holsapple, C.W., Sena, M.P.: ERP plans and decision-support benefits. Decis. Support Syst. **38**, 575–590 (2005). https://doi.org/10.1016/j.dss.2003.07.001
2. Bahrami, B., Jordan, E.: Utilizing enterprise resource planning in decision-making processes. In: Piazolo, F., Felderer, M. (eds.) Innovation and Future of Enterprise Information Systems. LNISO, vol. 4, pp. 153–168. Springer, Heidelberg (2013). https://doi.org/10.1007/978-3-642-37021-2_13

3. Hyndman, R.J., Makridakis, S., Wheelwright, S.C.: Forecasting—Methods and Applications. Wiley, New York (1998)
4. Browne, C., Geiger, T.: The Executive Opinion Survey: The Voice of the Business. Tourism, pp. 85–96 (2013)
5. Jacobs, R.F., Chase, R.B.: Operations and Supply Chain Management. McGraw-Hill, New York (2018)
6. Aslan, B., Stevenson, M., Hendry, L.C.: Enterprise resource planning systems: an assessment of applicability to make-to-order companies. Comput. Ind. **63**, 692–705 (2012). https://doi.org/10.1016/j.compind.2012.05.003
7. Gudac, I., Marovic, I., Hanak, T.: Sustainable optimization of winter road maintenance services under real-time information. Procedia Eng. **85**, 183–192 (2014). https://doi.org/10.1016/j.proeng.2014.10.543
8. Martino, J.P.: Technologies Forecasting for Decision Making. McGraw-Hill, Inc., New York (1972)
9. Güllü, R.: On the value of information in dynamic production/inventory problems under forecast evolution. Nav. Res. Logist. **43**, 289–303 (2004). https://doi.org/10.1002/(sici)1520-6750(199603)43:2<289::aid-nav8>3.0.co;2-6
10. Dalrymple, D.J.: Sales forecasting practices. Results from a United States survey. Int. J. Forecast. **3**, 379–391 (1987). https://doi.org/10.1016/0169-2070(87)90031-8
11. Wilkins, L., Moser, C.A.: Survey Methods in Social Investigation. Routledge, London (2007). https://doi.org/10.2307/587572
12. Brady, S.R.: Utilizing and adapting the Delphi method for use in qualitative research. Int. J. Qual. Methods **14** (2015). https://doi.org/10.1177/1609406915621381
13. Balboni, B., Terho, H.: Outward-looking and future-oriented customer value potential management: the sales force value appropriation role. Ind. Mark. Manag. **53**, 181–193 (2016). https://doi.org/10.1016/j.indmarman.2015.05.022
14. Zhang, Y.: Time Series Analysis. Oxford University Press, Oxford (2013). https://doi.org/10.1093/oxfordhb/9780199934898.013.0022
15. Hyndman, R.J., Athanasopoulos, G.: Forecasting: Principles and Practice. OTexts, Melbourne (2018)
16. Mundle, F.I.B., Makridakis, S., Wheelwright, S.: Forecasting methods for managers. J. Oper. Res. Soc. **29**, 282 (2006). https://doi.org/10.2307/3009460
17. Chatfield, C.: Time-series forecasting. Chapman and Hall/CRC, Boca Raton (2005). https://doi.org/10.1111/j.1740-9713.2005.00117.x
18. Conejo, A.J., Plazas, M.A., Espínola, R., Molina, A.B.: Day-ahead electricity price forecasting using the wavelet transform and ARIMA models. IEEE Trans. Power Syst. **20**, 1035–1042 (2005). https://doi.org/10.1109/TPWRS.2005.846054
19. Kourentzes, N.: On intermittent demand model optimization and selection. Int. J. Prod. Econ. **156**, 180–190 (2014). https://doi.org/10.1016/j.ijpe.2014.06.007
20. Makridakis, S.: ARMA models and the box-jenkins methodology. J. Forecast. **16**, 147–163 (1997)
21. Kraft, S., Pacheco-Sanchez, S., Casale, G., Dawson, S.: Estimating service resource consumption from response time measurements. In: Proceedings of the Fourth International ICST Conference on Performance Evaluation Methodologies and Tools, p. 48 (2012). https://doi.org/10.4108/icst.valuetools2009.7526
22. Nenni, M.E., Giustiniano, L., Pirolo, L.: Demand forecasting in the fashion industry: a review. Int. J. Eng. Bus. Manag. **5** (2013). https://doi.org/10.5772/56840
23. Belbag, S., Cimen, M., Tan, S., Tas, A.: A research on corporate Enterprise Resource Planning (ERP) systems used for supermarket supply chain inventory management in Turkey. Eur. J. Sci. Res. **38**, 486–499 (2009)

24. Gulyassy, F., Hoppe, M., Hermann, M., Kohler, O.: Materials planning with SAP. Galileo Press, München (2010)
25. Houghton, L., Kerr, D.V.: A study into the creation of feral information systems as a response to an ERP implementation within the supply chain of a large government-owned corporation. Int. J. Internet Enterp. Manag. **4**, 135 (2015). https://doi.org/10.1504/ijiem. 2006.010239
26. Sugiarto, V. C., Sarno, R., Sunaryono, D.: Sales forecasting using Holt-Winters in enterprise resource planning at sales and distribution module. In: 2016 International Conférence on Information & Communication Technology and Systems (ICTS), pp. 8–13 (2016)
27. Taylor, J.W.: Multi-item sales forecasting with total and split exponential smoothing. J. Oper. Res. Soc. **62**, 555–563 (2011). https://doi.org/10.1057/jors.2010.95
28. Grabis, J., Bondars, Ž., Kampars, J., Dobelis, Ē., Zaharčukovs, A.: Context-aware customizable routing solution for fleet management. In: Proceedings of the 19th International Conference on Enterprise Information Systems, ICEIS 2017, pp. 638–645 (2017). https://doi.org/10.5220/0006366006380645
29. Pindyck, R.S., Rubinfeld, D.L.: Econometric Models and Economic Forecasts, p. 664 (1998)
30. Zdravkovic, J., Kampars, J., Stirna, J.: Using open data to support organizational capabilities in dynamic business contexts. In: Matulevičius, R., Dijkman, R. (eds.) CAiSE 2018. LNBIP, vol. 316, pp. 28–39. Springer, Cham (2018). https://doi.org/10.1007/978-3-319-92898-2_3
31. Grabis, J., Minkēviča, V.: Context-aware multi-objective vehicle routing. In: Proceedings of 31st European Conference on Modelling and Simulation, pp. 235–239 (2017). https://doi.org/10.7148/2017-0235
32. Edwards, J.B.: Speed adjustment of motorway commuter traffic to inclement weather. Transp. Res. Part F Traffic Psychol. Behav. **2**, 1–14 (1999). https://doi.org/10.1016/S1369-8478(99)00003-0
33. Nguwi, Y.Y., Kouzani, A.Z.: Detection and classification of road signs in natural environments. Neural Comput. Appl. **17**, 265–289 (2008). https://doi.org/10.1007/s00521-007-0120-z
34. Jeffrey, S.J., Carter, J.O., Moodie, K.B., Beswick, A.R.: Using spatial interpolation to construct a comprehensive archive of Australian climate data. Environ. Model. Softw. **16**, 309–330 (2001). https://doi.org/10.1016/S1364-8152(01)00008-1
35. Kampars, J., Grabis, J.: Near real-time big-data processing for data driven applications. In: Proceedings of the 2017 International Conference on Big Data Innovations and Applications, Innovate-Data 2017, pp. 35–42. IEEE (2018). https://doi.org/10.1109/Innovate-Data.2017.11
36. Grabis, J., Kampars, J., Pinka, K., Pekša, J.: A data streams processing platform for matching information demand and data supply. In: Cappiello, C., Ruiz, M. (eds.) CAiSE 2019. LNBIP, vol. 350, pp. 111–119. Springer, Cham (2019). https://doi.org/10.1007/978-3-030-21297-1_10

Business Intelligence for Information and Software Systems: Special Session on Intelligent Methods for Data Analysis and Computer-Aided Software Engineering

TabbyXL: Rule-Based Spreadsheet Data Extraction and Transformation

Alexey Shigarov[1,2(✉)], Vasiliy Khristyuk[1], Andrey Mikhailov[1],
and Viacheslav Paramonov[1,2]

[1] Matrosov Institute for System Dynamics and Control Theory of SB RAS,
134 Lermontov st., Irkutsk, Russia
shigarov@icc.ru

[2] Institute of Mathematics, Economics and Informatics, Irkutsk State University,
20 Gagarin blvd., Irkutsk, Russia
http://cells.icc.ru

Abstract. This paper presents an approach to rule-based spreadsheet data extraction and transformation. We determine a table object model and domain-specific language of table analysis and interpretation rules. In contrast to the existing data transformation languages, we draw up this process as consecutive steps: role analysis, structural analysis, and interpretation. To the best of our knowledge, there are no languages for expressing rules for transforming tabular data into the relational form in terms of the table understanding. We also consider a tool for transforming spreadsheet data from arbitrary to relational tables. The performance evaluation has been done automatically for both (role and structural) stages of table analysis with the prepared ground-truth data. It shows high F-score from 95.82% to 99.04% for different recovered items in the existing dataset of 200 arbitrary tables of the same genre (government statistics).

Keywords: Data extraction · Data transformation · Table analysis · Rule-based programming · Spreadsheet

1 Introduction

A big volume of arbitrary tables (e.g. cross-tabulations, invoices, roadmaps, and data collection forms) circulates in spreadsheet-like formats. Mitlöhner et al. [28] estimate that about 10% of the resources in Open Data portals are labeled as CSV (Comma-Separated Values), a spreadsheet-like format. Barik et al. [2] extracted 0.25M unique spreadsheets from COMMON CRAWL[1] archive. Chen and Cafarella [6] reported about 0.4M spreadsheets of CLUEWEB09 CRAWL[2] archive.

---

[1] http://commoncrawl.org.
[2] http://lemurproject.org/clueweb09.

© Springer Nature Switzerland AG 2019
R. Damaševičius and G. Vasiljevienė (Eds.): ICIST 2019, CCIS 1078, pp. 59–75, 2019.
https://doi.org/10.1007/978-3-030-30275-7_6

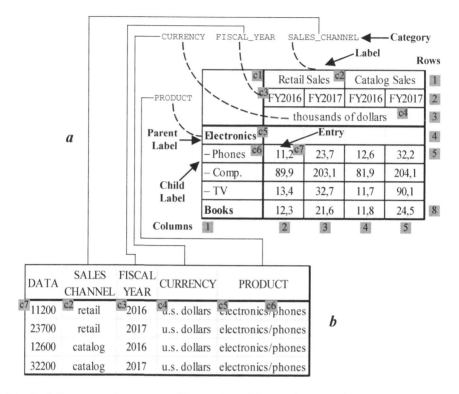

Fig. 1. A fragment of a source arbitrary spreadsheet table—*a*; a fragment of a target table in the relational (canonical) form generated from the source table—*b*.

Spreadsheets can be considered as a general form for representing tabular data with an explicitly presented layout (cellular structure) and style (graphical formatting). For example, HTML tables presented on web pages can be easily converted to spreadsheet formats. The arbitrary spreadsheet tables can be a valuable data source in business intelligence and data-driven research. However, difficulties that inevitably arise with extraction and integration of the tabular data often hinder the intensive use of them in the mentioned areas.

Many of arbitrary spreadsheet tables are an instance of weakly-structured and non-standardized data (Fig. 1, *a*). Unlike relational tables (Fig. 1, *b*), they are not organized in a predefined manner. They lack explicit semantics required for high-level computer interpretation such as SQL queries. To be accessible for data analysis and visualization, their data need to be extracted, transformed, and loaded (ETL) into databases. Since arbitrary tables can have various complex cell layouts (structures), often the familiar industrial ETL-tools are not sufficient to populate automatically a database with their data.

Researchers and developers faced with the tasks of spreadsheet data integration often use general-purpose tools. They often offer their own implementations of the same tasks. In such cases, domain-specific tools can reduce the complexity of software development in the domain of the spreadsheet data integration. This is especially important when a custom software for data extraction and transformation from heterogeneous arbitrary spreadsheet tables is implemented for a short time and with a lack of resources.

1.1 Related Work

There are several recent studies dealing with spreadsheet data converting. The tools [14–16,18,27,29,31] are devoted to issues of converting data presented in spreadsheets or web tables to RDF (Resource Description Framework) or OWL (Web Ontology Language) formats. The solutions for spreadsheet data extraction and transformation [1,3,17,19,22] are based on programming by examples. Some of the solutions also include own domain-specific languages: XLWRAP [27], M² [31], TABLEPROG [19], and FLARE [3].

Hung et al. [20] propose TRANSHEET, a spreadsheet-like formula language for specifying mappings between source spreadsheet data and a target schema. Embley et al. [13] propose an algorithmic end-to-end solution for transforming "header-indexed" tables in CSV format to a relational form ("category tables") based on header indexing. SENBAZURU, a spreadsheet database management system proposed by [5], provides extracting relational data from spreadsheets ("data frames"). HAEXCEL framework [10] enables migrating normalized data among spreadsheets and relational databases. MDSHEET framework [8,9] also implements a technique that automatically infers relational schemes from spreadsheets. The framework [7] constructs trained spreadsheet property (e.g. aggregation rows or hierarchical header) detectors based on rule-assisted active learning.

DEEXCELERATOR project [12] aims at the development of a framework for information extraction from partially structured documents such as spreadsheets and HTML tables. The framework exploits a set of heuristics based on features of tables published as Open Data. DEEXCELERATOR works as a predefined pipeline without any user interaction. Koci et al. [23–25] expand the covered spectrum of spreadsheets. They proposes a machine learning approach for table layout inference [24] and TIRS, a heuristic-based framework for automatic table identification and reconstruction in spreadsheets [25]. Their recent paper [23] introduces a novel approach to recognition of the functional regions in single- and multi-table spreadsheets.

The recent papers [4,39] develop domain-specific solutions. The work [39] proposes algorithms and accompanying software for automatic annotation of natural science spreadsheet tables. The tool proposed in [4] extracts RDF data from French government statistical spreadsheets and populates instances of their conceptual model. The system CACHECK [11] automatically detects and repairs "smelly" cell arrays by recovering their computational semantics. TaCLe [26] automatically identifies constraints (formulas and relations) in spreadsheets. The papers [41,42] suggest an approach to rule-based semantic extraction from tabular documents.

1.2 Contribution

Our work shows new possibilities in spreadsheet data transformation from arbitrary to relational tables based on rule-based programming for the following *table understanding* [21] stages:

- *Role analysis* extracts functional data items, entries (values) and labels (keys), from cell content.
- *Structural analysis* recovers relationships of functional data items (i.e. entry-label and label-label pairs).
- *Interpretation* binds recovered labels with categories (domains).

Our contribution consists in the following results:

- The two-layered table object model combines the physical (syntactic) and logical (semantic) table structure. Unlike others models, it is not based on using functional cell regions but determines that functional items can be placed anywhere in a table.
- The domain-specific language, CRL (Cells Rule Language), is intended for programming table analysis and interpretation rules. In contrast to the existing mapping languages, it expresses the spreadsheet data conversion in terms of table understanding.
- The tool for spreadsheet data extraction and transformation from an arbitrary (Fig. 1, a) to the relational (canonical) form (Fig. 1, b), TABBYXL[3], implements both the model and the language. Compared to the mentioned solutions it draws up this process as consecutive steps: role analysis, structural analysis, and interpretation.
- The CRL interpreter (CRL2J) provides the translation of CRL rules to JAVA code in the imperative style. It allows automatically generating JAVA source code from CRL rules and compile it to JAVA bytecode, and then runs generated JAVA programs. The interpreter uses CRL grammar implemented by ANTLR[4]. This ensures the correctness of CRL language grammar.
- The ruleset for transforming arbitrary tables of the same genre (government statistical websites) is implemented in three formats: CRL, DSLR (DROOLS[5]), and CLP (JESS[6]). The experimental results are reproduced and validated by using three different options: (i) CRL-to-JAVA translation; (ii) DROOLS rule engine; (iii) JESS rule engine. The results (recovered relational tables) are the same for all of these three options. This confirms the applicability of CRL language for expressing table analysis and interpretation rules.

This paper continues our series of works devoted the issues of table understanding in spreadsheets [33,34,37,38]. It combines and significantly expands our approach to table understanding based on executing rules for table analysis and interpretation with a business rule engine [34]. We briefly introduced

---

[3] https://github.com/tabbydoc/tabbyxl2.

[4] http://www.antlr.org.

[5] https://www.drools.org.

[6] http://www.jessrules.com.

the preliminary version of our domain-specific rule language first in [33]. The prototype of our tool for canonicalization of arbitrary tables in spreadsheets is discussed in [37]. This work extends the results presented in the paper [38] by adding the CRL interpreter for the CRL-to-JAVA translation, as well as by the implementation and validation of the ruleset by using the different options: CRL2J, DROOLS, and JESS.

The novelty of our current work consists in providing two rule-based ways to implement workflows of spreadsheet data extraction and transformation. In the first case, a ruleset for table analysis and interpretation is expressed in a general-purpose rule language and executed by a JSR-94-compatible rule engine (e.g. DROOLS or Jess). In the second case, our interpreter translates a ruleset expressed in CRL to JAVA source code that is complicated and executed by the JAVA development kit. This CRL-to-JAVA translation allows us to express rulesets without any instructions for management of the working memory such as updates of modified facts or blocks on the rule re-activation. The end-users can focus more on the logic of table analysis and interpretation than on the logic of the rule management and execution.

2   Table Object Model

The table object model is designed for representing both a physical structure and logical data items of an arbitrary table in the process of its analysis and interpretation (Fig. 2). Our model adopts the terminology of Wang's table model [40]. It includes two interrelated layers: *physical* (syntactic) represented by the collection of cells (Sect. 2.1) and *logical* (semantic) that consists of three collections of entries (values), labels (keys), and categories (concepts) (Sect. 2.2). We deliberately resort to the two-way references between the layers to provide convenient access to their objects in table analysis and interpretation rules.

2.1   Physical Layer

`Cell` object represents common features of a cell that can be presented in tagged documents of well-known formats, such as Excel, Word, or HTML. We define `Cell` object as a set of the following features:

- *Location*: `cl`—left column, `rt`—top row, `cr`—right column, and `rb`—bottom row. A cell located on several consecutive rows and columns covers a few grid tiles, which always compose a rectangle. Moreover, two cells cannot overlap each other.
- *Style*: `font`—font features including: `name`, `color`, `size`, etc.; `horzAlignment` and `vertAlignment`—horizontal and vertical alignment; `bgColor` and `fgColor`—background and foreground colors; `leftBorder`, `topBorder`, `rightBorder`, and `bottomBorder`—border features; `rotation`—text rotation.
- *Content*: `text`—textual content, `indent`—indentation, and `type`—its literal data type (`numeric`, `date`, `string`, etc.).

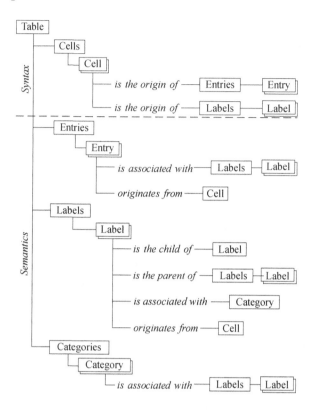

Fig. 2. Two-layered table object model.

- *Annotation*: mark—a user-defined word or phrase to annotate the cell.
- *Logical layer references*: entries (a set of entries) and labels (a set of labels) originated from this cell. Thus, a cell can contain several entries and labels.

For example, Fig. 3 presents an initial state of some cells (c1,..., c7) shown in Fig. 1, *a*.

2.2   Logical Layer

Entry object serves as a representation a data value of a table. It consists of the following attributes: value—a value (text), labels—a set of labels associated with this entry, and cell—the physical layer reference to a cell as its origin that serves as data provenance. An entry can be associated with only one label in each category.

Label represents a label (key) that addresses one or more entries (data values). It is defined as follows: value—a value (text), children—a set of labels which are children of this label, parent—its parent label, category—an associated category, cell—the physical layer reference to a cell as its origin (data provenance).

```
c1=(cl=1,rt=1,cr=1,rb=3,text=null)
c2=(cl=2,rt=1,cr=3,rb=1,text="Retail Sales")
c3=(cl=2,rt=2,cr=2,rb=2,text="FY2016")
c4=(cl=2,rt=3,cr=5,rb=3,text="thousands of dollars")
c5=(cl=1,rt=4,cr=1,rb=4,text="Electronics")
c6=(cl=1,rt=5,cr=1,rb=5,text="- Phones")
c7=(cl=2,rt=5,cr=2,rb=5,text="11.2",type=NUMERIC)
```

Fig. 3. Some initial facts (cells) for the table shown in Fig. 1, *a*.

```
e1=(value="11200",labels={l1,l2,l3,l5},cell=c7)
l1=(value="retail",category=d1,cell=c2)
l2=(value="2016",category=d2,cell=c3)
l3=(value="u.s. dollars",category=d3,cell=c4)
l4=(value="electronics",children={l5,...}, category=d4,cell=c5)
l5=(value="phones",parent=l4,category=d4,cell=c6)
d1=(name="SALE CHANNEL",labels={l1,...})
d2=(name="FISCAL YEAR",labels={l2,...})
d3=(name="CURRENCY",labels={l3,...})
d4=(name="PRODUCT",labels={l4,l5,...})
```

Fig. 4. Some recovered facts (functional items) for the table shown in Fig. 1, *a*.

`Category` models a category of labels as follows: `name`—an internal name, `URI`—a uniform resource identifier representing this category (concept) in an external vocabulary, `labels`—a set of its labels. Each label is associated with only one category. Labels combined into a category can be organized as one or more trees.

This layer allows representing items differently depending on target requirements of the table transformation. For example, Fig. 4 demonstrates a possible target state of the entry (`e1`), labels (`l1`,..., `l5`), and categories (`d1`,..., `d4`) recovered from the initial cells shown in Fig. 3. They can be presented as a tuple of a target relational Table 1, *b*.

3 CRL Language

The rules expressed in our language are intended to map explicit features (layout, style, and text of cells) of an arbitrary table into its implicit semantics (entries, labels, and categories). Figure 5 demonstrates the grammar of CRL, our domain-specific language, in Extended Backus-Naur form. This grammar is also presented in ANTLR format[7].

A rule begins with the keyword `rule` and ends with `end`. A number that follows the keyword `rule` determines the order of executing this rule.

```
rule #i
  when conditions
  then actions
end
```

---

[7] https://github.com/tabbydoc/tabbyxl2/blob/master/src/main/resources/crl_gram.g.

```
rule          = 'rule' <a Java integer literal> 'when' condition
                'then' action 'end' <EOL> {rule} <EOF>
condition     = query identifier [':' constraint {',' constraint}
                [',' assignment {',' assignment}]] <EOL> {condition}
constraint    = <a Java boolean expr>
assignment    = identifier ':' <a valid Java expr>
query         = 'cell' | 'entry' | 'label' | 'category' | 'no cells' |
                'no entries' | 'no labels' | 'no categories'
action        = merge | split | set text | set indent | set mark |
                new entry | new label | add label | set parent |
                set category | group <EOL> {action}
merge         = 'merge' identifier 'with' identifier
split         = 'split' identifier
set text      = 'set text' <a Java string expr> 'to' identifier
set indent    = 'set indent' <a Java integer expr> 'to' identifier
set mark      = 'set mark' <a Java string expr> 'to' identifier
new entry     = 'new entry' identifier ['as' <a Java string expr>]
new label     = 'new label' identifier ['as' <a Java string expr>]
add label     = 'add label' identifier | (<a Java string expr>
                'of' identifier | <a Java string expr>)
                'to' identifier
set parent    = 'set parent' identifier 'to' identifier
set category  = 'set category' identifier | <a Java string expr>
                'to' identifier
group         = 'group' identifier 'with' identifier
identifier    = <a Java identifier>
```

Fig. 5. Grammar of CRL language.

The left hand side (**when**) of a rule consists of one or more *conditions* that enable to query available facts which are cells, entries, labels, and categories of a table. Each of the conditions listed in the left hand side of a rule has to be true to execute its right hand side (**then**) that contains *actions* to modify the existed or to generate new facts about the table.

3.1 Conditions

We use two kinds of conditions. The first requires that there exists at least one fact of a specified data type, which satisfies a set of constraints:

```
cell var: constraints, assignments
entry var: constraints, assignments
label var: constraints, assignments
category var: constraints, assignments
```

The condition consists of three parts. In their order of occurrence, the first is a keyword that denotes one of the following fact types: cell, entry, label, or category. The second is variable, a variable of the specified fact type. The third optional part begins with the colon character. It defines constraints for restricting the requested facts and assignments for binding additional variables with values. A *constraint* is a boolean expression in JAVA. The comma character separating the constraints is the logical conjunction of them. An *assignment* (`variable: value`) sets a value (JAVA expression) to a variable. A condition without constraints allows querying all facts of specified type. The second kind of conditions determines that there exist no facts satisfied to specified constraints: The first part of these conditions is a keyword for satisfying a type of facts. The second part contains constraints on the facts.

3.2 Cell Cleansing

In practice, hand-coded tables often have messy layout (e.g. improperly split or merged cells) and content (e.g. typos, homoglyphs, or errors in indents). We address several actions to the issues of cell cleansing that can be used as the preprocessing stage.

- `merge`, the action combines two adjacent cells when they share one border.
- `split`, the action divides a merged cell that spans n-tiles into n-cells. Each of the n-cells completely copies content and style from the merged cell and coordinates from the corresponding tile.
- `set text`, the action provides modifying textual content of a cell. Some string processing (e.g. regular expressions and string matching algorithms) implemented as JAVA-methods can be involved in the action.
- `set indent`, the action modifies an indentation of a cell.

3.3 Role Analysis

This stage aims to recover entries and labels as functional data items presented in tables. We also enable associating cells with user-defined tags (marks) that can assist in both role and structural analysis.

- `set mark`, the action annotates a cell with a word or phrase. The assigned tag can substitute the corresponding constraints in subsequent rules. The typical practice is to set a tag to all cells, which play the same role or are located in the same table functional region. Thereafter, we can use these tags in subsequent rules instead of repeating constraints on cell location in the regions.
- `new entry`, the action generates an entry, using a specified cell as its origin. Usually, a value of the created entry is an expression obtained as a result of string processing for its textual content of the cell.
- `new label`, the action generates a label in a similar way.

3.4 Structural Analysis

The next stage recovers pairs of two kinds: entry-label and label-label.

- `add label`, the action binds an entry with an added label. A label can be specified as a value of a category indicated by its name.
- `set parent`, the action connects two labels as a parent and its child.

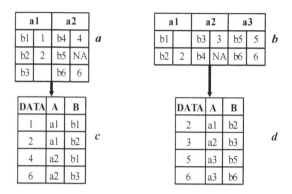

Fig. 6. Source tables—a and b; target canonicalized tables—c and d.

3.5 Interpretation

The stage includes actions for recovering label-category pairs.

- set category, the action associates a label with a category.
- group, the action places two labels in one group. Arbitrary tables often place all labels of one category in the same row or column. Consequently, we can suppose that the labels belong to a category without defining its name. In the cases, grouping two or more labels means that they all belong to an undefined category. All labels of a group can be associated with only one category.

3.6 Illustrative Example

Figure 6 depicts an example of a transformational task that consists in converting tables similar to ones (a and b) into the relational form (c and d). These tables satisfy the following assumptions: $1, \ldots, n$ are entries, $a_1, \ldots, a_m$ are column

```
(1) when cell $c: text == "NA"
    then set text "" to $c
(3) when cell $c: (cl % 2) == 1
    then new label $c
    when
(5)    entry $e
       label $l: cell.rt == $e.cell.rt, cell.cl == $e.cell.cl - 1
    then add label $l to $e
(6) when label $l: cell.rt == 1
    then set category "A" to $l
```

```
(2) when cell $c: (cl % 2) == 0, !blank
    then new entry $c
    when
(4)    entry $e
       label $l: cell.cr == $e.cell.cr
    then add label $l to $e

(7) when label $l: cell.rt > 1
    then set category "B" to $l
```

Fig. 7. A reference ruleset for transforming the source tables (Fig. 6, a, c) to the target canonical forms (Fig. 6, b, d).

labels of the category A, $b_1, \ldots, b_k$ are row labels of the category B. Figure 7 presents a reference ruleset implemented for this task. It contains only 7 rules that are executed in the following order: (1) data cleansing, (2) entry generation, (3) label generation, (4) associating entries with column labels, (5) associating entries with row labels, (6) categorizing column labels, and (7) categorizing row labels.

4 Implementation with Options

TABBYXL implements both the presented table object model and the rule-based approach to spreadsheet data extraction and transformation. It can process data, using one of the following options:

- CRL2J-*option* automatically generates JAVA source code from CRL rules and compile it to JAVA bytecode, and then runs the generated program. This option requires that ruleset is implemented in CRL language. We use ANTLR, the parser generator, to implement the CRL-to-JAVA translator. This allows to parse CRL rules and to build their object model which is then translated to JAVA source code.
- DROOLS-*option* relies on DROOLS EXPERT rule engine. The rules can be expressed in DRL (the general-purpose rule language that is native for DROOLS) or in a dialect of CRL that is implemented as a domain-specific language (DSL) in corresponding of DROOLS requirements. In the last case, CRL rules presented in DSLR format are automatically translated into DRL format through the DSL-specification that defines CRL-to-DRL mappings. Unlike the pure CRL, this dialect supports DRL attributes in rule declarations.
- JESS-*option* executes a ruleset with JESS rule engine. This option requires that a ruleset is represented in the well-known CLP (CLIPS) format.

Moreover, the current version of TABBYXL supports rule engines that are compatible with JAVA RULE ENGINE API (JSR94[8]). Therefore, it is possible to use not only DROOLS or JESS, but also others rule engines supporting JAVA RULE ENGINE API, and to represent the rules in their native formats. Any case, TABBYXL builds an instance of the table object model from source spreadsheet data. The cells of this instance are asserted as facts into the working memory of a rule engine. Optionally, some user-defined categories specified in YAML format can also be loaded and presented as facts. The rule engine matches asserted facts against the rules. While rules are executed, the instance of the table object model is augmented by recovered facts (entries, labels, and categories). At the end of the transformation process, the instance is exported as a flat file database.

---

[8] https://www.jcp.org/ja/jsr/detail?id=94.

Table 1. Experiment results on the role and structural analysis stages.

Metrics	Role analysis		Structural analysis	
	Type of instances			
	Entries	Labels	Entry-label pairs	Label-label pairs
recall	0.9813 $\frac{16602}{16918}$	0.9965 $\frac{4842}{4859}$	0.9773 $\frac{34270}{35066}$	0.9389 $\frac{1951}{2078}$
precision	0.9996 $\frac{16602}{16609}$	0.9364 $\frac{4842}{5171}$	0.9965 $\frac{34270}{34389}$	0.9784 $\frac{1951}{1994}$
F-score	0.9904	0.9655	0.9868	0.9582

5 Experimental Results

The purpose of the experiment is to show a possibility of using our tool for tables, which originate from various sources produced by different authors but pertain to the same document genre. The experiment includes two parts: (i) designing and implementing an experimental ruleset for tables of the same genre, and (ii) evaluating the performance of the ruleset on a set of these tables.

We used TROY200 [30], the existing dataset of tables, for the performance evaluation. It contains 200 arbitrary tables as CSV files collected from 10 different sources of the same genre, government statistical websites predominantly presented in English language.

We designed and implemented a ruleset that transforms TROY200 arbitrary tables to the relational form, using two formats: CRL and CLP (JESS). We also prepared ground-truth data, including reference entries, labels, entry-label, and label-label pairs extracted from TROY200 tables. Their form is designed for human readability. Moreover, they are independent of the presence of critical cells in tables. The performance evaluation is based on comparing the ground-truth data with the tables generated by executing the presented ruleset for the experiment dataset.

All tables of the dataset were automatically transformed into the relational form, using TABBYXL with three different options: CRL2J, DROOLS, and JESS. The results are the same for all of these three options.

We used the standard metrics: *recall*, *precision*, and *F-score*, to evaluate our ruleset for both role and structural analysis. We adapted them as follows. When R is a set of instances in a target table and S is a set of instances in the corresponding source table, then:

$$\text{recall} = \frac{|R \cap S|}{|S|} \quad \text{precision} = \frac{|R \cap S|}{|R|}$$

An instance refers to an entry, label, entry-label pair, or label-label pair. These metrics were separately calculated for each type of instances (entries, labels, entry-label pairs, and label-label pairs).

The experiment results are shown in Table 1. Among 200 tables of the dataset, only 25 are processed with errors (1256 false negatives in 25 tables, and 498 false positives in 14 ones). Only one table is not processed. This results in 948 false negative and 316 false positive errors, which amount to about 72% of all errors. In this case, entries are not recovered because they are not numeric as it is assumed in the used ruleset.

Table 2. Comparison of the running time by using the different options.

Running time of	CRL2J	DROOLS	JESS
Ruleset translation (t_1)	2108 ms	1711 ms	432 ms
Ruleset execution (t_2)	367 ms	1974 ms	4149 ms

Additionally, Table 2 presents a comparison of the running time for the ruleset translation and execution processes, using the implemented options. The ruleset translation time (t_1) is a time of translating an original ruleset into an executable form. The ruleset execution time (t_2) is a total time of executing the ruleset presented in the executable form that is required to process all 200 tables of the dataset. In the case of CRL2J option, t_1 is a time of parsing and compiling the original ruleset into a JAVA program, while t_2 is a time of executing the generated Java program. In the case of the use of a rule engine (DROOLS or JESS option), t_1 is a time of parsing the original ruleset and adding the result into a rule engine session. t_2 consists of a time of asserting initial facts into the working memory and a time of executing the ruleset by the rule engine. The results shown in Table 2 were obtained with the following computer: 3.2 GHz 4-core CPU and 8 GB RAM. The use of CRL2J option requires slightly more time for the translation of the ruleset. However, CRL2J is faster for the execution of the program (ruleset) compared to DROOLS or JESS rule engine.

All data and steps to reproduce the experiment results are publicly available as a dataset[9] [35]. It contains the following items: the relational tables obtained by TABBYXL; the ground-truth data; the mentioned CRL and CLP rulesets; the detailing of the performance evaluation. Some comparison of TABBYXL in its previous version with others solutions is discussed in the paper [38].

This experiment exemplifies the use of our language for developing task-specific rulesets. The performance evaluation confirms the applicability of the implemented ruleset in accomplishing the stated objectives of this application.

6 Conclusions and Further Work

The presented approach can be applied to develop software for extraction and transformation data of arbitrary spreadsheet tables. We expect TABBYXL to be useful in cases when data from a large number of tables appertaining to a few table types are required for populating a database.

We showed experimentally that rules for table analysis and interpretation can be expressed in a general-purpose rule-based language and executed with a

---

[9] https://data.mendeley.com/datasets/ydcr7mcrtp/3.

rule engine [34]. But only a few of its possibilities are sufficient for developing our rules. The exploration of these possibilities has led to development of CRL, a domain-specific rule language, which specializes in expressing only rules for table analysis and interpretation. Our language hides details which are inessential for us and allows to focus on the logic of table analysis and interpretation. There are two ways to use CRL rules. They can be executed with a rule engine (e.g. DROOLS or JESS) or be translated to programs presented in the imperative style (e.g. in JAVA language).

The experiment demonstrates that the tool can be used for developing programs for transformation of spreadsheet data into the relational form. One rule-set can process a wide range of tables of the same genre, e.g. government statistical websites. Our tool can be used for populating databases from arbitrary tables, which share common features.

The work focuses rather on table analysis than on issues of interpretation. We only recover categories as sets of labels, without binding them with an external taxonomy of concepts (e.g. Linked Open Data). The further work on table content conceptualization can overcome this limitation. Moreover, we observe that arbitrary tables can contain messy (e.g. non-standardized values or typos) and useless (e.g. aggregations or padding characters) data. It seems to be interesting for the further work to incorporate additional techniques of data cleansing in our tool. Another direction of development is to integrate the presented results with the tools for extracting tables from documents (e.g. untagged PDF documents [32,36]) in end-to-end systems for the table understanding.

Acknowledgment. This work is supported by the Russian Science Foundation under Grant No.: 18-71-10001.

References

1. Astrakhantsev, N., Turdakov, D., Vassilieva, N.: Semi-automatic data extraction from tables. In: Selected Papers of the 15th All-Russian Scientific Conference on Digital Libraries: Advanced Methods and Technologies, Digital Collections, pp. 14–20 (2013)
2. Barik, T., Lubick, K., Smith, J., Slankas, J., Murphy-Hill, E.: Fuse: a reproducible, extendable, internet-scale corpus of spreadsheets. In: Proceedings of the 12th Working Conference on Mining Software Repositories, pp. 486–489. IEEE Press (2015). https://doi.org/10.1109/MSR.2015.70
3. Barowy, D.W., Gulwani, S., Hart, T., Zorn, B.: FlashRelate: extracting relational data from semi-structured spreadsheets using examples. SIGPLAN Not. **50**(6), 218–228 (2015). https://doi.org/10.1145/2813885.2737952
4. Cao, T.D., Manolescu, I., Tannier, X.: Extracting linked data from statistic spreadsheets. In: Proceedings of the International Workshop on Semantic Big Data, pp. 5:1–5:5 (2017). https://doi.org/10.1145/3066911.3066914
5. Chen, Z.: Information extraction on para-relational data. Ph.D. thesis, University of Michigan, US (2016)
6. Chen, Z., Cafarella, M.: Automatic web spreadsheet data extraction. In: Proceedings of the 3rd International Workshop on Semantic Search Over the Web, pp. 1:1–1:8 (2013). https://doi.org/10.1145/2509908.2509909

7. Chen, Z., et al.: Spreadsheet property detection with rule-assisted active learning. Technical report CSE-TR-601-16 (2016). https://www.cse.umich.edu/techreports/cse/2016/CSE-TR-601-16.pdf

8. Cunha, J., Erwig, M., Mendes, J., Saraiva, J.: Model inference for spreadsheets. Autom. Softw. Eng. **23**(3), 361–392 (2016). https://doi.org/10.1007/s10515-014-0167-x

9. Cunha, J., Fernandes, J.P., Mendes, J., Saraiva, J.: Spreadsheet engineering. In: Zsók, V., Horváth, Z., Csató, L. (eds.) CEFP 2013. LNCS, vol. 8606, pp. 246–299. Springer, Cham (2015). https://doi.org/10.1007/978-3-319-15940-9_6

10. Cunha, J., Saraiva, J.a., Visser, J.: From spreadsheets to relational databases and back. In: Proceedings of the ACM SIGPLAN Workshop Partial Evaluation and Program Manipulation, pp. 179–188 (2009). https://doi.org/10.1145/1480945.1480972

11. Dou, W., Xu, C., Cheung, S.C., Wei, J.: CACheck: detecting and repairing cell arrays in spreadsheets. IEEE Trans. Software Eng. **43**(3), 226–251 (2017). https://doi.org/10.1109/TSE.2016.2584059

12. Eberius, J., Werner, C., Thiele, M., Braunschweig, K., Dannecker, L., Lehner, W.: DeExcelerator: a framework for extracting relational data from partially structured documents. In: Proceedings of the 22nd ACM International Conference on Information & Knowledge Management, pp. 2477–2480 (2013). https://doi.org/10.1145/2505515.2508210. http://doi.acm.org/10.1145/2505515.2508210

13. Embley, D.W., Krishnamoorthy, M.S., Nagy, G., Seth, S.: Converting heterogeneous statistical tables on the web to searchable databases. IJDAR **19**(2), 119–138 (2016). https://doi.org/10.1007/s10032-016-0259-1

14. Ermilov, I., Ngomo, A.-C.N.: TAIPAN: automatic property mapping for tabular data. In: Blomqvist, E., Ciancarini, P., Poggi, F., Vitali, F. (eds.) EKAW 2016. LNCS (LNAI), vol. 10024, pp. 163–179. Springer, Cham (2016). https://doi.org/10.1007/978-3-319-49004-5_11

15. Fiorelli, M., Lorenzetti, T., Pazienza, M.T., Stellato, A., Turbati, A.: Sheet2RDF: a flexible and dynamic spreadsheet import&lifting framework for RDF. In: Ali, M., Kwon, Y., Lee, C.H., Kim, J., Kim, Y. (eds.) IEA/AIE 2015. LNCS, vol. 9101, pp. 131–140. Springer, Cham (2015). https://doi.org/10.1007/978-3-319-19066-2_13

16. Galkin, M., Mouromtsev, D., Auer, S.: Identifying web tables: supporting a neglected type of content on the web. In: Klinov, P., Mouromtsev, D. (eds.) KESW 2015. CCIS, vol. 518, pp. 48–62. Springer, Cham (2015). https://doi.org/10.1007/978-3-319-24543-0_4

17. Gulwani, S., Harris, W.R., Singh, R.: Spreadsheet data manipulation using examples. Commun. ACM **55**(8), 97–105 (2012). https://doi.org/10.1145/2240236.2240260

18. Han, L., Finin, T., Parr, C., Sachs, J., Joshi, A.: RDF123: from spreadsheets to RDF. In: Sheth, A., et al. (eds.) ISWC 2008. LNCS, vol. 5318, pp. 451–466. Springer, Heidelberg (2008). https://doi.org/10.1007/978-3-540-88564-1_29

19. Harris, W.R., Gulwani, S.: Spreadsheet table transformations from examples. SIGPLAN Not. **46**(6), 317–328 (2011). https://doi.org/10.1145/1993316.1993536

20. Hung, V., Benatallah, B., Saint-Paul, R.: Spreadsheet-based complex data transformation. In: Proceedings of the 20th ACM International Conference on Information and Knowledge Management, pp. 1749–1754 (2011). https://doi.org/10.1145/2063576.2063829

21. Hurst, M.: Layout and language: challenges for table understanding on the web. In: Proceedings of the 1st International Workshop on Web Document Analysis, pp. 27–30 (2001)

22. Jin, Z., Anderson, M.R., Cafarella, M., Jagadish, H.V.: Foofah: transforming data by example. In: Proceedings of the ACM International Conference on Management of Data, pp. 683–698 (2017). https://doi.org/10.1145/3035918.3064034
23. Koci, E., Thiele, M., Lehner, W., Romero, O.: Table recognition in spreadsheets via a graph representation. In: 13th IAPR International Workshop on Document Analysis Systems, pp. 139–144 (2018). https://doi.org/10.1109/DAS.2018.48
24. Koci, E., Thiele, M., Romero, O., Lehner, W.: A machine learning approach for layout inference in spreadsheets. In: Proceedings of the 8th International Joint Conference on Knowledge Discovery, Knowledge Engineering and Knowledge Management, pp. 77–88 (2016). https://doi.org/10.5220/0006052200770088
25. Koci, E., Thiele, M., Romero, O., Lehner, W.: Table identification and reconstruction in spreadsheets. In: Dubois, E., Pohl, K. (eds.) CAiSE 2017. LNCS, vol. 10253, pp. 527–541. Springer, Cham (2017). https://doi.org/10.1007/978-3-319-59536-8_33
26. Kolb, S., Paramonov, S., Guns, T., De Raedt, L.: Learning constraints in spreadsheets and tabular data. Mach. Learn. **106**(9), 1441–1468 (2017). https://doi.org/10.1007/s10994-017-5640-x
27. Langegger, A., Wöß, W.: XLWrap – querying and integrating arbitrary spreadsheets with SPARQL. In: Bernstein, A., Karger, D.R., Heath, T., Feigenbaum, L., Maynard, D., Motta, E., Thirunarayan, K. (eds.) ISWC 2009. LNCS, vol. 5823, pp. 359–374. Springer, Heidelberg (2009). https://doi.org/10.1007/978-3-642-04930-9_23
28. Mitlöhner, J., Neumaier, S., Umbrich, J., Polleres, A.: Characteristics of open data CSV files. In: 2nd International Conference on Open and Big Data, pp. 72–79 (2016). https://doi.org/10.1109/OBD.2016.18
29. Mulwad, V., Finin, T., Joshi, A.: A domain independent framework for extracting linked semantic data from tables. In: Ceri, S., Brambilla, M. (eds.) Search Computing. LNCS, vol. 7538, pp. 16–33. Springer, Heidelberg (2012). https://doi.org/10.1007/978-3-642-34213-4_2
30. Nagy, G.: TANGO-DocLab web tables from international statistical sites (Troy_200), 1, ID: Troy_200_1 (2016). http://tc11.cvc.uab.es/datasets/Troy_200_1
31. O'Connor, M.J., Halaschek-Wiener, C., Musen, M.A.: Mapping master: a flexible approach for mapping spreadsheets to OWL. In: Patel-Schneider, P.F., et al. (eds.) ISWC 2010. LNCS, vol. 6497, pp. 194–208. Springer, Heidelberg (2010). https://doi.org/10.1007/978-3-642-17749-1_13
32. Shigarov, A., Altaev, A., Mikhailov, A., Paramonov, V., Cherkashin, E.: TabbyPDF: web-based system for PDF table extraction. In: Damaševičius, R., Vasiljevienė, G. (eds.) ICIST 2018. CCIS, vol. 920, pp. 257–269. Springer, Cham (2018). https://doi.org/10.1007/978-3-319-99972-2_20
33. Shigarov, A.: Rule-based table analysis and interpretation. In: Dregvaite, G., Damasevicius, R. (eds.) ICIST 2015. CCIS, vol. 538, pp. 175–186. Springer, Cham (2015). https://doi.org/10.1007/978-3-319-24770-0_16
34. Shigarov, A.: Table understanding using a rule engine. Expert Syst. Appl. **42**(2), 929–937 (2015). https://doi.org/10.1016/j.eswa.2014.08.045
35. Shigarov, A., Khristyuk, V.: TabbyXL2: experiment data. Mendeley Data, v2 (2018). https://doi.org/10.17632/ydcr7mcrtp.2
36. Shigarov, A., Mikhailov, A., Altaev, A.: Configurable table structure recognition in untagged PDF documents. In: Proceedings of the ACM Symposium on Document Engineering, pp. 119–122 (2016). https://doi.org/10.1145/2960811.2967152

37. Shigarov, A.O., Paramonov, V.V., Belykh, P.V., Bondarev, A.I.: Rule-based canonicalization of arbitrary tables in spreadsheets. In: Dregvaite, G., Damasevicius, R. (eds.) ICIST 2016. CCIS, vol. 639, pp. 78–91. Springer, Cham (2016). https://doi.org/10.1007/978-3-319-46254-7_7
38. Shigarov, A.O., Mikhailov, A.A.: Rule-based spreadsheet data transformation from arbitrary to relational tables. Inf. Syst. **71**, 123–136 (2017). https://doi.org/10.1016/j.is.2017.08.004
39. de Vos, M., Wielemaker, J., Rijgersberg, H., Schreiber, G., Wielinga, B., Top, J.: Combining information on structure and content to automatically annotate natural science spreadsheets. Int. J. Hum. Comput. Stud. **103**, 63–76 (2017). https://doi.org/10.1016/j.ijhcs.2017.02.006
40. Wang, X.: Tabular abstraction, editing, and formatting. Ph.D. thesis, University of Waterloo, Waterloo, Ontario, Canada (1996)
41. Yang, S., Guo, J., Wei, R.: Semantic interoperability with heterogeneous information systems on the internet through automatic tabular document exchange. Inf. Syst. **69**, 195–217 (2017). https://doi.org/10.1016/j.is.2016.10.010
42. Yang, S., Wei, R., Shigarov, A.: Semantic interoperability for electronic business through a novel cross-context semantic document exchange approach. In: Proceedings of the ACM Symposium on Document Engineering, pp. 28:1–28:10 (2018). https://doi.org/10.1145/3209280.3209523

Extending Interaction Flow Modeling Language (IFML) for Android User Interface Components

Iffat Fatima$^{(\boxtimes)}$, Muhammad Waseem Anwar, Farooque Azam,
Bilal Maqbool, and Hanny Tufail

Department of Computer and Software Engineering,
College of Electrical and Mechanical Engineering,
National University of Sciences and Technology (NUST), Islamabad, Pakistan
{iffat.fatima18, bilal.maqbool16,
hanny.tufail16}@ce.ceme.edu.pk,
{waseemanwar, farooq}@ceme.nust.edu.pk

Abstract. Interaction Flow Modeling Language (IFML) is an Object Management Group (OMG) standard for depicting front end behavior of software applications. It provides a platform independent description of graphical user interfaces for web as well as mobile applications. Mobile development has emerged as a vast area of research in the last decade. IFML meta-model caters for many generic user interface (UI) components but several characteristics of mobile application interface are found missing. This paper investigates the user interface characteristics of native android application user interface that are absent in the IFML meta-model. We then propose an extension of the identified characteristics using IFML to supplement usability in Android applications. This extended meta-model can be further used to generate Android platform specific code for user interfaces via model to code transformation.

Keywords: Android · IFML · Model-based · UI

1 Introduction

Model Driven Architecture (MDA) has been in use for user interface transformations which create Platform Independent Models (PIM) and convert them to Platform Specific Models (PSM) [1, 2]. OMG creates standards for different modeling techniques prevalent in the software industry and it adopted IFML as a standard for modeling software front end specification. IFML is used to create UI models for software applications which represents user interaction and behavior for UI of web and mobile applications. Model Driven (MD) is used to decrease the complexity specially for modelling of Android User Interface Components and IFML extension can facilitate to reduce complexity in the modelling of mobile User Inter-face Components [19].

© Springer Nature Switzerland AG 2019
R. Damaševičius and G. Vasiljevienė (Eds.): ICIST 2019, CCIS 1078, pp. 76–89, 2019.
https://doi.org/10.1007/978-3-030-30275-7_7

IFML defines several basic UI characteristics which can be used to represent front end of any software application. Some of these core components include a (1) View Container which is representation of a Window in web applications, (2) View Component which displays content or can accept data as input. (3) Event which can trigger (4) an Action that can alter the behavior of the UI component based on occurrence of that event. Apart from this there are many other components available which help enrich the application front end.

Smartphones have penetrated our lives very quickly in the last decade. In order to create an engaging user experience, design of UI is of vital importance. Keeping Android applications in perspective, IFML is still not enriched enough to include smartphone specific components. Many characteristics like styling and motion/touch events are missing in the IFML meta-model which can contribute to enhancement of application usability.

In this paper, we focus on applying the techniques of Model Driven Architecture (MDA) to enrich the UI of mobile applications specifically native Android applications through IFML meta-model extension. IFML has some core UI classes defined at the meta-model level. This model has been extended to represent many basic characteristics of the UI specific to web and mobile application. Here, we present an IFML meta-model extension specifically targeted towards Android application characteristics. We identify the Android specific missing characteristics in the IFML meta-model and model them as extensions of the IFML meta-model classes by defining their appropriate stereotypes. For this purpose, a modeling Profile is created for the proposed extension. This profile is then imported in the IFML Editor to create an IFML based model for a real-life use case of Android application in order to represent the usage of IFML extensions in real life Android applications.

The paper is organized as follows: Sect. 2 presents the Literature Review of the research papers relevant to the topic under research. Section 3 is Proposed Profile which gives description of meta-model extension. Section 4 describes a Case Study which validates the proposed solution. Section 5 includes Discussion of the above sections and future work. Section 6 presents Conclusion (Fig. 1).

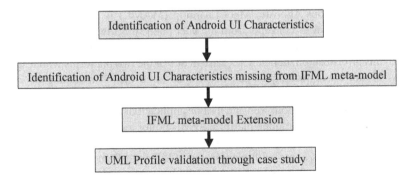

Fig. 1. Research overview

2 Literature Review

Research work of the recent years in domain of IFML was reviewed for the current paper. Many papers specific to use of IFML in mobile applications were reviewed as well, a summary of which will be presented in this section. IFML has a number of applications in mobile and web domain not only for modeling but providing a base for model transformation [3]. The literature review has been divided into different sections based on the model-based approaches for UI conceptualization.

2.1 Significance of IFML Concepts in Model to Code Transformations

IFML standards defined in OMG standard documentation are used to model different mobile and web application UI. These models can be further transformed to platform specific code using different tools. Many approaches and tools have been created to generate front-end code for web and mobile applications, few of which are as follows: In [4], several aspects of IFML were studied and semantics were provided by mapping IFML concepts to Place Chart Nets (PCN) in order to clarify the constructs like nested interfaces, View component computation and events. This mapping was modeled using model driven approach and the model was verified by a simulation of PCN. The approach was is further extended to generate code for the mobile and web applications. [5] presents a technique to create a platform independent IFML model for UI of a rich internet application. A platform specific model for the application is created in Java following the Model View Presenter architecture. These two models are used as input and output models for the query view transformation respectively. This approach is further verified by a case study. IFML can also be used to model cross platform mobile applications using WebRatio, which generates code for the end product. [6] discusses in detail how IFML meta-model can be extended to incorporate components specific to mobile applications. WebRatio is based on the IFML standards and it can be used to create IFML models, develop application and design interfaces for cross platform applications. As a result, a fully functional application can be created from this tool. [7] describes different tradeoffs between different strategies for generation of code from model in context of WebRatio. The best strategy was added to the WebRatio tool for mobile platform. Model Agnostic Meta Learning (MAML) is another alternative to IFML which has drawn its concepts from the later one [8]. Software developers wither use mobile first or web first approach while developing a cross platform application. As a result of this prioritization, deficiencies arise in one of the two platforms with respect to usability. Model based techniques can be used to align the UI modeling of various platforms through a single mode. [9] presents how a single platform independent IFML model can be used to create both web and mobile applications. MobML language is used to increase precision for the mobile platform. IFML Editor tool can be used to model UI of applications. [10] discusses prototype generation from the IFML Editor tool for web and mobile applications along with mapping of IFML with Perti Net based PCNs for simulation of model. Another tool called Adapt-UI is used for code generation of UIs for mobile applications which employs the IFML Editor plugin to create graphical models [11]. Hence, the concepts defined in the IFML meta-model can be directly used in any of the code generators to create UIs, thus proving their significance.

2.2 Limitations of IFML w.r.t. Usability

[12] discusses how IFML can be used to enhance presentation of the web application interfaces. As a result of this approach an HTML model is created at the end by combining Ontology Web Language (OWL) technology and IFML. As IFML is more strongly designed to represent UI interactions but it does not cover the design perspective very strongly, therefore, OWL can be used to compensate for that weakness. Before-referenced paper uses UI concepts defined in OWL to support IFML components. A similar approach can be applied on mobile applications as well. [13] presents an interesting approach to create UI components of mobile games using model driven engineering techniques. A UML model has been used in this approach to represent the game specific UI characteristics of mobile application including game specific interactions. A code generator is built in Java to generate executable JavaScript code for the UML model. Although UI components of mobile games differ from contemporary mobile applications, however, many features lie common between the two, which can be incorporated in the later. Usability is an important aspect of the software based products. [14] discusses how usability of applications can be understood in context of IFML UI modeling and how it is propagated further to the final platform specific interface. It discusses the limitations of IFML in modeling usability in terms of multi-level user interactions, undo/exit events, process progress visualization and feedback. Therefore, this is one of the areas of IFML that need to be explored and refined with details.

2.3 Modeling IFML Limitations

In order to create mobile specific UI components, their structure and behavior in the mobile environment needs to be analyzed. An approach has been developed to model some Android specific UI components using IFML. It involves reverse engineering approach by static analysis of android specific components that correspond to IFML container components. Constraints are extracted from these components like window transitions etc. These analyzed components are then modeled using IFML based on extracted constraints [15]. Stereotypes can be defined for UI modeling of web applications. [16] discusses how IFML, a PIM, can be extended to a PSM by definition of UI stereotypes using this approach. Hence, definition of stereotypes as extension of the modeling language meta-model [17] can be used to cater for the limitations of the language.

2.4 Research Gap

For current research, work done in IFML in the mobile application domain specifically Android applications was reviewed for the currently proposed idea. Some UI components of Android Applications like camera, audio recorder, custom lists etc. have been modeled by providing extensions of the IFML meta-model in [18]. But IFML is still limited in providing usability and presentation details. We are going to propose some of UI characteristics of Android application as extensions of the current IFML meta-model that will further enhance the Android UI components. Those characteristics have been divided into two categories based on the IFML components they will extend from. The categories are as follows:

1. Styled View Components: IFML currently does not include styling for components. Hence, we propose to extend styled UI components from the existing View Component meta class provided by IFML
2. Touch Events: Interaction with UI is done by Touch Events in Android applications which have not been currently modeled using IFML. Hence, we propose several Touch Events extensions from System Event meta class provided by IFML.

3 Proposed Profile

A UML class diagram has been chosen to create the IFML extension profile for the components identified in the previous section. This profile will consist of the following elements: (1) Metaclass which represents classes in this profile (2) Stereotype which represents class as an extension of the Metaclass (3) Tagged values which represent the attributes of the stereotype class (4) Operations which represent the behavior of the stereotype class. It allows us to extend stereotypes from meta-classes and generalize those stereotypes to create more stereotypes. In this paper, we present extension of the IFML meta-model for styling the UI components in Android applications along with touch events. The stereotypes defined in this paper have been created in accordance with the view hierarchy in native Android applications. Extended profile is given in Fig. 2.

Here we present the description of the stereotypes of the profile. The description will consist of stereotype name, description, base class from which stereotype is extended, tagged values along with their description. The description of stereotypes is as follows (Table 1):

View

Description: This component is a basic view containing fundamental UI attributes from which many other views of the UI will generalize.

Base Class: IFML::Core::ViewComponent

Table 1. Tagged values for View

Tagged value	Data type	Description
width	Integer	Width of view
height	Integer	Height of view
alpha	Integer	Transparency of view
visibility		Represents whether view is visible or not
background	Integer	Id of background of view
clickable		Represents whether view can be clicked or not
margin	Integer	Distance between this view's outer boundary and other views
padding	Integer	Distance between this view's outer boundary and inner content
rotation	Integer	The angle at which the view is to be rotated

Toast

Description: This component is used to display messages to user. It appears on top of all views and stays visible for a specific amount of time (Table 2).

Base Class: IFML::Core::ViewComponent

Table 2. Tagged values for Toast

Tagged value	Data type	Description
view	View	Represents customized view component will display
duration	Integer	Represents the time for which this view will appear

PopupMenu

Description: This component used to create popup dialogs on screens (Table 3)

Base Class: IFML::Core::ViewComponent

Table 3. Tagged values for PopupMenu

Tagged value	Data type	Description
view	View	Represents customized view component will display

StyledImageView

Description: This component is used to display images in UI (Table 4)

Base Class: IFML::Extensions::View

Table 4. Tagged values for Styled Image View

Tagged value	Data type	Description
src	View	Source image as drawable to be displayed in this view
scaleType	ScaleType	How image will be scaled in the enclosing view depending on its size
adjustViewBounds	Boolean	Which represents how the view will enclose the source
cropToPadding	Boolean	Which represents whether the image will be cropped to represent the view padding

StyledAnimaingProgressBar

Description: This component is used to display progress of processes in the UI (Table 5)

Base Class: IFML::Extensions::View

Table 5. Tagged values for StyledAnimatingProgressBar

Tagged value	Data type	Description
progress	Integer	Progress value to be displayed
progressTint	Color	Color of the progress completed
secondaryProgressTint	Color	Color of the progress under processing
indeterminate	Boolean	Whether this progress bar will keep on progressing for infinite amount of time or not
indeterminateDuration	Integer	Duration of indeterminate animation
animationResolution	Integer	Animation frame timeout

RatingBar

Description: This component is used to display rating as stars (Table 6)
Base Class: IFML::Extensions::View::StyledAnimaing ProgressBarClass

Table 6. Tagged values for RatingBar

Tagged value	Data type	Description
isIndicator	Boolean	Progress value to be displayed
numStars	Integer	Color of the progress completed
rating	Integer	Color of the progress under processing
stepSize	Integer	Progress bar will animate infinitely or not

StyledTextView

Description: This component is used to represent text in views (Table 7).
Base Class: IFML::Extensions::View

Table 7. Tagged values for StyledTextView

Tagged value	Data type	Description
textColor	Color	The color in which text will be displayed
textSize	Color	Font size of text
textStyle	Integer	Integer id of the custom style to be applied in this view
capitalized	Boolean	Whether text of this view is capitalized letters or lowercase
gravity	Integer	The alignment type of this view
typeface	Typeface	Font typeface applied on this text

StyledEditText

Description: This component is used to represent editable text in views.
Base Class: IFML::Extensions::View::StyledTextView

StyledButton

Description: This component is used to represent buttons in views.

Base Class: IFML::Extensions::View::StyledTextView
CompoundButton
Description: This component is a view generalized from StyledTextView Class. It is used to represent button or a group of buttons with icons in views.
Base Class: IFML::Extensions::View::StyledButton
Tagged Values: It contains following tagged value: checked:Boolean [1] which represented whether this view has been selected or not (Table 8)

Table 8. Tagged values for CompoundButton

Tagged value	Data type	Description
checked	Boolean	Represents whether this view has been selected or not

StyledCheckBox
Description: This component is used to select on or more options in a form
Base Class: IFML::Extensions::View::CompoundButton
StyledRadioButton
Description: This component is used to select one option out of many in a form
Base Class: IFML::Extensions::View::CompoundButton
Tagged Values: It contains following tagged value: thumb:Drawable [1] which represents what icon shape will appear for this button (Table 9)

Table 9. Tagged values for StyledRadioButton

Tagged value	Data type	Description
thumb	Drawable	Represents what icon shape will appear for this button

StyledSwitch
Description: This component is a UI representation of turning something on or off.
Base Class: IFML::Extensions::View::CompoundButton
Tagged Values: It contains following tagged value: checked:Boolean [1] which represented whether this view has been selected or not (Table 10)

Table 10. Tagged values for StyledSwitch

Tagged value	Data type	Description
checked	Boolean	Represents whether this view has been selected or not

TouchEvent
Description: This component is used to represent the Touch Events in Android application
Base Class: IFML::Core::SystemEvent

Tagged Values: It contains following tagged values: (1) coordinates: PointerCoordinates [1] which represents the position of the detected touch gesture, its orientation and area covered by touch

Operations: As touch events defines the behavior of the system therefore we have defined two operations for this stereotype (Table 11).

Table 11. Operations for TouchEvent

Operation	Return type	Description
isTouch	Boolean	returns a true value if the detected gesture is a valid touch event
obtainEvent (in coord: PointerCoordinates, in duration: Real, in pressure:Real)	void	captures the event and detects what type of event has occurred e.g. finger touch has been lifted, put down on screen etc.

Behavior of the following events will be determined by how the obtainEvent() operation is overloaded.

SingleTapEvent

Description: It can be used to detect the touch event in which user taps the screen one time.

Base Class: IFML::Extensions::TouchEvent

DoubleTapEvent

Description: This event can be used to detect the touch event in which user taps the screen two times with a threshold on duration between two consecutive taps.

Base Class: IFML::Extensions::TouchEvent

PinchAndZoomEvent

Description: This event can be used to detect the two finger event. It will be detected when user moved two fingers closer or apart

Base Class: IFML::Extensions::TouchEvent

DragAndDropEvent

Description: This event can be used to detect the touch event in which user touches one point on screen, drags the finger to other point and then releases

Base Class: IFML::Extensions::TouchEvent

PressAndHoldEvent

Description: This event can be used to detect the touch event in which user touches the screen once and let go of it after a specific time threshold. This is same as long press/touch of screen

Base Class: IFML::Extensions::TouchEvent

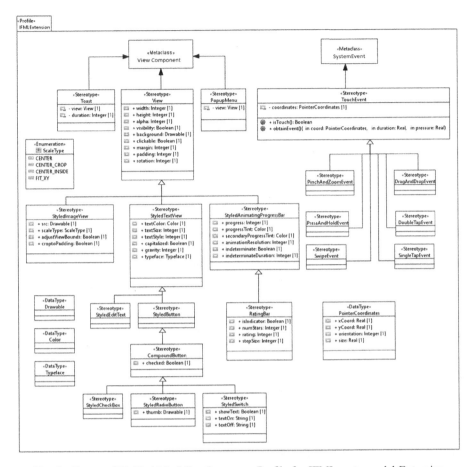

Fig. 2. Proposed Unified Modeling Language Profile for IFML meta-model Extension

SwipeEvent

Description: It can be used to detect the touch event in which user moves finger from one point to another on the screen based on a duration threshold. This can be single finger swipe or multi=finger swipe.

Base Class: IFML::Extensions::TouchEvent

IFML supports definition of datatypes similar to UML models. Following datatypes were defined in the profile for some of the tagged values:

ScaleType: It is an Enumeration which contains different literals which specify values for image scaleType are. Literals are as follows: CENTER_CROP, CEN-TER_INSIDE, CENTER_INSIDE, FIT_XY

Drawable: It is a DataType which is used to hold image resource and its behavior

Color: It is a DataType which holds the color values and properties for the views.

Typeface: It is a DataType which defines the font typeface and its properties (Table 12)

Table 12. Properties of PointerCoordinates

Properties	Return type	Description
xCoord	Real	contains the x-coordinate of the center point at which user has touched
yCoord	Real	contains the y-coordinate of the center point at which user has touched
orientation	Integer	the orientation of the touch gesture through an angle
Size	Real	value for touch area

4   Validation

Here, we present a design problem which can be catered using the styling and touch events defined in the previous section. We consider a set of requirements for an Android application UI that is responsible for displaying a form for online payment. The form consists of two screens: Payment Screen and Instructions Screen. Payment Screen consists of an instruction label, a field to enter amount, different options for payment method and a Pay button. User will enter amount in the field, select one of the options for payment and taps on Pay button. When the user taps on the button, Confirmation screen opens which contains a close button and open details label. If the user taps on the close button, the screen closes. If the user taps and holds on the open details label, a popup view appears on top of this view with transaction details.

Payment Screen and Confirmation Screen are created by default IFML::Core:: ViewComponent. The instruction label is created by using the IFML::Extension:: StyledTextView, field for payment amount can be styled by using IFML::Extension:: StyledEditText. Pay button and close button are created by using IFML::Extension:: StyledButton whereas the two payment options i.e. pay by cash and pay by credit card are created by IFML::Extension::StyledRadioButton. Details popup is created using the IFML::Extension::Popup. Two of the touch events are implemented by using the TouchEvents. Tap on pay button is done by IFML::Extensions::SingleTapEvent and press and hold on DetailsLabel is done by IFML::Extensions::PressAndHoldEvent. Default IFML::Core::Action is used to represent the actions triggered by our extended Events. In order to apply styling and touch events to this use case we use a subset of the stereotypes modeled in Fig. 2 on the before mentioned set of requirements for a UI.

Setting the values for the tagged values defined in the stereotypes of the View classes can help enhance user experience by providing styling information. Similarly, application can be navigated by using the Touch Events and their behavior can be defined by overriding the stereotype operations mentioned in Sect. 1. Figure 4 shows a graphical representation of this system modeled by IFML core components using our proposed extensions. Those IFML extensions can be seen in IFML Editor Tool palette in Fig. 3. Hence, any application can be easily modeled using the extensions in IFML Editor.

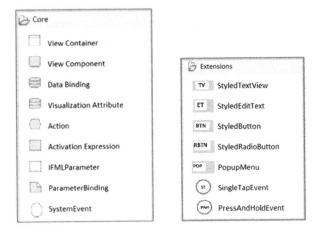

Fig. 3. IFML Editor Palette

5   Discussion

In this paper, an IFML extension model is provided which can be used to improve the presentation and usability of UIs of Android applications. This meta-model extension can be used to model a wide array of Android application UIs by means of IFML Editor Tool. This approach differs from [6, 7, 12, 18] as it provides details about the styling of user interface components for application presentation along with touch sensor interaction.

A case study was presented to validate usage of some of the defined UI extensions in the IFML Graphical Editor. The case study clearly shows how the extensions created in IFML can be used to model styling and touch events for Android application front-end. As IFML Editor is an open-source tool, hence any extensions created in IFML meta-model can be graphically represented by extending the tool in Sirius.

The IFML extensions created here can be used to generate code for custom UI classes which can directly be added to the XML layout files as supported by native Android platform.

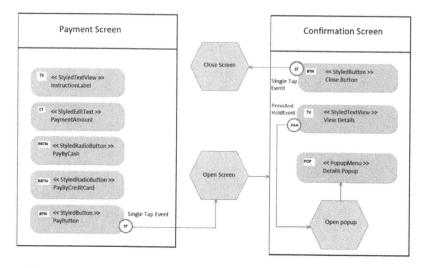

Fig. 4. Case study represented by user interface model created in IFML Editor

6 Conclusion

In this paper UI characteristics missing of Android applications in IFML were identified to create an IFML meta-model extension for Android application front-end. Several stereotypes were defined as extensions of the IFML View component to represent basic UI components used in mobile applications. Tagged values were used to introduce styling attributes of those views. Moreover, we defined Touch Event extension from IFML System Event to represent touch gestures in Android smartphones. Operations were used to represent the behavior of UI touch events. Currently, these elements are missing in the IFML meta-model. Addition of these styling and event characteristics to IFML can help enhance the usability of the user interfaces generated using IFML which was the one aspect missing in the modeling language. Hence, the extended model can be later used in model to text transformations.

References

1. Miao, G., Hongxing, L., Songyu, X., Juncai, L.: Research on user interface transformation method based on MDA. In: 2017 16th International Symposium on Distributed Computing and Applications to Business, Engineering and Science (DCABES) (2017)
2. Zouhaier, L., Hlaoui, Y.B., Ben Ayed, L.J.: Generating accessible multimodal user interfaces using MDA-based adaptation approach. In: 2014 IEEE 38th Annual Computer Software and Applications Conference (2014)
3. Hamdani, M., Butt, W.H., Anwar, M.W., Azam, F.: A systematic literature review on Interaction Flow Modeling Language (IFML). In: Proceedings of the 2018 2nd International Conference on Management Engineering, Software Engineering and Service Sciences, ICMSS 2018, pp. 134–138 (2018)

4. Bernaschina, C., Comai, S., Fraternali, P.: Formal semantics of OMG's Interaction Flow Modeling Language (IFML) for mobile and rich-client application model driven development. J. Syst. Softw. **137**, 239–260 (2018)

5. Laaz, N., Mbarki, S.: A model-driven approach for generating RIA interfaces using IFML and ontologies. In: 2016 4th IEEE International Colloquium on Information Science and Technology, pp. 83–88 (2017)

6. Acerbis, R., Bongio, A., Brambilla, M., Butti, S.: Model-driven development of cross-platform mobile applications with web ratio and IFML. In: Proceedings of the 2nd ACM International Conference on Mobile Software Engineering and Systems, MOBILESoft 2015, pp. 170–171 (2015)

7. Umuhoza, E., Ed-Douibi, H., Brambilla, M., Cabot, J., Bongio, A.: Automatic code generation for cross-platform, multi-device mobile apps: some reflections from an industrial experience. In: Proceedings of the 3rd International Workshop on Mobile Development Lifecycle, MobileDeLi 2015, pp. 37–44 (2015)

8. Rieger, C., Kuchen, H.: A process-oriented modeling approach for graphical development of mobile business apps. Comput. Lang. Syst. Struct. **53**, 43–58 (2018)

9. Brambilla, M., Mauri, A., Franzago, M., Muccini, H.: A model-based method for seamless web and mobile experience. In: Proceedings of the 1st Proceedings of the 1st International Workshop on Mobile Development, Mobile! 2016, pp. 33–40 (2016)

10. Bernaschina, C., Comai, S., Fraternali, P.: Online model editing, simulation and code generation for web and mobile applications. In: Proceedings of the 2017 IEEE/ACM 9th International Workshop on Modelling in Software Engineering, MiSE 2017, pp. 33–39 (2017)

11. Yigitbas, E., Sauer, S., Engels, G.: Adapt-UI. In: Proceedings of the ACM SIGCHI Symposium on Engineering Interactive Computing Systems, EICS 2017, pp. 99–104 (2017)

12. Laaz, N., Mbarki, S.: Integrating IFML models and owl ontologies to derive UIs web-Apps. In: 2016 International Conference on Information Technology for Organizations Development, IT4OD 2016, pp. 1–6 (2016)

13. Stürner, M., Brune, P.: Virtual worlds on demand? Model-driven development of Javascript-based virtual world UI components for mobile apps. In: Proceedings of the 4th International Conference on Model-Driven Engineering and Software Development, pp. 648–655 (2016)

14. Queiroz, R., Marques, A.B.: Evaluating usability of IFML models: how usability is perceived and propagated (2018)

15. Huang, A., Pan, M., Zhang, T., Li, X.: Static extraction of IFML models for android apps (2018)

16. Da Costa, S.L., Neto, V.V.G., De Oliveira, J.L.: A user interface stereotype to build Web portals. In: Proceedings of the 9th Latin American Web Congress, LA-WEB 2014, pp. 10–18 (2014)

17. Wakil, K., Jawawi, D.N.A.: Extensibility interaction flow modeling language metamodels to develop new web application concerns. Kurd. J. Appl. Res. **2**(3), 172–177 (2017)

18. Brambilla, M., Mauri, A., Umuhoza, E.: Extending the Interaction Flow Modeling Language (IFML) for model driven development of mobile applications front end. In: Awan, I., Younas, M., Franch, X., Quer, C. (eds.) MobiWIS 2014. LNCS, vol. 8640, pp. 176–191. Springer, Cham (2014). https://doi.org/10.1007/978-3-319-10359-4_15

19. Anwar, M.W., et al.: Model-based design verification for embedded systems through SVOCL: an OCL extension for SystemVerilog. Des. Autom. Embed. Syst. **21**(1), 1–36 (2017)

Directed Multi-target Search Based Unit Tests Generation

Greta Rudžionienė, Šarūnas Packevičius$^{(\boxtimes)}$, and Eduardas Bareiša$^{(\boxtimes)}$

Kaunas University of Technology, Kaunas, Lithuania
rd.greta@gmail.com, sarunas@ieee.org, eduardas.bareisa@ktu.lt

Abstract. Software testing costs are reduced by employing test automation. One of the automation activities is tests generation. The goal of
tests generation is to generate tests with large code coverage with the
efficient faults detection ability. Search-based tests generation methods
are analysed and their experimental comparison is provided in this paper.

The novel search-based unit tests generation approach directed by
multiple search targets to generate unit tests is presented. Introduced
method allows generating test data and oracles using static code analysis and code instrumentation. Oracles are created as assertions based on
system state after tests execution phase, thus making tests suitable for
regression testing.

The method was implemented as an experimental tool. It was
evaluated and compared against other search-based tests generation
tools/methods by using code coverage and mutation score metrics. The
experimental evaluation was performed on 124 classes from 3 open source
libraries.

Keywords: Unit tests generation · Unit testing ·
Search based software testing

1 Introduction

Users of software systems expect high quality software [1,2]. This is usually
achieved by software testing activities [3]. They include acceptance, system, integration, usability, components, units and other testing processes [4–6]. Many of
them require testers to manually define and implement tests. With the rise of
Continuous Integration/Continuous Delivery techniques [7] and DevOps culture,
unit testing has become crucial part to ensure high quality software. Automation tools can build and re-test software applications after each developer change
(regression testing) that involves automatically executing the whole test suite.

To ensure quality - high software coverage with unit tests and having effective
tests (tests with ability to detect as many defects as possible)[8] are needed. To
achieve those goals, it is necessary: (a) to have enough tests to cover all software
units, (b) tests must be self-checking (having oracles).

The "a" option is achieved by automatically generating unit tests [9,10]. The
"b" option is achieved by automatically adding test oracles to generated tests,

© Springer Nature Switzerland AG 2019
R. Damaševičius and G. Vasiljevienė (Eds.): ICIST 2019, CCIS 1078, pp. 90–109, 2019.
https://doi.org/10.1007/978-3-030-30275-7_8

accepting first tests run results as correct values (and using those as a basis for regression testing) [11], or using model based testing [12,13].

In most cases oracles in tests are defined manually. This requires having test data (tests) that is minimal and covering as much application as possible resulting in test suite optimization problem. Therefore, search-based tests generators must reach two goals: (a) reach as high code coverage as possible, (b) be as small as possible in terms of test suite size (number of test cases).

In this paper we are investigating a search-based unit tests generation approach directed by multiple search targets (objectives) to generate unit tests that cover those goals. Our approach uses static analysis and instrumentation to collect structural information before and during tests execution. To solve "a" we use evolutionary algorithm to find test sequences which cover as much code as possible. To solve "b" - we add assertions based on system state after tests execution so that tests can be used for regression testing. To reduce number of test cases generated - we have set multiple target objectives which might overlap, resulting in tests covering several targets. To further reduce size of each test case in terms of statements - we incrementally augment test sequences so that shorter solutions are selected first.

To sum up, this paper makes the following contributions:

- We propose search based tests generation technique guided by structural and run-time data
- We evaluate our technique in terms of code coverage and mutation score, comparing it with state of the art tools (Randoop [10] and EvoSuite [9]) using 124 benchmarks from 3 open source programs by using two time budgets

  Main research questions were:

- RQ1: How does proposed technique compete with other state of the art tools (Randoop [10] and EvoSuite [9]) in terms of instructions, complexity and branches coverage?
- RQ2: How does proposed technique compete with other state of the art tools (Randoop [10] and EvoSuite [9]) in terms of fault detection ability?

The remainder of paper is organized as follows: Sect. 2 summarizes background and related work. Section 3 describes new search-based tests generation method. Section 4 describes experimental study and results comparing presented method and tool with Evosuite [9] and Randoop [10]. Section 5 provides further work. Conclusions are presented in the Sect. 6.

2   Background and Related Work

Software testing is perceived as an expensive part of software development [14]. Many methods are developed for reducing testing costs [15–17]. Costs are usually reduced by using automation [18]. Automation covers two parts of testing: (a) tests execution and (b) tests creation.

Test execution automation covers topics defining tests as executable ones (for example, behaviour driven development and test definition language [19]) and executing one. Also, selecting the best test suite from existing tests set for current regression tests run is one of testing costs reduction methods [20,21]. However, this kind of automation requires already created test suites.

The automation of tests creation relies on automated tests generation [22–24]. Tests generation methods can be grouped into such categories: test data and oracles generation. Data generation methods concentrate only on test data generation and code coverage by those tests. This goal is usually achieved using search-based test generation methods [25–28]. To achieve oracle generation goal - model based testing methods are applied [29–33].

In this paper we consider that target of search based test generators is software unit tests creation. Nevertheless, it has been applied to create other kinds of tests [34] as well. Created unit tests later can be extended with test oracles [11] (if necessary) and used for testing software in automated or ad-hoc run activities.

Unit test is a series of method calls with fixed input data and a means to evaluate if executed sequence resulted in the expected behaviour. They can aid in defects location, bugs prevention, serve as documentation and facilitate understanding of the system [35].

Evolutionary techniques such as GA, symbolic execution have already been proven to be efficient in effective unit tests generation [36,37]. They are inspired by natural selection. Such algorithms try to find solutions which cover particular targets. They start by generating initial set of candidate solutions called population. Then repeatedly apply mutation and crossover operators to find better solutions. Then only fittest members are transferred to the next generation. Fitness of a candidate solution is measured using fitness function [25] measuring how far/distant solution is from reaching a target goal.

In context of unit testing, a candidate solution represents a single test case consisting of method sequences and input test data. Quality of unit tests is usually evaluated by measuring code coverage and mutation testing. Coverage shows which lines, branches or instructions have been executed [38]. And mutation testing - shows if tests are able to detect faults by introducing small changes into software and rerunning test suites to see if they fail (detect the regression) [39]. Thus these criterion are used in fitness function to evaluate how good candidate solution is.

In literature, there are multiple search-based approaches available. We will discuss only a few of them. Random based tools such as Randoop [10], GRT [40], JTexpert [41] employs random testing to generate tests. Randoop generates sequences of method calls and then based on execution results creates either regression or fault revealing tests [10]. However, one main limitation of such generation is that there are lots of tests generated, which might be hard to maintain. GRT [40] combines static and dynamic techniques to guide random tests generation. Their result show that random testing can achieve high coverage and detect previously unknown defects. JTexpert [41] also uses random approach to generate tests which cover all branches. Results show that it achieved high code coverage (70%) in less than ten seconds.

Another, state of the art tool is Evosuite. It applies search based techniques such as whole test suite [9], multi-target genetic algorithms such as DynaMosa [42], seeding [43] to generate Junit tests [44]. It uses fitness functions and their combinations such as method, line, branch, output, mutation and exception coverage [45].

In [46] an incremental genetic algorithm was proposed. At first it tries to find a population of solutions which exercise branches. After this - that population is used as initial population for incremental part. This allows reducing number of iterations and population size.

3   Proposed Method

In this paper we are investigating a search based algorithm for test cases generation. Basic structure is displayed in Fig. 1. It consists of 2 main phases - preprocessing and search. In the pre-processing phase - structural information about statements in classes is collected and instrumentation happens. Then search phase starts. It uses meta data information from previous phase for selecting target goals and instrumented SUT (System Under Test) to track execution. At first initial population of candidate solutions is generated. Then algorithm repetitively tries to update current population to find best candidate solutions. After time budget is exhausted - all found solutions by each target goals are collected and transformed to unit tests.

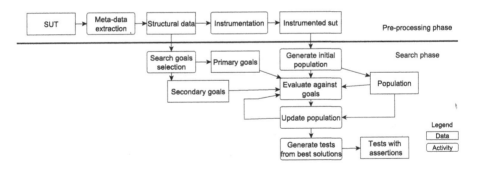

Fig. 1. High level overview of proposed method

Main parts are discussed in the next chapters.

3.1   Pre-processing Phase

Meta Data Extraction. In this step structural information about each CUT (Class Under Test) is extracted. It analyses all statements in CUT and collects information about their types, parameters and methods which contain them.

Instrumentation. This step is responsible for adding probing statements to each method in CUT. This allows tracking what values were used and which statements were executed during each method call in SUT. Figure 2 demonstrates an example of a method dividing CUT result value by passed argument *(v)* before instrumentation. And Fig. 3 contains an instrumented version. Line 8 shows a call to probe method with fully qualified method name, unique identifier and values which were used. Once this statement gets executed - tests generator collects data about a branch predicate which is going to be evaluated. On line 10 - there is another call to probe method with executed method name and unique identifier to indicate that a branch predicate was satisfied. Once such instrumented method gets executed - we know what kind of statements were called and what values were used allowing to guide search.

```
1   public class Calculator {
2           private double result = 0;
3           public Calculator divide(double v) {
4                   if (v != 0) {
5                           result /= v;
6                   }
7                   return this;
8           }
9   }
```

Fig. 2. Method before instrumentation

3.2   Candidate Solution Representation

Very important part in search based tests generation is candidate solution representation. In our method each solution contains two parts: sequence of method calls which need to be executed and input data for the sequence.

Sequence part contains definitions of constructor, writers and observers method calls. Constructor defines what kind of method and parameters are needed to create an instance of CUT. Writers contain a list of methods and parameters which will participate in crossover part. Those methods change CUT state or do some calculations. Observers are used in oracles generation as they return state of CUT without any side effects.

Input data part contains information what kind of values need to be passed when executing sequence methods. They are used in execution of methods. Mutation operation alters those values and generates new solutions with the intent that uncovered branches or statements will be executed.

3.3   Search Phase

Search phase is responsible for generating candidate solutions and finding best ones. Each solution is evaluated against target goal and if it satisfies required

```
1    public class Calculator {
2            private double result = 0;
3            public Calculator divide(double v)
4            {
5                    Object aug_test5, aug_test6;
6                    aug_test5 = Double.valueOf(0.0);
7                    aug_test6 = Double.valueOf(v);
8                    BranchesMonitor.INSTANCE.pre("<Calculator:_Calculator_
                             divide(double)>", 4, aug_test5, aug_test6);
9                    if (v − 0.0 != 0) {
10                           BranchesMonitor.INSTANCE.hit("<Calculator:_
                                     Calculator_divide(double)>", 4);
11                           result = result / v;
12                   }
13                   return this;
14           }
15   }
```

Fig. 3. Method after instrumentation

target or is better than already existing - internal target archive gets updated. The whole procedure is depicted in Algorithm 1.

It starts by generating initial population and target goals. Then while time has not run out - algorithm searches for best solutions. At first - solutions in current population are evaluated against target goals. Then with some random probability fixed number of solutions selected from population are stored in the archive. After this - depending on another probability either best candidates or archive items are selected for generating next generation. Then by applying either crossover or mutation operation - new candidate solutions are created. Crossover operation creates new solutions by updating list of writer methods in sequences. Mutation operator - only alters input data. This is discussed in further sections.

Initial Population Generation. Initial population is created by analysing CUT methods. They are classified as constructors (creating instances of CUT), observers (not changing class state) and writers (methods which change class state or do some calculations). Then Cartesian product of constructors and writers is created. Each such pair is augmented by calls to observer methods and default input data set forming a candidate solution. Such dynamic selection of initial population allows finding shorter sequences of method calls satisfying target goals because solutions are augmented only later by crossover operator with additional calls to writer methods.

Target Goals Selection. Target goals are responsible for selecting best candidate solutions which are later transformed to actual tests in form of tests.

Input : Time budget b, Sample count n, Probabilities $p_1, p_2, p3$, Class *class* under test, Structural classes information from pre-process phase *structInfo*

Output: Selected candidate solutions for tests output *solutions*

1   *population* ← *GenerateInitialPopulation(class, structInfo)*;
2   *archive* ← ∅;
3   *goals* ← *GenerateTargetGoals(class, structInfo)*;
4 **while** *Time budget b has not run out* **do**
5   EvaluatePopulation(*goals, population*) ;
6   p ← *RandomProbability()* ;
7   **if** $p \geq p_1$ **then**
8 | *archive* ← *archive* ∪ *SampleNItemsFrom(population, n)*;
9   **end**
10   **if** $p \geq p_2$ **then**
11 | *population* ← *SampleNItemsFrom(archive, n)*;
12   **end**
13   **else**
14 | *population* ← *GetBestCandidates(goals)*;
15   **end**
16   **if** $p \geq p_3$ **then**
17 | *population* ← *Crossover(population)*;
18   **end**
19   **else**
20 | *population* ← *Mutate(population)*;
21   **end**
22 **end**
23 *best* = *GetBestCandidatesSet(goals)*;
24 **return** *best*;

Algorithm 1: Search procedure

Algorithm analyses information gathered in the pre-processing phase and creates target goals. They represent what kind of condition does a solution need to satisfy in order to get selected in the final output. There are two types of goals - primary and secondary. Against primary goals - execution results are always evaluated as they guide search. While against secondary goals - only if goal does not have any solution or primary goal target was met in order to select better candidate. This allows controlling number of selected solutions as some of the candidates might cover multiple goals. After each evaluation if new solution is better than currently held, new solution replaces old one or is appended to the internal goal archive.

The following target goals are created:

– Branches - these goals require that a particular branch predicate is executed. To reduce inputs search space we have categorized branches into such types [47]:

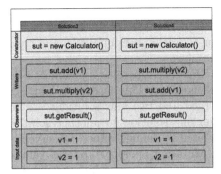

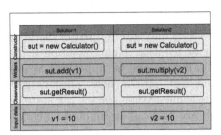

(a) Solutions for crossover   (b) Generated solutions

Fig. 4. Crossover operator

- Numeric branches (primary) - for which distance can be expressed as a real number. For example for branch $if(a \geq 5)$ if "a" value equals to 1, we calculate distance as $|1 - 5| = 4$
  * Branch predicate was executed and not satisfied, distance is larger than stored in the goal archive
  * Branch predicate was executed and not satisfied, distance is smaller than stored in the goal archive
  * Branch predicate was executed and satisfied, distance is smaller than stored in the goal archive
  * Branch predicate was executed and satisfied, distance is larger than stored in the goal archive
- Non-numeric branches (primary) - for which distance can be expressed only as boolean value, for example $if(a == null)$
  * Branch predicate was executed and not satisfied
  * Branch predicate was executed and satisfied
- Non void return statement (secondary) - this goal seeks to find a fixed number solutions which returned unique values
- Unexpected exception thrown (primary) - this goal tracks any unique exceptions that have not been thrown by throws statement
- Parameter value change (secondary) - this goal tracks parameter value change before and after method call. For example an array of numbers $[3, 2, 1]$ was passed as argument and after method execution array values were rearranged to $[1, 2, 3]$. If this happened and goal has not been satisfied yet - then such solution will get selected
- Other control statement execution (secondary) - this goal tracks if control flow statements were executed. This excludes all branching and return statements as they are covered by other goals.

3.4 Mutation and Crossover

Our algorithm uses mutation and crossover operators to generate new candidate solutions.

Crossover operator - generates new children by only altering writer methods in sequences. This is depicted in Fig. 4 where Solution 1 and Solution 2 are merged and two new solutions are created. This is done by appending writer from one solution to another solution. Input test data in new solutions gets updated to default values. Observers stay the same as they track CUT state.

Mutation operator updates values which are used as an input. In Fig. 5 a solution is depicted which used value 10 as an input for parameter $v1$ when calling method *add*. After mutation operator is applied - three new solutions are added to the population where value $v1$ is incremented (Solution 6) and decremented by 1 (Solution 7) and multiplied -1 (Solution 5).

3.5 Solutions Evaluation

In this step, each candidate solution is executed and its execution trace is evaluated against primary and secondary goals. Execution trace contains information about what kind of statements were executed. Whole process is depicted in Algorithm 2.

Input: Population of candidate solutions to evaluate *population* , target goals structure *goals* containing primary and secondary goals

```
 1 foreach candidate solution sol_i ∈ population do
 2      result = Execute(sol_i) ;
 3      solutionMatches = false ;
 4      foreach goal g_i ∈ goals.primaryGoals do
 5          if goal.isMatch(result) then
 6              goal.save(result);
 7              solutionMatches ← TRUE ;
 8          end
 9      end
10      foreach goal g_i ∈ goals.secondaryGoals do
11          if solutionMatches ∧ (¬g_i.hasAnySolutions()) then
12              if goal.isMatch(result) then
13                  goal.save(result) ;
14              end
15          end
16      end
17 end
```

Algorithm 2: Population evaluation

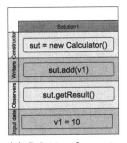

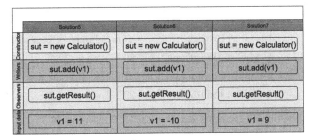

(a) Solution for mutation

(b) Generated solutions

Fig. 5. Mutation operator

4 Evaluation

4.1 Experimental Setup

This section presents evaluation of our method. We have developed ATG tool implementing technique suggested in previous section. It uses Soot framework[1] for pre-processing phase. For unit tests generation we used JavaParser framework[2].

We have compared tool performance on code coverage and fault detection ability with Evosuite (1.0.6 version) and Randoop (4.1.1 version) tools. In this study, we performed experiments using JUnit Tool Contest infrastructure[3]. Experiments were done using Docker image on AMD Ryzen physical machine with 16 GB RAM and Linux Debian OS. Java version 1.8 with maximum 12G heap size was used. We only specified time budgets for Evosuite and Randoop, leaving other parameter values to default ones.

Empirical Study Objects. The study was performed on 124 classes from 3 open source libraries. Each project was checked out from Github and built locally. Only public and non abstract classes were selected for tests generation. All used projects are described in Table 1. Column *Classes* shows a number of non abstract classes selected for benchmarking. *Methods* and *Branches* columns indicate number of methods and branches in the selected benchmark classes. In total 124 benchmarks were chosen.

Experimental Procedure. To answer both of the research questions (RQ1 and RQ2), we have generated tests using 10 and 30 s budget for all (124) selected classes using our tool, Evosuite and Randoop. We have repeated all these runs 5 times, totalling in 3720 (124 * 3 * 5 * 2) test generation tries. After that,

---

[1] https://github.com/Sable/soot.

[2] https://github.com/javaparser/javaparser.

[3] https://github.com/PROSRESEARCHCENTER/junitcontest.

Table 1. Experiment's items

Id	Project	Total classes	Classes	Methods	Branches
1-ALG	Algorithms[a]	89	85	343	879
3-COM	Commons-CLI[b]	27	20	245	588
1-JOD	Joda-Money[c]	29	19	345	675
Total		145	124	933	2142
Average		48,333	41,333	311	714

[a]https://github.com/pedrovgs/Algorithms,
ref: ed6f8a49948c09a21bfeb7bc38b4f24141795e38
[b]https://github.com/apache/commons-cli,
ref: 24113f46d2890f2aa972a2f88bb03dccb59c252a
[c]https://github.com/JodaOrg/joda-money,
ref: e1f2de75aa36610a695358696c8a88a18ca66cde

tests code was compiled. To answer question one - code coverage was measured with Jacoco[4] tool by running each generated test suite separately against each benchmark class. To answer question two - we ran mutation testing using Pit[5] tool with ALL mutators enabled the same way as we run test suites for code coverage measurement.

4.2 Results

In this section we summarize results from the study. In further tables column *Ev.* shows results from Evosuite, *Rn.* - Randoop and *ATG* from our tool.

Table 2 shows average number of tests generated during each run. When using 10 s budget - ATG tool generated 723 tests, Evosuite - 504 and Randoop - 18830 on average per project. During 30 s run - ATG generated around 823, Evosuite - 576 and Randoop - 59122 tests on average per project. The increase of generated tests is explained by the fact that ATG and Evosuite are search based tools. They try to find solutions which cover target goals. With increased budget, there is a chance that tests meeting target goals were found and generated in the final test suite. While large number of tests generated by Randoop is explained by the fact that tool randomly generates tests until search budget is exhausted. With bigger time budget, more tests are generated.

It is noticeable that Evosuite was not able to generate tests for 11 items during 10 s run. This number slightly decreased once time budget was increased to 30 s. ATG tool was not able to cover 2 objects, while Randoop - 7 during both runs. After manually investigating tests, we found out that ATG tool did not generate any tests for a single benchmark due to internal timeout for a single test execution (3 s) as initial population contained 39 sequences and only a few of them were executed. This could be facilitated by introducing dynamic allocation

---

[4] https://www.eclemma.org/jacoco/.
[5] http://pitest.org/.

of timeout for a single sequence. And another case was caused by a syntax error for complex data structure in the generated suite. Randoop did not generate any tests as it could not generate any sequences at all for skipped benchmarks. Evosuite did not generate tests due to the allocated budget timeout.

Table 2. Test counts by project, tool and budget

Project	Tool	10 s budget		30 s budget	
		Skipped	Avg. no. tests	Skipped	Avg. no. tests
0-ALG	atg	0	1086	0	1136
0-ALG	evosuite	10	463	6	532
0-ALG	randoop	6	34891	6	104327
1-JOD	atg	0	474	0	627
1-JOD	evosuite	0	649	0	725
1-JOD	randoop	0	10353	0	34321
3-COM	atg	2	611	2	707
3-COM	evosuite	1	400	0	473
3-COM	randoop	1	11246	1	38720
Total	atg	2	2171	2	2470
	evosuite	11	1512	6	1730
	randoop	7	56490	7	177368
Average	atg	0,667	723,667	0,667	823,333
	evosuite	3,667	504	2	576,667
	randoop	2,333	18830	2,333	59122,667

RQ1: Code Coverage. Figures 6, 7, 8 summarizes results for answering RQ1. They show how many instructions, complexity and branches were covered for each project's benchmark by every tool. All tools managed to cover more instructions, complexity and branches with an increased budget than compared to smaller time budget. Evosuite performed the best in terms of covering branches (88%), complexity (88%) and instructions (90%) during all runs. ATG tool managed to cover 64% branches, 64% complexity and 77% instructions. Resulting in better coverage than Randoop. It covered 48% branches, 60% complexity and 61% of instructions.

To further verify the findings, additional calculations using Vargha and Delaney effect size and Mann-Whitney U-test were performed as recommended by [48]. Results are represented in Table 3. $ATG \geq$ column shows how many percent of cases prototype tool managed to cover methods better or equally when compared with the other tool. Column $Avg., ATG \geq$ displays averages.

Table 3. Coverage statistics

Tool	Project	Counter	Budget	Ef. size	p-value	ATG>=	Avg., ATG>=
Ev.	0-ALG	BRANCH	10	0,43977	0,00564	82,184	55,18
Ev.	0-ALG	BRANCH	30	0,44066	0,00001	84,239	
Ev.	1-JOD	BRANCH	10	0,32414	0,00000	41,964	
Ev.	1-JOD	BRANCH	30	0,24916	0,00000	41,071	
Ev.	3-COM	BRANCH	10	0,23474	0,00000	32,812	
Ev.	3-COM	BRANCH	30	0,28174	0,00001	48,438	
Ev.	0-ALG	COMPLEXITY	10	0,47217	0,04442	89,199	664,292
Ev.	0-ALG	COMPLEXITY	30	0,46773	0,00011	90,615	
Ev.	1-JOD	COMPLEXITY	10	0,42908	0,00000	65,587	
Ev.	1-JOD	COMPLEXITY	30	0,36877	0,00000	65,992	
Ev.	3-COM	COMPLEXITY	10	0,17815	0,00000	28,846	
Ev.	3-COM	COMPLEXITY	30	0,24645	0,00000	45,513	
Ev.	0-ALG	INSTRUCTION	10	0,47382	0,08168	88,502	64,234
Ev.	0-ALG	INSTRUCTION	30	0,46346	0,00003	90,291	
Ev.	1-JOD	INSTRUCTION	10	0,44941	0,00000	68,421	
Ev.	1-JOD	INSTRUCTION	30	0,37417	0,00000	66,397	
Ev.	3-COM	INSTRUCTION	10	0,17558	0,00000	27,564	
Ev.	3-COM	INSTRUCTION	30	0,24762	0,00000	44,231	
Rn.	0-ALG	BRANCH	10	**0,75392**	**0,00000**	94,652	81,133
Rn.	0-ALG	BRANCH	30	**0,75713**	**0,00000**	95,722	
Rn.	1-JOD	BRANCH	10	**0,62580**	**0,00000**	83,929	
Rn.	1-JOD	BRANCH	30	**0,63951**	**0,00000**	87,5	
Rn.	3-COM	BRANCH	10	0,47083	0,55367	59,375	
Rn.	3-COM	BRANCH	30	0,52783	0,50323	65,625	
Rn.	0-ALG	COMPLEXITY	10	**0,67298**	**0,00000**	96,774	79,132
Rn.	0-ALG	COMPLEXITY	30	**0,67766**	**0,00000**	97,419	
Rn.	1-JOD	COMPLEXITY	10	**0,66341**	**0,00000**	91,498	
Rn.	1-JOD	COMPLEXITY	30	**0,67578**	**0,00000**	92,308	
Rn.	3-COM	COMPLEXITY	10	0,28893	0,00000	41,026	
Rn.	3-COM	COMPLEXITY	30	0,34759	0,00000	55,769	
Rn.	0-ALG	INSTRUCTION	10	**0,65491**	**0,00000**	96,129	79,159
Rn.	0-ALG	INSTRUCTION	30	**0,66361**	**0,00000**	97,419	
Rn.	1-JOD	INSTRUCTION	10	**0,66816**	**0,00000**	92,308	
Rn.	1-JOD	INSTRUCTION	30	**0,67948**	**0,00000**	92,308	
Rn.	3-COM	INSTRUCTION	10	0,28569	0,00000	41,026	
Rn.	3-COM	INSTRUCTION	30	0,35597	0,00001	55,769	

Based on performed calculations, we can see that ATG tool was not able to cover greater number of branches, complexity or instructions than Evosuite for all benchmarks. This could be explained by the fact that Evosuite is very mature tool. However, we can see that ATG tool performed better as effect

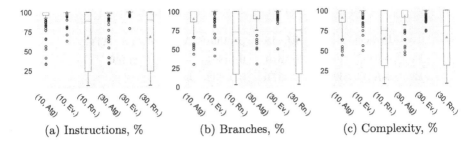

Fig. 6. Algorithms coverage

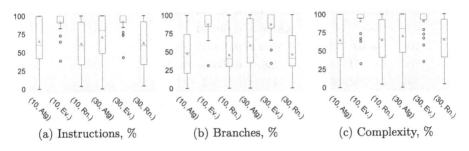

Fig. 7. Commons-CLI coverage

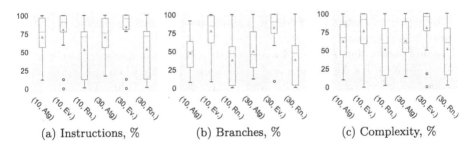

Fig. 8. Joda-Money coverage

size is over 0.5 and p-value less than 0.005 for the Algorithms and Joda-Money project when compared with Randoop. Prototype managed to cover around 90% branches, complexity and instructions better or equally than Randoop tool.

In general, prototype tool managed to cover equally or better 55% branches, 64% complexity, 64% instructions when compared to Evosuite. Comparison with Randoop shows that ATG was able to cover equally or better 79% of instructions, 79% complexity and 81% of branches on average.

RQ2: Fault Detection. To answer RQ2 mutation testing was performed. In total 1443040 mutants were executed. Figure 9 shows average number of achieved mutation score using different budgets. Mutation score is calculated as a ratio

Table 4. Mutation score statistics among tools

Tool	Project	Budget	Ef. size	p-value	ATG>=	Avg, ATG>=
Ev.	0-ALG	10	0,4619	0,14861	53,394	41,998
Ev.	0-ALG	30	0,43716	0,02432	54,583	
Ev.	1-JOD	10	0,42769	0,00000	50,698	
Ev.	1-JOD	30	0,39414	0,00000	49,693	
Ev.	3-COM	10	0,18716	0,00000	19,178	
Ev.	3-COM	30	0,218	0,00000	24,444	
Rn.	0-ALG	10	**0,66152**	**0,00000**	78,333	68,262
Rn.	0-ALG	30	**0,66208**	**0,00000**	78,750	
Rn.	1-JOD	10	**0,65962**	**0,00000**	82,326	
Rn.	1-JOD	30	**0,66964**	**0,00000**	83,028	
Rn.	3-COM	10	0,30684	0,00000	39,726	
Rn.	3-COM	30	0,34403	0,00003	47,407	

of killed (detected) mutants divided by total number of total mutants. Each mutant is a version of a cut with a small change (incorrect class version).

Evosuite was the best at detecting faults reaching average 65% mutation score overall. ATG detected 49% mutants. And - Randoop 39% on average.

To further validate these findings, non-parametric statistics were calculated as in previous section.

Table 4 shows that ATG tool managed to detect more mutants with statistical significance for Algorithms and Joda-Money project when compared with Randoop as effect size is over 0.5 and p-value less than 0.005. Overall, ATG managed to detect same amount or more mutants as Evosuite in 41% of cases. When compared to Randoop this number was even higher. In 68% of cases ATG performed same of better.

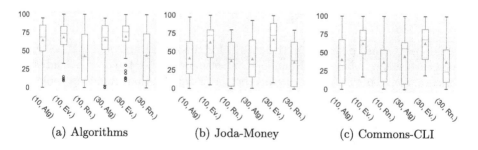

(a) Algorithms   (b) Joda-Money   (c) Commons-CLI

Fig. 9. Mutation score (%) by project

Summary. To sum up, our tool implementing proposed method managed to cover on average 64% instructions, 64% complexity, 55% branches equally or better than Evosuite. Results on comparison with Randoop are more promising as it managed to exercise 79% instructions and complexity, 81% branches equally or better. With regards to fault detection capability - our tool on average was better or equal to Evosuite in 41% and in 68% compared to Randoop in all runs. Altogether, these are great results having in mind that Evosuite and Randoop have been actively developed for over 5 years [10, 49].

5 Further Work

During experiments we have identified the following places for improvement - constants seeding, methods classification into pure/impure, object types support and parameter tuning.

Constants seeding has successfully been already implemented in Evosuite [43]. Results have shown increase in performance. Prototype used during experiments only supported seeding of String constants. Improving this area could allow our tool to cover more targets (i.e. branches) and find solutions faster.

With regards to purity [50] - ATG tool based on return type and number of arguments decides whether a method is pure or not. Pure methods act as observers, returning only object's state. Impure methods - are used to alter CUT state or do some calculations. Improvement in this area would allow generating better test suites in terms of coverage and mutation score as more CUT states would be covered. Randoop [10] already provides ability for the user to supply either a list of side-effect-free methods or add annotations to code.

Improved object types support would allow to generate shorter tests and improve coverage. As if tool would know that a particular interface is implemented by a concrete class, it could reused instead of instantiating an anonymous class object. This is already supported in Evosuite [43, 51]. Results confirm shorter tests length, improved coverage and mutation score.

And last but not the least, search based test techniques greatly depend on various parameters - population size, mutation and crossover probabilities and others. During experimentation we identified a case when no tests were generated, as initial tests population was not fully executed due to timeouts for a single test sequence. This could be facilitated by dynamic budget allocation for a single member execution. Improvements in this area could greatly impact test suites generation.

6 Conclusions

Search based testing is efficient in generating effective unit tests. In this paper we have evaluated a search based technique which uses multiple target goals for tests generation. Our approach is novel as it uses more granular set of fitness functions than other tools and uses crossover operator intelligently guide solutions search.

A comparison with other state of the art tools have shown that our method can generate tests which achieve same or higher coverage (in 80% cases) and mutants detection (in 68% cases) than Randoop. While results when comparing with very mature search based tests generation tool Evosuite, show that there is still place for improvement. Although our tool managed to reach higher or equal instructions coverage in 64% and complexity cases as Evosuite, but less amount of mutants were detected (only 41% cases were better or same).

References

1. Whittaker, J.A., Voas, J.M.: 50 years of software: key principles for quality. IT Prof. **4**(1520–9202), 28–35 (2002)
2. Misra, S., Adewumi, A., Maskeliūnas, R., Damaševičius, R., Cafer, F.: Unit testing in global software development environment. In: Panda, B., Sharma, S., Roy, N.R. (eds.) REDSET 2017. CCIS, vol. 799, pp. 309–317. Springer, Singapore (2018). https://doi.org/10.1007/978-981-10-8527-7_25
3. Myers, G.J., Sandler, C.: The Art of Software Testing. Wiley, New York (2004). ISBN 0471469122
4. Fitzgerald, B., Stol, K.-J.: Continuous software engineering and beyond: trends and challenges. In: Proceedings of the 1st International Workshop on Rapid Continuous Software Engineering, pp. 1–9. ACM, Hyderabad (2014). https://doi.org/10.1145/2593812.2593813. ISBN 978-1-4503-2856-2
5. Alhassan, J.K., Misra, S., Umar, A., Maskeliūnas, R., Damaševičius, R., Adewumi, A.: A fuzzy classifier-based penetration testing for web applications. In: Rocha, Á., Guarda, T. (eds.) ICITS 2018. AISC, vol. 721, pp. 95–104. Springer, Cham (2018). https://doi.org/10.1007/978-3-319-73450-7_10. ISBN 978-3-319-73449-1
6. Soltani, M., Panichella, A., van Deursen, A.: A guided genetic algorithm for automated crash reproduction. In: 2017 IEEE/ACM 39th International Conference on Software Engineering (ICSE), pp. 209–220, May 2017
7. Cobanoglu, C.: Adopting continuous delivery practices to increase efficiency: a case study (2017)
8. Gopi, P., Ramalingam, M., Arumugam, C.: Search based test data generation: a multi objective approach using MOPSO evolutionary algorithm. In: Proceedings of the 9th Annual ACM India Conference, pp. 137–140. ACM, Gandhinagar (2016). https://doi.org/10.1145/2998476.2998492. ISBN 978-1-4503-4808-9
9. Rojas, J.M., Vivanti, M., Arcuri, A., Fraser, G.: A detailed investigation of the effectiveness of whole test suite generation. Empir. Softw. Eng. **22**, 1–42 (2016). https://doi.org/10.1007/s10664-015-9424-2. ISSN 1573–7616
10. Pacheco, C., Ernst, M.D.: Randoop: feedback-directed random testing for Java. In: OOPSLA 2007 Companion, pp. 815–816. ACM (2007)
11. Danglot, B., Vera-Perez, O.L., Baudry, B., Monperrus, M.: Automatic test improvement with DSpot: a study with ten mature open-source projects. arXiv preprint arXiv:1811.08330 (2018)
12. Pretschner, A.: Model-based testing, St. Louis, MO, USA (2005). https://doi.org/10.1145/1062455.1062636
13. Barr, E.T., Harman, M., McMinn, P., Shahbaz, M., Yoo, S.: The Oracle problem in software testing: a survey. IEEE Trans. Softw. Eng. **41**, 507–525 (2015)
14. Jones, C., Bonsignour, O.: The Economics of Software Quality. Addison-Wesley Professional, Reading (2011)

15. Binkley, D.: Using semantic differencing to reduce the cost of regression testing. In: Proceedings Conference on Software Maintenance, pp. 41–50 (1992)

16. Eski, S., Buzluca, F.: An empirical study on object-oriented metrics and software evolution in order to reduce testing costs by predicting change-prone classes. In: 2011 IEEE Fourth International Conference on Software Testing, Verification and Validation Workshops, pp. 566–571 (2011)

17. Diaz, E., Tuya, J., Blanco, R.: Automated software testing using a meta-heuristic technique based on tabu search. In: 18th IEEE International Conference on Automated Software Engineering, Proceedings, pp. 310–313 (2003)

18. Karhu, K., Repo, T., Taipale, O., Smolander, K.: Empirical observations on software testing automation. In: 2009 International Conference on Software Testing Verification and Validation, pp. 201–209 (2009)

19. Solis, C., Wang, X.: A study of the characteristics of behaviour driven development. In: 2011 37th EUROMICRO Conference on Software Engineering and Advanced Applications, pp. 383–387 (2011)

20. Baudry, B., Fleurey, F., Le Traon, Y.: Improving test suites for efficient fault localization. In: Proceedings of the 28th International Conference on Software Engineering, pp. 82–91 (2006)

21. Lam, S.S.B., Raju, M.H.P., Ch, S., Srivastav, P.R., et al.: Automated generation of independent paths and test suite optimization using artificial bee colony. Procedia Eng. **30**, 191–200 (2012)

22. Korel, B.: Automated software test data generation. IEEE Trans. Softw. Eng. **16**, 870–879 (1990)

23. Zhang, S., Saff, D., Bu, Y., Ernst, M.D.: Combined static and dynamic automated test generation. In: Proceedings of the 2011 International Symposium on Software Testing and Analysis, pp. 353–363 (2011)

24. Chen, T., Zhang, X.-S., Guo, S.-Z., Li, H.-Y., Wu, Y.: State of the art: dynamic symbolic execution for automated test generation. Future Gener. Comput. Syst. **29**, 1758–1773 (2013)

25. McMinn, P.: Search-based software test data generation: a survey. Softw. Testing Verif. Reliab. **14**, 105–156 (2004)

26. Ali, S., Briand, L.C., Hemmati, H., Panesar-Walawege, R.K.: A systematic review of the application and empirical investigation of search-based test case generation. IEEE Trans. Softw. Eng. **36**, 742–762 (2010)

27. Lakhotia, K., Harman, M., McMinn, P.: A multi-objective approach to search-based test data generation. In: Proceedings of the 9th Annual Conference on Genetic and Evolutionary Computation, pp. 1098–1105 (2007)

28. Harman, M., Kim, S.G., Lakhotia, K., McMinn, P., Yoo, S.: Optimizing for the number of tests generated in search based test data generation with an application to the oracle cost problem. In: 2010 Third International Conference on Software Testing, Verification, and Validation Workshops, pp. 182–191 (2010)

29. Utting, M., Pretschner, A., Legeard, B.: A taxonomy of model-based testing approaches. Softw. Testing Verif. Reliab. **22**, 297–312 (2012)

30. Packevicius, S., et al.: Test data generation for complex data types using imprecise model constraints and constraint solving techniques. Inf. Technol. Control **42**, 191–204 (2013). ISSN 1392-124X

31. Packevičius, Š., Ušaniov, A., Bareiša, E.: Software testing using imprecise OCL constraints as oracles. In: Proceedings of the 2007 International Conference on Computer Systems and Technologies, CompSysTech 2007, Bulgaria, pp. 121:1–121:6. ACM, New York (2007). https://doi.org/10.1145/1330598.1330726

32. Pretschner, A., et al.: One evaluation of model-based testing and its automation. In: Proceedings of the 27th International Conference on Software Engineering, pp. 392–401 (2005)

33. Barisas, D., Bareiša, E., Packevičius, Š.: Automated method for software integration testing based on UML behavioral models. In: Skersys, T., Butleris, R., Butkiene, R. (eds.) ICIST 2013. CCIS, vol. 403, pp. 272–284. Springer, Heidelberg (2013). https://doi.org/10.1007/978-3-642-41947-8_23

34. Arcuri, A.: RESTful API automated test case generation with EvoMaster. ACM Trans. Softw. Eng. Methodol. **28**, 3:1–3:37 (2019). https://doi.org/10.1145/3293455. ISSN 1049–331X

35. Meszaros, G.: XUnit Test Patterns: Refactoring Test Code. Prentice Hall PTR, Upper Saddle River (2006). ISBN 0131495054

36. Almulla, H., Salahirad, A., Gay, G.: Using search-based test generation to discover real faults in Guava. In: Menzies, T., Petke, J. (eds.) SSBSE 2017. LNCS, vol. 10452, pp. 153–160. Springer, Cham (2017). https://doi.org/10.1007/978-3-319-66299-2_13

37. Campos, J., et al.: An empirical evaluation of evolutionary algorithms for unit test suite generation. Inf. Softw. Technol. **104**, 207–235 (2018). http://www.sciencedirect.com/science/article/pii/S0950584917304858. ISSN 0950–5849

38. Yang, Q., Li, J.J., Weiss, D.M.: A survey of coverage-based testing tools. Comput. J. **52**, 589–597 (2009)

39. Jia, Y., Harman, M.: An analysis and survey of the development of mutation testing. IEEE Trans. Softw. Eng. **37**, 649–678 (2011). ISSN 0098–5589

40. Ma, L., et al.: GRT: an automated test generator using orchestrated program analysis. In: 2015 30th IEEE/ACM International Conference on Automated Software Engineering (ASE), pp. 842–847, November 2015

41. Sakti, A., Pesant, G., Guéhéneuc, Y.: Instance generator and problem representation to improve object oriented code coverage. IEEE Trans. Softw. Eng. **41**, 294–313 (2015). ISSN 0098–5589

42. Panichella, A., Kifetew, F.M., Tonella, P.: Automated test case generation as a many-objective optimisation problem with dynamic selection of the targets. IEEE Trans. Softw. Eng. **44**, 122–158 (2018). ISSN 0098–5589

43. Rojas, J.M., Fraser, G., Arcuri, A.: Seeding strategies in search-based unit test generation. Softw. Testing Verif. Reliab. (2016). https://doi.org/10.1002/stvr.1601. ISSN 1099–1689

44. Fraser, G.: A tutorial on using and extending the EvoSuite search-based test generator. In: Colanzi, T.E., McMinn, P. (eds.) SSBSE 2018. LNCS, vol. 11036, pp. 106–130. Springer, Cham (2018). https://doi.org/10.1007/978-3-319-99241-9_5. ISBN 978-3-319-99240-2

45. Rojas, J.M., Campos, J., Vivanti, M., Fraser, G., Arcuri, A.: Combining multiple coverage criteria in search-based unit test generation. In: Barros, M., Labiche, Y. (eds.) SSBSE 2015. LNCS, vol. 9275, pp. 93–108. Springer, Cham (2015). https://doi.org/10.1007/978-3-319-22183-0_7

46. Manikumar, T., John Sanjeev Kumar, A., Maruthamuthu, R.: Automated test data generation for branch testing using incremental genetic algorithm. Sadhana 41, 959–976 (2016). https://doi.org/10.1007/s12046-016-0536-1. ISSN 0973–7677

47. Shamshiri, S., Rojas, J.M., Fraser, G., McMinn, P.: Random or genetic algorithm search for object-oriented test suite generation? In: Proceedings of the 2015 Annual Conference on Genetic and Evolutionary Computation, pp. 1367–1374. ACM, Madrid (2015). https://doi.org/10.1145/2739480.2754696. ISBN 978-1-4503-3472-3

48. Arcuri, A., Briand, L.C.: A Hitchhiker's guide to statistical tests for as sessing randomized algorithms in software engineering. Softw. Test. Verif. Reliab. **24**, 219–250 (2014)
49. Fraser, G., Zeller, A.: Mutation-driven generation of unit tests and Oracles. In: Proceedings of the ACM International Symposium on Software Testing and Analysis, pp. 147–158. ACM, Trento (2010). https://doi.org/10.1145/1831708.1831728. ISBN 978-1-60558-823-0
50. Stewart, A., Cardell-Oliver, R., Davies, R.: UWA-CSSE-14001 Side effect and purity checking in Java: a review (2014)
51. Fraser, G., Arcuri, A.: Automated test generation for Java generics. In: Winkler, D., Biffl, S., Bergsmann, J. (eds.) SWQD 2014. LNBIP, vol. 166, pp. 185–198. Springer, Cham (2014). https://doi.org/10.1007/978-3-319-03602-1_12

Motivational and Goal-Oriented Viewpoint for Architectural Modeling of Software Intensive Systems

Petr Sosnin$^{(\boxtimes)}$

Ulyanovsk State Technical University, Ulyanovsk 432027, Russia
sosnin@ulstu.ru

Abstract. The paper deals with the use of the design thinking approach in creating the architectural views considering the motivational excitement and goal setting in designing the software intensive systems (SIS). In this case, any architectural view is formed in work with the system of conceptual equations, solving of which is based on the designer's reasoning of the abductive type. In conditions of automated design thinking, such reasoning helps to define constructive relations binding motives, goals, and requirements integrated into the corresponding view. For all views included in the architectural description, these relations are useful to combine, visualize, and interpret as motivationally targeted view demonstrated which architectural decisions correspond to the intended goals.

Keywords: Architectural modeling · Design thinking · Goal · Motivational design · Software intensive system · Viewpoint

1 Introduction

Professionally mature development of modern SIS is unthinkable without the mandatory construction and operational use of an architecture description (AD). This artifact is a conceptual version of SIS, reflecting its understanding as a wholeness, which is in demand by stakeholders at all stages of the SIS life cycle. As a sample of verified structures and embedded understanding, AD plays a managerial role, providing the correspondence between this sample and the current state of the SIS in the design process. Should also be highlighted, this version is the first (earliest) representation of SIS as a wholeness, which can be tested to detect dangerous semantic errors.

Marked positives of AD were reasons for intensive accumulating the experience of architectural modeling that was generalized in several standards among which it should be noted the standard ISO/IEC/IEEE 42010: 2011. This standard assumes that the AD is the system $S(\{V_j\})$ of "architectural views" $\{V_j\}$, based on corresponding "viewpoints" $\{VP_k\}$, each of which specifies "the conventions (such as notations, languages, and types of models) for constructing a certain kind of view. That viewpoint can be applied to many systems. Each view is one such application" [1].

Thus, any viewpoint can be interpreted as a certain guide with necessary means that help to build the corresponding view or a set of views, any of which expresses the

© Springer Nature Switzerland AG 2019
R. Damaševičius and G. Vasiljevienė (Eds.): ICIST 2019, CCIS 1078, pp. 110–120, 2019.
https://doi.org/10.1007/978-3-030-30275-7_9

certain interest (concern C_i) in visualized forms that are understandable for the certain stakeholders involved in the corresponding project. Therefore, any new viewpoint is an artifact that should be developed, starting with the decision to take into account the important concern (or their group), the viewpoint for which is absent or must be modified.

In this paper, we offer a viewpoint created for the controlled objectification of such types of problems as "motives" and "goals" in the conditions of development of a certain SIS, whose life cycle begins with vague intentions. In this case, firstly, the developers must understand the work ahead, presenting it as a whole as a task that needs to be solved. In the course of such an understanding, designers will need to identify the main motives and goals that will govern their work in the design process.

Our proposal is based on principle relations among "Motives," "Goals" and "Tasks" as essences, each of them plays a special role in the work with project tasks that must be solved in developing the AD of the corresponding SIS. These relations lead to the architectural view demonstrating the goal setting and means that help to attain all intended goals. The offered viewpoint is intended for developing of such architectural view that we called a motivationally targeted view.

The remainder of the paper is structured as follows. Features of design thinking in the considered version of architectural modeling are presented in Sect. 2. Section 3 points out related works. An approach in the offered viewpoint is described in Sect. 4. In Sect. 5, we present an example of the motivationally targeted view, and the paper is concluded in Sect. 6.

2   Features of Goal Setting in Developing the Architectural Description

Architectural modeling is a kind of activity in which the designers most fully manifest the features of design thinking. To underline these features, for the typical reasoning used by designers, Dorst [2] suggests using the expression

$$\frac{WHAT}{(thing)} + \frac{HOW}{(working\,principle)}\,leads\,\frac{RESULT}{(observed)} \tag{1}$$

which can be fitted on problematic situations arisen in designer's work. In investigated design situations, a researcher should define and insert adequate 'constant' and/or 'variables' in this expression after which it can be interpreted as a specific 'equation.'

Such interpretation helped to Dorst to analyze the following kinds of equations:

- DEDUCTION $WHAT + HOW\,leads\,???$
- INDUCTION $WHAT +\; ???\,leads\,RESULT$
- ABDUCTION 1 $??? + HOW\,leads\,RESULT$
- ABDUCTION 2 $??? +\; ???\,leads\,RESULT$

According to the analysis, Dorst concluded that abductive types of reasoning define the nature of designing as a human activity in problematic situations. Moreover, for design practice, the most typical reasoning corresponds to conceptual equations of the fourth kind, which require the use of iterative reducing the uncertainties of 'unknowns' till their appropriate 'values.'

Such a way opens up the possibility for the reasoning of designers even in conditions

$$\frac{WHAT\,???}{(thing)} + \frac{HOW\,???}{(working\,principle)}\,leads\,\frac{RESULT\,???}{(observed)}, \qquad (2)$$

in which the designer iteratively sets intermediate values for two unknowns, calculating the third unknown in the conceptual equation to be solved.

Considering equations of all kinds are formed in different situations for diverse essences corresponded components of equations, but, in any case, they reflect cause-and-effect inferences that are intertwined in the design process. Among these inferences, solving the abductive equations occupy the principal place.

What has been said above is particularly important at early design steps, when designers try to express an arisen intention about achieving the conceived value. This intention implicitly concerns reasoning about the motives and goals of the project and their formulation or, by other words, it concerns the work, for example, with the following equation

$$\frac{Motives\,??}{(essences)} + \frac{HOW\,?}{(goal\,setting)}\,leads\,\frac{Goals\,???}{(intended)}, \qquad (3)$$

in which the quantity of question signs indicates on the different degree of uncertainty.

It should be noted, intentions, motives, and goals are typical concerns in architectural modeling, that prompt to bind with such modeling an appropriate view or views and a viewpoint or viewpoints. This paper devotes to defining of them, but, previously, we want to disclose some our positions that are based on the Vityaev's research [3], the content of which defines relations among motives and goals in the frame of the corresponding task and results of its solution.

In this publication based on the theory of functional systems (TFS, developed by P. Anokhin [4]), E. Vityaev describes features of the goal-directed behavior in conditions when a person is trying to solve the certain task. The discussed kind of behavior includes the following specific features:

1. Intrinsic and/or extrinsic stimulus (perceived by the person) lead to a motivational excitement that activates mechanisms of goal setting.
2. An initial definition of the intended goal "does not imply knowledge of how, by what means and when it can be attained."
3. The goal cannot be attained without having a criterion of its attainment.
4. "Between the concepts of goal and result, the following relationship holds: the result is obtained when the goal is attained, and the criterion of its availability is "triggered." But when the goal is being set, we have the goal but not the result."
5. Extending the description of the goal by conditions in which the expected result can be (possible hypothetically) obtained, leads to a description of what is called the "task.

Below, these features and described understanding of the design nature will be taken into account in our reasoning that will concern the work with project tasks that help to create the architecture of the SIS

3   Related Works

This section, we start with clarifying the kinds of actions that the designer has to perform in design thinking in work with any new task. To do this, we will return to the study of Dorst who notes the set of such actions includes *formulating, representing, moving, evaluating and managing* of components of reasoning in the conceptual space of the corresponding project [2]. Noting these actions, he means that they are performed in conditions of solving the equations among which the abductive equations occupy a fundamental place.

Another observation of Dorst [5] is the start of the project with an abductive equation

$$\frac{WHAT\ ?}{(thing)} + \frac{HOW\ leads\ to\ VALUE}{(frame)} \tag{4}$$

in conditions when designers have experience of designing that has similarity with a conceived project, and they can try to inherit the structural relationships between HOW and VALUE. For such inheritance, Dorst introduces the concept "framing," putting into it the following content "Framing is the key to design abduction. This is because the most logical way to approach a design problem is to work backward, as it were: starting from the only "known" in the equation, the desired value, and then adopting or developing a frame that is new to the problem situation." Similar cases also admit for the iterative search of the appropriate solutions, but at the level of reframing.

The important role of abductive reasoning in the design synthesis is discussed in [6] where its authors analyze the use of abductive transfers from a design intent to design targets, and to new design conceptions also. Additionally, they underline the possibility of an abductive diagnosis of violating design constraints or design axioms. The useful collection of patterns of abduction reasoning and inferences is considered and formalized in the paper [7].

Indicated type of equations suggests that their conceptual solutions are defined with the use of mechanisms of design thinking. Therefore, among related works, we mark publications that disclose some features of these mechanisms. Overview comparison of models and mechanisms at micro-, meso- and macro-levels of designing is conducted in the paper [8]. Several important mechanisms consider in the paper [9] that focuses on the evolutionary side of the explanatory design.

A very important group of related works includes papers devoted to relations between motives and goals. In the understanding of these relations, we follow the Goal Setting Theory Goa [10], some motivational aspect of which is constructively evolved in [11]. We took into account the way of the motivational design described in the papers [12, 13].

All papers indicated in this section were used as sources of requirements in developing the set of means included in the motivational and goal oriented viewpoint applied for building the motivationally targeted view on the SIS to be designed.

4 Goal-Oriented Architecture Modeling

The main intention of architectural modeling is to understand the SIS to be developed as a whole and as early as possible. Understanding is a naturally artificial process and its result, artificial part of which includes figuratively semantic scheme and coordinated verbal description. Strategic result of the necessary understanding is formed as an integrated complex of architectural views, each of which V_j can be considered as a result of solving the corresponding architectural task Z_j.

In this section, we present our version of attaining the necessary understanding that clarifies motivationally targeted view on designing the SIS. In the general case, work with any task Z_j begins with the conceptual equation

$$\frac{Motive(Z_J)\,??}{(essences)} + \frac{HOW1(Z_J)\,???}{(goal\ setting)}\ leads\ \frac{Goal(Z_J)\,?}{(intended)} \tag{5}$$

where, for simplifying the reasoning, we suppose that work with task Z_j is caused by one Motive (Z_j) and one Goal (Z_j).

Any goal is meaningful if there is a criterion whose application allows anybody to assess attaining the goal. Therefore, it needs to extend the Eq. (4) by adding the equation

$$\frac{Criterion(Goal(Z_J)\,??}{(essences)} + \frac{HOW2(Z_J)\,???}{(checking\ the\ attainment)}\ leads\ \frac{Goal(Z_J)\,?}{(intended)} \tag{6}$$

In its turn, needed checking the Goal (Z_j) is possible if the task Z_j is solved and the way of the solution is implemented as a minimum in conceptually-prototype version because only it opens the possibility for cause-and-effect understanding the solution of the task Z_j. Thus, it needs to add one more equation

$$\frac{TaskZ_J\,??}{(essences)} + \frac{HOW3(Z_J)\,???}{(solving\ the\ task)}\ leads\ \frac{Result(Z_J)\,?}{(obtained)} \tag{7}$$

which together with the Eqs. (3) and (4) forms a system of conceptual equations.

Note, components of these equations have conceptual nature, for example, component "Task Z_j" presents "statement of the task Z_j" in its current state. By other words, this component is a dynamic construction that is formed on the course of solving the indicated system of equations or conceptual solving the task Z_j.

In the process of solving, other components of the system of equations are also dynamic constructs that are formed in this process that leads to building the view V_j corresponding to the obtained Result (Z_j). The built view V_j integrates several important requirements $R_j = \{R_{jk}\}$, the composition of which correspond to the construct "Criterion (Goal(Z_j))." Thus, the built view V_j can be presented by the following symbolic expression

$$V_j = S_j(Motive(Z_j)), \; Goal(Z_j), Criterion(Z_j), Result(Z_j)). \qquad (8)$$

where any component of the expression is the conceptual object created on the course of solving the system of equation with the use of design thinking.

For such work, we developed and many times used our version of automated design thinking approach [14], the scheme of which is presented in Fig. 1.

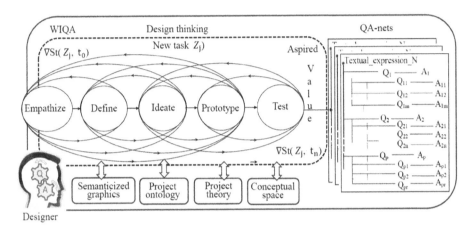

Fig. 1. The iterative process of design thinking

The scheme indicates that process of design thinking is implemented in the instrumental environment WIQA intended for conceptual designing the SIS in conditions when the designer can use such artifacts as Project ontology, Project theory and Conceptual space that are created on the course of designing in parallel with other designers' activity. The main attention of actions in the frame of the scheme focused on *formulating* the statement of the task and also on *representing, moving, evaluating, and managing* components of reasoning in forms of question-answer analysis. All these actions described in detail in the paper [15]. Additionally, actions include building the diagrammatic representation of the view (for example. the view V_j) and prototyping the solution of the task (for example, the task Z_j). So, the developed version of the DT-approach is the constructive way for solving the type of the systems of conceptual equations that are considered above.

Let us return to the stage of architectural modeling, the practice of which demonstrates that the artifact AD combines a set of coordinated views $\{V_j\}$. Therefore, in developing the AD, designers must solve a system of the system of conceptual equations or, the other words, they will create a system of the following artifacts

$$V_1 = S_1(Motive(Z_1)),\ Goal(Z_1),\ Criterion(Z_1),\ Result(Z_1)).$$
$$V_2 = S_2(Motive(Z_2)),\ Goal(Z_2),\ Criterion(Z_2),\ Result(Z_2)).$$
$$\dots\dots\dots\dots\dots\dots\dots\dots\dots\dots\dots\dots\dots\dots\dots\dots\dots$$
$$V_J = S_J(Motive(Z_J)),\ Goal(Z_J),\ Criterion(Z_J),\ Result(Z_J)).$$

$$(9)$$

We offer to bind with this system the integrated view that we called "motivationally targeted view" (or shortly, MT-view). In the general case, the diagrammatic representation of the MT-view will have the structure that conditionally shown in Fig. 2.

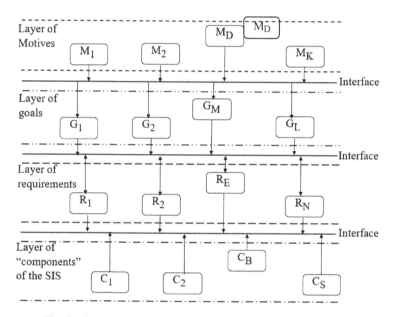

Fig. 2. Generalized structure of the motivationally targeted view

Any layer in this scheme presents components conditionally and in general. In the real MT-views, components of layers are combined in the net or tree. A similar way is used for combining the layers (in Fig. 2, this role is fulfilled by interfaces). What is especially important, after solving of all conceptual equations, components of any layer are strictly specified and expressed in understandable forms.

For the layer of motives, this means that the motivational design is implemented: internal and external motives are divided into groups; dominant motive M_D is highlighted; it is established cause-and-effects relations among motives and goals. In a set of goals, it is highlighted the main goal of G_M or their subset, and all relations of the subordinated types are defined and marked.

The layer of requirements (integrated into the AD) indicates, firstly, which criterions must be used for checking the attainment of goals defined in the layer above, and secondly, in which components of the SIS any requirement must be objectified. Thus, the motivationally targeted view reflects physical and conceptually algorithmic feasibility of the SIS that to be designed in accordance with initial intentions.

5 Motivationally Targeted View on Understanding

To fill the generalized scheme of the MT-view by the practical content, we consider some decisions bounded with our version of the automated design thinking that includes the component called "Semanticized graphics" or shortly SG. It was conceived for objectifying the mental imagination in conceptual experimenting applied in design thinking [15]. By other words, in this process, mental imagination is a source of intellectual "guessing" generated by the right hemisphere of the brain, and any result of such abductive guessing is useful to register in the graphical form reflected its structure as a wholeness. That is why the indicated component can help the designer in solving the conceptual equations described above.

Developing of this component was starting with the following motive:

M_D. In design thinking, explicit graphical registering the mental imagery will facilitate to increase the effectiveness of understanding activated when it is necessary for the designer.

Among possible ways of registering the appeared mental imagery, we chose those which is based on appropriate forms of programming that help to imitate the process of creating the result of registering ant its testing. Therefore, it was intended to realize the SG as a graphical editor oriented on creating the block-and-line schemes with features described just above. It should be noted that any of these schemes can be interpreted as an appropriate view of what the designer needs to understand.

This decision was expressed by the following main goal:

G_M. Means of the SG must help the designer to register the process and result of any act of understanding in observable and programmable forms that confirm the wholeness of the built block-and line scheme.

Understanding is a naturally artificial process and its result, as told just above, can be implemented with the use of appropriated views any of which (similarly architectural views) should be presented by the corresponding block-and-line scheme with a coordinated verbal description. Moreover, according to the goal G_M, any view on understanding must be accessible the designer in the appropriate program form. Such intention has led us to the following subordinated sub-goals:

G_1. For supporting the architectural forms of understanding, it is rational to apply the pictorial programming that helps to bind any block-and-line scheme with the program of its drawing for the repeatable activating the process and result of such form of understanding.

G_2. To provide the iterative coordination between the graphical side of the view and its verbal description, it is rational to apply the declarative programming (more exactly, Prolog-like description) that helps to discover errors and inconsistencies for their correcting in graphical and symbolic components of the artificial side of understanding.

G_3. To express cause-effect manifestations of understanding, it is rational to apply the model-driven approach to programming oriented on the use of UML.

Goals are defined correctly only if there are criteria for testing their achievement. As stated above, the role of such criteria can be assigned to requirements whose fulfillment confirms that the intended effects are observed. In real practice, some requirements can be reasons while effects are consequences.

In the considered case, awaited effects must be bound with a constructive expression of achieving the necessary understanding, the result of which is registered by the set of chosen views (block-and-line schemes and their descriptions). In developing the SG, achieving the necessary effects were caused by the following essential requirements:

R_E. To provide the programmable effects in the graphical components of views on understanding, it is necessary to extend the pseudocode language embedded in the WIQA toolkit so that it will support pictorial, declarative, and model-driven forms of programming.

R_1. For any element placed in the workspace of the graphical editor, means of pictorial programming must provide assigning an indexed link, the activation of which helps to switch to another scheme or call a program unit or switch to a specific application outside the WIQA toolkit.

R_2. For any textual unit and its semantic net, declarative programming must provide their automated iterative coordination with using the transition to Prolog-like description for its subsequent checking on errors and inconsistencies.

R_3. To objectify an algorithmic side of understanding that embeds in UML diagrams, it needs to provide their model-driven transformation to program codes helping to discover semantic errors and demonstrate dynamics of the corresponding process.

Coming from the declared motive, goals and requirements, at the conceptual stage of designing the graphical editor and other necessary means of its using for the achievement of intended goals, we developed the corresponding MT-view, the simplest scheme of which is shown in Fig. 3.

The choice of the simplest scheme is caused by demonstrating aims of this section. The SG was developed two years ago, and the final version of its MT-view was richer.

In the version, that is presented in Fig. 3; it is reflected only the kernel of the SG – its three modules providing the basic modes of creating and using the graphical editor. Each of these modes is responsible for the materialization of the corresponding requirement.

Additionally, the view indicates its dependence from the project ontology. Any label on the scheme that is drawn in the editor and any notion applied in the scheme description must be checked on the correspondence of the project language, and, therefore, on the correspondence of the project ontology. Furthermore, the module 2 is responsible for logical checking the applied textual units after their transformations in Prolog-like descriptions that must be corresponded the project ontology also.

The scheme in Fig. 3 presents not only the example of the MT-view but also the basic components of the motivationally and goal-oriented viewpoint for developing any MT-views. More detailly, this viewpoint includes means for implementing the following actions:

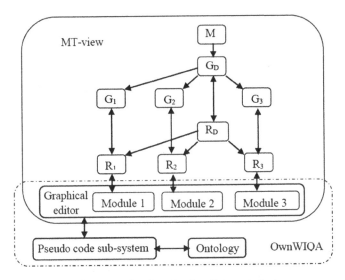

Fig. 3. Example of motivationally targeted view

- Preparation to drawing the MT-view (automated design thinking for solving the conceptual equations);
- Visualization for using the MY-view (graphical editor, project ontology, a complex of means for pseudo code programming, the library of program utilities for the SG-transformations and transitions).

If these actions are included in conceptual designing the certain SIS, they will facilitate to usefully objectifying the motivational and goal-oriented basis of the corresponding project in the visualized and understandable form.

6 Conclusion

In the paper, we demonstrate the purposefulness of including the MT-views in the practice of architectural modeling the SIS. For creating these views, the designers can use conceptual equations defined by K. Dorst to express the nature of design thinking. Such equations admit applying unknowns indicating on essences of different types, including motives and goals. Considering such essences leads to defining the systems of conceptual equations of the abductive types, for solving of which it is possible to use the appropriate version of the automated design thinking.

In several real projects, we have tested our version of automated design thinking in its application for building the MT-views. This version is implemented in the instrumental environment WIQA intended for conceptual designing the SIS in conditions when the designer can use means of the Semanticized Graphics and such artifacts as Project ontology, Project theory, and Conceptual space that are created on the course of designing in parallel with other designers' activity.

The paper includes the example of the MT-view that corresponds to the development of the SG-component, extending the potential of the WIQA toolkit. This component is intended for the architectural expression of understanding when it is necessary. Such necessity is especially important when it needs to create the architectural descriptions or, by other words, when it needs to create a system $S(\{V_j\})$ of architectural views. Any of this view expresses the embedded understanding. MT-view is one of them.

Acknowledgement. This work was supported by the Russian Fund for Basic Research (RFBR), Grant #18-07-00989a, Grant # 18-47-73001r-a, 18-47-732012 r_mk, and the State Contract No. 2.1534.2017/4.6.

References

1. Standard ISO/IEC/IEEE 42010 (2011). https://www.iso.org/standard/50508.html
2. Dorst, K.: The nature of design thinking, in DTRS8 interpreting design thinking. In: Proceeding of Design Thinking Research Symposium, pp. 131–139 (2010)
3. Vityaev, E.E.: Purposefulness as a principle of brain Activity. In: Nadin, M. (ed.) Anticipation: Learning from the Past. CSM, vol. 25, pp. 231–254. Springer, Cham (2015). https://doi.org/10.1007/978-3-319-19446-2_13
4. Sudakov, K.V.: The theory of functional systems: general postulates and principles of dynamic organization. Integr. Physiol. Behav. Sci. **32**(4), 392–414 (1997)
5. Dorst, K.: The core of 'design thinking' and its application. Des. Stud. **32**(6), 521–532 (2011)
6. Lu, S.C.-Y., Liu, A.: Abductive reasoning for design synthesis. USACIRP Ann. Manuf. Technol. **61**, 143–146 (2012)
7. Schurz, G.: Patterns of abduction **164**(2), 201–234 (2008)
8. Wynn, D.C., Clarkson, P.J.: Process models in design and development. Res. Eng. Design **29**(2), 161–202 (2018)
9. Nguyen, L., et al.: Evolutionary processes as models for exploratory design. In: Knippers, J., Nickel, K.G., Speck, T. (eds.) Biomimetic Research for Architecture and Building Construction. BS, vol. 8, pp. 295–318. Springer, Cham (2016). https://doi.org/10.1007/978-3-319-46374-2_15
10. Yurtkoru, E.S., Bozkurt, T., Bektas, F., Ahmed, M.J., Kola, V.: Application of goal setting theory. PressAcademia Procedia (PAP) **3**, 796–801 (2017)
11. Locke, E., Latham, G.: New directions in goal-setting theory. Assoc. Psychol. Sci. **15**(5), 265–268 (2006)
12. Lunenburg, F.P.: Goal-setting theory of motivation. Int. J. Manag. Bus. Adm. **15**, 1–6 (2011)
13. Keller, J.M.: Motivational Design for Learning and Performance the ARCS Model Approach. Springer, New York (2010). https://doi.org/10.1007/978-1-4419-1250-3
14. Sosnin, P.: Substantially evolutionary theorizing in designing software-intensive systems. Information **9**(4), 1–29 (2018)
15. Sosnin, P.: Automated design thinking oriented on innovatively personified projects communications in computer and information. Science **920**, 312–323 (2018)

Modeling Bimodal Social Networks Subject to Recommendation

Robert Albert Kłopotek[✉] [iD]

Faculty of Mathematics and Natural Sciences, School of Exact Sciences,
Cardinal Stefan Wyszyński University in Warsaw, Warsaw, Poland
r.klopotek@uksw.edu.pl

Abstract. This paper describes modeling of social networks subject to recommendation. Cold Start User-Item Model (CSUIM) of bipartite graph is considered, which simulates bipartite graph growth based on several parameters. An algorithm is proposed to compute parameters of this model from real graph data so that real graph and its model have similar graph metrics.

Keywords: Social Network Analysis · Recommendation ·
Network graphs · Bipartite graphs · Bipartite graph model ·
Graph growth simulation

1 Introduction

Much interest of researchers is attracted by social networks which can be modeled via bipartite graphs with users and items as such models can be applied to tasks like a recommendation. Both the actual graph structure and the graph dynamics and its development in time are important. Such growth models are vital in Social Network Analysis (SNA) as they allow e.g., to test which microoperations happening in the network may lead to the macrostructures that we can observe, to develop and test social network algorithms when real-world data are not numerous and the threat of overfitting is serious, and to perform what-if analysis on social networks without experimenting with real people. Many more reasons can be found. Hence one needs growth models that are sufficiently similar to real-world phenomena on the one hand and on the other hand one requires also a method of extracting model parameters from the actual real network in order to generate similar ones.

Over the last decade a number of growth models for bipartite graphs have been proposed [2,5,16], however, their bipartite graph generators have some limitations. They create bipartite graphs with limited reproduction of real-life graph properties and they create two graph structures which complicate the models a lot. A detailed discussion of the issues can be found in [3,7]. Recently Exponential Random Graph Models (ERGM) were revisited [8,12] which make use of advances in Monte Carlo simulation, in particular, MCMC (Markov chain Monte Carlo) techniques. Unfortunately, they can be applied to small networks (up to 50 nodes) due to its complexity (see [1]).

© Springer Nature Switzerland AG 2019
R. Damaševičius and G. Vasiljevienė (Eds.): ICIST 2019, CCIS 1078, pp. 121–135, 2019.
https://doi.org/10.1007/978-3-030-30275-7_10

In this paper we consider the graph generator *Cold Start User-Item Model (CSUIM)* that can be viewed as a graph growth model with seven parameters. In [3,6] it has been demonstrated that the model qualitatively reflects properties of real-life bipartite graphs quite well. Therefore, it has been used for qualitative studies of various phenomena. CSUIM model touches a very important problem of *cold start* in a recommendation of products to users and vice versa. The *cold start* problem concerns recommendation of products to a new user from whom we have no information in our system or we have no information about and we want to recommend it to users in our system.

Regrettably, no results are known so far for computing or estimating model parameters from the real-world data for CSUIM. With the current paper, we intend to close this gap. We present a method to capture the parameters from the actual graph and verify the similarity of metrics between the original graph and the one obtained from the model.

The paper is structured as follows: in Sect. 2 we briefly recall the CSIUM generator. In Sect. 3 we propose a method of parameter computation from a graph. In Sect. 4 we present experimental results on parameter recovery and model quality. Section 5 contains some concluding remarks.

2   CSUIM Bipartite Graph Generator

The bi-modal graph generator analyzed in [3,6] is more flexible than graph generators proposed in [2,5,16], though it cannot generate a disconnected graph with desired properties. Its advantage is the capability to create graphs with a broader range of clustering behavior via the so-called bouncing mechanism. The bouncing mechanism is an adaptation of a surfing mechanism in classical graphs (see [15]). The bouncing mechanism is used only to the edges which were created according to the preferential attachment.

In CSUIM we consider a graph with the set of vertices $W = U \cup V, U \cap V = \emptyset$, where the set U is called "users" and set V is called "items". We consider both the uniform attachment, where incoming nodes form links to existing nodes selected uniformly at random, and the preferential attachment, when probabilities are assigned proportional to the degrees of the existing nodes (see [4]). The generator has 7 parameters:

1. m — the initial number of edges, the initial number of vertices is $2m$
2. δ — the probability that a new vertex v added to a graph in the iteration t is a user $v \in U$, so $1 - \delta$ means probability that v is an item, $v \in I$
3. d_u — the number of edges added from the vertex of type user in one iteration (number of items bought by a single new user),
4. d_v — the number of edges added from the vertex of type item in one iteration (number of users that bought the same new item)
5. α — the probability of *item* preferential attachment, $1 - \alpha$ — the probability of *item* uniform attachment
6. β — the probability of *user* preferential attachment, $1 - \beta$ — the probability of *user* uniform attachment

7. γ — the fraction of edges attached in a preferential way which were created using the bouncing mechanism

CSUIM creates a node in the set of users with probability δ and $1 - \delta$ in the set of items. The newly created node is connected with nodes of the opposite modality. If the node is of type user it will be connected with d_u items and if it is of type item then it will be connected with d_v nodes of type user. To find the node to which the newly added node will be connected we use two mechanisms: the *uniform attachment* (UA) and the *preferential attachment* (PA). PA is drawn with probability α for items and β for users, otherwise, nodes are selected by UA. When PA is selected we have to choose fraction γ of edges that will be attached by the bouncing mechanism (see below).

Input: Parameters: $m \in Z^+$, $\delta \in (0; 1)$, $d_u \in Z^+$, $d_v \in Z^+$, $\alpha \in [0; 1]$, $\beta \in [0; 1]$ and $\gamma \in [0; 1]$

Step 1. Initialize the graph with m edges (we have $2m$ vertices).

Step 2. Add a new vertex to the graph of type *user* with probability δ, otherwise of type *item*.

Step 3. Choose a neighbor to join the new vertex according to the rules:

Step 3.a. If the new node is *item* then add d_v edges from this node to type *user* vertices using PA mechanism (with probability β) or UA (otherwise)

Step 3.b. If the new node is *user* then add d_u edges from this node to type *item* vertices using PA mechanism (with probability α) or UA (otherwise)

Step 3.c. Consider newly added vertex v_0 and edges from this node added by PA mechanism (nodes u_i and v_i are from different modalities). Select γ fraction of those end nodes. For each node u_1 from this set pick at random one of its neighbors v_2. From the randomly selected node v_2 select its neighbor u_3 at random again. Connect the new node v_0 to the node u_3 selected in this way instead of the original node u_1 obtained by PA.

Step 4. Repeat Steps 2 and 3 T times.

Output: Bipartite graph

Algorithm 1: Cold Start User-Item Model

The procedure for generating synthetic bipartite graphs is outlined in Algorithm 1. The step 3.c (*bouncing*) emulates the behavior called recommendation. One can imagine that a customer which is going to buy one of the products encounters another consumer that already purchased it and recommends him another product instead. The first consumer changes their mind and follows this recommendation with probability γ. By varying this parameter one can observe what happens when people are more or less sensible to the recommendation.

Selecting products by UA simulates consumers that do not bother which product to choose. PA simulates consumers that look for products on their own (e.g., dresses unseen frequently on street). Note that this model of graph growth simulates a very special purchase behavior — namely the behavior of only new consumers and new products. In spite of its limited applicability the model is very important because it concentrates on a very hard part of the recommendation process called "cold start". More detailed specifics of this hard problem were presented in [9,13].

It is easy to see that after t iterations with bouncing mechanism disabled ($\gamma = 0$) we have $|U(t)| = m + \delta t$ vertices of type *user* and $|V(t)| = m + (1 - \delta)t$ vertices of type *item*. Average number of edges attached in one iteration is $\eta = d_u \delta + (1 - \delta)d_v$. After large number of iterations we can skip m initial edges in further calculations. Thus, we can show that average number of vertices of type *user* and of type *item* depends only on iteration t and δ and does not depend on m, d_v, d_u. Total number of edges depends only on d_v, d_u and δ. This is not a good news, because we cannot use them to estimate all parameters of the generator, especially β, α and γ. Below we present a way around this problem.

3   Parameter Estimation

In this section, we propose algorithms for the computation of all CSUI model parameters. First we describe retrieval of parameters δ, m, d_u and d_v. Then we propose two algorithms. The first algorithm estimates α and β parameter using a distribution of node degree in each modality and linear regression. The second one uses modularity measure and linear regression for computation of γ parameter.

3.1   Parameter δ

The simplest parameter to estimate is δ, which is probability that new vertex v added to graph in iteration t is a user $v \in U$, so $1 - \delta$ means probability that new vertex v is an item $v \in V$: $\delta = \frac{|U|}{|U \cup V|}$, where $|U|$ cardinality is set of nodes user and V is set of nodes of type item.

3.2   Parameters d_u, d_v and m

There are two approaches to obtain d_u and d_v. The first and simples one is to set d_u as minimal degree in user set and analogously set d_v as minimal degree in item set.

The second way is more complicated. Average number of edges attached in one iteration is $\eta = d_u \delta + (1 - \delta)d_v$. η is easy to estimate from graph as $\eta = \frac{|E|}{|U \cup V|}$, where $|E|$ is total number of edges in graph. δ is computed from previous section. Most of vertex degree distribution mass is on lower degrees k, so we can make integer minimization of $d_u + d_v$ with additional restriction $d_u \delta + (1 - \delta)d_v - \eta = 0$. Another way is brute force approach. It is done based on vertex degree distribution in each modality. We fix some d_u and compute the value d_v from equation $|E| = d_u \cdot |U| + d_v \cdot |V|$.

m is the number of initial edges. It must be at least $\max(d_u, d_v)$. The better way is to set it for computation on $d_u + d_v$ because it speeds up a few initial steps when there are few nodes in a graph.

3.3   Parameters α and β

We have verified experimentally that there is a linear relation between $\ln P(k)$
and $\ln k$ where $P(k)$ is the probability of occurrence of a node of degree k (see
Fig. 1). We discovered that linear relation between $\ln P(k)$ and $\ln k$ almost does
not change when we fix β and change value of α from 0 to 0.99.

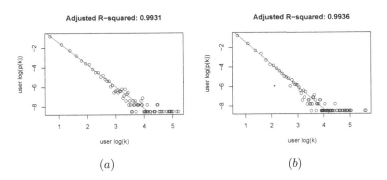

(a)   (b)

Fig. 1. Plot of experimental relation $\ln P(k)$ versus $\ln k$ for generated graph for modality users in 10K iterations, $\alpha = 0$ and $\beta = 0.99$ in (a), $\alpha = 0.99$ and $\beta = 0.99$ in (b),
$\delta = 0.5$ and $d_u = 2$, $d_v = 3$. Drawn line is regression line based on this relation for
$k = d_u, d_u + 1, ..., 2(d_u + d_v)$ which contains most of distribution mass.

Therefore, we looked at the relationship between α (analogously for β) and
the direction coefficient of the straight line approximating relationship between
$\ln(p_k)$ and $\ln k$ and draw it for various values of α (β). We observed that for a
wide range of values of α (β) this relationship is linear. This is (approximately)
in accordance with theoretical relationship derived in [3] (for β):

$$P(k_u) = \frac{\eta}{(1 - \delta)\beta d_v} \delta\beta \left(\frac{(1 - \beta)\eta + \delta\beta k}{(1 - \beta)\eta + \delta\beta d_u} \right)^{\frac{-\eta}{(1-\delta)\beta d_v}} \tag{1}$$

The preferential attachment has a power law distribution with a *heavy tail*
of node degrees and the uniform attachment has an exponential distribution of
node degrees, with a *light tail*. As demonstrated in [14], empirical mixture of
these two distributions can be approximated with the power law distribution.
Therefore, linear regression analysis had been used sometimes to evaluate the fit
of the power law distribution to data and to estimate the value of the exponent
and also to obtain the mixture parameter α. The rationale behind this approach
is that the heavy tail distribution dominates over the exponential distribution
for nodes of higher degree. This technique produces biased estimates (see [14]).

In the CSUI model when β grows, the probability of connecting new link with
preferential attachment grows as well. Thus, we can approximate distribution of
vertices degrees by power law distribution from experimental degree distribution
$p(k)$ and compute the exponent of this distribution. We have

$$p(k) = \exp(b) \cdot k^a \tag{2}$$

for some coefficients a and b. After applying ln function to both sites we get:

$$\ln(p(k)) = a \cdot \ln(k) + b \tag{3}$$

As we see in the experiments, it is unreliable for low values of α (β) (below 0.1) — see Fig. 2(a) (ln $P(k)$ vs ln(k)) and Fig. 2(b) (ln $P(k)$ vs k).

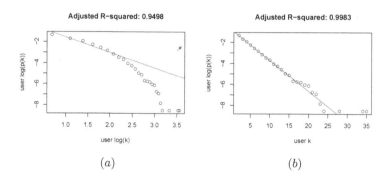

(a)   (b)

Fig. 2. Plot of experimental relation $\ln P(k)$ versus $\ln k$ (a) and versus k (b) for generated graph for modality users in 10K iterations, $\alpha = 0.02$, $\beta = 0.02$, $\delta = 0.5$ and $d_u = 2$, $d_v = 3$, where $P(k) = p_{k,UIM}$. Drawn line is regression line based on this relation for $k = d_u, d_u + 1, ..., 2(d_u + d_v)$ which contains most of distribution mass.

Therefore, combining this with theoretical derivation in [3], we can compute α and β from linear models. The method for this computation is presented in Algorithm 2.

3.4 Parameter γ

The bouncing parameter of the graph model may be used to model the behavior of users vulnerable to recommendations. We found out that this parameter is linearly correlated with graph metric called "optimal modularity" (see [10]).

Modularity is a measure of the quality of a clustering of nodes in a graph. *Optimal modularity* is the modularity of such a clustering of nodes for which the modularity is the highest among all the node clusterings of a given graph.

The Newman's optimal modularity tells us how much our graph differs from a random one. In a fully random graph edges are attached to some nodes at random from some distributions. The bouncing parameter γ of CSUI model gives us a kind of dependence of node linking to other nodes — selecting both ends of an edge. Value γ represents a fraction of edges attached in a preferential way which were created using the bouncing mechanism. The greater value of γ is, the stronger dependence in creating links in graph occurs. When we have some kind of dependence while creating links, the greater is the value of modularity.

Input: Bipartite graph $G = U \cup V$, where $U \cap V = \emptyset$.

Step 1. Compute exponent exp_U of degree distribution of user node set U and analogously exp_I of item node set V

Step 2. Compute δ from Subsect. 3.1 and d_u and d_v from Subsect. 3.2.

Step 3. Define the set $\mathbb{A} = \{\alpha_1, ..., \alpha_I\}$ and the set $\mathbb{B} = \{\beta_1, ..., \beta_J\}$, to be called grid of α and β later.

Step 4. For each pair (α_i, β_j) generate a bipartite graph with these parameters setting δ, d_u and d_v as computed in Sects. 3.1 and 3.2 and setting γ to zero. From the generated graph compute exponent $exp_{U_{ij}}$ of degree distribution of user set and analogously $exp_{I_{ij}}$ of item set.

Step 5. For the data set D_α consisting of $(\alpha_i, exp_{I_{ij}})$ perform linear regression creating m_α with response vector α and predictor variable exp_I.

Step 6. For the data set D_β consisting of $(\beta_j, exp_{U_{ij}})$ perform linear regression creating m_β with response vector β and predictor variable exp_U.

Step 7. Predict α from m_α based on exp_I obtained from graph G.

Step 8. Predict β value from m_β based on exp_U obtained from graph G.

Output: α and β values

Algorithm 2: Computation of α and β.

Let us consider bouncing from the newly created user vertex u (see Fig. 3). Firstly, the bouncing algorithm selects an item vertex i. From this vertex, we can go further to user modality through edges added in previous steps either by an edge added in one of the previous iterations by adding a user node or an item node. From the fact that we deal with power-law distribution of vertex degree we know that most of the distribution mass have vertices with the smallest degree. Thus, it is more probable that we go through the edge added by adding a user node u_2 and from this node to an item node i_k which is the end node of the edge e. So we created new edge (u, i_k). So the probability of creating edge (u, i_k) is:

$$P(i_k|u) \approx \sum_{u_2,i} P(i|u)P(u_2|i)P(i_k|u_2) \tag{4}$$

Equation (4) can be written in this form, because if we add a new vertex u to the graph then outgoing edges from this node are independent of each other. Because the node i has low degree, most of outgoing links from i_k are independent and analogously most of user nodes are of low degree, so outgoing links are independent. In general after "sufficient" time during the further evolution of network we get $P(i_k|u_2) = P(u_2|i_k)$, so we have:

$$P(i_k|u) = \sum_{u_2,i} P(i|u)P(u_2|i)P(i_k|u_2) = P(i_k|u_2) \underbrace{\sum_{u_2,i} P(i|u)P(u_2|i)}_{=1} = P(i_k|u_2)$$

$$\tag{5}$$

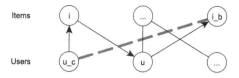

Fig. 3. Example of creating new edge (dashed line) from new node u using bouncing mechanism. Directed arrows indicate the following steps of bouncing mechanism in undirected bipartite graph.

Thus, the bouncing mechanism does not change distribution on most degrees (small degree) and can be considered separately from α and β parameters.

In Fig. 4(a) we see that this relationship seems to be linear even for small values of α and β. Unfortunately, when we add more edges in one step the linear relation gets weaker — see Fig. 4(b).

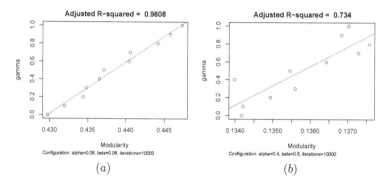

Fig. 4. Plot of modularity for prediction of γ. Test setting in (a): 10000 iterations, $d_u = 2$, $d_v = 3$, $\alpha = 0.06$, $\beta = 0.06$ and $\delta = 0.5$. Test setting in (b): 10000 iterations, $d_u = 10$, $d_v = 20$, $\alpha = 0.4$, $\beta = 0.6$ and $\delta = 0.5$. Drawn line is regression line.

As we had shown this relation is well approximated by a linear model to some extent. If $\alpha, \beta \in [0.1, 0.9]$ and $d_u, d_v \leq 5$ then *bouncing* parameter is predicted quite good from simple linear model. Thus, we constructed the Algorithm 3.

4   Experimental Results

We present experimental results on parameter recovery and model quality. We performed several simulations to validate theoretical relations involving parameters α and β described in Sect. 3.3 and parameter γ described in Sect. 3.4. Those simulations are presented in Sect. 4.1. After verifying theoretical properties, we tested how well parameters of CSUI model can be obtained from several real networks. The network generated from CSUI model and real network were compared based on a number of metrics described in Sect. 4.2.

Input: Bipartite graph $G = U \cup V$, where $U \cap V = \emptyset$.

Step 1. Compute α and β from Algorithm 2.

Step 2. Create grid of γ_i values.

Step 3. For each γ_i generate graph model and compute modularity.

Step 4. Make dataset D_γ containing γ_i values and modularity values.

Step 5. Make linear regression model $model_\gamma$ having response vector γ and one variable $modularity$.

Step 6. Predict γ value from $model_\gamma$ based on $modularity$ from graph G.

Output: γ value

Algorithm 3: Computation of γ.

4.1   Validity of Parameter Recovery Models

In this section we made several simulations generating networks from CSUI model to verify theoretical properties. Experiments with α and β were made based on Algorithm 2. Experimental results in Fig. 5(a) and (b) show, that α and β parameters do not depend on each other. Model $m1$ contains 2 variables: β and exp_I in Fig. 5(a), α and exp_U in Fig. 5(b). Model $m2$ contains only one variable — exp_I in Fig. 5(a) and exp_U in Fig. 5(b). On top of each plot is given p-value of ANOVA test of difference between model $m1$ and $m2$. Adjusted R-Squared values for models $m1$ and $m2$ in Fig. 5(a) are 0.94 and p-value of ANOVA test is 0.82. Adjusted R-Squared values for models $m1$ and $m2$ in Fig. 5(b) are around 0.86 and p-value of ANOVA test is 0.63. The p-value of the ANOVA test is greater than 0.05, so at this level of importance there is no statistically significant difference. Thus, α parameter does not depend on β parameter in Fig. 5(a) and β parameter does not depend on α parameter in Fig. 5(b).

The 2D plot of data obtained from experiment is given in Fig. 6(a) and Fig. 6(b) for 5000 and 50000 iterations respectively. We can see that with more iterations the spread of points for different values of the α parameter at the same value of β is getting smaller, which gives a better prediction of the parameter β. Moreover, with more iterations this independency gets stronger — greater p-value of ANOVA test. Thus, we can predict them separately.

Simulations with γ parameter were made based on Algorithm 3. Plots of data obtained from experiment for 10000 iterations and different values of α and β are given in Fig. 7. We can see almost ideal fit (adj. R-squared value above 0.98).

4.2   Retrieval of Parameters

In our experiments, we used StackExchange data dump from December 2011 (topical fora). Stack Exchange is a fast-growing network of question and answers sites on diverse topics from software programming to cooking to photography and gaming. We analyzed databases from forums: bicycles, drupalanswers, itsecurity, texlatex, theoreticalcomputerscience and webapplications — see Tables 1, 2 and 3 for detailed results. From this data bipartite graph for each dataset was created.

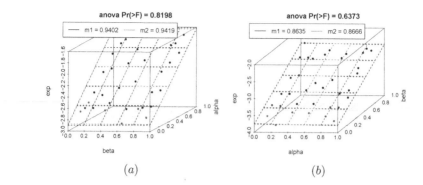

(a)   (b)

Fig. 5. 3D plot of exponent of distribution of item modality exp_I (a) and exp_U (b) for prediction of parameter α (a) and β (b). Test setting: 5000 iteration, $d_u = 3$, $d_v = 2$. Adjusted R-Squared values for (a) are around 0.94 and for (b) are around 0.86. P-value of ANOVA test of diff. between model $m1$ and $m2$ for (a) is 0.82 and for (b) is 0.63.

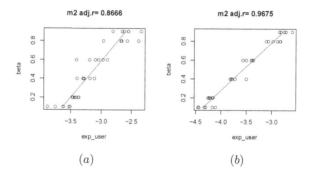

(a)   (b)

Fig. 6. 2D plot of exponent of distribution of user modality exp_U for prediction of parameter β. Test setting: 5000 (a) and 50000 (b) iterations, $d_u = 3$, $d_v = 2$. Adjusted R-Squared value for (a) is 0.87 and in (b) is 0.97. Drawn line is regression line.

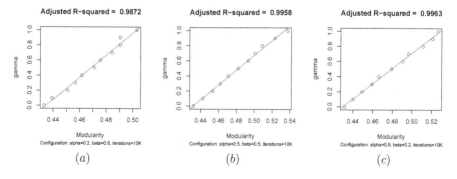

(a)   (b)   (c)

Fig. 7. Plot of modularity for prediction of γ. Test setting: 10000 iterations, $\alpha = 0.2$ and $\beta = 0.8$ (a), $\alpha = 0.5$ and $\beta = 0.5$ (b), $\alpha = 0.8$ and $\beta = 0.2$ (c). Drawn line is regression line.

In one modality there were users and in other topics. An edge was created, when a user participated in a topic by writing a post in this topic. The edge between user and topic was created only once. We interpret network structure as an undirected graph with no weights per edge.

Due to the limitation of CSUI model we took under consideration only the giant component (GC). Giant component is the biggest connected component in a graph. In a real-world graph, it contains 70% or more of the whole graph and influences the growth of the network (see [11]). From created bipartite graphs we calculated several graph and model properties and compared them to an artificial graph generated from CSUI model. Metrics used in experiments:

1. Total Nodes — the total number of nodes in GC.
2. Total Edges — the total number of edges in GC.
3. Average Degree — the average of node degree in GC.
4. Diameter — the maximal distance between all pairs of nodes in GC.
5. Radius — the radius[1] of GC.
6. Average Path Length — the average number of steps along the shortest paths for all possible pairs of network nodes. It is a measure of the efficiency of information or mass transport on a network.
7. Number Of Shortest Paths — the number of shortest paths in GC.
8. Communities Number — the number of communities from Neumann's modularity algorithm in GC.
9. Density — measures how close the network is to a complete graph. A complete graph has all possible edges and density equal to 1.
10. Modularity — the Neumann's modularity
11. Avg Item Clustering — the average value of BLCC[2] for modality items.
12. Avg User Clustering — the average value of BLCC for modality users — see footnote.
13. UsersCount — the number of nodes in modality users.
14. ItemsCount — the number of nodes in modality items.
15. User Average Degree — the average value of users node degree.
16. Item Average Degree — the average value of items node degree.

---

[1] The radius r of a graph is the minimum eccentricity of any vertex, $r = \min_{v \in W} \epsilon(v)$. The eccentricity $\epsilon(v)$ of a vertex v is the greatest geodesic distance between v and any other vertex.

[2] In bipartite graph for all vertices a, b in the same modality set we do not have any edges between them, so Local Clustering Coefficient (LCC) is always zero. Therefore, in [3] another suitable metric for clustering tendency was proposed — Bipartite Local Clustering Coefficient (BLCC). BLCC is defined as $BLCC(u) = 1 - \frac{|N_2(u)|}{\sum_{v \in N_1(u)}(k_v - 1)}$, where W denote set of all vertices. Then $N_s(n)$ is set of neighbours of vertex $n \in W$, which are $s \geq 1$ steps away. In other words $N_s(n) = \{a \in W : K(n, a) = s\}$, where $K(i, j)$ is minimal distance (number of edges) between vertices i and j. In [3] it is shown that graph metric LCC and $BLCC$ are similar in classical graphs.

17. gen alpha — value of parameter α from CSUI model. Computation is based on Algorithm 2 from Sect. 3.3. In the column 'Graph' it is computed based on a real graph and in the column 'Model' it is computed based on a generated network from CSUI model. This value is in $[0,1]$ interval. We give exact value from a linear model for demonstration purposes.

18. gen beta — value of parameter β from CSUI model. Computation is based on Algorithm 2 from Sect. 3.3. Interpretation as for gen alpha metric.

19. gen p add user — value of parameter δ from CSUI model. Computation is based on Sect. 3.1.

20. gen p bouncing — value of parameter γ from CSUI model. Computation is based on Algorithm 3 from Sect. 3.4.

21. ExpUserCoeff — the exponent of an exponential distribution of node degree of modality users.

22. ExpItemCoeff — the exponent of an exponential distribution of node degree of modality items.

23. graph eta — the average number of edges in one iteration, $\eta = \frac{|E|}{|U \cup V|}$

We extracted graph parameters as described in Sect. 3. It turned out (see Tables 1, 2 and 3) that the most crucial parameters were d_u and d_v. Values of these two parameters determine how the graph generated by the model will be similar to a real one. We used two methods for finding optimal values d_u and d_v: discrete optimization and brute force approach described in Sect. 3.2. The brute force approach gave us the best results in half of the cases.

Table 1. (a) Experimental results for dataset *bicycles* for $d_u = 2$ and $d_v = 2$. (b) Experimental results for dataset *drupalanswers* for $d_u = 3$ and $d_v = 1$.

Metric	Graph	Model	Relative error
Total Nodes	4111	4111	0.0000
Total Edges	7667	8210	0.0708
Average Degree	3.7300	3.9942	0.0708
Diameter	11	9	0.1818
Radius	6	6	0.0000
Average Path Length	4.2897	4.8359	0.1273
Number Of Shortest Paths	16896210	16896210	0.0000
Communities Number	27	31	0.1481
Density	0.0009	0.0010	0.0708
Modularity	0.5461	0.5484	0.0042
Avg Item Clustering	0.0219	0.0118	0.4614
Avg User Clustering	0.1172	0.1363	0.1626
UsersCount	636	669	0.0519
ItemsCount	3475	3442	0.0095
User Average Degree	12.0550	12.2720	0.0180
Item Average Degree	2.2063	2.3852	0.0811
gen alpha	1.2305	0.6683	0.4569
gen beta	0.5131	0.5999	0.1691
gen p add user	0.1547	0.1627	0.0519
gen p bouncing	0.3027	0.3326	0.0988
ExpUserCoeff	-0.8341	-1.0050	-0.2049
ExpItemCoeff	-3.1033	-4.3912	-0.4150
graph eta	1.8650	1.9971	0.0708

(a)

Metric	Graph	Model	Relative error
Total Nodes	6950	6950	0.0000
Total Edges	9862	9088	0.0785
Average Degree	2.8380	2.6153	0.0785
Diameter	15	12	0.2000
Radius	8	7	0.1250
Average Path Length	5.4024	7.0790	0.3103
Number Of Shortest Paths	48295550	48295550	0.0000
Communities Number	46	57	0.2391
Density	0.0004	0.0004	0.0785
Modularity	0.7090	0.7586	0.0699
Avg Item Clustering	0.0037	0.0002	0.9335
Avg User Clustering	0.0690	0.0048	0.9307
UsersCount	1071	1075	0.0037
ItemsCount	5879	5875	0.0007
User Average Degree	9.2082	8.4540	0.0819
Item Average Degree	1.6775	1.5469	0.0779
gen alpha	-0.7685	0.0916	-1.1192
gen beta	0.3099	0.3867	0.2480
gen p add user	0.1541	0.1547	0.0037
gen p bouncing	8.1270	0.0454	0.9944
ExpUserCoeff	-1.1052	-1.1859	-0.0730
ExpItemCoeff	-4.0796	-3.5429	-0.1316
graph eta	1.4190	1.3076	0.0785

(b)

Table 2. (a) Experimental results for dataset *itsecurity* for $d_u = 1$ and $d_v = 2$. (b) Experimental results for dataset *texlatex* for $d_u = 1$ and $d_v = 2$.

Metric	Graph	Model	Relative error
Total Nodes	5619	5619	0.0000
Total Edges	9572	10083	0.0534
Average Degree	3.4070	3.5889	0.0534
Diameter	14	11	0.2143
Radius	7	6	0.1429
Average Path Length	4.5853	4.9775	0.0855
Number Of Shortest Paths	31567542	31567542	0.0000
Communities Number	33	44	0.3333
Density	0.0006	0.0006	0.0534
Modularity	0.5976	0.5944	0.0052
Avg Item Clustering	0.0144	0.0120	0.1631
Avg User Clustering	0.0828	0.0953	0.1510
UsersCount	1148	1149	0.0009
ItemsCount	4471	4470	0.0002
User Average Degree	8.3380	8.7755	0.0525
Item Average Degree	2.1409	2.2557	0.0536
gen alpha	1.7195	0.6584	0.6171
gen beta	0.6432	0.5696	0.1144
gen p add user	0.2043	0.2045	0.0009
gen p bouncing	0.3335	0.2915	0.1261
ExpUserCoeff	-0.9237	-0.8275	-0.1042
ExpItemCoeff	-3.3054	-5.0719	-0.5344
graph eta	1.7035	1.7944	0.0534

(a)

Metric	Graph	Model	Relative error
Total Nodes	23668	23668	0.0000
Total Edges	44610	44443	0.0037
Average Degree	3.7696	3.7555	0.0037
Diameter	12	11	0.0833
Radius	7	6	0.1429
Average Path Length	4.4984	4.5038	0.0012
Number Of Shortest Paths	560150556	560150556	0.0000
Communities Number	38	65	0.7105
Density	0.0002	0.0002	0.0037
Modularity	0.5553	0.5587	0.0061
Avg Item Clustering	0.0102	0.0061	0.4059
Avg User Clustering	0.0997	0.1058	0.0613
UsersCount	2885	2887	0.0007
ItemsCount	20783	20781	0.0001
User Average Degree	15.4627	15.3942	0.0044
Item Average Degree	2.1465	2.1386	0.0036
gen alpha	2.0704	0.7445	0.6404
gen beta	0.8029	0.7750	0.0347
gen p add user	0.1219	0.1220	0.0007
gen p bouncing	0.2329	0.2363	0.0144
ExpUserCoeff	-0.8174	-0.8038	-0.0167
ExpItemCoeff	-4.1118	-6.2667	-0.5241
graph eta	1.8848	1.8778	0.0037

(b)

Table 3. (a) Experimental results for dataset *theoreticalcomputerscience* for $d_u = 3$ and $d_v = 2$. (b) Experimental results for dataset *webapplications* for $d_u = 2$ and $d_v = 1$.

Metric	Graph	Model	Relative error
Total Nodes	6114	6114	0.0000
Total Edges	12744	13273	0.0415
Average Degree	4.1688	4.3418	0.0415
Diameter	12	9	0.2500
Radius	7	6	0.1429
Average Path Length	4.2949	5.1327	0.1951
Number Of Shortest Paths	37374882	37374882	0.0000
Communities Number	29	39	0.3448
Density	0.0007	0.0007	0.0415
Modularity	0.5063	0.5081	0.0036
Avg Item Clustering	0.0296	0.0098	0.6682
Avg User Clustering	0.1130	0.0873	0.2275
UsersCount	1099	1065	0.0309
ItemsCount	5015	5049	0.0068
User Average Degree	11.5960	12.4629	0.0748
Item Average Degree	2.5412	2.6288	0.0345
gen alpha	1.4205	0.7093	0.5007
gen beta	0.3262	0.2598	0.2036
gen p add user	0.1798	0.1742	0.0309
gen p bouncing	0.2097	0.2987	0.4243
ExpUserCoeff	-0.8667	-0.7816	-0.0981
ExpItemCoeff	-3.1786	-3.7817	-0.1897
graph eta	2.0844	2.1709	0.0415

(a)

Metric	Graph	Model	Relative error
Total Nodes	6831	6831	0.0000
Total Edges	8897	8525	0.0418
Average Degree	2.6049	2.4960	0.0418
Diameter	20	14	0.3000
Radius	10	8	0.2000
Average Path Length	6.1617	7.7572	0.2589
Number Of Shortest Paths	46655730	46655730	0.0000
Communities Number	52	60	0.1538
Density	0.0004	0.0004	0.0418
Modularity	0.7654	0.7915	0.0341
Avg Item Clustering	0.0025	0.0003	0.8850
Avg User Clustering	0.0250	0.0020	0.9181
UsersCount	1691	1700	0.0053
ItemsCount	5140	5131	0.0018
User Average Degree	5.2614	5.0147	0.0469
Item Average Degree	1.7309	1.6615	0.0401
gen alpha	0.5000	0.5000	0.0000
gen beta	0.2695	0.2572	0.0456
gen p add user	0.2475	0.2489	0.0053
gen p bouncing	-0.3171	-0.0321	-0.8987
ExpUserCoeff	-1.2276	-1.2472	-0.0159
ExpItemCoeff	-3.7918	-2.4565	-0.3521
graph eta	1.3024	1.2480	0.0418

(b)

5   Conclusion

Cold Start User-Item Model (CSUIM) of bipartite graphs is very flexible and can be applied to many different problems. In this article, we showed that the parameters of this model can be obtained easily form an unknown bipartite graph. We presented several algorithms to estimate the most important parameters: δ, α, β, γ. We gave some advice about setting up the renaming parameters: m, d_u and d_v. Experimental result showed that CSUI model can be applied to some extent for modeling bipartite graph of users and user posts.

Moreover, we gave a theoretical basis for estimating parameters α and β based on the degree distribution in each of modalities. We showed that for small k (consuming most of the probability mass) and fixed α (or β) the value of $\ln(p_k)$ decreases nearly linearly with $\ln k$. The experiment presented in this paper proved that not only in theory but also in practice computing α does not depend on β value and vice versa. The sampling for linear regression models can be simply parallelized for more efficient computations. We also find out that the bouncing parameter γ is linearly correlated with Newman's optimal modularity. Experiments made on real-world graphs showed that from these theoretical relationships parameters α, β and γ can be extracted quite well.

Deep analysis of CSUI model provides a natural guide to future research concerning creating disconnected graphs. In general, it is a hard problem and to simplify one model's giant component of an analyzed graph. Although CSUI model can produce disconnected graphs by first initializing step, it can only merge disconnected components and does not produce (divide) new components, as it happens in real-world networks.

References

1. Chapter 12 - An Overview of Social Networks and Economic Applications. In: Handbook of Social Economics, vol. 1, pp. 511–585. North-Holland (2011)
2. Birmelé, E.: A scale-free graph model based on bipartite graphs. Discrete Appl. Math. **157**(10), 2267–2284 (2009)
3. Chojnacki, S.: Analiza technicznych własności systemów rekomenduj acych za pomoc a algorytmów losowych. Ph.D. thesis, Institute of Computer Science, Polish Academy of Sciences, Warsaw (2012)
4. Fotouhi, B., Rabbat, M.G.: Network growth with arbitrary initial conditions: analytical results for uniform and preferential attachment. CoRR abs/1212.0435
5. Guillaume, J.L., Latapy, M.: Bipartite structure of all complex networks. Inf. Process. Lett. **90**(5), 215–221 (2004)
6. Kłopotek, R.A.: Study on the estimation of the bipartite graph generator parameters. In: Kłopotek, M.A., Koronacki, J., Marciniak, M., Mykowiecka, A., Wierzchoń, S.T. (eds.) IIS 2013. LNCS, vol. 7912, pp. 234–244. Springer, Heidelberg (2013). https://doi.org/10.1007/978-3-642-38634-3_26
7. Kłopotek, R.A.: Invasive analysis of social networks. Ph.D. thesis, Institute of Computer Science, Polish Academy of Sciences, Warsaw (2014)
8. Koskinen, J.H., Robins, G.L., Pattison, P.E.: Analysing exponential random graph (p-star) models with missing data using bayesian data augmentation. Stat. Methodol. **7**(3), 366–384 (2010)

9. Lam, X.N., Vu, T., Le, T.D., Duong, A.D.: Addressing cold-start problem in recommendation systems. In: Proceedings of the 2nd International Conference on Ubiquitous Information Management and Communication, ICUIMC 2008, pp. 208–211. ACM (2008)

10. Newman, M.E.J., Girvan, M.: Finding and evaluating community structure in networks. Phys. Rev. E **69**, 026113 (2004)

11. Newman, M., Barabasi, A.L., Watts, D.J.: The Structure and Dynamics of Networks: (Princeton Studies in Complexity). Princeton University Press, Princeton (2006)

12. Robins, G., Snijders, T., Wang, P., Handcock, M., Pattison, P.: Recent developments in exponential random graph (p*) models for social networks. Soc. Netw. **29**(2), 192–215 (2007)

13. Schein, A.I., Popescul, A., Ungar, L.H., Pennock, D.M.: Methods and metrics for cold-start recommendations. In: Proceedings of the 25th Annual International ACM SIGIR Conference on Research and Development in Information Retrieval, SIGIR 2002, pp. 253–260. ACM, New York (2002)

14. Shatnawi, R., Althebyan, Q.: An empirical study of the effect of power law distribution on the interpretation of OO metrics. ISRN Softw. Eng. (2013)

15. Vázquez, A.: Growing network with local rules: preferential attachment, clustering hierarchy, and degree correlations. Phys. Rev. E **67**, 056104 (2003)

16. Zheleva, E., Sharara, H., Getoor, L.: Co-evolution of social and affiliation networks. In: Proceeding of the 15th ACM SIGKDD International Conference on Knowledge discovery and data mining, KDD 2009, pp. 1007–1016. ACM, New York (2009)

On Similarity Measures for a Graph-Based Recommender System

Zühal Kurt[1]([⊠]), Alper Bilge[2,3], Kemal Özkan[1],
and Ömer Nezih Gerek[3]

[1] Eskişehir Osmangazi University, 26480 Eskişehir, ES, Turkey
zkurt@ogu.edu.tr
[2] Computer Research and Application Centre, 26480 Eskişehir, ES, Turkey
[3] Eskişehir Technical University, 26480 Eskişehir, ES, Turkey

Abstract. Recommender systems are drawing increasing attention with several unresolved issues. These systems depend on personal user preferences on items via ratings and recommend items based on choices of similar users. A graph-based recommender system that has ratings of users on items can be shown as a bipartite graph in which vertices match users and items nodes, and edges correspond to ratings. Recommendation generation in a bipartite graph can be moderated as a sub-problem of link prediction. In the relevant literature, modified link prediction methods are employed to differentiate between fundamental relational dualities of like vs. dislike and similar vs. dissimilar. However, the similarity relationships between users/items are often ignored. We propose a new model that utilizes user-user and item-item similarity values with relational dualities in order to improve coverage and hits rate by carefully incorporating similarities. We compare five similarity measures in terms of hits rate and coverage while providing top-N recommendations. We scrutinize how such similarity measures perform with top-N item recommendation processes over the standard MovieLens Hetrec and MovieLens datasets. The experimental results show that hits rate and coverage can be improved by about 7% and 4%, respectively, with Jaccard and Adjusted-Cosine similarity measures being the best performing similarity measures. Significant differences/improvements are observed over the previous CORLP approach.

Keywords: Bipartite graph · Complex domain · Similarity measures

1 Introduction

Recommender systems are used in several different applications to help users survive in an overwhelming amount of data [1, 10, 13, 14]. Examples of such can be systems for recommending movies, TV shows, commercial products, or music.

There are numerous approaches for recommender systems that utilize either content, rating, or demographic information. Content-Based Filtering (CBF) and Collaborative Filtering (CF) methods are two of the widely-used techniques for constructing recommender systems [10–12]. CBF methods suggest items to users by analyzing the item descriptions to identify which items are of interest to a particular user. The recommendations of these systems are similar in content to the items in which the user

© Springer Nature Switzerland AG 2019
R. Damaševičius and G. Vasiljevienė (Eds.): ICIST 2019, CCIS 1078, pp. 136–147, 2019.
https://doi.org/10.1007/978-3-030-30275-7_11

was previously interested. CF-based recommender systems use rating information to identify a neighborhood of a particular user that has previously shown similar behavior. Then, this neighborhood is analyzed to identify new pieces of information that can be shared by a particular user. User neighborhood is constructed with information such as accessing to the same type of information, purchasing a similar set of products, liking/disliking a similar set of movies. Such approaches are referred to as user-based recommendation algorithms. An essential component of CF approaches is finding similarities between users effectively. However, rating data are usually not sufficient to find similarities, especially for the cold-start problem that refers to the severe degradation of recommendation quality when only a few ratings are available [15, 16]. Item-based CF recommender systems are constructed to deal with these deficiencies. The recommendation algorithms of these CF systems firstly determine the various itemset-item similarities and then combine them to determine the similarity between a user's list and a candidate recommender item [10, 16]. Many real-world implementations have used these CF recommendations approaches with traditional vector similarity measures, i.e., cosine or Pearson's correlation. While the overall efficiency of CF recommender systems is evident, there are some questions about whether traditional measures are suitable, and which measure is useful.

Various hybrid recommendation algorithms have been proposed to overcome unresolved problems in recommender systems and hybrid schemes combining CBF along with CF for recommendation models are becoming popular [3]. Modeling users and items as nodes in a graph structure yields superior results in applying CBF and CF algorithms in one framework [3, 6, 7]. A graph-based recommender system that has ratings of users on items can be represented as a graph where vertices correspond to users and items and edges to ratings. Such a model was proposed that depends on users' ratings, reviews, and social data to utilize various personalized information to improve recommendation accuracy in [22]. Recommendation generation in a graph can be considered as a link prediction problem. Link prediction algorithms perform well in correctly predicting high probable links even if the information about the graph structure is incomplete [22, 23].

Furthermore, link prediction approaches are used to distinguish between fundamental relational dualities of like/dislike and similar/dissimilar [2–7]. A link prediction algorithm based on the local similarity values of nodes is proposed to evaluate which measure performs better in the task of predicting the future links, which can be utilized for the propagation of information and opinion in social networks [23, 25]. However, the similarity relationships between users or items nodes are mostly disregarded. A new concept of the small world model is proposed to evaluate the similarity between objects/items in a graph, which provides better performance depending on similarity factors [24]. Similarity factor between every pair of nodes is obtained based on the random walk to identify the neighboring nodes for inclusion in the graph, [24]. Graph-based recommendation techniques first analyze the user-item interaction matrix to identify relationships between different users or items, then use these relationships to compute recommendations for users indirectly.

In this work, a graph-based recommender system is proposed that incorporates numerical ratings and similarity of items/users. Thus, the proposed model utilizes user-user and item-item similarity values with the relational dualities in order to improve the accuracy of the system by carefully incorporating similarities. We focus on a graph based recommendation model that relies on top-N recommendations. The similarity measurements referred to in this paper have been used in various item-based CF recommender systems [10, 16], but these systems tended to produce lower-quality recommendations when compared to the hybrid or graph-based approaches. The proposed graph model utilizes user-user and item-item similarities with the like/dislike dualities in order to improve the accuracy of the recommendation system. Unlike the earlier researches, which only consider complex numbers in like/dislike factors [6, 19], user-item interaction matrix is totally weighted with complex numbers. Since a complex number yields a natural algebraic link between real and imaginary values, the recommendation problem is viewed as a problem of link prediction. So, using the proposed method, other link prediction algorithms can still be directly incorporated. We assess the proposed representation's validity and efficiency by evaluating the performance of the proposed recommendation approach in two real-world datasets.

2 Background

A recommender system may be shown as a specific graph, called a bipartite graph. A simple directed graph, $G = (V, E)$, is composed of vertices connected by edges. Vertices, V, in a directed network are the nodes (items and users), whereas edges, E, refer to the links between the nodes, i.e., ratings. Let U be the set of users and I the set of items, respectively. Then, V is the combination of all users and items ($V = U \cup I$) and E is the link set of nodes. A path is notated as $(a_1, a_2, \ldots, a_{k+1})$ and the path length is represented by k, with two endpoints, a_1 and a_{k+1}, linked by the inner nodes of $a_i (i = 2, 3, \ldots, k)$. Here, k links are observed along the path of $(a_i, a_{i+1}) \in E$, where $i = 1, 2, \ldots, k$. When the length is one ($k = 1$), it means that there is a link to any inner nodes. We describe $N_u(i) = \{i | (u, i) \in E, i \in I\}$ as the set of items that user u rated and $N_i(u) = \{u | (u, i) \in E, u \in U\}$ as the set of users who rated item i. When there is a connection between two nodes, there need to be two links that connect this node-pair, one in each direction. Then, it is possible to reduce the recommendation effort to predict a link in the graph between a user and a specific item exists. A prediction that indicates the relevance degree of any item to a particular user is calculated by using a link prediction algorithm in graph-based recommender systems [6].

2.1 Link Prediction Functions

Polynomials; It is possible to use any polynomial with only odd powers and non-negative weights as a recommendation algorithm: $p(A) = aA + b \cdot A^3 + c \cdot A^5 + \ldots$.

Rank Reduction; involves finding a matrix that has the maximum rank of r, which corresponds to the nearest one to the given adjacency matrix (via SVD of A).

Hyperbolic sine; The hyperbolic sine of the matrix naturally provides odd powers: $sinh(A) = A + (1/6) \cdot A^3 + (1/120) \cdot A^5 + \ldots$

Newman kernel; The geometric (or Newman) series represents the Newman kernel; $(I - \alpha A)^{-1} = I + \alpha A + \alpha^2 \cdot A^2 + \alpha^3 \cdot A^3 + \ldots$, where the inverse of the largest singular value of A must be larger than the constant α. Restricting the Newman kernel to odd powers only ends up with the odd Newman kernel;

$$\alpha A (I - \alpha^2 A^2)^{-1} = I + \alpha A + \alpha^3 \cdot A^3 + \alpha^5 \cdot A^5 + \ldots, \tag{1}$$

which is used in bipartite networks [7].

2.2 Similarity Metrics

Several standard similarity metrics used in recommender systems are discussed here. Each similarity formula uses an m-by-n user-item interaction matrix.

Cosine similarity; Two items are shown as x and y vectors in the m-D user-space, and the similarity is defined as the cosine of the angle between these two vectors.

$$sim(x, y) = \cos(x, y) = \frac{x \cdot y}{\|x\|_2 * \|y\|_2} \tag{2}$$

Adjusted cosine similarity; This is a modified cosine similarity, considering rating behaviors of different users [10]. The average ratings for each user u, $\overline{R_u}$ is subtracted from each user's ratings $R_{u,x}$ for the item x to get:

$$sim(x, y) = acos(x, y) = \frac{\sum_{u \in U} (R_{u,x} - \overline{R_u})(R_{u,y} - \overline{R_u})}{\sqrt{\sum_{u \in U} (R_{u,x} - \overline{R_u})^2} \sqrt{\sum_{u \in U} (R_{u,y} - \overline{R_u})^2}} \tag{3}$$

Jaccard similarity index; It compares ratings for two users' rating vectors to find out which ratings are common and which are not, ranging between 0% and 100%. The idea is that users are more similar as they have more common ratings. The higher the percentage of *Jaccard index*, the more the number of common ratings between two users. $Jaccard(I_u, I_v) = |I_u| \cap |I_v| / |I_u| \cup |I_v|$, where $|I_u|$ and $|I_u|$ are the cardinality of items rated by users u and v.

Pearson correlation coefficient; Corresponds to the simple correlation coefficient between item sequences $X = \{x_i : i = 1, \ldots, n\}$ $Y = \{y_i : i = 1, \ldots, n\}$, defined as

$$pearson(X, Y) = r = \frac{\sum_{i=1}^{n} (x_i - \bar{x})(y_i - \bar{y})}{\sqrt{\sum_{i=1}^{n} (x_i - \bar{x})^2} \sqrt{\sum_{i=1}^{n} (y_i - \bar{y})^2}}, \text{ where } \bar{x} = \frac{1}{n} \sum_{i=1}^{n} x_i, \bar{y} = \frac{1}{n} \sum_{i=1}^{n} y_i.$$

Spearman similarity coefficient; is obtained by applying the Pearson coefficient to rank-transformed data: $spearman(X, Y) = \rho = \frac{6 \cdot \sum_{i=1}^{n} [R(x_i) - R(y_i)]^2}{n \cdot (n^2 - 1)}$, where $R(x_i)$ and $R(y_i)$ represent ranks of x_i and y_i in item sequences of X and Y.

Adamic-Adar (AA) Coefficient; favors the common neighbors that have fewer neighbors, hence measures how strong the relationship between a common neighbor and the evaluated pair of nodes is [25]: $AA(x, y) = \sum_{z \in |\Gamma(x) \cap \Gamma(y)|} \frac{1}{\log(|\Gamma(z)|)}$, where $\Gamma(x), \Gamma(y)$ are the set of neighbors of node x and y, and $|\Gamma(z)|$ is the degree of the node z.

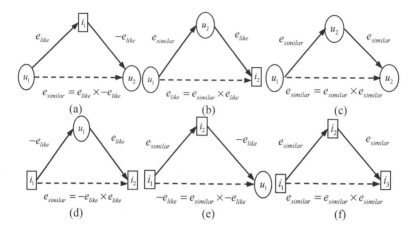

Fig. 1. The triangle closing multiplication rule set, (a, d) show that the same interest of users/items produces similarity, (b, e) show that similar users/items will have similar interest (c, f) show that user/item similarity is transitive among users/items.

2.3 Triangle Closing

Nodes in a user-item bipartite graph may have two kinds of relationships: similarity and like/dislike. Similarity factor ($e_{similar}$) may be for user-user and item-item links. User-item links may have e_{like} factor (with $-e_{like}$ for item-user link association). Finally, the triangle closing rule is formed as described in Fig. 1. The rule includes two components: users displaying the same interest in shared items may be similar (Fig. 1a), similar users will be similarly interested in the same item (Fig. 1b), and user similarity is transitive among users (Fig. 1c). The items liked by associated users may be similar (Fig. 1d), users tend to be interested in similar items (Fig. 1e), and item similarity is transitive among items (Fig. 1f), all of which form the main points of CF, providing the following are the mathematical principles:

$$e_{similar} = -e_{like}^2, \; e_{like} = e_{similar} \times e_{like}, \; e_{similar} = e_{similar}^2 \tag{4}$$

The solution of this system of equations yields results for $e_{similar}$ and e_{like}, which can attain complex values: $e_{like} = j$ and $e_{similar} = 1$, where j is the imaginary unit.

2.4 Adjacency Matrix

The adjacency matrix is shown as $A \in \mathbb{R}^{|V| \times |V|}$ given by: $A(u, i) = \begin{cases} 1 \; if \, (u, i) \in E \\ 0 \; if \, (u, i) \notin E \end{cases}$ when $G = (V, E)$ denotes an undirected and unweighted network. The adjacency matrix A is symmetric and square. Thus, the number of paths connecting two nodes can be derived by computing the powers of the matrices in unweighted networks. Furthermore, the number of common neighbors between two nodes u and i ($u, i \in V$) can be formulated by taking the square of the adjacency matrix: $N(u, i) = A^2(u, i)$, which applies basic triangle closing and may be explained as the number of paths with a length of two among them. This formulization has a key point: these two nodes will be closer the bigger the entry of the square of the adjacency matrix is. The number of paths of any length k from node u to node i can be expressed by the components of $A^k(u, i)$. Therefore, the closeness of the two nodes may be computed by the weighted sum of powers of the adjacency matrix A. Such an example of a link prediction method to merge these results is the matrix exponential: $exp(A) = I + A + 1/2 \cdot A^2 + \ldots$. This function considers that all powers of A involve all the paths between two nodes. The real numbers are used to represent the user-user and item-item relationships, and the complex numbers are used to express the user-item interactions. The adjacency matrix A of the user-item graph G is given as follows:

$$A(u, i) = \begin{cases} 1 \; if \; u \; similar \; i \\ -1 \; if \; u \; dissimilar \; i \\ j \; if \; u \; likes \; i \; or \; i \; dislikes \; u \\ -j \; if \; u \; dislikes \; i \; or \; i \; likes \; u \\ 0 \; if \; (u, i) \notin E \end{cases} \tag{5}$$

where $A(u, i)$ is the value of row u and column i of the matrix A. The matrix A may be conveniently given as: $\begin{bmatrix} A_{UU} & A_{UI} \\ A_{IU} & A_{II} \end{bmatrix}$, where A_{II} and A_{UU} are the item-item and user-user similarity matrices, A_{UI} and A_{IU} are the user-item preference matrices, also the conjugate transpose of A_{IU} can be described as, $A_{IU} = -A_{UI}^T$. The preference matrices are complex matrices, whereas the similarity matrices are real matrices. In the Complex Representation-based Link Prediction (CORLP) method [10], the authors do not take into account the relationships between users or items; they represent the bipartite graph as G and the adjacency matrix as A, corresponding to $A = \begin{bmatrix} 0 & A_{UI} \\ -A_{UI}^T & 0 \end{bmatrix}$. As per the representation of the adjacency matrix A, each entry in the preference matrix A_{UI} has only three values: j, $-j$ and 0. Furthermore B, the biadjacency matrix of bipartite graph corresponding to A, is a real matrix. Then A can be given as $\begin{bmatrix} 0 & jB \\ -jB^T & 0 \end{bmatrix}$

Based on the path counting process in the unweighted and undirected networks, the weighted path counting process for paths of length k can be derived by A^k. If we only consider the relationships between users and items, the kth power of the adjacency matrix may be further mathematically expressed as in Eq. 6. Thus, any sum of the powers of the adjacency matrix A may be divided into components that are even and odd, but only the odd components are effective for final recommendation. Therefore, a general application of the to A produces $P(A) = \lambda \cdot A + \lambda_3 \cdot A^3 + \lambda_5 \cdot A^5 + \lambda_7 \cdot A^7 + \lambda_9 \cdot A^9 + \ldots$. To ensure that shorter paths yield more to the predictions, $\{\lambda_1, \lambda_2, \lambda_3, \ldots\}$ is a decreasingly weighted sequence.

$$A(u, i) = \begin{cases} \begin{bmatrix} (BB^T)^n & 0 \\ 0 & (B^TB)^n \end{bmatrix} where\ k = 2n \\ j \times \begin{bmatrix} 0 & (BB^T)^nB \\ -(B^TB)^nB^T & 0 \end{bmatrix} where\ k = 2n+1 \end{cases} \quad (6)$$

The proposed similarity-inclusive link prediction method (SIMLP) varies from the CORLP method [6] in modeling of the adjacency matrix, calculating the powers of the adjacency matrix, and yielding the final recommendation. After the combination of user and item matrices, the main adjacency matrix is constructed as shown in Eq. (7).

$$A = \begin{pmatrix} u_{11} & \cdots & u_{1n} & r_{11} & \cdots & r_{1n} \\ \vdots & \ddots & \vdots & \vdots & \ddots & \vdots \\ u_{m1} & \cdots & u_{mn} & r_{m1} & \cdots & r_{mn} \\ -r_{11} & \cdots & -r_{1n} & k_{11} & \cdots & k_{1n} \\ \vdots & \ddots & \vdots & \vdots & \ddots & \vdots \\ -r_{m1} & \cdots & -r_{mn} & k_{m1} & \cdots & k_{mn} \end{pmatrix}, \quad (7)$$

where u_{ij} denotes the similarity between the ith and j^{th} users, k_{ij} denotes the similarity between the ith and j^{th} items, r_{ij} represents as the like/dislike relationship between the ith user and j^{th} item.

3   Recommendation Methodology

We use a testing methodology similar to that of [6]. The ratings are split to test and training sets and the 10-fold cross-validation method is used. At each fold, the test set is forced to include only 5-star ratings to assure validity [6, 19].

Here, the adjacency matrix's generation of our proposed method requires rating conversion, where the ratings in the training set are converted to j (like) or $-j$ (dislike), according to whether the rating is greater than or equal to 3, or not, respectively. If the (u, i) pair is excluded in the training set, the value in the adjacency matrix is zero. Since recommendation error is irrelevant for this problem, hits rate and coverage values are used for comparison [6, 17, 18]. Regarding the top-N recommendations, the overall hits rate and coverage are described by averaging all test cases: $hits\ rate(N) = \frac{\#hits}{|T|}$, $coverage(N) = \frac{|\cup recommend(N,u)|}{\#items}$. When the item i is included in the user u's top-N recommendations list for each pair (u, i) in the test set, it will get one hit. The overall hit is shown as $\#hits$, and the number of test pairs is shown as $|T|$. Thus, the hits rate can be expressed as the capability to recommend relevant items to users. Another quality indicator is coverage, which is equal to the percentage of items that the system can recommend. It is useful in models which recommend a limited but highly accurate number of items. An algorithm is argued to perform well if both metrics are high.

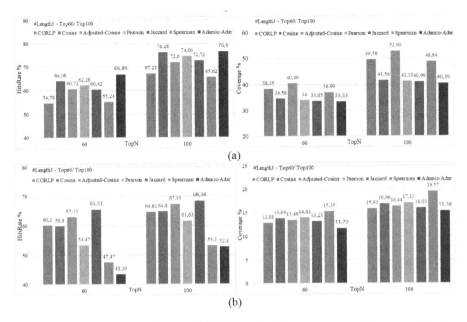

Fig. 2. Comparison of the CORLP and SIMLP methods by coverage and hits rate with using different similarity metrics for top-N recommendation on MovieLens (a) and Hetrec (b) datasets.

4 Experimental Results and Datasets

We employed the tests in two real-world datasets: MovieLens (100,000 ratings ranging from 1-to-5 from 943 users on 1,682 movies) and MovieLens Hetrec (855,598 ratings ranging from 1-to-5 from 2,113 users on 10,197 movies) [8, 9]. First, ratings in these datasets were converted into complex numbers to form biadjacency matrices. Then, similarity measurements were applied to the user-item rating matrices. Finally, the user-user similarity matrices and item-item similarity matrices of rating matrices of these datasets were determined. Combining all these matrices, main adjacency matrices were constructed for these two datasets as in Eq. (7). The hyperbolic-sine function is applied to the adjacency matrices as a link prediction function, as in [6]. The results of the SIMLP method by using various similarity metrics for top-N recommendations are given in Fig. 2. The results of SIMLP algorithm are measured with path length 3 to compare with CORLP method, since CORLP has the best results in path length 3. Figure 2 shows that the proposed SIMLP method achieves higher hits rate and coverage when using Adjusted Cosine similarity metric. Figure 2 also shows that SIMLP method yields better results than CORLP when SIMLP is modified with the proposed similarity metrics, with an exception of Spearman similarity metric.

We propose to modify the CORLP and SIMLP algorithms with using the Neumann Kernel as a link prediction function, in order to investigate SIMLP and CORLP methods' behaviors after changing link prediction algorithms. Hence, the Neumann Kernel is used as a link prediction function, that formulated as in Eq. (1). We set $\alpha = 0.001$ and $\alpha = 0.0001$ in Eq. (1) respectively for the experiments on both datasets.

As the same as, the results of the SIMLP and CORLP algorithm are measured with path length 3. The results of the CORLP and SIMLP method by using various similarity metrics for top-N recommendation tasks are illustrated in Fig. 3. The results indicate that the proposed SIMLP method obtains higher hits rate and coverage than CORLP method when SIMLP utilized with similarity metrics defined in this study.

In this study, we try to answer two questions: Does the proposed SIMLP approach that utilizes various similarities perform better than CORLP approach? Which similarity metrics improve the performance of SIMLP for top-N recommendation task? We use hits rate and coverage as the primary measures to compute the performance of the proposed recommendation algorithm. Two-factor Anova test is conducted to further evaluate performance differences among SIMLP and CORLP approaches, [20, 21]. Thus, the specific hypotheses examined in our study are:

- H1: The SIMLP based recommendation approach achieves higher hits rate than the CORLP based recommendation approach does.
- H2: The SIMLP based recommendation approach achieves higher coverage than the CORLP based recommendation approach does.

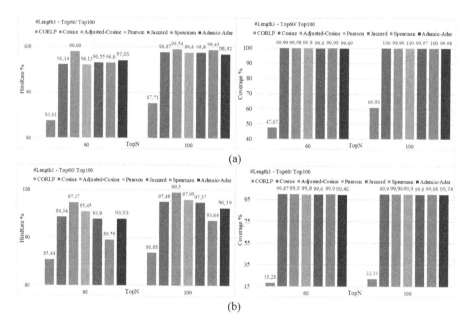

Fig. 3. Comparison of SIMLP and CORLP methods by coverage and hits rate utilizing Neumann link prediction kernel for top-N recommendation on MovieLens (a) and Hetrec (b) datasets.

Table 1 includes the only one p-value that reflects no significant differences among CORLP and SIMLP (that utilizes Spearman similarities) methods with respect to hits-rate on MovieLens dataset. Table 1 demonstrates that there are statistically significant differences between CORLP and SIMLP methods with respect to hits rate. The hypotheses

H1 are supported for each similarity metrics defined in this paper with the exception of Spearman similarity measurement by our experimental results. As shown in Table 2, there are no significant differences between CORLP and SIMLP (that utilizes Spearman, Jaccard and adjusted-cosine similarities) methods with respect to coverage on MovieLens and Hetrec dataset. The other p-values in Table 2 demonstrate that statistically significant differences are observed between CORLP and SIMLP methods with respect to coverage. The hypotheses H2 are supported for each similarity metrics defined in this paper with the exception of Spearman and adjusted-cosine similarity measurements by our experimental results.

Table 1. The p-values of the comparison of the CORLP and the SIMLP methods for each similarity metrics with regards to hits rate on MovieLens and Hetrec datasets.

Dataset	Similarity measure					
	Cosine	Adjusted-Cosine	Pearson	Jaccard	Spearman	Adamic-Adar
Movielens	0.0007	0.0061	0.0060	0.0113	0.6744	0.0132
Hetrec	0.0183	0.0176	0.0002	0.0009	0.00001	0.0006

Table 2. The p-values of the comparison of the CORLP and the SIMLP methods for each similarity metrics with regards to coverage on MovieLens and Hetrec datasets.

Dataset	Similarity measure					
	Cosine	Adjusted-Cosine	Pearson	Jaccard	Spearman	Adamic-Adar
Movielens	0.0081	0.1286	0.0045	0.0025	0.7488	0.0077
Hetrec	0.0351	0.1471	0.0235	0.4518	0.0013	0.0088

Table 3. The p-values of the comparison of the SIMLP and the CORLP methods that utilize Neumann link prediction kernel with regards to hits rate on MovieLens and Hetrec datasets.

Dataset	Similarity measure					
	Cosine	Adjusted-Cosine	Pearson	Jaccard	Spearman	Adamic-Adar
Movielens	0.0001	0.0001	0.0001	0.00004	0.0001	0.0006
Hetrec	0.0212	0.0969	0.0012	0.0244	0.7266	0.001

Table 4. The p-values of the comparison of the SIMLP and the CORLP methods that utilize Neumann link prediction kernel with regards to coverage on MovieLens and Hetrec datasets.

Dataset	Similarity measure					
	Cosine	Adjusted-Cosine	Pearson	Jaccard	Spearman	Adamic-Adar
Movielens	6×10^{-11}	5×10^{-11}	6×10^{-11}	9×10^{-11}	5×10^{-11}	1×10^{-10}
Hetrec	5×10^{-14}	4×10^{-14}	1×10^{-14}	1×10^{-14}	1×10^{-14}	1×10^{-14}

The p-values of the comparison between the SIMLP and the CORLP methods that utilize Neumann link prediction kernel with regards to hits rate and coverage on MovieLens and Hetrec datasets are given in Tables 3 and 4. The two p-values, that reflect no significant differences between CORLP and SIMLP (that utilizes Spearman and adjusted-cosine similarities) methods with respect to hits rate on Hetrec dataset, are given in Table 3. The other p-values in Table 3 indicate that there are statistically significant differences between CORLP and SIMLP methods with respect to hits rate. The hypotheses H1 are supported for each similarity metrics defined in this study with the exception of Spearman and adjusted-cosine similarity measurements by our experimental results. Table 4 demonstrates that there are statistically significant differences between CORLP and SIMLP methods with respect to coverage. Then, the hypotheses H2 are supported for each similarity metrics defined in this paper.

5 Conclusion

The proposed recommendation method relies on the link prediction approach in the weighted graph model, and complex numbers denote the weights in the graph. This algorithm can accurately differentiate "similarity" between two users (or two items) and the "like" between a user and an item. We have improved this algorithm by incorporating similarity factors among users and items. The experimental results show that the proposed SIMLP method provides better efficiency for the top-N recommendation task. The results also show that Jaccard and Adjusted cosine similarity measures outperform their alternatives. We have observed that using two quality metrics (coverage and hits rate on the MovieLens Hetrec and MovieLens datasets), the proposed SIMLP method performs better than the CORLP method. The proposed method provides about %7 higher hits rate and about %4 better coverage than the CORLP method based on the k-fold results. Besides, we have examined the SIMLP and CORLP method by modifying the link prediction function as Neumann kernel. About %12 better hits rate and about %40 better coverage are obtained with SIMLP as opposed to CORLP, both in MovieLens and Hetrec datasets. From two-factor anova test analysis, the proposed algorithm is observed to be significantly superior to CORLP. We conclude that the proposed SIMLP method resolves the accuracy and sparsity problems in graph-based recommender systems, rendering the proposed recommender system a better algorithmic option.

References

1. Huang, Z., Zeng, D., Chen, H.: A comparative study of recommendation algorithms in E-commerce applications. IEEE Intell. Syst. **22**, 68–78 (2007)
2. Zhou, T., Ren, J., Medo, M., Zhang, Y.C.: Bipartite network projection and personal recommendation. Phys. Rev. **76**(4), 046–115 (2007)
3. Li, X., Chen, H.: Recommendation as link prediction in bipartite graphs: a graph kernel-based machine learning approach. Decis. Support Syst. **54**(2), 880–890 (2013)
4. Getoor, L., Diehl, C.P.: Link mining: a survey. ACM SIGKDD Explor. Newslett. **7**(2), 3–12 (2005)

5. Liben-Nowell, D., Kleinberg, J.: The link-prediction problem for social networks. J. Am. Soc. Inf. Sci. Technol. **58**(7), 1019–1031 (2007)
6. Xie, F., Chen, Z., Shang, J., Feng, X., Li, J.: A link prediction approach for item recommendation with complex number. Knowl. Based Syst. **81**, 148–158 (2015)
7. Kunegis, J., De Luca, E.W., Albayrak, S.: The link prediction problem in bipartite networks. In: Hüllermeier, E., Kruse, R., Hoffmann, F. (eds.) IPMU 2010. LNCS (LNAI), vol. 6178, pp. 380–389. Springer, Heidelberg (2010). https://doi.org/10.1007/978-3-642-14049-5_39
8. Harper, F.M., Konstan, J.A.: The MovieLens datasets: History and context. ACM Trans. Interact. Intell. Syst. **5**(4), 1–19 (2016)
9. GroupLens Research Group, May 2011. https://grouplens.org/datasets/hetrec-2011/
10. Sarwar, B.M., Karypis, G., Konstan, J.A., Riedl, J.: Item-based collaborative filtering recommendation algorithms. In: Proceedings of the 10th International Conference on World Wide Web, pp. 285–295. ACM, New York (2001)
11. Pazzani, M.J., Billsus, D.: Content-based recommendation systems. In: Brusilovsky, P., Kobsa, A., Nejdl, W. (eds.) The Adaptive Web. LNCS, vol. 4321, pp. 325–341. Springer, Heidelberg (2007). https://doi.org/10.1007/978-3-540-72079-9_10
12. Pazzani, M.J.: A framework for collaborative, content-based and demographic filtering. Artif. Intell. Rev. **13**(5–6), 393–408 (1999)
13. Beeferman, D., Berger, A.: Agglomerative clustering of a search engine query log. In: Proceedings of the 6th ACM SIGKDD International Conference on Knowledge Discovery & Data Mining, pp. 407–415. ACM, New York (2000)
14. Kitts, B., Freed, D., Vrieze, M.: Cross-sell: a fast promotion-tunable customer–item recommendation method based on conditional independent probabilities. In: Proceedings of the 10th International Conference on Proceedings of ACM SIGKDD, pp. 437–446. ACM, New York (2000)
15. Ahn, H.J.: A new similarity measure for collaborative filtering to alleviate the new user cold-starting problem. Inf. Sci. **178**(1), 37–51 (2008)
16. Deshpande, M., Karypis, G.: Item-based top-N recommendation algorithms. ACM Trans. Inf. Syst. (TOIS) **22**(1), 143–177 (2004)
17. Cremonesi, P., Koren, Y., Turrin, R.: Performance of recommender algorithms on top-N recommendation tasks. In: 4th Proceedings on ACM Conference on RecSys, pp. 39–46. ACM, Barcelona (2010)
18. Gedikli, F., Jannach, D.: Recommendation based on rating frequencies. In: 4th Proceedings on ACM Conference on RecSys, pp. 26–30. ACM, Barcelona (2010)
19. Kurt, Z., Özkan, K., Bilge, A., Gerek, Ö.N.: A similarity-inclusive link prediction based recommender system approach. Elektronika IR Elektrotechnika (2019, to appear)
20. Kurt, Z.: Graph based hybrid recommender systems. (PhD thesis), Anadolu University, Eskişehir (2019)
21. Huang, Z., Chung, W., Ong, T.H., Chen, H.: A graph-based recommender system for digital library. In: Proceedings of the 2nd ACM/IEEE-CS Joint Conference on Digital Libraries, pp. 65–73. ACM, Oregon (2002)
22. Ji, Z., Pi, H., Wei, W., Xiong, B., Wozniak, M., Damasevicius, R.: Recommendation based on review texts and social communities: a hybrid model. IEEE Access **7**, 40416–40427 (2019)
23. Martinčić-Ipšić, S., Močibob, E., Perc, M.: Link prediction on Twitter. PLoS ONE **12**(7), e0181079 (2017)
24. Behera, R., Rath, S., Misra, S., Damaševičius, R., Maskeliūnas, R.: Large scale community detection using a small world model. Appl. Sci. **7**(11), 1173 (2017)
25. De SaÂ, H.R., Prudêncio, R.B.: Supervised link prediction in weighted networks. In: International Joint Conference on Neural Network, pp. 2281–2288. IEEE, USA (2011)

Run-Time Class Generation: Algorithms for Union of Homogeneous and Inhomogeneous Classes

Dmytro O. Terletskyi[✉]

Taras Shevchenko National University of Kyiv, Kyiv 03022, Ukraine
dmytro.terletskyi@gmail.com

Abstract. Run-time code (class) generation is a way to develop adaptive intelligent systems, which can dynamically modify their source codes and knowledge bases up to challenges of the working environment. The example of such challenges is a task of integration of new extracted or acquired knowledge into the knowledge base avoiding redundancy of their representation. To execute it effectively the system should be able to analyze and generate (create) new classes of objects dynamically. Therefore algorithms for dynamic creation of new classes of objects via computing the union of homogeneous and inhomogeneous and union of two inhomogeneous classes of objects are proposed in the paper. Proposed algorithms provide an opportunity for knowledge-based systems to generate new classes, which define heterogeneous collections of objects at the run-time; to determine connection between new and previously acquired knowledge; to conclude thematic relevance and connection level of new knowledge with particular theme, category or domain; to integrate new knowledge into the knowledge base. Developed algorithms have quadratic polynomial time complexity and linear space complexity. They can be adapted and integrated into particular object-oriented programming language or knowledge representation model.

Keywords: Run-time code generation (RTCG) ·
Run-time class generation (RTClG) ·
Universal union exploiter of classes · Union of classes

1 Introduction

One of the important features of intelligent systems is their ability to adapt dynamically to challenges of the working environment. It means that the systems should be able to modify their own source codes and knowledge bases dynamically, when required. Such functionality can be implemented via dynamic analysis, modification and generation of program codes and knowledge representation structures on the implementation and conceptual level correspondingly.

According to [9–11, 19], there are two main approaches to code generation – static or *compile-time code generation (CTCG)* and dynamic or *run-time code generation (RTCG)*. Within static code generation a compiler analyzes and

© Springer Nature Switzerland AG 2019
R. Damaševičius and G. Vasiljevienė (Eds.): ICIST 2019, CCIS 1078, pp. 148–160, 2019.
https://doi.org/10.1007/978-3-030-30275-7_12

transforms the program metastructure to corresponding executable machine codes during program compilation. Within dynamic code generation an interpreter analyzes and modifies program codes during execution of particular program instructions. Consequently, program metastructure is inaccessible at the run-time in the first case and always accessible in the second one.

In addition, as it was noted in [19], metaprogramming systems can be divided on *homogeneous systems*, where the meta-language and the object language are the same, and *heterogeneous systems*, where the meta-language differs from the object-language. In the first case the system uses single type system for meta-language as well as for object-language, where both are sublanguages of particular programming language. In the second case meta-language and object-language can use different type systems and interaction between meta-level and object-level requires development of correspondent translator. Finally, only homogeneous meta-systems can support reflection, what makes run-time code generation possible. Therefore dynamic approach to analysis and generation of program codes within homogeneous meta-system is suitable for implementation of mechanisms of dynamic adaptation of the system to challenges of its working environment.

Generally, way of code generation implementing depends on chosen programming paradigm and language. Nowadays the most popular programming paradigm is the object-oriented programming (OOP), which is supported by majority of modern programming languages. Within the class-based OOP task of code generation can be reduced to generation of particular program constructions, such as classes or hierarchies of classes. Consequently, as it was noted in [24], the task of *run-time code generation (RTCG)* can be reformulated as the task of *run-time class generation (RTClG)*. Some of interpreted programming languages with dynamic typing (e.g. Python, Ruby, etc.) have such internal metaprogramming constructions as metaclasses, which provide dynamic creation of classes at the run-time. However, to use this approach it is required to define correspondent metaclasses within program codes of the system beforehand.

Among the variety of intelligent systems, *knowledge-based systems (KBSs)* form one of the biggest classes. The set of the main tasks for KBSs includes *knowledge acquisition, extraction, representation, integration, reasoning, transferring, exchange*, etc. To solve these tasks a KBS should be capable to analyze and dynamically generate knowledge representation structures, in particular those, which are previously undefined within the system. Dynamic generation of knowledge representation structures depends on particular knowledge representation model, which belongs to some knowledge representation paradigm and uses certain representation structures. Therefore task of run-time code generation can be interpreted in terms of knowledge management as *run-time knowledge generation (RTKG)*.

2   Object-Oriented Dynamic Analysis of Knowledge

Within the object-oriented approach knowledge management is reduced to manipulations with three main representation structures – objects, classes and relations among them [4,18]. Therefore, task of dynamic generation of particular knowledge representation structure has at least three different variations. As it was noted in [24], one of them can be defined as *dynamic generation of classes* or *run-time class generation (RTClG)*.

A KBS can use the ability to generate classes dynamically as a tool to response to challenges of its working environment. However, a KBS should be able to perform dynamic analysis of knowledge, which can include such tasks as: determination of connection between old and new knowledge; conclusion about their thematic relevance; evaluation of their connection with particular theme, category or domain; evaluation of novelty level of acquired or extracted knowledge; etc. Such analysis can be used for effective integration of new acquired or extracted knowledge into the knowledge base avoiding redundancy of their representation and storing.

According to [16], *knowledge integration* is defined as a task of incorporating new information into a knowledge base, which requires elaborating new information and resolving inconsistencies with existing knowledge. As it was noted in [14,17], this task is essential for developing knowledge-based systems and crucial to automated knowledge acquisition in systems with multifunctional knowledge bases. Therefore Murray and Porter developed knowledge acquisition tool KI which main aim is to help knowledge engineers to extend the knowledge bases. They proposed computational model of knowledge integration [14–17], which includes three main phases:

1. *Recognition* of novelty of acquired or extracted knowledge.
2. *Elaboration* of the consequences of acquired or extracted knowledge.
3. *Adaptation* of elaborated knowledge, via modifying the knowledge base for their accommodation.

During the first phase a KBS should identify knowledge structures within the knowledge base, which are relevant to acquired or extracted knowledge. If such structures are found, then new obtained knowledge in some context are relevant to knowledge from the system knowledge base, otherwise they are completely new for a KBS. To implement this phase within the object-oriented approach, a KBS should be able to compare new and old knowledge. As specifications and signatures of objects and classes are sets, then the comparison can be achieved via performing of adapted set-theoretic operations over classes and (or) objects, such as union, intersection, difference, equivalence and inclusion checking, etc. However, these operations should be adopted to particular class concepts and implemented as correspondent algorithms.

The purpose of the second phase is to determine how the new obtained knowledge interact with existing knowledge, according to recognized context, and how they can affect them. The influence can be different, it can cause incompleteness, inconsistencies and contradictions of the knowledge base. As it was noted in [16,17], KI uses system of frames interpreted in semantic network context as the knowledge representation model. To execute the elaboration phase, it uses inference rules to propagate the effects of the new knowledge. Within the object-oriented approach this phase can be considered as the reasoning over classes hierarchy, where integration of particular classes into the hierarchy can affect it and process of reasoning in general. Therefore during this phase all anomalies, which can occur as the result of such integration, should be discovered.

During the third phase a KBS should resolve all anomalies within the knowledge base, which occurred after elaboration phase. Since this process is non-deterministic, and therefore it is hard to automatize it via algorithmic approach, in the expert systems it is usually performed by an expert. Within the object-oriented approach this phase can be interpreted as refinement of classes hierarchy, therefore integration of new classes into the hierarchy should be performed avoiding anomalies occurrence and representation redundancy.

3   Classes Within Object-Oriented Programming

Nowadays, concept of class is the one of basic notions within class-based object-oriented programming (OOP) and inalienable syntactic construction for all modern programming languages, which support this paradigm. Despite this, currently there is no single generally accepted definition for this concept, instead of this a number of different interpretations of a class were proposed, according to which, a class can be considered as:

- *a set of objects that share a common structure, common behavior, and common semantics*, i.e. a collection of related entities or objects with common properties and behavior, i.e. class defines the collection of objects of the same kind [2,3,6];
- *a blueprint or a template for objects*, i.e. abstract prototype for creation of particular objects, consequently all objects created using the same blueprint or template have the equivalent structure and behavior [5,13,28];
- *a data type equipped with a possibly partial implementation*, i.e. a complex abstract and encapsulated data type, which defines collection of typical data-entities (instances of the class), and its implementation can be hidden for users [6,12];
- *a factory-like entity which creates objects*, i.e. a factory which produces objects of the same kind, i.e. all objects of the class have equivalent structure and behavior [6,13];
- *a program structure or module*, i.e. a container, which encapsulates within itself types, data and operations over them [6].

Usually a set of properties (i.e. *specification*) and (or) a set of methods defined over the specification (i.e. *signature*) form the internal representation of a class. However, there are classes which have more complex internal structure, that includes nested classes. In such cases, outer classes aggregate a set of smaller classes, which have their own specifications and signatures.

Since specification and signature of a class within the OOP provides the same structure and behavior for all its objects, such classes can define only *homogeneous sets* of objects. It is a significant functional restriction for classes within the OOP, because it is frequently necessary to work with heterogeneous collections of objects, which contain objects of different types. As the result, it is impossible to represent similar but simultaneously not equivalent types of objects without duplication of their equivalent parts, using homogeneous classes.

Nevertheless, all these restrictions can be removed by using inheritance mechanism and creation of correspondent class hierarchies. However, according to [1,27], there are such problems as problem of exceptions, redundancy, ambiguity and semantic incompatibility, etc. which can occur during construction of class hierarchies and reasoning over them, using mechanism of inheritance.

4   Classes Within Object-Oriented Dynamic Networks

Taking into account the idea of a class within the OOP, alternative concepts of classes were proposed in [25,26], within such object-oriented knowledge representation model as object-oriented dynamic networks (OODNs). Unlike the homogeneous classes within the OOP, classes within OODNs divided on two kinds – *homogeneous* and *inhomogeneous* (or *heterogeneous*) ones.

4.1   Homogeneous Classes

In general, concepts of homogeneous classes within OODNs are similar to analog within the OOP, and can be defined as a tuple $T = (P(T), F(T))$, where $P(T)$ is a specification of the class T and $F(T)$ is its signature. However, as it was shown in [20,21,25,26], OODNs exploit another conception of classes and objects attributes, which allows definition of quantitative and qualitative properties. Such approach provides an opportunity to describe (represent) particular essences, their classes and relations among them, within a domain more precisely. Nevertheless, similarly to analogs within the OOP, homogeneous classes within the OODNs allow only definition of *homogeneous sets of objects*. Therefore, the notion of *inhomogeneous classes*, which provides an opportunity to define classes of heterogeneous collections, was introduced in [25,26].

4.2   Single-Core Inhomogeneous Classes

It is known that inhomogeneous (heterogeneous) collections of objects contain objects of different types (classes). Within the OOP such collections can be defined using *union types*, which denote set-theoretic union of some types, which are viewed as sets of instances that belong to those types and behave as their the least common supertype [7,8]. It means that union types can be used for definition of heterogeneous collections of objects, where classes of objects belong to the same hierarchy. However, as it was noted in [7,8], union types cannot be used to instantiate objects. Moreover, even suppose it possible, the least common supertype (superclass) can define only parts of the structure and behavior, which are common for all members of the hierarchy. It cannot define the specifics of each member of the hierarchy, consequently it is impossible to create all objects of the heterogeneous collection using it. The root of the problem is the unitarity of the homogeneous classes, which can define only one type of objects within the class.

As it was noted in [6], concepts of class and type within the OOP are often thought as the same thing and the unitarity of homogeneous classes is the one of reasons why it is so. Concept of inhomogeneous classes within the OODNs introduces the difference between these notions, according to which a type defines a set of homogeneous objects, while a class can define two and more similar and (or) different types. It is possible, because inhomogeneous classes of objects have specific structure formed by cores and projections. Cores define the common parts of the structure and behavior for the set of types, while projections define unique parts for each type.

Depending on similarity of types, inhomogeneous classes can have different number of cores and (or) projections, however the simplest form of inhomogeneous class of objects is a *single-core inhomogeneous class (SCIC)*, which was introduced in [20], then generalized in [21]. The structure of SCIC is formed by single core and set of projections, therefore such classes define heterogeneous collections of objects and show the difference between notion of the class and the type within OODNs. In addition, SCICs allow definition of sets of types, which have and (or) do not have an intersection.

4.3   Multi-Core Inhomogeneous Classes

SCICs are useful kind of inhomogeneous classes of objects, however different pairs of types can have different intersections, therefore in these cases various pairs of projections can have intersections, in particular inequivalent ones. It means that using of SCICs in some cases can cause redundant representation of types. To avoid this problem, the notion of *core of level m* of inhomogeneous class of objects was introduced in [21].

Cores of level m allow definition of common subtypes for different types, in such a way avoiding representation redundancy. The possible number of cores of level m within inhomogeneous class, which defines n types of objects, equals to k, where $0 \leq k \leq C_n^m$. Using concept of core of level m, notion of SCIC was generalized to *multi-core inhomogeneous class of objects (MCIC)* in [21]. MCICs define heterogeneous collections of objects of particular types and eliminate redundancy of their representation, which can occurs as the result of using SCICs.

Comparing concepts of classes and types within OODNs, it is possible to conclude that concept of type is equivalent to concept of homogeneous class, while inhomogeneous classes are more general, because they simultaneously define more than one type of objects.

5   Development of Union Algorithms

In contrast to other set-theoretic operation, union operation allows effective integration of new knowledge into the knowledge base, avoiding redundancy of their representation. In addition, if inhomogeneous classes of objects obtained via union operation have at least one core, it means that new knowledge are somehow connected with previously acquired ones. A number of created cores for such classes determines the level of connection between new and previously obtained knowledge, which can be used to infer about thematic relevance between these knowledge. Moreover, it can be used to determine the level of membership of knowledge to particular theme, category or domain. Therefore adaptation of union operation for homogeneous and inhomogeneous classes of objects and development of corresponding algorithms for its implementation are topical issues.

The basis for all set-theoretic operations is checking of equivalence between element of sets, which helps to distinguish elements from each other. Therefore, equivalence of properties (quantitative and qualitative) and methods of classes, within OODNs, were defined in [23], after that corresponding algorithms were proposed in [24].

5.1   Union Exploiter of Classes

The concept of set-theoretical union was adopted within the OODNs as the universal union exploiter of classes, which was proposed in [20], then generalized in [23].

Definition 1. *Union $T_1 \cup \cdots \cup T_n$ of classes of objects $T_1, \ldots, T_n$, $n \geq 2$, which define $l_1 \geq 1, \ldots, l_n \geq 1$ types of objects correspondingly, is a class $T_{1\ldots m}$, which defines types of objects $t_1, \ldots, t_m$, such that $\forall t_{w_1}, t_{w_2} \mid w_1 \neq w_2$, and $Eq(t_{w_1}, t_{w_2}) = 0$, where $w_1, w_2 = \overline{1, m}$, $1 \leq m \leq l_1 + \cdots + l_n$, and satisfy the following condition $\left(\forall t_i^k, \exists! t_j^{1\ldots m} \right) \wedge \left(\forall t_j^{1\ldots m}, \exists t_i^k \right) \mid Eq\left(t_i^k, t_j^{1\ldots m} \right) = 1$, where t_i^k is a i-th type of class T_k, where $i = \overline{1, l_k}$, $k = \overline{1, n}$, and $t_j^{1\ldots m}$ is a j-th type of class $T_{1\ldots m}$, $j = \overline{1, m}$.*

This exploiter gives an opportunity to compute the union of n classes, via creating new class of objects $T = T_1 \cup \cdots \cup T_n$, which can be homogeneous or heterogeneous, depending on equivalence and level of heterogeneity of classes $T_1, \ldots, T_n$.

Since classes within the OODNs are divided on homogeneous and inhomogeneous (heterogeneous), which have different structures, it requires to consider three possible cases of classes union:

1. homogeneous class $\cup$ homogeneous class;
2. homogeneous class $\cup$ inhomogeneous class;
3. inhomogeneous class $\cup$ inhomogeneous class.

Correspondent algorithm for the first case was proposed in [22]. It requires two homogeneous classes of objects as the input data, and returns inhomogeneous class of objects, which can be single-core or zero-core inhomogeneous[1] one, depending on existence of intersections among classes. Let us develop the appropriate algorithms for the second ans third cases.

5.2 Union of Homogeneous and Inhomogeneous Classes

According to idea of the universal union exploiter of classes, computation of union $T_1 \cup T_{t_1,...,t_n}$, where T_1 is a homogeneous class of objects and $T_{t_1,...,t_n}$ is a multi-core inhomogeneous class of objects, requires to overview their structures and to check the existence of equivalent properties and methods. In addition, construction of such union requires to create new cores and projections dynamically as parts of resulting multi-core inhomogeneous class of objects. Equivalent properties and (or) methods should form new cores of the class $T_{t_1,...,t_m}$, while inequivalent ones should form its new projections. These ideas were implemented within the corresponding union algorithm Algorithm 1.

As we can see, Algorithm 1 uses homogeneous class T_1 and multi-core inhomogeneous class T_2 as the input data and returns new multi-core inhomogeneous class T, which is a result of corresponding union $T_1 \cup T_2$. Polymorphic function $Eq()$ returns 1 if properties $p_1(T_1)$, $p_2(T_2)$ or methods $f_1(T_1)$, $f_2(T_2)$ are equivalent, and 0 in opposite case. Function $get\_level()$ returns level of selected core or projection[2]. Function $get\_max\_id\_of\_core\_level\_m(T, l)$ returns maximum id of core of level l in the class T. Function $get\_max\_pr\_id(T)$ returns maximum projection index among projections within the class T if they exist, and 0 in opposite case.

5.3 Union of Homogeneous Classes

Similarly to previous algorithm, the implementation of union $T_{t_1,...,t_n} \cup T_{t_1,...,t_m}$ of two multi-core inhomogeneous classes $T_{t_1,...,t_n}$ and $T_{t_1,...,t_m}$ also requires to overview their structures and to check the existence of equivalent properties and methods. Moreover, construction of such union also requires dynamically to create new cores and projections of resulting multi-core inhomogeneous class $T_{t_1,...,t_k} = T_{t_1,...,t_n} \cup T_{t_1,...,t_m}$. These ideas were implemented within the corresponding union algorithm Algorithm 2 as the generalization of Algorithm 1.

As we can see, Algorithm 2 uses two multi-core inhomogeneous class T_1 and T_2 as the input data and returns new multi-core inhomogeneous class T, which is a result of corresponding union $T_1 \cup T_2$. All functions which are used in the algorithm have the same meaning as in Algorithm 1.

5.4 Complexity Analysis

Analyzing pseudocodes of proposed algorithms, we can see that they perform:

---

[1] When there is no intersection among classes, their union contains only projections of types.

[2] Since any projection contains only unique properties and (or) methods of particular type, then a projection level is always equals to 1.

Algorithm 1. Union of homogeneous and inhomogeneous classes of objects.

Require: T_1 is a HC, T_2 is a MCIC

Ensure: $T = T_1 \cup T_2$

1: $T := \{\}$;
2: $T_2^c := copy(T_2)$;
3: **for all** $p_1 \in P(T_1)$ **do**
4:    **for all** $p_2 \in P\left(Core_j^i(T_2)\right)$ **or** $P(pr_k(T_2))$ **do**
5:       $eq\_element := Eq(p_1, p_2)$;
6:       **if** $eq\_element = 1$ **then**
7:         $l := get\_level\left(Core_j^i \text{ or } pr_k\right) + 1$;
8:         $max\_cid\_T_1 := get\_max\_id\_of\_core\_level\_m(T_1, l)$;
9:         $max\_cid\_T_2 := get\_max\_id\_of\_core\_level\_m(T_2, l)$;
10:        $cid := max(max\_cid\_T_1, max\_cid\_T_2)$;
11:       **if** $Core_{cid}^l \notin T$ **then**
12:         $Core_{cid}^l := \{\}$;
13:         $P := \{\}$;
14:         $Core_{cid}^l.append(P)$;
15:         $T.append\left(Core_{cid}^l\right)$;
16:       $P\left(Core_{cid}^l(T)\right).append(p_1)$;
17:       $\left(P\left(Core_j^i(T_2^c)\right) \text{ or } P(pr_k(T_2^c))\right).remove(p_2)$;
18:       **if** $P\left(Core_j^i(T_2^c)\right) \text{ or } P(pr_k(T_2^c)) = \{\}$ **then**
19:         $T_2^c.remove\left(P\left(Core_j^i(T_2^c)\right) \text{ or } P(pr_k(T_2^c))\right)$;
20:       **if** $\left(Core_j^i(T_2^c) \text{ or } pr_k(T_2^c)\right) = \{\}$ **then**
21:         $T_2^c.remove\left(Core_j^i(T_2^c) \text{ or } pr_k(T_2^c)\right)$;
22:       **break**;
23:    **if** $eq\_element = 0$ **then**
24:       $pid := get\_max\_pr\_id(T_2) + 1$;
25:       **if** $pr_{pid} \notin T$ **then**
26:         $pr_{pid} := \{\}$;
27:         $P := \{\}$;
28:         $pr_{pid}.append(P)$;
29:         $T.append(pr_{pid})$;
30:       $P(pr_{pid}(T)).append(p_1)$;

   ... {The same procedure over methods of classes}

31: **for all** $Core_j^i(T_2^c) \in T_2^c$ **or** $pr_k(T_2^c) \in T_2^c$ **do**
32:    $T.append\left(Core_j^i(T_2^c) \text{ or } pr_k(T_2^c)\right)$;
33: $delete(T_2^c)$;
34: **return** T;

- $D(T_1) \times D(T_2) = n \times m$ checks of properties equivalence,
- $D(T_2) = q_{cp}$ operations of properties copying,
- $D(T_2) = q_{rp}$ operations of properties removing,
- $func(T_1) \times func(T_2) = k \times w$ checks of methods equivalence,
- $func(T_2) = q_{cf}$ operations of methods copying,
- $func(T_2) = q_{rf}$ operations of methods removing,

Algorithm 2. Union of inhomogeneous classes of objects.

Require: T_1, T_2 are MCICs
Ensure: $T = T_1 \cup T_2$
1: $T := \{\}$;
2: $T_2^c := copy(T_2)$;
3: **for all** $Core_i^n(T_1) \in T_1$ **or** $pr_q(T_1) \in T_1$ **do**
4:     **for all** $p_1 \in P\left(Core_i^n(T_1)\right)$ **or** $P(pr_q(T_1))$ **do**
5:         **for all** $Core_j^m(T_2) \in T_2$ **or** $pr_w(T_2) \in T_2$ **do**
6:             **for all** $p_2 \in P\left(Core_j^m(T_2)\right)$ **or** $P(pr_w(T_2))$ **do**
7:                 $eq\_element := Eq(p_1, p_2)$;
8:                 **if** $eq\_element = 1$ **then**
9:                     $l := get\_level\left(Core_i^n \text{ or } pr_q\right) + get\_level\left(Core_j^m \text{ or } pr_w\right)$;
10:                     $cid := get\_max\_id\_of\_core\_level\_m(T, l)$;
11:                     **if** $Core_{cid}^l \notin T$ **then**
12:                         $Core_{cid}^l := \{\}$;
13:                         $P := \{\}$;
14:                         $Core_{cid}^l.append(P)$;
15:                         $T.append\left(Core_{cid}^l\right)$;
16:                     $P\left(Core_{cid}^l(T)\right).append(p_1)$;
17:                     $\left(P\left(Core_j^m(T_2^c)\right) \text{ or } P(pr_w(T_2^c))\right).remove(p_2)$;
18:                     **if** $P\left(Core_j^m(T_2^c)\right)$ **or** $P\left(pr_w(T_2^c)\right) = \{\}$ **then**
19:                       $T_2^c.remove\left(P\left(Core_j^m(T_2^c)\right) \text{ or } P\left(pr_w(T_2^c)\right)\right)$;
20:                     **if** $\left(Core_j^m(T_2^c) \text{ or } pr_w(T_2^c)\right) = \{\}$ **then**
21:                       $T_2^c.remove\left(Core_j^m(T_2^c) \text{ or } pr_w(T_2^c)\right)$;
22:                     **break**;
23:             **if** $eq\_element = 1$ **then**
24:                 **break**;
25:         **if** $eq\_element = 0$ **then**
26:             **if** $is\_core(Core_i^n(T_1) \in T_1 \text{ or } pr_q(T_1) \in T_1) = 0$ **then**
27:                 **if** $pr_k(T_1) \notin T$ **then**
28:                     $T.append\left(pr_k(T_1)\right)$;
29:                 $P(pr_k(T)).append(p_1)$;
30:         **else**
31:             $l := get\_level(Core_i^n(T_1) \in T_1 \text{ or } pr_q(T_1) \in T_1)$;
32:             $cid := get\_max\_id\_of\_core\_level\_m(T, l)$;
33:             **if** $Core_{cid}^l \notin T$ **then**
34:                 $Core_{cid}^l := \{\}$;
35:                 $P := \{\}$;
36:                 $Core_{cid}^l.append(P)$;
37:                 $T.append\left(Core_{cid}^l\right)$;
38:             $P\left(Core_{cid}^l(T)\right).append(p_1)$;
    ... {The same procedure over methods of classes}

where $D(T)$ is a number of properties of the class T and $funct(T)$ is a number of its methods, therefore their time complexity is equal to

$$O(n \times m + q_{cp} + q_{rp}) + O(k \times w + q_{cf} + q_{rf}) \approx O(n^2 + k^2 + q_c + q_r).$$

39: **for all** $Core_j^i(T_2^c) \in T_2^c$ **or** $pr_k(T_2^c) \in T_2^c$ **do**
40:   **if** $is\_core(Core_j^i(T_2^c)$ **or** $pr_k(T_2^c)) = 1$ **then**
41:     $l := get\_level(Core_j^i(T_2^c)$ **or** $pr_k(T_2^c))$;
42:     $cid := get\_max\_id\_of\_core\_level\_m(T, l)$;
43:     $T.append\left(Core_{cid}^l(T_2^c)\right)$;
44:   **else**
45:     $pid := D(T_1) + get_pid(Core_j^i(T_2^c)$ **or** $pr_k(T_2^c))$;
46:     $T.append\left(pr_{pid}^l(T_2^c)\right)$;
47: $delete(T_2^c)$;
48: **return** T;

In addition, algorithms use:

- t memory for storing class T,
- t_2 memory for storing copy of the class T_2,

therefore their space complexity is equal to $O(t + t_2)$.

6 Conclusions

For solving such tasks as dynamic knowledge analysis and integration, KBSs should be able to analyze new obtained knowledge, in particular to compare them dynamically with previously acquired or extracted ones, and to generate required knowledge structures for representation of specific knowledge, which are not defined within the system previously. Such opportunities for KBSs can be implemented via adaptation of set-theoretic operations over knowledge representation structures and development of correspondent algorithms for their practical realizations.

Union operation provides certain mechanisms for determination of connection between old and new knowledge; conclusion about their thematic relevance; evaluation of their connection with particular theme, category or domain; evaluation of novelty level of acquired or extracted knowledge. Therefore, corresponding algorithms, which compute union of homogeneous and inhomogeneous and union of two homogeneous classes of objects, were developed and described in the paper. Both algorithms implement concept of universal union exploiter of classes, introduced in [23], and have quadratic polynomial time complexity and linear space complexity. Such implementation gives following opportunities:

- *to generate new knowledge representation structures, which are not defined within the system* – by computing union of classes, algorithms dynamically generate new classes of objects, which are not previously defined within the system, still they can be generated when required;
- *to determine connection between old and new knowledge* – if inhomogeneous class of objects, which is a result of classes union, has cores, then new obtained knowledge are connected in some context to previously acquired ones;
- *to conclude their thematic relevance* – if inhomogeneous class of objects, which is the result of classes union, has cores which are common for new obtained knowledge and previously acquired, then they are thematically relevant;

- *to evaluate the novelty level of acquired or extracted knowledge* – existence of cores within the inhomogeneous class of objects, which is a result of classes union, determines the novelty level of obtained knowledge;
- *to integrate arbitrary knowledge into the knowledge base without redundancy of their representation* – according to concept of universal union exploiter of classes, algorithms decompose all new classes on particular types and integrate them within structures of new classes in the proper way.

Development of these algorithms is one more step to implement an ability of KBSs to react on challenges of the working environment dynamically. Proposed algorithms, as well as concept of inhomogeneous classes of objects, can be adapted for particular object-oriented programming language or knowledge representation model and then integrated into it. However, despite all benefits, proposed algorithms require further analysis and optimization.

References

1. Al-Asady, R.: Inheritance Theory: An Artificial Intelligence Approach. Ablex Publishing Corporation, Norwood (1995)
2. Ashrafi, N., Ashrafi, H.: Object Oriented Systems Analysis and Design, 1st edn. Pearson Education Limited, Harlow (2014)
3. Booch, G., et al.: Object-Oriented Analysis and Design with Applications, 3rd edn. Wesley, Boston (2007)
4. Brachman, R.J., Levesque, H.J.: Knowledge Representation and Reasoning. Morgan Kaufmann Publishers, San Francisco (2004)
5. Bruce, K.B.: Foundations of Object-Oriented Languages: Types and Semantics. The MIT Press, Cambridge (2002)
6. Craig, I.D.: Object-Oriented Programming Languages: Interpretation. UTCS. Springer, London (2007)
7. Igarashi, A., Nagira, H.: Union Types for Object-Oriented Programming. In: Proceedings of ACM Symposium on Applied Computing, Dijon, France, pp. 1435–1441, April 2006
8. Igarashi, A., Nagira, H.: Union types for object-oriented programming. J. Object Technol. **6**(2), 47–68 (2007)
9. Kamin, S.: Routine run-time code generation. ACM SIGPLAN Not. **38**(12), 208–220 (2003)
10. Keppel, D., Eggers, S.J., Henry, R.R.: A case for runtime code generation. Technical report 91-11-04, University of Washington, Department of Computer Science and Engineering, January 1991
11. Leone, M., Lee, P.: Lightweight run-time code generation. In: Proceedings of ACM SIGPLAN Workshop on Partial Evaluation and Semantics-Based Program Manipulation, Orlando, FL, USA, pp. 97–106 (June 1994)
12. Meyer, B.: Object-Oriented Software Construction, 2nd edn. Prentice Hall, Santa Barbara (1997)
13. Mezini, M.: Variational Object-Oriented Programming Beyond Classes and Inheritance. SECS, vol. 470. Springer, Boston (1998)
14. Murray, K.S.: Learning as knowledge integration. Ph.D. thesis, Faculty of the Graduate School, University of Texas at Austin, Austin, Texas, USA (May 1995)

15. Murray, K.S.: KI: a tool for knowledge integration. In: Proceedings of the 13th National Conference on Artificial Intelligence, AAAI 1996, Portland, Oregon, USA, pp. 835–842, August 1996

16. Murray, K.S., Porter, B.W.: Controlling search for the consequences of new information during knowledge integration. In: Proceedings of the 6th International Workshop on Machine Learning, New York, USA, pp. 290–295, June 1989

17. Murray, K.S., Porter, B.W.: Developing a tool for knowledge integration: initial results. Int. J. Man Mach. Stud. **33**(4), 373–383 (1990)

18. Negnevitsky, M.: Artificial Intelligence: A Guide to Intelligent Systems, 2nd edn. Wesley, Harlow (2004)

19. Sheard, T.: Accomplishments and research challenges in meta-programming. In: Taha, W. (ed.) SAIG 2001. LNCS, vol. 2196, pp. 2–44. Springer, Heidelberg (2001). https://doi.org/10.1007/3-540-44806-3_2

20. Terletskyi, D.O.: Exploiters-based knowledge extraction in object-oriented knowledge representation. In: Suraj, Z., Czaja, L. (eds.) Proceedins of the 24th International Workshop, Concurrency, Specification & Programming, CS&P 2015, vol. 2, pp. 211–221. Rzeszow University, Rzeszow, September 2015

21. Terletskyi, D.: Object-oriented knowledge representation and data storage using inhomogeneous classes. In: Damaševičius, R., Mikašytė, V. (eds.) ICIST 2017. CCIS, vol. 756, pp. 48–61. Springer, Cham (2017). https://doi.org/10.1007/978-3-319-67642-5_5

22. Terletskyi, D.O.: Algorithms for runtime generation of homogeneous classes of objects. In: Proceedings of the International Conference on Cyber Security and Computer Science, ICONCS 2018, Safranbolu, Turkey, pp. 160–164, October 2018

23. Terletskyi, D.O.: Object-oriented dynamic model of knowledge representation within intelligent software systems. Ph.D. thesis, Faculty of Computer Science and Cybernetics, Taras Shevchenko National University of Kyiv, Kyiv, Ukraine, April 2018

24. Terletskyi, D.O.: Run-time class generation: algorithms for intersection of homogeneous and inhomogeneous classes. In: Proceedings of the International Workshop on Information Modeling, Data and Knowledge Engineering, IWIMDKE 2019, Lviv, Ukraine, September 2019. This Workshop is a Part of XIV International Scientific and Technical Conference Computer Science and Information Technologies. http://csit.lp.edu.ua/

25. Terletskyi, D.O., Provotar, O.I.: Mathematical foundations for designing and development of intelligent systems of information analysis. Sci. J. Probl. in Program. **16**(2–3), 233–241 (2014)

26. Terletskyi, D.O., Provotar, O.I.: Object-oriented dynamic networks. In: Setlak, G., Markov, K. (eds.) Computational Models for Business and Engineering Domains, IBS IS&C, vol. 30, 1 edn., pp. 123–136. ITHEA (2014)

27. Touretzky, D.S.: The Mathematics of Inheritance Systems. Morgan Kaufmann Publishers, Los Altos (1986)

28. Weisfeld, M.: The Object-Oriented Thought Process. Developer's Library, 4th edn. Wesley, Boston (2013)

Modelling Patterns for Business Processes

Prima Gustiené[✉] and Remigijus Gustas

Karlstad Business School, Karlstad University, Karlstad, Sweden
{prima.gustiene, remigijus.gustas}@kau.se

Abstract. Analysis patterns are the groups of elements that represent a common construction in business modelling. Patterns are established with the aim to define and visualize the fundamental requirements that arise during business process modelling. There are a lot of patterns that describe the behaviour of business processes. Patterns enable stakeholders to communicate more effectively, with greater conciseness and less ambiguity. The problem with the existing business process patterns is that these patterns leave aside the static aspects of business processes. It is not enough to provide patterns just for processes or actions, it is necessary to show how data is integrated into business processes. This integration is important for flexible business processes, where stakeholders have more freedom to handle the sequence of actions in order to accomplish a given goal. The lack of an integrated modelling approach creates problems in rethinking and changing business processes. It is necessary to have a modelling approach which enables to manage necessary changes in business processes and data. The patterns for business processes should support the integration of static (data) and dynamic aspects (interaction and state changes of data) of the system as well to provide possibilities to model alternative actions in business processes. The paper presents Semantically Integrated Conceptual Modelling method (SICM) and how the method is applied for two modelling patterns that enables integration of both static and dynamic aspects of the system.

Keywords: Business process modelling · Modelling patterns ·
Conceptual Modelling · Modelling methods ·
Semantically Integrated Conceptual Modelling (SICM) method

1 Introduction

Business process modelling is the analytical illustration of an organization's business process. Modelling processes are critical for effective business process management [20]. Analysis patterns are groups of concepts that represent common constructions in business modelling [9]. These patterns are similar to workflow patterns, which were established with the aim to define business process modelling on a recurring basis [22]. Modelling patterns for system analysis and design are important for two main reasons. Firstly, they can be used for demonstrating the interplay of fundamental constructs that are used in system analysis and design process [12]. Secondly, patterns are important for the evaluation of the expressive power of semantic modelling languages [21].

© Springer Nature Switzerland AG 2019
R. Damaševičius and G. Vasiljevienė (Eds.): ICIST 2019, CCIS 1078, pp. 161–172, 2019.
https://doi.org/10.1007/978-3-030-30275-7_13

Patterns are established with the aim to define and visualize the fundamental requirements that arise during business process modelling. Patterns enable stakeholders to communicate more effectively, with greater conciseness and less ambiguity. Most patterns are created to define just the behaviour of business processes. Workflow patterns are usually defined by using Business Process Modelling Notation (BPMN) [2] for business process diagram and Unified Modelling Language (UML) activity diagram from Object management Group (OMG) [23]. Both notations are able to visualize process behaviour, but do not explicitly show how data changes, when some actions take place [15]. A concept represent data that is an input and an output to and from a process. Gunasekaran and Kobu [17] provided the literature review on different Business Process Modelling techniques. All these techniques define different aspects of the system using different types of diagrams therefor to reach semantic integration among different diagrams is difficult. The lack of the conceptual modelling method that provides the way to integrate static and dynamic aspects of business process specification is one of the reasons for BPR project failures [16].

The lack of flexibility in workflow modelling is one of the problems in business process modelling. According to Carvalho [3] a flexible process is not static and can have several different executions, which can be influenced by different situations. It is also very important that business modelling provides possibilities to model changes or alternative actions. According to van der Aalst [1], there are several problems concerning the lack of flexibility in workflow modelling. Firstly, the workflow approach is rigid and inflexible, because it focuses on what *should* be modelled instead of what *can* be done. Another problem is that workflow systems are focused on control flow and data aspect, which represents the context, does not receive enough importance. There is often semantic discontinuity, incompleteness and overlapping in system specifications, because static and dynamic constructs do not fit perfectly. In this case to manage verification of semantic integrity between business processes and business data becomes very difficult [16]. This leads to integrity problems, which imply semantic inconsistency and incompleteness of conceptual representations on various levels of abstraction. Integrated models should contribute to the process of validation and verification [4]. If just dynamic aspects are taken into consideration, then the quantity of patterns increases [15].

This paper is the continuation of the research on modelling patterns. The purpose of this paper is to introduce two new analysis patterns applying SICM method. The paper is organized as follows. Section 1 is introduction part. Section 2 presents the basic pattern of transaction. Section 3 presents SICM method the basic patterns of Transaction. Section 4 presents two new modelling patterns. The concluding Sect. 5 outlines the results of the paper.

2 The Basic Pattern of Transaction

The basic pattern of transaction [6] can be seen as a basic pattern of service interaction. A simple interaction loop between two actors can be vied as the basic construct of any communication process [5]. The transaction was chosen, because any transaction illustrates how enterprise actors performs actions; *production and coordination acts* [6].

Coordination acts are necessary to make commitment regarding the corresponding production act, which is supposed to bring value flow to service requester. *Production acts* are normally performed by service provider and are always associated with value flows. Both acts are important for the distinctions of responsibilities and fulfilments of the tasks that different actors are involved. It is critically important to motivate which actors should be involved in some specific interaction and why. Every intention of a coordination act that is performed by one actor should be motivated by goals stated at the business-oriented level. Goals dictate and motivate which enterprise actors interact for the purpose to achieve the goals. It is important to define the structure of every goal (data and processes) in order to know which actors have responsibility to perform some actions. Sometimes it is necessary to introduce some alternative actions, or actions which require some more interactions. It could be some unexpected intensions from different actors involved. It is necessary to have a method and a model that enables visualization of different unexpected actions. According to Dietz [6] the four cancelation patterns are necessary to allow for all possible rollback requirements.

SICM method is based on the ontological perspective of communication process. We see every communication or interaction process as a service. Service is a dynamic action of doing something, providing value, to somebody. Every business process can be analysed as a service, because every business process involves actors, humans, organisational or technical components, which communicated to provide value to another actor. Every interaction or communication between service requester and service provider must be motivated by the resulting value flow. SICM method is used to define the new facts, which results from the actions of the basic transaction pattern [6]. We will show how creation, termination or reclassification constructs of SICM method [15] can be used to specify the new facts that result after every action. Figure 1 presents the basic pattern of a transaction.

The basic element of interaction is a closed loop between service requester and service performer. It is called a service interaction loop [15]. Service provider promises to satisfy request of a service requester. The loop consists of four stages. *First,* the service requester makes a request to service performer. *Second,* they negotiate on the service requester conditions, which will result in a promise made by the service performer. The promise may imply the contract to fulfil those conditions. *Third,* the service performer does the work. *Forth,* the service requester accepts what has been promised. It signifies that one half of contract has been fulfilled, which means completion of a service interaction loop.

Every communication action is supposed to produce nought worthy facts, in form of data. New results from four basic actions, presented in Fig. 1, can be represented by such classes of objects *as Request, Promise, Stated Result and Accepted Result.* This can be represented by various classes of objects. For instance, when the *Request* action between service requester and service provider is activated and the action stores all the necessary details, it means that the object of **Request** is created. Such concepts are representing data at rest and the graph they are represented by rectangles. The example can be taken from the hotel reservation request, when someone requested the room. If a room is supposed to be delivered, then *Promise* action creates a **Promise** object. In the next service interaction loop, the object of **Promise** is reclassified to the object **Stated Result**. This reclassification is performed by the *State* action. This result may be finally

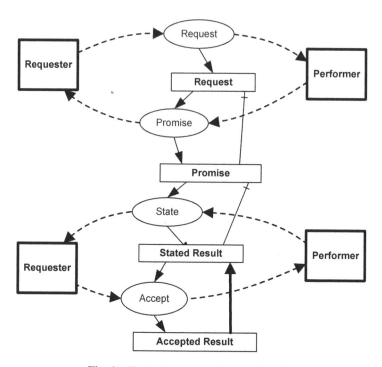

Fig. 1. The basic pattern of transaction [6]

accepted by the service requester by the *Accept* action. It produces the **Accepted Result.** This fact is linked by the inheritance arrow to the concept of **Stated Result**, which is produced by service performer. It signifies that the first half of the service exchange was performed.

3   SICM Method

In order to create a new artefact, it is necessary that this artefact not just can help people to fulfil their needs, overcome their problems and grasp new opportunities [19], but also provide the process how to use this new artefact. Design science is one of the paradigms in Information Systems (IS) research. This paradigm seeks to create new and innovative artefacts, which help the analysis, design, and implementation as well as use of IS more effectively and efficiently [18]. This is very important when creating a new artefact for IS development. There are seven guidelines that characterize the principles of design science [18] according to which it is important to evaluate a new artefact and show how a new artefact contribute to. SICM method [15, 16] contributes with prescriptive knowledge [19], which consists of prescriptive model and method that help solving practical problems. Prescriptive models can be seen as blueprints for developing artefacts. The modelling methods should provide guidelines and steps that can help to work in systematic and integrated way.

SICM method challenges the existing integration problems among interactive, behavioural and structural aspects [14] of IS. To capture the holistic structure of a system, it is necessary to understand how various components are related. Various aspects of a system should be integrated in order to ensure consistency and completeness of the overall system specifications [25]. The problems arise when different models are used to define various aspects of a system. The integration is crucial for successful reasoning, motivation and solving the problems that occur during system analysis and design [12]. Integration depends critically on a clear definition of the meta-model and modelling language [8]. SICM method provides the model, modelling language and modelling process that enables integration of static and dynamic aspects of the system. As all traditional modelling approaches lack such possibility.

The ontological foundation of the SICM model or construct is based on the philosophy of the concept of service. The ontological foundation of service has no direct relation to technological solutions. The objective of the service is to provide the description of *what* is happening in a model without any bias for implementation issues [12]. It is not 'a service' which is delivered and has value to the service requester, but the value of the content [7]. The content cannot be achieved without the dynamic process, without an interaction between some actors, the result of which creates a value to the actors that have some specific goal [10]. The interaction process that is incorporated in the concept of service has possibility to integrate two perspectives of a process; intersubjective and objective perspectives that are coming from communication understating. Communication action is constructed from intersubjective and objective perspectives [13]. Philosophical and ontological foundations of a service as a communication or interaction, provides us with an understanding how to make a construct that enables integration of static and dynamic aspects of the system.

The behavioural and structural dimensions of interactions are analysed in terms of creation, termination and reclassification actions. The internal changes of objects are expressed by using transition links between various classes of objects. The reclassification of object is defined as termination event in one class and creation of object in another class. Unbroken transition arrows represent the control flow of creation and termination events. A creation event is denoted by the outgoing transition arrow to a class. A termination event is represented by the transition dependency directed from a class. Figure 2 presents the main construct of SICM method. SICM construct provides possibility to integrate data and processes using one diagram.

The main elements of the construct are the following; *actors, interaction dependencies, flows and actions* [15]. Interaction dependencies (┅▶) represent moving flows such as information, decision, or resource. Actors involved in interaction loop may view all moving flows either as coordination or value flows such as materials or financial resources. When action take place it makes some changes to data (objects). The action can create a new object, delete or reclassify the object. Objects have attributes. Actors, which are active objects [24] can be linked to other actors using different dependencies. Available actions can be viewed as responsibilities, rights, obligations or claims. Visualisation of the business process 'Apply for a job' is presented in Fig. 3. From the basic pattern of transaction perspective (see Fig. 1) this example visualize just the half of the basic pattern of transaction. It represents just actions *Request* and *Promise* as well as objects *Request* and *Promise,* which are created

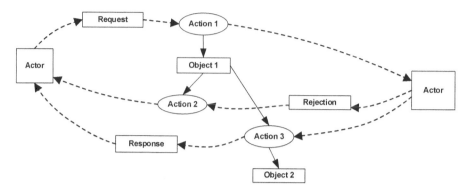

Fig. 2. The main SICM construct

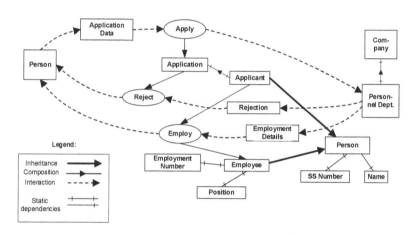

Fig. 3. Visualization of business process

when actions take place. The alternative actions can be visualized using SICM construct as well (see Action 2 in Fig. 2).

The example presents the business process how a person sends job application to the company. There are two actors involved: a **Person** and a **Company**. A dependency link between actors, Company and Personal Department, is composition. It is a strong type of aggregation. In SICM method we use just composition dependency. When a **Person** sends application data to a **Company,** *Apply* action creates an **Application** object that has one **Applicant** related to the **Application**. Inheritance dependency between an **Applicant** and a **Person** indicates that an **Applicant** is a **Person** that has two attributes name and social security number. A **Company** has an obligation to replay. A **Company** has two alternatives, either to employ a person or reject application. If an application will be rejected, rejection message will be sent to a person. If a person will be employed, an **Applicant** will be reclassified from an **Applicant** to an **Employee**. When the action *Employ* is activated, it removes the object **Applicant** and creates a new object of **Employee**, who is also a **Person** (please follow the inheritance link) who has the same attributes name and social security number as well as he gets one more attribute and it is Employment, that defines that he became an **Employee.** Inheritance dependency provides us possibility to avoid redundant data, when the same data is attached to the different objects.

4 Two Modelling Patterns

In previous research, the construct of SICM model was applied to represent such patterns as *sequence, synchronization, iteration, selection and search patterns* [11, 12] alternative pattern, with possibilities to define *underlying, overlying, overriding* and *enclosing* interaction loops [15]. Sequences, underlying, enclosing, overriding and overlying interaction loops between actors provides the foundation for composition of different scenarios. In this paper we present two more patterns. The first pattern is the extended universal pattern for transaction. The diagram includes the standard transaction pattern and four cancelation patterns. Every cancellation action can be performed if the corresponding facts exists. For example, a requester may withdraw his own request, a provider may withdraw his promise, a provider may cancel his own stated result or a requester may cancel his own acceptance. These four cancellation patterns may lead to partial or complete rollback of a transaction. These four cancellation patterns, should be integrated into a universal interaction pattern. A provider has also possibility to create a new *Offer* on a basis of created Request, which can be transformed into a counter request or it can be accepted by requester. All these possible outcomes are represented in the extended universal pattern, which is shown in Fig. 4.

The presented diagram includes the standard transaction pattern [6] and four cancellation patterns. It also includes **Offer** and **Counter Request** actions, which are taken from the conversation for action schema [26]. Every cancellation action can be performed if the corresponding fact exists. For instance, the **Withdraw Request** action can be triggered, if a request object was created by the Request action. Request cancellation event may occur when the customer finds for instance a better or cheaper room in another hotel. Request cancellation must be sent before a promise is created, because there will be no request when it is transformed to the promise. A **Withdraw Promise** action may take place if a Promise for some reason cannot be fulfilled by Performer. For instance, a Hotel Room was damaged as a consequence of some unexpected event. The requester may agree or disagree to accept the consequences of the **Withdraw Promise** action. Please note that **Withdraw Promise** action terminates the *Promise* object and preserves the *Request* object. So, the Requester will be forced to *Withdraw Request* or to cope with three possible alternatives of communication actions such as *Promise, Reject* or *Offer*. All these alternatives are clearly visible in our new universal interaction pattern in Fig. 4.

If we want to extend a not standard procedure with the negotiation cases, which are presented in Fig. 4 it can be done by including the offer by service provider and two responses from service requester such as *Accept Offer* or *Counter Request*. This is represented by pattern, which is shown in Fig. 5.

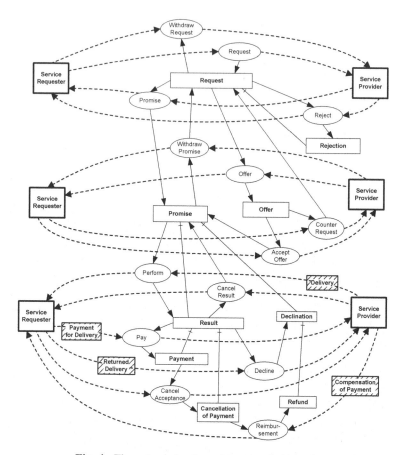

Fig. 4. The extended universal pattern of transaction

Interaction loops can be composed into more complex interaction loops. If these loops can be properly distinguished, they provide a natural mechanism for separation of concerns. Two dependent interaction loops can be interconnected by using the same created object. Each two loops can be in the sequence, overlaying, overriding, enclosing and underlying each other. When service interaction loops are composed in sequence, an object is created in the first loop, and then is consumed in the next interaction loop. Objects are inputs and outputs of the actions that take place in the loops. In some cases, requests and responses are delegated to more general or more specific actors, which are linked by inheritance or composition links. For instance, a Room Guest is a specialisation of a Customer and Hotel is composition of a Hotel Reservation System. If Customer requests to reserve a room, then the Hotel Reservation System creates a Reservation. Reservation consists of a number of reserved rooms. In the next interaction loop, the Hotel assigns each room to the corresponding room quest. Thus, each reserved room is removed and the assigned room is created. Service interaction loops can be decomposed into more specific underlying loops. Decomposition is typically performed by using a separate composition relation for

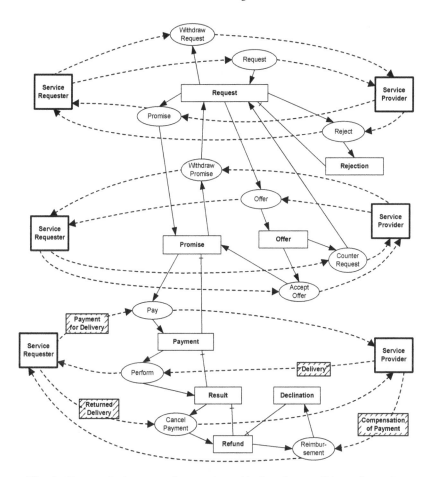

Fig. 5. Not standard pattern of transaction with changing conditions of promise

consumed and for created objects. It allows synchronization of an underlying interaction loop with the primary loop.

Organizational actor is a unit of functionality exposed to environment that is
conceptualized for representation of an enterprise subsystem. It depends on the individual actor role and his goals whether he considers some received information or
materials as value flows. So, value flow is relative notion. Ideally, any elementary
interaction must be motivated by the resulting value flow and vice versa. A value flow
typically requires the initiation of some coordinating interactions, which are necessary
for the provision of value flows. Service interactions take place between service
requester and service providers. A service provider can be also viewed as service
requester. He makes secondary requests, so that the network of performers comes into
play in fulfilling the primary request. The resulting interconnected loops between
requesters and providers caries out a business process. Interactions are composed into
webs of constituent loops until every role in the organization is accounted for. Secondary loops may arise in any place. The network of loops thus represents the network

of commitments in organization. Those processes may span several partnerships. A problem is that incomplete interaction flows may cause breakdowns or discontinuity in business process. It gives rise to customer complains that interfere with the purpose of work to satisfy requirements of service requester. Interaction loops can be broken in following cases:

(1) If a service requester makes an unclear request. It can be done in an unexpected way to the service provider.
(2) If a service provider does not decline a request clearly, leaving a service requester with a wrong feeling that something will happen. In that case a service provider may give no response and ignore the request.
(3) If a service provider delivers dubious result or may not deliver the result. A service requester may fail to receive a message about that.
(4) If a service provider fails to find out that a service requester is not satisfied.

Any of these breakdowns may leave service requester expecting some work that service provider will not deliver. Such breakdowns cannot be avoided. Many organizational problems are connected to persistently incomplete interaction loops that are caused by breakdowns. They are caused by processes that are missing entirely. Redesigning interaction loops is not just the problem of deployment of information technology in right places, but sometimes technology can be used to introduce required changes into design.

5   Conclusions

The purpose of the paper was to introduce two analysis patterns for business process modelling, which were created applying Semantically Integrated Conceptual Modelling (SICM) method. The essence of the method is based on providing a construct which enables integration of static and dynamic aspects of the system. Separation of static and dynamic aspects create two fundamental difficulties when presenting analysis patterns: (1) if just dynamic aspects are presented in the patterns, the number of patterns increases. (2) if static aspects are not taken into consideration, then the patters would be more complex. SICM construct is based on interaction loops. Interaction loops can be composed into sequences, they can enclose, overlay, underlie and override each other. The method has a sufficient expressive semantic power for modelling the patters for sequential, iterative, parallel and alternative behaviour. It was shown in this paper that applying the same construct it is possible to create two more patterns; one an extended universal pattern of transaction and another not standard pattern of transaction with changing conditions of promise. Having a modelling method and model that enables integration of static and dynamic aspects of the system, enrichers the research of analysis patterns. Analysis patters created using SICM method saves time for system analysis and design, as well as the method increases communication and learning process among stakeholders.

References

1. Van der Aalst, W.M., Weske, M., Grnbauer, D.: Case handling: a new paradigm for business process support. Data Knowl. Eng. **53**(2), 129–162 (2005)
2. BPMN. Business Process Modelling Notation (2019). http://www.bpmn.org
3. De Carvalho, R., Mili, H., Gonzalez-Huerta, J., Boubaker, A, Leshob, A.: Comparing ConDec to CMMN. Towards a Common Language for Flexible Processes (2016)
4. Chester, M., Athwall, A.: Basic Information Systems Analysis and Design. McGraw-Hill, London (2002)
5. Denning, P.J., Medina-Mora, R.: Completing the loops. Interfaces **25**(3), 42–57 (1995)
6. Dietz, J.: Enterprise Ontology: Theory and Methodology. Springer, Berlin (2006). https://doi.org/10.1007/3-540-33149-2
7. Ferrario, R., Guarino, N.: Towards an ontological foundation for services science. In: Domingue, J., Fensel, D., Traverso, P. (eds.) FIS 2008. LNCS, vol. 5468, pp. 152–169. Springer, Heidelberg (2009). https://doi.org/10.1007/978-3-642-00985-3_13
8. Finkelstein, C.: Enterprise integration using enterprise architecture. In: Linger, H. (ed.) Constructing the Infrastructure for the Knowledge Economy, pp. 43–81. Kluwer, New York (2004)
9. Fowler, M.: Analysis Patterns: Reusable Object Models. Addison-Wesley, Menlo Park (1997)
10. Gordijn, J., Yu, E., van der Raadt, B.: e-Service design Using i* and e3 value modeling. IEEE Softw. **23**(3), 26–33 (2006)
11. Gustas, R., Gustiene, P.: Service-Oriented Foundation and Analysis Patterns for Conceptual Modelling of Information Systems. Inf. Syst. Dev. Challenges Pract. Theory Educ. **1**, 249–265 (2009)
12. Gustiené, P.: Development of a new service-oriented modelling method for information systems analysis and design. Doctoral Thesis, Karlstad University Studies, Karlstad (2010)
13. Gustiené, P., Carlsson, S.: How models and methods for analysis and design of information systems can be improved to better support communication and learning. In: Pankowska, M. (ed.) Infonomics for Distributed Business and Decision-Making Environment: Creating Information system Ecology, pp. 44–63. IGI Global, New York (2010)
14. Gustas, R., Gustiené, P.: Conceptual modeling method for separation of concerns and integration of structure and behavior. Int. J. Inf. Syst. Model. Des. **3**(1), 48–77 (2012)
15. Gustas, R., Gustiené, P.: Semantically integrated conceptual modeling method and modeling patterns. In: Mehdi Khosrow-Pour, D.B.A (ed.) Systems and Software Development, Modeling, and Analysis: New Perspectives and Methodologies, pp. 1–33. IG Global, USA (2014)
16. Gustas, R., Gustiené, P.: Principles of semantically integrated conceptual modelling method. In: Shishkov, B. (ed.) BMSD 2016. LNBIP, vol. 275, pp. 1–26. Springer, Cham (2017). https://doi.org/10.1007/978-3-319-57222-2_1. ISBN 978-3-319-57221-5, ISBN 978-3-319-57222-2 (eBook)
17. Gunasekaran, A., Kobu, B.: Modelling and analysis of business process reengineering. Int. J. Prod. Res. **40**(11), 2521–2546 (2002)
18. Hevner, A.R., March, S.T., Park, J., Ram, S.: Design science in information systems research. MIS Q. **28**(1), 75–105 (2004)
19. Johannesson, Paul, Perjons, Erik: An Introduction to Design Science. Springer, Cham (2014). https://doi.org/10.1007/978-3-319-10632-8
20. Kissflow (kissflow.com). The Why and How of Business Process Modeling (2019). https://kissflow.com/bpm/business-process-modeling/

21. Rad, A.A., Benyoucef, M., Kuziemsky, C.E.: An evaluation framework for business process modelling languages in healthcare. J. Theoret. Appl. Electron. Commer. Res. **4**(2), 189–202 (2009)
22. Russell, N., Hofstede, A.H.M., Aalst, W.M.P., Mulyar, N.: Workflow control-flow patterns: a revised view (BPM Centre Report BPR-06-22) (2019). http://www.workflowpatterns.com/documentation/documents/BPM-06-22.pdf
23. OMG: Unified Modeling Language Superstructure, version 2.2 (2009). www.omg.org/spec/UML/2.2
24. Wagner, G.: The agent-object-relationship metamodel: towards unified view of state and behaviour. Inf. Syst. **28**(5), 475–504 (2003)
25. Whitten, J.L., Bentley, L.D.: System Analysis and Design Methods. McGraw Hill, London (1998)
26. Winograd, T., Flores, F.: Understanding Computers and Cognition: A New Foundation for Design. Ablex, Norwood (1986)

Design and Implementation of Rule Execution Mechanism for an eGuide Gamification Web Service

Artur Kulpa and Jakub Swacha$^{(\boxtimes)}$

Faculty of Economics and Management, University of Szczecin,
Szczecin, Poland
{artur.kulpa, jakub.swacha}@usz.edu.pl

Abstract. Gamification can be applied to multimedia visitor guidance systems (also known as eGuides) for the sake of raising engagement and improving experiences of their users. It involves the use of dedicated software for managing the game state and processing the game rules. This paper addresses the problems of an effective implementation of the latter element, proposing a rule execution mechanism dedicated for an eGuide gamification web service. It describes the architecture of the mechanism, its main algorithm, and the technology of implementation. The presented results of performance testing in a simulated environment show that the developed solution can effectively handle a volume of requests characteristic even for large tourist attractions.

Keywords: Gamification as a service · Gamification rule engine ·
Rule processing

1 Introduction

Gamification, which can be defined as "the use of game-design and game psychology in non-game settings to engage the target audience and motivate specific behaviors" [1], has a broad range of applications [2]. One of the areas which are highly suitable for the application of gamification is tourism [3], and a particularly convenient point of application for gamification in tourism are multimedia visitor guidance systems, also known as eGuides.

Practical implementation of gamification to eGuides requires a number of challenges to be solved. These may regard both the high-level aspects of implementation – such as the choice of gamification elements and patterns (see e.g. [4]) to be applied and their adaptation and combination, so that the desirable change in user experience and/or behavior is achieved – and the low-level ones, that is the technology necessary to implement the gamification in eGuides. The scientific reports on the implementation of gamification to eGuides tend to focus on the former kind of aspects (see e.g. [5, 6, 7]), while in our opinion, sharing the findings on the low-level, technological aspects of gamification implementation is also a matter of importance, as it can help in the development of better technological solutions and, as a result, may lead to more

© Springer Nature Switzerland AG 2019
R. Damaševičius and G. Vasiljevienė (Eds.): ICIST 2019, CCIS 1078, pp. 173–181, 2019.
https://doi.org/10.1007/978-3-030-30275-7_14

efficient gamification systems (in terms of required processing power and network resources).

In our prior work, we identified a number of components of gamification system in the technological perspective, including: event processing layer of the gamified system, gamification presentation layer of the gamified system, game state, game state maintenance subsystem, gamification management system, system of gamification rules and gamification rule processing system (note the separation of the rule specifications and the software that processes them) [8], each one introducing technological problems of its own. In this paper, we focus at the last of the above-mentioned components, and investigate the design and implementation of the gamification rule processing system developed as a part of a eGuide gamification web service [9] within a framework of an international project [10]. This is a direct continuation of our recent work, in which we proposed a scheme for description of events generated by eGuide users which conveys their key properties of relevance for gamification (such as context, actor, action, object, location and time) and a notation using this description for an effective specification of gamification rules depending only on the content of the generated stream of events [11]. Here, we extend this research by showing an effective means of processing such an event stream for the sake of application of relevant game rules.

2   Related Work

As noted in the introduction, while there is rich literature on applications of gamification, only few authors provide insight into how they implement rule execution mechanisms.

One of those providing such description is Herzig in his thesis on gamification as a service [12]. In his platform design, he proposes an event processing agent, defined as "a domain-independent component that is capable of rule and complex event processing based on the events received from the enterprise information systems" [12, p. 95], employing a complex procedure for processing the rules [12, p. 88–89].

In their thesis on designing enterprise gamification architectures, Stagliano and Stefanoni define a set of three components for handling rule processing, comprising:

- Gamification Adapter, collecting all the events generated by the gamified application and performing initial filtering of them,
- Event Detection module, performing the filtering and composition of the events through the use of monitored event rules defined by a gamification designer,
- Game Logic Analyzer, checking if the conditions of a particular set of rules defining particular gamification reactions are satisfied and, if it is the case, dispatching the event to the appropriate module able to handle it [13, pp. 25–26].

Another way of handling the gamification rule processing is to delegate it to an external rule processing engine, developed for purposes other than gamification, such as the Drools Business Rules Management System [14]. Such an approach has been implemented, e.g., in the gamification-based framework for acceptance requirements developed by Piras [15, p. 67].

The problem of rule processing engine development has obviously been studied also in contexts other than gamification. One such area are the task automation services, in which rules define data processing within workflows connecting various web applications and services. A detailed description of rule processing in such a system, featuring a central component called Semantic Rule Engine is provided by Barrios [16, pp. 38–40]. Note though its focus on interoperability, as the task automation rules pertain to data of various kind and coming from various systems – whereas the data dealt with by the rule engine described in this paper are much more strictly defined (gamification-related data generated by eGuide applications).

3   Rule Execution Mechanism

The investigated eGuide gamification web service [9] is accessed by eGuide applications via an API point call. The role of the eGuide applications is to register user actions and submit a request every time a potentially gamification-relevant event happens. The task of the rule execution mechanism is to analyze each submitted event whether all the conditions necessary for triggering any of the defined rules have been met. If so, the rule is processed having the event description as input and returning the rule result to the API client.

The critical issue was the decision on how to process event data for the sake of applying the defined gamification rules. One considered option was to process them in the background through an independent process, which, having finished, would send the results back to the eGuide application. With this approach, the user would not have to wait for the event and rule processing to continue using the application. The two main disadvantages of this solution were the complexity of the back-end it would require and expected problems with providing data access authorization. Moreover, the eGuide user expects to see the results of his or her activity right after it is performed, not when he or she is already engaged in another activity. In such circumstances, the advantage of not blocking the user is of dubious value.

The second considered option was an "on-the-fly" event processing, right after its data are received. The user after performing an action in an eGuide application has to wait for the system to process the event and relevant rules before he or she can continue. The obvious risk of this approach is whether the system coping with multiple requests would not degrade performance to the level noticeable by the user, with user experience affected negatively by the ensuing delays. There was a reason for such concerns, as the event and rule processing goes beyond standard CRUD actions, and involves not only the data contained in the event description, but also the current state of the game, affected by previous user actions.

Nonetheless the second option has been chosen. As the web service is implemented using Django REST Framework (DRF) [17], based on the MVC design pattern, the events are handled using the *genericViewSet* view modified by the *CreateModelMixin* class. In this scheme, the system automatically handles the initial processing of an API request by validating the transmitted data and recording them in the database for further processing. When processing received event data, the rule processing is initiated. The used *CreateModelMixin* class provides the *perform_create* method, thanks to which further processing can be started after the *Event* class object is saved to the database (see Fig. 1).

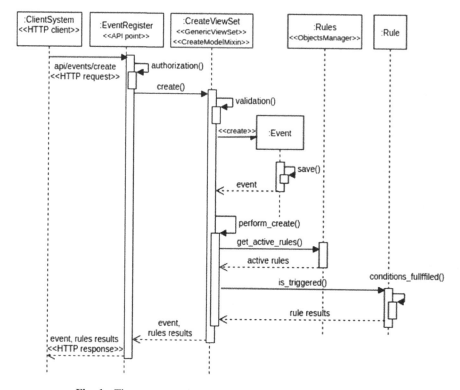

Fig. 1. The sequence diagram for the rule execution mechanism

The subsequent processing consists of two phases. The first phase is to search for all the rules that could potentially be triggered by the processed event, and load them into the rule cache. Only the rules that have been loaded to the cache are considered in the second phase, in which the conditions for triggering each of them are checked respectively. If the processed event meets all the conditions of a given rule, the relevant rule result specification is processed, and the obtained results are saved in the database and sent as a response to the client eGuide application. Note that the number of rules triggered by a single event may vary, depending only on the rule specifications (there are no technical limits).

4   Experimental Results

In order to verify the practical usability of the chosen approach, considering the concerns expressed in the previous section, its implementation has been subject to thorough performance tests.

Fifteen gamification rules were employed in the tests. They partly come from an early eGuide prototype developed within the BalticMuseums: Love IT! project [10], partly were developed specifically for the tests (to include some complex rules that were not found in the used eGuide prototype). All these rules, specified according to the format described in [11], are listed in Table 1.

Table 1. Specification of gamification rules triggered by the test requests.

Rule conditions	Rule results
action type in [Visit]	points: 12
date = [2019-05-09]	
action in [001_visit]	text: Hello
location in [Alligator gar, Amazonia]	badge: Captain Nemo:Captain Nemo
date >= [2019-05-01]	
date <= [2019-05-31]	
variable [todo] < value [5]	badge: Deep sea Explorer:Deep sea Explorer
item in [Puzzle to solve]	
location in [Amazonia]	badge: Young Sea Enthusiast:Young Sea Enthusiast
route in [For children]	
timestamp < [2019-05-01 12:00:00]	text: Exit
	points: 2
action type in [Play, Visit]	badge: Captain Nemo:Captain Nemo
location type not in [Exposition]	points: 3
route not in [For children]	points: 22
time > [08:00:00]	badge: Deep sea Explorer:Deep sea Explorer
time <= [16:00:00]	
item in [Puzzle for the youngest kids]	text: Great!
date = [2019-05-24]	badge: Young Sea Enthusiast:Young Sea Enthusiast
area in [Aquarium]	text: TO DO list
item not in [Quiz - game 1]	points: -5
item in [Quiz - game 1]	points: 1
	text: Win
	badge: Captain Nemo:Captain Nemo
variable [points] > value [20]	points: 5
variable [pionts] < value [5]	points: -10
	text: Game Over
location in [Zostera marina]	text: Bye!

The tests used randomly generated event descriptions that were submitted to the web service using HTTP POST method. In order to simulate many users using eGuide applications simultaneously, the requests were sent to the server in batches of 10, 40, and 80 at the same time using multiple threads. The Python code that has been used to perform the tests is presented in the Appendix. The tests were administered using the Multi-Mechanize Performance Test Framework version 1.2.0.1 [18].

The test platform used FreeBSD 11.2-RELEASE-p4 operating system, PostgreSQL 9.6.10 database management system, nginx 1.14.0 web server, Python 3.6.6 interpreter, Django 2.1.2 and Django Rest 3.9.1 frameworks as well as requests 1.2.3 Python module. The software was running on a machine featuring two Intel Xeon E5-2620 v4 2.10 GHz processors, 256 GB of RAM and 12 fast SSD drives within a virtualized environment limited to 2 GB of RAM, 45 GB of disk space, and 45 simultaneously running processes.

The measured processing times are presented in Table 2.

Table 2. Processing times measured in the test.

	Average	Median	Std. Dev.
10 events submitted simultaneously (160 test repetitions, 1600 samples)			
Retrieving relevant rules	0.003	0.002	0.001
Processing triggered rules	0.006	0.005	0.014
Storing rule results	0.004	0.003	0.007
Total request processing	0.105	0.098	0.054
40 events submitted simultaneously (40 test repetitions, 1600 samples)			
Retrieving relevant rules	0.003	0.002	0.001
Processing triggered rules	0.006	0.006	0.004
Storing rule results	0.004	0.000	0.006
Total request processing	0.109	0.104	0.034
80 events submitted simultaneously (20 test repetitions, 1600 samples)			
Retrieving relevant rules	0.003	0.003	0.001
Processing triggered rules	0.007	0.006	0.012
Storing rule results	0.007	0.001	0.032
Total request processing	0.126	0.111	0.067

As the experimental results show, the processing times measured in the test environment are acceptable for most practical purposes. Even in the most stressed scenario, with 80 events submitted simultaneously, the total request processing times barely surpassed 0.1 s, and the processing done with regard to the described mechanism constituted, on average, 12% of the total request processing time which means that it is not the main factor responsible for the delay perceived by end users.

Nonetheless, the delays measured in the test should be acceptable for the expected needs of user experience: considering that (1) the gamification-relevant actions take many seconds to perform (hence a single user cannot generate many requests in one second) and (2) even if an eGuide application is being used in a very large tourist attraction by several hundred users simultaneously, the probability of many of them submitting requests at the exactly same time is very low, the results should be interpreted positively for the proposed mechanism.

There are some limitations for such an interpretation due to the methodology of the performed test, though. The main one is the inability to predict how the processing time will scale with the growth of the database of processed events. The other refer to the possibility of many very complex rules defined in a single attraction, which, however seem to be very low in reality. On the other hand, the server resources employed in the tests were also limited, and they could be scaled up if such a need would arise.

5   Conclusion

The range of gamification applications broadens every year. One of its progression areas is tourism, where it can be used to raise engagement and improve experiences of eGuide users. The practical implementation of gamification relies on software systems supporting it to manage the game state and process the rules [8].

In this paper, we focused on the latter element, describing a mechanism for execution of gamification rules implemented in a web service providing gamification to eGuide applications [9]. We have applied an "on-the-fly" approach to event processing, in which the rules are processed immediately after the event data are received, and the user has to wait for rule processing to finish before he or she can continue to use the eGuide application. We have implemented the rule execution mechanism as a web service using Django REST Framework.

The presented results of its empirical verification based on performance tests confirm that the proposed approach could be effectively used in practice. In simulated yet realistic conditions, we positively verified its ability to handle a number of simultaneous randomly generated requests that matches the needs of even a large tourist attraction, making use only of server resources limited to a level available from inexpensive hosting providers.

Our next future work will be to test the presented mechanism in real-world conditions, using data generated by actual eGuide users which will be possible as soon as the eGuides using our gamification web service [9] are introduced in the museums.

Acknowledgement. BalticMuseums: Love IT! project is part-financed from the European Regional Development Fund within the Interreg South Baltic Programme.

Appendix. The Python Code Used to Perform the Tests

```
import time
import requests
import json
from random import randint, choice
import string


class Transaction(object):
    def __init__(self):
        self.custom_timers = {}

    def generate_description(self, size = 6,
chars = string.ascii_uppercase + string.digits):
        return("".join(choice(chars) \
for _ in range(size)))

    def run(self):
        post_body={
            "action": str(randint(1, 56)),
            "description": self.generate_description(
size = randint(1, 256)),}
        headers = {"Content-Type": "application/json",
"Authorization": "Bearer xxx"}
        url =
"http://bsgdevel.radak.usermd.net/api/events/"
        assert((resp.status_code == "201"),
"Bad Response: HTTP %s" % resp.status_code)
```

References

1. Marczewski, A.: Defining gamification – what do people really think? http://www.gamified.uk/2014/04/16/defining-gamification-people-really-think. Accessed 25 May 2019
2. Yu-Kai, C.: A comprehensive list of 90+ gamification cases with ROI stats. http://yukaichou.com/gamification-examples/gamification-stats-figures/#.VzCedYSLSUk. Accessed 25 May 2019
3. Bulencea, P., Egger, R.: Gamification in Tourism. Designing Memorable Experiences. Books on Demand, Norderstedt (2015)
4. Ašeriškis, D., Damaševičius, R.: Gamification Patterns for Gamification Applications. Procedia Comput. Sci. **39**, 83–90 (2014)

5. Papathanasiou-Zuhrt, D., Weiss-Ibanez, D.-F., Di Russo, A.: The gamification of heritage in the UNESCO enlisted medieval town of Rhodes. In: Proceedings of the 1st International GamiFIN Conference, pp. 60–70, Pori, Finland (2017)
6. Cesário, V., Radeta, M., Matos, S., Nisi, V.: The ocean game: assessing children's engagement and learning in a museum setting using a treasure-hunt game. In: CHI PLAY 2017 Extended Abstracts, pp. 99–109. ACM, Amsterdam, Netherlands (2017)
7. Signoretti, A., et al.: Trip 4 all: a gamified app to provide a new way to elderly people to travel. Procedia Comput. Sci. **67**, 301–311 (2015)
8. Swacha, J.: Architecture of a dispersed gamification system for tourist attractions. Information **10**(1), 33 (2019)
9. Swacha, J., Kulpa, A.: A cloud-based service for gamification of eGuides. In: 2018 6th International Conference on Future Internet of Things and Cloud Workshops, pp. 220–224. IEEE, Barcelona, Spain (2018)
10. BalticMuseums: Love IT! Project. www.balticmuseums.info. Accessed 25 May 2019
11. Swacha, J.: Representation of events and rules in gamification systems. Procedia Comput. Sci. **126**, 2040–2049 (2018)
12. Herzig, P.: Gamification as a service: conceptualization of a generic enterprise gamification platform. Ph.D. Thesis, Dresden University of Technology, Dresden, Germany (2014). http://nbn-resolving.de/urn:nbn:de:bsz:14-qucosa-148108
13. Stagliano, L., Stefanoni, G.: Designing enterprise gamification architectures. M.Sc Thesis, Politecnico di Milano, Milan, Italy (2013). https://www.politesi.polimi.it/bitstream/10589/86122/1/2013_12_Stagliano_Stefanoni.pdf. Accessed 25 May 2019
14. Drools. https://www.drools.org/. Accessed 25 May 2019
15. Piras, L.: Agon: a gamification-based framework for acceptance requirements. Ph.D. Thesis, University of Trento, Trento, Italy (2018). http://eprints-phd.biblio.unitn.it/3424/1/Luca_Piras_PhD_Thesis_FINAL_VERSION.pdf. Accessed 25 May 2019
16. Barrios, M.C.: A personal agent architecture for task automation in the web of data. bringing intelligence to everyday tasks. Ph.D Thesis, Universidad Politécnica de Madrid, Madrid (2016). http://oa.upm.es/39654. Accessed 09 June 2019
17. Christie, T.: Django REST framework. http://www.tomchristie.com/rest-framework-2-docs. Accessed 25 May 2019
18. Goldberg, C.: Multi-mechanize performance test framework. https://multi-mechanize. readthedocs.io/en/latest/. Accessed 25 May 2019

Challenges for Automated, Model-Based Test Scenario Generation

Alexander Kolchin[1(✉)], Stepan Potiyenko[1], and Thomas Weigert[2]

[1] V.M. Glushkov Institute of Cybernetics NAS of Ukraine, Kyiv, Ukraine
kolchin_av@yahoo.com
[2] Uniquesoft LLC, Palatine, IL, USA
thomas.weigert@uniquesoft.com

Abstract. This paper focuses on challenges to automatic test suite generation from formal models of software systems. Popular tools and methods and their limitations are discussed. Data cohesion, meaningfulness of derived behavior, usefulness for debugging, coverage evenness, coverage overlap, fault detection ability, and size of the generated test suite are considered as quality indicators for generated tests. A novel composite weight-based heuristic method for improving the quality of automatically generated test scenarios is proposed.

Keywords: Model-based testing · Data flow · Tests quality

1 Introduction

While the current maturity level of formal methods enables powerful tools for automated test data generation, producing effective test scenarios is still a challenging task [1]. Most test generation approaches use structural coverage criteria and focus on achieving high coverage as the main goal [2]. These tests may be useful in checking of implicit requirements, such as the absence of hanging, uncaught exceptions, or abnormal terminations, but not for revealing of inconsistencies between implementation and specification [3–5]. Much research has been dedicated to the comparison of the efficiency of different coverage types [2, 6], but questions about how to derive meaningful scenarios representing use-cases for conformance testing remain unconsidered.

Many empirical studies [3, 7–13] suggest that the level of structural coverage itself is not a good indicator of the effectiveness of a test suite. A generated counterexample path using conventional off-the-shelf model checkers is just an artifact of its search strategy, and thus, the sequence of events in such tests is the result of the order of enumeration of possible alternatives encountered during search rather than the logical interaction between them, leading to:

- Lack of data cohesion: tests often lack semantic content resulting in unclear test purposes, intricate behavior, as well as redundant or obfuscated behavior. A test path may terminate when a coverage item has been encountered without reaching its logical completion (for example, some value is computed, but then is never displayed or stored because the test scenario completes at an unrelated, already covered location).

R. Damaševičius and G. Vasiljevienė (Eds.): ICIST 2019, CCIS 1078, pp. 182–194, 2019.
https://doi.org/10.1007/978-3-030-30275-7_15

- Test overlap: automatically generated tests often suffer from a high level of overlap between test cases, resulting in uneven test coverage due to common path prefixes (some paths will be exercised more than thoroughly, but other paths will be exercised in just a single test case).

In order to alleviate these problems, the proposed method will consider test quality metrics, in particular data cohesion and coverage overlap, in addition to coverage level. The main goal is to achieve better test quality while maintaining the same level of computational complexity and resulting size of the test suite. This method focuses on test scenario generation from formal models (abstracting from code-specific technical detail) and aims to be an optimization complementing existing test generation approaches.

The paper is organized as follows: Sect. 2 discusses related work and motivation. Section 3 presents a brief overview of existing methods and problems of automatically generated test suites. The proposed weight-based test suite quality improving heuristic method is described in Sect. 4 and is empirically evaluated in Sect. 5.

2 Related Work

The level of code coverage is frequently used as a proxy measure for the "quality" of a test suite. Many software testing approaches are guided by coverage [2] and industry standards mandate that high levels of coverage be achieved [6]. Coverage gives us some level of completeness of the test suite, but there are other characteristics of a good test suite, such as its ability to detect faults, its usefulness in debugging [14, 15], its maintainability, and so on. These characteristics have not been extensively studied; for example, whether or which coverage criterion best guides software testing towards fault detection remains a controversial and open question [7, 12].

Heimdahl et al. [8] found that test cases produced using counterexample-based generation using structural criteria were less effective than test inputs generated randomly. They concluded that satisfying even a highly rigorous coverage criterion such as MC/DC is not a trustworthy indication of test suite effectiveness. In [10], the authors analyzed the efficiency of automatically generated tests for the avionics domain. They point out a need for reliable methods of assessing test quality and better test goal targeting. [7] presents an empirical evaluation of different structural coverage criteria and evaluates fault detection effectiveness using mutation testing. The authors claim that the level of coverage, while useful for identification of under-tested parts of a program, is not a good indicator of test suite effectiveness and thus should not be used as a quality target.

Most related to this paper is approach [17], where the authors suggest using cohesion and coupling metrics as objectives in addition to coverage criteria in order to improve the quality of a developed test suite code.

3 Test Suite Generation Challenges

Problems with decidability and performance encountered in the development of automating software testing techniques have stimulated different research approaches [1, 9]: Stochastic and combinatorial methods are easy to implement and are fast, but result in poor coverage and high redundancy. Genetic algorithms [16, 17] enhance coverage by selecting more promising test populations. Many systems implement hybrid and heuristic strategies. For example, systematic methods [5, 18–22], including the proposed approach, extract constraints for executing model paths and obtain test inputs that direct model behavior along these paths.

Test suite generation using model checking. For model-based test generation, a test goal with regards to a chosen coverage criterion could be specified through a temporal logic formula. Test generation is then solved as a reachability problem. Such a formula is typically represented in the form "always not p", and referred to as "trap property". Using different methods of model checking [18–21], it is possible to produce a counterexample trace, which violates the required property p. For example, Rayadurgam and Heimdahl [21] proposed a method to specify test goals for the MC/DC criterion [6] in linear temporal logic LTL.

Data-flow testing concentrates on how a variable is defined and used in the model, which can result in more efficient and targeted test suites [2, 16, 22]. Occurrences of a variable in a model are associated with its definition and use: The definition location (def) is a statement where a value is assigned to a variable; the usage location (use) is a statement where the value of the variable is read. A path is def-clear with respect to a variable if it contains no new definition of that variable. Data flow analysis identifies the defs of every variable in the program and the uses that might be affected by these defs (referred to as du-pairs). Rapps and Weyuker [23] propose the all-uses criterion for data flow testing, which requires each computation and condition affected by each definition to be tested.

A du-pair of a variable x, which is defined at location v and used at location v' (denoted $v \xrightarrow{x} v'$), can be characterized by the following LTL formula [20]:

$$ltl(v \xrightarrow{x} v') = F(v \wedge X[\neg def(x) \, U(v' \wedge Ff)])$$

where a finite path π will be a test sequence for $v \xrightarrow{x} v'$ if and only if there exist $0 \leq i < j \leq k$, such that $\pi(i) \models v$, $\pi(l) \models \neg def(x)$. for all $i < l \leq j$, $\pi(j) \models v'$ and $\pi(k) \models f$, f is a final state. The all-uses criterion is satisfied by set of paths, specified by $\bigcup_{v(\xrightarrow{x} v')} ltl(v \xrightarrow{x} v')$.

The drawback of such approach is that a generated test case is not necessarily a good reflection of the tested property; a counterexample path might not even contain a state where the antecedent of the required property becomes true.

Reachability analysis can be augmented by automata based models, where the information about du-pairs to be covered is maintained in auxiliary automata. For example, in [22] a specialized decision procedure for early termination of path unfolding is proposed, which allows exploration of a state only if it might increase the requested data flow coverage, resulting in more efficient state-space exploration.

For conformance testing it is important to achieve a high level of descriptive adequacy between the desired behavior and the test case obtained, allowing the validation of functional specifications through test cases. For this purpose, a formal model may be augmented with information describing user-defined reference behaviors, for example, in terms of sequence of important events [1]. In [11], the user-defined scenario stipulates a path property in form of a set of locations (check points), optionally ordered and extended with conditions over variables, such that a path satisfies the scenario if it includes all of its checkpoints. Unlike existing methods, which result in only one counterexample path per specified property, this method generates aggregate information about all satisfiable paths. This feature plays the role of an interactive path constructor, which prompts all satisfiable behavior alternatives, so that the user can find a desired path on-the-fly by iteratively specifying checkpoints and observe corresponding updates. Visualization of the cumulative coverage assists with desired test case generation and simplifies the identification of undesired behavior among the possible alternatives.

Efficiency Problem. Combinatorial explosion has proven to be a fundamental obstacle preventing the integration of model-based formal methods into industrial software development. Even a small model with binary attributes and a finite number of processes may produce a prohibitive (with respect to time and/or memory available) number of states to be explored [18–22]. BDD-based approaches are very sensitive to variable ordering, and in the worst case, the number of nodes grows exponentially. Bounded Model Checking is sensitive to non-trivial loops and in many cases fails to prove unreachability. As an example, consider the program listing in Fig. 1 which is analogous to fragments we observed in real industrial projects. Variables p1, ..., pN are not initialized and used as input parameters. The task is to check reachability of the ERROR label (which is actually unreachable). The initial model was simplified leveraging common state-space reduction methods; nevertheless, verification complexity remains exponential.

Experiments were conducted using different methods and tools: BDD (SMV, NuSMV), CEGAR (VCEGAR, BLAST), SMT(CBMC, Boogie), explicit model checking (SPIN), automata-based (UPPAAL), symbolic execution (SPF, PEX, KLEE). The test program was faithfully translated into the specification language of each tool.

```
int p1, ..., pN, k1=0, ..., kN=0, s=0;
 if(p1 == 1)k1 = 1;
 ...
 if(pN == 1)kN = 1;
L:
 if(s==0  &&  k1==1){s=s+1; goto L;}
 ...
 if(s==N-1 && kN==1){s=s+1; goto L;}
 if((s==N && (k1==0 ||... kN==0)) ||
   (s<N  && (k1==1 &&... kN==1))
   )goto ERROR;
```

Fig. 1. Example of a C program with messy loops

For SPF, the Java program was simplified by removing goto statements. Execution time (and, correspondingly, memory consumed) for all tools demonstrated exponential growth with an increase in the number of parameters, and none of them could successfully process a program with more than 18 parameters.

Test Suite Quality Problem. Conventional approaches to test suite generation mainly focus on attaining higher level of coverage as their primary objective. This strategy often leads to that tests reach their coverage items via confusing paths, resulting in subsequent problems with debugging and an increased cost of producing an oracle.

Tests produced by depth-first search (DFS) usually suffer from a high level of overlap between test cases and uneven coverage. This is due to the traversal mechanism: DFS chooses an alternative from the very beginning, and all reachable coverage items will be tested via that alternative. This shortcoming results in two main problems: highly unbalanced exercise of model behavior and complicated maintenance (a minor change in the source model may affect a significant part of the test suite).

A breath-first search (BFS) strategy often results in poor fault detection due to early termination. For example, experiments conducted in [8] show that randomly generated tests reveal more mutants than tests with MC/DC and branch coverage obtained using BFS.

Consider the example code snippet in Fig. 2.

```
int foo(int n, int q, int err){
01.    int res = 0;
02.    if(q == 1)
03.        res = featureQ();
04.    if(n == 1)
05.        res = 11;
06.    if(n == 2)
07.        res = 12;
....    ...
20.    if(n == 9)
21.        res = 19;
22.    if(err == 0)
23.        print("OK");
24.    else
25.        return -1;
26.    print_result(res);
27.    return res; }
```

DFS-based generated test suite:
```
foo(1,1,0):11
foo(2,1,0):12
...
foo(9,1,0):19
foo(9,1,1):-1
foo(1,0,0):11
```

BFS-based generated test suite:
```
foo(0,0,1):-1
foo(0,0,0):0
foo(1,0,1):-1
...
foo(9,0,1):-1
foo(0,1,1):-1
```

Fig. 2. Example of a program to test   **Fig. 3.** Tests

Branch-targeted DFS-based methods will produce a test suite (Fig. 3) highly overlapping on featureQ: all tests except the last one will contain this call; BFS-based strategies exhibit early termination and low data cohesion: almost all tests will finish with the result '−1' and fail to make the value of 'res' observable. Note also that both approaches fail to make the result returned by featureQ observable, which is possible using the inputs (0, 1, 0).

Test Suite Size and Faults Detection Ability Problems. The effectiveness of a test suite is usually associated with its fault detection ability. The efficiency of a test suite is reflected by the ratio of the number of tests over the number of faults detected. A widely used method of estimating the ability to reveal faults is mutation analysis [24]. It deliberately introduces artificially-generated faults ('mutants') into the original model. A test case is said to kill a mutant, if it fails during execution on a model with that mutant.

While automated tools are able to generate a huge number of tests [25] (the 'test explosion' problem), it may not be practical to maintain and run such tests. Due to available test execution time and other resource constraints, a test suite must be of reasonable size [26]. Redundancy in randomly generated test suites may exceed 75% [27]. Studies analyzing the fault detection ability using different test coverage criteria suspect that the effectiveness of a test suite is closely related to its size [28]. [29] reported that minimizing test suites while maintaining MC/DC coverage reduced their fault detection ability significantly. Similarly, in [7] the authors observed a significant correlation between the effectiveness of a test suite and its size.

Concretization with Boundary Values. Symbolic test generation approaches apply existential abstraction, which result in symbolic test scenarios, where variables are represented by constraints (e.g., 'x > 0'). Such tests need to be concretized before execution, that is, values of parameters must be substituted with admissible concrete values [30]. Using boundary values in concretization typically increases the probability of fault detection [31].

4 Weight-Based Test Suite Quality Improving Heuristic

Data-Flow Coverage. The proposed method relies on the observation that manually written tests representing use-cases of the SUT tend to have tight data dependencies with clear cause-effect relationships, resulting in increased data flow coverage when compared to test suites generated automatically using control-flow-oriented criteria [32, 33]. For example, experiments described in [16] indicate that data-flow testing achieves significantly higher mutation metrics versus test suites targeting branch coverage.

Another important characteristic of a test case is its usefulness for debugging. Debugging in essence is an attempt to find a dynamic slice with respect to a failure point. Such slice can be viewed as a data dependency sub-graph, and it is highly desirable to avoid including elements which do not belong to the slice in a test case [34]. Such elements will be redundant or will even obfuscate the test.

Heuristics not aimed at coverage. Search heuristics are a popular technique to steer the exploration of behavior towards the most promising paths in the model [35]. Data cohesion within each test case and overlap between test cases are practical parameters of guiding heuristics [17]. Average data cohesion may be computed as the mean number of du-pairs each test case covers; a higher score means more thorough cause-effect examination and thus higher level of semantic content. An overlap metric may be computed as follows:

$$\text{Overlap}(ts_a) = \sum \text{sim}(ts_a, ts_k) / (n - 1), \; ts_a \neq ts_k,$$

where ts_a is the test scenario under analysis, $T = \{ts_1, \ldots, ts_n\}$ is the test suite, n is size of T, and sim (ts_a, ts_k) denotes the similarity between ts_a and another test scenario $ts_k \in T$. The resulting value of the metric lies between $[0,1]$; a higher score means a higher overlap between ts_a and other scenarios.

The authors of [17] use similar cohesion and overlap metrics in addition to coverage criteria. Their method starts from a test suite generated for branch coverage and attempts to improve the quality of this test suite using a genetic algorithm. Computing cohesion is based on textual analysis of tests. They found that the incorporation of cohesion and coupling (overlap) into weight-based prioritization during test suite generation helps improve the overall quality of the generated tests.

Prioritization and prolongation. A key insight which aids in increasing data cohesion for individual tests is the observation of coherence between variables inherent to particular coverage items in hand-developed tests: The variables most likely to be in a backward slice of the coverage item and a test designed to cover this slice will also cover appropriate du-pairs in the proximity of the item. In other words, they will cover some branch in the cause-effect graph of the SUT. Another necessity is to cause possible faults to be visible [36]. In view of this observation, a test scenario which aims to cover some item should include events on both backward and forward slices with respect to the location of the item and be free of other events, as far as possible.

```
For each coverage item c in Coverage Goal,
   Construct Backward Slice(c);
   Identify set of defs(c), which belongs to
   Backward Slice(c).

During search for coverage item c,
   At each location with non-deterministic choice of
   transitions alternatives {t₁, …, tₙ},
      For each tᵢ ∈ {t₁, …, tₙ},
      Compute DU-priority(tᵢ) := number of reachable uses of active
                                 definitions from defs(c);
      Compute Overlap Level(tᵢ) := number of occurrences of tᵢ in
                                   whole test produced so far;
      Re-order the set of transitions to be fired wrt DU-priority and
   then apply Overlap Level inside subsets with equal score of DU-
   priority.
```

Fig. 4. Data-flow–based prioritization principle

```
For each coverage item c in Coverage Goal,    Construct Forward
Slice(c);
   Identify set of Observation Points, which belongs to Forward Slice(c).

During prolongation of path to coverage item c,
   At each location with non-deterministic choice of
   transitions alternatives {t₁, …, tₙ},
      For each tᵢ ∈ {t₁, …, tₙ},
         Compute Observation Proximity := number of transitions on control
                              flow graph to the nearest Observation Point.
         Compute DU-priority(tᵢ) := number of reachable uses of active
                              definitions from def(c);
         Compute Overlap Level(tᵢ) := number of occurrences of tᵢ in whole
                              suite produced so far;
      Re-order the set of transitions to be fired wrt Observation Prox-
imity, and then apply DU-priority and Overlap Level inside subsets with
equal score of Observation Proximity.
```

Fig. 5. Data- and Control-flow–based prolongation principle

After the intended coverage item is reached, the scenario-under-construction is prolonged up to some observation point (a selected output of the SUT). In order to observe the effect of the coverage item, the chosen observation points must belong to the forward slice of the coverage item. The data-flow-based prioritization and the prolongation procedure are described in Figs. 4 and 5, respectively.

Example. The test suite generated for the code sample in Fig. 2 following the proposed heuristic is presented in Fig. 6. The test $(0, 1, 0)$ which was missed by the test suite listed in Fig. 3 is produced because the definition of the variable 'res' on line 03 has usages on lines 26 and 27, and therefore the prolongation procedure will avoid re-definitions of 'res' at lines 05, 07, etc., yielding parameter values $n = 0$ and $err = 0$, and return the value computed by featureQ (denoted 'fQ').

```
foo(0,0,0):0
foo(0,1,0):fQ
foo(1,0,0):11
foo(2,0,0):12

...

foo(9,0,0):19
foo(9,0,1):-1
```

Fig. 6. Test suite with prioritization

Test Suite Minimization. A test suite may exhibit substantial levels of redundancy, as each test likely covers several coverage items. In general, the minimization task is NP-complete, so greedy approximation is used in practice [26]. The greedy algorithm selects the test scenario that covers the largest number of items not covered by the previously selected tests. In order to increase test suite efficiency, mutation analysis [24] is applied before test suite minimization. A mutation metric provides information regarding the generated mutants each test will kill. Each test scenario produced also includes information about the coverage items it covers together with an overall def-use metric. These metrics are used for the prioritization of test scenarios during test suite minimization as shown in Fig. 7.

```
Reset Mutants Killed Set;
Reset Covered DU Set;
Reset Minimized Test Suite;
For each coverage item c in Coverage Goal,
   For each ts in Original Test Suite that covers c,
   Compute score(ts) := number of mutants it kills not yet
                        included in Mutants Killed Set    +
                      + number of du-pairs it covers not yet
                        included in Covered DU Set;
   Add ts with the highest score to Minimized Test Suite;
   Add all mutants killed by ts with the highest score to
       Mutants Killed Set;
   Add all du-pairs covered by ts with the highest score to
       Covered DU Set;
```

Fig. 7. Test suite minimization principle

The coverage items in the outer loop are increased with respect to the number of generated test scenarios that cover it. Such ordering increases selection fairness: if, for example, some coverage item is covered by only one scenario, then the scenario will necessarily be added to the resulting test suite, and the set of mutants it kills and the du-pairs it covers will not be taken into account when evaluating subsequent scenarios.

Note that the resulting test suite may still contain redundancies with respect to the coverage criterion and the test suite could further be reduced to some pre-defined size using a threshold of the computed metrics. Our experiments have shown that aiming at branch coverage leaves around 15% redundancy while aiming at def-use coverage leaves less than 10% in comparison to a greedy minimization algorithm aimed at coverage alone. This overhead in coverage appears worthwhile taking into account the fault detection ability, as the number of mutants not killed is reduced by roughly 30%. The authors of [37] came to a similar conclusion when stating that while the number of coverage items for mutation testing is much larger than that needed for statement or branch coverage, it did not require significantly more tests.

5   Empirical Evaluation

This section describes an empirical study aimed at evaluating the effect of the proposed prioritization heuristics for achieving branch coverage. This study was guided by the following research questions:

RQ1: Does the prioritization heuristic produce more (data) cohesive and less overlapping tests?
RQ2: Does the prioritization heuristic affect the size of the produced tests?
RQ3: Does the prioritization heuristic affect fault detection ability?

RQ1 aims at not only to show a statistically relevant improvement in the metrics, but also concerns qualitative improvements in the resulting test suites with respect to readability, logical connectedness, diversity of exercised behavior, usefulness for debugging, and more. RQ2 examines whether the prioritization heuristic results in significant changes of the test suite when compared with a strategy aimed at branch coverage only. Test suite size will be assessed as the sum of all events (transitions) in all tests. RQ3 concerns test suite efficiency, which was not a direct goal of the proposed method but is nevertheless a desirable objective.

Experimental Procedure. For this study, seven different medium-sized models were taken from the telecom, automotive, and finance domains and are described in Table 1. For each model, a set of mutants was generated inducing typical faults: operator reference fault ('∨' is replaced by '∧', or vice versa), negation fault (a variable of a subformula is replaced by its negation), associative shift fault (change to the associativity of operators, e.g., $x1 \land (x2 \lor x3)$ vs. $(x1 \land x2) \lor x3$), missing variable fault (omission of a condition in a formula, e.g., $x1 \lor x2$ implemented as $x1$), missing assignment fault (some assignment is omitted, leaving the previous variable value). In order to prune untestable mutants, data flow analysis [22] was applied: a mutant, which had no reachable usage was removed as 'equivalent'. Only feasible du-pairs were taken into account.

Table 1. Models used in experiment

Characteristics	Model id						
	1	2	3	4	5	6	7
Number of attributes	19	37	211	72	54	112	297
Conditions (i.e., branches)	53	103	215	107	119	128	207
Assignments	98	212	506	174	256	544	426
Number of du-pairs	151	284	1013	493	541	1218	1322
Mutants generated	303	635	1233	814	758	1182	2026

For each model, two experiments aimed at branch coverage were conducted, one using ordinary test generation without prioritization (labeled NP below) and one with state-space traversal prioritization heuristics and mutation-score based minimization applied (WP).

Results and Analysis. Table 2 summarizes the observed results. Mutants killed max (maximal oracle) refers to that a test fails to pass due to some transition having become inapplicable (therefore, the whole scenario is determined to be infeasible) or a mismatch detected in input parameters. Mutants killed oo (output only oracle) refers to that a mismatch is detected either in the sequence or values of input parameters. These results indicate that heuristic prioritization positively affects the level of data cohesion of each test and the level of overlap in the test suite. The improvement in mutation metrics is achieved mainly due to the post-generation minimization procedure: in more than 25% of tests, mutation-based assessment plays a decisive role in comparison. Remarkably, besides the quantitative statistical improvements, the produced results often show resemblance with 'hand-made' test scenarios.

Table 2. Test generation results

Statistics	Model id						
	1	2	3	4	5	6	7
Test suite size NP	19	33	70	32	29	35	132
Test suite size WP	17	35	76	30	24	38	153
Def-use score NP	73	89	324	165	226	479	495
Def-use score WP	96	159	683	306	311	612	733
Mut. killed max% NP	159	365	554	467	452	548	959
Mut. killed max% WP	215	471	767	603	528	736	1371
Mut. killed oo% NP	118	298	370	298	304	346	688
Mut. killed oo% WP	193	380	677	492	431	558	1119
Average cohesion NP	10	9	13	26	18	23	31
Average cohesion WP	13	14	14	31	22	27	36
Overlap NP	0.62	0.57	0.41	0.47	0.43	0.56	0.65
Overlap WP	0.43	0.41	0.32	0.36	0.30	0.44	0.45

Incorporation of cohesion and overlap into prioritization during test suite generation helps to improve the overall quality of the test cases, which as a consequence are more (data) cohesive and overlap less (RQ1). The size of the test suite is not affected by prioritization (RQ2), while its ability to reveal faults has been improved (RQ3).

6 Conclusions

This paper addressed problems of quality and efficiency of test cases generated from formal models. The proposed method uses data flow analysis for measuring and reinforcing data cohesion within each test. Overlap is measured through global statement and branch coverage statistics of the resulting test suite. Fault detection ability is computed using a mutation-based approach and is applied during test suite minimization.

Based on the proposed method a prototype has been implemented and evaluated. This method extends state space traversal [18, 19] with a composite weight-based prioritization heuristic. Upon detecting of a new coverage item, the path prolongation procedure finds a path suffix leading to a point where the effect of the coverage item can be observed. During state space traversal, an alternative is assigned a higher priority if it can lead to greater number of uses of active definitions belonging to the backward slice with respect to the coverage item. This method can complement popular test case generation approaches.

Empirical results demonstrate a positive impact on the quality (readability, maintainability, usefulness in debugging, etc.) of test suites produced without negative impact on the size of the resulting test suite.

References

1. Utting, M., Legeard, B.: Practical Model-Based Testing: A Tools Approach, p. 456. Morgan-Kaufmann, San Francisco (2010)
2. Dssouli, R., et al.: Testing the control-flow, data-flow, and time aspects of communication systems: a survey. Adv. Comput. **107**, 95–155 (2017)
3. Gay, G., Staats, M., Whalen, M., Heimdahl, M.: The risks of coverage-directed test case generation. IEEE Trans. Softw. Eng. **41**, 803–819 (2015)
4. Fraser, G., Arcuri, A.: 1600 faults in 100 projects: automatically finding faults while achieving high coverage with Evosuite. Empir. Softw. Eng. **20**(3), 611–639 (2015)
5. Cseppento, L., Micskei, Z.: Evaluating symbolic execution-based test tools. In: IEEE Conference on Software Testing, Verification and Validation, pp. 1–10 (2015). http://doi.org/10.1109/ICST.2015.7102587
6. Chilenski, J., Millner, S.: Applicability of modified condition/decision coverage to software testing. Softw. Eng. J. **9**, 193–200 (1994)
7. Inozemtseva, L., Holmes, R.: Coverage is not strongly correlated with test suite effectiveness. In: Proceedings of ACM ICSE 2014, pp. 435–445 (2015). http://doi.org/10.1145/2568225.2568271
8. Heimdahl, M., Devaraj, G.: Specification test coverage adequacy criteria = specification test generation inadequacy criteria? In: IEEE Computer Society, HASE, pp. 178–186 (2004)
9. Rushby, J.: Automated test generation and verified software. In: Meyer, B., Woodcock, J. (eds.) VSTTE 2005. LNCS, vol. 4171, pp. 161–172. Springer, Heidelberg (2008). https://doi.org/10.1007/978-3-540-69149-5_18
10. Staats, M., Gay, G., Whalen, M., Heimdahl, M.: On the danger of coverage directed test case generation. In: de Lara, J., Zisman, A. (eds.) FASE 2012. LNCS, vol. 7212, pp. 409–424. Springer, Heidelberg (2012). https://doi.org/10.1007/978-3-642-28872-2_28
11. Kolchin, A.: Interactive method for cumulative analysis of software formal models behavior. In: Proceedings of the 11th International Conference of Programming UkrPROG 2018, vol. 2139–2018. pp. 115–123. CEUR-WS (2018)
12. Chekam, T., et. al.: An empirical study on mutation, statement and branch coverage fault revelation that avoids unreliable clean program assumption. In: IEEE-ACM 39th International Conference on Software Engineering, 12 p. (2017). http://doi.org/10.1109/ICSE.2017.61
13. Mustafa, A., et al.: Comparative evaluation of the state-of-art requirements-based test case generation approaches. Int. J. Adv. Sci. Eng. Inf. Technol. **7**, 1567–1573 (2017)
14. Ceccato, M., et al.: Do automatically generated test cases make debugging easier? an experimental assessment of debugging effectiveness and efficiency. ACM Trans. Softw. Eng. Methodol. **25**(1), 1–38 (2015). https://doi.org/10.1145/2768829
15. Groce, A., et al.: Cause reduction: delta debugging, even without bugs. Softw. Test. Verif. Reliab., 1–30 (2015). http://doi.org/10.1002/stvr.1574
16. Vivanti, M., et al.: Search-based data-flow test generation. In: IEEE International Symposium on Software Reliability Engineering, vol. 10 (2013). http://doi.org/10.1109/ISSRE.2013.6698890
17. Palomba, F., et al.: Automatic test case generation: what if test code quality matters? In: Proceedings of International Symposium on Software Testing and Analysis, pp. 130–141 (2016)
18. Cadar, C., Sen, K.: Symbolic execution for software testing: three decades later. Commun. ACM **56**(2), 82–90 (2013). https://doi.org/10.1145/2408776.2408795
19. Kolchin, A.V.: An automatic method for the dynamic construction of abstractions of states of a formal model. Cybern. Syst. Anal. **46**(4), 583–601 (2010). https://doi.org/10.1007/s10559-010-9235-9

20. Hong, H.S., Ural, H.: Dependence testing: extending data flow testing with control dependence. In: Khendek, F., Dssouli, R. (eds.) TestCom 2005. LNCS, vol. 3502, pp. 23–39. Springer, Heidelberg (2005). https://doi.org/10.1007/11430230_3

21. Rayadurgam, S., Heimdahl, M.: Coverage based test-case generation using model checkers. In: Proceedings of IEEE International Conference on the Engineering of Computer Based Systems, pp. 83–91 (2001)

22. Kolchin, A.: A novel algorithm for attacking path explosion in model-based test generation for data flow coverage. In: Proceedings of IEEE 1st International Conference on System Analysis and Intelligent Computing, SAIC 2018, 5 p. (2018). http://doi.org/10.1109/SAIC.2018.8516824

23. Rapps, S., Weyuker, E.: Data flow analysis techniques for test data selection. In: Proceedings of International Conference of Software Engineering, pp. 272–278 (1982)

24. Morell, L.J.: A theory of fault-based testing. IEEE Trans. Softw. Eng. **16**(8), 844–857 (1990). https://doi.org/10.1109/32.57623

25. Kotlyarov, V., Drobintsev, P., Voinov, N., Selin, I., Tolstoles, A.: Technology and tools for developing industrial software test suites based on formal models and implementing scalable testing process on supercomputer. In: Itsykson, V., Scedrov, A., Zakharov, V. (eds.) TMPA 2017. CCIS, vol. 779, pp. 51–63. Springer, Cham (2018). https://doi.org/10.1007/978-3-319-71734-0_5

26. Tallam, S., Gupta, N.: A concept analysis inspired greedy algorithm for test suite minimization. ACM Softw. Eng. Notes **31**(1), 35–42 (2006). https://doi.org/10.1145/1108768.1108802

27. Lei, Y., Andrews, J.: Minimization of randomized unit test cases. In: International Symposium on Software Reliability Engineering, pp. 267–276 (2005). http://doi.org/10.1109/ISSRE.2005.28

28. Namin, A., Andrews, J.: The influence of size and coverage on test suite effectiveness. In: Proceedings of International Symposium on Software Testing, pp. 57–68 (2009). http://doi.org/10.1145/1572272.1572280

29. Heimdahl, M., et al.: Test-suite reduction for model based tests: effects on test quality and implications for testing. In: ASE Conference, pp. 176–185 (2004). http://doi.org/10.1109/ASE.2004.1342735

30. Kolchin, A., et al.: An approach to creating concretized test scenarios within test automation technology for industrial software projects. Autom. Control Comput. Sci., pp. 433–442 (2013). http://doi.org/10.3103/S0146411613070213

31. Myers, G.J.: The Art Of Software Testing, 254 p. Wiley, New York (2004)

32. Herman, P.M.: A data flow analysis approach to program testing. Aust. Comput. J. **8**(3), 92–97 (1976)

33. Su, T. et. al. A survey on data-flow testing. ACM Comput. Surv. **50**, 35 p. (2017)

34. Beer, I., et al.: Explaining counterexamples using causality. Formal Methods Syst. Des. **40**(1), 20–40 (2012). https://doi.org/10.1007/s10703-011-0132-2

35. Neetu, J., Rabins, P.: Automated test data generation applying heuristic approaches—a survey. Softw. Eng., pp. 699–708 (2019). http://doi.org/10.1007/978-981-10-8848-3_68

36. Barr, E., et al.: The oracle problem in software testing: a survey. IEEE Trans. Softw. Eng. **41**, 507–525 (2015). https://doi.org/10.1109/TSE.2014.2372785

37. Li, N., Offut J.: An experimental comparison of four unit test criteria: mutation, edge-pair, all-uses and prime path coverage. In: IEEE International Conference on Software Testing, Verification and Validation, pp. 220–229 (2009). http://doi.org/10.1109/ICSTW.2009.30

Information Technology Applications: Special Session on Information Technology Security

Investigation of Matrix Power Asymmetric Cipher Resistant to Linear Algebra Attack

Aleksejus Mihalkovich$^{(\boxtimes)}$ ⓘ and Matas Levinskas

Kaunas University of Technology, Kaunas, LT, Lithuania
aleksejus.michalkovich@ktu.lt,
matas.levinskas@ktu.edu

Abstract. This paper continues our research of the so-called matrix power function and its application to cryptography. We consider the simplest case of the improved matrix power asymmetric cypher (MPAC). We show that our protocol is resistant to linear algebra attack, which can be applied to the initial version of MPAC to break it in polynomial time. Our main goal is to present the general idea for the choice of public parameters of MPAC protocol to avoid this attack while also avoiding exhaustive search attack.

Keywords: Non-commutative cryptography · Matrix power function · Security analysis

1 Introduction

After the sound paper [1] asymmetric cryptography has been rapidly developing. Widely used protocols like RSA, El-Gamal and others were presented. These protocols were based on the complexity of discrete exponent function, i.e. calculating the inverse action called the discrete logarithm. However, due to efforts of Shor, who showed that this problem can be solved in polynomial time using a quantum computer, cryptographers turned their attention to non-commutative algorithms. Early attempt to apply unsolvability of the word problem for cryptographic purposes was made in 1985 in [2]. Since then other protocols like Ko-Lee key exchange [3] and Anshel-Anshel-Goldfeld key exchange [4] were suggested. It was shown by Spilrain and Ushakov in [5], that instead of solving CSP an adversary can try to solve a much easier decomposition problem. Hence the Anchel-Anchel-Goldfeld scheme is reckoned being more advanced. But nevertheless this scheme has a disadvantage, since it is using tuples of generators of private keys and hence is increasing memory requirements.

Our contribution to this branch of cryptography is based on the function, which is applied to matrices defined in some matrix semigroup. The definition of our function is somewhat similar to matrix multiplication, however it uses nonlinear operations to obtain a value. For this purpose, we considered a commuting multiplicative semigroup S and a numerical ring R. It is important to note, that the cardinality of R depends on the maximal multiplicative order of elements of S. Using these algebraic structures we defined the matrix semigroup M_S and the matrix ring M_R, where all matrices are square

R. Damaševičius and G. Vasiljevienė (Eds.): ICIST 2019, CCIS 1078, pp. 197–208, 2019.
https://doi.org/10.1007/978-3-030-30275-7_16

of order m with entries selected from S and R respectively. We call the matrix semigroup M_S a *platform semigroup* and the matrix ring M_R a *power ring*.

Hence, matrix power function (MPF) is a mapping $F(X, Y) : M_R \times M_R \mapsto M_S$ denoted in a following way:

$$^XQ^Y = E, \tag{1}$$

where $Q = \{q_{ij}\}$, $X = \{x_{ij}\}$, $Y = \{y_{ij}\}$ and $E = \{e_{ij}\}$ are square matrices of order m. Furthermore, matrices X and Y are chosen from a power ring M_R, whereas matrix Q is chosen from a platform semigroup M_S. The entries of matrix E are calculated by the formula:

$$e_{ij} = \prod_{k=1}^{m} \prod_{l=1}^{m} q_{kl}^{x_{ik}y_{lj}}. \tag{2}$$

It is clear, that matrix $E \in M_S$. Properties of this function were considered in our previous papers [6–8]. We also investigated statistical properties of MPF and concluded, that it is a candidate one-way function [9].

Previously we proposed several cryptographic primitives based on this function [7, 8, 10]. In this paper we consider the so-called matrix power asymmetric cypher (MPAC) which was presented in [8]. In this paper we consider the resistance of the modified MPAC protocol to linear algebra cryptanalysis and its safe parameter values.

The rest of the paper is organized as follows: in the next section we briefly recall our previous work, we analyze the resistance of MPAC to linear algebra attack in Sect. 3 and present experimental results in Sect. 4. Conclusions are presented at the end of the paper.

2 Our Previous Work

In 2012 MPF was used for constructing an asymmetric cipher, which was presented in [8]. We briefly recall this protocol:

Let Q be a public matrix selected over platform group and let Z be a public matrix, selected over power ring. Alice has her private key – a pair $(X, U) = PrK_A$, where X is a randomly selected non-singular matrix and matrix U is a polynomial of Z i.e. $U = P_U(Z)$. Her public key is $PuK_A = (E = {}^XQ^U, A = XZX^{-1})$. Assume, that Bob is interested in sending a secret message M to Alice. He encrypts a message M by using Alice's PuK_A and performing following actions:

1. Bob generates his private and public data, i.e. he chooses at random a non-singular matrix Y and a set of coefficients of polynomial $P_V(\cdot)$. He computes matrices $F = {}^VQ^Y$ and $B = Y^{-1}ZY$. His public key is $PuK_B = (F, B)$. Note, that $V = P_V(Z)$.
2. Bob uses Alice's public key to compute the common key $K_B = {}^{XV}Q^{UY}$.
3. The ciphertext is $C = K_B \oplus M$, where $\oplus$ denotes XOR operation. Bob sends the pair (C, PuK_B) to Alice.

To decrypt Bob's message Alice calculates the decryption key $K_A = {}^{XV}Q^{UY}$ using Bob's public data. Since $K_A = K_B$, the message $M = K_A \oplus C$.

However, in 2016 this version of MPAC protocol was attacked. In their paper authors of [11] have shown, that our protocol was vulnerable to an attack based on linear algebra. The critical points C1 and C2 of this attack are the following:

- C1: Existence of matrix discrete logarithm – a mapping, which transforms identity (1) to the form:

$$X\left(\mathrm{ld}_g Q\right)Y = \mathrm{ld}_g E, \tag{3}$$

where $\mathrm{ld}_g(\cdot)$ is the discrete logarithm function applied elementwise to matrices Q and E;

- C2: A publically known basis of the set of polynomials, which, according to [12] can be calculated in polynomial time.

The initial version of the protocol was improved in our other papers [10, 13] to aggravate computation of the private matrices U and V. Our approach now uses private functions $f_U(x, y)$ and $f_V(x, y)$ of two non-commuting arguments x and y to define these matrices. Hence Alice publishes a triplet $PuK_A = (E = {}^X Q^U, A_1 = XZ_1X^{-1}, A_2 = XZ_2X^{-1})$, where $U = f_U(Z_1, Z_2)$, as her public key. Bob modifies step 1 of the protocol to reflect the changes made.

The benefit of using two public non-commuting matrices Z_1 and Z_2 to calculate matrix U instead of a single matrix Z is the fact, that a basis of the set of values of the function $f(Z_1, Z_2)$ is an open problem and hence the critical point C2 cannot be satisfied thus eliminating the possibility of linear algebra attack.

Due to this fact we focus on the improved version of MPAC protocol. Our goal is to propose a general idea about the choice of public matrices Z_1 and Z_2, which provides us with sufficient security against linear algebra attack while also being resistant to brute force attack, i.e. exploring all possible choices of private matrices has to be infeasible.

3   Resistance of MPAC to Linear Algebra Attack

The main idea for breaking the initial version of our protocol is the fact, that matrix U can be eliminated, i.e. an attacker can replace this matrix with the set of coefficients of the polynomial, which was used to calculate it.

In [13] we have improved the initial protocol by introducing two public non-commuting matrices Z_1 and Z_2 to calculate matrix U. Hence to recover Alice's private key an adversary has to solve the following system of equations:

$$\begin{cases} {}^X Q^U = E \\ XZ_1X^{-1} = A_1 \\ XZ_2X^{-1} = A_2 \end{cases}, \tag{4}$$

where matrix $U = f(Z_1, Z_2)$ and $f(x, y)$ is some function. An adversary may attempt to recover Alice's private key by applying the discrete logarithm function to the first equation of system (4). Furthermore, he can consider Bob's public data as well and hence recover the encryption key $K = {}^{XV}Q^{UY}$ by solving the following problem:

$$\begin{cases} X\left(\mathrm{ld}_g Q\right) U = \mathrm{ld}_g E \\ X Z_1 X^{-1} = A_1 \\ X Z_2 X^{-1} = A_2 \\ Y^{-1} Z_1 Y = B_1 \\ Y^{-1} Z_2 Y = B_2 \\ U = f(Z_1, Z_2) \end{cases} \tag{5}$$

where $\mathrm{ld}_g Q$ and $\mathrm{ld}_g E$ are discrete logarithms of matrices Q and E respectively, $f(Z_1, Z_2)$ is some randomly selected unknown function. This approach is similar to the one described in [11]. Note, that the following proposition holds:

Proposition 1. If the basis of the set of values of the function $f(Z_1, Z_2)$ can be found in reasonable time, then matrix U can be eliminated from the system (5).

Corollary 1. If the basis of the set of values of the function $f(Z_1, Z_2)$ can be found in reasonable time, then MPAC protocol can be broken in polynomial time.

Hence to achieve a sufficient level of security we have to enlarge the cardinality of the set of values of function $f(Z_1, Z_2)$. Onwards we will denote this set by S_f.

Note, however, that we cannot evaluate the exact value of cardinality of S_f since calculating the basis of this set is an open problem. Due to this fact we turn our attention to a certain subset of S_f which can be obtained by considering the following linear span:

$$\mathrm{Span}\left(I, Z_1, \ldots, Z_1^{k_1}, Z_2, \ldots, Z_2^{k_2}, Z_1 Z_2, \ldots Z_1 Z_2^{k_2}, Z_1^2 Z_2, \ldots, Z_1^{k_1} Z_2^{k_2}, Z_2 Z_1, \ldots, Z_2^{k_2} Z_1^{k_1}\right),$$

$$\tag{6}$$

where matrices $Z_1, \ldots, Z_1^{k_1}$ are linearly independent, matrices $Z_2, \ldots, Z_2^{k_2}$ are linearly independent whereas matrices $Z_1^{k_1+1}$ and $Z_2^{k_2+1}$ can be expressed as a linear combination of lower powers of matrices Z_1 and Z_2 respectively. Based on the basis of this linear span we aim to estimate a lower bound of cardinality of S_f.

Let us now consider the subsystem of conjugation equation in system (5) i.e.

$$\begin{cases} X Z_1 X^{-1} = A_1 \\ X Z_2 X^{-1} = A_2 \end{cases}. \tag{7}$$

This system can be solved in polynomial time, since it can be transformed to the following system of linear equations:

$$\begin{cases} X Z_1 = A_1 X \\ X Z_2 = A_2 X \end{cases}. \tag{8}$$

However, it is clear, that a single conjugation equation has a set of solutions, which can be obtained by using Gauss elimination. Hence the set of solutions of system (7) can be obtained by calculating a union of sets of solutions for each individual equations. Onwards we denote the set of solutions of the conjugation system by $S_C(Z_1, Z_2, A_1, A_2)$ or S_C for short. Note, that since system (5) clearly has two independent conjugation subsystems we have

$$S_C(Z_1, Z_2, A_1, A_2) \neq S_C(Z_1, Z_2, B_1, B_2).$$

To achieve sufficient level of security we have to enlarge the cardinalities of both sets $S_C(Z_1, Z_2, A_1, A_2)$ and $S_C(Z_1, Z_2, B_1, B_2)$, since otherwise our protocol may be vulnerable to brute force attacks.

Due to results of this section we perform experiments to find such non-commuting matrices Z_1 and Z_2, that

$$\begin{cases} |S_f| \to \max \\ |S_C| \to \max \end{cases}, \qquad (9)$$

where $|\;|$ denotes the cardinality of the set. Note, that we focus only on public matrices Z_1 and Z_2, since matrices A_1 and A_2 (or B_1 and B_2) are calculated during the protocol and hence the conjugation system (7) has at least one solution.

4 Construction of Public Matrices

In this section we consider the improved MPAC protocol, which was previously presented in [13]. We focus on the following simplified version of this protocol:

- The platform structure consisting of all possible base matrices is defined over the Sylow group with prime order p;
- The power structure consisting of all possible power matrices is defined over the numerical field $\mathbf{Z}_p$, where p is a prime number.

Note, that since all elements of Sylow group are generators (excluding the neutral element) the discrete logarithm function can always be applied to Eq. (1) to obtain Eq. (3). Hence to break the MPAC protocol we consider system (5) defined over the field $\mathbf{Z}_p$.

As mentioned above, to aggravate the adversary's task we construct matrices Z_1 and Z_2 satisfying conditions (9). We start by considering two randomly generated non-commuting matrices Z_1 and Z_2, i.e. the entries of these matrices are selected at random from $\mathbf{Z}_p$ with uniform distribution. Due to the structure of matrices Z_1 and Z_2 suggested in [13], without loss of generosity we assume, that these matrices have canonical form, i.e. each matrix can be expressed as follows:

$$Z_k = J_1 \oplus J_2 \oplus \ldots \oplus J_l, \qquad (10)$$

where $k \in [1, 2]$, $\oplus$ is the direct sum and $J_1, J_2, \ldots, J_l$ are Jordan blocks of sizes respectively $m_1, m_2, \ldots, m_l$, such that $\sum_{i=1}^{l} m_i = m$.

Let us consider the conjugation subsystem (7). Using the linear form (8) of this system we construct the following equation:

$$L\vec{X} = \vec{W}, \tag{11}$$

where L is the coefficients matrix, $\vec{X}$ is the stretch of the matrix X and $\vec{W} = \left(\overrightarrow{A_1}, \overrightarrow{A_2} \right)$ is a concatenation of two stretches of matrices A_1 and A_2. The coefficient matrix L can be conveniently expressed as follows:

$$L = \begin{pmatrix} I_m \otimes Z_1^T - A_1 \otimes I_m \\ I_m \otimes Z_2^T - A_2 \otimes I_m \end{pmatrix}, \tag{12}$$

where $\otimes$ is the Kronecker product. This method is explained in detail in [11]. We can now apply Gauss elimination to the matrix L to find the rank and defect of system of linear Equations (11) and hence find all solutions of conjugation system (7). Note, that we also have to check if the selected solution is invertible and reject singular matrices.

Hence, for a randomly selected stretch $\overrightarrow{X'}$ satisfying matrix Equation (11), we have to calculate $\det X'$ modulo p. Clearly, the value of $|S_C|$ is a multiple of the Euler's totient function $\phi = \phi(p)$ since we can multiply any solution of system (7) $\widetilde{X}$ by an invertible element $a \in Z_p$ while also multiplying matrix $\widetilde{X}^{-1}$ by a^{-1} to obtain another solution of the same system.

The experiments were performed as follows:

1. We fixed the order of square matrices m and a prime modulo p;
2. We chose the number of Jordan blocks for each matrix Z_1 and Z_2 at random. We also randomly selected an eigenvalue for each of the blocks from Z_p.
3. We generated a solvable conjugation system (7) by selecting a nonsingular matrix X with entries from Z_p and calculating matrices A_1 and A_2.
4. Using the method, described above, we solved the obtained system (7) defined over Z_p with respect to an unknown matrix X.

For each of the fixed pair of positive integers m and p we constructed 1000 solvable systems and analyzed the frequency of possible values of cardinality $|S_C|$. Here we present the experimental results for the case of $m = 4$, $p = 3$:

Hence, we can see from Table 1, that the value of cardinality $|S_C|$ greatly varies from the minimal value ϕ to the significantly large value $\phi^5 \cdot p^3$. Furthermore, some values of $|S_C|$ are more frequent than others. Due to problem (9) we aim to maximize the value $|S_C|$ and hence we have to generate system (7) based on some pre-defined stable template while also ensuring a large enough value of $|S_f|$.

Table 1. Experimental results for system (7) with parameters $m = 4$, $p = 3$.

Formula	$\lvert S_C \rvert$	Percentage	Formula	$\lvert S_C \rvert$	Percentage
ϕ	2	40.6	$\phi^3 p$	24	0.9
ϕ^2	4	6.2	$\phi^2 p^2$	36	1.7
ϕp	6	24.9	$\phi^3 p^2$	72	0.3
ϕ^3	8	0.1	$\phi^2 p^3$	108	2.7
$\phi^2 p$	12	16.2	$\phi^3 p^3$	216	0.5
ϕp^2	18	5.7	$\phi^5 p^3$	864	0.4

Through experiments we found that following pair is a suitable template (see Appendix 1):

$$T_3^{(1)} = \begin{pmatrix} t_1 & 1 & & & & 0 \\ & t_1 & 1 & & & \\ & & t_1 & 0 & & \\ & & & t_1 & \ddots & \\ & & & & \ddots & 0 \\ 0 & & & & & t_1 \end{pmatrix}, T_3^{(2)} = \begin{pmatrix} t_2 & & & & 0 \\ & t_3 & & & \\ & & t_2 & & \\ & & & t_2 & \\ & & & & \ddots \\ 0 & & & & t_2 \end{pmatrix}.$$

where $t_1, t_2, t_3 \in \mathbf{Z}_p$ are non-zero entries with $t_2 \neq t_3$. Other templates are also possible. Note, however, that matrices from distinct templates $T_i = \left\{ T_i^{(1)}, T_i^{(2)} \right\}$ and $T_j = \left\{ T_j^{(1)}, T_j^{(2)} \right\}$ cannot be used to generate conjugation system (7). The presented template provides us with stable value of cardinality $\lvert S_C \rvert$, i.e. this value does not depend on the chosen eigenvalues t_1, t_2, t_3. We evaluated the relation between square matrix order and approximate value of $\lvert S_C \rvert$. The results are presented in Table 2:

Table 2. Relation between matrix order and cardinality $\lvert S_C \rvert$.

m	3	4	5	6	7	8	9	10
$\log_p \lvert S_C \rvert$	2	5	11	19	23	37	50	64

We can see from Table 2, that the cardinality $\lvert S_C \rvert$ grows with rate close to exponential. However, despite this growth, the cardinality $\lvert S_f \rvert$ remains the same, i.e.

$$\lvert S_f \rvert = p^5 - 1. \tag{13}$$

We found other stable templates, which are presented in Appendix 1. For each of the templates found we evaluated both cardinalities considered. Due to presented results we can see, that the two separate goals ($\lvert S_f \rvert \to$ max and $\lvert S_C \rvert \to$ max) contradict with each other, i.e. larger values of $|S_f|$ correspond to smaller values of $|S_C|$. Hence the solution of problem (9) is a balance of these cardinalities rather than maximal values, i.e. we search for public matrices Z_1 and Z_2 satisfying the following property:

$$|S_f| \approx |S_C| \qquad (14)$$

The latter result is valid for both presented templates and is approximately equal to the value of $|S_C|$ in the case of $m = 4$. However, since our goal is to balance out the cardinalities $|S_C|$ and $|S_f|$ in case of larger matrices we choose the following structure of public matrices Z_1 and Z_2:

$$Z_1 = \begin{pmatrix} T_{i_1}^{(j_1)} & & & 0 \\ & T_{i_2}^{(j_2)} & & \\ & & \ddots & \\ 0 & & & T_{i_l}^{(j_l)} \end{pmatrix}, Z_2 = \begin{pmatrix} T_{i_1}^{(3-j_1)} & & & 0 \\ & T_{i_2}^{(3-j_2)} & & \\ & & \ddots & \\ 0 & & & T_{i_l}^{(3-j_l)} \end{pmatrix}, \qquad (15)$$

i.e. the pair of block matrices $\left\{ T_{i_l}^{(j_l)}, T_{i_l}^{(3-j_l)} \right\} = T_{i_l}$, l is the number of blocks, i_l denotes the index of a template and $j_l \in \{1, 2\}$.

The estimation of the lower bound of $|S_C|$ comes from the fact, that we can consider the block diagonal structure of private matrix X, i.e.

$$X = \begin{pmatrix} X_1 & 0 \\ 0 & X_2 \end{pmatrix},$$

where X_1 and X_2 are solutions of two independent conjugation systems. Since these solutions are independent, we can obtain the required estimation in the following way:

$$|S_C| \geq |(S_C)_1| \cdot |(S_C)_2|,$$

where $|(S_C)_1|$ and $|(S_C)_2|$ are cardinalities of solution sets of the corresponding conjugation systems.

Our evaluation of cardinality $|S_f|$ relies on the search of basis of linear span (6).

Empirically we found, that the best possible value of cardinality $|S_f|$ relies on the choice of templates and the choice of eigenvalues. More precisely, to achieve the best possible value of $|S_f|$ we have to choose eigenvalues in matrices Z_1 and Z_2 to be as distinct as possible, while also mixing template matrices in the block structure (15).

Hence, in general, for a combination of templates $T_{i_1}, T_{i_2}, \ldots, T_{i_l}$ we have the following lower estimates:

$$|S_C| \geq \prod_j \left|(S_C)_{i_j}\right|, \quad |S_f| \geq p^{\sum_j \alpha_j - 1} - 1,$$

where i_j indicates the template, α_j defines the value of cardinality $\left|(S_f)_{i_j}\right| = p^{\alpha_j} - 1$.

Based on the results of this section we suggest the following algorithm to generate public matrices Z_1 and Z_2 in a general case:

1. Select l templates from a preset list and randomly distribute template Jordan blocks between matrices $\widetilde{Z}_1$ and $\widetilde{Z}_2$;
2. Relying on the obtained estimation of lower bounds of both cardinalities find a secure value of p;
3. Generate an invertible matrix H and set $Z_1 = H\widetilde{Z}_1 H^{-1}$ and $Z_2 = H\widetilde{Z}_2 H^{-1}$ thus hiding the block structure of matrices $\widetilde{Z}_1$ and $\widetilde{Z}_2$.

Alice and Bob can now execute the MPAC protocol as presented in [10]. Note, that the conjugation subsystem (7) can be rewritten as follows:

$$\begin{cases} XH\widetilde{Z}_1 H^{-1} X^{-1} = A_1 \\ XH\widetilde{Z}_2 H^{-1} X^{-1} = A_2 \end{cases}.$$

We can see from the latter system of equations, that the block structure (15) defines cardinalities $|S_C|$ and $|S_f|$, since we can set $\widetilde{X} = XH$ and $\widetilde{X}^{-1} = H^{-1}X^{-1}$ to obtain system (7).

To demonstrate efficiency of our protocol we compared it with RSA asymmetric encryption by considering execution time of 3 major steps of both protocols, i.e. key generation, encryption and decryption. Our comparison is based on the key length of both protocols, i.e. secret exponent of RSA protocol and a pair of matrices (X, U) both consist of roughly the same amount of bits. RSA protocol was executed using imported javax.crypto package class cypher. Description of Java cryptography library functions is available online (see [14]). For MPAC execution we fixed the public parameters: MPAC-2048 ($p = 7$, $m = 12$), MPAC-4096 ($p = 11$, $m = 14$).

Experiments were performed using Matlab R2016b on a computer with the following system parameters:

- Processor: Intel Core i7-8750H 2.20 GHz;
- Memory (RAM): 8.00 GB;
- 64-bit Operating System.

The comparison results are presented in Table 3.

Table 3. The comparison of RSA and MPAC execution time (s) based on private key lengths.

	RSA-2048	RSA-4096	MPAC-2048	MPAC-4096
Key Generation	3.2896	40.3034	0.1584	0.225
Encryption	0.0338	0.236	0.2604	0.4414
Decryption	0.0016	0.0028	0.1432	0.2588
Full protocol time	3.325	40.5422	0.562	0.9252

We can see from the presented results, that even though RSA algorithm has an advantage over MPAC at encryption and decryption steps, the execution time of key generation procedure is the main advantage of MPAC protocol whereas the other steps are performed in a reasonable time. Hence we claim, that MPAC protocol is more efficient as compared with RSA asymmetric encryption.

5 Conclusions

The resistance of the improved version of MPAC protocol to linear algebra attack relies on the fact, that the private matrix U cannot be eliminated from the system (5) and hence the critical point C2 is not valid. However, the complexity of basis search problem is currently unknown to us. We believe that this problem is hard due to the fact, that the amount of functions $f(Z_1, Z_2)$ is far greater than the amount explored in this paper.

Based on the experimental results we found out, that in order to avoid exhaustive key search we have to find a balance between two cardinalities $|S_C|$ and $|S_f|$, which is achievable by using templates for the block structure of matrices Z_1 and Z_2. We also presented the general algorithm for choosing these public matrices while also hiding this structure from the plain sight of adversaries.

Appendix

See Table 4.

Table 4. Comparison of Jordan block templates

Template		$\log_p |S_C|$	$\log_p |S_f|$
$T_1^{(1)} = \begin{pmatrix} t_1 & 0 & 0 & 0 \\ 0 & t_1 & 0 & 0 \\ 0 & 0 & t_2 & 0 \\ 0 & 0 & 0 & t_1 \end{pmatrix}$	$T_1^{(2)} = \begin{pmatrix} t_3 & 0 & 0 & 0 \\ 0 & t_3 & 1 & 0 \\ 0 & 0 & t_3 & 0 \\ 0 & 0 & 0 & t_3 \end{pmatrix}$	8	3
$T_2^{(1)} = \begin{pmatrix} t_1 & 1 & 0 & 0 \\ 0 & t_1 & 0 & 0 \\ 0 & 0 & t_1 & 1 \\ 0 & 0 & 0 & t_1 \end{pmatrix}$	$T_2^{(2)} = \begin{pmatrix} t_2 & 0 & 0 & 0 \\ 0 & t_2 & 0 & 0 \\ 0 & 0 & t_2 & 0 \\ 0 & 0 & 0 & t_3 \end{pmatrix}$	4	4
$T_3^{(1)} = \begin{pmatrix} t_1 & 1 & 0 & 0 \\ 0 & t_1 & 1 & 0 \\ 0 & 0 & t_1 & 0 \\ 0 & 0 & 0 & t_1 \end{pmatrix}$	$T_3^{(2)} = \begin{pmatrix} t_2 & 0 & 0 & 0 \\ 0 & t_3 & 0 & 0 \\ 0 & 0 & t_2 & 0 \\ 0 & 0 & 0 & t_2 \end{pmatrix}$	5	5

(*continued*)

Table 4. (*continued*)

Template	$\log_p \lvert S_C \rvert$	$\log_p \lvert S_f \rvert$
$T_4^{(1)} = \begin{pmatrix} t_1 & 1 & 0 & 0 \\ 0 & t_1 & 1 & 0 \\ 0 & 0 & t_1 & 0 \\ 0 & 0 & 0 & t_1 \end{pmatrix}, T_4^{(2)} = \begin{pmatrix} t_2 & 1 & 0 & 0 \\ 0 & t_2 & 0 & 0 \\ 0 & 0 & t_2 & 0 \\ 0 & 0 & 0 & t_2 \end{pmatrix}$	5	5
$T_5^{(1)} = \begin{pmatrix} t_1 & 1 & 0 & 0 \\ 0 & t_1 & 1 & 0 \\ 0 & 0 & t_1 & 1 \\ 0 & 0 & 0 & t_1 \end{pmatrix}, T_5^{(2)} = \begin{pmatrix} t_2 & 1 & 0 & 0 \\ 0 & t_2 & 0 & 0 \\ 0 & 0 & t_2 & 1 \\ 0 & 0 & 0 & t_2 \end{pmatrix}$	3	6
$T_6^{(1)} = \begin{pmatrix} t_1 & 1 & 0 & 0 \\ 0 & t_1 & 1 & 0 \\ 0 & 0 & t_1 & 0 \\ 0 & 0 & 0 & t_1 \end{pmatrix}, T_6^{(2)} = \begin{pmatrix} t_2 & 1 & 0 & 0 \\ 0 & t_2 & 0 & 0 \\ 0 & 0 & t_2 & 0 \\ 0 & 0 & 0 & t_3 \end{pmatrix}$	3	7
$T_7^{(1)} = \begin{pmatrix} t_1 & 1 & 0 & 0 \\ 0 & t_1 & 1 & 0 \\ 0 & 0 & t_1 & 1 \\ 0 & 0 & 0 & t_1 \end{pmatrix}, T_7^{(2)} = \begin{pmatrix} t_2 & 1 & 0 & 0 \\ 0 & t_2 & 1 & 0 \\ 0 & 0 & t_2 & 0 \\ 0 & 0 & 0 & t_2 \end{pmatrix}$	2	7
$T_8^{(1)} = \begin{pmatrix} t_1 & 0 & 0 & 0 \\ 0 & t_1 & 1 & 0 \\ 0 & 0 & t_1 & 1 \\ 0 & 0 & 0 & t_1 \end{pmatrix}, T_8^{(2)} = \begin{pmatrix} t_2 & 1 & 0 & 0 \\ 0 & t_2 & 0 & 0 \\ 0 & 0 & t_2 & 0 \\ 0 & 0 & 0 & t_3 \end{pmatrix}$	1	8

References

1. Diffie, W., Hellman, M.: New directions in cryptography. IEEE Trans. Inf. Theory **22**(6), 644–654 (1976)
2. Wagner, N.R., Magyarik, M.R.: A Public-key cryptosystem based on the word problem. In: Blakley, G.R., Chaum, D. (eds.) Advances in Cryptology, CRYPTO 1984. Lecture Notes in Computer Science, vol. 196, pp. 19–36. Springer, Berlin (1985)
3. Ko, K.H., Lee, S.J., Cheon, J.H., Han, J.W., Kang, J., Park, C.: New public-key cryptosystem using braid groups. In: Bellare, M. (ed.) Advances in Cryptology — CRYPTO 2000, CRYPTO 2000. Lecture Notes in Computer Science, vol. 1880, pp. 166–183. Springer, Berlin (2000)
4. Anshel, I., Anshel, M., Goldfeld, D.: An algebraic method for public-key cryptography. Math. Res. Lett. **6**, 287–292 (1999)
5. Shpilrain, V., Ushakov, A.: The conjugacy search problem in public key cryptography: unnecessary and insufficient. Appl. Algebra Eng. Commun. Comput. **17**(3–4), 285–289 (2006)
6. Sakalauskas, E., Luksys, K.: Matrix power function and its application to block cipher S-box construction. Int. J. Innovative Comput. Inf. Control **8**(4), 2655–2664 (2012)
7. Sakalauskas, E., Listopadskis, N., Tvarijonas, P.: Key agreement protocol (KAP) based on matrix power function. In: Sixth International Conference on Information Research and Applications – i.Tech 2008, Varna, Bulgaria (2008)

8. Mihalkovič, A., Sakalauskas, E.: Asymmetric cipher based on MPF and its security parameters evaluation. In: Proceedings of the Lithuanian Mathematical Society, Series A, vol. 53, pp. 72–77 (2012)
9. Sakalauskas, E., Mihalkovich, A.: Candidate one-way function based on matrix power function with conjugation constraints. In: Proceedings of the Bulgarian Cryptography Days, pp. 29–37 (2012)
10. Sakalauskas, E., Mihalkovich, A.: New asymmetric cipher of non-commuting cryptography class based on matrix power function. Informatica 25(2), 283–298 (2014)
11. Liu, J., Zhang, H., Jia, J.: A linear algebra attack on the non-commuting cryptography class based on matrix power function. In: Chen, K., Lin, D., Yung, M. (eds.) Information Security and Cryptology, Inscrypt 2016. Lecture Notes in Computer Science, vol. 10143, pp. 343–354. Springer, Cham (2017)
12. Gantmakher, F.R.: The theory of matrices, vol. 131. American Mathematical Soc. (2000)
13. Sakalauskas, E., Mihalkovich, A.: Improved asymmetric cipher based on matrix power function resistant to linear algebra attack. Informatica 28(3), 517–524 (2017)
14. Jenkov.com Tech and Media Labs. http://tutorials.jenkov.com/java-cryptography/index.html

Using r-indiscernibility Relations to Hide the Presence of Information for the Least Significant Bit Steganography Technique

Piotr Artiemjew[(✉)] and Aleksandra Kislak-Malinowska

Faculty of Mathematics and Computer Science,
University of Warmia and Mazury in Olsztyn, Olsztyn, Poland
artem@matman.uwm.edu.pl, akis@uwm.edu.pl

Abstract. The paper presents some preliminary results concerning modification of the least significant bit steganography method. Using r - indiscernibility relations one can embed some information in the container in a semi-random way, whereas it can be reconstructed in a deterministic way. The combination of bits of RGB Bytes allows the bits of information to be hidden by means of a fixed mask. Each Byte of a pixel that contains a fixed combination of bits indiscernible in the fixed ratio with the mask may store the bit of information in the least significant bit. The bits indiscernible in other ratios form random gaps that leads to hiding the presence of information. In the paper we have implemented some steganography systems to test our approach by hiding the image in a cover picture.

Keywords: Steganography · Least significant bit ·
Indiscernibility relation · Rough sets

1 Introduction

The motivation to conduct this research was the assumption concerning potential application of partial indiscernibility in hiding the information presence. The obvious application seems to be in steganography systems. For our preliminary study the least significant bit technique and partial indiscernibility have been chosen for implementation. It has turned out that taking into consideration the combination of bits - using fixed mask - we can hide the information in a semi-random way. It is because there is a set of combinations that are indiscernible in the same fixed ratio r with the mask. r-indiscernible combinations point the Bytes that are containers to hide the bits information in the least significant bits. The Bytes that are indiscernible in other ratio are omitted during the information embedding. Intuitively, this technique hinders any statistical analysis of data with hidden messages. r-indiscernibility ratio is defined in terms of rough set theory. The rough set theory, founded by Pawlak in 1982 [11], is one of the most significant data mining theories to deals with data as information and

© Springer Nature Switzerland AG 2019
R. Damaševičius and G. Vasiljevienė (Eds.): ICIST 2019, CCIS 1078, pp. 209–220, 2019.
https://doi.org/10.1007/978-3-030-30275-7_17

decision systems. The information system is the set of objects described in some considered context. The decision system is the set of resolved problems described in a unified way. Rough sets theory provides a lot of useful tools. An important paradigm of rough set theory is a granular rough computing that is the recent paradigm in which one deals with granules - the groups of objects connected together by some form of similarity. This kind of computations was proposed by Zadeh [20]. In the paper some modified r-indiscernible relations were used - the special case of rough inclusions which are the internal part of granulation process proposed by Polkowski [12–15]. The paper is constructed as follows. In Sect. 2 there is an introduction to r indiscernibility relations. In Sect. 3 a short introduction to Cryptology by prism of steganography. In Sect. 4 the least significant bit technique is presented. Our method based on r indiscernibility relations is described in Sect. 5. Section 6 is an experimental part followed by Sect. 7 with conclusions.

2 r-indiscernibility Relations - Theoretical Background

Theoretical background of rough inclusions can be found in Polkowski [12–15], a detailed discussion may be found in Polkowski [16].

For given decision system (U, A, d), where U is the set of objects, A the set of conditional attributes, and d the decision attribute. Considering objects $u, v \in U$ - the standard rough inclusion μ is defined as

$$\mu(v, u, r) \Leftrightarrow \frac{|IND(u, v)|}{|A|} \geq r \tag{1}$$

r-indiscernible mask is defined as:

$$if\ \mu(v, u, r) \Leftrightarrow \frac{|IND(u, v)|}{|A|} = r,\ hide\ message\ bit\ in\ LSB, \tag{2}$$

$$if\ \mu(v, u, r) \Leftrightarrow \frac{|IND(u, v)|}{|A|} \neq r\ skip\ the\ Byte, \tag{3}$$

$$IND(u, v) = \{a \in A : a(u) = a(v)\}, \tag{4}$$

The parameter r is the *granulation radius* from the set $\{0, \frac{1}{|A|}, \frac{2}{|A|}, ..., 1\}$.

In the next section we have short introduction to the parent domain of steganography.

3   Cryptology Through the Prism of Steganography

Cryptology is the parent domain for cryptography and cryptanalysis, where the cryptography contains a subfield - called steganography. In the classical cryptography the information should be encrypted but their presence is not necessarily hidden. In steganography we usually hide information inside another information, where the presence of information should be hidden and the information is not necessary encrypted.

3.1   From Historical Use of Steganography to Modern Digital Techniques

Steganography is really an old field, discovered thousands of years ago. Let us describe their selected historical usage. 5000 years ago in ancient Egypt and China people had used sympathetic ink: (milk plus lemon) (milk, vinegar, fruit juices), the trace of which was seen on paper only after heating or treating with a special chemical reagent. In Ancient times in order to send the hidden message the wooden plates with an engraved message covered with dark wax were used. In Greece V at. p. during the Greco-Persian War - the information was sent on the tattooed head of a slave. In the Middle Ages The Cardano Grille method was discovered - some sheet of material were used with accidentally cut rectangles when the card is placed on a sheet of paper, the message is placed by writing one of several letters of the message in these rectangles. Then it takes off and the sender fills the remaining space with letters or words to create a message to send. During the Franco-Prussian War in 1871 the Micro-dots, Micro-points Technique were used - sending photographs of the size of dots, having the transparency of machine-printing). There are only few exemplary techniques.

In modern steganography one of the most popular techniques are digital techniques - where the data are embedded in digital covers - the pictures, the music files, etc. The full tree of the most popular techniques can be found in Fig. 1. In the paper we use digital - picture - cover to hide the information. The reader can find general workflow of steganographic system in Fig. 2.

3.2   Fundamental Rules of Steganography

Steganographic system is broken when:
The attacker will notice the use of steganography,
Read the embedded message.

The steganographic system is safe when:
The container is not significantly modified so that the human eye will not notice changes,
Embedded data is resistant to damage, compression, reformatting, sampling,
Hidden information can be extracted, even if the container is damaged.

3.3   A Few Words About Stegoanalisys

There are plenty of techniques to try to find the presence of hidden messages in data [5,7,8] the selected ones are below:

- stego-only attack: Steganographic media are the only things available for analysis,

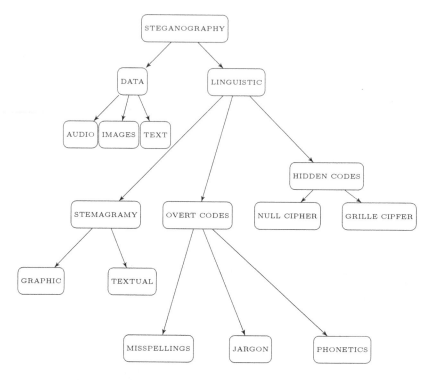

Fig. 1. Steganography techniques tree

- Known-cover attack: Container and media are available for analysis,
- Known-message attack: The hidden message is recognized,
- Chosen-steganography attack: The medium and the steganographic algorithm are recognized,
- Chosen-message attack: A message is known. A steganographic medium is created for analysis and comparison,
- Known-steganography attack - Container and steganographic carrier and algorithm are known,
- Statistical analysis: Detecting steganography in audio and graphics involves looking for data deviations from the accepted standards. A small deviation can show the information content,
- Structural analysis: File structure study. It consists among others of comparing the size of files, searching the file for content incompatible with features typical for its type, checking the checksum,
- Signature analysis: File test for the presence of standards. The advantage: we do not require a comparative material, it allows to identify the software used to hide the message. The disadvantage: we must have a database of patterns and often it should be active. It is enough to modify the footprint and the signature database will be ineffective. In our work we have performed Chi-square attack on our system to check the safety of the information hidden-the result can be found in Fig. 7.

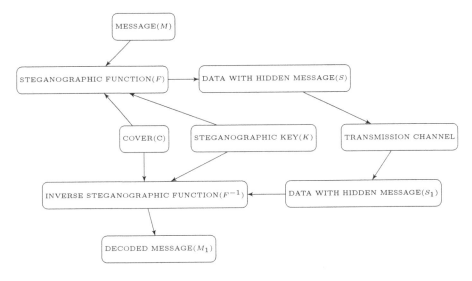

Fig. 2. Communication process - steganographic system

3.4   Steganography in Digital, Picture Cover

Digital steganography uses natural limitations of human perception. Considering the human eye vision limitations we can modify the shades of colors obtaining the same appearance of the pictures for a human eye (Fig. 3).

3.5   Features of the Human Eye and Its Limitations

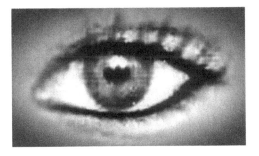

Fig. 3. Picture prepared using [21] (Color figure online)

- distinguishes between 5–10 thousand shades of a still image
- 250 degrees of gray, 64 shades of gray
- stamens recognize black and white contours of the image
- suppositories, which are 20 times less recognizable by color images, black and white image is received with a higher frequency
- suppositories respond better to yellow-green than blue-green.
- around the pupil of the eye we have the largest density of suppositories $(166000/\text{mm}^2)$
- The human eye is able to distinguish two points at a distance of 50 s.
- RGB Eye sensitivity 3: 1: 5

Considering the limitations we can change three bits in R Byte, one in G and five in B. In this way, in one of 24 bits pixel we can encode the whole byte of the secret information.

3.6 Digital Picture Representation

A computer image is a rectangular array of numbers that represent the illumination of light in different pixels. A typical image can consist of 256 colors and contain 8 bits per pixel. Images with 24-bits per pixel can also be used to hide data, there is more space to hide data.

There are plenty techniques exploiting these limitation - the basic one is inserting the least significant bit (LSB) [4,9]. Additionally one can use algorithms and transformations to hide the presence of information. The message saves to (LSB) changing the last bit of the binary pixel representation, the color changes in a way unnoticeable to the human eye.

Images in the black and white palette (GRAY-SCALE). Black and white graphics contain about 256 shades of gray, the human eye distinguishes about 64, changing the least significant bit we can encode the message unnoticeable to the eye. Sample change $01101011 \Rightarrow 01101010$.

Images in the color palette (256 colors) (24bits True Color). A typical image of 640×480 pixels while presenting each pixel with 256 colors can be saved in 8 bits (this image is up to 300 KB). In True Color mode the image of one pixel is represented in a 24-bit form. In the 24-bit image each pixel is described by means of 3 Bytes. These bytes may be in hexadecimal, decimal or binary form. White color is presented as Hexadecimal $FFFFFF_{HEX}$, Decimal $(255, 255, 255)_{DEC}$, Binary $(11111111, 11111111, 11111111)_{BIN}$. 24 bit files have a large size and there is a big field for coding information.

In the next section we describe one of the most popular technique based on limitations described.

4   Introduction to the Least Significant Bit Steganography Technique

The least significant steganography is the technique exploiting shortcomings of human vision where a massive set of information changing hue of red green or blue part of RGB pixel can be hidden. Here the red green and blue pixels are in a form of bits triples. For example, one can encode 750 characters in a 100×200 pixel image. How to hide A letter in a 24 bit image? Let us assume that our original bits are as follows:

$$00100110 \ 01011011 \ 10101110 \ 11101111$$

$$01010100 \ 01111010 \ 10011001 \ 00010111$$

The binary form of the letter A is **01000001**, we change the last bits of our eight bytes to hide the letter.

$$00100110 \ 01011011 \ 10101110 \ 11101110$$

$$01010100 \ 01111010 \ 10011000 \ 00010111$$

Note that we have only changed two bits of the image. The LSB can be detected by examining characteristic statistical color distributions. The solution to this problem is a steganographic key describing the positions of the modified pixels according to which the statistics will not be so clearly changed. The steganography key in our work is the usage of r indiscernibility relations. Let us introduce the way we make use this tool.

5 r Indiscernibility Relation Mask for the Least Significant Bit Method

In this section we present our modification of the least significant bit technique. For the given set of RGB pixels, $p_1, p_2, ..., p_k$, where each pixel is defined as:

$$p_i = (p_i^{red} \ p_i^{green} \ p_i^{blue}) :$$
$$p_i^{red} = b_1^{p_i^{red}} \ b_2^{p_i^{red}}, b_3^{p_i^{red}}, b_4^{p_i^{red}}, b_5^{p_i^{red}}, b_6^{p_i^{red}}, b_7^{p_i^{red}}, b_8^{p_i^{red}}$$
$$p_i^{green} = b_1^{p_i^{green}} \ b_2^{p_i^{green}}, b_3^{p_i^{green}}, b_4^{p_i^{green}}, b_5^{p_i^{green}}, b_6^{p_i^{green}}, b_7^{p_i^{green}}, b_8^{p_i^{green}}$$
$$p_i^{blue} = b_1^{p_i^{blue}} \ b_2^{p_i^{blue}}, b_3^{p_i^{blue}}, b_4^{p_i^{blue}}, b_5^{p_i^{blue}}, b_6^{p_i^{blue}}, b_7^{p_i^{blue}}, b_8^{p_i^{blue}}$$

A bit of the message can be hidden in the Byte (p_i^{color}) of pixel p_i if for fixed mask as a combination: $mask = (mask_1, mask_2, ..., mask_k)$, $k < 8$, the following condition is fulfilled:

$$\frac{IND(p_i^{color}, mask)}{card\{mask\}} = r \quad (5)$$

$$IND(p_i^{color}, mask) = \{bits \in Byte : bit(p_i^{color}) = bit(mask)\} \qquad (6)$$

with the assumption that bits of Bytes and mask bits are compared in the same positions in Byte.

Using such methodology we obtain a random set of masks that allow us for embedding the bits of message. The possibility of message embedding based on fixed mask can be checked before it is applied.

6   Experimental Session

We have implemented our method in C++ with use of Platform Independent Bitmap Image Reader Writer Library - bitmap_image.hpp - see [10]. In container from Fig. 4 we have 2592×4608 pixels, there are available 2592∗4608∗3 35831808 the least significant bits. The information to hide from Fig. 5 contain 451 × 500 pixels thus we have to hide 5412048 bits. Using exemplary mask = 11 or mask = 00 as two penultimate bits, and indiscernibility ratio equal 0.5 we have obtained 5902737 empty slots. Using the mask there are 2672541 changes in the container - the data are hidden indirectly by r indiscernibility mask. The mask never changes any Bytes of the container. Using masks 10 or 01 we have obtained 4953445 indiscernibility dependent gaps with 2678792 changes in the container.

One can ask how the size of hidden image is stored in the container. In our exemplary implementation the dimensions are hidden in a fixed pair of pixels of a cover picture. The pixels are in 24bits RGB format thus numbering Bytes of the pixels as $B_1, B_2, ..., B_6$ the size of a hidden image can be computed as

$$height = bin\_to\_dec(B_1) * bin\_to\_dec(B_2) + bin\_to\_dec(B_3) \qquad (7)$$

$$width = bin\_to\_dec(B_4) * bin\_to\_dec(B_5) + bin\_to\_dec(B_6) \qquad (8)$$

Fig. 4. Container

Fig. 5. Picture to hide - source [1]

Fig. 6. Container with hidden data - as we expected there is no visible difference with Fig. 4 - the human eye cannot detect it

Even if the size is readable there is a great difficulty to find which Bytes contain the hidden pictures because of indiscernibility mask application (Fig. 6). The size of the picture can be also hidden using indiscernibility mask. The only information to start the message recovery is to apply the proper indiscernibility mask. We have performed Chi-square attack test [18] - see Fig. 7 - using the tool [3] - to check if the embedded message disturbed statistics of cover image. The result confirms our assumption concerning difficulty of detecting the hidden information presence (Fig. 8).

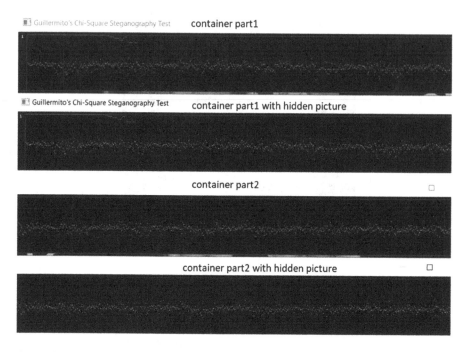

Fig. 7. Chi-Square attack on hidden data - there is no visible difference between tests, the presence of message is hidden

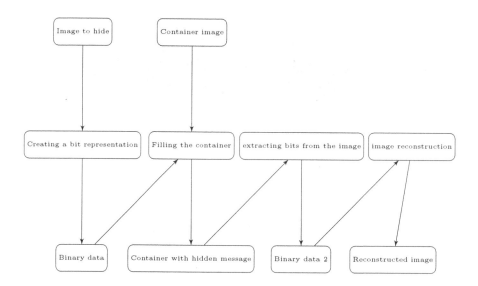

Fig. 8. Hiding picture inside the other one - our system design

7 Conclusions

In the paper we have presented the application of r indiscernibility relation as a steganography key for the least significant bit technique. According to our assumptions using the indiscernibility mask allows to hide the bits of information in a semi-random way that hides its presence. A number of experiments have been carried out to show how to apply the method proposed. In our example the information has been successfully embedded with the use of pairs of bit that are indiscernible in ratio 0.5. In the data a large number of random gaps appears because the r indiscernible bits in Bytes show non-deterministic character. In case of longer combinations the randomization of message bits position is expected to be higher. In future work we would like to optimize our technique and use the smallest possible number of bits to hide the message in a non-deterministic way. Another possible extension is the application of longer masks to check randomization levels. And finally it may be interesting to check different kinds of digital covers.

Acknowledgements. The research has been supported by grant 23.610.007-300 from Ministry of Science and Higher Education of the Republic of Poland.

References

1. Artiemjew, L.: "Lost in time" - wooden bas-relief from the collection of Lech Artiemjew artistic activity. https://www.facebook.com/lech.artiemjew
2. Baluja, S.: Hiding images within images. IEEE Trans. Pattern Anal. Mach. Intell. (2019)
3. Guillermito: BMP chi-square attack v0.1
4. Morkel, T., Eloff, J.H., Olivier, M.S.: An overview of image steganography. In: ISSA, pp. 1–11 (2005)
5. Krenn, R.: Steganography and steganalysis. http://www.krenn.nl/univ/cry/steg/article.pdf
6. Johnson, N.F., Jajodia, S.: Exploring steganography: seeing the unseen. Computer **31**(2), 26–34 (1998)
7. Wang, H., Wang, S.: Cyber warfare: steganography vs. steganalysis. Commun. ACM **47**(10), 76–82 (2004)
8. Silman, J.: Steganography and steganalysis: an overview, Sans Institute. https://www.researchgate.net/publication/242743284_Steganography_and_Steganalysis_An_Overview
9. Neeta, D., Snehal, K., Jacobs, D.: Implementation of LSB steganography and its evaluation for various bits. In: 1st International Conference on Digital Information Management, Portugal, pp. 173–178, 19–21 September 2006
10. Partow, A.: C++ Bitmap Library. http://partow.net/programming/bitmap/index.html
11. Pawlak, Z.: Rough sets. Int. J. Comput. Inf. Sci. **11**, 341–356 (1982)
12. Polkowski, L.: Rough Sets: Mathematical Foundations. Physica Verlag, Heidelberg (2002)

13. Polkowski, L.: Formal granular calculi based on rough inclusions. In: Proceedings of IEEE 2005 Conference on Granular Computing, GrC 2005, Beijing, China, pp. 57–62. IEEE Press (2005)
14. Polkowski, L.: Granulation of knowledge in decision systems: the approach based on rough inclusions. The method and its applications. In: Kryszkiewicz, M., Peters, J.F., Rybinski, H., Skowron, A. (eds.) RSEISP 2007. LNCS (LNAI), vol. 4585, pp. 69–79. Springer, Heidelberg (2007). https://doi.org/10.1007/978-3-540-73451-2_9
15. Polkowski, L.: A unified approach to granulation of knowledge and granular computing based on rough mereology: a survey. In: Pedrycz, W., Skowron, A., Kreinovich, V. (eds.) Handbook of Granular Computing, pp. 375–400. Wiley, Chichester (2008)
16. Polkowski, L.: Approximate Reasoning by Parts: An Introduction to Rough Mereology. Intelligent Systems Reference Library. Springer, Heidelberg (2011). https://doi.org/10.1007/978-3-642-22279-5
17. Polkowski, L., Artiemjew, P.: Granular Computing in Decision Approximation - An Application of Rough Mereology. ISRL. Springer, Cham (2015). https://doi.org/10.1007/978-3-319-12880-1
18. Westfeld, A., Pfitzmann, A.: Attacks on steganographic systems. In: Pfitzmann, A. (ed.) IH 1999. LNCS, vol. 1768, pp. 61–76. Springer, Heidelberg (2000). https://doi.org/10.1007/10719724_5
19. Wozniak, M., Polap, D.: Object detection and recognition via clustered features. Neurocomputing **320**, 76–84 (2018)
20. Zadeh, L.A.: Fuzzy sets and information granularity. In: Gupta, M., Ragade, R., Yager, R.R. (eds.) Advances in Fuzzy Set Theory and Applications, pp. 3–18. North-Holland, Amsterdam (1979)
21. BeFunky's all-in-one online Creative Platform - Photo Editing and Graphic Design Made for Everyone. https://www.befunky.com/

LRC-256, an Efficient and Secure LFSR Based Stream Cipher

Mohammadreza Ashouri$^{(\boxtimes)}$ (ID)

University of Potsdam, Potsdam, Germany
`ashouri@uni-potsdam.de`

Abstract. In this work we introduce LRC-256, a new hardware-based stream cipher that is designed based on an irregular clock-controlled combination generator with a unique mechanism of altering steps. Our proposed algorithm uses a 256-bit main key and a 32-bit message key. The most important measures we consider in designing LRC-256 are maximum period, high linear complexity, resistance to standard attacks, and secure statistical properties. The base component of our algorithm is a clock-controlled combination generator with a 1-bit memory.

In order to demonstrate the usefulness and performance of our proposed stream cipher, we implemented LRC-256 on a standard FPGA simulator, and we compared it with 12 standard and well-known stream and block ciphers, such as RC4, RC6, AES, 3DES, W7, Snow 2.0 LILI-II, and Helix. The result of our comparison proves that LRC-256 has higher efficiency and better security. Hence, LRC-256 is a proper option for resource-constrained devices where efficiency and safety are the most important metrics.

Keywords: Stream cipher · LFSR · Correlation immunity · Nonlinearity · Linear complexity · Computational security · Resilient function

1 Introduction

Stream ciphers are one of the most important form of symmetric encryption algorithms. Symmetric ciphers can be either block ciphers or stream ciphers. Block ciphers combine chunks of plaintext bits with key bits to generate pieces of ciphertext of the same size, typically 64 or 128 bits. Stream ciphers, on the other hand, do not mix plaintext and key bits; alternately, they produce pseudorandom bits from the key and encrypt the plaintext by XORing it with the pseudorandom bits, in the same style as the one-time pad [28].

Stream ciphers are more similar to deterministic random bit generators (DRBGs) than they are to full-fledged pseudorandom number generators (PRNGs) because, like DRBGs, stream ciphers are deterministic. Stream ciphers' determinism enables users to decrypt by regenerating the pseudorandom bits used to encrypt. With a PRNG, we can encrypt but never decrypt (which is secure), but useless. What sets stream ciphers apart from DRBGs is that DRBGs

© Springer Nature Switzerland AG 2019
R. Damaševičius and G. Vasiljevienė (Eds.): ICIST 2019, CCIS 1078, pp. 221–242, 2019.
https://doi.org/10.1007/978-3-030-30275-7_18

take a single input value whereas stream ciphers take two values: a key and a nonce[1]. The key should be secret and is usually 128 or 256 bits. The nonce does not need to be secret, except it should be unique for each key and is generally between 64 and 128 bits.

Stream ciphers generate a pseudorandom stream of bits called **keystream**. The keystream is XORed to plaintext to encrypt it and then XORed again to the ciphertext to decrypt it.

Although the design of stream ciphers seems to be simple, producing a secure stream cipher in the real world condition is one of the long-standing challenges in cryptography. The low performance and security defects of previous algorithms have been discovered over time, and it has even caused a lot of losses in the computer network world [38] (e.g. RC4 vulnerability). Therefore, scientists are continually looking for safer and faster algorithms for different applications and devices.

In this work we introduce LRC-256, an efficient and secure hardware-based stream cipher. Using linear-feedback shift registers (LFSR) as the central element in our design, help us in constructing a highly reliable, hardware efficient and low-cost stream cipher which make LRC-256 attractive for embedded devices, such as mobile phones, video game consoles, digital cameras, DVD players, and GPS devices.

The key contributions in LRC-256 are as follows:

- **Low implementation cost.** In order to reduce the cost of implementation, we minimized the size of the internal memory in LRC-256. Therefore, we used LFSR in the cipher which offers several advantages, such as high performance and low implementation cost [37].
- **Maximum period and high linear complexity.** Having a long period in our random code generator proposes a high linear complexity for the cipher, which makes it resist to conventional cipher attacks, such as correlation, algebraic and time-memory trade-off (TMTO) attacks [22].
- **Proper statistical characteristics.** Bits generated by our keystream generator are very similar to truly random sequences that makes LRC-256 secure against divide and conquer attacks [47].
- **High algebraic degree and nonlinearity.** In our proposed algorithm we have a strong avalanche effect [34] (message key on the main key). Using the substitution-permutation boxes [23], and Boolean functions with appropriate cryptographic properties have increased the algebraic degree and nonlinearity of LRC-256 so that our cipher is secure against distinguishing [35] and AIDA/cube attacks [4].

2 Stream Ciphers

In a basic stream cipher encryption operation, where SC is the stream cipher algorithm, KS the keystream, P the plaintext, and C the ciphertext. A stream

---

[1] The name nonce is short for number used only nonce. In the context of stream ciphers, it is sometimes termed the IV, for initial value.

cipher computes $KS = SC(K, N)$, encrypts as $C = P \oplus KS$, and decrypts as $P = C \oplus KS$. The encryption and decryption functions are the same because both do the same thing–namely, XOR bits with the keystream [3].

Stream ciphers enable us to encrypt a message with key $K1$ and nonce $N1$ and then encrypt a different message with key $K1$ and nonce $N2$ that is different from $N1$, or with key $K2$, which is different from $K1$ and nonce $N1$. However, we should never again encrypt with $K1$ and $N1$, because we would then use twice the same keystream KS. We would then have a first ciphertext $C1 = P1 \oplus KS$ a second ciphertext $C2 = P2 \oplus KS$, and if we have $P1$, then we can determine $P2 = C1 \oplus C2 \oplus P1$.

From a high-level outlook, there are two models of stream ciphers, stateful and counter based:

– Stateful stream ciphers have a secret internal state that evolves throughout keystream generation. The cipher initializes the state from the key and the nonce and then calls an update function to update the state value and produce one or more keystream bits from the state. For example, the famous RC4 [21] is a stateful cipher.
– Counter-based stream ciphers produce pieces of keystream from a key, a nonce, and a counter value. Unlike stateful stream ciphers, such as Salsa20 [5], no secret state is memorized during keystream generation.

These two procedures describe the high-level architecture of stream ciphers. Regardless how the kernel algorithms work, the internals of stream ciphers fall into two classes of hardware and software oriented.

2.1 Hardware-Oriented Stream Ciphers

Hardware in this context means application specific integrated circuits (ASICs), programmable logic devices (PLDs), and field-programmable gate arrays (FPGAs). The implementation of hardware-oriented stream ciphers is an electronic circuit that implements the cryptographic algorithm at the bit level, and that cannot be used for anything else. In other words, the circuit is a dedicated hardware. However, the software implementations of cryptographic algorithms command microprocessors what instructions to execute in order to run the algorithm. These instructions operate on bytes or words and then call pieces of an electronic circuit that implement general-purpose operations such as addition and multiplication. Software deals with bytes or words of 32 or 64 bits, whereas hardware deals with bits.

The main reason why stream ciphers are commonly use hardware implementations is because hardware oriented stream ciphers are usually cheaper in comparison with block ciphers [26]. Also, hardware oriented stream ciphers use smaller memory and fewer logical gates in compare to block ciphers, and therefore occupied a smaller area on an integrated circuit, which reduced the fabrication costs.

2.2   Feedback Shift Registers

Many stream ciphers use FSRs due to the simplicity of using them [2]. An FSR is an array of bits provided with an update feedback function, which we denote as f. The FSR's state is stored in the array, or register, and each update of the FSR uses the feedback function to change the state's value and to generate one output bit. In practice, an FSR works like this: if R_0 is the initial value of the FSR, the next state, R_1, is defined as R_0 left-shifted by 1 bit, where the bit leaving the register is returned as output, and where the empty position is filled with $f(R_0)$. The same rule is repeated to compute the subsequent state values R_2, R_3, and so on. That is given R_t, the FSR's state at time t, the next state, R_{t+1}, is the following:

$$R_{i+1} = (R_t << 1) | f(R_t) \tag{1}$$

In this equation $|$ is the logical OR operator and $<<$ is the shift operator (similar to the C language).

2.3   Boolean Functions in Stream Ciphers

Boolean functions play an important role in designing stream ciphers. These functions are commonly used in stream ciphers in order to combine the output of LFSRs, and their output is a sequences of pseudorandom bits (after a transient state) [40].

Definition 1: The Boolean function of n variables f is a function of the set F_2^n (all binary vectors with the length of n, such as $x = (x_1, \cdots, x_n)$) to the field $F_2 = \{0, 1\}$. It should be noted that finding proper Boolean functions with n variables for cryptographic usages is very time-consuming, particularly for large n in exhaustive search (the number of Boolean functions with n variables is 2^{2n}).

Definition 2: f is a Boolean function with n variables, so the following form is called the algebraic normal form (ANF) of f,

$$f(x_1, \cdots, x_n) = a_0 \oplus \left(\bigoplus a_i x_i \right) \oplus \left(\bigoplus a_{ij} x_i x_j \right) \cdots \oplus a_{12 \ldots n} x_1 \cdots x_n \tag{2}$$

where the coefficients a_i belong to the set $F_2 = \{0, 1\}$.

3   Design Criteria

The classic methods for designing Boolean functions can be divided into two approaches:

– In the first approach, we do not consider the algebraic degree and assume that the number of variables and the correlation immunity order are fixed. Thus, we attempt to select the functions with the maximum nonlinearity.

– In the second approach, we consider the algebraic degree; however, due to Siegenthaler inequality [41], the maximum degree of the algebraic value of an m-resilient function (with n variables) is equal to $n - m - 1$. The functions that achieve this degree are optimal, so this approach looks for optimal functions with high nonlinearity.

In general, the necessary conditions for designing Boolean functions in stream ciphers are as follow:

1. Balanceness: The Boolean function f with n variable is called a balanced function if its Hamming weight was 2^{n-1}.
2. Nonlinearity: $nl(f)$, the nonlinearity of the Boolean function f is defined as the Hamming distance f of the set of all Affin functions with n variables (the function f is an Affin function if $deg(f) \leq 1$).
3. Algebraic Degree: The maximum degree of the algebraic normal form is called an algebraic degree (it is represented by $deg(f)$). The maximum algebraic degree of a balanced function with n variables is $n - 1$. The Boolean functions used in stream ciphers should have a high algebraic degree. Otherwise, the linear complexity of the system will be reduced and broken.
4. The boolean function with n variables $f(x_1, \cdots, x_n)$, is called the correlation-immune of order m, if for any choice $i_1, \cdots, i_m$ of set $1, \cdots, n$, and any choice $c_1 \in \{0, 1\}$, we have:

$$Prob(f = 1 | x_{i1} = c_1, \cdots, x_{im} = c_m) = Prob(f = 1) \qquad (3)$$

The balanced and correlation-immune functions of order m are called m-resilient. Concerning the aforementioned mentioned properties [8, 16, 27, 36, 40], we design the best possible Boolean functions in the LRC-256 (because they have a complex algebraic normal form with the maximum nonlinearity, the maximum algebraic degree, and at the same time, a proper hardware implementation).

Generally, the following 5 criteria must be addressed in designing Boolean functions [7]:

1. Bijection
2. Strict avalanche criterion (SAC)
3. Bit independence criterion (BIC)
4. Nonlinearity
5. Balance

These criteria will meet in most of the standards set provided by the National Institute of Standards and Technology (NIST)[2]. Nevertheless, it is impossible to achieve all the criteria to their full potential. Their conflicting nature forces us to compromise some of the criteria [10], for example, correlation immunity conflicts with high nonlinearity, and maximum nonlinearity conflicts with balance.

---

[2] https://www.nist.gov/.

The main criteria of a proper Boolean function (S-Box) are:

– It should have balanced component functions,
– The non-linearity of its component functions should be high,
– The non-zero linear combinations of its component functions should be balanced and highly non-linear,
– It should satisfy SAC (strict avalanche criterion),
– It should have a high algebraic degree.

Since it is impossible to achieve all the above objectives, we consider the following properties for designing ideal S-Box in LRC-256:

– All linear combinations of s-box columns are bent.
– The s-box satisfies MOSAC (Maximum order SAC).
– The s-box satisfies MOBIC (Maximum order BIC).
– The set of weights of rows has a binomial distribution with mean $m/2$.
– The set of weights of all pairs of rows has a binomial distribution with mean $m/2$.
– The columns each have Hamming weight 2^{n-1}.

4   Overview of LRC-256

The base structure of the LRC-256 algorithm is a clock-controlled combination generator with memory [30, 40]. Figure 1 shows a simple combination generator.

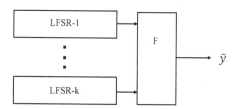

Fig. 1. Simple combination generator

So far, using this combination and the proper design of the F function and LFSRs, we obtain maximum period, high linear complexity, as well as the appropriate statistical properties [18, 24], but several attacks against this structure are applicable yet, such as algebraic and correlation attacks. In the following, we explain how we protect the structure of LRC-256 against the attacks:

4.1   Correlation Immunity

Combination generators are vulnerable to the various types of correlation attacks [24]. So, to make these attacks infeasible, the combining function F should have a high correlation-immunity order [14]. However, there exists a trade-off between the correlation-immunity order and the algebraic degree of a Boolean function. We can use memory to conquer this trade-off [41–43]. Using a bit of memory, correlation immunity is obtained, and we used this solution in the LRC-256 algorithm. Considering this property and the output F function is essential to keep secure the cipher against correlation attack. Figure 2 shows a combination generator with memory, where k is the number of inputs to the function f and m is the number of inputs to memory.

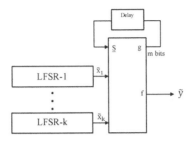

Fig. 2. Combination generator with memory

In Fig. 2, the function f generates the final output of the algorithm, using the $n = m + k$ input bits, and the vector function g makes the next m bits, using the same $m + k$ input bits. In a linear attack, ab adversary can find a linear combination of at most $m + 1$ consecutive output bits and a linear combination of maximum $m + 1$ input vector sequences for an m-bits memory combination generator that correlate with each other. These linear combinations are also referred to as Feed-forward linear transformations. The main part of the linear attack [42], which is one of the most advanced correlation attacks, is the LSCA[3] algorithm for finding these linear transformations that have a complexity of order $2k + m$. This algorithm is much faster than the exhaustive search in finding a linear relation. Although it does not have the optimal correlation coefficient, it obtains a good one. In general, k (the number of LFSRs) is small and we have to choose a large m. For example, if we want the complexity order is around 2^{128}, the number of memory bits should be 128.

Even though at first glance it may be practical, it should be noted that such functions are difficult to design, and the implementation of such a system, both in software and hardware is currently infeasible. In fact, we either need to save the truth tables with 128 variables (which requires 128×2^{128} bits of memory), or we need to implement the functions and their algebraic normal form, which requires 128×2^{128} algebraic normal form.

---

[3] Linear Sequential Circuit Approximation.

Considering the practical limitations, it is necessary to choose the value of m as small as possible and prevent the severe reduction of operational complexity of the linear attack with another trick which we describe it in the next section.

Another important point is how to design and select f and g functions. These functions should have proper characteristics [17] as follows:

1. The function f, the component functions of the vector function g, and also the linear combinations of these component functions should be balanced for any given fixed values of the input values $x_1, \cdots, x_k$.
2. The function f, the component functions of the vector function g, and the linear combinations of these component functions should be balanced for any given fixed values of memory variables $\underline{S}$.
3. The function f, the component functions of the vector function g, and the linear combinations of these component functions should have high non-linearity.

Finding the function f that has all above features, is relatively simple. For instance, if we consider a stronger condition that the function f is an $(n, 1, t)$-resilient function, in which $t = max(m, k)$, then conditions 1 and 2 are easily satisfied for the function f. So, it is enough to find functions among the $(n, 1, t)$-resilient functions that has a high non-linearity degree. To find these functions, Tarannikov's algorithm [29] can be used recursively to generate resilient functions with the maximum nonlinearity degree. However, it is more complicated regarding the function g. Thus, in this case we can ignore the mentioned strong and sufficient condition and fulfill the conditions 1, 2 and 3.

5   Implementation

Creating the initial vector in LRC-256 is one of the important challenges in the implementation phase. A functional stream cipher should be able to construct an infinite (computationally) pseudo-random sequence, using a finite-length random sequence. Since the main key is 256 bit (shorter than the initial state with 1600 bit), the main key must be extended by a fitting method to create the initial vector.

The second challenge is that we need a new key to encrypt each message in LRC-256. However, we cannot change the main key for each message. Therefore, we design a unique key generation component that produces the initial vector by combining the main key and a new key (we would call it message key). Hence, in order to implement this component we make a session key along with the message key and the main key. Next, we expand the generated session key to 1600 bit (the initial vector size). Figure 3 presents the process of generating the initial vector.

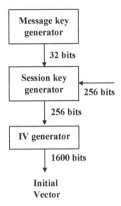

Fig. 3. Initial vector generation in LRC-256

5.1   Message Key Generator

In order to have proper random features in LRC-256, we should generate the message key in a way it does not repeat throughout a period of changing the main key. For instance, If we suppose to use LRC-256 for 24 h without interruption, and for every second we require a 32 bits message key, after 4.25 years, a full period of the message key will be generated. Hence, the **changeover period** of the main key will be up to 4.25 years. However, due to the common applications of stream ciphers, there is not security issue regarding repeating the session keys after this long period of time. We use an 32bit LFSR in order to generate the message key. The following primitive polynomial is the feedback function of the message key:

$$C(x) = x^{32} + x^{29} + x^{24} + x^{23} + x^{21} + x^{19} + x^{17} + x^{16} + x^{14} + x^{13} + x^{11} + x^9 + x^6 + x^3 + 1 \tag{4}$$

5.2   Session Key Generator

As we earlier mentioned, we need to design a proper **scramble function** in order to affect all bits of message keys. Our designed function must works based on a fixed main key, so that the changing of the bits of the message keys and the main key must be accomplished by the average probability of 50% (Avalanche effect).

Thus, we created our scramble function by helping of substitution-permutation network (SPN). So, whenever a 32-bit message key is entered into a permutation box (P-Box), a new 32-bit sequence will be produced. The resulting 32-bit sequence will be divided into 8 4-bit portions, and each portion will be entered into a substitution box (S-box 4 × 4). The outputs of these S-boxes are concatenated respectively and produce a 32-bit sequence. In order to produce sufficient diffusion on all output bits via input changes, this operation must be revolved at least 5 times. The function of the process is called Scram-5, which is shown in Figs. 4 and 5, respectively.

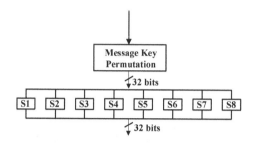

Fig. 4. Scram-5 function

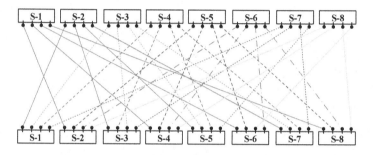

Fig. 5. Permutation box of the function Scram-5

Since in LRC-256 the size of main key size is 256 bits, we use our Scram-5 function for 8 times to produce a 256-bit sequence. Also, the session key is generated by **bit-wise XOR** operation on the sequence along with the main key. Figures 6 and 7 show the session key generator and the message key expansion, respectively.

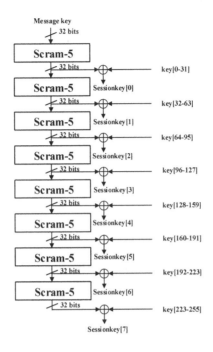

Fig. 6. Scram-5 in session key generator

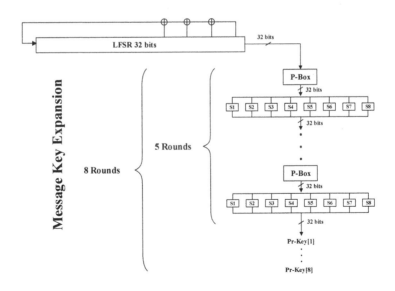

Fig. 7. Message key expansion

5.3   Initial Vector Generator

Because the size of the LFSRs used in our keystream generator is 1600 bits, LRC-256 generates a 1600-bit sequence for their initial state. As it is shown in Fig. 8, we use a 256-bit LFSR, a primitive polynomial (with the degree of 256), and 4 S-boxes to generate the state of initial vector.

The initial state of the LFSR is the session key (256-bit) that generates 8 bits at any clock. Four 64-bit (8×8) S-boxes are embedded in the feedback function of the LFSR, and one of them is selected and used for proper input-output diffusion.

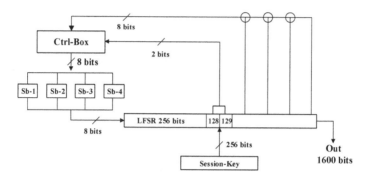

Fig. 8. Initial Vector Generator

We use the content of stage 128 and 129 in order to pick one of the S-boxes (e.g., the sequence 00 selects the first S-box, 01 selects the second S-box, 10 selects the third S-box, and 11 selects the fourth S-box). After generating 320 bits sequence (40 clocks), the diffusion will be achieved with 95% confidence. Hence, we discard the first 320 bits and take the next 1600 bits as the initial state of our keystream generator.

5.4   How to Initialize the Keystream Generator

In order to initialize 8 LFSRs used in the keystream generator, we divide the first 165 bits of the session key into 163 3-bit sets as follows:

$$\{1,2,3\},\{2,3,4\},\{3,4,5\},\cdots,\{163,164,165\}$$

Each set represents a decimal number from 0 to 7 and specifies one of the 8 LFSRs. For example, if the first set is 5, then the first bit of the initial vector should be placed in the first stage of the 6th LFSR. Similarly, 163 bits of the initial vector is replaced in 8 LFSRs. Then, the remaining **1437** bits of the initial vector is substituted in the empty stages of the LFSRs. We only use these routine for the first message key at the beginning of the communication. While the message key is being sent frequently for synchronization between the receiver and the transmitter, in the next message keys, the initial vector will be XORed to the content of each LFSR from 1 to 8.

5.5   Keystream Generator

Our keystream generator has 8 LFSRs with different sizes (239-bit, 163-bit, 223-bit, 181-bit, 199-bit, 173-bit, 193-bit, 229-bit) that are prime to each other. The LFSRs are clocked irregularly [14] so that one of the 64-bit S-boxes that was used in the initial vector generator will be selected. In order to select that S-box, we XOR the output bits of the 1st, 3rd, 5th and 7th LFSR, then we move the result to the left side. also, the output bits of the 2nd, 4th, 6th and 8th LFSR will be XORed and move to the right side. As a result, a 2-bit sequence will be obtained, a binary number between 0 and 3, that selects one of the S-boxes out of 4. The input of the selected S-box is in fact the output bits of the 8th LFSRs. The output of this S-box (8-bit) determines which LFSRs must be clocked in the next steps (the least significant bit of the S-box output, corresponds to 8th LFSR, and the most significant bit corresponds to the 1st LFSR). Next, via using **Majority Function**, LRC-256 determines which of these LFSRs must be clocked.

For Instance, if the output of the S-boxes is 10111001, the 1st, 3rd, 4th, 5th, and 8th LFSR will be clocked and generate a new bit, and those LFSRs with 0, retain their previous value. Please noted that since the number of the LFSRs is even, all of the LFSRs will be clocked in the case of equality (0000 and 1111). Figure 9 represents the general architecture of the keystream generator.

We consider the 8 bits of different stages of these LFSRs as the input for the 8 nonlinear Boolean functions with non-linearity number of 6 and correlation-immunity order of 2. Each of these functions has 9 input variables, and the value of the 9th variable of each of these is 1 bit out of 8 bits (S-box output). The least significant bit of the output goes to the function $F_{1,...}$, and the most significant

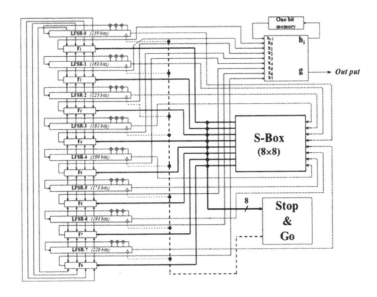

Fig. 9. The general architecture of the keystream generator in LRC-256

bit goes to the function F_8. The output of these 8 functions go to the 9th variable function g, which has the highest correlation immunity order.

Moreover, we use the output of the previous step of the nonlinear function h (which is used as the 9th variable of the function g). The output of the function g is the keystream, which we XOR it with the message bits (plain text). The feedback polynomials of the LFSRs have half size of their LFSR (in order to resist against fast correlation attacks).

6   Security Analysis of LRC-256

In LRC-256, each of the $2^n - 1$ non-zero initial states of the non-singular LFSRs (length n) produces an output sequence with maximum possible period $2^n - 1$ (note that the feedback functions of the LFSRs are primitive polynomials [11]). Hence, the lengths of all LFSRs are chosen from the prime numbers. Also, considering LRC-256 structure, its period is at least is 2^{1600}. Apparently, this large number of states makes LRC-256 secure against of the time-memory and trade-off attacks.

6.1   Correlation Immunity and Non-linearity of Boolean Functions

A non-linear function (without memory) and with n variables will have the correlation immunity of order m, if the mutual information between the output variable Z and any subset of m input variable is equal to 0.

$$I(Z; x_{i1}, \cdots, x_{im}) = 0 \ , \quad 0 \leq i_1 \leq i_2 < \cdots < i_m \leq n - 1 \tag{5}$$

There is always a trade-off between the non-linearity of the function f, i.e. k, with the correlation immunity order m. If n is the number of the input variables of the function f, then we have $k + m \leq n$. Note that this is necessary that the random output variable Z has a uniform distribution (which is essential in cryptography), so the trade-off will be:

$$k + m \leq n \text{ for } m = 0 \text{ or } m = n - 1$$

$$k + m \leq n - 1 \text{ for } 1 \leq m \leq n - 2$$

Via increasing the order of correlation immunity and the non-linearity order of the function f, the linear complexity of the generator will be decreased (and vice versa). Using a trick, one can get a function that has the maximum order of correlation immunity and maximum non-linearity order at the same time. In fact, this trade-off can be eliminated by using a single-bit memory in the input variables of the function. Moreover, there is no constraint on the non-linearity of the function f, so it can be selected freely. Hence, the output combiner of the LRC-256 - namely g and h functions are designed in this way. The algebraic form of these functions is as follows:

$$h_i = X_1 + X_2 + X_5 + X_5X_3 + X_6X_4 + X_7X_0 + X_7X_1 + X_7X_5 + X_8X_0 +$$
$$X_8X_2 + X_8X_7X_0 + X_8X_7X_1 + X_8X_7X_3X_2 + X_8X_7X_4X_2 + X_8X_7X_4X_3X_2 +$$

$X_8X_7X_5X_2$ + $X_8X_7X_5X_3X_2$ + $X_8X_7X_5X_4X_2$ + $X_8X_7X_5X_4X_3X_2+$
$X_8X_7X_6X_2 + X_8X_7X_6X_3X_2 + X_8X_7X_6X_4 + X_8X_7X_6X_4X_2+ X_8X_7X_6X_4X_3 +$
$X_8X_7X_6X_4X_3X_2$ + $X_8X_7X_6X_5$ + $X_8X_7X_6X_5X_2$ + $X_8X_7X_6X_5X_3+$
$X_8X_7X_6X_5X_3X_2 + X_8X_7X_6X_5X_4 + X_8X_7X_6X_5X_4X_2 + X_8X_7X_6X_5X_4X_3+$
$X_8X_7X_6X_5X_4X_3X_2$

$$g = X_0 + X_1 + X_2 + X_3 + X_4 + X_5 + X_6 + X_7 + h_{i-1} \qquad (6)$$

Please note that, in order to increase the speed of software implementation, the truth table of the above functions can be used in the form of lookup tables.

6.2   Correlation Immunity in LRC-256

Correlation attack is on the well-known and common attacks on stream ciphers, which attempts to discover the initial state of the cipher and hijacks the main key [22]. This attack can be carried out in two methods, namely statistical and analytical methods. In the statistical method, the correlation between the outputs of every LFSR with the final output will be determined.

Fortunately, based on to the results of our test in LRC-256, there is no statistical correlation between the output of the LFSRs and the final output of the our proposed algorithm. To prove the security of LRC-256 against of correlation attack, we first calculate the total number of possible keys for constructing the initial state. Hence, per each LFSR in our structure we compute the number of available feedback polynomials and the number of possible initial states. So, the number of feedback polynomials of degree L_i is:

$$U_i = \frac{\varphi(2^{L_i} - 1)}{L_i}$$

Note that, $\varphi(n)$ is **Euler's Totient function** that counts the positive integers up to a given integer n that are relatively prime to n. So, the total number of the keys will be:

$$\prod U_i \times (2^{L_i} - 1) \qquad (7)$$

If we assume that the initial state and polynomial feedback of each of the LFSRs can be calculated separately, the total number of keys will be equal to:

$$\sum U_i \times (2^{L_i} - 1) \qquad (8)$$

As a result, the total number of the keys is equal to:

$$2^{238} \times (2^{239} - 1) + \cdots + 2^{228} \times (2^{229} - 1) > 2^{477}$$

Therefore, we could confirm that LRC-256 is secure against correlation attack because finding the initiate state (and consequently the main key) is impossible due to computational limitations. Moreover, any kind of fast correlation attack against the LRC-256 is impractical due to the clock control structure of our algorithm, using dense feedback polynomials, correlation immune, nonlinear functions with having a large (1600 bits) initial state.

6.3 Algebraic Attack

Algebraic attack is one of the most successful attacks on the stream ciphers which used to be considered secure [1]. This attack attempts to construct the keystream of the algorithm by detecting the relationship between the input and output bits of stream ciphers.

Therefore, in order to have a secure cipher finding any relation between the input and the output must be impossible [31]. In LRC-256, we consider different arrangements to cope with this attack. For example, we have a powerful the initialization method, irregular clock structure, and we use the output of non-linear functions (instead of direct use of the LFSRs outputs on the input of the function g); hence, we create all necessary complexities to secure our proposed stream cipher against Algebraic, so potential attackers cannot find a relationship between input and output bits, because the initial location of the bits, LFSR's number, stage and clock of LFSRs are unclear in output sequence.

6.4 Time-Memory Trade-Off (TMTO) Attack

Time-Memory Trade-Off (TMTO) attacks propose a generic technique to reverse one-way functions, where one can trade off time and memory costs and which are mainly effective against stream ciphers [46]. This attack works based on **Birthday Paradox** which is often used to show how much data should be stored in memory to achieve a certain probability of success in the attack [19]. Through taking n random bits as the initial state, it produces n bits of keystream and compares it with the content that previously stored in memory (2^m n-bit output sequence, $m = n/2$). If the match was found, the state of the system is already taken. In it fails, a new n random bit will be used until finding the match. The memory and computational order of this attack can be calculated from the following relationships:

$$T = O(n + m^2)(2^m + 2^{n-m}) \tag{9}$$

$$M = O(n + m)(2^m) \tag{10}$$

Since we know the initial state of LRC-256 is 1600 bits and the value of m is equal to 800. Hence, the memory and computational order of implementing TMTO will be equal to:

$T = O(1600 + 800^2)(2^{800} + 2^{1600-800}) = 2^{820}$ $M = O(1600 + 800)(2^{800}) = 2^{810}$

Apparently, this massive memory and high computational order are sufficient to make the TMTO attack impossible in LRC-256.

6.5 Divide and Conquer Attack

Divide and conquer attack works based on the idea of time-memory trade-off attack [6]. According to the earlier proofs and the impractical requirements (e.g., reprocessing time, processing volume, and memory requirements) this attack cannot perform successfully on LRC-256; therefore without further analysis, we consider that LRC-256 is secure against Divide and conquer attack.

6.6 Distinguishing Attack

A distinguishing attack is an attack in which the adversary attempts to discover whether a known cipher generates a given sequence or if it comes to be a random sequence. In some cases, a distinguishing attack can be used to generate a key recovery attack [35].

More precisely, this attack attempts to get the initial state of the stream cipher by taking a long sequence of output bits. Since the linear complexity of LRC-256 is higher than 10^{480}, considering that our algorithm generates 10^{12} bits per second, after 1000 years, the adversary will only have 10^{22} output bits. Therefore, LRC-256 is highly secure against this attack.

6.7 AIDA/Cube Attacks

AIDA/ Cube attacks are actually generic key-recovery attacks that can be applied to encryption algorithms without having the internal structure of stream ciphers [12]. The necessary condition for these attacks is that the output from the generator can be represented as a low-degree decomposition multivariate polynomial in the standard algebraic form in the key and the plaintext [20].

We assume an adversary is permitted to ask the master polynomial (which is a chosen-plaintext and a chosen-IV setting) by her choice. Also, she achieves the resulting bit from the master polynomial. As a result, the adversary gains the system of polynomial equations. Thes, the purpose of the attack is to determine the system of equations that exposes the key variables [4].

This attack may be performed on LRC-256 if the output of the keystream was denoted by a low degree multivariate polynomial. In other words, this attack is successful when applied to random polynomials of degree d over n secret variables while the number m of public variables exceeds $d + \log_n d$. So, the complexity will be $2^{d-1}n + n^2$ bit operations, which is polynomial in n and low when d is small. The polynomials in LRC-256 have degrees from 163 to 239. Thus, the complexity of this attack will be at least 2^{162} bit operations that practically make it impossible to be performed in a reasonable time. Accordingly, we can confirm that LRC-256 is secure against this attack as well.

7 Comparison with Related Work

In order to analyze the performance of LRC-256, we compare it with 12 standard and popular ciphers including 5 stream ciphers: RC4 [33], HELIX [15], W7 [45], LILI-2 [9] and Snow 2.0 [13] as well as 7 important block ciphers: RC6, IDEA, SHACAL-1, 3DES, ICEBERG, Rijndael, and AES.

The hardware implementations of W7 and LILI-2 are straightforward since their hardware architectures are described in [9,45]. Also, for the efficient implementation of RC4 on FPGA, we adopted the parameterized implementation of [25] which helps to specify variable key lengths. Moreover, the details of block ciphers mentioned above can be found in Standaert's PhD thesis [39].

We represent the results of our comparison analysis in terms of throughput and efficiency (**Throughput/Nbr. of slices**) in Table 1.

Table 1. The results of performance and area comparison

Cipher	Throughput (Mbits/sec)	Number of slices	Throughput/Nbr. of slices
LILI-2	243	866	0.28
W7	768	608	1.26
Helix	1024.0	418	2.45
SNOW 2.0	5659	1015	5.57
RC4	120.8	140	0.86
LRC-256	**4021,62**	**691**	**5.82**
RC6	4800	7456	0.64
IDEA	6800	9793	0.69
SHACAL-1	17021	13729	1.24
3DES	917	604	1.51
ICEBERG	5659	4946	3.51
Rijndael	358	146	2.45
AES	358	146	2.45

In Table 1 we summarize our results and compares them with specific new stream and block ciphers on FPGAs. We have chosen FGPA for the implementation because its flexibility, logic and routing resources and low cost which make it one of the best options for implementing stream ciphers [32,44,48].

Remark that strict comparisons are made tough since these designs relate to various contexts (e.g. encryption/decryption designs, loop architectures or unrolled architectures for block ciphers). Looking at these results, the most effective of all the ciphers is LRC-256. Concerning other stream ciphers, Helix seems to be effective, but it requires some software precomputations, which may not be a practical solution for any context where the complete cipher has to be embedded on a single platform. LILI-2 is not competing with new block ciphers, and its expensive synchronization process largely restricts its efficiency. Eventually, SNOW 2.0 has the second best efficiency after LRC-256.

8   Limitations and Future Work

There are a few constraints to our approach that we try to solve in the future extension of this work. For example, we are aware that the initialization process is relatively complicated, which increase the security of our algorithm for the majority applications of hardware-based stream ciphers. However, this might have a slight impact on some applications where frequent re-keying is required such as mobile telephony. Also, even though LFSRs are a super efficient and low-cost component for designing hardware based stream ciphers, they are still suspected to be vulnerable against Side Channel Attacks.

9   Conclusion

Due to the extensive use of the stream cipher systems in the various applications in the embedded devices, in this paper we introduce LRC-256 as a hardware-oriented stream cipher that uses a clock-controlled generator with a novel mechanism of altering levels. The Length of the main key is 256 bits; however, it can be extended to 512 or 1024 bits with a little change in the initial vector generator. The essential criteria considered in our algorithm are the maximum period, high linear complexity, resistance to known attacks and safe statistical characteristics. The main structure of the LRC-256 contains a clock-controlled combination generator with internal memory.

The keystream, as the core component of LRC-256, generates unpredictable sequences that make our cipher system immune to the wide range of attacks. The result of our evaluation confirms the advantage of LRC-256 in comparing with similar works for lightweight memory devices such as embedded systems. Moreover, the result of our measurement demonstrates the optimality of LRC-256 in comparing with other well-known stream and block ciphers.

References

1. Armknecht, F.: Algebraic attacks on stream ciphers. In: European Congress on Computational Methods in Applied Sciences and Engineering, ECCOMAS, pp. 24–28 (2004)
2. Armknecht, F., Mikhalev, V.: On lightweight stream ciphers with shorter internal states. In: Leander, G. (ed.) FSE 2015. LNCS, vol. 9054, pp. 451–470. Springer, Heidelberg (2015). https://doi.org/10.1007/978-3-662-48116-5_22
3. Aumasson, J.-P.: Serious Cryptography. No Starch Press, San Francisco (2017)
4. Bard, G.V., Courtois, N.T., Nakahara, J., Sepehrdad, P., Zhang, B.: Algebraic, AIDA/cube and side channel analysis of KATAN family of block ciphers. In: Gong, G., Gupta, K.C. (eds.) INDOCRYPT 2010. LNCS, vol. 6498, pp. 176–196. Springer, Heidelberg (2010). https://doi.org/10.1007/978-3-642-17401-8_14
5. Bernstein, D.J.: Snuffle 2005: the Salsa20 encryption function (2015)
6. Bokhari, M.U., Alam, S., Masoodi, F.S.: Cryptanalysis techniques for stream cipher: a survey. Int. J. Comput. Appl. 60(9), 29–33 (2012)
7. Adams, C., Tavares, S.: The structured design of cryptographically good s-boxes. J. Cryptology 3(1), 27–41 (1990)
8. Chee, S., Lee, S., Lee, D., Sung, S.H.: On the correlation immune functions and their nonlinearity. In: Kim, K., Matsumoto, T. (eds.) ASIACRYPT 1996. LNCS, vol. 1163, pp. 232–243. Springer, Heidelberg (1996). https://doi.org/10.1007/BFb0034850

9. Clark, A., Dawson, E., Fuller, J., Golić, J., Lee, H.-J., Millan, W., Moon, S.-J., Simpson, L.: The LILI-II keystream generator. In: Batten, L., Seberry, J. (eds.) ACISP 2002. LNCS, vol. 2384, pp. 25–39. Springer, Heidelberg (2002). https://doi.org/10.1007/3-540-45450-0_3

10. Cobas, J.D.G., Brugos, J.A.L.: Complexity-theoretical approaches to the design and analysis of cryptographical boolean functions. In: Moreno Díaz, R., Pichler, F., Quesada Arencibia, A. (eds.) EUROCAST 2005. LNCS, vol. 3643, pp. 337–345. Springer, Heidelberg (2005). https://doi.org/10.1007/11556985_44

11. Deb, S., Biswas, B., Kar, N.: Study of NLFSR and reasonable security improvement on Trivium cipher. In: Mandal, J.K., Satapathy, S.C., Sanyal, M.K., Sarkar, P.P., Mukhopadhyay, A. (eds.) Information Systems Design and Intelligent Applications. AISC, vol. 339, pp. 731–739. Springer, New Delhi (2015). https://doi.org/10.1007/978-81-322-2250-7_73

12. Dinur, I., Shamir, A.: Cube attacks on tweakable black box polynomials. In: Joux, A. (ed.) EUROCRYPT 2009. LNCS, vol. 5479, pp. 278–299. Springer, Heidelberg (2009). https://doi.org/10.1007/978-3-642-01001-9_16

13. Ekdahl, P., Johansson, T.: A new version of the stream cipher SNOW. In: Nyberg, K., Heys, H. (eds.) SAC 2002. LNCS, vol. 2595, pp. 47–61. Springer, Heidelberg (2003). https://doi.org/10.1007/3-540-36492-7_5

14. Omar, A.E.A., Kholaif, S.M.A., El Hennawy, H.M.: LEA: link encryption algorithm proposed stream cipher algorithm. Ain Shams Eng. J. 6(1), 57–65 (2015)

15. Ferguson, N., Whiting, D., Schneier, B., Kelsey, J., Lucks, S., Kohno, T.: Helix: fast encryption and authentication in a single cryptographic primitive. In: Johansson, T. (ed.) FSE 2003. LNCS, vol. 2887, pp. 330–346. Springer, Heidelberg (2003). https://doi.org/10.1007/978-3-540-39887-5_24

16. Filiol, E., Fontaine, C.: Highly nonlinear balanced Boolean functions with a good correlation-immunity. In: Nyberg, K. (ed.) EUROCRYPT 1998. LNCS, vol. 1403, pp. 475–488. Springer, Heidelberg (1998). https://doi.org/10.1007/BFb0054147

17. Golic, J.: Correlation properties of a general binary combiner with memory. J. Cryptol. 9, 111–126 (1996)

18. Chambers, W.G., Gollmann, D.: Clock-controlled shift registers: a review. IEEE J. Sel. Areas Commun. 7(4), 525–533 (1989)

19. Hamann, M., Krause, M., Meier, W., Zhang, B.: Time-memory-data tradeoff attacks against small-state stream ciphers. IACR Cryptology ePrint Archive 2017, 384 (2017)

20. Islam, S., Afzal, M., Rashdi, A.: On the security of LBlock against the cube attack and side channel cube attack. In: Cuzzocrea, A., Kittl, C., Simos, D.E., Weippl, E., Xu, L. (eds.) CD-ARES 2013. LNCS, vol. 8128, pp. 105–121. Springer, Heidelberg (2013). https://doi.org/10.1007/978-3-642-40588-4_8

21. Jindal, P., Singh, B.: A survey on RC4 stream cipher. J. Comput. Netw. Inf. Secur. 7, 37–45 (2015)

22. Mostafa, S., Saad, H., Jaber, M.M., Ali, M.H., Dhafer, K.: The design trends of keystream generator for stream cipher for high immunity attacks. In: Sulaiman, H.A., Othman, M.A., Othman, M.F.I., Rahim, Y.A., Pee, N.C. (eds.) Advanced Computer and Communication Engineering Technology. LNEE, vol. 362, pp. 877–889. Springer, Cham (2016). https://doi.org/10.1007/978-3-319-24584-3_74

23. Kashmar, A.H., Ismail, E.S.: Blostream: a high speed stream cipher. J. Eng. Sci. Technol. 12(4), 1111–1128 (2017)

24. Khan, A.A., Mirza, F., Khan, M.A.: Transform domain analysis of sequences (2015)

25. Kitsos, P., Kostopoulos, G., Sklavos, N., Koufopavlou, O.: Hardware implementation of the RC4 stream cipher. In: 2003 46th Midwest Symposium on Circuits and Systems, vol. 3, pp. 1363–1366. IEEE (2003)
26. Kumar, S., Lemke, K., Paar, C., et al.: Some thoughts about implementation properties of stream ciphers. In: The State of the Art of Stream Ciphers, SASC 2004, pp. 14–15 (2004)
27. Maitra, S., Sarkar, P.: Highly nonlinear resilient functions optimizing siegenthaler's inequality. In: Wiener, M. (ed.) CRYPTO 1999. LNCS, vol. 1666, pp. 198–215. Springer, Heidelberg (1999). https://doi.org/10.1007/3-540-48405-1_13
28. Manifavas, C., Hatzivasilis, G., Fysarakis, K., Papaefstathiou, Y.: A survey of lightweight stream ciphers for embedded systems. Secur. Commun. Netw. 9(10), 1226–1246 (2016)
29. Mariot, L., Leporati, A.: A genetic algorithm for evolving plateaued cryptographic Boolean functions. In: Dediu, A.-H., Magdalena, L., Martín-Vide, C. (eds.) TPNC 2015. LNCS, vol. 9477, pp. 33–45. Springer, Cham (2015). https://doi.org/10.1007/978-3-319-26841-5_3
30. Vanstone, S., Menezes, A., Van Oorschot, P.: Handbook of Applied Cryptography. CRC Press, Boca Raton (1997)
31. Courtois, N.T.: Fast algebraic attacks on stream ciphers with linear feedback. In: Boneh, D. (ed.) CRYPTO 2003. LNCS, vol. 2729, pp. 176–194. Springer, Heidelberg (2003). https://doi.org/10.1007/978-3-540-45146-4_11
32. Pal, S., Pandian, K.K.S., Ray, K.C.: FPGA implementation of stream cipher using Toeplitz Hash Function. In: 2014 International Conference on Advances in Computing, Communications and Informatics, ICACCI, pp. 1834–1838. IEEE (2014)
33. Paul, G., Maitra, S.: RC4 Stream Cipher and Its Variants. CRC Press, Boca Raton (2011)
34. Ramanujam, S., Karuppiah, M.: Designing an algorithm with high avalanche effect. IJCSNS Int. J. Comput. Sci. Netw. Secur. 11(1), 106–111 (2011)
35. Rose, G., Hawkes, P.: On the applicability of distinguishing attacks against stream ciphers. IACR Cryptology ePrint Archive, 2002:142 (2002)
36. Seberry, J., Zhang, X.-M., Zheng, Y.: On constructions and nonlinearity of correlation immune functions. In: Helleseth, T. (ed.) EUROCRYPT 1993. LNCS, vol. 765, pp. 181–199. Springer, Heidelberg (1994). https://doi.org/10.1007/3-540-48285-7_16
37. Shah, T., Upadhyay, D., Sharma, P.: A comparative analysis of different LFSR-based ciphers and parallel computing platforms for development of generic cipher compatible on both hardware and software platforms. In: Afzalpulkar, N., Srivastava, V., Singh, G., Bhatnagar, D. (eds.) Proceedings of the International Conference on Recent Cognizance in Wireless Communication & Image Processing, pp. 305–316. Springer, New Delhi (2016). https://doi.org/10.1007/978-81-322-2638-3_35
38. Sriadhi, S., Rahim, R., Ahmar, A.S.: Rc4 algorithm visualization for cryptography education. J. Phys: Conf. Ser. 1028, 012057 (2018)
39. Standaert, F.-X.: Secure and efficient use of reconfigurable hardware devices in symmetric cryptography. Ph.D. thesis, Faculté des sciences appliquées, Université catholique de Louvain (2004)
40. Deb, S., Bhuyan, B., Gupta, N.C.: Design and analysis of LFSR-based stream cipher. In: Mandal, J.K., Saha, G., Kandar, D., Maji, A.K. (eds.) Proceedings of the International Conference on Computing and Communication Systems. LNNS, vol. 24, pp. 631–639. Springer, Singapore (2018). https://doi.org/10.1007/978-981-10-6890-4_61

41. Siegenthaler, T.: Correlation-immunity of nonlinear combining functions for cryptographic applications. IEEE Trans. Inform. Theory **30**, 776–780 (1984)
42. Siegenthaler, T.: Decrypting a class of stream ciphers using ciphertext only. IEEE Trans. Comput. **34**, 81–85 (1985)
43. Siegenthaler, T.: Design of combiners to prevent divide and conquer attacks. In: Williams, H.C. (ed.) CRYPTO 1985. LNCS, vol. 218, pp. 273–279. Springer, Heidelberg (1986). https://doi.org/10.1007/3-540-39799-X_21
44. Taqieddin, E., Abu-Rjei, O., Mhaidat, K., Bani-Hani, R.: Efficient FPGA implementation of the RC4 stream cipher using block ram and pipelining. Procedia Comput. Sci. **63**, 8–15 (2015)
45. Thomas, S., Anthony, D., Berson, T., Gong, G.: The W7 stream cipher algorithm (2003)
46. van den Broek, F., Poll, E.: A comparison of time-memory trade-off attacks on stream ciphers. In: Youssef, A., Nitaj, A., Hassanien, A.E. (eds.) AFRICACRYPT 2013. LNCS, vol. 7918, pp. 406–423. Springer, Heidelberg (2013). https://doi.org/10.1007/978-3-642-38553-7_24
47. Vorobets, H., Vorobets, O., Horditsa, V., Tarasenko, V., Vorobets, O.: Features of synthesis and statistical properties of the modified stream encoder with dynamic key correction. In: 2018 IEEE 9th International Conference on Dependable Systems, Services and Technologies (DESSERT), pp. 153–158. IEEE (2018)
48. Wollinger, T., Paar, C.: How secure are FPGAs in cryptographic applications? In: Y. K. Cheung, P., Constantinides, G.A. (eds.) FPL 2003. LNCS, vol. 2778, pp. 91–100. Springer, Heidelberg (2003). https://doi.org/10.1007/978-3-540-45234-8_10

AbsoluteSecure: A Tri-Layered Data Security System

Oluwafemi Osho[1], Farouk A. Musa[2], Sanjay Misra[3(✉)],
Andrew A. Uduimoh[1], Adewole Adewunmi[3], and Ravin Ahuja[4]

[1] Federal University of Technology, Minna, Nigeria
{femi.osho, a.uduimoh}@futminna.edu.ng
[2] DigitalJewels, Lagos, Nigeria
faroukm@digitaljewel.net
[3] Covenant University, Ota, Nigeria
{sanjay.misra,
wole.adewunmi}@covenantuniversity.edu.ng
[4] Vishwakarma Skill University Gurugram, Gurugram, Hariyana, India

Abstract. Data has been touted as the new oil. This attests to the level of importance it has garnered over the years. With increased proliferation of and advancements in technology, data is bound to play more prominent role. The need for data security, therefore, cannot be overstated. Existing systems for securing data often rely on one or combination of biometric, cryptography, and steganography. In this paper, we propose AbsoluteSecure, a data security system that combines the three techniques to enhance the security of data. The system is implemented using C#. To evaluate its performance, experiments are performed to assess its usability and security. Specifically, on usability, its capacity to successfully enroll a new user's fingerprint and authenticate an enrolled user are evaluated. On the other hand, to ascertain its security, we measure how much it can detect and deny access to unauthorized users, both at the authentication and usage levels. The results of the experiments show that AbsoluteSecure can ensure the confidentiality, integrity, and availability of data.

Keywords: Cryptography · Steganography · Biometric · Multi-layer security

1 Introduction

In recent times, the world has indeed experienced much technological progress. This has helped to improve the way we carry out various operations, thereby saving computational time and resources, leading to improved results. However, these improvements in technology have posed their attendant challenges, such as the need to secure highly-priced data. This is due to the activities of attackers who continue to develop and deploy increasingly sophisticated tools and methods, to carry out different attacks against users' data. Some of the attacks include data modification, deletion, denial of service, impersonation, eavesdropping, and identity theft [1, 2]. According to a survey by Ponemon Institute in 2018, the estimated average total cost of a data breach was $3.86 million. This was an increase of 6.4% when compared to the preceding year.

© Springer Nature Switzerland AG 2019
R. Damaševičius and G. Vasiljevienė (Eds.): ICIST 2019, CCIS 1078, pp. 243–255, 2019.
https://doi.org/10.1007/978-3-030-30275-7_19

The report also forecasted the likelihood of reoccurrence of breach over the next two years as 27.8% [3].

Security of confidential data is unarguably very important. It is the sole foundation of data confidentiality, integrity and availability, which are paramount in the transmission of data in data systems [4].

Table 1. Summary of existing studies

Category	Method	Scheme	Work
Single	Cryptography	RSA	Jamgekar et al. [6] Osho et al. [7]
		AES	Elfakharany [8]
	Steganography	Audio	Verma et al. [9]
		Image	Kamath [10]
		Video	Bodhak et al. [11]
	Biometrics	Brain	Damasevicius [12]
		Fingerprint	Patel [13]
		Gait	Damasevicius [14]
		Voice	Paunovic et al. [15]
Hybrid	Cryptography + Biometrics	AES + Fingerprint	Ojeniyi et al. [4]
	Cryptography + Steganography	Blowfish + Image	Dixit et al. [16]
		Image + RSA	Gupta et al. [17]
		Visual Cryptography + Text	Roy et al. [18]
	Biometrics + Steganography	Fingerprint + Face + Image	Paul et al. [19]
		Fingerprint + Image	Shubhangi et al. [20]
		Skin + Image	Shejul et al. [21]
	Multimodal biometrics	Face + fingerprint	Shanthini et al. [22]

To improve data security, many systems have been proposed (Table 1). These systems make use of different techniques individually or in combination, such as cryptography, steganography, and biometrics, to enhance the security of data. Each of these techniques, however, have some limitations. For instance, in cryptography, the cipertext, if intercepted by an adversary, could be subjected to cryptanalysis. Similarly, a message concealed using steganography could be exposed if subjected to steganalysis. Consequently, a data security system that one of or combines both cryptographic and steganographic techniques would need further improvement. One option is to integrate both techniques with biometrics. Biometrics leverages the uniqueness in the physical or behavioural attributes of an individual or entity [5]. Table 2 presents the performance of different mitigation mechanisms using one, two or combination of the three techniques against different attacks.

Table 2. A summary of data attacks and performance of different mitigating techniques

Category	Attack	Cryptography	Cryptography + Steganography	Cryptography + Steganography + Biometrics
Confidentiality	Data theft	No	No	Yes
	Cryptanalysis	No	No	Yes
	Brute force	No	No	Yes
	Sniffing	No	Yes	Yes
	Eavesdropping	Yes	Yes	Yes
	Man in the middle	Yes	Yes	Yes
	Key logging	No	No	Yes
Integrity	Data diddling	Yes	Yes	Yes
	Data modification	Yes	Yes	Yes
	Masquerading	No	No	Yes
	Salami attack	No	Yes	Yes
Availability	Denial of service	No	No	Yes
	Data deletion	No	No	Yes
	Buffer overflow	No	No	No

This study proposes and implements a secure data security system that demonstrates the integration of cryptography, steganography and biometrics for enhancing security of data.

The rest of the study is organized as follows: in section two, we review related concepts. Section three presents the proposed system. A proof-of-concept and evaluation of the performance of the system are presented in sections four and five respectively. Section six concludes the study.

2   Literature Review

2.1   Cryptography

Cryptography is a technique used to secure digital information or communication from unauthorized access. It is used for providing access control mechanism in systems and preventing attackers, who gain unauthorized access to systems, from accessing confidential information. It has been widely adopted by the intelligence organisations, government, individuals and also the military.

Cryptography exists in two categories: symmetric (also called private key cryptography) and asymmetric cryptography (also known as public key cryptography). In symmetric cryptography, the same key is used for the sending and receiving of messages, that is, the same key is employed for encryption and decryption [23] The key is known to both the sending and the receiving parties. Examples are Data Encryption Standard (DES) and Advanced Encryption Standards (AES).

In Asymmetric, also known as public key, cryptography, two different keys are generated for the encryption and decryption process. The key used for encryption, known as the public key, is known to any encrypter, hence it being termed public. The key used for decrypting is called the private key. One of the most popular is the RSA cryptosystem. It is widely used in various protocols and platforms. Others include Rabin, ElGamal, NTRU, and Paillie.

Cryptography is indeed a very sustainable means of securing data and communication lines. However, irrespective of the strength of a cryptosystem, it can still be exposed to cryptanalysis in the event of interception by an unauthorized party [24].

2.2   Steganography

Steganography has been used over the years to protect valuable data through obscurity. In steganography, data is protected by concealing it in a covert medium, which masks the existence of the data. Data undergoes steganography to produce a stego-object [25]. The stego-object comprises of a cover medium and the payload. The cover medium is the media used to mask the data. The data that is being masked is called the payload.

Steganography is widely used by intellectual property holders, using a technique known as watermarking, to protect their works against piracy [20]. It can also be combined with cryptography to attain improved security of data [16]. Modern steganography uses a wider variety of media as the cover medium. These include audio, video, image, and text.

It is important to note that steganography does not modify or transform a given data, it merely masks the data with a specified medium (cover medium) in such a way that makes it unable to be noticed by anyone. Therefore, the security of a steganographic process depends entirely on the eradication of the possibility of it being identified by an adversary [26].

2.3   Biometrics

Biometrics involves the various techniques used to identify individuals using their unique psychological or behavioural qualities. These qualities include the human voice, signature, face, fingerprint, DNA, retina, iris, and ear shape [13, 15, 27–30].

Biometrics as a form of authentication has been in usage since the 1890s. It was used in Argentina where a fingerprint template was created. Fingerprint biometrics then became an official measure for identifying humans in the 1900s.

Biometric features of individuals are extremely unique and the possibility of counterfeiting biometric traits is quite impossible. That makes it an efficient technique for human identification, hence its common use for authentication [5].

Biometric systems generally consists of three units, viz., the sensor, the data processing unit and the user application. The sensor refers to any component used to collect the minutiae data from the individual. The data processing component handles the collection and matching of user biometric trait. The user application gives the user the interface to interact with [27].

Authentication in biometric systems follow three steps. The biometric sample of the user is first collected and stored. At authentication, the matching algorithm collects a test sample, which is compared with the stored one. A mathematical value is then generated and the degree of similarity and dissimilarity is calculated. A match is met when the mathematical degree reaches a biometric mean set by the matching algorithm [27].

3   Proposed Tri-Layered Data Security System

Analysis of existing data security systems revealed the use or one or combination of cryptographic, biometric, and steganographic techniques for securing data. Each of these techniques has its own limitations, as well as combining any two of them.

3.1   Requirement Definition

There are some core and basic functional and non-functional requirements a data security system must satisfy to effectively secure data. These include the following:

- The data security system should ensure new users are successfully enrolled.
- The data security system should ensure unauthorized persons cannot gain access to authorized users' data.
- The data security system should ensure a legitimate user cannot gain unauthorized access to the data of other users.
- The data security system should be easy to use.

3.2   Framework of Proposed System

To enhance data security, we propose AbsoluteSecure, a tri-layered data security system that leverages biometrics, cryptography and steganography for securing data. The system combines fingerprint biometrics, Advanced Encryption Standard (AES), and LSB image steganography. The proposed system is presented in Fig. 1.

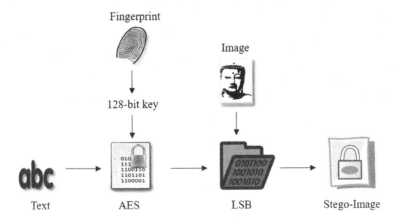

Fig. 1. Proposed tri-layered data security system

The fingerprint biometrics component serves two purposes: authentication and generation of a 128-bit key used for both encrypting and decrypting messages. The key is generated using the minutiae points extracted from the fingerprint. To extract the minutiae points, the steps include [31, 32]:

- Image preprocessing using histogram equalization.
- Segmentation of the preprocessed fingerprint.
- Orientation field estimation, which helps in the recognition of poor quality latents.
- Image enhancement. This is done before minutiae extraction for the purpose of further enhancing the fingerprint image. Methods used include Gaussian Low-Pass Filter and Gabor Filter.
- Region of Interest (ROI) selection using binarization and morphological operators.
- Thinning.

The system uses the Advanced Encryption System (AES) to encrypt/decrypt the data. The AES uses a 128 bit key length, generated from the user's fingerprint biometric features. It consists of layers, which manipulate a 4 by 4 array of bytes, or 128 bits of data path, commonly called the state. Every round of AES undergoes four stages: key addition, byte substitution, permutation of the data on a byte level (ShiftRows), and mixing blocks of four bytes (MixColumn) [33, 34]. The block diagram of the AES is presented in Fig. 2.

3.3   Process Design

To use our proposed tri-layered data security system, a user would need to be enrolled on the system. The enrollment and usage processes are described below.

Enrollment
Enrolment of a new user is usually facilitated by the administrator. The new user specifies a user name and password. Thereafter, the biometric details are captured. Once this process is complete the user subsequently can use the system.

Usage
Depending on the user, there are two level of access: administrator and ordinary user. While both categories of users have access to use the system for securing their data, the administrator has the additional privilege of facilitating the enrolment of new users. Figure 3 depicts an activity diagram of levels of usage our proposed system.

To secure a piece of data, a user can either load a text from memory, or manually type the text into the text field. The user is then prompted to select a recipient. The next stage entails selecting a cover image from memory, which is used to produce the stego-image

Retrieval of data follows a reverse order. After logging in to the system, the user loads the stego-image from memory, then extracts the ciphertext, and finally decrypts the ciphertext to get the plaintext. The sequence of process involved in both securing and retrieving data is illustrated in Fig. 4.

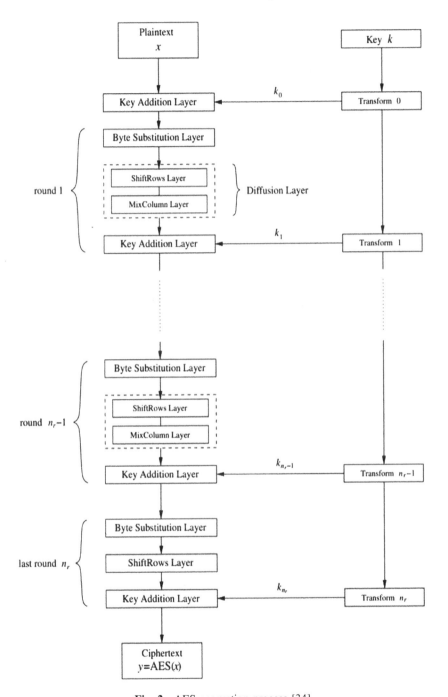

Fig. 2. AES encryption process [34]

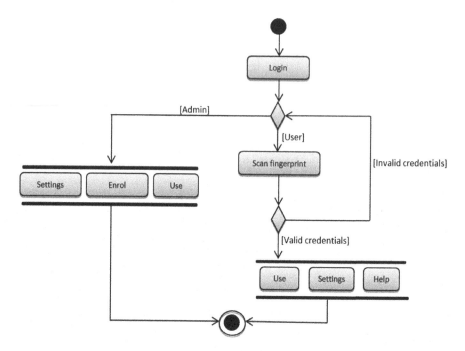

Fig. 3. Activity diagram of levels of usage

4 System Implementation

To implement AbsoluteSecure, the following hardware and software resources were used:

- C#: the programming language.
- Microsoft Visual Studio 2010: the integrated development environment, for coding, debugging and executing of source codes.
- DigitalPersona U.are.U 4000B fingerprint reader and software development kit: for fingerprint biometric enrolment and authentication.
- A Sony VAIO VPCEA45FA Laptop (Specification: 4 GB RAM, Core i3 Intel processor, 2.53 GHz Dual Core processor speed, 320 GB Hard Drive, and Windows 8 Operating System: for testing the system.

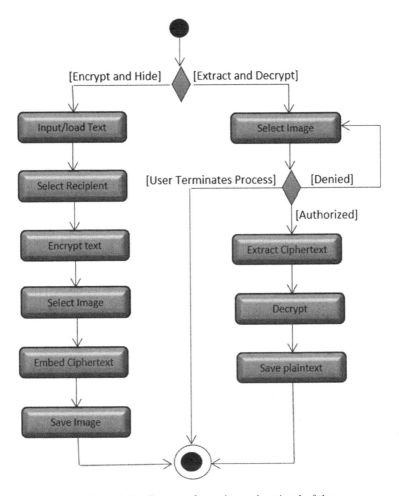

Fig. 4. Activity diagram of securing and retrieval of data

5 Performance Evaluation

To use the system, an enrolled user is presented with the login interface, which accepts the individual's username and password. If the credentials match one of the records in the database, the individual is then allowed to submit a fingerprint sample via a fingerprint scanner. If the sample matches the username and password combination, the individual is granted access to the corresponding profile.

To evaluate the performance of the system, we considered its usability and security. Twenty individuals were used, comprising ten enrolled and ten illegitimate users.

5.1 System Usability

To determine if our system was usable, we evaluated its capacity to successfully enroll the fingerprint of a new user and not reject a legitimate user. These were used to determine the failure to enroll rate (FER) and false rejection rate (FRR). The experiments were performed using ten individuals.

Failure to Enroll Rate (FER)
This implies the rate at which the biometric system fails to enroll a new user. We denote this as FER, and is calculated as:

$$\text{FER} = \frac{\text{Number of times a system refused to enrol user}}{\text{Number of trials}} \times 100 \qquad (1)$$

For each of the ten individuals, there were five enrollment attempts. Out of a total of fifty trials, we recorded two instances where the fingerprint of a user was not enrolled by the system. This gives an FER of 4%.

False Rejection Rate (FRR)
This calculates the likelihood of a legitimate user being denied access. We considered the FRR at the authentication level, denoted by FRR_{Auth}, to evaluate the rate at which the enrolled users were denied login access to their respective profiles. On the other hand, the FRR_{Usg} indicates the rate at which the legitimate users could not access their data and other system functionality. In both cases, for each of the ten users, five attempts were made.

The FRR is represented mathematically as:

$$FRR = \frac{\text{Number of times an enrolled user was not recognised}}{\text{Total number of trials}} \times 100 \qquad (2)$$

From our experiments, both FRR_{Auth} and FRR_{Usg} were 0%, i.e. there were no instances recorded where legitimate users could not be authenticated by the system nor allowed access to their data.

5.2 System Security

To assess how secure the system is against unauthorized access, we evaluated its capacity to detect and deny access to unauthorized users, both at the authentication and usage levels. The experiments consisted of the use of ten legitimate and ten illegitimate users.

False Acceptance Rate (FAR)
The FAR was first evaluated at the authentication stage. Denoted as FAR_{Auth}, this amounts to the rate at which illegitimate users were accepted as legitimate and successfully authenticated. Five of them were given the username and password of legitimate users. This was used to simulate a situation where the username and password of some legitimate users are known to attackers. One means of achieving this is through social engineering. The remaining five were not given any details. In real life,

these represent attackers with no prior knowledge of any legitimate users' details, who would try to brute-force to gain access to the system. Each of the test users were asked to make five login attempts.

The second experiment, represented as FAR_{Usg}, implies measuring the likelihood of users accessing the data of other users without authorization. To determine this, we asked each of the ten legitimate users to try, in five attempts, to access data belonging to other users.

Mathematically, the FAR is calculated using the formula:

$$FAR = \frac{\text{Number of times the system accepts an illegitimate user}}{\text{Total number of trials}} \times 100 \quad (3)$$

From results obtained, both FAR_{Auth} and FAR_{Usg} were 0%. None of the illegitimate users was successfully authenticated by the system. Also, not one of the legitimate users could gain access to any other user's data.

Table 3 provides a summary of the different results from the five experiments. In terms of enrolling new users, the system recorded a success rate of 96%. On the other hand, analysis of the results suggests its immense capacity to effectively secure users' data.

The system ensures confidentiality of users' information first by preventing unauthorized access by un-enrolled individual at the authentication level. Even when the username and password associated with a legitimate user are known by an un-enrolled individual, at the biometric level authentication is denied. In the same vein, for a user enrolled on the system, the likelihood of an unauthorized access to other users' data, as demonstrated by the system, was zero. It also supports confidentiality by encrypting the stored data and hiding them in an image.

Table 3. Performance evaluation of AbsoluteSecure

Metric	Rate
FER_{Auth}	4%
FRR_{Auth}	0%
FRR_{Usg}	0%
FAR_{Auth}	0%
FAR_{Usg}	0%

One of the consequences of successfully preventing unauthorized access to the stored data is the guarantee of integrity of information. As long as an attacker cannot gain unauthorized access to users' data, it cannot be modified.

Our proposed system also guarantee availability of data by preventing data deletion by unauthorized individuals. This is equally achieved by denying unauthorized users access to data belonging to legitimate users.

6 Conclusion

In this study, we proposed a multi-layer data security system that leverages on bio-metric, cryptography, and steganography for securing data. The system can be deployed both as a standalone or network application. The proposed system was implemented and tested. Based on the results of experiments performed to evaluate its usability and security, we demonstrated the capacity of AbsoluteSecure to provide effective security of data, ensuring confidentiality, integrity, and availability of data. Specifically, while ensuring that enrolled users are successfully authenticated and able to access their data all the time, the system ensured zero likelihood of unauthorized access to users' data.

The main focus of this study was demonstrating the integration of cryptographic, biometric, and steganographic techniques to secure data. As much as this was achieved, there are areas that were not covered. For example, the performance of the system under high-volume data could be explored in further studies. Another area worth investigating is how the integrated techniques influence hardware resources.

References

1. Ahmad, A.: Types of security threats and it's preventions. Int. J. Comput. Technol. Appl. **3**(3), 720–752 (2012)
2. Microsoft: Common Types of Network Attacks [Internet]. Microsoft Technet (2011). [cited 17 Aug 2015]
3. Ponemon Institute: 2018 Cost of a Data Breach Study: Global Overview (2018)
4. Ojeniyi, J.A., Waziri, V.O., Suleiman, I.: Improved data security framework based on advanced encryption standard and fingerprint. In: Proceedings of the International Conference on Science, Technology, Education, Arts, Management and Social Sciences (iSTEAMS), pp. 111–120. iSTEAMS Research Nexus (2014)
5. Jain, A.K., Ross, A., Nandakumar, K.: An introduction to biometrics. In: 2008 19th International Conference on Pattern Recognition, Tampa, Florida. IEEE (2008)
6. Jamgekar, R.S., Joshi, G.S.: File encryption and decryption using secure RSA. Int. J. Emerg. Sci. Eng. **1**(4), 11–14 (2013)
7. Osho, O., Zubair, Y.O., Ojeniyi, J.A., Osho, L.O.: A simple encryption and decryption system. In: International Conference on Science, Technology, Education, Arts, Management and Social Sciences (iSTEAMS), Ado-Ekiti, Nigeria, pp. 77–84. iSTEAMS Research Nexus (2014)
8. Elfakharany, S.: Secure mobile payment protocol using asymmetric encryption for authorization. J. Netw. Commun. Emerg. Technol. **2**(2), 34–40 (2015)
9. Verma, T.G., Hasan, Z., Verma, G.: A unique approach for data hiding using audio steganography. Int. J. Mod. Eng. Res. (IJMER) **3**(4), 2098–2101 (2013)
10. Kamath, P.R.: A secure and high capacity image, steganography technique. Int. J. Signal Image Process. (SIPIJ) **4**(1), 83–89 (2013)
11. Bodhak, P.V., Gunjal, B.L.: Improved protection in video steganography. Int. J. Eng. Innov. Technol. (IJEIT) **1**(4), 31–37 (2012)
12. Damaševicius, R., Maskeliunas, R., Kazanavicius, E., Wozniak, M.: Combining cryptography with EEG biometrics. Comput. Intell. Neurosci. **2018**, 1–11 (2018)
13. Patel, U.: A study on fingerprint biometrics recognition. Int. J. Eng. Sci. **1**(2), 1–6 (2015)

14. Damasevicius, R., Maskeliunas, R., Venckauskas, A., Wozniak, M.: Smartphone user identity verification using gait characteristics robertas. Symmetry **8**(100), 1–20 (2016)
15. Paunović, S., Nešić, L., Kovačević, J.: Application of voice biometrics in protection systems and crime fighting. J. Inf. Technol. Appl. **4**(2), 59–67 (2012)
16. Dixit, P.H., Waskar, K.B., Bombale, U.L.: Multilevel network security combining cryptography and steganography on ARM platform. J. Embed. Syst. **3**(1), 11–15 (2015)
17. Gupta, S., Ankur, G., Bhushan, B.: Information hiding using least significant bit steganography and cryptography. Int. J. Mod. Educ. Comput. Sci. **6**(1), 27–34 (2012)
18. Roy, S., Venkateswaran, P.: Online payment system using steganography and visual cryptography. In: 2014 IEEE Students' Conference on Electrical, Electronics and Computer Science, SCEECS 2014, pp. 1–5 (2014)
19. Paul, L., Anilkumar, M.: Authentication for online voting using steganography and biometrics. Int. J. Adv. Res. **1**(10), 26–32 (2012)
20. Shubhangi, D.C., Malipatil, M.: Authentication watermarking for transmission of hidden data using biometrics technique. Int. J. Emerg. Technol. Adv. Eng. **2**(5), 1–6 (2012)
21. Shejul, A.A., Kulkarni, U.L.: A DWT based approach for steganography using biometrics. In: 2010 International Conference on Data Storage and Data Engineering (DSDE), pp. 39–43 (2010)
22. Shanthini, B., Swamynathan, S.: Multimodal biometric-based secured authentication system using steganography. J. Comput. Sci. **8**(7), 1012–1021 (2012)
23. Dorst, K., Stewart, S., Staudinger, I., Paton, B.: Symmetric cryptography. In: Dagstuhl Reports Conference, pp. 1–16 (2012)
24. Atul, K.: Cryptography and Network Security, 2nd edn. Tata McGraw-Hill Education (2008)
25. Amirtharaj, R., Rayappan, J.B.B.: Steganography-time to time: a review. Res. J. Inf. Technol. **5**(2), 53–66 (2013)
26. Jayaram, P., Ranganatha, H.R., Anupama, H.S.: Information hiding using audio steganography - a survey. Int. J. Multimed. Appl. **3**, 86–96 (2011)
27. Singhal, R., Jain, P.: Biometrics: enhancing security. Asian J. Comput. Sci. Inf. Technol. **3**, 89–92 (2011)
28. Bowyer, K.W., Hollingsworth, K.P., Flynn, P.J.: A survey of iris biometrics research: 2008–2010. In: Handbook of Iris Recognition, pp. 15–54 (2013)
29. Li, Z., Park, U., Jain, A.K.: A discriminative model for age invariant face recognition. IEEE Trans. Inf. Forensics Secur. **6**(3), 1028–1037 (2011)
30. Aronowitz, H., Hoory, R., Pelecanos, J., Nahamoo, D.: New developments in voice biometrics for user authentication. In: Proceedings of the Annual Conference of the International Speech Communication Association, INTERSPEECH, pp. 17–20 (2011)
31. Shodhganga: Design of Secured Key Generation Algorithm using Fingerprint Based Biometric Modality
32. Jagadeesan, A., Duraiswamy, K.: Secured cryptographic key generation from multimodal biometrics: feature level fusion of fingerprint and iris. Int. J. Comput. Sci. Inf. Secur. **7**(1), 296–305 (2010)
33. Katz, J., Lindell, Y.: Introduction to Modern Cryptography, pp. 1–498. CRC Press, Boca Raton (2007)
34. Paar, C., Pelzl, J.: Understanding Cryptography, pp. 1–372. Springer, Heidelberg (2010). https://doi.org/10.1007/978-3-642-04101-3

Visual Analytics for Cyber Security Domain: State-of-the-Art and Challenges

Robertas Damaševičius[✉], Jevgenijus Toldinas,
Algimantas Venčkauskas, Šarūnas Grigaliūnas, Nerijus Morkevičius,
and Vaidas Jukavičius

Department of Computer Science, Kaunas University of Technology,
Kaunas, Lithuania
robertas.damasevicius@ktu.lt

Abstract. Visual Analytics is a complex sub-field of data analytics that concentrates on the use of the information visualization methods for facilitating effective analysis of data by employing visual and graphical representation. In cyber security domain, Effective visualization of the data allows to infer valuable insights that enable domain analysts to construct successful strategies to mitigate cyber attacks and provide decision support. We perform a survey of the state-of-the-art in the cyber security domain, analyze main challenges and discuss future trends. We summarize a large number of cyber security and digital forensics visualization works using the Five Question Method of Five W's and How (Why, Who, What, How, When, and Where) approach as a methodological background. We perform analysis of the works using J. Bertin's Semiotic Theory of Graphics, and VIS4ML ontology as a theoretical foundation of visual analytics. As a result, we formulate the main challenges for the development of this area of research in the future.

Keywords: Visual analytics · Visualization · Cyber security ·
Digital forensics · Decision support

1 Introduction

Visual Analytics is a complex sub-field of data analytics that focuses on the use of the information visualization methods for facilitating effective analysis of data by employing visual and graphical representation [1]. Visualization defines a defining role in the field of multi-attribute, multi-dimensional data analysis and cognition.

Visual data analysis helps to identify structures, repetitions, anomalies, patterns, and trends, and exceptions in complex data [2]. The aim of cyber security data visualization is to support domain experts in decision-making in order to improve the safety and security of our cyber infrastructures by providing effective tools and environments [3].

Information visualization methods started be employed in information security, especially for visualizing network traffic and cyber attacks [4]. These visualization techniques are particularly useful for situational awareness [5]. Effective visualization of the data allows to infer valuable insights that enables domain analysts to construct

© Springer Nature Switzerland AG 2019
R. Damaševičius and G. Vasiljevienė (Eds.): ICIST 2019, CCIS 1078, pp. 256–270, 2019.
https://doi.org/10.1007/978-3-030-30275-7_20

successful strategies and make informed decisions [6]. In case of cyber attack or post-attack investigation, identifying who (users) and what (applications) are responsible for the attack is a non-trivial task. Cyber security stakeholders need effective visualization methods and tools that supports them in exploring and analyzing very large amounts of logs in a visual and interactive way with least effort.

In this survey, we summarize a large number of cyber security and digital forensics visualization works using the Five Question Method of Five W's and How (Why, Who, What, How, When, and Where) approach as a methodological background [7].

A similar approach was employed in [8] to organize a survey of visual analytics in deep learning domain. By constructing the survey in this way, many known research papers could be analyzed. Such structural organization captures the requirements, stakeholders, and methods of cyber security visualization, and positions works of other authors in the context of known literature. We conclude by outlining current research challenges.

We expect that this survey will serve for researchers and practitioners to provide understanding how visualization contributes research and decision making in cyber security domain.

2 Methodology

We present a comprehensive overview on visualization and visual analytics in cyber security research, using a Five Questions approach [7], which allows us to position each analyzed research contribution with respect to the following questions: Why, Who, What, How, When, and Where, and at the same time to discuss and emphasize multifaceted contributions known research contributions.

To emphasize and analyze the impact of visual analytics on the cyber security domain, our survey analyzes most relevant works from the intersection of cyber security, digital forensics, human-computer interaction, usability engineering and computer vision domains. We highlight how visual analytics has become indispensable in solving some of largest problems of cyber security and digital forensics, such as interpretation of network data flows.

For paper searching, we use Clarivate Analytics Web of Science, Scopus, IEEE Xplore, and ACM Digital Library databases. For each work, we analyzed metadata, abstract, explicit contributions, and challenges and requirements formulated (if any). With this information, we used the Five Questions Framework to analyze the existing works on visualization and visual analytics in cyber security as follows:

Why do we want to use visualization in cyber security domain?
Who are the stakeholders that use and benefit from cyber security visualization?
What data, features, and relationships can we visualize in cyber security?
How can we visualize cyber security data?
When visualization used in cyber security?
Where is cyber security visualization being used?

Our further analysis is based on the J. Bertin's Semiotic Theory of Graphics [9]. This theory is based on common understanding that communication involves the use of meaningful signs for sharing knowledge. Bertin outlined main visual variables (i.e., color, size, shape, hue, texture, and orientation) and suggested ways how to apply visual variables to represent different types of information such as quantitative, ordinal, selective, or associative.

While the abovementioned theoretical frameworks provided many useful suggestions and guidelines for visualization, in practice they lack of conceptual operationalization for the use in specific domains such as cyber security domain [10]. A methodological approach is provided by VIS4ML ontology as a theoretical foundation of visual analytics [11].

3   Findings and Results

3.1   Why: Motivation for Visualization in Cyber Security

One of the most important reasons why cyber security stakeholders want to visualize data in cyber security domain is to understand and explain large amounts of data, which otherwise overwhelms an expert due to its huge size. To cope with the scale and complexity of the challenges posed by these data, cyber security analysts have powerful analytical and visualization tools [12].

Data visualization is often integrated into cyber security platforms, offering an intuitive way to view activities that lead to more efficient cyber operations. One way to find insights about high warnings is to identify an anomaly. Models and trends are interesting, but more often cyber analysts need to find exceptional results. Seeing data related to many cases or alerts at the same time can reveal unusual patterns of activity that require further investigation.

3.2   Who: Users of Visualization in Cyber Security

User-based assessment provides effective evidence of the measurable benefits of data visualization systems and the impact of visualization tools on achieving security goals. Analysts rely on graphics visualization to provide a global and/or local view of their connected data. For cyber security visualization experts, it's primary role is decision support [13]. Matching these goals is difficult and sometimes impossible, so it is necessary to understand the compromise between evaluating the use of different datasets or systems.

3.3   What: Cyber Security Data Used for Visualization

Graphic visualization is an important part of any cyber security strategy. Analysts are trying to disclose insights from complex logs that limit their investigative powers and leave systems vulnerable. The cyber data visualization system is required to assist analysts in the decision-maker's location and create customized network visualization results that allow analysts to explore data at their own pace and scale. Analysts must be able to share data insights. Adequate visualization functionality, including filtering, temporal analysis, geospatial visualization, anomaly detection, social network analysis, and node grouping, is required. In case of a cyber attack, a data analyst cannot prevent an attack, but visualization of the graphics can still help them understand and prevent recurrence of an attack.

Visual data system objects obtained in collaboration with real users are often convincing examples of practice, as they may disclose previously unknown information within an organization. The most important thing is the layout, filtering and social networking of the performers, but it must be combined with a powerful rendering engine. However, real-life data sets are rarely published even anonymously, so it is difficult to carry out a meta-analysis in later studies [14].

The size and complexity of these sets of data objects are also uncontrollable and cannot be considered equivalent to data sets in other organizations. Therefore, in order to support future research, the characteristics of actual visualized data object sets should describe its characteristics and attributes.

3.4   How: Visualization Metaphors and Techniques

Icons visualize data items as pictures and map data to visual elements. Icons can utilize shapes (such as lines, bands, or bars) and visual features such as color, texture, or diameter of shapes. The representation can e supplemented by textures and animation [15]. For example, in VisSecAnalyzer [16], each network object is visualized by an icon, while the background color of the icon encodes values of the security metrics computed for a network host, such as Risk Level, Mortality, or Criticality (Fig. 1).

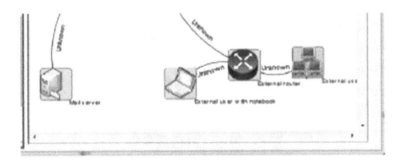

Fig. 1. Example of visualization of data is cyber security domain based on geometric icons in VisSecAnalyzer [16].

Radial icons are based on a wheel-metaphor which uses a radial layout to reflect spatial distribution and multidimensional attributes. An example is IDSRadar, a visualization framework used to visualize Intrusion Detection System (IDS) alerts in real-time [17]. Here a wheel demonstrates its advantages for compact layout, when visualizing large amounts of network data (Fig. 2).

Word clouds are a keyword-based text visualization technique, where each visual feature represents a text chunk (e.g., labels) in a document. For example, in TagsNet [18], word clouds are used for forensic triage of email network narratives (Fig. 3).

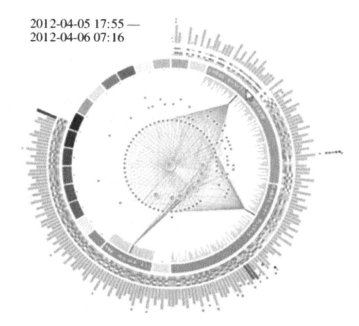

Fig. 2. Example of visualization of data is cybersecurity domain based on a wheel metaphor in IDSRadar [17].

Fig. 3. Example of visualization of data is digital forensics domain based on a word cloud metaphor in TagsNet [18].

Heatmap (or density map) combines discrete data points into a continuous representation according to the distribution of the data. Heatmap handles the overlapping issue well, and fits well for qualitative analysis. For example, in SemanticPrism [19], heatmap is used to show the geospatial distribution of a policy or an activity (Fig. 4).

Graphs can be used to visualize the dynamics and similarities in complex networks. While graphs can naturally represent computer networks, graphs generally have scalability problems. TO alleviate these problems, additional visualization methods such as

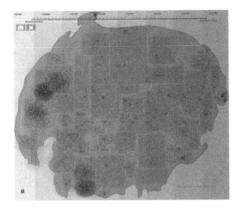

Fig. 4. Example of visualization of data is digital forensics domain based on a heatmap metaphor in SemanticPrism [19].

graph clustering or node coloring can be used. For example, in ENAVis [20] to effectively represent the activities in the computer network (Fig. 5).

Fig. 5. Example of visualization of data is digital forensics domain based on a graph metaphor in ENAVis [20].

Bubble charts are effective for identifying clusters and outliers, in the data, and is independent from the size of the dataset. For example, in BubbleNet [21], bubble charts are combined with cartographic maps identify and summarize patterns within the geographical distribution of cybersecurity data (Fig. 6).

Fig. 6. Example of visualization of data is digital forensics domain based on a bubble map metaphor in BubbleNet [21].

Icicle Plots are a method for presenting hierarchical/clustered data. For example, in LifeFlow [22t], icicle plots are used to visualize the temporal distribution of sequential events (Fig. 7).

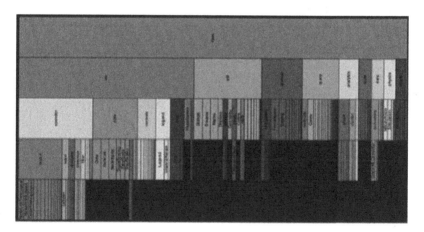

Fig. 7. Example of visualization of data is digital forensics domain based on a icicle plot metaphor in LifeFlow [22].

An interactive lens (or semantic zoom) lets the user to emphasize different characteristics of big dataset at different scales at different zoom levels in order to provide interactive analysis capability. For example, in Portvis [23] semantic zoom allows to present information in detail by providing zooming in and out (Fig. 8).

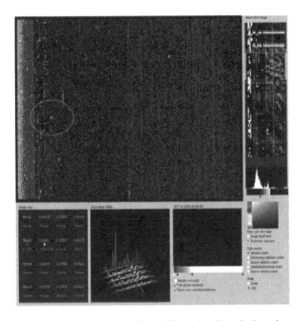

Fig. 8. Example of visualization of data is digital forensics domain based on a semantic zoom metaphor in Portvis [23].

The metaphor of a 'river' is applied in temporal visualizations with information flow representing the procession of time from left to right. The river metaphor can be implemented as alluvial plot. For example, in [24] such visualization indicates temporal variation (Fig. 9).

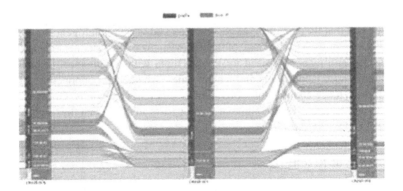

Fig. 9. Example of visualization of data is digital forensics domain based on a river metaphor in [24].

Tree map provides a hierarchical view on data using a group of tiles of various sizes and colors. It presents a global view of complex multi-dimensional inter-related data. For example, in Prefuse visualization toolkit [25], treemap visualization is used for the showing the hierarchical organization of the source code, while color represents the date of last modification (Fig. 10).

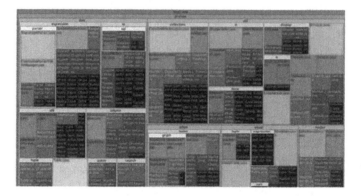

Fig. 10. Example of visualization of data is digital forensics domain based on tree map in prefuse visualization toolkit [25].

3.5   When: When Visualization Used in Cyber Security?

Most commonly, visualization is used for historical analysis of cybersecurity data, e.g., for post-attack digital forensics. A growing amount of works address the problem of real-time analysis and visualization of data, e.g., to detect cyber attacks or spread of malware in-real time [17]. Finally, a third stream of research addresses the problem of predicting cyber attacks in the future [26].

3.6   Where: Where Is Cyber Security Visualization Being Used?

Cyber threat intelligence objects can be any of the attributes in the data file. All of this is due to the fact that these data are large, complex and varied. Intelligence is evidence-based knowledge of threats. The task of the data visualization system is to help the user make decisions and react. We need to provide them with intelligence - whether it is technical information about tools and technologies, whether the opponent is using, or contextual intelligence about actor motivation or different campaigns. Graphics are the ideal way to deliver such scale, complexity, and variety in a way that the user can easily manage [27].

3.7   Summary of Results

The results of our survey are summarized in Table 1 based on the characteristics of Visual Variables [9] as follows:

Table 1. Comparison of visualization capabilities of visual analytics platforms and tools for cybersecurity according to Bertin's [9] visual variables (Y = yes; N = no; G = good; M = marginal; P = poor; NA = not applicable)

Tool	Syntactic	Size	Shape	Orientation	Color Hue	Color value	Text-ure	Reference
CRUMBS	A	N	Y	Y	Y	N	Y	[28]
	S	Y	N	Y	Y	Y	Y	
	O	P	P	M	G	G	M	
	N	P	P	M	P	P	P	
Taggle	A	N	N	Y	Y	Y	N	[29]
	S	N	N	Y	Y	N	N	
	O	G	P	P	M	M	P	
	N	P	M	M	G	P	P	
Bespoke	A	N	N	N	N	Y	N	[30]
	S	Y	N	N	N	Y	N	
	O	P	P	P	P	M	P	
	N	P	P	P	P	P	P	
FLUKES	A	N	N	N	Y	Y	N	[31]
	S	N	N	N	Y	Y	N	
	O	P	P	P	G	P	P	
	N	P	P	P	G	P	P	
Visualdrives	A	Y	N	N	Y	N	N	[32]
	S	Y	N	N	Y	N	N	
	O	G	P	P	G	M	P	
	N	G	P	P	G	M	P	
Insight	A	N	N	N	Y	N	N	[33]
	S	N	N	N	Y	N	N	
	O	P	P	P	M	P	P	
	N	P	P	P	M	P	P	
CyberForensic TimeLab	A	N	N	Y	N	N	N	[34]
	S	N	N	Y	Y	N	N	
	O	P	P	G	M	P	P	
	N	p	p	G	M	P	P	
BubbleNet	A	Y	N	Y	Y	Y	N	[35]
	S	Y	N	Y	Y	N	N	
	O	G	P	P	G	G	P	
	N	G	P	P	G	G	P	
Change-Link 2.0	A	N	N	N	Y	Y	N	[36]
	S	N	N	N	Y	Y	N	
	O	P	M	P	G	G	P	
	N	P	M	P	G	G	P	

(*continued*)

Table 1. (*continued*)

Tool	Syntactic	Size	Shape	Orientation	Color Hue	Color value	Text-ure	Reference
LogAnalysis	A	Y	Y	Y	Y	Y	N	[37]
	S	Y	Y	Y	Y	Y	N	
	O	G	G	G	G	G	P	
	N	G	G	G	G	G	P	
Topic models	A	N	N	N	Y	N	N	[38]
	S	N	N	N	Y	Y	N	
	O	P	P	P	G	M	P	
	N	P	P	P	G	M	P	
ContraVis	A	Y	Y	N	Y	Y	N	[39]
	S	Y	Y	N	Y	Y	N	
	O	G	G	M	G	G	P	
	N	G	G	M	G	G	P	
XFake	A	N	N	N	Y	Y	N	[40]
	S	N	N	N	Y	N	N	
	O	P	P	P	G	M	P	
	N	P	P	P	G	G	P	
ExplorViz	A	N	N	N	Y	Y	N	[41]
	S	N	N	N	Y	Y	N	
	O	P	P	M	G	G	P	
	N	P	P	M	G	G	P	

Associative (A): Is change in this visual variable enough to allow us to perceive them as a group?

Selective (S): Is change in this visual variable alone enough to allow us to select it from a group?

Ordinal (O): Are changes in this variable perceived as ordered?

Numerical (N): Is there a numerical reading obtainable from changes in this visual variable?

4   Conclusions

This paper provided an overview of visual analytics methods and techniques for cyber security domain data. Based on the results and findings from our analysis, we summarize the key challenges of the future visual analytics research in the cyber security domain.

Scalability. The growth of data available for analysis presents an overwhelming challenge to visualizing cyber security data effectively. Most of visual analytics techniques are not scalable to extreme-scale data. To address scalability problems, the capability of effectively handling very large amounts of network data, visual analytics methods such as VAST [42] have been proposed. Despite this scalability of visualization will continue to attract increased interest in the future.

Report Generation. Report generation methods have attracted much attention over the past several years in cyber security domain. Visual analytics tools often allow creating reports on the results of the analysis. Report (or insight) generation from visualizations can provide insights into patterns of data found during the analysis [43]. Nevertheless, report generation from visualization is still in its infancy, while the methods used are heuristic and subjective, leaving much room for researchers to study.

Reliability. Uncertainty modeling is critical in ensuring reliability and trustworthiness of visual analytics and supporting making informed decisions. Few approaches allow to display the uncertainty information in cyber security domain visually [44]. However, there are still no widely acknowledged techniques.

Heterogeneous Data Analysis: Security analysts often obtain information by analyzing different sources of information such as operating system logs and social networks. Although a wide variety of techniques have been proposed to visualize data sources individually, the development of a consistent and concise interaction mechanism between these views still remains challenging [27].

Collaborative Intelligence. Incident response teams often have to work closely together when trying to resolve a system breach. Collaborative visual analytics [45, 46] emphasizes the importance of sharing and exchanging knowledge and insight between collaborating cyber security experts working remotely on the same problem. The need for integration of visual displays of data between different tools and stakeholder will continue to be highly relevant in the future.

Situation Awareness. Large volume of data extracted from computer networks and high complexity of relations between data inhibits achieving situational awareness by an expert. The final aim is to present a bird's view on the security events to cyber security experts for decision support and situation awareness [47, 48].

Usability. To provide efficient decision support, visualization interfaces should have the general look of the system well designed and aesthetically pleasing while ensuring the requirements of target audience of a system are satisfied? Main user experience components including familiarity, learnability, responsiveness, performance, intuitiveness, efficiency, helpfulness, and satisfactoriness [49] must be ensured.

Privacy. Security visualization systems should ensure the protection of private user data when user privacy is top priority, while analyzing user behavior through checking network traffic or analyzing logs.

Human Factors. Effective use of colour, texture, shape, and motion, etc., can effectively capture human attention, which is highly relevant for real-time monitoring tasks [50].

Acknowledgement. This paper is supported in part by European Union's Horizon 2020 research and innovation programme under Grant Agreement No. 830892, project "Strategic programs for advanced research and technology in Europe" (SPARTA).

References

1. Keim, D., Andrienko, G., Fekete, J.-D., Görg, C., Kohlhammer, J., Melançon, G.: Visual analytics: definition, process, and challenges. In: Kerren, A., Stasko, J.T., Fekete, J.-D., North, C. (eds.) Information Visualization. LNCS, vol. 4950, pp. 154–175. Springer, Heidelberg (2008). https://doi.org/10.1007/978-3-540-70956-5_7
2. Shiravi, H., Shiravi, A., Ghorbani, A.A.: A survey of visualization systems for network security. IEEE Trans. Vis. Comput. Graph. **18**(8), 1313–1329 (2012). https://doi.org/10.1109/tvcg.2011.144
3. Fink, G.A., North, C.L., Endert, A., Rose, S.: Visualizing cyber security: usable workspaces. In: 2009 6th International Workshop on Visualization for Cyber Security. IEEE (2009). https://doi.org/10.1109/vizsec.2009.5375542
4. Khanh Dang, T., Tri Dang, T.: A survey on security visualization techniques for web information systems. Int. J. Web Inf. Syst. **9**(1), 6–31 (2013). https://doi.org/10.1108/17440081311316361
5. Tianfield, H.: Cyber security situational awareness. In: 2016 IEEE International Conference on Internet of Things (iThings) and IEEE Green Computing and Communications (GreenCom) and IEEE Cyber, Physical and Social Computing (CPSCom) and IEEE Smart Data (SmartData) (2016). https://doi.org/10.1109/ithings-greencom-cpscom-smartdata.2016.165
6. Marty, R.: Cyber security: how visual analytics unlock insight. In: 19th ACM SIGKDD International Conference on Knowledge Discovery and Data Mining, KDD 2013. ACM Press (2013). https://doi.org/10.1145/2487575.2491132
7. McCaslin, M.L., Scott, K.W.: The five-question method for framing a qualitative research study. Qual. Rep. **8**(3), 447–461 (2003)
8. Hohman, F.M., Kahng, M., Pienta, R., Chau, D.H.: Visual analytics in deep learning: An interrogative survey for the next frontiers. IEEE Trans. Vis. Comput. Graph. (2018). https://doi.org/10.1109/TVCG.2018.2843369
9. Bertin, J.: Graphische Semiologie: Diagramme, Netze, Karten; Translated from the 2nd French Edition (1973). Walter de Gruyter, Berlin, Germany (1974). ISBN 3-11-003660-6
10. Störrle, H., Fish, A.: Towards an operationalization of the "Physics of Notations" for the analysis of visual languages. In: Moreira, A., Schätz, B., Gray, J., Vallecillo, A., Clarke, P. (eds.) MODELS 2013. LNCS, vol. 8107, pp. 104–120. Springer, Heidelberg (2013). https://doi.org/10.1007/978-3-642-41533-3_7
11. Sacha, D., Kraus, M., Keim, D.A., Chen, M.: VIS4ML: an ontology for visual analytics assisted machine learning. IEEE Trans. Vis. Comput. Graph. **25**(1), 385–395 (2019). https://doi.org/10.1109/TVCG.2018.2864838
12. Staheli, D., et al.: Visualization evaluation for cyber security. In: Eleventh Workshop on Visualization for Cyber Security, VizSec 2014. ACM Press (2014). https://doi.org/10.1145/2671491.2671492
13. de Bruijn, H., Janssen, M.: Building cybersecurity awareness: the need for evidence-based framing strategies. Gov. Inf. Q. **34**(1), 1–7 (2017). https://doi.org/10.1016/j.giq.2017.02.007
14. Zheng, M., Robbins, H., Chai, Z., Thapa, P., Moore, T.: Cybersecurity research datasets: taxonomy and empirical analysis. In: 11th USENIX Conference on Cyber Security Experimentation and Test (CSET 2018), p. 2. USENIX Association, Berkeley (2018)
15. He, J., Chen, H., Chen, Y., Tang, X., Zou, Y.: Diverse visualization techniques and methods of moving-object-trajectory data: a review. ISPRS Int. J. Geo-Inf. **8**(2), 63 (2019). https://doi.org/10.3390/ijgi8020063

16. Kotenko, I., Novikova, E.: VisSecAnalyzer: a visual analytics tool for network security assessment. In: Cuzzocrea, A., Kittl, C., Simos, D.E., Weippl, E., Xu, L. (eds.) CD-ARES 2013. LNCS, vol. 8128, pp. 345–360. Springer, Heidelberg (2013). https://doi.org/10.1007/978-3-642-40588-4_24

17. Zhao, Y., Zhou, F., Fan, X., Liang, X., Liu, Y.: IDSRadar: a real-time visualization framework for IDS alerts. Sci. China Inf. Sci. 56(8), 1–12 (2013). https://doi.org/10.1007/s11432-013-4891-9

18. Haggerty, J., Haggerty, S., Taylor, M.: Forensic triage of email network narratives through visualisation. Inf. Manag. Comput. Secur. 22(4), 358–370 (2014). https://doi.org/10.1108/IMCS-11-2013-0080

19. Chen, V.Y., Razip, A.M., Ko, S., Qian, C.Z., Ebert, D.S.: Multi-aspect visual analytics on large-scale high-dimensional cyber security data. Inf. Vis. 14(1), 62–75 (2013). https://doi.org/10.1177/1473871613488573

20. Liao, Q., Striegel, A., Chawla, N.: Visualizing graph dynamics and similarity for enterprise network security and management. In: 7th International Symposium on Visualization for Cyber Security (VizSec 2010), pp. 34–45 (2010). https://doi.org/10.1145/1850795.1850799

21. McKenna, S., Staheli, D., Fulcher, C., Meyer, M.: BubbleNet: a cyber security dashboard for visualizing patterns. Comput. Graph. Forum 35(3), 281–290 (2016). https://doi.org/10.1111/cgf.12904

22. Wongsuphasawat, K., Guerra Gómez, J.A., Plaisant, C., Wang, T., Taieb-Maimon, M., Shneiderman, B.: LifeFlow. In: Annual Conference Extended abstracts on Human Factors in Computing Systems - CHI EA 2011. ACM Press (2011). https://doi.org/10.1145/1979742.1979557

23. McPherson, J., Ma, K.-L., Krystosk, P., Bartoletti, T., Christensen, M.: PortVis. In: Proceedings of the 2004 ACM Workshop on Visualization and Data Mining for Computer Security - VizSEC/DMSEC 2004. ACM Press (2004). https://doi.org/10.1145/1029208.1029220

24. Qiu, H.S.: Streaming data visualization for network security. Ph.D. thesis, Princeton University (2017)

25. Goodall, J.R.: Introduction to visualization for computer security. In: Goodall, J.R., Conti, G., Ma, K.L. (eds.) VizSEC 2007. Mathematics and Visualization, pp. 1–17. Springer, Heidelberg (2008). https://doi.org/10.1007/978-3-540-78243-8_1

26. Hu, H., Zhang, H., Liu, Y., Wang, Y.: Quantitative method for network security situation based on attack prediction. Secur. Commun. Netw. 2017, 19 (2017). https://doi.org/10.1155/2017/3407642. Article ID 3407642

27. Scheepens, R., Michels, S., van de Wetering, H., van Wijk, J.J.: Rationale visualization for safety and security. Comput. Graph. Forum 34, 191–200 (2015)

28. Angelini, M., Blasilli, G., Lenti, S., Santucci, G.: Visual exploration and analysis of the Italian cybersecurity framework. In: Workshop on Advanced Visual Interfaces AVI (2018). https://doi.org/10.1145/3206505.3206579

29. Furmanova, K., et al.: Taggle: Combining Overview and Details in Tabular Data Visualizations, 14 p. (2019). arXiv:1712.05944v3 [cs.HC]

30. Tillekens, A., Le-Khac, N.-A., Thi, T.T.P.: A Bespoke forensics GIS tool. In: 2016 International Conference on Computational Science and Computational Intelligence, pp. 987–992. IEEE (2016). https://doi.org/10.1109/csci.2016.188

31. Aldwairi, M., Alsaadi, H.H.: FLUKES: autonomous log forensics, intelligence and visualization tool. In: Proceedings of ICFNDS 2017, Cambridge, United Kingdom, 19–20 July 2017, 6 p. (2017). https://doi.org/10.1145/3102304.3102337

32. Tuncel, M.A., Francis, H., Taylor, M., Jones, D.L.: Visualdrives forensic tool. In: International Conference on Developments of E-Systems Engineering (DeSE), Burj Khalifa, Dubai, United Arab Emirates, 13–15 December 2015. https://doi.org/10.1109/dese.2015.68
33. Hales, G., Ferguson, I., Archibald, J.: Insight: an application of information visualisation techniques to digital forensics investigations. Int. J. Cyber Situat. Aware. 2(1), 100–118 (2017)
34. Olsson, J., Boldt, M.: Computer forensic timeline visualization tool. Digit. Investig., S78–S87 (2009). https://doi.org/10.1016/j.diin.2009.06.008
35. McKenna, S., Staheli, D., Fulcher, C., Meyer, M.: BubbleNet: a cyber security dashboard for visualizing patterns. In: Eurographics Conference on Visualization (EuroVis), vol. 35(3), pp. 281–290 (2016). https://doi.org/10.1111/cgf.12904
36. Leschke, T.R., Nicholas, C.: Change-Link 2.0: a digital forensic tool for visualizing changes to shadow volume data. In: VizSec 2013, Atlanta, GA, USA, 14 October 2013, pp. 17–24 (2013)
37. Catanese, S.A., Fiumara, G.: A visual tool for forensic analysis of mobile phone traffic. In: MiFOR 2010, Firenze, Italy, 29 October 2010, pp. 71–76 (2010)
38. Goswami, A., Mohapatra, D.P., Zhai, C.: Qu antifying and visualizing the demand and supply gap from e-commerce search data using topic models. In: WWW 2019 Companion, San Francisco, CA, USA, 13–17 May 2019, pp. 348–353 (2019)
39. Le, T.V.M., Akoglu, L.: ContraVis: contrastive and visual topic modeling for comparing document collections. In: Proceedings of the 2019 World Wide Web Conference (WWW 2019), San Francisco, CA, USA, 13–17 May 2019, 11 p. ACM, New York (2019). https://doi.org/10.1145/3308558.3313617
40. Yang, F., et al.: XFake: explainable fake news detector with visualizations. In: WWW 2019, San Francisco, CA, USA, 13–17 May 2019. https://doi.org/10.1145/3308558.3314119
41. Fittkau, F., Krause, A., Hasselbring, W.: Software landscape and application visualization or system comprehension with ExplorViz. Inf. Softw. Technol. 87(2017), 259–277 (2017). https://doi.org/10.1016/j.infsof.2016.07.004
42. Vallentin, M., Paxson, V., Sommer, R.: VAST: a unified platform for interactive network forensics. In: 13th Usenix Conference on Networked Systems Design and Implementation (NSDI 2016), pp. 345–362. USENIX Association, Berkeley (2016)
43. Baráth, J., Harakaľ, M.: Protocols for exchange of cyber security information. In: Security and Protection of Information (2013)
44. Bonneau, G.-P., Hege, H.-C., Johnson, C.R., Oliveira, M.M., Potter, K., Rheingans, P., Schultz, T.: Overview and state-of-the-art of uncertainty visualization. In: Hansen, Charles D., Chen, M., Johnson, C.R., Kaufman, A.E., Hagen, H. (eds.) Scientific Visualization. MV, pp. 3–27. Springer, London (2014). https://doi.org/10.1007/978-1-4471-6497-5_1
45. Zhong, Z., et al.: A user-centered multi-space collaborative visual analysis for cyber security. Chin. J. Electron. 27(5), 910–919 (2018). https://doi.org/10.1049/cje.2017.09.021
46. Kabil, A., Duval, T., Cuppens, N., Le Comte, G., Halgand, Y., et al.: Why should we use 3D collaborative virtual environments for cyber security? In: IEEE 4th VR International Workshop on Collaborative Virtual Environments (IEEEVR 2018) (2018)
47. Erbacher, R.F., Frincke, D.A., Wong, P.C., Moody, S., Fink, G.: A multi-phase network situational awareness cognitive task analysis. Inf. Vis. 9, 204–219 (2010)
48. Angelini, M., Santucci, G.: Cyber situational awareness: from geographical alerts to high-level management. J. Vis. 20(3), 453–459 (2017). https://doi.org/10.1007/s12650-016-0377-3
49. Nielsen, J.: Usability Engineering. Academic Press, London (1993)
50. Dasgupta, A., Arendt, D.L., Franklin, L.R., Wong, P.C., Cook, K.A.: Human factors in streaming data analysis: challenges and opportunities for information visualization. Comput. Graph. Forum 37(1), 254–272 (2018). https://doi.org/10.1111/cgf.13264

Software Engineering: Special Session on Software and Model Metrics and Measurements

A Novel Unsupervised Learning Approach for Assessing Web Services Refactoring

Guillermo Rodriguez[1], Cristian Mateos[1], Luciano Listorti[2],
Brian Hammer[2], and Sanjay Misra[3(✉)]

[1] ISISTAN-UNICEN-CONICET, Tandil, Argentina
{guillermo.rodriguez,cristian.mateos}@isistan.unicen.edu.ar
[2] UNICEN, Tandil, Argentina
[3] Covenant University, Ota, Nigeria
ssopam@gmail.com

Abstract. During the last years, the development of Service-Oriented applications has become a trend. Given the characteristics and challenges posed by current systems, it has become essential to adopt this solution since it provides a great performance in distributed and heterogeneous environments. At the same time, the necessity of flexibility and great capacity of adaptation introduce a process of constant modifications and growth. Thus, developers easily make mistakes such as code duplication or unnecessary code, generating a negative impact on quality attributes such as performance and maintainability. Refactoring is considered a technique that greatly improves the quality of software and provides a solution to this issue. In this context, our work proposes an approach for comparing manual service groupings and automatic groupings that allows analyzing, evaluating and validating clustering techniques applied to improve service cohesion and fragmentation. We used V-Measure with homogeneity and completeness as the evaluation metrics. Additionally, we have performed improvements in existing clustering techniques of a previous work, VizSOC, that reach 20% of gain regarding the aforementioned metrics. Moreover, we added an implementation of the COBWEB clustering algorithm yielding fruitful results.

Keywords: Software refactoring · Web services · Service grouping ·
Text mining · Unsupervised machine learning

1 Introduction

Currently, the Service-Oriented Computing (SOC) paradigm has gained considerably attention by the software industry. This paradigm is commonly built on the architectural style called Service-Oriented Architecture (SOA). SOA solutions have emerged due to their low implementation costs, their prompt response and adaptation to business changes, and the ease and flexibility of integration with legacy systems [1]. The goal of this paradigm is to develop a system as a set of small software components, each one executing in its own process and communicating with each other through (lightweight) mechanisms. In this style

© Springer Nature Switzerland AG 2019
R. Damaševičius and G. Vasiljevienė (Eds.): ICIST 2019, CCIS 1078, pp. 273–284, 2019.
https://doi.org/10.1007/978-3-030-30275-7_21

there are nodes that play the role of providers making their resources available to other nodes called consumers. Consumers have access to remote services in a standardized way. The exchange of data is done through a set of protocols such as SOAP (Simple Object Access Protocol), which is based on the use of a data structuring language such as XML, or REST (REpresentational State Transfer), which generally uses the JSON format.

A WSDL (Web Service Description Language) document is, on the other hand, an XML-based description of the functional requirements necessary to establish communication [2]. A WSDL document provides a Web Service description of how the service can be called, what parameters it expects and what data structure it returns as a response, among other characteristics.

The flexibility of implementing SOA solutions in heterogeneous environments and the ability to adapt to give quick responses in situations in which changing business objectives are presented, also entails a system growth that makes the maintenance by developers imperative. In particular, the growth of a system in an SOA context can reveal design problems within WSDL documents, such as operations that should be in the same document but are in separate documents or operations with different names but which actually do the same, among other problems [3].

In this context, refactoring is considered a technique that greatly improves the quality of the software and the productivity of the developers, which facilitates the maintenance and understanding of the system. The use of semi-automatic tools that use the first contract services development approach [4], like Apache Axis2 for Java, can produce duplication of unnecessary code or inside WSDL documents. A possible solution is to detect common practices that reduce syntactic information within a WSDL document and define solutions that eliminate the problems introduced in the WSDL by using the semi-automatic tools. However, WSDL documents are usually extensive and require a meticulous reading, since they are based on XML, which can be arduous, tedious and leads to not distinguishing possible opportunities for refactoring or even more worrying, not detecting errors in the architecture and the system code.

This problem in WSDL documents could have a negative impact on quality of service (QoS) of service-oriented applications [23], such as performance and maintenance and evolving capacity, among others. In this context, there are grouping and visualization techniques that aim to solve or alleviate the aforementioned problems, and in this way, facilitate the task of the developers when they detect opportunities to refactor documents and hence services. There are certain approaches [4–7] that have focused on studying the WSDL documents in isolation instead of analyzing them together in the context of the whole SOA application.

To alleviate this issue, we enrich our previous tool called VizSOC [8] by incorporating a set of metrics for measuring the quality of refactoring opportunities in comparison with manual refactoring conducted by expert software developers (ground truth). Furthermore, we added another clustering technique to VizSOC, which has impacted considerably on the clustering performance, i.e. COBWEB. To address the first issue, we searched for a set of WSDL document clusters present in an SOA architecture, resulting from manual refactoring, which presented the best grouping. The term "best grouping" in this context means those sets of clusters that are more "similar" to those obtained as a result of applying the unsupervised learning techniques. That is to say, the distances between the manual groupings and the automatic ones were measured, and then a comparative analysis was made to decide which manual refactoring should be chosen. To do this, the V-measure metric was used along with its sub-metrics homogeneity and completeness [9].

As for the second issue, the purpose of the present work is to achieve an improvement of the clustering techniques through heuristics, modifications and new grouping algorithms that assist the software developers in the detection of opportunities for refactoring Web Services being analyzed. The new modifications are based on improving the modeling of the problem and its representation through the use of text mining techniques, such as word splitting and word filtering. In addition to this, we also propose to include a new clustering algorithm, namely COBWEB.

To evaluate our approach, we carried comparisons between different manual groupings and automatic groupings. As a basis for the implementation of the solution, we have the web tool VizSOC [8] and a set of manual refactorings applied to a case study of 211 WSDL documents, taken from a Web Services dataset obtained from the migration of a real legacy system [6].

The remaining of this paper is organized as follows. Section 2 describes the background. Section 3 presents the related work. Section 4 presents the proposed approach. The empirical evaluation of the approach is explained and summarized in Sect. 5. Finally, conclusions and future lines of research are stated in Sect. 6.

2 Background

The Service-Oriented Computing paradigm promotes the efficient development and deployment of an application in terms of cost and time. To flexibly enable the composition of applications Web Services are utilized as building blocks [10]. Several software applications have started a refactoring process towards service-oriented software applications. Refactoring aims at increasing understandability, flexibility, and dependability, while at the same time preserving the functional behavior of the artifact in order to make it more maintainable [21]. Furthemore, refactoring might achieve better modularization and generalization of the components [22]. In this context, Web Services are usually described by means of WSDL documents. This language is an XML format that allows software developers to describe service functionality and communication protocols to be accessed through the Internet [4]. The main conceptual elements in WSDL documents are Types, Messages, PortTypes, Bindings and Services. Types contain the definitions of the types of data that will be used in/out the service. To specify types, an XML schema is utilized. Each data type defines an element with a complexType inside it, which lists a series of elements of basic types (built-in).

Messages define the contents of a message abstractly by using data types defined in *wsdl:types*. Each message consists of one or more parts that will make use of an element or complexType, referencing them with the element and type message attributes respectively. There will be as many *wsdl:message* tags as necessary.

A PortType is a set of abstract operations that indicate which abstract messages are received and sent. WSDL supports several operational patterns including one-way (receives a message), request-response (receives a message, then sends one in response), request-response (sends a message, then receives one in response) and notification.

To define operations, their messages are detailed by means of the *wsdl:operation tag*. The fact that they are request-response operations are specified implicitly by firstly placing the *wsdl:input* tag and then *wsdl:output*. Bindings provide the format and protocol details for the messages and operations of a PortType. For example, the operations might be accessed by means of the protocol SOAP, and then a specific SOAP binding is declared in the document [11]. Finally, Services are a set of related ports under the same name. Each port defines a particular and concrete endpoint of the communication, linking a binding with a location address.

3   Related work

In this section we analyze different research works that propose alternatives to facilitate the detection of refactoring opportunities in SOA applications and different approaches to achieve the grouping of services, using several clustering techniques. VizSOC [8] is a web tool based on unsupervised learning that aims to assist software developers in detecting refactoring opportunities in SOA applications. VizSOC analyzes the WSDL documents belonging to an SOA application, detecting anti-patterns present in these contracts, suggesting how to solve them and applying clustering techniques (K-Means, Expectation Maximization and hierarchical algorithms) to detect refactoring opportunities, such as for example, reducing duplicate functionality. The tool exploits the advantages of the Hierarchical Edge Bundle (HEB) visualization technique to help developers understand the clusters generated by VizSOC [8].

Dong et al. [12] propose a set of algorithms to implement similarity searches for Web Service operations. Each structure of the services is explored, and grouping mechanisms are used in terms of the descriptions of Web Services operations and the names of the parameters of the operations. The main factor of the algorithm proposed here is the use of a technique that creates clusters of parameter names that are mapped to semantically significant concepts. Along this line, [13] propose an approach that uses key features (types, messages, ports, content, and service name) extracted from WSDL documents with the aim of grouping Web Services based on similar functionalities. These features describe and reveal the functionality of a Web Service. From these features, Web Services are grouped in similar groups.

[14] propose the use of the code-first or bottom-up method to avoid common design errors when generating WSDL contracts and to measure the impact of the approach in the discovery of services. This is done through the use of language-specific tools such as Axis' Java2WSDL or the Visual Studio WSDL tool. The main contributions of this article are the presentation of statistical evidence showing that WSDL contracts using code-first, can get rid of the same antipatterns, simply looking at the classic code metrics and the empirically demonstrated viability of the metric directed refactorings to improve the visibility of services.

However, there is a research line pursuing attention regarding the comparison between manual and automatic groupings that allows analyzing and validating the refactorings generated by automatic techniques. Furthermore, current approaches might take advantage from a mechanism to facilitate the additional improvement out of clustering techniques.

4   Our Approach

In light of the aforementioned gaps in the literature, we present a novel approach useful for assessing refactoring of SOA-based software applications. We aim to compare manual with automated refactoring when using unsupervised learning. Figure 1 illustrates our approach, which is divided into two stages. The first one will result in what is commonly known as ground truth, that is, an automatic refactoring of a WSDL document dataset that presents the best grouping (as judged by human developers). This grouping will be used as input to the second stage, in which it will act as a reference (ideal to achieve grouping) in the process of designing automatic grouping algorithms.

4.1   First Stage

These manual refactorings arise from the work carried out by advanced students in the Systems Engineering BSc program at the Faculty of Exact Sciences (Universidad Nacional del Centro de la Provincia de Buenos Aires). These students had elementary knowledge of development of service-oriented applications and software refactoring.

The objective of these works was to analyze the above-mentioned case study to group operations in new services according to students' criteria. These refactorings followed criteria that analyze the names of the operations, the input and output parameters, the code repetition, among others, in order to determine if the grouping is adequate.

It is important to emphasize that, initially, there were 8 manual refactorings, which after a process of analysis, only 3 of them were viable for their use. The two main problems detected, which have been decisive in deciding discarding the remaining 5, were the lack of operations and the impossibility of accurately determining the correspondence of certain operations in manual refactorings with those of the original case study.

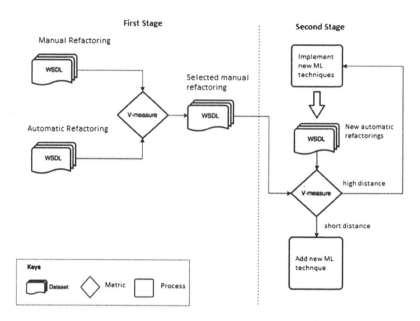

Fig. 1. Description of our Machine Learning-powered (ML) approach.

Once the 3 useful manual refactorings have been selected, the process of comparative analysis of these with the refactorings resulting from applying automatic clustering techniques to the case study was initiated. We explored the following clustering techniques: K-Means [15], COBWEB [16], Hierarchical [17] and Expectation Maximization (EM) [18]. To measure the similarity between two groupings (manual and automatic), the V-Measure metric is utilized.

4.2 Second Stage

The second stage aims to achieve a set of improvements to the automatic clustering techniques implemented in the extended VizSOC tool through a comparative analysis similar to the first stage. This process could be schematically described through the following steps:

– Define and design an improvement of a technique, new algorithm or heuristic.
– Implement this modification in the VizSOC tool.
– Carry out the grouping of services with the new modification.
– Measure through V-Measure the distance between the ground truth (obtained from the first stage) and the grouping with the improvement and without the improvement.

By conducting this workflow (Fig. 1), we intend to improve the automatic techniques implemented in the tool by using the results obtained in the first stage. The manual refactoring chosen in the first stage is an ideal service grouping that will allow determining if the new technique can be considered as an improvement or not. Finally, if the new modification outperforms the existing ones, it will be implemented in the tool to facilitate the task of developers when detecting refactoring opportunities [19].

5 Experimental evaluation

This section evaluates the effectiveness of our approach to assess clustering techniques applied to refactoring of service-oriented applications.

To carry out the first stage, we considered a WSDL dataset taken from the ISISTAN software library, which was produced by migrating a Mill Sales Management system implemented in COBOL to SOA. The system provides support for sales transaction management between clients, suppliers and creditors, and comprises 211 COBOL programs and an extra COBOL program acting as a program selector (menu). No databases or CICS transactions are involved, since data storage is programmatically handled via ".dat" files. An independent file (COMMAREA) is used for data definition of each COBOL program. First, direct migration was done, generating 211 Web Services with 252 operations by wrapping each COBOL program via a 1-to-1 mapping strategy [20]. WSDL interfaces were also generated by building a thin service layer. From this single dataset, 3 new datasets were generated by applying manual refactorings, mainly removing duplicate operations and merging/joining operations were appropriate.

Having implemented the modifications, the comparison process consisted in calculating the V-Measure between automatic and manual refactoring. Tables 1 and 2 show the comparative process described above. The only difference between the tables is that Table 1 uses k = 38 (number of clusters) for the automatic algorithms that need it (K-Means and EM) and Table 2 shows the number of clusters contained in the manual refactoring that is being used.

Table 1. Distances between manual and automatic refactorings using V-Measure with k = 38.

k = 38	K-Means	Hierarchical	EM
Manual refactoring A	0.657	0.472	0.645
Manual refactoring B	0.727	0.549	0.722
Manual refactoring C	0.736	0.546	0.725

Observing the results and emphasizing the distances obtained, Manual Refactoring A can be discarded, since it looses in all the comparisons. On the other hand, Manual Refactoring C outperformed all the algorithms and it should be considered as ground truth. Only in the Hierarchical algorithm Manual Refactoring B obtained better results, although being such a small difference it was considered that it should not affect the final decision.

Table 2. Distances between manual and automatic refactorings using V-Measure with k = No. of groups of manual refactoring.

k = #manual groups	K-Means	Hierarchical	EM
Manual refactoring A k = 52	0.719	0.472	0.691
Manual refactoring B k = 130	0.884	0.549	0.883
Manual refactoring C k = 144	0.904	0.546	0.898

As for the second stage, the results obtained with the application of improvements and modifications are described. The Manual Refactoring C with 144 clusters is used for all the comparison tests, and for the sake of simplicity, the algorithms that need a k (number of clusters) used the value returned by the Hierarchical algorithm (38 clusters).

Table 3 shows the results in terms of V-Measure of the application of text mining strategies, which are based on the separation and filtering of terms, on K-Means and EM algorithms. Remarkably, the results obtained in terms of V-Measure after applying text mining strategies were better than the application of bare clustering algorithms.

Table 3. Distances between the manual and automatic refactoring with and without text mining strategies: splitting and filtering of words.

	K-Means	EM
Without modifications	0.736	0.725
With modifications	**0.784**	**0.775**

Once the implementation of the grouping at the WSDL level has been carried out by means of text mining strategies, two clustering algorithms were run. The first one is applied in the first division and generates datasets of WSDLs, whereas the second one is applied to each dataset individually. Table 4 depicts the results in terms of V-Measure after running K-Means, EM and COBWEB as clustering algorithms corresponding to the first run.

Table 4. Distances between the manual and automatic refactoring at WSDL grouping level.

	K-Means	COBWEB	EM
Without modifications	**0.784**	0.643	0.775

Secondly, for the second grouping (at the operation level) it is unfeasible to use algorithms that receive a number of cluster beforehand. This stems from the fact that datasets to which the algorithm is applied have an unknown length, since they depend on the result of the first algorithm used. Therefore, we decided to use the Hierarchical and COBWEB clustering algorithms only.

For the sake of clarity, Table 5 illustrates the results in terms of V-Measure of the comparisons between Hierarchical and COBWEB algorithms including text mining strategies. The results indicate the COBWEB outperforms considerably the Hierarchical clustering algorithm.

Table 5. Distances between Hierarchical and COBWEB algorithms with text mining strategies.

	Hierarchical	COBWEB
With modifications	0.909	**0.923**

To sum up, Table 6 presents web service architectures before and after applying refactoring (original dataset, manual refactoring A, manual refactoring B and manual refactoring C). We utilized the following metrics to visualize the before-after effect: Number of WSDL documents (WSDLs), Number of Operations (Operations), Average of Operations per WSDL (Operations per WSDL (Avg.)), Lines of Code (LOC) and Average of Lines of Code per WSDL (LOC per WSDL (Avg.)).

Table 6. Web service architectures before and after applying refactoring.

Dataset	Original	Refactoring A	Refactoring B	Refactoring C
WSDLs	211	52	144	130
Operations	252	140	201	186
Operations per WSDL (Avg.)	1.19	2.69	1.39	1.43
Lines of Code (LOC)	44627	14201	28205	26658
LOC per WSDL (Avg.)	211.5	273.09	195.86	205.06

6 Conclusions and future work

The work presented an approach for assessing automatic refactoring of Web Services. The approach utilized the results of comparisons between manual and automatic groupings as a means of validating the clustering techniques, which have been improved with text mining strategies.

In addition, alternatives are proposed to facilitate the detection of refactoring opportunities in SOA applications and different approaches to achieve the grouping of services, using clustering. These alternatives and improvements showed favorable results by 20%, with V-Measure scores as high as 0.92.

On the other hand, it is important to emphasize that the implementation of the approach developed in this work continued with the original design principles. This means that it is perfectly feasible to apply both the new improvements and the comparison in new cases of studies. In this sense, VizSOC operates as a testbed where new grouping schemes can be empirically studied. The grouping of similar operations manually in these cases can become a tedious task, with a very high time demand in many cases. Our approach aimed to solve this problem, automating the clustering of similar operations in seconds. With this, developers would have a powerful tool when designing refactorings in contexts with numerous services and operations. To this end, integrating our approach with the VizSOC web tool is also crucial.

As future work, we will address three important limitations of our current approach. First, there is a need to enhance the proposed text mining strategies to exploit semantic similarity metrics between terms in operations in order to propose refactorings, since at present we only exploit syntactic approaches. For example, we could use metrics such as Google's Normalized Distance. Second, we plan to incorporate reverse engineering to reduce efforts in maintaining refactored legacy systems documented by means of visual representations [24]. Last but not least, we also need to validate the approach with more datasets coming from SOA contexts in order to ensure generality, for which another COBOL-to-SOA dataset from a governmental institution is available [20].

Acknowledgment. We acknowledge the anonymous referees for their comments to improve the paper. We also thank the people who helped us with the manual refactorings.

References

1. Erickson, J., Siau, K.: Web services, service-oriented computing, and service-oriented architecture: separating hype from reality. In: Principle Advancements in Database Management Technologies: New Applications and Frameworks, p. 176 (2009)
2. Christensen, E., Curbera, F., Meredith, G., Weerawarana, S.: Web services description language (WSDL) 1.1. (2001)
3. Rodríguez, G., Soria, Á., Teyseyre, A., Berdun, L., Campo, M.: Unsupervised learning for detecting refactoring opportunities in service-oriented applications. In: Hartmann, S., Ma, H. (eds.) DEXA 2016. LNCS, vol. 9828, pp. 335–342. Springer, Cham (2016). https://doi.org/10.1007/978-3-319-44406-2_27
4. Mateos, C., Crasso, M., Zunino, A., Ordiales Coscia, J.L.: Revising WSDL documents: why and how - Part II. IEEE Internet Comput. **17**(5), 46–53 (2013)
5. Rodriguez, J.M., Crasso, M., Mateos, C., Zunino, A.: Best practices for describing, consuming, and discovering web services: a comprehensive toolset. Softw. Pract. Experience **43**(6), 613–639 (2013)
6. Mateos, C., Rodriguez, J., Zunino, A.: A tool to improve code-first web services discoverability through text mining techniques. Softw. Pract. Experience **45**(7), 925–948 (2015)

7. Webster, D., Townend, P., Xu, J.: Interface refactoring in performance-constrained web services. In: 2012 IEEE 15th International Symposium on Object/Component/Service-Oriented Real-Time Distributed Computing (ISORC), pp. 111–118. IEEE (2012)
8. Rodriguez, G., Teyseyre, A., Soria, A., Berdun, L.: A Visualization Tool to Detect Refactoring Opportunities in SOA Applications. In: XLIII Latin American Conference on Informatics. IEEE (2017)
9. Cohen, A.R., Vitanyi, P.M.: Normalized Google Distance of Multisets with Applications. arXiv preprint arXiv:1308.3177 (2013)
10. Ezenwoke, A., Misra, S., Adigun, M.O.: An approach for e-Commerce on-demand service-oriented product line development. Acta Polytechnica Hungarica 10(2), 69–87 (2013)
11. Which style of WSDL should I use? 24 May 2005. https://www.ibm.com/developerworks/library/ws-whichwsdl/. Accessed 3 July 2017
12. Dong, X., Halevy, A., Madhavan, J., Nemes, E., Zhang, J.: Similarity search for web services. In: 30th International Conference on Very large data bases, pp. 372–383. VLDB Endowment (2004)
13. Elgazzar, K., Hassan, A.E., Martin, P.: Clustering wsdl documents to bootstrap the discovery of web services. In: IEEE International Conference on Web Services, pp. 147–154. IEEE (2010)
14. Rodriguez, J.M., Crasso, M., Mateos, C., Zunino, A., Campo, M.: Bottom-up and top-down cobol system migration to web services. IEEE Internet Comput. 17(2), 44–51 (2013)
15. MacQueen, J.: Some methods for classification and analysis of multivariate observations. In: Proceedings of the fifth Berkeley symposium on mathematical statistics and probability, vol. 1, no. 14, pp. 281–297 (1967)
16. Fisher, D.H.: Knowledge acquisition via incremental conceptual clustering. Mach. Learn. 2(2), 139–172 (1987)
17. Ward Jr., J.H.: Hierarchical grouping to optimize an objective function. J. Am. Stat. Assoc. 58(301), 236–244 (1963)
18. Nigam, K., McCallum, A.K., Thrun, S., Mitchell, T.: Text classification from labeled and unlabeled documents using EM. Mach. Learn. 39(2–3), 103–134 (2000)
19. Kim, M., Zimmermann, T., Nagappan, N.: A field study of refactoring challenges and benefits. In: Proceedings of the ACM SIGSOFT 20th International Symposium on the Foundations of Software Engineering, p. 50. ACM (2012)
20. Mateos, C., Zunino, A., Flores, A., Misra, S.: COBOL systems migration to SOA: assessing antipatterns and complexity. Information Technology and Control (2019, in press)
21. Damaševičius, R.: Refactoring of learning objects for mobile learning. In: Papadopoulos, G., Wojtkowski, W., Wojtkowski, G., Wrycza, S., Zupancic, J. (eds.) Information Systems Development, pp. 839–847. Springer, Boston (2009). https://doi.org/10.1007/b137171_88
22. Valincius, K., Stuikys, V., Damasevicius, R.: Understanding of e-commerce is through feature models and their metrics. In: Proceedings of the IADIS International Conference Information Systems, IS, pp. 55–62 (2013)

23. Venckauskas, A., Stuikys, V., Damasevicius, R., Jusas, N.: Modelling of Internet of Things units for estimating security-energy-performance relationships for quality of service and environment awareness. Secur. Commun. Networks **9**(16), 3324–3339 (2016)
24. Ceponienė, L., Drungilas, V., Jurgelaitis, M., čeponis, J.: Method for reverse engineering UML use case model for websites. Inf. Technol. Control **47**(4), 623–638 (2018)

Comparing Static and Dynamic Weighted Software Coupling Metrics

Henning Schnoor[(✉)] and Wilhelm Hasselbring

Software Engineering Group, Kiel University, Kiel, Germany
{hs,wha}@informatik.uni-kiel.de

Abstract. Coupling metrics are an established way to measure software architecture quality with respect to modularity. Static coupling metrics are obtained from the source or compiled code of a program, while dynamic metrics use runtime data gathered e.g., by monitoring a system in production. We study *weighted* dynamic coupling that takes into account how often a connection is executed during a system's run. We investigate the correlation between dynamic weighted metrics and their static counterparts. We use data collected from four different experiments, each monitoring production use of a commercial software system over a period of four weeks. We observe an unexpected level of correlation between the static and the weighted dynamic case as well as revealing differences between class- and package-level analyses.

Keywords: Software metrics · Monitoring · Dynamic analysis · Static analysis

1 Introduction

Coupling [14,31]—the number of inter-module connections in software systems—has long been identified as a software architecture quality metric for modularity [29]. Taking coupling metrics into account during development of a software system can help to increase the system's maintainability and understandability [7], in particular for microservice architectures [24]. As a consequence, aiming for high cohesion and low coupling is accepted as a design guideline in software engineering [11].

In the literature, there exists a wide range of different approaches to measuring coupling. Usually, the coupling degree of a module (class or package) indicates the number of "connections" it has to different system modules. A "connection" between modules **A** and **B** can be, among others, a method call from **A** to **B** or an exception of type **B** thrown by **A**. Many notions of coupling can be measured statically, based on either source code or compiled code.

Static analysis is attractive since it can be performed immediately on source code or on a compiled program. However, it has been observed [5,12,15] that for object-oriented software, static analysis does not suffice, as it often fails to account for effects of inheritance with polymorphism and dynamic binding. This is addressed by dynamic analysis, where monitoring logs are generated while running the software.

© Springer Nature Switzerland AG 2019
R. Damaševičius and G. Vasiljevienė (Eds.): ICIST 2019, CCIS 1078, pp. 285–298, 2019.
https://doi.org/10.1007/978-3-030-30275-7_22

The results obtained by dynamic analysis depend on the workload used for the run of the system yielding the monitoring data. Hence the availability of representative workload for the system under test is crucial for dynamic analysis. As a consequence, dynamic analysis is more expensive than static analysis.

Dynamic analysis is often used to improve upon the accuracy of static coupling analysis [16]. Dynamic analysis uses monitoring data to find, e.g., all classes **B** whose methods are called by the class **A**. In this case, the *individual relationship* between two classes **A** and **B** is *qualitative*: The analysis only determines whether there is a connection between **A** and **B**, and does not take its strength (e.g., number of calls during a system's run) into account. In contrast, a *quantitative* coupling measurement quantifies the strength of the connection between **A** and **B** by assigning it a concrete number.

The coupling metrics we consider in this paper are defined using a *dependency graph*. The nodes of such a graph are program modules (classes or packages). Edges between modules express call relationships. They can be labelled with *weights*, which are integers denoting the number of occurrences of the call represented by the edge. Depending on whether coupling metrics take these weights into account or not, we call the metrics *weighted* or *unweighted*. The main two metrics we consider are the following:

1. Unweighted static coupling, where an edge from **A** to **B** is present in the dependency graph if some method from **B** is called from **A** in the (source or compiled) program code,
2. Weighted dynamic coupling, where an edge from **A** to **B** is present in the graph if such a call actually occurs during the monitored run of the system, and is attributed with the number of such calls observed.

Dynamic weighted coupling measures cannot replace their static counterparts in their role to e.g., indicate maintainability of software projects. However, we expect dynamic weighted coupling measures to be highly relevant for software restructuring: In contrast to static coupling measures, weighted dynamic measures can reflect the runtime communication "hot spots" within a system, and therefore may be helpful in establishing performance predictions of restructuring steps. For example, method calls that happen infrequently may be replaced by a sequence of nested calls or with a network query without relevant performance impacts. Since static coupling measures are often used as basis for restructuring decisions [11,26], dynamic weighted coupling measures can potentially complement their static counterparts in the restructuring process. This possible application leads to the following question: Do dynamic coupling measures yield additional information beyond what we can obtain from static analysis?

Initially, we expected static and dynamic coupling degrees to be almost unrelated: A module **A** has high static coupling degree if there are many method calls from **A** to methods outside of **A** or vice versa in the program code. On the other hand, **A** has high dynamic weighted coupling degree if during the observed run of the system, there are many runtime method calls between **A** and other parts of the system. Since a single occurrence of a method call in the code can be executed millions of times—or not at all—during a run of the program, static and weighted dynamic coupling degrees do not need to correlate. Thus, our initial hypothesis was to not observe a high correlation between static and weighted dynamic metrics.

Our main research question is: **Are static coupling degrees and dynamic weighted coupling degrees statistically independent? If we observe correlation, can we quantify the correlation?**

To answer these questions, we compare the two coupling measures. We use dynamically collected data to compute weighted metrics that take into account the number of function calls during the system's run. We obtained the data from a series of four experiments. Each experiment consists of monitoring real production usage of a commercial software system (Atlassian Jira [6]) over a period of four weeks each. Our monitoring data contains more than three billion method calls. We compare the results from our dynamic analysis to computations of static coupling degrees.

Directly comparing static and weighted dynamic coupling degrees is of little value, as these are fundamentally different measurements: For instance, the absolute value of dynamic weighted degrees depends on the duration of the monitored program run, which clearly is not the case for the static measures. We therefore instead compare *coupling orders*, i.e., the ranking obtained by ordering all program modules by their coupling degree using the Kendall Tau[1] metric [21]. This also allows to quantify the difference between such orders.

Our answer to the above stated research questions is that static and (weighted) dynamic coupling degrees are *not* statistically independent. A possible interpretation of this result is that dynamic weighted coupling degrees give additional, but related information compared to the static case. In addition to this result, we observe insightful differences between class- and package-level analyses.

Contributions
The results and contributions of this paper are:[2]

- Using a unified framework, we introduce precise definitions of static and dynamic coupling measures.
- To investigate our main research question, we performed four experiments involving real users of a commercial software product (the Atlassian Jira project and issue tracking tool [6]) over a period of four weeks each. The software was instrumented via the dynamic monitoring framework Kieker [20] based on AspectJ [22]. From the collected data, we computed our dynamic coupling measures. We compared the obtained results, using the Kendall-Tau metric [8], to coupling measures we obtained by static analysis.

---

[1] See [19] for a discussion of the relationship between this metric and Spearman's correlation.

[2] A replication package inlcuding the collected data of our experiments will soon be published on Zenodo, to allow other researchers to repeat and extend our work.

- The results show that all coupling metrics we investigate are correlated, but there are also significant differences. In particular, when considering package-level coupling, the correlation is significantly stronger than for class-level coupling. As reason we assume that effects like polymorphism and dynamic binding often do not cross package boundaries.

Finally, we note that this paper is an extension of a previous short poster paper [30] in which a high-level overview of the research approach and the first data set are presented. The current paper extends the previous short poster paper (2 pages in length) as follows:

- This paper contains an in-depth explanation of the research approach, including a precise definition of our coupling metrics.
- We report on the statistical properties of the data collected during the experiments.
- We report on the findings of four experiments whereas the short paper only discusses the first of our four data sets.

Paper Organization

The remainder of the paper is organized as follows: In Sect. 2, we discuss related work. Section 3 provides our definition of weighted dynamic coupling. In Sect. 4, we explain our approach to static and dynamic analysis. Section 5 then describes the setting of our experiment. The results are presented and discussed in Sect. 6. In Sect. 7, we discuss threats to validity and conclude in Sect. 8 with a discussion of possible future work.

2   Related Work

There is extensive literature on using coupling metrics to analyse software quality, see, e.g., Fregnan et al. [17] for an overview. Briand et al. [10] propose a repeatable analysis procedure to investigate coupling relationships. Nagappan et al. [27] show correlation between metrics and external code quality (failure prediction). They argue that no single metric provides enough information (see also Voas and Kuhn [32]), but that for each project a specific set of metrics can be found that can then be used in this project to predict failures for new or changed classes. Misra et al. [25] propose a framework for the evaluation and validation of software complexity measures. Briand and Wüst [9] study the relationship between software quality models to external qualities like reliability and maintainability. They conclude that, among others, import and export coupling appear to be useful predictors of fault-proneness. Static weighted coupling measures have been considered by Offutt et al. [28]. Allier et al. [2] compare static and unweighted dynamic metrics.

Our approach is different: We do not study correlation between software metrics and software quality, but correlation between different software metrics.

Dynamic (unweighted) metrics have been investigated in numerous papers (see, e.g., Arisholm et al. [5] as a starting point, also the surveys by Chhabra and Gupta [13] and Geetika and Singh [18]). None of these approaches considers dynamic *weighted* metrics, as we do.

Dynamic analysis is often used to complement static analysis. As an notable exception, Yacoub et al. [33] use weighted metrics. However, to obtain the data, they do not use runtime instrumentation—as we do—but "early-stage executable models." They also assume a fixed number of objects during the software's runtime.

Arisholm et al. [5] study dynamic metrics for object-oriented software. Our dynamic coupling metrics are based on their *dynamic messages* metric. The difference is as follows: Their metric counts only distinct messages, i.e., each method call is only counted once, even if it appears many times in a concrete run of the system. The main feature of our *weighted* metrics is that the number of occurrences of each call during the run of a system is counted. The *dynamic messages* metric from [5] corresponds to our unweighted dynamic coupling metrics (see below).

3   Dynamic, Weighted Coupling

3.1   Dependency Graphs

We performed our analyses with two different levels of granularity: on the (Java) class and package levels. In the following we use the term *module* for either class or package, depending on the granularity of the analysis. The output of either types of analyses (dynamic and static) is a labeled, directed graph G, where the nodes represent program modules (i.e., classes or packages), and the labels are integers which we refer to as *weights* of the edges. An edge from **A** to **B** has label (weight) $n_{A,B}$, this denotes that the number of *directed interactions* between **A** and **B** occurring in the analysis is $n_{A,B}$.

In the case of a static analysis, this means that there are $n_{A,B}$ places in the code of **A** where some method from **B** is called. For dynamic analysis, this means that during the monitored run of the system, there were $n_{A,B}$ run-time invocations of methods from **B** by methods from **A**.

Our graph G is a *weighted dependency graph*, hence we call the coupling metrics we define below *weighted* metrics. When we disregard the numbers $n_{A,B}$, the graph G is a plain *dependency graph*, i.e., a directed graph where the edges reflect function calls between the modules. We refer to metrics defined on the unweighted dependency graph—i.e., metrics that do not take the weights $n_{A.B}$ into account—as *unweighted* metrics. We study the following three conceptually different approaches to measure coupling dependency between program modules:

1. The first approach is *static analysis*, which identifies method calls by analyzing the compiled code (we used BCEL to analyze Java `.class` and `.jar` files). Here we do not take weights into account. We therefore compute our static coupling measures from an unweighted dependency graph.

2. Our second approach is *unweighted dynamic analysis*. This analysis identifies method calls between modules as they appear in an actual run of the system (the data is obtained by monitoring), but does not take the weights $n_{A,B}$ into account. It therefore does not distinguish between cases where a module **A** calls another module **B** a million times or just once. This metric is essentially the *dynamic messages* metric from [5].
3. Our third approach is *weighted dynamic analysis*, which differs from its unweighted counterpart only by taking the weights $n_{A,B}$ into account.

The distinctions between static/dynamic analyses and unweighted/weighted analyses are orthogonal choices. In particular, we omit in the present paper a weighted, static analysis, since our main motivation is the comparison of dynamic, weighted metrics unweighted, static metrics.

3.2   Definition of Coupling Metrics

We now define the coupling measures we study. Our measures assign a *coupling degree* to a program module (i.e., a class or a package). We consider 18 different ways to measure coupling, resulting from the following three orthogonal choices:

1. The first choice is between **c**lass-level and **p**ackage-level granularity. Depending on this choice, a **module** is either a (Java) class or a (Java) package.
2. The second choice is between one of our three basic measurement approaches: static, dynamic **u**nweighted, or dynamic **w**eighted analysis.
3. The third choice is to measure **i**mport- **e**xport- or **c**ombined coupling.

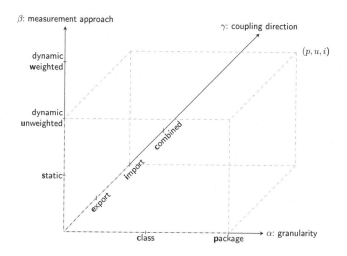

Fig. 1. Dimensions of analyses

To distinguish these 18 types of measurement, we use triples (α, β, γ), where α is **c** or **p** and indicates the granularity, β is **s**, **u**, or **w** and indicates the basic measurement approach, and γ is **i**, **e**, or **c**, indicating the direction of couplings taken into account. Figure 1 illustrates these three orthogonal choices: The example triple (p, u, i) denotes an analysis with granularity **p**ackage-level, using dynamic **u**nweighted analysis, and considers coupling in the **i**mport direction.

Our coupling measures can be computed from the two dependency graphs resulting from our two analyses (static and dynamic). For a module **A**, and a choice of measure (α, β, γ), the (α, β, γ)-*coupling degree of* **A**, denoted with $\mathsf{coupdeg}_{\alpha,\beta,\gamma}(\mathbf{A})$, is computed as follows:

- We compute $G_{\alpha,\beta}$. This is the weighted dependency graph between classes (if $\alpha = c$) or packages (if $\alpha = p$) obtained by static analysis (if $\beta = s$) or dynamic analysis (if $\beta = u$ or $\beta = w$), where each weight $n_{A,B}$ is replaced with 1 if the analysis is static or (dynamic) unweighted (i.e., if $\beta \in \{s, u\}$).
- Then, $\mathsf{coupdeg}_{\alpha,\beta,\gamma}(\mathbf{A})$ is the out-degree of **A**, in-degree of **A**, or sum of these, depending on whether $\gamma = i$, $\gamma = e$, or $\gamma = c$. The in (out) degree of **A** is the sum of the weights of its incoming (outgoing) edges in the graph.

4   Static and Dynamic Analysis

We perform our static analysis (using the Apache BCEL [4]) on the compiled code. This also implies that some optimizations have already performed by the compiler, such as removal of dead code. Therefore, our static and dynamic analyses are performed on the exact same code, without differences introduced in the compilation process. For the dynamic analysis, we use the Kieker framework [20] that allows to register every method call. Kieker uses AspectJ's [22] load-time weaver to instrument the analyzed software automatically at load-time. In order to reduce the performance impact of monitoring, we restricted the monitoring to a subset of the system, and adjusted the static analysis accordingly.

5   Experiment Design

We analyzed the software Atlassian Jira, versions 7.3.0, 7.4.3, and 7.7.1 [6]. The system was instrumented using AspectJ technology. For each method call, we recorded the time stamp, the class name of caller and of the callee.

To perform our analysis with realistic workload, we conducted four experiments with real users using a software system (Atlassian Jira [6]) in production. Jira was used by students participating in a mandatory programming course of our computer science curriculum. In the course, the students develop a software using the Kanban process management method [1]. The time span of the project is four weeks, with full time participation by the students.

We report on four experiment runs, from February and September of 2017 and 2018. Each time, the software ran for a four-week period. The collected monitoring data from each run includes the startup sequence, basic configuration such as database access, initial tasks as user registration and setup of the Kanban boards, and day-to-day usage. No person-related data is used for our analysis. In Table 1, we list the number of method calls recorded as well as the number of users of our Jira installation in each of the three experiment runs.

Obviously, there are differences between the four runs of the software that we analyze. For example, different students took parts in the course each time, the focus of the project required using different features of the Jira software in each iteration, and we also instructed them to use more features of the tool in the later iterations (this is

Table 1. Number of users and monitored method calls

#	date	users	method calls
1	February 2017	19	196,442,044
2	September 2017	48	854,657,027
3	February 2018	16	475,357,185
4	September 2018	58	2,409,688,701

one reason why the number of method calls per student is higher in the later runs of the experiment). Therefore, our four experiments—even though they are conducted using the same software system—give us slightly more variation in the data than running the exact same software with the exact same group of users. However, our main analysis results do not vary significantly between the different runs of the experiment, indicating that our findings are invariant under small changes of the experiment setup.

6   Experiment Results

Compared Measures We compare the coupling degrees computed by these different approaches. Comparing the actual "raw" values of $\mathsf{coupdeg}_{\alpha,\beta,\gamma}(\mathbf{A})$ for different combinations of α, β, γ and some class or package $\mathbf{A}$ does not make much sense: The weighted values depend on the length of the measurement run of the system, whereas the static analysis does not.

However, the absolute coupling values are usually not the most interesting results of such an analysis. For a developer, the identification of the modules with the highest coupling degree is among the most interesting results of applying a software metric. Therefore, a useful approach is to study the relationship between the *orders* among the modules in the different analyses: Each analysis yields an ordering of the classes or packages from the ones with the highest coupling degree to the ones with the lowest one; we call these orders *coupling orders*. These orders can be compared between different analyses of varying measurement durations.

Given our coupling measure definitions, we have the following choices for a left-hand-side (LHS) and a right-hand-side (RHS) analysis:

- The first choice is whether to consider class or package analyses (both the LHS and the RHS should consider the same type of module).
- The second choice is which two of our three basic measurement approaches (see Sect. 3.1) we intend to compare: *static* analysis, (dynamic) *unweighted* analysis, and (dynamic) *weighted* analysis. There are three possible choices: s vs. u, s vs. w, and u vs. w.
- For each combination, we consider import, export, and combined coupling.

Hence, there are 18 comparisons we can perform in each of our four data sets, leading to 72 different comparisons.

Kendall-Tau Distance To study the difference between our different basic measurement approaches, we compare the coupling orders of the analyses using the Kendall-Tau distance [8]: For a finite base set S with size n, the metric compares two linear orders $<_1$ and $<_2$. The Kendall-Tau distance $\tau(<_1, <_2)$ is the number of swaps needed to obtain the order $<_1$ from $<_2$, normalized by dividing by number of possible swaps $\frac{n(n-1)}{2}$. Hence $\tau(<_1, <_2)$ is always between 0 (if $<_1$ and $<_2$ are identical) and 1 (if $<_1$ is "reverse" of $<_2$). Values smaller than 0.5 indicate that the orders are closer together than expected from two random orders, while values larger than 0.5 indicate the opposite.

Distance Values To present our results, we use the following notation to specify the LHS and RHS analyses: We use a triple $\alpha : \beta_1 \leftrightarrow \beta_2$, where $-\alpha$ is c or p expressing **c**lass or **p**ackage coupling, $-\beta_1$ is s or u expressing whether the LHS analysis is **s**tatic or (dynamic) **u**nweighted, $-\beta_2$ is u or w expressing whether the RHS analysis is (dynamic) **u**nweighted or (dynamic) **w**eighted.

For each of these combinations, we consider export, import, and combined coupling analyses. This results in 18 comparisons for each data set, which are presented in Tables 2, 3, 4, and 5 for our four experiments.

Statistical Significance To measure statistical significance, we computed the absolute z-scores of our experiments. The smallest observed absolute z-score among all our experiments is 9.41, and all but two absolute values are above 10. As a point of reference, the corresponding likelihood for z-score 10 is $7.6 \cdot 10^{-24}$, this is the probability to observe the amount of correlation seen in our dataset under the assumption that the compared orders are in fact independent. This indicates a huge degree of statistical significance, which is due to the large number of program units appearing in our analysis.

Discussion The first obvious take-away from the values presented in Tables 2, 3, 4-5 is that all 72 reported distances (and of course also the average values) are below 0.5, many of them significantly so. This indicates that there is a significant similarity between the coupling orders of the static and the two dynamic analyses. This was not to be expected: While in small runs of a system, one could

Table 2. Coupling analyses (data set 1)

	$c : s \leftrightarrow u$	$c : s \leftrightarrow w$	$c : u \leftrightarrow w$	$p : s \leftrightarrow u$	$p : s \leftrightarrow w$	$p : u \leftrightarrow w$
import	0:31	0:36	0:13	0:33	0:36	0:08
export	0:41	0:41	0:24	0:30	0:32	0:21
combined	0:35	0:41	0:29	0:29	0:33	0:23
average	0:35	0:39	0:22	0:31	0:33	0:17

Table 3. Coupling analyses (data set 2)

	$c : s \leftrightarrow u$	$c : s \leftrightarrow w$	$c : u \leftrightarrow w$	$p : s \leftrightarrow u$	$p : s \leftrightarrow w$	$p : u \leftrightarrow w$
import	0:30	0:36	0:14	0:31	0:35	0:09
export	0:41	0:43	0:26	0:30	0:33	0:22
combined	0:34	0:41	0:31	0:28	0:33	0:23
average	0:35	0:40	0:24	0:30	0:33	0:18

Table 4. Coupling analyses (data set 3)

	$c : s \leftrightarrow u$	$c : s \leftrightarrow w$	$c : u \leftrightarrow w$	$p : s \leftrightarrow u$	$p : s \leftrightarrow w$	$p : u \leftrightarrow w$
import	0:38	0:42	0:12	0:37	0:39	0:06
export	0:38	0:40	0:22	0:28	0:31	0:20
combined	0:36	0:40	0:28	0:30	0:33	0:23
average	0:37	0:41	0:21	0:32	0:35	0:17

Table 5. Coupling analyses (data set 4)

	$c : s \leftrightarrow u$	$c : s \leftrightarrow w$	$c : u \leftrightarrow w$	$p : s \leftrightarrow u$	$p : s \leftrightarrow w$	$p : u \leftrightarrow w$
import	0:37	0:42	0:12	0:36	0:39	0:06
export	0:38	0:40	0:23	0:28	0:32	0:20
combined	0:35	0:40	0:29	0:30	0:33	0:24
average	0:37	0:41	0:21	0:31	0:35	0:17

possibly conjecture that there might not be a large difference between the static and dynamic notions of coupling, this changes when we analyze longer system runs: In our longest experiment, we analyzed more than 2.4 billion method calls. The dynamic, weighted coupling degree of a class **A** is the number of calls from or to methods from **A** among these 2.4 billion calls, while its static, unweighted coupling degree is the number of classes **B** such that the compiled code of the software contains a call from **A** to **B** or vice versa. A single method call in the code is only counted once in an unweighted analysis, but this call can be executed millions of times during the experiment, and each of these executions is counted in the weighted, dynamic coupling analysis. Therefore, it was not necessarily to be expected that we observe correlation between unweighted static and weighted dynamic coupling degrees.

However, our results suggest that all of the three types of analyses that we performed are correlated, with different degrees of significance. In particular, dynamic weighted coupling degrees seem to give additional, but not unrelated information compared to the static case.

The static coupling order is closer to the dynamic unweighted than to the dynamic weighted order in almost all cases. This was expected: In an hypothetical "complete run" of a system, and in the absence of issues resulting from object-oriented features these measures would coincide. On the other hand, the dynamic weighted analysis is very different from the static one by design.

A very interesting observation is that in all 36 cases except for 3 cases involving import coupling in our first two data sets, comparing $c : \beta \leftrightarrow \gamma$ for some coupling measure with $\beta \in \{s, u, w\}$ and $\gamma \in \{i, e, c\}$.

To $p : \beta \leftrightarrow \gamma$ shows that the distance from the analysis of the package case is smaller than the corresponding distance in the class case, sometimes significantly so. A possible explanation is that in the package case, the object-oriented effects that are often cited as the main reasons for performing dynamic analysis are less present, as, e.g., inheritance relationships are often between classes residing in the same package.

7   Threats to Validity

Concerning external validity, our analysis is limited by the fact that we covered only four runs, each with four weeks, of only one software system (Atlassian Jira). To address this threat, we plan to monitor additional software tools such as Jenkins and Tomcat (which are also used in the course). Concerning internal validity, our dynamic analysis omits some of Jira's classes in order to maintain sufficient performance of the system. To ensure that our comparisons in Sect. 6 are conclusive, we only considered the classes and packages covered by both the static and dynamic analysis in the computation of the Kendall Tau distances. Additionally, different interpretations of what is considered as coupling between the static and in the dynamic analyses are always possible. However, since our notion of coupling is rather simple (method calls between different classes), we are confident that our static and dynamic analysis in fact use the same notion of coupling. Finally, as discussed in Sect. 4, we examine compiled code, not source code. When performing a similar analysis on source code, the differences between the static and the dynamic analyses would likely increase, as the dynamic analysis of course also uses compiled code. However, this can also be seen as an advantage, since this allows us to focus on the differences between static code and a running system, which is the goal of this study.

8   Conclusions and Future Work

We studied three different basic measurement approaches: Static coupling, unweighted dynamic coupling, and weighted dynamic coupling. We performed four runs of an experiment that allows to compare these metrics to static coupling measurements. Our results, as discussed in Sect. 6, suggest that dynamic coupling metrics complement their static counterparts: Despite the large (and expected) difference, there is also a statistically significant correlation. This suggests that further study of dynamic weighted coupling and its relationship with other coupling metrics is an interesting line of research.

A key question is how the additional information given by weighted dynamic coupling measurements can be used to evaluate the architectural quality of software systems, or more generally, to assist a software engineer in her design decisions. Coupling metrics can be used as recommenders for restructuring [11], and for static coupling measures, correlation between coupling and external quality has been observed [23]. A study of the relationship between static coupling measures and changeability and code comprehension has been performed in [33]. In [3], it is argued that unweighted dynamic metrics can be used for maintenance prediction. Since dynamic weighted metrics contain additional information compared to their unweighted counterparts, it will be interesting to study whether and how this additional information can be used in these contexts.

References

1. Ahmad, M.O., Markkula, J., Oivo, M.: Kanban in software development: a systematic literature review. In: 2013 39th Euromicro Conference on Software Engineering and Advanced Applications, pp. 9–16, September 2013. https://doi.org/10.1109/SEAA.2013.28
2. Allier, S., Vaucher, S., Dufour, B., Sahraoui, H.A.: Deriving coupling metrics from call graphs. In: Tenth IEEE International Working Conference on Source Code Analysis and Manipulation, SCAM 2010, Timisoara, Romania, pp. 43–52, 12–13 September 2010. IEEE Computer Society (2010). https://doi.org/10.1109/SCAM.2010.25
3. Chug, A., Sharma, H.: Dynamic metrics are superior than static metrics in maintainability prediction: an empirical case study. In: 2015 4th International Conference on Reliability, Infocom Technologies and Optimization (ICRITO)(Trends and Future Directions), pp. 1–6. IEEE (2015)
4. Apache Software Foundation: Commons BCEL: Byte code engineering library (2016). https://commons.apache.org/proper/commons-bcel/
5. Arisholm, E., Briand, L.C., Føyen, A.: Dynamic coupling measurement for object-oriented software. IEEE Trans. Software Eng. **30**(8), 491–506 (2004). https://doi.org/10.1109/TSE.2004.41
6. Atlassian: JIRA project and issue tracking (2017). https://www.atlassian.com/software/jira/
7. Bogner, J., Wagner, S., Zimmermann, A.: Automatically measuring the maintainability of service-and microservice-based systems: a literature review. In: Proceedings of the 27th International Workshop on Software Measurement and 12th International Conference on Software Process and Product Measurement, pp. 107–115. ACM (2017)
8. Briand, L., Emam, K.E., Morasca, S.: On the application of measurement theory in software engineering. Empirical Softw. Eng. **1**(1), 61–88 (1996). https://doi.org/10.1007/BF00125812
9. Briand, L.C., Wüst, J.: Empirical studies of quality models in object-oriented systems. Adv. Comput. **56**, 97–166 (2002). https://doi.org/10.1016/S0065-2458(02)80005-5
10. Briand, L.C., Wüst, J., Daly, J.W., Porter, D.V.: Exploring the relationships between design measures and software quality in object-oriented systems. J. Syst. Softw. **51**(3), 245–273 (2000). https://doi.org/10.1016/S0164-1212(99)00102-8
11. Candela, I., Bavota, G., Russo, B., Oliveto, R.: Using cohesion and coupling for software remodularization: is it enough? ACM Trans. Softw. Eng. Methodol. **25**(3), 24:1–24:28 (2016). https://doi.org/10.1145/2928268
12. Carver, R.H., Counsell, S., Nithi, R.V.: An evaluation of the MOOD set of object-oriented software metrics. IEEE Trans. Software Eng. **24**(6), 491–496 (1998). https://doi.org/10.1109/32.689404
13. Chhabra, J.K., Gupta, V.: A survey of dynamic software metrics. J. Comput. Sci. Technol. **25**(5), 1016–1029 (2010). https://doi.org/10.1007/s11390-010-9384-3
14. Chidamber, S.R., Kemerer, C.F.: Towards a metrics suite for object oriented design. In: OOPSLA, pp. 197–211. ACM (1991)
15. Chidamber, S.R., Kemerer, C.F.: A metrics suite for object oriented design. IEEE Trans. Software Eng. **20**(6), 476–493 (1994). https://doi.org/10.1109/32.295895
16. Cornelissen, B., Zaidman, A., van Deursen, A., Moonen, L., Koschke, R.: A systematic survey of program comprehension through dynamic analysis. IEEE Trans. Software Eng. **35**(5), 684–702 (2009)

17. Fregnan, E., Baum, T., Palomba, F., Bacchelli, A.: A survey on software coupling relations and tools. Inf. Softw. Technol. **107**, 159–178 (2019). https://doi.org/10.1016/j.infsof.2018.11.008

18. Geetika, R., Singh, P.: Dynamic coupling metrics for object oriented software systems: a survey. SIGSOFT Softw. Eng. Notes **39**(2), 1–8 (2014). https://doi.org/10.1145/2579281.2579296

19. Gilpin, A.R.: Table for conversion of Kendall's tau to Spearman's rho within the context of measures of magnitude of effect for meta-analysis. Educ. Psychol. Measur. **53**, 87–92 (1993). https://doi.org/10.1177/0013164493053001007

20. van Hoorn, A., Waller, J., Hasselbring, W.: Kieker: a framework for application performance monitoring and dynamic software analysis. In: Proceedings of the 3rd ACM/SPEC International Conference on Performance Engineering (ICPE 2012), pp. 247–248. ACM, April 2012. https://doi.org/10.1145/2188286.2188326

21. Kendall, M.G.: A new measure of rank correlation. Biometrika **30**(1/2), 81–93 (1938)

22. Kiczales, G., Hilsdale, E., Hugunin, J., Kersten, M., Palm, J., Griswold, W.G.: An overview of aspectJ. In: Knudsen, J.L. (ed.) ECOOP 2001. LNCS, vol. 2072, pp. 327–354. Springer, Heidelberg (2001). https://doi.org/10.1007/3-540-45337-7_18

23. Kirbas, S., et al.: The relationship between evolutionary coupling and defects in large industrial software. J. Softw. Evol. Process **29**(4), e1842-n/a (2017). https://doi.org/10.1002/smr.1842,e1842smr.1842

24. Knoche, H., Hasselbring, W.: Drivers and barriers for microservice adoption - a survey among professionals in Germany. Enterp. Model. Inf. Syst. Architectures (EMISAJ-Int. J. Conceptual Model.) **14**(1), 1–35 (2019). https://doi.org/10.18417/emisa.14.1

25. Misra, S., Akman, I., Palacios, R.C.: Framework for evaluation and validation of software complexity measures. IET Software **6**(4), 323–334 (2012). https://doi.org/10.1049/iet-sen.2011.0206

26. Mitchell, B.S., Mancoridis, S.: Comparing the decompositions produced by software clustering algorithms using similarity measurements. In: 2001 International Conference on Software Maintenance, ICSM 2001, Florence, Italy, pp. 744–753, 6–10 November 2001. IEEE Computer Society (2001). https://doi.org/10.1109/ICSM.2001.972795

27. Nagappan, N., Ball, T., Zeller, A.: Mining metrics to predict component failures. In: Proceedings of the 28th international conference on Software engineering (ICSE 2006), pp. 452–461. ACM (2006). https://doi.org/10.1145/1134285.1134349

28. Offutt, J., Abdurazik, A., Schach, S.R.: Quantitatively measuring object-oriented couplings. Software Qual. J. **16**(4), 489–512 (2008). https://doi.org/10.1007/s11219-008-9051-x

29. Parnas, D.L.: On the criteria to be used in decomposing systems into modules. Commun. ACM **15**(12), 1053–1058 (1972). https://doi.org/10.1145/361598.361623

30. Schnoor, H., Hasselbring, W.: Toward measuring software coupling via weighted dynamic metrics. In: Chaudron, M., Crnkovic, I., Chechik, M., Harman, M. (eds.) Proceedings of the 40th International Conference on Software Engineering: Companion Proceeedings, ICSE 2018, Gothenburg, Sweden, pp. 342–343, May 27 - June 03 2018. ACM (2018). https://doi.org/10.1145/3183440.3195000

31. Stevens, W., Myers, G., Constantine, L.: Structured design. In: Yourdon, E.N. (ed.) Classics in Software Engineering, pp. 205–232. Yourdon Press, Upper Saddle River (1979)

32. Voas, J.M., Kuhn, R.: What happened to software metrics? IEEE Comput. **50**(5), 88–98 (2017). https://doi.org/10.1109/MC.2017.144
33. Yacoub, S.M., Ammar, H.H., Robinson, T.: Dynamic metrics for object oriented designs. In: 6th IEEE International Software Metrics Symposium (METRICS 1999), Boca Raton, FL, USA, pp. 50–61, 4–6 November 1999. IEEE Computer Society (1999). https://doi.org/10.1109/METRIC.1999.809725

Empirical Study on the Distribution of Object-Oriented Metrics in Software Systems

K. Muthukumaran[1](✉), N. L. Bhanu Murthy[2], and P. Sarguna Janani[2]

[1] School of Computing and Information Technology,
Manipal University Jaipur, Jaipur, India
`muthukumaran.kasinathan@jaipur.manipal.edu`
[2] Department of Computer Science and Information Systems,
BITS Pilani Hyderabad Campus, Hyderabad, India
{`bhanu,f2012148`}`@hyderabad.bits-pilani.ac.in`

Abstract. We attempt to model the probability distribution of object-oriented software metrics. We employ 5 distribution models to find out the distributions the metrics follow. We use AIC, BIC and RMSE as goodness-of-fit measures. Though the past studies have shown that the software projects frequently follow power law, having a Pareto distribution, we seek to study more number of software systems and distribution models to infer more generalizable results, since they occasionally seem to follow Log-normal or Gamma distribution as well. Apart from these three models we have also considered Weibull distribution and Generalized Pareto Distribution (GPD). In this study, we have made an attempt to answer the hypothesis that the object-oriented software metrics follow a particular distribution by comparing various distributions applied over a large number of projects using a recognized statistical framework.

Keywords: Object-oriented metrics · Software metrics distribution · Software quality · Model selection

1 Introduction

Object-oriented software development offers a mechanisms to model the real world which makes the software systems more understandable, maintainable and reusable [5,23]. Metrics that measure the properties of software systems provide means to the managers and developers to track and achieve the goals of software development [24]. The CK metric suite by Chidambar and Kemerer has gained an industry-wide acceptance as a set of such metrics. It provides a formal suite of metrics to track the process of software design by providing quantitative measures to aid in understanding design integrity, detecting potential flaws and identifying targets for redesigning. They are also used in predicting certain external software qualities such as software defects [9,19,33], testing and maintenance effort. The metrics help the management in selecting the suitable

© Springer Nature Switzerland AG 2019
R. Damaševičius and G. Vasiljevienė (Eds.): ICIST 2019, CCIS 1078, pp. 299–317, 2019.
https://doi.org/10.1007/978-3-030-30275-7_23

object-oriented design by allowing them to optimize the factor according to the goals of the organization, such as minimizing the cost of development, testing and maintenance over the life of application. Such optimizations and estimations can be computed better if we know the distributions each of these metrics follow.

The distributions followed by the object-oriented metrics is a starting point to explore the stochastic process that the development of a software project follows. Though the process of software development adopts a design and coding process with the primary goal of implementing the functionalities effectively and efficiently, the entire process has an apparent randomness, however the resulting software system metrics have statistical regularities. The distribution followed by metrics indicates the underlying generative process involved. Each of the distributions have their own generative processes. Mitzenmacher [25] has listed six unrelated, independent generative models that can result in power law. Similarly Concas et al. [8] has provided the generative process for Log-normal distribution and Normal distribution. We have considered these generative models and have attempted to reason if these generative processes could indeed explain the process of the development of the project attributes.

We have considered five models in our study. Past studies have shown that the software projects frequently follow power law. They occasionally seem to follow Log-normal or Gamma distribution [8,14,31]. Apart from these three models, we have also considered Weibull distribution and Generalized Pareto Distribution (GPD). The intuitions for considering the distributions have been discussed in Sect. 3.2. The number of projects that were considered in past studies are not sufficient to infer a more generalizable conclusion. In this study, an attempt has been made to perform an exhaustive comparison over a large number of projects that shall provide a more definitive conclusion to the hypothesis that the metric follows a particular distribution or set of distributions. The CK metrics that have been considered in the study are Weighted Methods per Class (WMC), Depth of Inheritance Tree (DIT), Response For Class (RFC), Lack of Cohesion of Methods (LCOM), Coupling Between Objects (CBO) and Number of Children (NOC). Apart from these metrics we have also considered Lines of Code (LOC). The process of choosing the most appropriate model involves parameter fitting followed by comparison of models using one of the goodness-of-fit statistics. Studies [8,14,31] generally involve parameter fitting using one or more of the following methods: Maximum Likelihood Estimate (MLE), Least Square Estimate (LSE) or Method of Moments (MoM) and compare the models using the goodness-of-fit measures like KS Distance, R^2(Coefficient of Determination) or Pearson χ^2 test. However using these measures have few drawbacks and Akaike Information Criterion (AIC) is a better statistic to compare the models [34], and this shall be discussed in Sect. 3.3. Therefore the objectives of the study are to propose the distribution that best fits each of CK metrics and to reason out the generative model followed by the metric.

The rest of the paper has been organized as follows. In Sect. 2, we have discussed the previous work that have been reported on the distribution followed by CK Metrics and related fields, thereby discussing the motivation of our study.

Section 3 describes the dataset that has been used and also the models that have been considered. Further we have explained the intuition behind choosing each of the models. It also provides the advantages of using AIC as a goodness-of-fit statistic and how it addresses the drawbacks of other commonly used statistics. We have discussed Friedman test and Nemenyi Test which were used to compare the models across various datasets. The experiments and results have been discussed in Sect. 4. We have listed our observations and future direction for this work in Sect. 5.

2 Related Work

The pervasiveness of power law in Software systems has been actively explored in various studies. Louridas et al. [22] have explored in depth the ubiquity of power laws in various levels of abstraction of software systems. It was established that power law was not only existent at class and function level but also in the distribution of packages and libraries in different systems and languages. The measurement of procedural complexity of software system has been done using fan-in and fan-out. The power law distribution was fitted using linear regression on the log-log data plots and the benchmark used to determine the goodness-of-fit was R^2. Studies focused on the distribution based on not only file-dependencies but other attributes as well. Baxter et al. [4] studied the key structural attributes of about 56 Java programs and fitted power law using weighted least squares fit. It was concluded that while most of the 17 attributes followed power law, few of them followed Log-normal or stretched exponential. It was checked whether each fit was consistent with the data at different confidence intervals, and then the best fit was decided.

Concas et al. [8] focused on the CK metric properties of the implementation of a Smalltalk system (VisualWorks Smalltalk). They validated whether the data follow a Log-normal or a Pareto distribution using Maximum Likelihood Estimations. They have found that most studied metrics followed a power law distribution except for the number of methods metric (i.e., the WMC metric), the number of all instance variables metric, and the CBO metric, which follow a Log-normal distribution. Though the study performed was quite detailed, the number of projects considered was too less to arrive at concrete conclusions and also the study was performed on SmallTalk programs, the OOP principles of which vary considerably from the more commonly used languages of Java and C++. Shatnawi et al. [31] focused on fitting CK metrics to power law distribution using Maximum Likelihood Estimation and have proposed initial statistical tests (based on Kurtosis and skewness) that can be used as initial screening test to rule out power law Distribution. They have considered 5 Java software projects. Herraiz et al. [14] based their study on the Qualitas Corpus, measuring the CK metrics suite values for every file of every Java project in the corpus. They concluded that the range of high values for the different metrics follows a power law distribution, whereas the rest of the range follows a Log-normal distribution. They fitted the distribution using the Kolmogorov-Smirnov distance as a measurement of the goodness-of-fit.

Among the distributions that follow power law, the prominent one is Pareto distribution. Other specific distributions have been considered quite often in studies pertaining to software systems. Grbac et al. [13] have considered Weibull distribution and Pareto distribution among others while studying the probability distribution of faults in software systems. Adamic et al. [1] provide the analytical derivation of Pareto 80-20 principle by converting power law to rank size distribution. This has been used by Louridas et al. [22] to come up with more appreciable interpretations of the fitted distribution by providing conclusions like the richest 'a' percent of the items have 'b' percent of the resources where 'a' and 'b' are analytically calculated.

Studies have also attempted to explore the generative models of various distributions. Mitzenmacher [25] discovered that Log-normal and power law distributions are connected quite naturally, and hence it is not surprising to state that Log-normal distributions could be a possible alternative to power law distributions across many fields contributing significantly to the debate over whether file size distributions are best modeled by a power law distribution or a Log-normal distribution. Further, these model have been used to explain the stochastic process involved in software development. Concas et al. [8] have also tried to justify the possible generation process that could have resulted in the statistical distribution. The models considered by them are: Random and Independent increments leading to Normal distribution, Random and proportional increments paving way to Log-normal distribution and finally Preferential Attachment resulting in power law.

While most of these studies almost ubiquitously used goodness-of-fit tests like KS Distance or Chi-Square test, Vose [34] provides reasoning to why Akaike Information Criterion (AIC) is a better goodness-of-fit measure. Among the reasons stated, the prominent one is that AIC is based on calculating the log likelihood of the fitted distribution producing the set of observations. This allows one to use maximum likelihood as the fitting method and be consistent with the goodness-of-fit statistic. Also, the information criteria penalize distributions with greater number of parameters, and thus help avoid the over-fitting problem [2]. Li et al. [21] also adopt AIC as the goodness-of-fit measure while choosing the distribution that models the number of defect occurrences in each time period over the lifetime of a release of a widely deployed software project. After comparing the AIC values it was concluded that Weibull performed the best and Theil statistics values were derived and analyzed to validate the Weibull model.

In this work, we have considered 5 possible distribution which have been fit over each of the CK metrics of 50 projects. When the number of datasets is huge as in our case, analysis becomes intractable. Therefore statistical methods like Nemenyi tests are employed to summarize results across the multiple datasets [10]. The process was employed by Lessman et al. [20] in order to determine the significantly better classifier in a large-scale empirical comparison of 22 classifiers over 10 datasets while benchmarking classification models for software defect prediction.

Nemenyi test and Friedman test provide a concrete results on whether a model is significantly outperforming other models. And thereby we can eliminate the threats of human error and statistical inaccuracy. The details of the methodology used and its theoretical motivations are provided in the model selection section. We aim to check if a model is significantly better in fitting the metric distribution over all the project. In the instances where such a model exists, we have discussed the possible stochastic generative process that could have resulted in the distribution and also reasoned if such an inference is valid.

3 Background

3.1 Datasets

Most of the earlier studies have relied on CK metric data from relatively fewer software systems. However we attempt to generalize the results using larger datasets consisting of the public Eclipse dataset [26] and the public data collected by Jureczko et al. [17]. We have used the CK Metric values of 50 versions of various software systems that have been listed in Table 2.

Apart from the open source projects, six proprietary softwares have been considered. Of them, five are custom software systems built for companies in the insurance domain and the sixth is a standard tool that supports quality assurances in software development. All six were built by the same company.

3.2 Probability Distributions

In total we have considered five models which have been discussed below.

Table 1. Software metrics

Name	Description
Lines of Code (LOC)	Number of non-commented lines of code for each software component (e.g., in a class)
Weighted Methods per Class (WMC)	Number of methods contained in a class including public, private and protected methods
Coupling Between Objects (CBO)	Number of classes to which a class is coupled
Depth of Inheritance (DIT)	Maximum inheritance path from the class to the root class
Number Of Children (NOC)	Number of immediate sub-classes of a class
Response For a Class (RFC)	Number of methods that can be invoked for an object of given class
Lack of Cohesion among Methods (LCOM)	Number of methods in a class that are not related through the sharing of some of the class fields

Table 2. Software projects under study

S. no.	Project name	Version	Number of modules	S. no.	Project name	Version	Number of modules
1	Apache Ant	1.3	126	23	Apache Lucene	2.2	248
2		1.4	179	24		2.4	341
3		1.5	294	25	Apache POI	1.5	238
4		1.6	352	26		2	315
5		1.7	746	27		2.5	386
6		1	340	28		3	443
7	Apache Camel	1.2	609	29	Apache Synapse	1	158
8		1.4	873	30		1.1	223
9		1.6	966	31		1.2	257
10	Apache Ivy	1.1	112	32	Apache Velocity	1.4	197
11		1.2	242	33		1.5	215
12		1.3	353	34		1.6	230
13	jEdit	3.2	273	35	Xalan Java	2.4	724
14		4	307	36		2.5	804
15		4.1	313	37		2.6	886
16		4.2	368	38		2.7	910
17		4.3	493	39	Apache Xerces	init	163
18	Apache Tomcat	1	859	40		1.2	441
19	Apache Log4j	1	136	41		1.3	454
20		1.1	110	42		1.4	589
21		1.2	206	43	Redaktor	1	176
22	Apache Lucene	2	196	44	ArcPlatform	1	234

Pareto Distribution. The first distribution that has been considered in the study is the heavy tailed Pareto distribution, which follows power law [27]. Named after the economist Vilfredo Pareto, the Pareto principle was first conceived to model the distribution of resources in a population, the famous 80-20 principle [29]. Formally the Pareto distribution has the following probability distribution,

$$\frac{\alpha x_m^a}{x^{\alpha+1}} \quad for \quad x \geq x_m \tag{1}$$

where $x_m > 0$ is the scale (real) parameter and $\alpha > 0$ is the shape (real) parameter.

Its CDF can be described as,

$$1 - \left(\frac{x_m}{x}\right)^\alpha \quad for \quad x \geq x_m \tag{2}$$

Pareto distribution is reported to be ubiquitous when it comes to the properties of software systems. Fenton et al. [11] performed a quantitative analysis of fault distributions and confirmed that the number of defects in software systems follow Pareto distribution. The same was replicated and confirmed by Andersson et al. [3].

Concas et al. [8] have concluded that the software properties systematically followed Pareto distribution in the SmallTalk project, Visual Works.

The Pareto distribution is the most common power law distribution. Its statistical distribution can thus be generated by the different stochastic processes listed by Mitzenmacher [25]. Preferential Attachment is the simplest and most common explanation of all different stochastic processes [8].

Preferential Attachment. It is the phenomena where new objects tend to attach to popular objects. That means, the probability of choosing an entity to modify (increment) is directly proportional to the present size of the entity and the increment value is independent of the entity size. In the software systems, the objects can be files (classes) and the properties are the metric values. The probability of modifying a larger file can intuitively be considered to be higher. The preferential attachment may thus apply in our context.

Log-Normal Distribution. The next distribution that we have considered, a common contender to fit the software metrics, is Log-normal distribution. Previous studies have considered Log-normal distribution and found that few metrics follow this distribution [8,14,31]. The Log-normal distribution has the following probability distribution,

$$\frac{1}{x\sigma\sqrt{2\pi}}e^{-\frac{(ln\,x-\mu)^2}{2\sigma^2}} \tag{3}$$

where $\mu\epsilon\mathbb{R}$ is the location parameter and $\sigma > 0$ is the scale parameter. And its CDF is as follows.

$$\frac{1}{2} + \frac{1}{2}erf\left[\frac{ln\,x - \mu}{\sqrt{2}\sigma}\right] \tag{4}$$

Law of Proportional Effect: Gibrat's law proposed by Gibrat [12], also known as the law of Proportional Effect provides the stochastic process that results in Log-normal distribution. It states that the probability of change (increment) is same for all modules (files), independent of their size, however the increment is proportional to their present property value. In our context, it means that the probability of a particular file being chosen for increment is the same as other files. However the magnitude of the increment of metric is proportional to its current value. A major drawback of this stochastic model is that it cannot fit the metric value to a file/module (or any other granularity) which is newly introduced and has no metric value yet.

Weibull Distribution. Another distribution we have considered is the Weibull distribution, named after the Swedish mathematician Waloddi Weibull. The distribution has found widespread application in the field of reliability engineering where we fit the distribution of failure times of a product. In such cases the shape parameter (k), provides the rate of failure. The value of k is used to determine if the product faces 'Infant Mortality' or 'Aging'. If the shape parameter k < 1, then failure rate decreases with time. And Weibull distribution is said to be fat-tailed in this case. This is the case that we come across in our study.

Weibull distribution is also used to describe the strength of material with shape factor being the shape module. Weibull distribution is widely adopted in predicting the reliability of software systems in the software development life cycle where the cumulative number of faults was plotted against weeks after deployment [21]. Further, Zhang et al. [36] explored the modeling the distribution of faults over file with Weibull distribution and have found it to perform better than Pareto distribution. As the software metrics are correlated with the fault distribution in modules [16], we consider Weibull distribution in our study. The probability distribution of Weibull is:

$$
f(x) = \begin{cases} \frac{k}{\lambda}\left(\frac{x}{\lambda}\right)^{k-1} e^{-\left(\frac{x}{\lambda}\right)^k} & x \geq 0 \\ 0 & x < 0 \end{cases}
\tag{5}
$$

where $\lambda \epsilon (0, +\infty)$ is the scale parameter and $k \epsilon (0, +\infty)$ is the shape parameter. While the CDF of Weibull distribution is given as:

$$
CDF = \begin{cases} 1 - e^{-\left(\frac{x}{\lambda}\right)^k} & x \geq 0 \\ 0 & x < 0 \end{cases}
\tag{6}
$$

Generalized Pareto Distribution (GPD). We have also considered Generalized Pareto Distribution (GPD) as another possible candidate distribution. The GPD was introduced by Pickands [30] and since then it found applications in reliability engineering. The GPD is mainly used for the analysis of extreme events as it provides the complex model to describe the full range of data, especially the tail data. The probability distribution function of GPD is given by:

$$
\frac{1}{\sigma}(1 + \xi z)^{-\left(\frac{1}{\xi+1}\right)}
\tag{7}
$$

where $z = \frac{x-\mu}{\sigma}$, where $\mu \epsilon (-\infty, \infty)$ is the location parameter, $\sigma \epsilon (0, \infty)$ and $\xi \epsilon (-\infty, \infty)$ is the shape parameter and CDF is given by

$$
1 - (1 + \xi z)^{-\frac{1}{\xi}}
\tag{8}
$$

The distribution provides a wide and continuous range of possible shapes with exponential and Pareto distributions as the special cases. The form of GPD depends upon the value of its shape parameter (k).

- when k = 0, GPD reduces to exponential function
- when k = 1, GPD reduces to uniform distribution
- when k < 0, GPD reduces to Pareto distribution of second kind.

GPD too is not new to the field of software engineering as well, Kolassa et al. [18] proposed GPD to define commit sizes in open source projects.

Gamma Distribution. Another distribution that has been considered is Gamma distribution. In their study, Concas et al. [8] observed that one of the software metrics followed Gamma distribution.

Let's consider a Poisson process with 'points' occurring randomly in time. The sequence of inter-arrival times in the process is a sequence of independent random variables, each of which has exponential distribution. And the distribution of the nth interval is said to follow Gamma distribution. This formal generative process is however unintuitive to realize in our study. The probability density function is given as

$$\frac{1}{\Gamma(k)\,\theta^k} x^{k-1} e^{-\frac{x}{\theta}} \tag{9}$$

The CDF is given as

$$\frac{1}{\Gamma(k)} \gamma\left(k, \frac{x}{\theta}\right) \tag{10}$$

In the following section we explain in detail how the models are fit to the dataset and what was the basis of selection of the best model.

3.3 Model Selection

We note that, earlier works in this field uses goodness-of-fit (GoF) statistics for model selection. While using GoF, over-fitting are significant and might mislead a model selection algorithm [32]. Huang et al. attempted to combat some of these by including three methods of parameter estimation and ten goodness-of-fit measures [15]. However, multiple parameter estimation methods and goodness-of-fit statistics does not address the over-fitting problems. Further, they resort to qualitative means to summarize the results across the multiple dimensions of variations i.e. the goodness-of-fit statistics and methods of parameter estimation. The Akaike and Bayesian information criteria penalize the model for complexity in terms of the number of parameters. The more parameters a model has more likely it is to over-fit, and this is reflected in the increasing penalty term that seeks to eliminate this overfitting. Hence, we make use of information criteria (AIC, BIC).

Root Mean Square Error (RMSE) is a frequently used statistic to calculate the difference between the observed values and predicted values.

$$RMSE = \sqrt{\frac{1}{n} \sum_{i=1}^{n} (X_i - O_i)^2} \tag{11}$$

where O_i is the set of observed values and X_i is the set of respective predicted values. The above equation suggests that a low value of the metric indicates better fit. We use the statistic not to compare various models but to check how well the best model as proposed by the AIC actually fits the given data distribution.

The method that we have adopted in our study to test the null hypothesis is Friedman test and then we proceed with Nemenyi post-hoc test in case the null hypothesis is rejected. The post-hoc test is conducted to find whether there is a significant difference among the models performance. Post-hoc test is conducted on any two models, which is actually testing the null hypothesis that their means are similar. If the difference between the means ranks is more than the critical difference, the null hypothesis is rejected. The Friedman's test statistic is defined as follows,

$$\chi_F^2 = \frac{12K}{L(L+1)} \left[\sum_{i=1}^{L} AR_i^2 - \frac{L(L+1)^2}{4} \right] \tag{12}$$

where L is the number of models and K represents the number of datasets. The critical difference is calculated as follows,

$$CD = q_{a;\infty;L} \sqrt{\frac{L(L+1)}{12K}} \tag{13}$$

The value $q_{a;\infty;L}$ is based on the studentized range statistic.

4   Experiments and Results

We have conducted experiments on 50 versions of software systems and the details of these projects are described in Sect. 3.1. For each of the version, AIC and BIC values are computed for each of five models and six metrics. We then performed Friedman's test to reject or accept the null hypothesis which states that *"there is no significant difference between the five models"*. We reject the null hypothesis at 0.01 level of significance. If null hypothesis is rejected, we perform the post-hoc test (Nemenyi) and plot the Nemenyi diagram. The diagram has the models on X axis and their mean rank on Y axis. The Critical Difference (CD), which is used to determine if a model is performing better than the rest, is denoted as a vertical line extending above the mean rank. If a model M1 has a higher mean rank than the highest point of the CD interval line of another model M2 then we can say that M2 outperforms M1 with statistical significance. The Nemenyi plots for different metrics have been plotted and discussed in the next section. The AIC, BIC and RMSE values obtained for each of the metrics is listed in Tables 3, 4 and 5.

Table 3. Mean AIC values

Distribution/Metrics	Gamma	GPD	LNORM	Pareto	Weibull
CBO	12529.01	12554.24	12900.62	12554.16	12555.20
DIT	6006.38	7113.30	6077.51	7100.89	6012.88
LCOM	8647.76	7649.41	7579.94	7652.89	7821.39
LOC	22590.38	21002.44	21005.10	21002.43	21138.05
NOC	592.32	−2220.51	−2765.89	−2220.51	−699.13
RFC	12131.79	12209.30	12373.95	12208.77	12160.73
WMC	9584.81	9601.52	9343.66	9602.98	9662.59

Table 4. Mean BIC values

Distribution/Metrics	Gamma	GPD	LNORM	Pareto	Weibull
CBO	12537.32	12562.55	12908.93	12562.47	12563.51
DIT	6014.70	7121.61	6085.83	7109.20	6021.19
LCOM	8655.79	7657.44	7587.97	7660.92	7829.42
LOC	22598.69	21010.75	21013.41	21010.75	21146.36
NOC	600.76	−2212.07	−2757.45	−2212.07	−690.70
RFC	12139.94	12217.46	12382.11	12216.92	12168.89
WMC	9593.12	9609.83	9351.97	9611.30	9670.90

Table 5. Mean RMSE values

Distribution/Metrics	Gamma	GPD	LNORM	Pareto	Weibull
CBO	0.048	0.055	0.052	0.055	0.052
DIT	0.156	0.120	0.157	0.119	0.151
LCOM	0.093	0.074	0.067	0.075	0.086
LOC	0.156	0.170	0.150	0.170	0.183
NOC	0.030	0.022	0.032	0.022	0.018
RFC	0.041	0.042	0.054	0.042	0.040
WMC	0.043	0.045	0.036	0.045	0.043

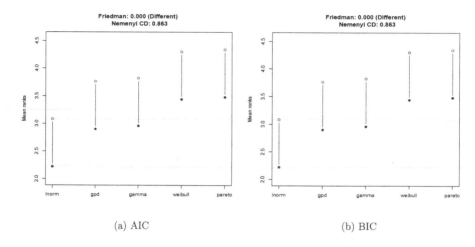

(a) AIC   (b) BIC

Fig. 1. Nemenyi plots - WMC

4.1   Weighted Method per Class (WMC)

For WMC, the null hypothesis is rejected. This means that not all the models have performed equally and thus we can conclude that one or few of the models performs significantly better than others. Nemenyi plots are shown in Fig. 1. On performing the Nemenyi test, we observe that the Log-normal model fits better, closely followed by Gamma and Generalized Pareto models.

Wheedlen et al. observed that WMC follows power law behavior [35]. Concas et al. observed that the distribution of WMC for a Small Talk project followed a Log-normal distribution. Our result is in agreement with the observations [7]. However, Law of Proportionate increment is too rough to model the generative process for the metric distribution. Most of the methods are written at one go according to the class design that was drawn initially. Therefore it is too much of a generalization if we say that the class is selected at random and the increment in the number of methods in class is proportional to the existing number of methods.

4.2   Coupling Between Objects (CBO)

The null hypothesis is not rejected for CBO and hence there is no significant difference among five models.

Many attempts have made to represent a software project as a graph, and observe the scale free behavior shown by the distribution of edges, which is the characteristic of any system following power law. Louridas et al. [22] have seen software project with such a perspective, links representing the use of a class by another class, and have concluded it to follow power law.

CBO is a metric closely related to these links. It is the count of the number of classes that are coupled to a particular class which means that the methods of one class call and access the variables of other. These calls are counted in both the directions. Therefore CBO of a class A includes both, the classes referenced by this class and also the classes referencing class A. CBO is (Number of Links)/(Number of Classes in the module) where the links represent dependence and composition between modules. Therefore it was intuitively expected that CBO metric shall follow power law, with Pareto model fitting the distribution well. Our experiment shows all the models (including Pareto) perform equally and no model performs significantly better than the rest.

4.3   Response For Class (RFC)

Response for Class is the number of distinct methods and constructors invoked by a class. It includes the methods defined in the class and also the methods called by the methods of the class. The null hypothesis is rejected for RFC, suggesting significant difference in the performance of the models. Nemenyi diagram is shown in Fig. 2. From the diagram we observe that Gamma, Pareto, Weibull and Generalized Pareto models fit RFC better than Log-normal.

Like CBO, RFC is a metric that deals with the relationship between classes. In our experiment, we observe that the four out of five models, performed no better than each other. Thus we shall not be able to pinpoint the generative model that may have led to the current distribution.

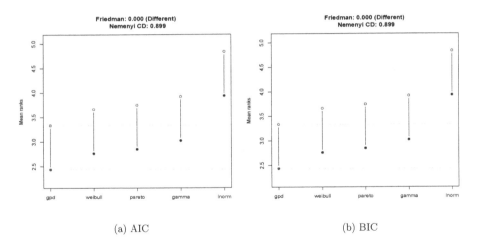

(a) AIC   (b) BIC

Fig. 2. Nemenyi plots - RFC

4.4   Depth of Inheritance Tree (DIT)

The null hypothesis is rejected and therefore we proceeded to perform the Nemenyi test. Figure 3 shows the Nemenyi diagram generated using AIC, BIC values for models, fitting DIT metrics of various projects.

From the Nemenyi diagram we can see that the two best fitting models are Log-normal and Gamma. Their respective RMSE values are 0.0156 and 0.0157 respectively.

The law of proportionate effect doesn't seem to be applicable though our experiments reveal that DIT follows Log-normal. It would be highly impractical to say that the increment of the depth in inheritance tree is proportional to the present depth value. Every time a programmer makes the inheritance tree of a class deeper, it is by a single unit. Therefore increments are constant rather than proportional. It seems unrealistic to say that all the files will be chosen with equal probability. And at the same time it is equally extreme to say that the probability of choosing a file is proportional to its existing value. Thus, though experiments show Lognormal and Gamma Distributions to be fitting the metric distribution well, their generative processes are too complicated to be intuitively conceived. Also, since the dynamics exhibited by the metric data is very limited, the result may be misleading. Hence we cease to explore further possibilities.

4.5   Lack of Cohesion of Methods (LCOM)

LCOM gives the correlation between the methods and local variables of a class. High cohesion suggests good class division. The null hypothesis is rejected, indicating that there is significant difference between the performance of models. Therefore Nemenyi test is performed and it is observed that Log-normal distribution is the best performer among the models. Figure 4 shows the plotted graph. The average value of RMSE for the fit of Log-normal distribution is 0.067.

Pani and Concas observed that the Log-normal model fit the LCOM metric distribution the best in case of the Java project Eclipse [28]. In our study we notice that this observation can be generalized to all Java projects.

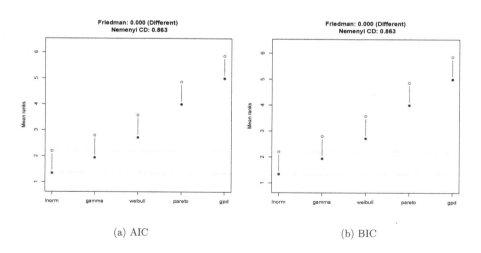

(a) AIC   (b) BIC

Fig. 3. Nemenyi plots - DIT

LCOM metric as originally proposed by Chidamber and Kemerer is as follows [6]. Let a class C have n methods $M_1, M_2, M_3, ...M_n$. Let I_i be the set of instance variables used by method M_i. Let $P = \{(I_i, I_j) | I_i \cap I_j = \phi\}$ and $Q = \{(I_i, I_j) | I_i \cap I_j \neq \phi\}$ then,

$$LCOM = |P| - |Q|, \, if \, |P| > |Q|$$
$$= 0 \quad otherwise$$

(14)

The above definition shows that a higher LCOM value suggests the splitting of a class as there is a lack of cohesion. This suggests that $|P| > |Q|$ which means that more pairs of methods don't have a common instance variable. An increase in the LCOM value can be achieved in the following ways: Increasing $|P|$, i.e., introducing a method that doesn't share a common instance variable with more than half of the existing methods. Decreasing $|Q|$, i.e., deleting a method that shares a common instance variable with more that half of the existing methods. In the process of software development, deletion of methods is highly rare when compared to addition of new methods. Therefore we focus on the 1st scenario.

Consider 2 classes C1 and C2 with the LCOM value 10 and 20 respectively. This means that C1 has 10 more pairs of incoherent methods than coherent ones and C2 has 20 more pairs. This means that the C2 has more 'clusters' of methods that are incoherent with each other. If we introduce a incoherent method to each of these 'clusters', the magnitude of increase in the LCOM value of C2 will be higher than that of C1. The possible magnitude of increase is approximately proportional to the LCOM value of the class. Hence we can identify the presence of 'Law of Proportional Effect' which leads to the Log-normal distribution that the metric follows.

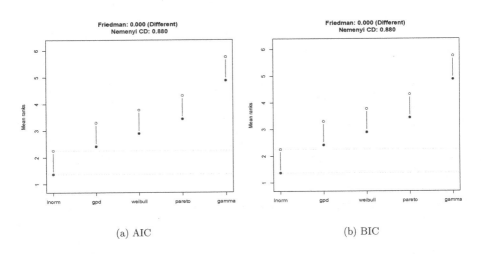

(a) AIC   (b) BIC

Fig. 4. Nemenyi plots - LCOM

4.6 Number of Children (NOC)

For NOC, the null hypothesis is rejected and hence Nemenyi test is employed. The nemenyi plots are shown in Fig. 5. It is observed that Log-normal fits NOC better than other models. The average RMSE for the Log-normal fit is 0.0323 which suggests that not only is the Lognormal model relatively better than other model, but also it fits the data distribution well in absolute sense too.

It seems unrealistic to say that the metric distribution might have been generated by Law of Proportional effect, i.e., the classes being chosen with equal probability and the magnitude of increment in number of children for a class being proportional to its present metric value. Thus, though experiments show Log-normal model to be fitting the metric distribution well, its generative process is too complicated to be intuitively obtained.

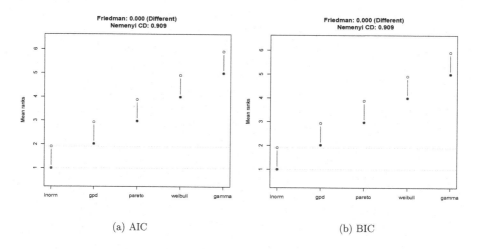

(a) AIC   (b) BIC

Fig. 5. Nemenyi plots - NOC

4.7 Lines of Code (LOC)

Though this is not one of the original CK metric, Lines of Code is a commonly used metric to understand the size and growth of the software systems. In an attempt to find the distribution followed by the metric, we fit five models and compare them with their respective AIC values. The null hypothesis is rejected and hence one or few of the models fit significantly better than the rest. We further proceeded to perform the Nemenyi test and found that GPD and Weibull models fit the data equally well and are better than the other models with a statistical significance. We then observed the RMSE values for the fits, in order to estimate how well the models actually fit the data, and find the score to be 0.170 and 0.183 for GPD and Weibull respectively. This significant value suggests that though the models are better among the models that we have considered, they can not be considered to fit the given distribution well.

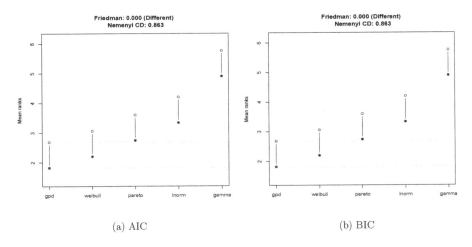

(a) AIC   (b) BIC

Fig. 6. Nemenyi plots - LOC

5   Conclusion

Understanding the distributions of CK metrics will help us in predicting the evolutions and efforts required to maintain such systems. It will also be useful to estimate the quality attributes of software projects. As these metrics frequently follow power law, they are also shown to follow Log-normal or Gamma distributions occasionally. In our attempt to model the distribution of six object-oriented metrics and LOC, we have found that, with respect to AIC and BIC, WMC, DIT, LCOM and NOC metrics follow the Log-normal distribution. On the contrary, it is not clear in RFC and CBO's case, as the distribution models that fit the RFC and CBO are not significantly better than each other. GPD and Weibull models fit the LOC metric significantly better than other three distributions but with respect to RMSE, GPD and weibull performances are observed to be poor. With the probability distributions that the object-oriented metrics follow, we have also explored the generative processes and made an attempt to reason if these processes could indeed explain the software development process. In some cases, though we find the distributions that the metrics follow, the generative processes are too complex to be explained intuitively. Hence, a study on the relationship between the generative processes and the software development activities will move the field forward. The study will help the researchers to choose more intuitive and reasonable probability distribution model for the object-oriented metrics.

References

1. Adamic, L.A., Huberman, B.A.: Zipf's law and the internet. Glottometrics **3**(1), 143–150 (2002)
2. Akaike, H.: A new look at the statistical model identification. IEEE Trans. Autom. Control **19**(6), 716–723 (1974)
3. Andersson, C., Runeson, P.: A replicated quantitative analysis of fault distributions in complex software systems. IEEE Trans. Soft. Eng. **33**(5), 273–286 (2007)
4. Baxter, G., Frean, M., Noble, J., Rickerby, M., Smith, H., Visser, M., Melton, H., Tempero, E.: Understanding the shape of Java software. ACM Sigplan Not. **41**, 397–412 (2006)
5. Booch, G.: Object-oriented development. IEEE Trans. Software Eng. **2**, 211–221 (1986)
6. Chidamber, S.R., Kemerer, C.F.: A metrics suite for object oriented design. IEEE Trans. Software Eng. **20**(6), 476–493 (1994)
7. Concas, G., Marchesi, M., Murgia, A., Tonelli, R., Turnu, I.: On the distribution of bugs in the eclipse system. IEEE Trans. Software Eng. **37**(6), 872–877 (2011)
8. Concas, G., Marchesi, M., Pinna, S., Serra, N.: Power-laws in a large object-oriented software system. IEEE Trans. Software Eng. **33**(10), 687–708 (2007)
9. D'Ambros, M., Lanza, M., Robbes, R.: Evaluating defect prediction approaches: a benchmark and an extensive comparison. Empirical Soft. Eng. **17**(4–5), 531–577 (2012)
10. Demšar, J.: Statistical comparisons of classifiers over multiple data sets. J. Mach. Learn. Res. **7**, 1–30 (2006)
11. Fenton, N.E., Ohlsson, N.: Quantitative analysis of faults and failures in a complex software system. IEEE Trans. Softw. Eng. **26**(8), 797–814 (2000)
12. Gibrat, R.: Les inégalités économiques: applications: aux inégalitês des richesses, à la concentration des entreprises, aux populations des villes, aux statistiques des familles, etc: d'une loi nouvelle: la loi de l'effet proportionnel. Librairie du Recueil Sirey (1931)
13. Grbac, T.G., Huljenić, D.: On the probability distribution of faults in complex software systems. Inf. Softw. Technol. **58**, 250–258 (2015)
14. Herraiz, I., Rodriguez, D., Harrison, R.: On the statistical distribution of object-oriented system properties. In: 2012 3rd International Workshop on Emerging Trends in Software Metrics (WETSoM), pp. 56–62. IEEE (2012)
15. Huang, C.Y., Kuo, C.S., Luan, S.P.: Evaluation and application of bounded generalized pareto analysis to fault distributions in open source software. IEEE Trans. Reliab. **63**(1), 309–319 (2013)
16. Jureczko, M.: Significance of different software metrics in defect prediction. Soft. Eng. Int. J. **1**(1), 86–95 (2011)
17. Jureczko, M., Madeyski, L.: Towards identifying software project clusters with regard to defect prediction. In: Proceedings of the 6th International Conference on Predictive Models in Software Engineering, p. 9. ACM (2010)
18. Kolassa, C., Riehle, D., Salim, M.A.: A model of the commit size distribution of open source. In: van Emde Boas, P., Groen, F.C.A., Italiano, G.F., Nawrocki, J., Sack, H. (eds.) SOFSEM 2013. LNCS, vol. 7741, pp. 52–66. Springer, Heidelberg (2013). https://doi.org/10.1007/978-3-642-35843-2_6
19. Kumar, L., Misra, S., Rath, S.K.: An empirical analysis of the effectiveness of software metrics and fault prediction model for identifying faulty classes. Comput. Stand. & Interfaces **53**, 1–32 (2017)

20. Lessmann, S., Baesens, B., Mues, C., Pietsch, S.: Benchmarking classification models for software defect prediction: a proposed framework and novel findings. IEEE Trans. Soft. Eng. **34**(4), 485–496 (2008)
21. Li, P.L., Shaw, M., Herbsleb, J., Ray, B., Santhanam, P.: Empirical evaluation of defect projection models for widely-deployed production software systems. ACM SIGSOFT Soft. Eng. Notes **29**, 263–272 (2004)
22. Louridas, P., Spinellis, D., Vlachos, V.: Power laws in software. ACM Trans. Soft. Eng. Methodol. (TOSEM) **18**(1), 2 (2008)
23. Meyer, B.: Object-Oriented Software Construction, vol. 2. Prentice hall, New York (1988)
24. Misra, S., Adewumi, A., Fernandez-Sanz, L., Damasevicius, R.: A suite of object oriented cognitive complexity metrics. IEEE Access **6**, 8782–8796 (2018)
25. Mitzenmacher, M.: A brief history of generative models for power law and lognormal distributions. Internet Math. **1**(2), 226–251 (2004)
26. Murgia, A., Concas, G., Marchesi, M., Tonelli, R., Turnu, I.: An analysis of bug distribution in object oriented systems. arXiv preprint arXiv:0905.3296 (2009)
27. Newman, M.E.: Power laws, pareto distributions and Zipf's law. Contemp. Phys. **46**(5), 323–351 (2005)
28. Pani, F.E., Concas, G.: Stochastic models of software development activities. In: Proceedings of WSEAS International Conference. Recent Advances in Computer Engineering Series, No. 7 (2012)
29. Pareto, V., Page, A.N.: Translation of manuale di economia politica ("manual of political economy"). AM Kelley, New York (1971)
30. Pickands III, J.: Statistical inference using extreme order statistics. Ann. Stat. **3**, 119–131 (1975)
31. Shatnawi, R., Althebyan, Q.: An empirical study of the effect of power law distribution on the interpretation of OO metrics. ISRN Soft. Eng. **2013** (2013)
32. Shriram, C., Muthukumaran, K., Bhanu Murthy, N.: Empirical study on the distribution of bugs in software systems. Int. J. Soft. Eng. Knowl. Eng. **28**(01), 97–122 (2018)
33. Shukla, S., Radhakrishnan, T., Muthukumaran, K., Neti, L.B.M.: Multi-objective cross-version defect prediction. Soft Comput. **22**(6), 1959–1980 (2018)
34. Vose, D.: Fitting distributions to data (2010)
35. Wheeldon, R., Counsell, S.: Power law distributions in class relationships. In: 2003 Proceedings of 3rd IEEE International Workshop on Source Code Analysis and Manipulation, pp. 45–54. IEEE (2003)
36. Zhang, H.: On the distribution of software faults. IEEE Trans. Soft. Eng. **34**(2), 301 (2008)

Information Technology Applications: Special Session on Language Technologies

Identification of Age and Gender in Pinterest by Combining Textual and Deep Visual Features

Sandra-Pamela Bravo-Marmolejo, Jorge Moreno, Juan Carlos Gomez[✉],
Claudia Pérez-Martínez, Mario-Alberto Ibarra-Manzano,
and Dora-Luz Almanza-Ojeda

Departamento de Ingeniería Electrónica, División de Ingenierías Campus
Irapuato-Salamanca, Universidad de Guanajuato, Salamanca, Mexico
{sp.bravomarmolejo,je.morenomoreno,jc.gomez,perez.claudia,ibarram,
dora.almanza}@ugto.mx

Abstract. In social media users share a lot of content, such as comments, news, photos, videos, etc. This information can be used by automated systems to segment the users to provide them with specific recommendations or focused content. One of the most popular way to segment the users is by age and gender. Nevertheless, such demographic variables are frequently hidden, and thus becomes useful to indirectly infer them. Commonly, these variables are learned using the text comments the users publish, analyzing the style of writing or frequency of words. In this paper, we present a study of several machine learning models that employ user generated images and text trying to exploit both types of information to infer the age and gender for Pinterest users. We experiment with the models using a dataset composed of 548,761 pins, posted by 264 users. Each pin is a combination of an image and a short comment. We transformed the images to a deep visual representation using the pretrained convolutional neural network ResNet-50, and transformed the comments using the tf-idf method. We compare the models among them and between the types of information using different performance metrics. Our experiments show interesting results and the viability of employing the user generated image and text content to characterize users.

Keywords: Social media · Data mining · Machine learning ·
Big data · Pinterest

1 Introduction

In the last decade, the use of social networks has increased substantially, mainly due to the flexibility of the sites to be accessed in multiple languages and countries. For example by 2018, Facebook, the most widely used social network,

© Springer Nature Switzerland AG 2019
R. Damaševičius and G. Vasiljevienė (Eds.): ICIST 2019, CCIS 1078, pp. 321–332, 2019.
https://doi.org/10.1007/978-3-030-30275-7_24

reached about 2.7 billion of active monthly users[1]. Pinterest, a relatively new social network (launched in 2010) has had an interesting increasing of audience in recent years, reaching 250 million of monthly active users[2].

The large amount of social media users generates a massive amount of data presented in different formats like photos, text comments, videos, audios, etc. All the stylish, format and frequency in which the users express themselves represent a set of characteristics that describes the users behaviours, demographics, preferences, opinions and personalities. This description is very important for the tasks of author profiling and author identification, which are widely implemented in several areas like forensics [1], security [2], business, marketing, among others. Ads and other social media information are interpreted differently and people might behave accordingly [3,4]. For those reasons, many companies and organizations use the author profiling analysis to determinate what kind of content to provide for advertising, marketing and recommendations; but also for costumer segmentation, political campaigns, social security programs, etc. Most of studies in author profiling are focused on age and gender detection, but there are some others that incorporate less common tasks like predicting authors degree of religiosity and IT background status [5].

In recent years, PAN (Plagiarism Analysis, Authorship Identification, and Near Duplicate Detection)[3] labs had presented a set of relevant tasks on digital text forensics and stylometry for author profiling, as part of the CLEF Conferences. The tasks have been about predicting gender, age, native language and personality [6–9]. Among them, age and gender identification has been the most popular and relevant task.

In the literature, most of the works on age and gender identification in social media are based on the text the users generate as part of their publications. The features extracted from text and used in such works could be separated in two groups, content-based and style-based. Meaning, the topics that the author usually communicate and the style that he or she implement, which includes grammar and the frequency of words. Using text from social networks to identify age and gender has several issues, for example, the lack of access to all users' publications; the lack of consistent data, given that in social media users write very short messages; and the highly unstructured data, since the messages usually contain non-standard language [10].

Regarding image data, most of the studies in social media are focused on author identification using face images [11]. Nevertheless, in a real implementation, looking for photos where a face appear and assure that the face is from the publication author deals a big challenge. Some works merge user generated images with metadata like tags on images description in order to infer the author [12].

---

[1] https://www.statista.com/statistics/272014/global-social-networks-ranked-by-number-of-users/.

[2] https://business.pinterest.com/en.

[3] https://pan.webis.de/tasks.html.

In this work we present a study of different machine learning models for age and gender identification for Pinterest users. For building the models we employ user generated data in the form of images and text, trying to exploit both types of information. For experimenting, we employ an imbalanced dataset extracted from Pinterest, with a total of 548,761 pins corresponding to 264 users. Our dataset reflects the real distribution of data on Pinterest, where around 81% of Pinterest users are women and the majority of active Pinterest users are below 40 years old.[4] In Pinterest a pin is the basic information unit, and is a tuple composed by an image and a short comment.

We process the images using the pretrained Convolutional Neural Network (CNN) ResNet-50 to transform them into a reduce set of deep visual descriptive features, avoiding the high dimensionality of the data. Additionally, we use the term-document-inverse-document-frequency (tf-idf) method to transform the text comments, obtaining a sparse matrix that contains the relationship between each term and each user.

We perform several experiments for each type of transformed data independently and then as a combination using six machine learning models, Logistic Regression, Linear Support Vector Machine, Multinomial Naïve Bayes, Random Forest, K-Nearest Neighbours and Nearest Centroid Classifier. The models performance is compare with three metrics, accuracy, macro F1 and Cohen's Kappa.

Our research questions in this paper are two. For predicting age and gender for users of social media employing image and text data: (1) How different approaches of machine learning models perform depending on the type of information? (2) What type (or combination) of information performs the best?

The rest of the paper is organized as follows. In Sect. 2 we present relevant works for age and gender identification for social media users. In Sect. 3 we present the methodology to process the image and text data and the evaluation of the models with both types of information. In Sect. 4 we describe the results obtained by the classification models using the aforementioned performance metrics. Finally, in Sect. 5 we describe the conclusions of this research.

2   Related Work

Age and gender identification for users of social media has been study through different approaches and for several purposes. In [13], the authors base their research on personal face images employing a Support Vector Machine (SVM) classifier, with three types of features, Local Binary Pattern, Scale Invariant Feature Transform (SIFT) and Color Histogram. In [14], the authors use Independent Component Analysis and Active Appearance models to extract features from personal face and full body images to identify author's gender, age, facial expressions and identity. Deep learning models have also been implemented in [15] using the Lithuanian embedding words with Long-Short Term Memory (LSTM) and Convolutional Neural Networks (CNN) models, which results do not outperform the traditional machine learning methods.

---

[4] www.omnicoreagency.com/pinterest-statistics/.

Nonetheless, the availability of personal images is sometimes complicate in social networks, since many users do not post personal information or the networks hide such information. Because of that, researchers have started focused on predicting age and gender from the users' generated content. Regarding images, in [16] the authors used a Bag of Visual Words approach in combination with SIFT features to predict users' genders from their posted images. For text, in [10] the authors applied a SVM with words and n-grams features for age and gender identification on a corpus of chat texts extracted from the Belgian social network Netlog. Also with text, in [17] the authors described how online behavior like wording, stylistic choices and lexical content, can be used to predict age.

Most of the relevant works for age and gender identification have been conducted as part of the series of tasks hosted by PAN. Until 2017 the tasks employed different Twitter datasets containing exclusively text. In [18], the authors collected data from different contexts like blogs, tweets and hotels reviews, and built a model where the output of a gender classifier is used as an input for a age classifier. In [19], the authors focused in sub-profiles and aim to build document vectors that represent with detail the relationship between documents and sub-profiles. In [20], the authors implemented a tf-idf-based model for language variety classification and a CNN for gender classification. In [21] researchers use a graph-base approach, based on the hypothesis that the way users express their emotions about topics depends on their age and gender.

In PAN 2018, the PAN task introduced the possibility to work with images and text simultaneously to predict gender and age, but just a few researchers used the image data. For example, in [22], the authors implemented a CNN to find and classify faces in images by gender and emotion. In [23], the authors proposed the Text Image Fusion Neural Network model which consider the synergy of texts and images.

An important remark about the PAN tasks for predicting age and gender, is that the organizers provide balanced datasets, with about the same number of users for each gender. This can be a problem to real world analysis since there actually exists some non uniform distribution among the groups. On the other hand, using unbalanced distributions of users can generate a bias problem in some classification models.

3 Methodology

3.1 Dataset Description

Initially, we randomly collected around 1.2 million pins from 674 users by crawling the Pinterest site. A pin is a tuple of an image and a text comment, and they are organized in boards, but for the purposes of this article, the board information was ignored. Figure 1 shows examples of common pins in Pinterest which represents our dataset. The original data was cleaned by discarding users with less than 500 pins and removing pins whose text were in a different language than English. Finally, we removed users for whom we could not identify their genders and ages. This last filter was performed by three judges, whom manually accessed the users' profile and selected and labeled only those that they were able to identify by gender and age group. A final judge chose the final age and gender group by majority vote. After cleaning, we ended up with a dataset of 264 users and a total of 548,761 pins, with an average of 2078 pins per users. For this research we consider the whole pins information, meaning the images and their text comments. The dataset was labeled for each user with two classes for gender, male and female, and four classes for age, 18–24, 25–34, 35–49 and 50+.

Tree Tunnel.   Times Square.

Fig. 1. Example of two pins (images and text comments) from Pinterest.

Table 1 shows the distribution of users along the classes for gender and age. We observe that there is a imbalance among the classes, with a majority of female users (~75%) and a majority of middle age adults in the group of 35–49 years (~38%).

Table 1. User distribution for gender and age in our Pinterest dataset

Age	Male	Female	Total
[18–24]	1	19	20
[25–34]	11	72	83
[35–49]	34	65	99
[50+)	21	41	62
Total	67	197	264

3.2 Data Processing

Text. We cleaned the text data by removing HTML tags, very short words (length < 3), very long words (length > 35) and stopwords. For that, we used the Python libraries Beautiful soup and NLTK. After cleaning, all the pins comments from a user were concatenate in a single long document (user document).

Afterwards, we extracted two types of content features for each user document, words (sequences of alphabetical characters plus the '-' and '_' symbols to captures composed words) and emojis/emoticons. Research has shown that emotions offer some new information to the classifiers and very useful combined with other features [24,25]. For extracting words we used a regular expression, whilst for emoticons we used the Python library Emoji.

We used the tf-idf method to transform the user documents into a sparse matrix of size $n \times m$ expressing the relationship of importance between each term and each user, where n is the number of users and m the size of the vocabulary. For building such matrix, the method has first to extract the vocabulary and compute the idf for each word in it. To avoid mixing the test data during the process, we apply first the tf-idf over the training set to extract the vocabulary and the idfs, and then use such elements to transform the test set. Since we use a 10-fold cross validation, tf-idf is applied independently over each fold.

Images. We processed the image data by first resizing all the pin images to a fixed size of 224 × 224 pixels. This size allows fast extraction of deep features while not loosing to much resolution. We then extracted deep features using a CNN architecture ResNet-50 that was pre-trained over the categories of the Imagenet dataset [26]. We pass each image through the ResNet-50 network and obtained the output of the final layer, that is, before the classification layer, to represent the image as a vector of 2,048 features. After processing all the images, we ended with a matrix of dimensions $n \times m$ were n is the number of total pins (548,761) and m represents the number of features extracted per image (2048). In this case, we can not concatenate all the images from a single user, since the number of images varies per user, whilst the number of deep features is fixed.

3.3   Classification Models

We implemented six classification models that have been largely used for age and gender identification. We selected two linear discriminative classifiers, Logistic Regression (LR) and Linear Support Vector Machine (LSVM), a probabilistic classifier, Multinomial Naïve Bayes (MNB), a classifier based on decision trees, Random Forest (RF) and two instance-based classifier, K-Nearest Neighbors (KNN) and Nearest Centroid Classifier (NCC). In our experiments, we used KNN only for text, and NCC only for images. This was because KNN is an expensive model when working with large numbers of examples. For the instance-based classifiers we used the cosine similarity as the metric to measure distances with both types of information.

We trained and tested each model with the two types of information and with a combination of the two. With each classifier and type of information, we performed a 10-fold cross-validation to obtain robust average results regarding the independence between the training and test sets.

In the case of text, as mentioned above, for each training part in each fold, we extract a vocabulary as a set of unique words and emojis/emoticons, and compute the idfs for each term in it. Using the vocabulary and the idfs weights we transform the training and the test sets to produce two document-terms sparse matrices. Finally all document vectors in both matrices are normalized to the unit using the $l2$ Euclidean norm. Images were transformed using and independent model, so no test data could be mixed during the process.

With text, the data split for the folds and the prediction by the models could be done directly at the user level, since all the text information from one user is concatenated. In this way is possible to predict the age and gender variables directly. In the case of images, the split is done at the user level, but the prediction is done at the pin level. That is, when forming the folds, a user is considered as a set of all his/her pins, but during the test phase, we predict the variables for each pin of a user independently. To reach a final decision with a model for a given user, we take the majority class among all his/her pins.

For the combination of the two types of information, we took the probability outputs from the same classification models for each type of information and apply the following equation.

$$p_{md,c,u} = p_{md,c,u,text} + p_{md,c,u,image} \tag{1}$$

where $p_{md,c,u,text}$ is the probability computed by a model (md) for a class (c) for a user (u) using text; $p_{md,c,u,image}$ is the probability computed by a model for a class for a user using images; and $p_{md,c,u}$ is the total probability. For text, the output from a model correspond directly to a user; for images, we take the average of the probabilities for the pins of the majority class. For a user, with one model we computed the probabilities for all the classes and we selected the class with the highest probability.

Finally, most methods have a hyper-parameter (HP) that influences their classification performance. We optimized for each HP by conducting an internal 3-fold cross validation for each external fold for each possible value of the HP. This is a form a linear search, where we vary the value of each HP an try a 3-fold cross validation, trying to maximize the F1 metric. In Table 2 we show the HPs and their values considered for optimization.

Table 2. Hyper-parameter to optimize in each model

Model	HP	Description	Values
LR	C	Regularization parameter	[0.1, 1, 10, 100]
LSVM	C	Regularization parameter	[0.1, 1,10, 100]
RF	n	Number of trees in the forest	[5,10,15,20]
KNN	k	Number of neighbors	[1,2,3,5,10]

3.4   Performance Metrics

The models were evaluated using three metrics: Accuracy, F1 (macro) and Cohen's Kappa. Accuracy is defined as $Accuracy = \frac{TP+TN}{TP+FP+FN+TN}$. F1 is defined as: $F1 = 2 \cdot \frac{Precision \cdot Recall}{Precision + Recall}$. Precision is defined as $Precision = \frac{TP}{TP+FP}$. Recall is defined as: $Recall = \frac{TP}{TP+FN}$. In these equations, TP, TN, FP and FN are compute for each class. TP is the true positives, TN is the true negatives, FP is the false positives and FN the false negatives.

An important remark is that accuracy is not a good metric for unbalance datasets. Commonly, in such cases a classification model tends to classify all the data with the majority class, reaching a good accuracy, but generating a misguided data description. On the other hand, macro F1 is a very helpful metric for unbalance data. In this version, F1 is computed per class and then average over all the classes, given the same weight to each class independently of its size. Accuracy and F1 goes from 0 (worst) to 1 (best).

The Cohen's kappa coefficient is defined as $\kappa = \frac{p_o - p_e}{1 - p_e}$, where p_o is the relative observed agreement among raters, and p_e is the hypothetical probability of chance agreement among raters. κ takes values between -1 (worst) and 1 (best), measuring the level of agreement between the predicted classes by a classifier and the real classes.

4   Results

In the following tables we present the results of our experiments. The results are split per gender and age identification, and per type of information (text, images and the combination of both). Each cell in the tables shows the average and the standard deviation of the 10-folds per model and per performance metric. The numbers in bold represent the best values for each metric in the corresponding table. The last row in each table indicates the average for each column.

To understand the values in accuracy and macro F1 with an unbalanced dataset, we can consider a classifier that always assign the majority class. Our dataset contains a majority of female users (197 out of 264, ~75%) and a majority of users between 35–49 years (99 out of 264, ~0.38%). Thus, the majority class classifier has a baseline accuracy of 0.75 for gender and 0.38 for age; and a baseline macro F1 of 0.43 for gender and 0.14 for age. As we already pointed out, accuracy is not a good metric for unbalanced dataset and macro F1 is preferred for comparisons.

Table 3 show the results for gender (left) and age (right) identification, using the pins text data. For gender, the best result for accuracy is given by LR, whilst KNN gives the best result for F1; and LSVM and KNN present the best values for κ, but LSVM presents less variation along the different test folds. For age, LR presents the best results for all the metrics. In both tables, we can notice that LR and LSVM obtain very similar values for all the metrics.

Table 4 present the results for gender (left) and age (right) identification, respectively, using the pins image data. For gender, the best accuracy is obtained by LR and LSVM; the best F1 by MNB and NCC; and the best κ by NCC. For age, RF produces the best results for all the metrics, with LSVM producing also the best results for F1 and κ, but with a larger variation along the test folds.

Table 3. Results for gender and age with user generated text

Model	Gender			Age		
	Accuracy	F1	κ	Accuracy	F1	κ
LR	**0.77**(0.13)	0.60(0.19)	0.24(0.39)	**0.47**(0.10)	**0.39**(0.19)	**0.21**(0.15)
LSVM	0.76(0.13)	0.61(0.19)	**0.25**(0.27)	0.46(0.14)	0.38(0.18)	0.20(0.20)
MNB	0.75(0.02)	0.43(0.01)	0.00(0.00)	0.39(0.08)	0.16(0.09)	0.03(0.12)
RF	0.76(0.08)	0.54(0.22)	0.14(0.38)	0.37(0.13)	0.27(0.10)	0.06(0.22)
KNN	0.74(0.08)	**0.62**(0.22)	**0.25**(0.38)	0.41(0.16)	0.35(0.21)	0.16(0.23)
Avg.	0.76(0.09)	0.56(0.17)	0.18(0.28)	0.42(0.12)	0.31(0.15)	0.13(0.18)

As a summary, with image data NCC is a good model to identify gender, whilst RFC is good to identify age.

Table 5 show the results for gender (left) and age (right) identification, respectively, when using a combination of text and image data. For gender, the combination of KNN(text)+NCC(images) obtains the best results for all the metrics. This models surpass the others for 30% with F1 and 40% with κ. For age, the best model for accuracy is LR; whilst for the other two metrics the best model is the combination of KNN+NCC. If we compare the results with the individual tables for each type of information, we observe that only the combination of KNN+NCC produces better results that using only one type of information. The rest of the models perform better with only one type of information, that could be text or images.

Table 6 shows the summary of the best models for each type of information, considering the F1 metric. In this table, we can observe that the KNN+NCC model produces the best results for both gender and age identification. We guess the combination of the instance-based classifier is better to discriminate among classes because it combines a fine grain exploration (KNN) with a summary exploration (NCC), which helps to partially avoid the noise in the test data.

Table 4. Results for gender with user generated images

Model	Gender			Age		
	Accuracy	F1	κ	Accuracy	F1	κ
LR	**0.75**(0.02)	0.43(0.01)	0.00(0.00)	0.37(0.17)	0.27(0.14)	0.10(0.24)
LSVM	**0.75**(0.05)	0.47(0.20)	0.06(0.32)	0.39(0.16)	**0.29**(0.13)	**0.13**(0.22)
MNB	0.72(0.20)	**0.67**(0.25)	0.35(0.48)	0.29(0.17)	0.26(0.17)	0.08(0.19)
RF	0.74(0.02)	0.43(0.01)	−0.01(0.04)	**0.41**(0.11)	**0.29**(0.10)	**0.13**(0.15)
NCC	0.71(0.20)	**0.67**(0.23)	**0.36**(0.45)	0.28(0.16)	0.26(0.16)	0.08(0.19)
Avg.	0.73(0.10)	0.53(0.14)	0.15(0.26)	0.35(0.15)	0.27(0.14)	0.10(0.20)

Table 5. Results for gender when combining user generated text and images

Model	Gender			Age		
	Accuracy	F1	κ	Accuracy	F1	κ
LR	0.75(0.02)	0.43(0.01)	0.00(0.00)	**0.44**(0.14)	0.32(0.11)	0.17(0.20)
LSVM	0.75(0.02)	0.43(0.01)	0.00(0.00)	0.42(0.25)	0.39(0.30)	0.18(0.29)
MNB	0.75(0.07)	0.47(0.17)	0.05(0.29)	0.36(0.15)	0.23(0.16)	0.04(0.21)
RF	0.75(0.06)	0.48(0.14)	0.07(0.22)	0.40(0.21)	0.27(0.21)	0.09(0.33)
KNN+NCC	**0.79**(0.20)	**0.73**(0.24)	**0.47**(0.48)	0.43(0.18)	**0.40**(0.24)	**0.20**(0.26)
Avg.	0.76(0.07)	0.51(0.11)	0.12(0.20)	0.41(0.19)	0.32(0.20)	0.14(0.26)

In all the cases, the models produce a better performance for macro F1 than a majority baseline model.

Table 6. Summary of the best results with F1 for gender and age

Problem	Text		Images		Text+Images	
	Model	F1	Model	F1	Model	F1
Gender	KNN	0.62(0.22)	NCC	0.67(0.23)	KNN+NCC	**0.73**(0.24)
Age	LR	0.39(0.19)	RF	0.29(0.10)	KNN+NCC	**0.40**(0.24)

5   Conclusions and Future Work Directions

In this paper we presented a study of age and gender identification based on user generated text and images, considering a dataset collected from Pinterest with an unbalanced distribution of users.

We tested our dataset with six well knows classification methods used for age and gender classification, and measured their performance using three performance metrics.

From the results of the experiments we can draw the following conclusions:

- Age identification is a more complex task than gender identification, mainly due to the number of categories. But it also means that there is a difference of content published between male and females users and an overlapping of content posted among age categories, meaning that users of different age classes could share similar topics.
- Instanced based classifiers perform as good models for gender identification, either when using text data (KNN), image data (NCC) or both.
- For age identification the performance of the models varies depending of the data used. With text data, only LR gives the best results; with image data, RF and LSVM have the best values; finally, when combining both types of information, KNN+NCC performs the best.

- Averaging the results of all the models over F1, for gender identification using text data or the combination of text and images produces the best results; whilst for age identification the combination of text and images produces the best results.
- Not all the classification models could exploit the use of both types of information, meaning that for several of them the decision surface produced when combining the probabilities overlap among classes.

Some ideas for further research include the use of a different schema to combine the outputs from the independent classifiers from text and image data. Another idea is to combine the data using methods such as Canonical Correlation Analysis or Bi-Lingual Topic Models, to transform both data to a single correlated space.

References

1. Orebaugh, A., Allnutt, J.: Classification of instant messaging communications for forensics analysis. Int. J. Forensic Comput. Sci. **1**, 22–28 (2009)
2. Argamon, S., Koppel, M., Pennebaker, J.W., Schler, J.: Automatically profiling the author of an anonymous text. Commun. ACM **52**(2), 119–123 (2009)
3. Liaudanskaitė, G., Saulytė, G., Jakutavičius, J., Vaičiukynaitė, E., Zailskaitė-Jakštė, L., Damaševičius, R.: Analysis of affective and gender factors in image comprehension of visual advertisement. In: Silhavy, R. (ed.) CSOC 2018. Advances in Intelligent Systems and Computing, vol. 764, pp. 1–11. Springer, Cham (2018). https://doi.org/10.1007/978-3-319-91189-2_1
4. Zailskaitė-Jakštė, L., Damaševičius, R.: Gender-related differences in brand-related social media content: an empirical investigation. In: 13th International Computer Engineering Conference (ICENCO), pp. 118–123. IEEE, December 2017
5. Hsieh, F., Dias, R., Paraboni, I.: Author profiling from Facebook corpora. In: Proceedings of the Eleventh International Conference on Language Resources and Evaluation (LREC-2018) (2018)
6. Rangel Pardo, F.M., Celli, F., Rosso, P., Potthast, M., Stein, B., Daelemans, W.: Overview of the 3rd author profiling task at PAN 2015. In: CLEF 2015 Evaluation Labs and Workshop Working Notes Papers, pp. 1–8 (2015)
7. Rangel, F., Rosso, P., Verhoeven, B., Daelemans, W., Potthast, M., Stein, B.: Overview of the 4th author profiling task at PAN 2016: cross-genre evaluations. In: Balog, K., et al. (ed.) Working Notes Papers of the CLEF 2016 Evaluation Labs. CEUR Workshop Proceedings, pp. 750–784 (2016)
8. Rangel, F., Rosso, P., Potthast, M., Stein, B.: Overview of the 5th author profiling task at pan 2017: gender and language variety identification in Twitter. Working Notes Papers of the CLEF (2017)
9. Rangel, F., Rosso, P., Montes-y-Gómez, M., Potthast, M., Stein, B.: Overview of the 6th author profiling task at PAN 2018: multimodal gender identification in Twitter. Working Notes Papers of the CLEF (2018)
10. Peersman, C., Daelemans, W., Van Vaerenbergh, L.: Predicting age and gender in online social networks. In: Proceedings of the 3rd International Workshop on Search and Mining User-Generated Contents, pp. 37–44. ACM, October 2011
11. Lyons, M.J., Budynek, J., Akamatsu, S.: Automatic classification of single facial images. IEEE Trans. Pattern Anal. Mach. Intell. **21**(12), 1357–1362 (1999)

12. McAuley, J., Leskovec, J.: Image labeling on a network: using social-network meta-data for image classification. In: Fitzgibbon, A., Lazebnik, S., Perona, P., Sato, Y., Schmid, C. (eds.) ECCV 2012. LNCS, vol. 7575, pp. 828–841. Springer, Heidelberg (2012). https://doi.org/10.1007/978-3-642-33765-9_59
13. Fazl-Ersi, E., Mousa-Pasandi, M.E., Laganiere, R., Awad, M.: Age and gender recognition using informative features of various types. In: IEEE International Conference on Image Processing (ICIP), pp. 5891–5895. IEEE, October 2014
14. Wilhelm, T., Böhme, H.J., Gross, H.M.: Classification of face images for gender, age, facial expression, and identity. In: Duch, W., Kacprzyk, J., Oja, E., Zadrożny, S. (eds.) ICANN 2005. LNCS, vol. 3696, pp. 569–574. Springer, Heidelberg (2005). https://doi.org/10.1007/11550822_89
15. Kapočiūtė-Dzikicnė, J., Damaševičius, R.: Lithuanian author profiling with the deep learning. In: Federated Conference on Computer Science and Information Systems (FedCSIS), pp. 169–172. IEEE, September 2018
16. You, Q., Bhatia, S., Sun, T., Luo, J.: The eyes of the beholder: gender prediction using images posted in online social networks. In: IEEE International Conference on Data Mining Workshop, pp. 1026–1030. IEEE, December 2014
17. Rosenthal, S., McKeown, K.: Age prediction in blogs: a study of style, content, and online behavior in pre-and post-social media generations. In: Proceedings of the 49th Annual Meeting of the Association for Computational Linguistics: Human Language Technologies-Volume 1, pp. 763–772. Association for Computational Linguistics, June 2011
18. Marquardt, J., et al.: Age and gender identification in social media. In: CLEF (Working Notes), pp. 1129–1136, September 2014
19. López-Monroy, A.P., Montes-y-Gómez, M., Escalante, H.J., Pineda, L.V.: Using intra-profile information for author profiling. In: CLEF (Working Notes), pp. 1116–1120, September 2014
20. Schaetti, N.: UniNE at CLEF 2017: TF-IDF and deep-learning for author profiling. In: CLEF (Working Notes) (2017)
21. Rangel, F., Rosso, P.: On the impact of emotions on author profiling. Inf. Process. Manage. 52(1), 73–92 (2016)
22. Nieuwenhuis, M., Wilkens, J.: Twitter text and image gender classification with a logistic regression n-gram model. In: Proceedings of the Ninth International Conference of the CLEF Association (CLEF 2018), September 2018
23. Takahashi, T., Tahara, T., Nagatani, K., Miura, Y., Taniguchi, T., Ohkuma, T.: Text and image synergy with feature cross technique for gender identification. Working Notes Papers of the CLEF (2018)
24. Martinc, M., Skrjanec, I., Zupan, K., Pollak, S.: PAN 2017: author profiling-gender and language variety prediction. In: CLEF (Working Notes) (2017)
25. Lopez-Santamaria, L.-M., Gomez, J.C., Ibarra-Manzano, M.-A., Almanza-Ojeda, D.-L.: Age and gender identification in unbalanced social media. In: Proceedings of the 29th International Conference on Electronics, Communications and Computers (CONIELECOMP 2019), pp. 74–80 (2019)
26. Deng, J., Dong, W., Socher, R., Li, L.J., Li, K., Fei-Fei, L.: Imagenet: a large-scale hierarchical image database. In: IEEE Conference on Computer Vision and Pattern Recognition, pp. 248–255. IEEE, June 2009

Analysis of Dispersion and Principal Component Analysis of Babblings' Signals from Moderate Preterm and Term Infants

Ana-Catalina Muñoz-Arbeláez[1(✉)], Leonor Jaimes-Cerveleón[1,2], and Javier-Darío Fenández-Ledesma[1]

[1] Universidad Pontificia Bolivariana, Circular 1ª, 70-01 Medellín, Colombia
ana.munozar@upb.edu.co
[2] Universidad de Pamplona, km 1 vía Bucaramanga, Pamplona Norte de Santander, Colombia

Abstract. There are different milestones expected to achieve in each month while infants are growing. During the first year of live they produce vocal sounds known as crying and babbling, which requires the coordination and development of different systems. These productions are being studied to find patterns which can be used to identify infants with developmental impairments or with normal development. Previous studies focused on crying signals, even though, none of the methodologies used have been established as a reliable method for clinical diagnosis of developmental impairments. This paper proposes a statistical analysis of babblings' signals in order to identify patterns to differentiate between infants' patients and controls. The size of the sample was 180 signals, 55 from 8 moderate preterm infants, and 125 from 22 term infants. A short-time Fourier transform was applied to each signal and a statistical validation was made using analysis of dispersion and principal component analysis. The results indicate ranges with significant difference between patients and controls sets.

Keywords: Speech development · Preterm infants · Babbling signal analysis · Short-time Fourier transform

1 Introduction

As infants are growing produce vocal sounds known as cooing, gooing, crying, squealing and babbling, which represent the product of speech development during the first year of life [1–3]. Despite global scale assessments are used by pediatricians and healthcare professionals to measure infants' development, the application of these scales are biases by the clinical observations, the clinician expertise and the parents report of the achieve milestones seem in infants [4]. For this reason, early diagnoses are rarely done [5], instead, only general early warnings are made. Since the last two decades, researchers are looking for acoustic patterns in infants' vocal sounds indicating developmental delays in order to identify specific markers for different diseases related to developmental impairments [6, 7].

© Springer Nature Switzerland AG 2019
R. Damaševičius and G. Vasiljevienė (Eds.): ICIST 2019, CCIS 1078, pp. 333–342, 2019.
https://doi.org/10.1007/978-3-030-30275-7_25

A.-C. Muñoz-Arbeláez et al.

Studies has focused on crying signals [8], as these signals may indicate information about the reason for crying, and about a possible physiological or physical impairment [8, 9]. Moreover, it can be used as an input to design non-invasive tools for developmental impairment diagnoses [10–12]. The methodologies used are based on two stages: (i) feature extraction and (ii) pattern classification [8, 11]. However, it seems that crying cannot be an accurate signal to classify between normal and non-normal development, because it is difficult to identify the original and real cause of each crying [8], also, the cry infant classification, for clinical diagnoses or developmental stage, represents a multiclass problem [8, 10, 12].

Another obstacle of previous studies is databases used lack of heterogeneous features and large samples. From reviewed studies, less than 200 infants have been recorded per research, and even several of them have used the same database. Additionally, each signal has been divided into multiple signals of 1 s [4, 8–15]. Although classification algorithms have been trained with large data, it does not correspond to a heterogeneous population, and more data and research are needed to design more accurate automated analysis models of infant's vocal sounds [16]. Furthermore, appropriate signal features extraction process needs to be improved [9] in order to gather only the most representative acoustic patterns; given better extracted samples and reducing the compute cost of the classification algorithms.

Delays on the onset of expected babbling patterns is considered as a predictor of developmental impairment [17], for the reason speech depends on the coordination of breathing, phonation and articulation systems [1, 3]. Thus, altered patterns in vocal sounds are due to disorders or damage in one or more systems. As well, since these systems are modulated by the central nervous system, sometimes, they may fail due to injuries, genetic defects or developmental disorders that affect the complex brain function [9]. Therefore, recognition of patterns in babblings signals may give information about infants' normal development.

As previous studies do not report statistical validation of the stage of feature extraction and crying classification has not been selected as a tool yet, this paper proposes the data analysis of babblings' signals, instead of crying, in order to identify possible patterns which can differentiate between two groups: moderate preterm and term infants. The first group was called patients and the second one controls. The analysis of dispersion and principal component analysis (PCA) were the two statistical procedures used.

2 Methodology

A total of 30 subjects between 0 and 12 months of age from Medellín-Colombia participated: 8 Patients ($\overline{age} = 6$) and 22 Controls ($\overline{age} = 7$). Each infant's parents signed the inform consent, where was explained the purpose of the research, the bioethical principles, the needed data, and the babbling recording method. The instruments used to record the babblings were smartphones, which have at least a 44100 Hz sampling rate. From each infant were collected 2 min of babbling sounds, and data related to the biological age and to the term birth. The last data were used to identify the target: patient for the moderate preterm and control for the term infants.

Each recorded audio was cleaned, noise filtered and normalized. Then, signals of 10 s of length were cut. The final database reached 55 signals of patients and 125 signals of controls, each one with 10 s of length. The short-time Fourier transform (STFT) algorithm were applied to each data in the database as follows:

$$P_v = \sum x[n] e^{-\frac{2\pi jkn}{N}} Q_v[n] \tag{1}$$

$$Q_v[n] = \phi[n - s] \tag{2}$$

$$s = [1024, 1024 + 512, \ldots, N - 512]$$

$$v = [2, 3, 4, 5, \ldots, 862]$$

$$Q_1[n] = \begin{vmatrix} 1 & 0 \leq n \leq \tau \\ 0 & others \end{vmatrix} \tag{3}$$

$$\tau = 512$$

P_v = short-time Fourier transform
Q_v = Fourier window
N = Signal length
X = Babbling signal

For each window of the STFT an analysis of the dispersion was made. This analysis was also applied in five different subgroups characterize by having data with only one age in months: 3, 6, 7, 9, and 10 months. For this analysis was used the standard deviation equation:

$$SD_{sample} = \sqrt{\frac{\sum |x - \bar{x}|^2}{N - 1}} \tag{4}$$

X = Fourier signal
$\bar{X}$ = Mean of each signal
N = Vector length

Finally, a principal component analysis was used to explore a set of minimum values linearly uncorrelated which can describe the babblings signals.

3   Results

From the literature is known clinicians observe changes in babblings to point out delays. However, it is difficult to diagnose just listening those changes. The analysis of the babblings' signals explains possible range of significant differences between preterm and term infants. A short-time Fourier transform was applied to each babbling signal to consider the frequencies involved in the differentiation of patients and controls. From each signal were obtained a matrix of (862, 1025), where 862 are the total windows where the Fourier transform was applied, and 1025 is the size of each window.

3.1   Analysis of Dispersion

The analysis of dispersion was applied for each window obtained in each set: patients and controls. Also, the difference between dispersions of controls and patients was calculated. A total of 862 values of dispersion per set are presented. As observed in Fig. 1. The window 759 has a control set dispersion of 4.11 and a patient set dispersion of 1.18, which represents the higher difference of dispersion (2.93) found.

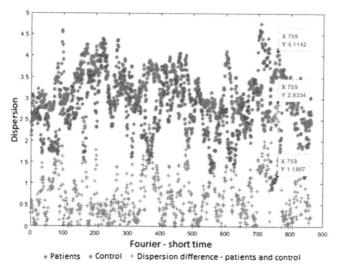

Fig. 1. Analysis of dispersion of the values for each window of the STFT algorithm applied to each data in the database. Blue points represent the patient set and red points the control set. Pink mark represents the difference between the dispersion of patients and controls in a specific window. (Color figure online)

In order to observe the change of dispersion through ages in patients, five different subgroups characterize by having data with only one age in months (3, 6, 7, 9, and 10 months) are presented in Figs. 2, 3, 4, 5 and 6. Figure 2 illustrates the comparison between 3 patients with 3 months of age and total controls. It seems patients with 3 months have more dispersion in the production of babblings' signals. This possibly evidences a higher activation in the exploration of random movements to produce babblings and little feedback in the learning of specific vocal sounds mapping to specific movements. Moreover, it is important to highlighted there is sampling bias due to the few signals gathered from patients with 3 months.

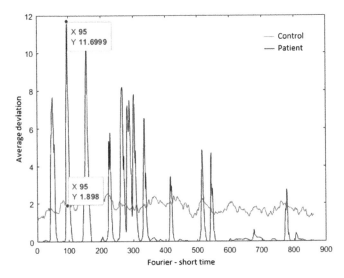

Fig. 2. Comparison between patients with 3 months of age and total controls of the analysis of dispersion of the values for each window of the STFT algorithm applied to each data in the database. Black line represents the patient set and red line the control set. (Color figure online)

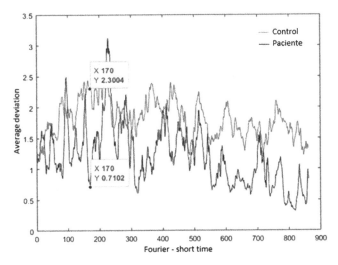

Fig. 3. Comparison between patients with 6 months of age and total controls of the analysis of dispersion of the values for each window of the short-time Fourier transform (STFT) algorithm applied to each data in the database. Black line represents the patient set and red line the control set. (Color figure online)

Figure 3 illustrates the comparison between 30 patients with 6 months of age and total controls. The dispersions from both sets appear to be close, however, the dispersion line of patients represents points with less values than the control line. It probably means patients do not change as much as controls in the production of different range of frequencies as did in previous ages.

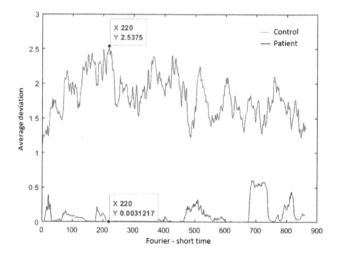

Fig. 4. Comparison between patients with 7 months of age and total controls of the analysis of dispersion of the values for each window of the STFT algorithm applied to each data in the database. Black line represents the patient set and red line the control set. (Color figure online)

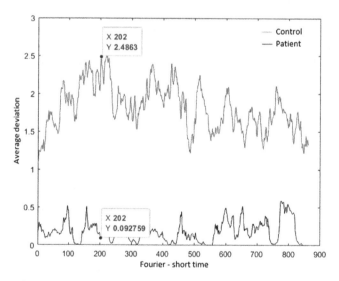

Fig. 5. Comparison between patients with 9 months of age and total controls of the analysis of dispersion of the values for each window of the STFT algorithm applied to each data in the database. Black line represents the patient set and red line the control set. (Color figure online)

Figures 4, 5 and 6 illustrate the comparison between 5 patients with 7 months of age, 5 patients with 9 months of age and 11 patients with 10 months of age respectively, and total controls. As in Fig. 3, the line of the patient dispersion is under the control line. These results may be consisted with delays in the onset of expected patterns during development in patients due to impairments related to preterm birth.

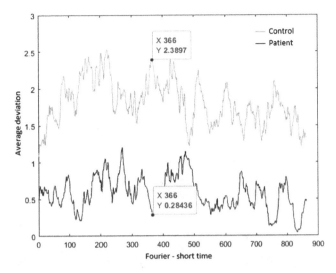

Fig. 6. Comparison between patients with 10 months of age and total controls of the analysis of dispersion of the values for each window of the STFT algorithm applied to each data in the database. Black line represents the patient set and red line the control set. (Color figure online)

3.2 Principal Component Analysis

The principal component analysis showed a 98.095% representation of the total information in data with the sum of the first 140 components. This means the 833850 data per babbling signal can be describe with a 98% of accuracy with only 140 components. According to Fig. 7 component 2 has a representation percentage of 2.91.

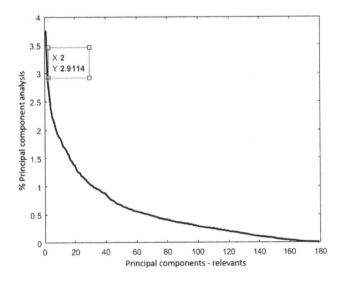

Fig. 7. Sedimentation graph

Figure 8 illustrates the found components in the PCA. After the dimensionality reduction it is concluded the total data matrix has a final size of 180 * 140 with a 98.09% of information resolution.

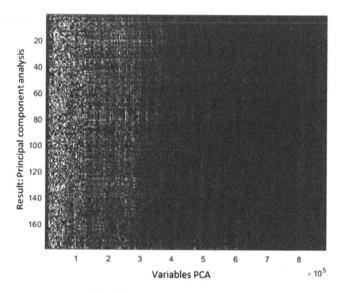

Fig. 8. New data in PCA space

4 Discussion

The theory of speech development explains that the delays on the onset of milestones and clinical patterns in babblings suggest neurodevelopmental impairment in infants [6]. Thus, different acoustic patterns in the babblings' signals may indicate possible impairments. In this paper babblings signals are proposed as a reliable marker of neurodevelopment instead of crying signals. A total of 180 signals (55 from patients and 125 from controls) were analyzed through statistical procedures to validate the hypothesis: there are patterns in babblings signals which differentiate infants' patients from controls.

According to the results of the analysis of dispersion for each window of the short-time Fourier transform (STFT), it can be concluded there is a significant difference between patients and controls, having some windows more relevant than others. This means that frequencies related to those relevant windows should be explore in future studies in order to identify the specific range of frequencies which can describe the babbling signal of a patient or a control.

Furthermore, considering the separate analysis of the five subgroups, characterize by the patients' ages (3, 6, 7, 9 and 10 months), it seems a better difference between patients and controls as the ages are 7 months or higher. These results are possibly explained by the learning process of the coordination and development of the systems involved in the vocal production. During the first months may be harder to identify patterns in the babbling signals because the complex system of vocal production has not received enough feedback to develop and to make evident a delay in any of the systems implicated. Despite of it, here was found significant difference in some ranges in subjects with 3 months or under. Those differences probably indicate the known delays of moderate preterm infants related to the not complete weeks of gestation.

Nonetheless as infants grow some delays are expected to see clearer in the babblings' signals of preterm infants. Therefore, here are presented results that evidence higher differences between patients and controls while patients' subjects have higher ages. The development of the systems related to the vocal production influence the final signal produce. Consequently, when an infant has a neurodevelopmental delay or impairment, the babbling signal is likely to be different from one produce by a healthy infant. More exploration of the range of frequencies with significant differences and statistical analysis are needed to find frequencies range correlated to specific neurodevelopmental impairments and chronological age.

Finally, the results of the principal component analysis suggest the 98.09% of the babblings' signals are described by 140 components. More studies are necessary to validate which components are statistically representative in order to describe the babblings' signals according to the minimum data needed to correlate them with neurodevelopmental delays or impairments.

5 Conclusion

This study explored the analysis of babblings signals as possible marker of the neurodevelopment. Babblings from moderate preterm and term infants were recorded. The results indicate significant difference between patients and controls across some ranges in the signals. Future studies should explore which ranges are more significant to characterized neurodevelopmental stages. There was also found 140 components as minimum uncorrelated values explaining the babblings' signals. It is important to continue exploring the main components implicated in the differentiation of patients and controls. Furthermore, is it highlighted the importance to consider the chronological age of each infant in future approaches.

References

1. Kent, R., Hustad, K.: Speech production: development. In: Squire, L. (ed.) Encyclopedia of Neuroscience, pp. 255–264. Academic Press, Oxford (2009). https://doi.org/10.1016/B978-008045046-9.09002-1. Science Direct 9366
2. Najnin, S., Banerjee, B.: A predictive coding framework for a developmental agent: speech motor skill acquisition and speech production. Speech Commun. **92**(Supplement C), 24–41 (2017). https://doi.org/10.1016/j.specom.2017.05.002
3. I. of-Medicine-&-National-Academies-of Sciences-Engineering-&-Medicine, Speech and Language Disorders in Children: Implications for the Social Security Administration's Supplemental Security Income Program, pp. 43–80. The National Academies Press, Washington, DC (2016). https://doi.org/10.17226/21872

4. Cruz, M., Reyes, C., Altamirano, L.: On the implementation of a method for automatic detection of infant cry units. Procedia Eng. **35**, 217–222 (2012). https://doi.org/10.1016/j. proeng.2012.04.183. International Meeting of Electrical Engineering Research 2012

5. Pontificia-Universidad-Javeriana, F. de Medicina, D. de Epidemiología-Clínica-Bioestadística, Escala Abreviada de desarrollo 3, Bogotá (2016)

6. Chittora, A., Patil, H.: Data collection of infant cries for research and analysis. J. Voice **31** (2), 252.e15–252.e26 (2017). https://doi.org/10.1016/j.jvoice.2016.07.007

7. Oller, D., et al.: Automated vocal analysis of naturalistic recordings from children with autism, language delay, and typical development. Proc. Nat. Acad. Sci. U.S.A. **107**(30), 13354–13359 (2010). https://doi.org/10.1073/pnas.1003882107

8. Saraswathy, J., Hariharan, M., Yaacob, S., Khairunizam, W.: Automatic classification of infant cry: a review. In: International Conference on Biomedical Engineering (ICoBE), pp. 543–548 (2012)

9. Hariharan, M., et al.: Improved binary dragonfly optimization algorithm and wavelet packet based non-linear features for infant cry classification. Comput. Methods Programs Biomed. **155**, 39–51 (2018). https://doi.org/10.1016/j.cmpb.2017.11.021

10. Sahin, M., et al.: Utilizing infant cry acoustics to determine gestational age. J. Voice **31**(4), 506.e1–506.e6 (2017). https://doi.org/10.1016/j.jvoice.2016.10.005

11. Rosales-Pérez, A., Reyes-García, C., Gonzalez, J., Reyes-Galaviz, O., Escalante, H., Orlando, S.: Classifying infant cry patterns by the genetic selection of a fuzzy model. Biomed. Signal Process. Control **17**, 38–46 (2015). https://doi.org/10.1016/j.bspc.2014.10. 002. mAVEBA 2013

12. Hariharan, M., Saraswathy, J., Sindhu, R., Khairunizam Yaacob, W.: Infant cry classification to identify asphyxia using time-frequency analysis and radial basis neural networks. Expert Syst. Appl. **39**(10), 9515–9523 (2012). https://doi.org/10.1016/j.eswa.2012.02.102

13. Oller, D.: The Emergence of the Speech Capacity. Taylor & Francis, New York (2014)

14. Chaiwachiragompol, A., Suwannata, N.: The features extraction of infants cries by using discrete wavelet transform techniques. Procedia Comput. Sci. **86**, 285–288 (2016). https:// doi.org/10.1016/j.procs.2016.05.073

15. Saraswathy, J., Hariharan, M., Khairunizam, W., Yaacob, S., Thiyagar, N.: Infant cry classification: time frequency analysis. In: IEEE International Conference on Control System, Computing and Engineering, pp. 499–504 (2013). https://doi.org/10.1109/iccsce. 2013.6720016

16. Beckman, M., Plummer, A., Munson, B., Reidy, P.: Methods for eliciting, annotating, and analyzing databases for child speech development. Comput. Speech Lang. **45**(Suppl. C), 278–299 (2017). https://doi.org/10.1016/j.csl.2017.02.010

17. Molemans, I., Van-Den-Berg, R., Van-Severen, L., Gillis, S.: How to measure the onset of babbling reliably? J. Child Lang. **39**(3), 523–552 (2012). https://doi.org/10.1017/ s0305000911000171

A Graph-Based Approach to Topic Clustering of Tourist Attraction Reviews

Nuttha Sirilertworakul[1(✉)] and Boonsit Yimwadsana[1,2]

[1] Faculty of Information and Communication Technology, Mahidol University,
999 Phuttamonthon 4 Road, Salaya 73170, Nakhon Pathom, Thailand
nuttha.sii@student.mahidol.ac.th, boonsit.yim@mahidol.ac.th
[2] Integrated Computational BioScience Center, Office of the President,
Mahidol University, 999 Phuttamonthon 4 Road,
Salaya 73170, Nakhon Pathom, Thailand

Abstract. A large volume of user reviews on tourist attractions can prohibit travel businesses from acquiring overall consumers' expectations and consumers themselves from seeing the big picture and making thoughtful decisions on trip planning. Summarization of the reviews allows both parties to catch the main themes and underlying tones of the attractions. In this paper, we address the task of topic clustering, by applying a graph-based approach to group the reviews into clusters. To interpret the resulting review clusters, WordNet and Inverse Document Frequency (IDF) are utilized to extract keywords from each cluster which represents the topic. We evaluate the graph-based clustering approach against gold standard data annotated by human and the results are compared against Latent Dirichlet Allocation (LDA), a widely used algorithm for topic discovery. The approach is shown to be competitive to LDA in terms of clustering user reviews on tourist attractions. The graph-based approach, unlike LDA which requires the number of clusters as an input, can dynamically clusters the reviews into groups, revealing the number of clusters.

Keywords: Text mining · Text summarization · Topic clustering · Graph clustering · User reviews

1 Introduction

User reviews on tourist attractions provide travel businesses and consumers with a mixture of fact and opinion which are significant to their decision making [15]. While businesses require user reviews for product and service improvement, consumers need them for trip planning. Summarizing the reviews allows both parties to catch the main themes and underlying tones of the attractions.

Summarization can be performed by discovering patterns of words in a collection of documents which reflect its underlying topics [2]. Not only topic discovery reveals general ideas of the documents, there are several applications based on it. Some examples are topic-based searching [9], contextual advertising [17], and recommender systems [12].

R. Damaševičius and G. Vasiljevienė (Eds.): ICIST 2019, CCIS 1078, pp. 343–354, 2019.
https://doi.org/10.1007/978-3-030-30275-7_26

In this paper, we apply Soft-Regularized Markov Clustering (SR-MCL) [20] to cluster user reviews and extract keywords from each resulting cluster which represents the topic, through the utilization of WordNet[1] and Inverse Document Frequency (IDF). The advantage of the graph-based approach over Latent Dirichlet Allocation (LDA) [5] is its ability to dynamically group reviews into clusters and thus provide the number of clusters which is usually unknown and varies depending on the nature of the data.

2   Related Work

2.1   Text Summarization

Text summarization is the task of "grouping together of similar information and describing those groups" [16]. The resulting groups can be described using either *extractive* or *abstractive* approach. Extractive summarization uses units of text, such as words and sentences, from data in the group to represent the group while abstractive summarization represents the group with a new description, similar to the approach taken by human.

As described in [16], we explore extractive summarization which includes two main tasks: (1) topic clustering which groups similar reviews into clusters and (2) keyword extraction which draws keywords from the resulting clusters to represent the topics. In this paper, the focus is on the task of topic clustering and its evaluation against LDA clustering. For the task of keyword extraction, we investigate the utilization of WordNet and IDF to semantically draw meaningful words from each cluster, representing a topic.

2.2   Markov Clustering

Soft-Regularized Markov Clustering (SR-MCL) [20] is a graph clustering algorithm which is a variant of Markov Clustering (MCL) [7] and Regularized Markov Clustering (R-MCL) [18]. MCL runs two operations, *Expand* and *Inflate*, iteratively on a stochastic matrix, M, which describes the transition probabilities from each of the nodes in the graph to the others. The Expand operation is $M := M \times M$, and the Inflate operation raises each cell in the matrix by the Inflate parameter (r), and re-normalizes the sum of each column to 1, representing the transition probabilities.

R-MCL later modified MCL by replacing the Expand operation with *Regularize* operation which is $M := M \times M_G$, where M_G is a canonical stochastic matrix storing the original transition probabilities of the nodes within the graph. The Regularize and Inflate operations are run iteratively, spreading more flows within the same cluster than between clusters as intuitively there are more paths between nodes within the same cluster. The algorithm is terminated when there is no change in the matrix M or the number of iterations is reached. After the termination, nodes that flow to the same 'attractor node' belong to the same

---

[1] Lexical database which measures the relatedness of terms.

Algorithm 1. SR-MCL [20]

Input: The canonical stochastic matrix M_G, the balance parameter b, the inflation parameter r, the penalized ratio β and the number of iterations t.

Output: A set of clusters C.

1: $C = \{\}$
2: $count = \{0, 0, ..., 0\}$
3: **for** $iter \to t$ **do**
4:     **repeat**
5:         $M_R = RegularizationMatrix(M, M_G, b)$
6:         $M = M * M_R$ ▷ Regularize
7:         $M = Inflate(M, r, count, \beta)$ ▷ Inflate
8:         $M = Prune(M)$
9:     **until** M converges   ▷ iter-time execution of R-MCL
10:    $T_{iter} = attractors(M)$ ▷ Resulting attractor nodes
      from iter-time execution of R-MCL
11:    **for all** $v_i \in T_{iter}$ **do**
12:       $count[i] = count[i] + 1$
13:    **end for**
14:    $C_{iter} = clusters(M)$ ▷ Resulting clusters from iter-time execution of R-MCL
15:    $C = C \cup C_{iter}$
16: **end for**
17: $C = post\text{-}process...(C)$ ▷ Extract qualified clusters

---

cluster. Additionally, a balance parameter (b), is introduced in [19] to inhibit the flow to an attractor node which attracts a large number of nodes. This produces the resulting clusters which are more balanced in size.

In SR-MCL, the idea is to "iteratively re-execute R-MCL while ensuring that the resulting clusters are not always the same" [20] by introducing a penalty parameter (β) in the Inflate operation. The parameter decreases the flow to a node which has been an attractor x times in the previous iterations by raising the node (i.e., the corresponding column in the matrix M) to $r \times \beta^x$", where $\beta > 1$. After the algorithm is terminated, post-processing step removes redundant and low-quality clusters according to the quality function. The default quality function is density multiply by the square root of size. The advantage of SR-MCL over MCL and R-MCL is its soft-clustering property which means a node can belong to more than one cluster. The SR-MCL process is shown in Algorithm 1.

Typical applications of MCL and its variants are in clustering biological networks such as protein-protein interaction networks [20]. Few applications are also found in text corpora. In [8], MCL is applied to automatically discover word senses from text. In [13], a technique to classify Arabic documents is proposed through a combination of MCL and Deep Belief Networks. Another closely related work is topic clustering of comments on online news [1] which applied MCL to group comments and the resulting clusters are labeled by incorporating information from DBpedia. One limitation on topic clustering of this approach is that MCL is a hard-clustering algorithm (i.e., each comment is assigned to only one cluster).

This paper applied SR-MCL which is a soft-clustering algorithm to cluster user reviews on tourist attractions, allowing the reviews to belong to more than one cluster. This corresponds with the nature of a review which is usually composed of more than one topic.

3 Dataset

English written reviews from 4 popular tourist attractions in Bangkok, Thailand of different categories are downloaded from TripAdvisor[2]. The four attractions are Lumphini Park (nature), Wat Pho (landmarks), Jim Thomson (museums), and Siam Paragon (shopping). Each attraction contains more than 3000 reviews. All of the reviews in each attraction are used to generate a separate set of review clusters and topics.

To evaluate the resulting clusters, a gold standard dataset is created by human annotators using a similar approach as in [1]. Using a 95% confidence level and $\pm 10\%$ margin of error, a set of 100 random reviews from each of the four attractions are provided to two annotators to group them into clusters by following the steps as: (1) Read the reviews and come up with topics labeled by a word or phrase. For instance, an annotator may come up with topics Food, Shopping, and Transportation when provided with reviews from a shopping attraction. (2) Assign the reviews to one or more created topics (i.e., clusters). On average, an annotator creates 9.31 clusters per attraction.

4 Method

4.1 Document Clustering

Since our approach applied SR-MCL which is a graph algorithm to perform document clustering, a set of reviews from each tourist attraction is represented as a graph. The graph is denoted as $G(V, E, W)$ where V is a set of nodes which represent the reviews and E is a set of edges which connect the nodes (i.e., reviews).

The set of edges, E, has a corresponding set of weights, W. The weight $w_{i,j}$ on an edge $e_{i,j}$ is a cosine similarity value between nodes v_i and v_j. In our approach, there is an edge, $e_{i,j}$, between nodes v_i and v_j if the similarity value between the two nodes is greater than or equal to a similarity threshold, x, ranging from $(0, 1)$.

In practice, the graph is constructed from the reviews on each attraction as: (1) Data preprocessing is performed by tokenizing each review into terms, converting all terms to lowercases, removing non-alphabetic characters and stopwords, and stemming the terms into their root forms. This step generates a bag of words from the input reviews. (2) Feature extraction constructs a term-document matrix (e.g., TF-IDF matrix), which stores the occurrences of each

---

[2] https://www.tripadvisor.com/.

term within each review. (3) Cosine similarity measure is applied to the term-document matrix to find a similarity score between each pair of reviews, forming a pairwise similarity matrix, S. (4) The adjacency matrix, A, which corresponds to a graph, is computed by pruning the similarity matrix according to the similarity threshold (x) discussed in the previous paragraph:

$$a_{i,j} = \begin{cases} s_{i,j}, & \text{if } s_{i,j} \geq x \\ 0, & \text{otherwise} \end{cases} \tag{1}$$

The adjacency matrix is then re-normalized by columns. The result is a stochastic matrix which is parsed to SR-MCL algorithm shown in Algorithm 1. The implementation[3] of SR-MCL used by this work is provided by [6].

4.2   Topic Extraction

SR-MCL returns a set of review clusters. To extract a topic which is represented as keywords from each review cluster, WordNet and Inverse Document Frequency (IDF) are applied.

Since keywords of the topic are semantically similar to other probable words within the cluster, WordNet is used to give more weight to those words [3]. Given $n(w, t)$ be a function which returns the total count of word w from documents in cluster t, C_t be a set of words from documents in cluster t, and $PS(w, v)$ be a function which returns path similarity[4] between the words w and v in WordNet which ranges between $[0, 1]$. The word count $WN(w, t)$ of word w in topic t is updated as:

$$WN(w, t) = n(w, t) + \sum_{v \neq w \in C_t} n(v, t) \times PS(w, v) \tag{2}$$

Then IDF is applied at the cluster level (i.e., reviews in the same cluster are treated as a single document) to reduce the importance of words which occur in many clusters. Given $IDF(w)$ be a function which returns inverse document frequency of word w. The term-topic score of word w in topic t is calculated by multiplying the probability of the updated word count by IDF as:

$$Term\text{-}Topic(w, t) = \frac{WN(w, t)}{\sum_{v \in C_t} WN(v, t)} \times IDF(w) \tag{3}$$

Lastly, the words in each cluster are arranged by their term-topic scores in descending order which reflects the importance of words within the cluster, representing the topic.

---

[3] https://github.com/koadman/proxigenomics.
[4] Path similarity computes the shortest path between two word senses. Word senses are more similar when their path distance is closer to 1.

4.3 Topic Tagging

Each document is tagged with generated topics, together with their probabilities distributed over the document. Let W_t be a set of top-N words from topic t, W_d be a set of words from document d, T_d be a set of topics document d is composed of (i.e., a set of clusters document d belongs to), and $TFIDF(w, d)$ be a function which returns term frequency-inverse document frequency of word w in document d. The probability distribution of topic t on document d is computed:

$$Topic\text{-}Doc(t, d) = \frac{\sum_{w \in W_d \cap W_t} TFIDF(w, d)}{\sum_{k \in T_d} \left(\sum_{v \in W_d \cap W_k} TFIDF(v, d) \right)} \tag{4}$$

5   Experiments and Results

5.1   Cluster Granularity in SR-MCL

Instead of being supplied with the number of clusters as in LDA, SR-MCL has the Inflate parameter (r) which reflects cluster granularity. Figure 1 shows the BCubed[5] precision, recall, and the number of clusters as we varied r between 1.1 and 2.5. The precision varies slightly around 0.70 while the recall fluctuates strongly when the value of r is higher. A larger value of r also results in finer granularity and thus more clusters are generated.

In the following experiments, r is set to 1.5 as in [1] to demonstrate the robustness of the parameter against different text corpora.

5.2   Comparison with Latent Dirichlet Allocation

The approach is compared against LDA, a widely used algorithm for topic discovery. An LDA model is created for each set of reviews. Since LDA requires a predetermined number of topics, it is set to the average number of clusters [1] within the gold standard dataset mentioned in Sect. 3. The average number of topics is 9.31, so the number of topics is set to 9 topics for each LDA model created. For the LDA hyperparameters β and α, they are set respectively to 0.1 and 50/T, where T is the number of topics as suggested in [10]. Since LDA distributes multiple topics as probabilities over a document, a threshold is used to determine the topics of which a certain document is made. In this work, a threshold is set to be $1/T$, where T is the number of topics. For SR-MCL configurations, r is set to 1.5 as preciously tuned in [1] to work with text corpora. The other parameters are set to default values [20].

For evaluation, the SR-MCL clusters and LDA clusters are compared with the gold standard dataset described in Sect. 3. BCubed precision, recall, and F-measure are used as evaluation metrics since they fulfill the formal cluster constraints: cluster homogeneity, completeness, rag bag, and cluster size versus quantity [4].

---

[5] BCubed is an evaluation metric which compares the resulting clusters generated by an algorithm with the gold standard clusters.

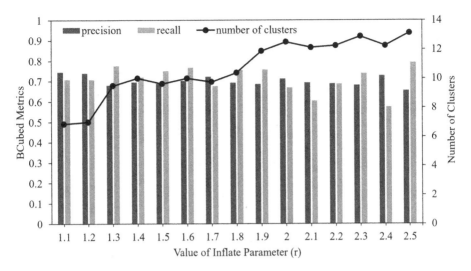

Fig. 1. BCubed precision, recall, and the number of generated clusters when the Inflate parameter is varied.

Using BCubed to estimate the fit between two sets of clusters X and Y at an item level, precision measures a proportion of items sharing a cluster with a particular item i in X which appears in its cluster in Y and recall measures a proportion of items sharing a cluster in Y with the item i which appears in its cluster in X [14]. For F-measure, we use F1 score which is the harmonic mean of precision and recall. The evaluation employed follows the BCubed definition discussed in [4].

The clustering evaluation results are shown in Table 1. The fit between Human1-Human2 clusters, according to BCubed metrics, is around 0.73. To compare the fits of SR-MCL-to-human and LDA-to-human clusters, a paired t-test is performed. According to the test, we cannot reject the hypothesis that SR-MCL clustering performs better than LDA clustering in terms of precision ($p = 0.28$). Yet, the mean recall and F-measure of SR-MCL clustering are significantly[6] higher than those of LDA clustering, with p-values of 0.01 and 0.04 respectively.

Table 1. Average BCubed Precision, Recall, and F-measure metrics.

Metric	Human1-Human2	SR-MCL-Human	LDA-Human
BCubed Precision	0.76	0.79	0.82
BCubed Recall	0.71	0.63	0.48
BCubed F-measure	0.73	0.69	0.60

---

[6] There is a statistically significant difference between the two results if p-value is less than 0.05 ($p < 0.05$).

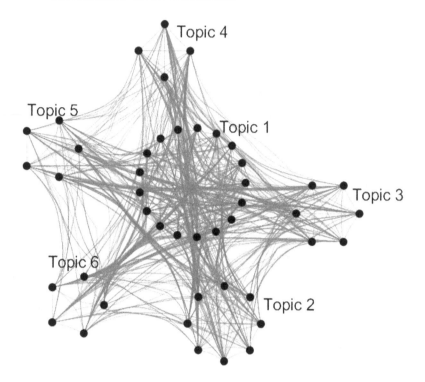

Fig. 2. Document-topic relationship

5.3 Identifying Document-Topic Relationship

Aiming to ease the interpretation of clustering results, we illustrate document clustering as a graph with nodes representing the reviews. Each node has an attribute, most-likely topic, which indicates the topic the review is made up of with the highest probability as computed using Eq. 4. The edges connect the nodes sharing one or more clusters (i.e., topics). The weight on an edge indicates the number of topics shared by the two reviews.

Figure 2 illustrates an example of the graph using Cytoscape[7], a graph visualization tool. The nodes, whose most-likely topics are the same, are circularly grouped together and the edges are bundled using a built-in algorithm invented by [11] to reduce the clutter within the graph and highlight the connectivity strengths between the reviews and the topics.

---

[7] https://cytoscape.org/.

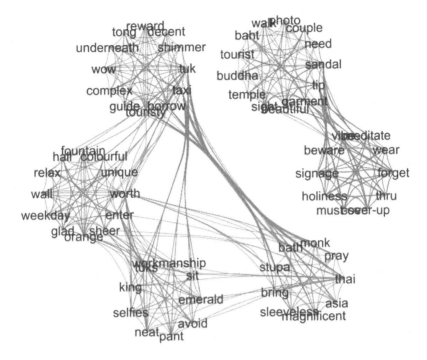

Fig. 3. Word-topic relationship

5.4   Identifying Term-Topic Relationship

Similar to Sect. 5.3 with the aim of investigating the semantics, we present the relationship between words and topics as a graph with nodes representing the words. Each node has most-likely topic as an attribute, stating the topic the word resides and has the highest term-topic score among its scores in other topics. The edges connect the nodes which share one or more topics. The weight on an edge is an average of term-topic score multiplication of the two words co-occurring within the same clusters. Let avg_t be a function which returns an average of the series where t is the topic(s) the two words co-occur and $Term\text{-}Topic(w,t)$ be a function which returns term-topic score of word w in topic t. The weight of edge between word w and word v is computed as:

$$W(w,v) = avg_t(Term\text{-}Topic(w,t) \times Term\text{-}Topic(v,t)) \qquad (5)$$

Figure 3 shows an example of the graph with nodes circularly grouped by their most-likely topics and edges bundled, highlighting the connectivity strengths between the words and the topics.

6   Discussion

The results of topic clustering based on SR-MCL demonstrate that the approach is an alternative to LDA to cluster reviews of tourist attractions. Unlike LDA,

SR-MCL does not require the number of clusters as prior knowledge. Yet, its Inflate parameter affects the number of clusters. To demonstrate its robustness against different text corpora, we adopted a previously tuned value [1]. The value results in relatively high precision and recall when compared with other values of r.

The limitation of the demonstrated graph-based topic clustering is in its several parameters of SR-MCL which are set to default values in the experiments. Changing of these parameter values could affect the clustering results.

For topic extraction, WordNet and IDF are used to extract semantically-similar keywords from each cluster to represent a topic. The results are visualized using graphs to investigate the relationships between reviews sharing the same topics and between keywords co-occurring within the same and different topics. Highly overlapped topics are detected by bunches of edges within the graphs.

7   Conclusion

In this paper, a topic clustering approach based on SR-MCL is applied to cluster user reviews on tourist attractions. Using BCubed metrics to determine the fit between the resulting clusters and those of the gold standard dataset, we found that the approach is competitive to LDA in terms of clustering user reviews.

While LDA explicitly requires the number of clusters as prior knowledge, SR-MCL relies on the Inflate parameter (r) to dynamically determine the number of clusters. The higher value of r results in more clusters being generated. We set r to 1.5 as in [1] to demonstrate the robustness of the parameter against different text corpora. This value of r results in relatively high precision and recall.

For topic extraction, WordNet and IDF are utilized to extract keywords from each cluster which represents a topic. To explore the resulting topics and investigate their semantic relationships, we illustrate document-topic and term-topic relationships as graphs. The term-topic relationship, moreover, allows the consumers to possibly catch the main themes within the attractions.

Our future work focuses on semantic improvement and exploration on the effects of other SR-MCL parameters on the dataset.

Acknowledgments. This research project was supported by Faculty of Information and Communication Technology, Mahidol University. The study was carried out under the research framework of Mahidol University.

References

1. Aker, A., et al.: A graph-based approach to topic clustering for online comments to news. In: Ferro, N., et al. (eds.) ECIR 2016. LNCS, vol. 9626, pp. 15–29. Springer, Cham (2016). https://doi.org/10.1007/978-3-319-30671-1_2
2. Alghamdi, R., Alfalqi, K.: A survey of topic modeling in text mining. Int. J. Adv. Comput. Sci. Appl. **6** (2015). https://doi.org/10.14569/IJACSA.2015.060121

3. Alkhodair, S.A., Fung, B.C.M., Rahman, O., Hung, P.C.K.: Improving interpretations of topic modeling in microblogs. J. Assoc. Inf. Sci. Technol. **69**(4), 528–540 (2018). https://doi.org/10.1002/asi.23980
4. Amigó, E., Gonzalo, J., Artiles, J., Verdejo, F.: A comparison of extrinsic clustering evaluation metrics based on formal constraints. Inf. Retrieval **12**(4), 461–486 (2009). https://doi.org/10.1007/s10791-008-9066-8
5. Blei, D.M., Ng, A.Y., Jordan, M.I.: Latent Dirichlet allocation. J. Mach. Learn. Res. **3**, 993–1022 (2003). http://dl.acm.org/citation.cfm?id=944919.944937
6. DeMaere, M.Z., Darling, A.E.: Deconvoluting simulated metagenomes: the performance of hard- and soft- clustering algorithms applied to metagenomic chromosome conformation capture (3C). PeerJ **4**, e2676 (2016). https://doi.org/10.7717/peerj.2676
7. van Dongen, S.M.: Graph clustering by flow simulation. Ph.D. thesis, University of Utrecht, The Netherlands (2000). https://dspace.library.uu.nl/handle/1874/848
8. Dorow, B., Widdows, D.: Discovering corpus-specific word senses. In: 10th Conference of the European Chapter of the Association for Computational Linguistics (2003). http://aclweb.org/anthology/E03-1020
9. Grant, C.E., George, C.P., Kanjilal, V., Nirkhiwale, S., Wilson, J.N., Wang, D.Z.: A topic-based search, visualization, and exploration system. In: FLAIRS Conference (2015)
10. Griffiths, T.L., Steyvers, M.: Finding scientific topics. In: Proceedings of the National Academy of Sciences, vol. 101, pp. 5228–5235. National Academy of Sciences (2004). https://doi.org/10.1073/pnas.0307752101
11. Holten, D., van Wijk, J.J.: Force-directed edge bundling for graph visualization. In: Proceedings of the 11th Eurographics/IEEE - VGTC Conference on Visualization, EuroVis 2009, pp. 983–998. The Eurographics Association and Wiley, Chichester (2009). https://doi.org/10.1111/j.1467-8659.2009.01450.x
12. Ji, Z., Pi, H., Wei, W., Xiong, B., Woźniak, M., Damasevicius, R.: Recommendation based on review texts and social communities. A hybrid model. IEEE Access **7**, 40416–40427 (2019). https://doi.org/10.1109/ACCESS.2019.2897586
13. Jindal, V.: A personalized Markov clustering and deep learning approach for Arabic text categorization. In: Proceedings of the ACL 2016 Student Research Workshop, pp. 145–151. Association for Computational Linguistics (2016). https://doi.org/10.18653/v1/P16-3022
14. Jurgens, D., Klapaftis, I.: SemEval-2013 task 13: word sense induction for graded and non-graded senses. In: Second Joint Conference on Lexical and Computational Semantics (*SEM), Volume 2: Proceedings of the Seventh International Workshop on Semantic Evaluation (SemEval 2013), pp. 290–299. Association for Computational Linguistics (2013). http://aclweb.org/anthology/S13-2049
15. Litvin, S., Hoffman, L.M.: Responses to consumer-generated media in the hospitality marketplace: an empirical study. J. Vacation Mark. **18**, 135–145 (2012). https://doi.org/10.1177/1356766712443467
16. Llewellyn, C., Grover, C., Oberlander, J.: Improving topic model clustering of newspaper comments for summarisation. In: Proceedings of the ACL 2016 Student Research Workshop, pp. 43–50. Association for Computational Linguistics, Berlin, August 2016. http://anthology.aclweb.org/P/P16/P16-3007
17. Phuong, D.V., Phuong, T.M.: A keyword-topic model for contextual advertising. In: Proceedings of the Third Symposium on Information and Communication Technology, SoICT 2012, pp. 63–70 (2012). https://doi.org/10.1145/2350716.2350728

18. Satuluri, V., Parthasarathy, S.: Scalable graph clustering using stochastic flows: applications to community discovery. In: Proceedings of the 15th ACM SIGKDD International Conference on Knowledge Discovery and Data Mining, KDD 2009, pp. 737–746. ACM, New York (2009). https://doi.org/10.1145/1557019.1557101
19. Satuluri, V., Parthasarathy, S., Ucar, D.: Markov clustering of protein interaction networks with improved balance and scalability. In: Proceedings of the First ACM International Conference on Bioinformatics and Computational Biology, BCB 2010, pp. 247–256. ACM, New York (2010). https://doi.org/10.1145/1854776.1854812
20. Shih, Y.K., Parthasarathy, S.: Identifying functional modules in interaction networks through overlapping Markov clustering. Bioinformatics **28**(18), i473–i479 (2012). https://doi.org/10.1093/bioinformatics/bts370

Short Text Computing Based on Lexical Similarity Model

Arifah Che Alhadi[1(✉)], Aziz Deraman[1], Masita@Masila Abdul Jalil[1],
Wan Nural Jawahir Wan Yussof[1], and Shahrul Azman Mohd Noah[2]

[1] Faculty of Ocean Engineering Technology and Informatics,
Universiti Malaysia Terengganu, 21030 Kuala Nerus, Terengganu, Malaysia
{arifah_hadi,a.d,masita,wannurwy}@umt.edu.my
http://www.umt.edu.my
[2] Center for Artificial Intelligence Technology (CAIT), Faculty of Information Science
and Technology, Universiti Kebangsaan Malaysia, 43600 Bangi, Selangor, Malaysia
shahrul@ukm.edu.my
http://www.ukm.my/

Abstract. Short text similarity deals with determining the closeness
of two text mean the same thing by lexical or semantic. Various short
text similarity approaches have been proposed which are based on lexical
matching, semantic knowledge background or combining models. Lexical based model does not capture the actual meaning behind the words.
However, semantic approach are relying on knowledge background or corpus which cannot be assumed to be available in handling such huge new
word of data sparseness and noise in short text. This work are focusing
on lexical-based similarity models for analysing the unstructured short
text. The term-based and edit distance model are used in comparing the
applicability of these model to compute the similarity value of short text.
The experimental results shows that each model have their key strengths
and limitations in computing similarity value of short text.

Keywords: Lexical-based model · Damerau-Levenshtein distance ·
Levenshtein Distance · Cosine · Short text

1 Introduction

Text similarity is important in many task of information retrieval such as search,
information extraction, document clustering, categorization or classification, language modeling and ontology mapping. In line with the popularity of social
media platform, short text similarity models play an increasingly important role
in analyzing the short text that contains a lot of valuable information.

A range of short text similarity approaches have been proposed and effectively
used analysing between queries [24], documents [14], text snippets [34], short
segment [24], tweets [28], sentence [19,21,26,27] or question answer (QA) [31].

Computing similarity between short texts is a challenging task for natural
language processing. This is due to complexity of the short text structure and

© Springer Nature Switzerland AG 2019
R. Damaševičius and G. Vasiljevienė (Eds.): ICIST 2019, CCIS 1078, pp. 355–366, 2019.
https://doi.org/10.1007/978-3-030-30275-7_27

typically represented by very limited words with data sparsity and noises [3,12]. Its usually containing abbreviations, acronyms, slang, unusual terms, and emoticons due to limitations in short textual lengths [25,33,35]. This communication is a highly creative and unique form of language that has never been seen before.

In addition, users also create 'new languages' which combine words, unique spelling and punctuation in social media [33]. However, the modification of this text sometimes leads to the formation of informal short texts, written with grammatical errors and contains many spelling mistakes [35].

A variety of lexical-based model exist for text similarity analysis. These include term and character-based similarity models [10]. While these models has achieved some success in document similarity, however the ability to analysis the short has not been fully explored.

The main interest of this study is a comparison of different lexical-based models for measurement of similarity between unstructured short text. The purpose of this comparison between lexical-based model is to evaluate which techniques are effective in short text similarity analysis. The remainder of the paper is laid as follows. Section 2 presents an overview of lexical models for text similarity which cover the term or token-based and character-based model. The extensive experiment carried out is described in Sect. 3. The applicability of selective models and results obtained are discussed in Sect. 4. Finally, the last section concludes with an overview of current work.

2 Related Work

Lexical-based similarity model was originally applied to identify the words with similar string sequences and character compositions [10]. The lexical model however does not consider the actual meaning behind the words or the entire phrases in context. This model is divided into two sub categories; which are term or token-based and character-based similarities measure.

2.1 Term or Token-Based Similarities

The term or token-based model are very widely used in different areas such as in term matching, entity extraction, QA analysis and much more. Term or token-based Metrics is a similarity metric that separate string into words and symbols called tokens by using separator such as spaces, line breaks, hyphens, punctuations or special characters. The similarities between the two token sets are later computed [8]. Token-based analyse text as a set of tokens or words and therefore allowed it to consider the semantic meaning of the words and processes massive texts. The token-based convert the strings into words. The well known token-based metrics used is cosine model.

Cosine model has been used in several studies to analyse the short texts such as question and answer [4], sentences [19,26,27,29], tweets [28] and record of DBLP and Music track [17].

Cong et al. [4] has implemented three different models which are cosine, sequential pattern and graph based propagation. The sequential pattern is used as feature to differentiate between questions and non-questions. The presence of question marks and classical features (5W1H words) was applied to identify the questions. The identification and ranking of candidate answers for the questions in same thread was performed using the graph based propagation method. Finally the cosine model was used to generate the similarity score between Q&A pairs.

A similar work by Lee et al. [17] also used token based similarity approaches which proposed an efficient algorithm for cosine similarity joins over weight vectors namely as MMJoin algorithm. MMJoin also improved the prefix filtering by proposing new filtering technique called length filtering. They performed series of empirical evaluations on large-scale datasets and concluded that the technique efficiently filters out dissimilar pairs of objects.

Another method to analyse the text similarity is based on the similarity in words' orders. Noah et al. [26] used this model to analyse Malay sentences. The vector similarity measurement (cosine) was applied for calculating the similarities in words' orders. They also followed and modified the approach of [19] by forming a joint distinct word set for two sentences. The overlap edge cutting-based method that was previously proposed by Lesk [18] was applied. An open dictionary was chosen as lexical database for Malay.

Rong et al. [29] considered the length of sentences and position of the terms in their studies. A solution for string similarities joined with different similarities thresholds was proposed and two indexing techniques namely partition based indexing and similarity aware indexing in order to support different thresholds was devised. New index probing techniques and filtering methods and index were proposed in order to improve the join performance by applying different lexical models which are the Cosine, Jaccard and Dice model.

Narrative reviews of lexical-based model yet disclose that it possess many barriers and drawbacks. The major limitations of these models is depended on exact term match occurring in short text and do not consider the noise inside. The problem of this model is as the noise increased, the similarity value of the texts pair is decreased. Some work apply pre-processing such as stemming to overcome the limitation. However works by [13, 23, 30] and [9] claimed that stop word removal and stemming process negatively impacts the performance of short text analysis.

2.2   Character-Based Model

Character-based model measuring the distance (inverse similarity) between two strings and is useful in the case of typographical errors [15]. Numerous character similarities have been proposed. The character similarities can be measured by calculating the longest length of the common subsequent, the distance factor or by comparing n-grams from each character in two strings.

The edit distance also has been applied for analysing similarities of Japanese [16] and Arabic [1, 5] languages. Jones et al. [16] have applied edit distance model for Japanese web search queries. In their study, the characteristics of Japanese search query logs and manual query reformulations descriptions, carried out by Japanese web searchers was given. The variety of edit distance measures was considered to detect pairs whose substitutability was explained by changes in writing system and applied Levenshtein distance to each of normalized Japanese writing forms.

Another work on the application of edit distance model was by El-Shishtawy [5], who applied this model for matching Arabic names sing a large Arabic dataset. A new hybrid sequential algorithm, which combined the advantage of token-based and edits distance approach, was introduced to improve the qualities of Arabic name matching.

3   Short Text Similarity with Lexical-Based

Text similarity can be measured at different levels or angles, lexical or semantic, ranging from words and phrases, to paragraphs and documents. The research is focusing on computing the similarity value sim $(s,t$ between two given texts s and t based on different types of lexical models. The final outcome of the evaluation process is the ability to identify the similarity between the two input of short texts using only lexical-based model.

In this experiment, similarities between the short text which consider different texts structure and includes some noise are also calculated to compare with the short text which free noise. The various conditions of texts from online dataset [6] were prepared as shown in Table 1. The different structure or conditions is needed to find the strength and limitation of each selected lexical-based model. It is due to cosine is based on word frequency but edit distance is character based distance.

Table 1. Sentences with different conditions

Condition	Example of Sentences
Similar sentences with similar structure	
	- James decided to quit smoking but it was not an easy decision.
	- James decided to quit smoking. However, it was not an easy decision.
Similar sentences with similar structure but contain noise	
	- James decided to quit smoking but it was not an easy decision.
	- James decided to quick smoking. However, it was x an ez decision.
Similar sentences with different structure	
	- James decided to quit smoking. However, it was not an easy decision.
	- Though it was not an easy decision, James decided to quit smoking.
Similar sentences with different structure but contain noise	
	- James decided to quit smoking. However, it was not an easy decision.
	- Though it was x an ez decision, James decided to quick smoking.

3.1 Cosine Similarity

Using cosine similarity, sentence will be tokenized for splitting a sentence into words, phrases or symbols [22]. Then each sentences are represented as tokens and is organized in terms-document matrix. In a term-document matrix, a document vectors is represent the frequency of terms occurrence in document collections. The rows of the matrix represent to the documents in the collections and columns corresponds to term. The zero value is assigned for terms that does not appear in the document and a non-zero value for every word terms occurs in the document. The non-zero values of each entry in the matrix are set based on frequency of terms occurrence within a document using *tf-idf* scheme. The frequencies of terms in a document tend to indicate the relevance or similarity of the document to each other.

A collection of documents m that represent n in term-document matrix (4). The term weight (w) corresponds to an entry in the matrix. w is equal to zero if the terms doesn't exist in the document.

$$
\begin{array}{c}
\begin{array}{cccccc} T_1 & T_2 & T_3 & \cdots & \cdots & T_n \end{array} \\
\begin{array}{c} D_1 \\ D_2 \\ \vdots \\ \vdots \\ D_m \end{array}
\begin{pmatrix}
w_{T1} & w_{T1} & w_{T1} & \cdots & \cdots & w_{Tn} \\
w_{T1} & w_{T1} & w_{T1} & \cdots & \cdots & w_{Tn} \\
\cdots & \cdots & \cdots & \cdots & \cdots & \cdots \\
\cdots & \cdots & \cdots & \cdots & \cdots & \cdots \\
W_{Tm} & W_{Tm} & \cdots & \cdots & \cdots & W_{tn}
\end{pmatrix}
\end{array}
\tag{1}
$$

Weight of each word is then calculated based on the *Inverse Document Frequencies*. Then similarity value is computed using cosine defined as follow:

$$
cos(s,t) = \frac{s \cdot t}{\|s\|\|t\|}
\tag{2}
$$

where $s \cdot t$ is the dot product of the sentence s and target sentence t vectors. $\|s\|$ $\|t\|$ are the Euclidean norms vectors of s and t. The Euclidean norm is calculated as follows:

$$
\|s\|\|t\| = \sqrt{\sum_{i=1}^{n}(s_i)^2} \times \sqrt{\sum_{i=1}^{n}(t_i)^2}
\tag{3}
$$

The similarity scores between short texts is automatically generated. Normally in short text, term-frequency vectors are typically very sparse as example the terms have many 0 values. Data sparseness means the text contains several features and few words co-occurrences which also affect the similarity analysis [3].

3.2 Edit Distance Model

Levenshtein Distance and Damerau-Levenshtein distance as used as the baseline models. The *ed(s,t)* between short texts *(s)* and *(t)* is defined as minimum number of insertions, deletions, replacements and transposition of characters necessary to make two strings equal. The bigger the return value is, the less similar the two texts are because different texts take more edits than similar texts.

In the following discussion, let $s = i_1, i_2, \ldots i_n$ be a short text of length n and $t = j_1, j_2, \ldots j_m$ a short text of length m. To derive the LD for s and t, the string s vs string t matrix 1 is constructed as follows:

$$
M = \begin{matrix} & st & 0 & 1 & 2 & 3 & \cdots & \cdots & n \\ 0 & & M_{0,0} & M_{0,j} & M_{0,j+1} & M_{0,j+2} & \cdot & \cdots & M_{0,n} \\ 1 & & M_{i,0} & M_{i,j} & M_{0,j+1} & M_{0,j+2} & \cdot & \cdots & M_{i,n} \\ \vdots & & \cdots & \cdots & \cdots & \cdots & \cdots & \cdots & \cdots \\ \vdots & & \cdots & \cdots & \cdots & \cdots & \cdots & \cdots & \cdots \\ \vdots & & \vdots & \vdots & \vdots & \vdots & \vdots & \ddots & \vdots \\ m & & M_{m,0} & M_{m,j} & M_{m,j+1} & M_{m,j+2} & \cdots & \cdots & M_{m,n} \end{matrix}
\tag{4}
$$

M_{ij} is a matrix of string s compared with string t. The the cell M_{ij} contains the value ed(s[1..i], t[1..j]). The recursion value of $M[i-1, j-1]$ is 0 if $s[i]$ and $t[j]$ are the same strings. Otherwise if $s[i] \neq t[j]$, the recursion value Levenshtein Distance is computed using the following conditions:

$$
1 + min(M[i-1, j-1], M[i-1, j], M[i, j-1])
\tag{5}
$$

The Damerau-Levenshtein distance can be computed otherwise identically as the Levenshtein edit distance, but using the following recursion:

$$
M[i,j] = \begin{cases} M[i-1, j-1] \ if \ s[i] = t[j] \\ 1 + (M[i-2, j-2]) \ if \ s[i] = t[j-1] \ and \ s[i-1] = t[j] \\ 1 + min(M[i-1, j-1], M[i-1, j], M[i, j-1]), otherwise \end{cases}
\tag{6}
$$

The similarity score is calculated after retrieving the distance of Levenshtein and Damerau-Levenshtein distance, by using the following formula:

$$
Sim_{ed}(s, t) = 1 - \frac{edDist(s, t)}{max(|s|, |t|)}
\tag{7}
$$

where max is the length of the longest of the two given texts (s,t) and ed is the Levenshtein or Damerau-Levenshtein distance. Thus the similarity value of s and t is calculated. A large value means the strings are very similar.

4   Result and Discussion

This section describes the data that were used in this experiments using real data, online resource and benchmark dataset prepared by other researchers. The short text classification show that the size of labeled sample can reflect the performance of classifier and the validity of the research is higher. Besides that, the increasing size of labeled sample can effect the confidence and reliability of the confidence interval.

However, due to the sparsity of short text, its hard to identify the size of labeled sample is acceptable for short text classifier training [35]. The texts is too short, sparse or low frequencies of features to provide enough information for classifying/clustering the text (similar/dissimilar). The test dataset used in this experiment was provided by Li et al. [6,19]. In both dataset, the lexical-based models are compare each other for measuring the similarity for short texts.

For each dataset, sentences with noise were added for testing the lexical-based models. This noise was prepared by five bachelor students of Software Engineering, Faculty of Ocean Engineering Technology and Informatics, Universiti Malaysia Terengganu. The students were asked to add spelling error or standard and non-standard short form as the noise to the dataset. The reason for this steps is taken due to nonexistence of benchmark dataset of text similarity which containing noises.

The lack of suitable short text evaluation dataset which contains noise is greatest obstacle that hinders for evaluating the selected lexical-based model. Li et al. [19] dataset is used because this dataset is also commonly used in many studies for short text analysis [7,11,29,32]. Its contains 65 sentence pairs which include the value of mean $(\overline{X})$ and standard deviations of sentences ratings. The value of $\overline{X}$ is a rating scales between 0 to 4. The liner transformation is used by rescale the value $\overline{X}$ column by dividing by 4 which mean the scale between 0 to 1. The scale between 0 to 1 is normally use to measure the similarity.

The results of the 65 sentence pairs by Li et al. [19] was represented by graph as shown in Fig. 1. The result indicates that the similarity value of sentences pair are effected by the length of terms or characters within the sentences.

Online dataset contain a set of similar sentences. It divided into four categories, similar sentences but with different sentence patterns, similar sentence to show contrast, similar sentence to show cause and effect and similar sentences to state condition. For each categories, the noise is added in the sentences for experiments purposes.

Table 2 summarizes the results of each model. From this table, the comparison of results for cosine, LD and DLD shows the strength and limitation of each single model. The first condition is comparison with similar short text with similar structure but contain noise. As example, for the input short text *'Jane was unhappy because she had lost her job.'* is compared with target short text 3, the similarity values of LD and DLD are same (0.84) which are still higher than the cosine values of 0.67, despite of the presence of noises in the input short text. The same results are also obtained for the eight comparison which are LD and DLD (0.74) and cosine (0.58).

However, for target text 2, *'James decided to quit smoking but it was not an easy decision'*, results for the fifth to seventh shows that LD and DLD give very low similarity values compared to cosine. All the short text are similar but with difference short text structures. LD and DLD computes how far two strings are

Table 2. Pair of sentences with cosine, LD and DLD similarity value

Conditions	Sentences compared	$Cos\theta$	LD	DLD
Different sentence patterns				
Jane was unhappy because she had lost her job.				
1.	As Jane had lost her job she was unhappy.	0.78	0.31	0.31
2.	Jane had lost her job and that made her unhappy.	0.56	0.33	0.33
3.	Jane was unheppi becoz she had lost her job.	0.84	0.67	0.67
Show contrast				
James decided to quit smoking but it was not an easy decision.				
4.	James decided to quit smoking. However, it was not an easy decision.	0.83	0.87	0.87
5.	Though it was not an easy decision, James decided to quit smoking.	0.83	0.15	0.15
6.	Even though it was an easy decision, James decided to quit smoking.	0.75	0.17	0.17
7.	In spite of it not being an easy decision, James decided to quit smoking	0.69	0.22	0.22
8.	James decided to quick smoking. However, it was x an ez decision.	0.58	0.74	0.74
9.	Though it was x an ez decision, James decided to quick smoking.	0.58	0.16	0.16
Show cause and effect				
Susie wanted to win the first prize so she worked hard.				
10.	Because Susie wanted to win the first prize, she worked hard.	0.78	0.82	0.82
11.	Susie wanted to win the first prize. Therefore so she worked hard.	0.78	0.82	0.82
State condition				
You must work hard, or you won't win.				
12.	If you don't work hard, you won't win.	0.77	0.65	0.65
13.	Unless you work hard, you won't win.	0.78	0.82	0.82
14.	You must work hard. Otherwise you won't win.	0.71	0.82	0.82

from one another. This implies that small strings will be near to one another and larger strings will be further from each other. Furthermore, since LD and DLD compares the direct distance, it is very sensitive to the structure of the text. It may show low similarity value if the subjects of two short texts are the same, but have different ordering of the text structure.

In addition, the DLD and LD calculation gives a high similarity value for sentences that are much the same, in the sense of word utilization and structural build-up or direct copies. It is also restricted in the way that the compared sentence have to be really equal in length, or else the difference in length will contribute towards dissimilarity. Therefore, comparing a little string to a huge string will therefore yield a small similarity score. This is the weakness of edit distance model.

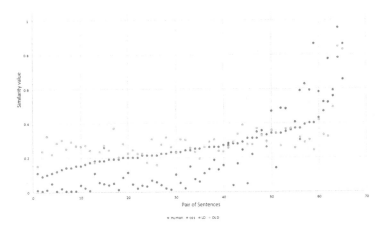

Fig. 1. Comparison similarity value by lexical-base model for Li et al. [19] dataset

The cosine similarity works poorly because the measure is based on the occurrence and frequency of term. Due to the character limit of short text, it's contain few words and hardly ever contain a word multiple times in a single short sentence. The length of the document will effect the similarity measure value. However, for target sentence 7, the cosine model give the value 0.69 of similarity value if the short text are free from noise. It is because this model does not consider the sentence structure but only use the term occurrence and frequency as the measure. Therefore the results does not affect the similarity values of compared sentences.

The comparison also have been made between DLD and LD. With the same sentence example, the similarity value of LD is lower than DLD if involve the transposition operation of the characters. Otherwise, without transposition operation the similarity values will be the same for both LD and DLD. However, the difference value obtained still impact the rank of search results.

5   Conclusions and Future Work

This paper presented comparative analysis between several lexical-based similarity existing models. The following models have been applied which are (i) cosine, (ii) Damerau-Lavenshtein and (iii) Lavenshtein distance. All the models are useful to calculate the lexical similarities of short texts.

The cosine similarity model only considered the terms occurred in both sentences. However, users tend to compact the short text in social media platform by using emoticons, abbreviations, acronyms, phonetic substitutions, slang, misspellings, new words, URL and symbols to fulfill the text limitations [2,20]. Since the cosine model depends on term occurrence and exact match, the term 'tomorrow' and '2morrow', will be assumed as a totally different term.

Whereas, LD and DLD models used the edit distance to overcome the noise in short text which gave better similarity value compared to the cosine model.

For instance, the term *'tomorrow'* and *'2morrow'* will have high similarity value because its distance is only 2. However, if the similar sentence with different structure, the similarity value for both models will decrease. Some the limitations of the edit distance model is its dependency on the sentence structure for calculating the similarity value.

The results of this studies show that, strengths and limitations of each lexical-based models were identified. The outcome of the experiments of short texts which contained noise shows that the strengths and limitations of each lexical-based models will result in increasing and decreasing similarity value depends on text structure and terms occurrence. It shows that the finding will affect the retrieval and ranking results.

Based on the experiment also, the similarity values obtained from each models determined the suitability of these selected lexical-based models to be used and shows the applicability in analysis the short text. This work provides a baseline model for further experiment in ensemble the model. Hence, this study continuing planning to fill the gap by combining these models to cope with data sparseness and noise in short text.

Acknowledgment. This research is sponsored by the Ministry of Higher Education, under the Fundamental Research Grants Scheme vot 59467.

References

1. Alabbas, M., Ramsay, A.: Natural language inference for Arabic using extended tree edit distance with subtrees. J. Artif. Intell. Res. **48**, 1–22 (2013)
2. Anson, S., Watson, H., Wadhwa, K., Metz, K.: Analysing social media data for disaster preparedness: understanding the opportunities and barriers faced by humanitarian actors. Int. J. Disaster Risk Reduction **21**, 131–139 (2017)
3. Boom, C.D., Canneyt, S.V., Bohez, S., Demeester, T., Dhoedt, B.: Learning semantic similarity for very short texts. CoRR abs/1512.00765 (2015)
4. Cong, G., Wang, L., Lin, C.Y., Song, Y.I., Sun, Y.: Finding question-answer pairs from online forums. In: Proceedings of the 31st Annual International ACM SIGIR Conference on Research and Development in Information Retrieval, SIGIR 2008, pp. 467–474 (2008)
5. El-Shishtawy, T.: A hybrid algorithm for matching Arabic names. CoRR abs/1309.5657 (2013)
6. EnglishPractice.com: Writing similar sentences (2019). https://www.englishpractice.com/
7. Ferreira, R., Lins, R.D., Simske, S.J., Freitas, F., Riss, M.: Assessing sentence similarity through lexical, syntactic and semantic analysis. Comput. Speech Lang. **39**(C), 1–28 (2016)
8. Gali, N., Mariescu-Istodor, R., FrÃnti, P.: Similarity measures for title matching. In: 23rd International Conference on Pattern Recognition (ICPR), pp. 1548–1553, December 2016
9. Gao, L., Zhou, S., Guan, J.: Effectively classifying short texts by structured sparse representation with dictionary filtering. Inf. Sci. **323**(C), 130–142 (2015)
10. Gomaa, W.H., Fahmy, A.A.: A survey of text similarity approaches. Int. J. Comput. Appl. **68**(13), 13–18 (2013)

11. Harispe, S., Ranwez, S., Janaqi, S., Montmain, J.: Semantic similarity from natural language and ontology analysis. CoRR abs/1704.05295 (2017)
12. Hasan, A.A., Tiun, S., Yusof, M.M., Mokhtar, U.A., Jambari, D.I.: Enhanced feature for short document classification. J. Eng. Appl. Sci. **12**(13), 3534–3540 (2017)
13. Hu, X., Tang, L., Tang, J., Liu, H.: Exploiting social relations for sentiment analysis in microblogging. In: Proceedings of the Sixth ACM International Conference on Web Search and Data Mining, WSDM 2013, pp. 537–546. ACM, New York (2013)
14. Huang, A.: Similarity measures for text document clustering. In: Proceedings of the Sixth New Zealand Computer Science Research Student Conference (NZCSRSC 2008), Christchurch, pp. 49–56 (2008)
15. Jiang, Y., Li, G., Feng, J., Li, W.S.: String similarity joins: an experimental evaluation. Proc. VLDB Endow. **7**(8), 625–636 (2014)
16. Jones, R., Bartz, K., Subasic, P., Rey, B.: Automatically generating related queries in Japanese. Lang. Resour. Eval. **40**(3), 219–232 (2006)
17. Lee, D., Park, J., Shim, J., Lee, S.G.: Efficient filtering techniques for cosine similarity joins. Inf. Int. Interdisc. J. **14**, 1265 (2011)
18. Lesk, M.: Automatic sense disambiguation using machine readable dictionaries: how to tell a pine cone from an ice cream cone. In: Proceedings of the 5th Annual International Conference on Systems Documentation, SIGDOC 1986, pp. 24–26. ACM, New York (1986)
19. Li, Y., McLean, D., Bandar, Z.A., O'Shea, J.D., Crockett, K.: Sentence similarity based on semantic nets and corpus statistics. IEEE Trans. Knowl. Data Eng. **18**(8), 1138–1150 (2006)
20. Lochter, J.V., Zanetti, R.F., Reller, D., Almeida, T.A.: Short text opinion detection using ensemble of classifiers and semantic indexing. Expert Syst. Appl. **62**, 243–249 (2016)
21. Ma, W., Suel, T.: Structural sentence similarity estimation for short texts. In: Proceedings of the Twenty-Ninth International Florida Artificial Intelligence Research Society Conference, FLAIRS 2016, Key Largo, 16–18 May 2016, pp. 232–237 (2016)
22. Manning, C.D., Raghavan, P., Schütze, H.: Introduction to Information Retrieval. Cambridge University Press, New York (2008)
23. Martínez-Cámara, E., Montejo-Ráez, A., Martín-Valdivia, M.T.: Ureña López, L.A.: SINAI: machine learning and emotion of the crowd for sentiment analysis in microblogs. In: Second Joint Conference on Lexical and Computational Semantics (*SEM). Volume 2: Proceedings of the Seventh International Workshop on Semantic Evaluation (SemEval 2013), pp. 402–407. Association for Computational Linguistics, Atlanta, June 2013
24. Metzler, D., Dumais, S., Meek, C.: Similarity measures for short segments of text. In: Amati, G., Carpineto, C., Romano, G. (eds.) ECIR 2007. LNCS, vol. 4425, pp. 16–27. Springer, Heidelberg (2007). https://doi.org/10.1007/978-3-540-71496-5_5
25. Nakov, P., et al.: Developing a successful SemEval task in sentiment analysis of Twitter and other social media texts. Lang. Resour. Eval. **50**(1), 35–65 (2016)
26. Noah, S.A., Amruddin, A.Y., Omar, N.: Semantic similarity measures for Malay sentences. In: Goh, D.H.-L., Cao, T.H., Sølvberg, I.T., Rasmussen, E. (eds.) ICADL 2007. LNCS, vol. 4822, pp. 117–126. Springer, Heidelberg (2007). https://doi.org/10.1007/978-3-540-77094-7_19
27. Noah, S.A., Omar, N., Amruddin, A.Y.: Evaluation of lexical-based approaches to the semantic similarity of Malay sentences. J. Quantit. Linguist. **22**(2), 135–156 (2015)

28. Rizzo Irfan, M., Fauzi, M., Tibyani, T., Dyah Mentari, N.: Twitter sentiment analysis on 2013 curriculum using ensemble features and k-nearest neighbor. Int. J. Electr. Comput. Eng. (IJECE) **8**, 5409 (2018)
29. Rong, C., Silva, Y.N., Li, C.: String similarity join with different similarity thresholds based on novel indexing techniques. Front. Comput. Sci. **11**(2), 307–319 (2017)
30. Saif, H., Fernandez, M., He, Y., Alani, H.: On stopwords, filtering and data sparsity for sentiment analysis of Twitter. In: Calzolari, N., et al. (eds.) Proceedings of the Ninth International Conference on Language Resources and Evaluation (LREC 2014). European Language Resources Association (ELRA), Reykjavik, May 2014
31. Severyn, A., Moschitti, A.: Learning to rank short text pairs with convolutional deep neural networks. In: Proceedings of the 38th International ACM SIGIR Conference on Research and Development in Information Retrieval, SIGIR 2015, pp. 373–382. ACM, New York (2015)
32. Tsatsaronis, G., Varlamis, I., Vazirgiannis, M.: Text relatedness based on a word thesaurus. J. Artif. Int. Res. **37**(1), 1–40 (2010)
33. Varnhagen, C.K., McFall, G.P., Pugh, N., Routledge, L., Sumida-MacDonald, H., Kwong, T.E.: lol: new language and spelling in instant messaging. Read. Writ. **23**(6), 719–733 (2010)
34. Wenyin, L., Quan, X., Feng, M., Qiu, B.: A short text modeling method combining semantic and statistical information. Inf. Sci. **180**(20), 4031–4041 (2010)
35. Yan, L., Zheng, Y., Cao, J.: Few-shot learning for short text classification. Multimed. Tools Appl. **77**(22), 29799–29810 (2018)

Information Technology Applications: Special Session on Smart e-Learning Technologies and Applications

Gamified Evaluation in STEAM

Pavel Boytchev[1]([✉])[iD] and Svetla Boytcheva[2][iD]

[1] Faculty of Mathematics and Informatics - KIT,
Sofia University "St. Kliment Ohridski", Sofia, Bulgaria
boytchev@fmi.uni-sofia.bg
[2] Institute of Information and Communication Technologies,
Bulgarian Academy of Sciences, Sofia, Bulgaria
svetla.boytcheva@gmail.com

Abstract. The process of converting non-game educational content and processes into game-like educational content and processes is called gamification. This paper describes issues regarding gamification of students' evaluation in STEAM. The characteristics of such gamification pose unique requirements for the learning tools, which cannot be handled by general learning management systems. The proposed system extends an existing gamified learning environment and includes the evaluation as integral component of the gaming. To facilitate adequate evaluation the system builds and manages competence profiles of students', based on continuous stream of vectored scores generated during the gameplay. The most popular metrics for calculating grades fail on streamed scores, so we proposed a new aggregation method *temporal average*, which is easy to calculate, supports streaming scores and captures temporal tendencies of competence development.

Keywords: Gamification in education · STEAM education ·
Educational software · Student evaluation

1 Introduction

Technology Enhanced Learning (TEL) uses various approaches and methods for increasing the effectiveness of education via modern technologies. The mere use of any piece of technology is not sufficient to enhance learning [4]. Instruction Based Learning (IBL) and Project Based Learning (PBL) are two of the most spread TEL approaches. They are being introduced in the education of pupils and young students as a way to provide a fruitful context for learning. The education of university students and adults may also benefit from IBL and PBL, however, it

The research is partially supported by the National Scientific Program "Information and Communication Technologies in Science, Education and Security" (ICTinSES) financed by the Ministry of Education and Science; and by Sofia University "St. Kliment Ohridski" research science fund project N80-10-75/12.04.2019 "Use of high performance computing technological tools for competence development for applying the inquiry-based approach in STEM education at secondary school".

© Springer Nature Switzerland AG 2019
R. Damaševičius and G. Vasiljevienė (Eds.): ICIST 2019, CCIS 1078, pp. 369–382, 2019.
https://doi.org/10.1007/978-3-030-30275-7_28

is possible to enrich the approach by using Game Based Learning (GBL). The introduction of GBL closes the loop between children and adult education – Fig. 1. The adult education provides IBL and PBL to children education, while children education provides gamification to adult education.

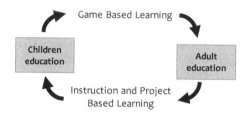

Fig. 1. IBP, PBL and GBL approaches

The process of converting non-game educational content and processes into game-like educational content and processes is called gamification. Gamification is not a new method in education and has traditionally been used in various levels and subjects in education [8]. Kim et al. [13] examine how gamification was employed in different science, technology, engineering and mathematics (STEM) learning - namely in chemistry, biology, general science explorations, computer programming, anatomy, genetics, mathematics, etc. Effective learning through gamification needs adequate implementation, taking into account the subject specifics, the educational goals and the student's needs. Problems of gamification implementation are analyzed in [18] as well as, why it fails in some cases and how it can be improved. The authors propose nine gamification heuristics that acknowledge the importance of design, system properties, contextual demands and user characteristics.

The Lithuanian case study [17] presents preschool children education in music by using the game "Happy piano sounds". The game is based on metaphorization, fuzzification and gamification. The evaluation of such gamification is a challenging task, because the participants are 4–7 years old children. The chosen method is the Child-Initiated Pretend Play Assessment [19]. The assessment results show promising and positive results of application of gamification in preschool children education in music.

Active student participation in the course material comprehension is the most effective way of learning. Some widely used methods are inquiry based learning, learning by doing, project based learning, and gamification. The active learning approaches show significant improvement in course material comprehension and student motivation to study the subject. Freeman et al. [9] test this hypothesis and present meta-analysis of 255 studies that include student performance data in undergraduate STEM courses, comparing traditional lecturing versus active learning. The reported results show that the risk of course failure is 50% higher in traditional courses then in those providing active learning, and the later one report on average 6% higher scores in examination. Tembo and Lee [20] show the positive effect in motivation of high school students in Malaysia to study physics by using interactive simulations. Blazauskas et al. [3] discuss virtual reality models application in subjects other than STEM – history education. The evaluation results show increasing comprehension of the course material and attractiveness of the subject.

There are many examples for successful implementation of gamification in university STEM courses covering a broad range of topics like Computer Organization [12], Software Engineering [1], C–programming [11], Computer Graphics with WebGL [21], Game Development [15], Emerging Technology of Cloud Computing [12]. Some patterns in gamification for different applications can be identified [2]. That allows definition of an abstract formal model for unification of common characteristics of gamification applications, like data, users, rules, actions and interfaces.

Although IBL, PBL and GBL could be implemented without use of any modern technology, this paper will focus on an approach of GBL, which relies on technology and contributes to TEL. All these new active learning methods require also development of new methodology for student evaluation. In this paper we discuss the main aspects of gamification of students' evaluation and assessment and propose new complex evaluation method.

The initial goal is to capture and automatically evaluate streaming scores generated by students as they play in a specially designed educational gaming environment. In this respect the proposed gaming evaluation will be approbated with a single game. However, the methodology could be applied to other games, which deal with competences and real-time streaming of scores. For the practical application of the proposed gamified evaluation the existing educational environment in Sofia University will be extended by gamification modules, and then linked to the existing learning management system.

This paper is structured as follows: Sect. 2 describes main characteristics of evaluation in gamification; Sect. 3 outlines the methodology; Sect. 4 presents implementation of the gamified evaluation system; Sect. 5 defines student competences profiles presentation and evaluation; Sect. 6 presents the formal model for aggregation of streaming evaluation; Sect. 7 summarizes the presented evaluation method and briefly sketches plans for further work.

2   Gamification of Evaluation

The evaluation of students is a component of the learning process, which can naturally be gamified. For example, quizzes and tests could be converted into applied games by providing a suitable gaming environment. One of the side effects of the gamification of evaluation is that it is expected to reduce the urge for cheating and plagiarism. The other side effect is that it will blend evaluation and assessment into a single activity.

Zichermann and Cunningham [23] describe the classical evaluation methods in gamification, the so called *game mechanics*: points (experience, redeemable, skill, karma, reputation), badges, levels, progress bars, leader boards, virtual currency and avatars. Usually, traditional lecturing is combined with gamification in blended learning format, which includes both teacher monitoring and self-assessment evaluation methods [13]. Such approach allows to use more complex models for student evaluation. Hamari and Eranti [10] present framework for gamification achievements for student evaluation making a parallel to academic achievements during the course completion. In [1] are used some game mechanics like badges and leaderboards in a Software Engineering course.

In contrast with multi-agent gamification systems [22], our proposed solution does not allow grades and tasks to be shared among the agents (students). Each student is assigned an individual task, and students can not cooperate for solving tasks. Another restriction is that agents (students) cannot collide during their exploration of the gaming environment. In [16] is proposed gamification evaluation based on the idea of simulated annealing algorithm that plans next movements of agents in the system in order to avoid collision.

In our previous research we presented how traditional lecturing in Computer Graphics courses can be enhanced by gamification methods and some game mechanics like badges can be implemented in student evaluation [5].

3   Methodology

This sections presents the development methodology of a gamified evaluation for the specific educational goals of Fundamentals of Computer Graphics.

A gamified evaluation is a continuous activity which eliminates the "gambling" aspect of tests. Playing a educational game has a learning outcome when succeeding and when failing. Students have immediate visual feedback on their current and overall achievements. From pedagogical point of view a gamified evaluation could embed the same topics in different gaming situations leading to better learning and understanding. The main characteristics of gamified evaluation are presented in Table 1.

The design of the system relies on already existing software – the Meiro virtual environment and the learning management system Moodle. The software development started with the implementation of a gamified environment based on extended Meiro. Real-time tests of the environment with over 140 students is planned from December 2019 to February 2020. There will also be students' surveys of their experience with the system. Then we will analyse the log files from the gameplay of each student and the estimated evaluation, proposed by the system. This evaluation will be compared to the evaluation if more traditional testing methods would have been used. The result of the analyses will be used to improve the software, to fine-tune the automatic gamified evaluation and to get detailed insight on the performance of the characteristics of the gamified evaluation in Table 1 from technological and from educational viewpoints.

Table 1. Characteristics of gamified evaluation

Parameter	Description
Time	No restriction. Evaluation could be performed at any time both during classes and as extra class activity
Location	No restriction. Evaluation could be performed at school, at home or even while commuting
Hardware	Practically no restriction. Modern computers and smartphones are power enough to support online 3D graphics for game environments
Software	Practically no restriction. Modern operating systems support both native and online gaming environments including in browsers
Number of evaluations	No restriction. Evaluations could be made multiple times similarly to making several attempts to pass a level in a computer game
Sharing evaluation	Off-game sharing of evaluation experience is highly encouraged. This is includes tips and suggestion for solving problems, as well as achievements

4   Implementation Architecture

This section describes the implementation of a gamified evaluation system, which is based on the gamified educational environment Meiro, and Moodle – a popular Learning Management System (LMS).

Meiro is a multilevel 3D maze containing interactive models about Computer Graphics. The left snapshot in Fig. 2 shows central projection on a plane. The right snapshot is from a model demonstrating embedded matrix manipulations between adjacent layers in layered objects. The current implementation of Meiro can generate gaming environments of various complexities. There are over 270 interactive 3D models which can be configured and placed in Meiro. These models are used in the Fundamentals of Computer Graphics course in the Faculty of Mathematics and Informatics at Sofia University.

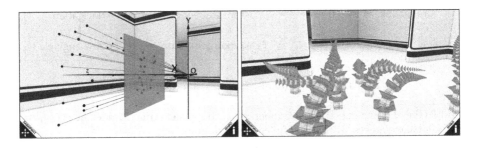

Fig. 2. Examples of 3D models in a Meiro maze

The conversion of Meiro from a learning environment into an evaluation environment requires modification of its internal architecture by adding new modules: *evaluation models, evaluation configurator* and *evaluation reporter*. Authentication, profile management and grading records are supported by the LMS. There are two approaches of combining existing LMS with the newly developed evaluation software. The straightforward approach is to rely on the grading functionality of the LMS [14]. The current implementation of Meiro-Moodle communication is via external modules through Learning Tools Interoperability (LTI) interface[1]. The first official version of LTI is proposed in 2010 based on BasicLTI[2]. The main advantage of using LTI is that externally developed educational tools can communicate with LMS systems. Unfortunately, this also bridges some disadvantages. For example, if the LMS has specific limitations, they will also affect the functionality of the external tool.

This prompts the design of another approach, which provides its own grading module supporting the specific grading functionality required by the gamification. Figure 3 shows the proposed architecture. The new modules are the following:

- Customizable 3D evaluation models that are positioned inside the maze. Each model represents one problem to solve.
- The Evaluation configurator takes a model and fine-tunes its configuration to achieve a balance between the learning goals and the current student's skills. As a result, the same model could represent simple and complex problems.
- Real-time results from playing a game are sent to the Evaluation generator. This module converts user's interactions into evaluation-aware values.
- Finally, the evaluation results are stored in the Custom gradebook, and after aggregation are delivered back to the LMS's gradebook.

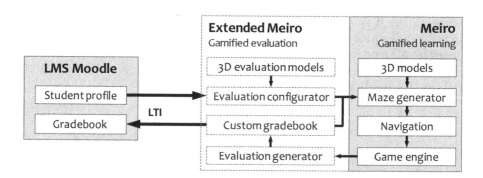

Fig. 3. Architecture of gamified evaluation in Meiro

[1] IMS Global Learning Tools Interoperability Implementation Guide: http://www.imsglobal.org/specs/ltiv1p1p1/implementation-guide.

[2] Marc, A., Jordi, P., and Severance, C. (2010, June). basiclti4moodle: https://code.google.com/archive/p/basiclti4moodle/.

The main advantage of the proposed architecture is that it provides functionality, which is not available in the currently used LMS. Namely:

– Streaming evaluation: During the gameplay students walk in the maze, solve many problems in any order and replay some of the 3D models several times. As long as each activity is transparently converted into a grade score, the gameplay effectively generates a continuous stream of scores.
– *Vector evaluation*: Moodle and other LMS support general gradebooks which have individual grading score per activity (scalar evaluation). The nature of a gamified evaluation is to generate multiple scores for each activity, capturing the different personalities and competences of players.
– *In-game visualization*: The stream of vector grades is a collection of data, which can be properly consolidated and visualized as a 3D model inside the game. This allows students to monitor and comprehend their learning progress within the gaming environment.

5   Competence Profiles and Evaluation

The vectorization of evaluation is useful to capture both students' competences and problems' competences. In the context of Fundamentals of Computer Graphics the term *competence* does not have the meaning defined in DigComp 2.0[3], but is tailored to computer graphics. The newer DigComp 2.1 contains 5 dimensions [6], 21 competences at 8 qualification levels. As some of these competences are irrelevant to the course, we propose a new set of 17 competences, grouped in Mathematics, Computer Science, Physics and Art zones as shown in Table 2. These competences may reuse the 8-level qualification of DigComp 2.1.

Table 2. Computer graphics competences

1. Mathematics	2. Computer Sciences
1.1. Math objects	2.1. Rasterization
1.2. Equations	2.2. Geometrical data
1.3. Parameters and properties	2.3. Motion and animation
1.4. Discovering relations	2.4. Graphical objects
1.5. Approximating relations	
3. Physics	4. Art
3.1. Physics laws	4.1. Colours and palettes
3.2. Simulation of phenomena	4.2. Geometric shapes
3.3. Representation of phenomena	4.3. Orientation in 3D
	4.4. Synchronization
	4.5. Graphical effects

---

[3] European Union. (2017, April 20). The Digital Competence Framework 2.0: https://ec.europa.eu/jrc/en/digcomp/digital-competence-framework.

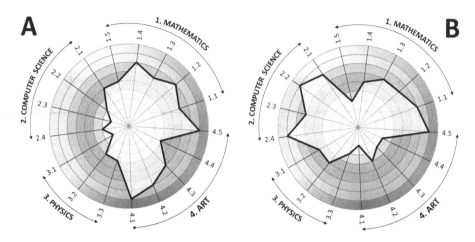

Fig. 4. Radar diagram of competence profiles of two students

The competence set of a person can be visualized in the game as a star or radar diagram [7], which represents a competence profile. Figure 4 shows competence profiles of two students – A and B. Competences are locating along the perimeter, while the qualification grid is radial and the lowest competence level is at the inner-most ring of the diagram. According to the shown diagrams, student A has competence in the mathematical and the artistic aspects of computer graphics, while student B is strong in Mathematics and Computer Sciences (CS).

The vectored evaluation via radar diagrams has two main advantages over the traditional scalar evaluation: it reflects the individuality of students (some are more artistic, others prefer abstract math), and it indicates competence gaps of students, which can be used for selection of appropriate problems.

The same approach of radar visualization can be applied to problems given to students. A problem may be related to several competences at once with levels, represented in a radar diagram. The same structure of students' and problems' competence profiles enables their mapping. Figure 5 shows the competence profiles of students A and B, and the competence profile of a typical CS problem. The mapping of these profiles establishes a direct notion of the potential effect of the problem to the students.

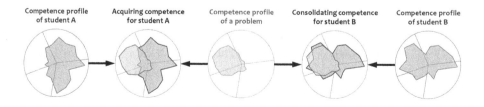

Fig. 5. Mapping competence profiles of students and problems

The mapping onto A's profile indicates that for A this problem will develop new competences, because A lacks sufficient CS skills. As for B, whose competence profile show CS skills, the same problem will consolidate B's knowledge. As long as the competence profiles of both students and problems can be represented with vectors of the same cardinality, mapping profiles is straightforward. When the vectors are compared, the differences between corresponding values indicate competence gaps – either positive or negative. For example, if a student has reached level 5 at competence "Approximating relations" (#1.5 in Table 2), but a problem has level 8 at the same competence, then the competence gap in respect to competence #1.5 is 3. If another problem has level 1 of this competence, then there is a negative competence gap of −4. This means that the second problem will not develop competence #1.5 of the student.

Competence profile mapping can produce valuable results even when profiles are of the same type as mapped. For example, mapping competence profiles of problems in a given maze will produce the overall profile of the whole maze. Similarly, if students take part in group-based learning activity, then each group may have members of mutually complementary competence profiles – visually this means that the union of the profiles spans in all radar directions.

6   Aggregation of Streaming Evaluation

One of the characteristics of the gamified evaluation, as listed in Table 1, is that students can explore the same 3D model (or problem) many times. This generates a significant volume of data which refers to the same set of competences. Traditionally, LMS provides simple functions for calculating aggregated score X_n of n scores $\{x_1, x_2, \ldots, x_n\}$. Table 3 presents some of the popular functions and why they are not suitable for streaming scores. For example, the evaluation of moda requires access to all scores, but only one of them is actually used. Also, moda is not affected by the ordering of scores, i.e. if their order is changed, moda will be the same. A good aggregation function would have three "yes" values in Table 3.

Table 3. Popular aggregation functions

Function X_n	Function name	Incremental calculation	Uses all x_i values	Captures tendencies
$X_n = x_1$	First score	Yes	No	No
$X_n = x_n$	Last score	Yes	No	No
$X_n = maxValue\{x_i\}$	Max score	Yes	No	No
$X_n = \frac{1}{n}\sum x_i$	Average	Yes	Yes	No
$X_n = midValue\{x_i\}$	Median	No	No	No
$X_n = maxOccur\{x_i\}$	Moda	No	No	No

The desired properties of the aggregation function in a gamified evaluation with streaming vectored scores can be summarized as this:

- Easy calculation from performance point of view.
- Respectful to individual scores, yet suppressing incidental fluctuations.
- Incremental nature, which allows updating the score as new scores arrive, without the need to access all previous scores.
- Captures tendencies (or development) of score results over time.

We propose a metric, which is provisionally called *temporal average*. It is easy to calculate, sensitivity to fluctuations can be controlled (via parameter $\alpha \in (0, 1)$) and it allows incremental updates:

$$X_n = (1 - \alpha) \sum_{i=1}^{n} \alpha^{n-i} x_i \tag{1}$$

The practical implementation of temporal average uses its recurrent representation, which defines the temporal average as a liner combination between the previous aggregated score and the new individual score:

$$X_0 = 0, X_n = (1 - \alpha) x_n + \alpha X_{n-1} \tag{2}$$

To bring up the properties of average temporal let consider the multiple gradings of three students over the course of 15 academic weeks – see Fig. 6. Student A plays a problem 7 times and the scores at the beginning (weeks 1 and 3) are excellent. Student B plays the same problem only three times and performs relatively consistently. Student C starts with low grades, but improves the result towards the end. The pedagogical question is what should the final score be for these three students?

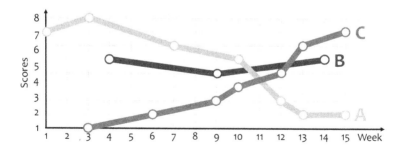

Fig. 6. Exemplary multiple scores of three students

Table 4 compares the aggregated scores of the popular methods (listed in Table 3) and the temporal average with $\alpha = 0.7$. The competences of student C should be evaluated with higher scores, because C shows spectacular tendency of improvement the score – from 0 in week 3 to 7 in week 15.

Table 4. Comparison of the popular aggregation functions and the temporal average in the last column

Student grades	First	Last	Max	Avg	Med	Moda	TAvg
A {7, 8, 6, 5, 2, 1, 1}	7.00	1.00	8.00	4.29	5.00	1.00	2.40
B {5, 4, 5}	5.00	5.00	5.00	4.67	4.00	5.00	3.08
C {0, 1, 2, 3, 4, 6, 7}	0.00	7.00	7.00	3.29	3.00	N/A	4.45

The average score of student A is better than that of student C, however, the tendency of degrading result of A leads to a significantly lower temporal average score of 2.40. As for student B, the results are steady, but their temporal average 3.08 is lower than C's 4.45, because student B has only 3 scores (weeks 4, 9 and 14), which are not enough to generate a credible overall score.

The temporal average score could be explained in terms of different weights of scores depending on time – recent scores are "heavier" and have greater impact than scores, achieved long ago. Similar methods are used in computer graphics and digital video production to represent fast motion – *motion blur* and *temporal smooth*. They overlap and blend several frames into one by applying higher transparency to distant frames and higher opacity to nearby frames.

The α coefficient in Eqs. 1 and 2 defines the sensitivity of the temporal average and it has different interpretation when the number of attempts is low or high:

- When α is close to 0: just a few attempts are sufficient to achieve a credible score; however, if there are many attempts, only the last few of them have a noticeable impact on the aggregated score.
- When α is close to 1: many attempts are needed to achieve a credible score and most of them will affect the final score, as a result, when there are few attempts, the aggregated score will be low due to the lack of credibility.

In an extreme case (similar to the consistent results of student B), when all scores are equal, i.e. $x_1 = \cdots = x_n = k$, the value of the aggregated score is:

$$X_n = (1 - \alpha) \sum_{i=1}^{n} \alpha^{n-i} k = (1 - \alpha)\frac{1 - \alpha^n}{1 - \alpha}k = (1 - \alpha^n)k \tag{3}$$

A credibility of 90% means that the final score is at least 90% of the individual scores, i.e. $X_n >= 0.9\,k$. When $\alpha = 0.1$ the first score reaches 90% credibility, when $\alpha = 0.5$ it requires 4 scores, and when $\alpha = 0.9$ it takes 22 individual scores to reach 90%.

It is not possible to determine the optimal value for α because this depends on the person who designs the evaluation process and decides the importance of individual scores. Too low values for α will increase the sensibility, so incidental fluctuation of the students' performance will easily affect their final scores. On the other hand, too high values for α will force students to play and replay the evaluation game too many times in order to accumulate some credible score.

Although the proposed temporal average is easy and incremental to calculate, it respects individual scores, protects against incidental fluctuations and captures tendencies, it is not feasible to use it whenever there are many students' scores to be aggregated into a single score. Temporal average provides meaningful results only if the same student solves multiple times one or more problems with compatible competence profiles.

If the problems are not compatible at competence level (i.e. their competence profiles do not overlap), than the series of scores do not represent the learning curve of the student and the calculated temporal average score will have no pedagogical value. Similarly, if many students solve the same problem, the collection of their scores should not be aggregated by a temporal average, because the individual scores in the collection do not represent the development of any competences over time.

In Sect. 2 we stated that a gamified evaluation could also be used for students' assessment. A gamified evaluation produces enough data (individual scores of playing many games) to generate the competency profile of a student – see Fig. 7. The profile is the boundary that encompasses all achieved competences and skills. In this respect, the interior area of the profile determines the evaluation of the student. The exterior area defines the assessment of the student in individual competences, because the profile is not a scalar, but a vector. This delivers sufficient pedagogical information as to decide what further steps are necessary in order to improve the overall results.

When the competence profile is compressed to a single number in the LMS gradebook, then the shape of the profile is lost as well as all information, useful for assessment. This means that the extraction of assessment-aware data should be done before the generation of a single grade number. In a gamified evaluation the extraction could be performed at any time during a gameplay, thus providing a real-time continuous evaluation and assessment of students.

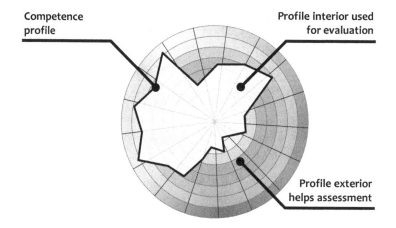

Fig. 7. Blending evaluation and assessment

7   Conclusion and Further Work

This paper presents a method for gamified evaluation based on students' competence profiles. The system allows quantitative analysis of student experience, competencies, skills and achievement from different points of view. The trends of the course progress allow to predict the overall student success in course completion. Especially in computer graphics course, where evaluation of diverse range of competences, knowledge and skills is required, the proposed students' profiles provide an effective way to capture the diversity of students' achievements.

Meiro has hundreds of 3D models, but its extension focuses on models for gamified evaluation and on the visual in-game representation of competences, described in Sects. 5 and 6. The proposed gamified evaluation will be tested in December 2019 with over 140 undergraduate students, providing us with data about the applicability and the limitation of the temporal average. We expect it should only be used to aggregate the scores of individual students, because the temporal average of scores of two or more students will not provide any meaningful information about the development of each of them. The real-time approbation with students will answer one important pedagogical question: Could students apply specific game strategies to control their automatic evaluations?

The result from the tests will provide confirmation whether the temporal average is a suitable evaluation metric. If the gamified evaluation proves to be successful, Meiro will outreach and cover other disciplines in Sofia University, especially those that already use virtual programming environments, like the courses *Educational Languages and Environments*, *Geometry of Motion* and the soon to be offered *Virtual and Augmented Reality*.

References

1. de Almeida Souza, M.R., Constantino, K.F., Veado, L.F., Figueiredo, E.M.L.: Gamification in software engineering education: an empirical study. In: 2017 IEEE 30th Conference on Software Engineering Education and Training (CSEE&T), pp. 276–284. IEEE (2017)
2. Ašeriškis, D., Damaševičius, R.: Gamification patterns for gamification applications. Procedia Comput. Sci. **39**, 83–90 (2014)
3. Blazauskas, T., Maskeliunas, R., Bartkute, R., Kersiene, V., Jurkeviciute, I., Dubosas, M.: Virtual reality in education: new ways to learn. In: Damaševičius, R., Mikašytė, V. (eds.) ICIST 2017. CCIS, vol. 756, pp. 457–465. Springer, Cham (2017). https://doi.org/10.1007/978-3-319-67642-5_38
4. Boytchev, P.: Technology enhanced technology enhanced learning. J. e-Learn. Knowl. Soc. **6**(2), 13–26 (2010)
5. Boytchev, P., Boytcheva, S.: Evaluation and assessment in TEL courses. In: AIP Conference Proceedings, vol. 2048, no. 1, p. 020035 (2018)
6. Carretero, S., Vuorikari, R., Punie, Y., et al.: DigComp 2.1: the digital competence framework for citizens with eight proficiency levels and examples of use. Technical report. Joint Research Centre (Seville site) (2017)
7. Chambers, J.M.: Graphical Methods for Data Analysis. Chapman and Hall/CRC, Boca Raton (2017)

8. Dicheva, D., Dichev, C., Agre, G., Angelova, G.: Gamification in education: a systematic mapping study. J. Educ. Technol. Soc. **18**(3), 75–88 (2015)
9. Freeman, S., et al.: Active learning increases student performance in science, engineering, and mathematics. Proc. Nat. Acad. Sci. **111**(23), 8410–8415 (2014)
10. Hamari, J., Eranti, V.: Framework for designing and evaluating game achievements. In: Digra Conference. Citeseer (2011)
11. Ibáñez, M.B., Di-Serio, A., Delgado-Kloos, C.: Gamification for engaging computer science students in learning activities: a case study. IEEE Trans. Learn. Technol. **7**(3), 291–301 (2014)
12. Iosup, A., Epema, D.: An experience report on using gamification in technical higher education. In: Proceedings of the 45th ACM Technical Symposium on Computer Science Education, pp. 27–32. ACM (2014)
13. Kim, S., Song, K., Lockee, B., Burton, J.: Gamification cases in education. Gamification in Learning and Education. AGL, pp. 117–123. Springer, Cham (2018). https://doi.org/10.1007/978-3-319-47283-6_10
14. Lekova, M., Boytchev, P.: Virtual learning environment for computer graphics university course. In: Proceedings of 12th International Technology, Education and Development Conference, pp. 3301–3309. IATED Academy (2018)
15. O'Donovan, S., Gain, J., Marais, P.: A case study in the gamification of a university-level games development course. In: Proceedings of the South African Institute for Computer Scientists and Information Technologists Conference, pp. 242–251. ACM (2013)
16. Połap, D., Woźniak, M.: The impact of the cost function on the operation of the intelligent agent in 2D games. In: Damaševičius, R., Vasiljevienė, G. (eds.) ICIST 2018. CCIS, vol. 920, pp. 293–302. Springer, Cham (2018). https://doi.org/10.1007/978-3-319-99972-2_23
17. Raziūnaitė, P., Miliūnaitė, A., Maskeliūnas, R., Damaševičius, R., Sidekerskienė, T., Narkevičienė, B.: Designing an educational music game for digital game based learning: a Lithuanian case study. In: 2018 41st International Convention on Information and Communication Technology, Electronics and Microelectronics (MIPRO), pp. 0800–0805. IEEE (2018)
18. van Roy, R., Zaman, B.: Why gamification fails in education and how to make it successful: introducing nine gamification heuristics based on self-determination theory. In: Ma, M., Oikonomou, A. (eds.) Serious Games and Edutainment Applications, pp. 485–509. Springer, Cham (2017). https://doi.org/10.1007/978-3-319-51645-5_22
19. Stagnitti, K., Unsworth, C., Rodger, S.: Development of an assessment to identify play behaviours that discriminate between the play of typical preschoolers and preschoolers with pre-academic problems. Can. J. Occup. Ther. **67**(5), 291–303 (2000)
20. Tembo, T.M.T., Lee, C.S.: Using 2D simulation applications to motivate students to learn steam. In: 25th International Conference on Computers in Education: Technology and Innovation: Computer-Based Educational Systems for the 21st Century, Workshop Proceedings, pp. 403–409 (2017)
21. Villagrasa, S., Duran, J.: Gamification for learning 3D computer graphics arts. In: Proceedings of the First International Conference on Technological Ecosystem for Enhancing Multiculturality, pp. 429–433. ACM (2013)
22. Winnicka, A., Kęsik, K., Połap, D., Woźniak, M., Marszałek, Z.: A multi-agent gamification system for managing smart homes. Sensors **19**(5), 1249 (2019)
23. Zichermann, G., Cunningham, C.: Gamification by Design: Implementing Game Mechanics in Web and Mobile Apps. O'Reilly Media Inc., Sebastopol (2011)

Development of Virtual Laboratory Works for Technical and Computer Sciences

Bohdan Sus[1](✉) [iD], Nataliia Tmienova[1] [iD], Ilona Revenchuk[2] [iD],
and Vira Vialkova[1] [iD]

[1] Taras Shevchenko National University, 60 Volodymyrska Street,
Kyiv 01103, Ukraine
bnsuse@gmail.com, tmyenovox@gmail.com,
veravialkova@gmail.com
[2] Kharkiv National University of Radio Electronics, Nauky Avenue 14,
Kharkiv 61166, Ukraine
ilona.revenchuk@nure.ua

Abstract. The most effective way of development process of electronic virtual laboratory activities in physics and information technologies has been presented. In the described virtual laboratory work the mathematical modeling, hardware-in-the-loop simulation, electrical emulation of sensors were effectively combined with didactic requirements such as formalization, application of mathematical terminology, development of dimensional imagination, modeling and dynamics of physical processes. The main steps of development and execution of virtual laboratory work in preparation for the real experiment with unique equipment and created software for modern material science and microelectronics have been described in detail. Improvement of the virtual simulators to create the results of observations with the addition of random errors and delays typical of real measuring devices have been implemented. It is shown that student can clearly see the kinetics of studied processes taking place in the volume of the sample. It was demonstrated that immersion environment provides the ability of interaction with virtual objects and tools much more efficiently to show the researcher the functioning of automatic methods especially with complex and unique equipment. The computer demonstrations as important didactic means at study of engineering and physics in systems of electronic education can be introduced by the simulation of a physical process through animation and video of the real experiment.

Keywords: Virtual laboratory work · Simulator · Remote labs ·
Computer based support · Cognitive activity · Virtual device · Adaptive model

1 Introduction

Distance learning and open universities become more popular and widely used for teaching and learning. However, because of the specific nature of the subject area, the teaching of science and engineering is still relatively backward in terms of using the implementation of new technological approaches, in particular, for online distance learning. The main reason for this inconsistency is that engineering and technical

© Springer Nature Switzerland AG 2019
R. Damaševičius and G. Vasiljevienė (Eds.): ICIST 2019, CCIS 1078, pp. 383–394, 2019.
https://doi.org/10.1007/978-3-030-30275-7_29

subjects often require laboratory activities to ensure effective acquisition of skills and practical experience. Practical experience has a key role in high technologies. Modern semiconductor devices, especially intelligent sensors with integrated processor units and Space-based solar power elements are created by methods of planar technology in a thin, near-surface layer of silicon plates. In these processes, in the near-surface layer of plates, areas of n-type and p-type are formed, the surface of the plates is oxidized, layers of metallization and passivation are applied and various chemical treatments are carried out. In some cases, technological process can create the negative or dangerous conditions for the test engineer. Therefore, the process of development of special virtual laboratory works became very relevant. Control of the state of semiconductor wafers and the results of their physical and chemical treatments is important at all stages of the production of planar electronic devices and can determine the quality of the final product. In this connection, special methods of modeling for control are acquired of special importance, which can be included in the chain of feedback control of technological operations and promptly affect their progress.

Virtual laboratory works and simulators are a welcome first step in the STEM training, recognizing that students will still need practical experience with real equipment. Integration of virtual laboratories into the virtual world is one of the major challenges for future research and development [1]. Virtual laboratory work is computer program that allows performing experiments and getting results without using real laboratory installations and instruments. We create an interactive model of the laboratory setup, including virtual instruments and tools. The computer model allows the student to consistently perform the steps of the laboratory work program. Virtual laboratory work, which involves the mathematical modeling, can be called a virtual simulator.

Computer support of the educational process provides opportunities for independent work of students and their work in classrooms and laboratories. By using network technologies and electronic educational tutorials with interactive demonstrations, a student can learn the subject, perform tests, prepare for the actual research and perform remote and virtual laboratory work independently.

At the same time, work with modern scientific or technological equipment often deals with the computer, which helps the student to control the hardware, obtain the data and perform calculations without directly observing the object of research, his reaction to the effects of experimental factors or change the course of the study [2]. In this case, computer simulation techniques provide great advantages in creating a dynamic visual picture of the physical experiment or phenomena, including such that it is impossible or difficult to observe in the real experiment and a great opportunity to improve methods of laboratory work. Therefore, it allows stating that further improvement of the programs of virtual laboratory work by adding the elements of a real experiment with instrumental errors, diversifying model of investigation and taking into account the principles of didactics enable the creation of virtual laboratory works very similar to real ones [3].

There are a number of projects for the development of virtual laboratory works in natural science. The main objectives of the research are the development, testing, implementation and distribution of educational modules, teaching methods and pedagogical strategies based on the use of virtual devices in various fields of science (physics, chemistry, biology) to help students through the availability of virtual tools in classes. Virtual instruments combined with dynamic models of physical laws allow simulating learning skills in a virtual lab. TEALSIM is an open source environment for creating, presenting and managing different simulations area [4]. It was developed by the TEAL Active Learning Technology project at Massachusetts Institute of Technology. TEALSIM software helps us to increase the student's conceptual and analytical understanding of nature and dynamics of electromagnetic phenomena. TEALSIM is a very useful instrument especially in topics of electricity and magnetism. It helps students to visualize phenomena and allows them to see invisible in real conditions lines of the magnetic field. It is not always possible to perform measurements during physical experiments when the source data were obtained. In recent years, it has become clear that we can significantly improve the study of measuring techniques and methods through interactive technologies and augmented reality. This allows future researchers to perform measurements of samples of a virtual environment and explore their features manually. Data can be represented as models of virtual objects. A user can view data representation in different forms and control elements of the virtual world by the means of different methods of interaction [5]. The virtual lab provides an opportunity for researchers to interact with physical experiments and simulations by the means of interactive tools for visualizing, measuring, analyzing and modeling experimental data. For example, a virtual environment tracking tool for biological imaging [6] allows researchers to manually measure the length of fibers in sets of data about volume. System that uses a virtual protractor and caliper to measure angles and distances from stereo pairs created by a scanning electron microscope is described in [7]. However, the discussed above lab activities are quite similar and do not involve interdisciplinary approach during the work with high-tech equipment.

Performance of the analysis of experimental data may be subject to the execution of laboratory work even without a real or virtual experiment. The described laboratory work may be an experimental analysis of numerous samples, the calculations and comparative analysis of their characteristics. In this case, the calculation of the laboratory work can be closer to real scientific research and even lead to the discovery of new effects or patterns. A brilliant example of remote research is work with huge array observations of orbital telescope Hubble that in 15 years of work photographed more than 700,000 images of 22,000 celestial objects [8].

The main objectives of the research are the development of virtual laboratory work on natural science with modeling of dynamics of physical processes to provide the highest standards of e-learning. It supposes the implementation of principles of adaptive and active learning, as well as modeling of virtual measurements during the development process. Since every student is learning in a different way, multi-step algorithms are used in the development of laboratory work, which evaluates the effectiveness of actions based on decisions and offers different types of multimedia forms and adaptive learning scenarios for each student. Much of the assignments and experiments can be performed using simulation programs or on the basis of remote access to real equipment. Such laboratory works are safe to use and make it possible for students to do some research a hundred times. Modeling of natural science processes and adaptive tasks lead to an increase in the mental activity and competencies of students. It is encouraging research students to learn essential skills and tools especially required for further work with unique samples to correctly use the equipment and methods of measurements.

To achieve the main objectives of the research, it is necessary to perform the following steps:

- to create an algorithm of measurements in the virtual simulator;
- to develop special virtual simulator;
- to create and visualize virtual laboratory work.

2 Main Results of Research

2.1 Realization of Virtual Laboratory Work

To improve methods of virtual laboratory work wide use of interactivity with the implementation of the principles of activity and interdisciplinary approaches to learning is required. In the case of laboratory work, the essence of these approaches is to diversify ways of virtual laboratory work on each step, the presence of self-control and methods of evaluation of results. During laboratory work, students have to fulfill a task of conscious choice and means of experiment operation. This may be the choice from the available list of virtual instruments, conditions of the experiment, design equations etc. It increases creativity and curiosity of students [3, 9, 10].

Often in laboratory activity in modern physics the student must specify the temperature range of measurements of voltages and currents, values of the magnetic or electric fields required for the study. At this step student should define the sample parameters required to research and set accuracy and measurement step values. Student should show knowledge of devices, based on the given experimental conditions.

The user interface of virtual laboratory work looks like as in real hardware. By pressing the appropriate buttons, student receives data reproduced on the monitor in the form of plots or tables. The measured values are taken from the database of real obtained or simulated settings. During "experimental" data, receiving the result of each "measurement" can be defined by data interpolation and the addition of random errors, time delay, like in real measurements. Error value based on the characteristics of the devices can be set by the teacher in advance. If the student chose too large or too small measurement step, due to delays in the virtual devices, experimental data receiving time could increase vastly. This makes the student to repeat the study with different parameters of the experiment. Therefore, the student faces the same problem as in real experiment, and he gets the skills and experience. It is advisable to use of virtual laboratory activities in preparation for the real experiment, especially with complex and unique equipment. Artificial reduction of device delays helps to quickly obtain the necessary skills to work with the equipment.

After the virtual experiment, students should evaluate the obtained data and determine their validity for further mathematical processing. In the case of not properly selected conditions and parameters of the research, settings of the devices and step measuring range experimental data obtained will not contain the necessary information. A set of software tools for studying and solving the direct research needs of materials science, semiconductor electronics, and information technologies has been developed. The interactive selection of modes, samples or devices is implemented by the means of an adaptive model. The implementation of an adaptive model can be done using neural networks, which make it possible to determine the optimal dependence of performance on the passing of tests. An adaptive model scenario of the virtual electronic laboratory work is shown on Fig. 1.

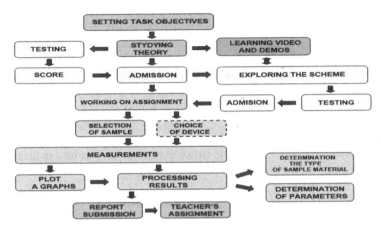

Fig. 1. Adaptive model of virtual electronic laboratory work

Tasks are executed in real time, with the visualization of complex processes and interactively measure additional data. At any stage of the process, the user can analyze the data from the current set of measurements. Each component of the virtual device can exchange data with other components of the virtual laboratory work and external programs by the means of shared memory. For rapid application development of an efficient user interface and the provision of main aspects of its operation, the virtual library of the environment window (VEWL) with a set of tools has been used [11].

2.2 Modelling of Virtual Measurements

One of the problems that arises during development of a virtual simulator is the identical repeatability of the results of work, with the same output data and experiment parameters. This reduces the possibilities of virtual simulators, allows guessing of the right answer for testing and minimizing work resemblance to real simulator studies. One of the ways to improve the virtual simulator is to create the results of observations with the addition of random errors and delays typical of real measuring devices. Measuring instruments are characterized by errors, which have additive and multiplicative components. The values of these components depend on the value of the measured parameter - f_0, and the range of the instrument on which measurements are made. The same errors are inherent in the value of the argument x on which depends the parameter f_0. It includes calculations of the current value of the argument x, the corresponding value f_0 and the result of the observation $f(x_j)$, taking into account the measurement errors. Initially, calculations of the current value of the argument x, the corresponding value f_0 and the result of the observation $f(x_j)$, taking into account the measurement error are performed. The results of $f(x_j)$ are displayed with delays characteristic of the equipment selected at the beginning of operation. The peculiarity of a virtual experiment is that the initial dependence on the basis of which the result is generated contains a finite number of values of the measured value f_0 and only for completely certain values of the argument x. Therefore, in a virtual simulator, for finding the observation results $f(x_j)$ corresponding to a given x, an interpolation of the source file data is implemented and an error value is added. Moreover, as in the real experiment, the value x is verified equal to the nearest multiple quantization level for the selected instrument. When the results of measurements carried out and a small step of the argument change x are used to form the database, linear interpolation can be applied in the virtual simulator. If values x are exceeded beyond the data contained in the output file, an extrapolation is applied or an error message is generated. The virtual simulator reports an attempt at expanding the range of virtual measurements to an area of values x outside the range allowed for the selected device at the stage of entering the experiment parameters. The result of the virtual measurement is formed in the form of a tabulated function:

$$f(x) = f_0(x) + \mu(f_0(x)) + add \tag{1}$$

where: $f_0(x)$ - Interpolated output data, $\mu(f_0(x))$ - multiplicative error of the device, add - additive error of the device. Values of $\mu(f_0(x))$ and add, were calculated on the basis of the Box-Muller pseudo-random number sampling transform, which simulates the values distributed under the normal law:

$$\mu(f_0(x)) = \sigma_\mu(f_0(x)) \cdot \sin(2\pi * \varphi) \cdot \sqrt{-2 \cdot \ln(r)} \tag{2}$$

$$add = \sigma_a \cdot \sin(2\pi * \varphi) \cdot \sqrt{-2 \cdot \ln(r)}, \tag{3}$$

where: φ, r, are independent random variables that evenly distributed in the range $[0, 1]$, σ_μ and - σ_a the variance of the multiplicative and additive components of the instrument error. Values σ_μ and σ_a for each of the instrument used in the virtual simulators are predefined and stored in the appropriate simulator database. The definition of σ_μ and σ_a, according to the data given in the technical documentation for the devices, is a complex mathematical task inverse to the problem of finding a dispersion in a known data set and can not always be solved. In this case, and where the law of error distribution is unknown, it is possible to use the simplest, uniform distribution:

$$\mu(f_0(x)) = error \cdot (1 - 2 \cdot \varphi_0) \cdot f_0(x), \tag{4}$$

$$add = \varepsilon \cdot (1 - 2 \cdot r_0) \tag{5}$$

where: $error$ - maximum multiplicative error, ε - maximum value of additive error, φ_0, r_0 - independent random variables are evenly distributed in the range $[0, 1]$. For the values of ε and $error$ accepted maximum values of errors, presented in the technical datasheets. When averaging the measurement results for some value of the argument x_j for the selected amount of observations n, the value

$$f(x_j) = \frac{1}{n} \cdot \left(\sum_{i=1}^{n} f_i(x_j) \right) \qquad (6)$$

Therefore, for the same source data file, the results of two virtual measurements will vary even under the same conditions of the virtual experiment (the step of changing the argument x and the number of averaging n). With the increase of n the difference in the results decreases and they approach to the data of the output file. If $n \rightarrow \infty$ $f(x) \rightarrow f_0(x)$ and does not depend on the law of distribution of error and absolute values of ε and *error*. About an attempt to extend the range of virtual measurements to the range of values x outside the range allowed for the selected device, the virtual simulator reports immediately, at the stage of entering the experiment parameters. The discussed algorithm of measurements in the virtual simulator has been implemented in a number of laboratory activities. For illustration, the results of simulation on a virtual simulator, which determined the lifetime of carriers τ in their recombination through deep levels via measurements of noise spectral density in the semiconductor resistor s_i on the frequency f are presented. As the initial data, the theoretical dependence of $s_i(f)$ was taken at temperature T = 320 K, in which the generation-recombination component of noise was present, which corresponded to two deep levels with the time of life $\tau_1 = 5{,}625 \cdot 10^{-5}$ and $\tau_2 = 4{,}15 \cdot 10^{-3}$ accordingly. Also, the thermal noise and 1/T - type noise were taken into account. The values of τ_1 and τ_2 were taken from real measurements conducted on semiconductor samples. When performing modeling treated the problem of finding the number of deep levels that exist in the sample and calculation of lifetime that characterizes these levels. The simulation included the choice of measurement accuracy and the steps of the frequency measurements. The choice of the student for the high accuracy of measurements and the number of experimental points, could give the correct result, but in this case, the increased time of calculations became unacceptable. Therefore, the student, as in the real study, had to perform tasks of finding and optimizing the parameters of the experiment. Implementation of the dependence of the spectral density of the s_i current noise on the frequency f for the semiconductor resistor is shown on Fig. 2. The typical realizations of the dependence of $s_i(f)$ on the logarithmic scale are obtained with errors of 10% and 50%, respectively.

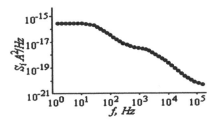

Fig. 2. Error of measurement is 10%

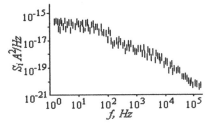

Fig. 3. Error of measurement is 50%.

The approximate magnitude of the distribution of the obtained values of deviation realizations, on which depended the accuracy of the definition is indicated by the marks of different sizes. It can be seen that dependence $s_i(f)$ has two characteristic areas for the generation-recombination noise. The transition from the saturation to the $s_i(f) \sim 1/f^2$ dependence is described. In the future, to calculate the lifetime τ of each level, it is necessary to determine the number of such areas and make approximation of the obtained dependences by the theoretical values to determine τ_1 and τ_2. With an increase of measurement error up to 50%, the presence of the generic-recombinant noise areas characteristic is becoming uncertain, and the task of determining the quantity and parameters of the levels become considerably more complicated. Similarly, an excessive increase in the measurement step for the f_i/f_{i-1} frequency, especially in the large error of measurement, leads to a substantial complication, or even impossibility, to determine the number of levels and their parameters. Since the realization of the dependence of $s_i(f)$ is random, the determined values are also random. So the definition of the 10 realizations of $s_i(f)$ with an error of 10% and a measurement step $f_i/f_{i-1} \leq 1,1$ led to the distribution of δ values of τ in the range of 2%, and with an error of 50%, $\delta \approx 20\%$. At the same values of measurement errors, increasing the step by frequency to $f_i/f_{i-1} \leq 2,3$ led to the distribution of values to 20 and 1000 percent, respectively. Similar research results are also observed in real experiments. This is a great advantage of virtual laboratory work.

2.3   Example of Created Virtual Laboratory Work

In the result of our research a number of virtual laboratory works have been developed. As an example, we will discuss virtual laboratory work of modern Semiconductor Physics and nano electronics. It provides the bulk lifetime measurement of charge carriers in Silicon by the method of conductivity modulation. Laboratory work based on automated research installation. This laboratory work is the relevant for the course. The method of measurement is based on the measuring the lifetime via modulation of conductivity of sample, which varies with the injection of non-equilibrium charge carriers due to a sharp metal probe in contact with the semiconductor wafer (Fig. 4).

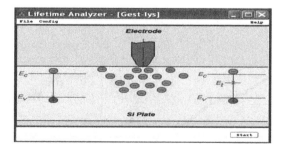

Fig. 4. Animation frame, which schematically shows the processes of diffusion and recombination of charge carriers.

Initially, the probe get a short pulse of current, which leads to injection of charge carriers and the increase of the conductivity of the sample in the area around the probe. After some time on probe, second pulse is used to measure the lifetime value. Then the time interval between the first and second pulse and the voltage drop across the sample during the two pulses are measured.

Since conductivity of the sample increases during the first pulse due to injection of charge carriers, the voltage drop on the sample decreases. In the sample, the carrier concentration decreases and the resistance of the sample increases again due to the processes of diffusion and recombination. Monitoring of the dependence of the amplitude of the second measuring voltage pulse depending on the delay of the second pulse relative to the first it is possible to determine the kinetics of change of conductivity type and the lifetime of non-equilibrium charge carriers.

The interface of the main window is shown on Fig. 5. Using item "Oscilloscope" student makes virtual measurements in automatic or manual modes.

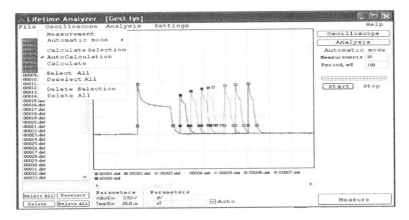

Fig. 5. The interface of the window of virtual laboratory work.

Number of each experimental point is shown in the list (left side of the interface). Visual image is shown on a virtual oscilloscope screen located in the center. Student should select from the list of oscillograms valid experimental points suitable for further mathematical processing and delete unsuitable ones. Student may perform measurement in accelerated mode and evaluate the influence of selected parameters of experiment on the result and its accuracy.

After front-end processing of data, final calculations are carried out. After click "Analysis" button (Fig. 5) appears the "results analysis" is shown in Fig. 6.

Calculation of the effective lifetime τ_{eff} is held by the slope of linear plot of the experimental curve based on formulas $\tau_{eff} = dt/d(\ln U)$, bulk τ_v by the formula.

$$1/\tau_v = 1/\tau_{eff} - 1/\left(\frac{d^2}{\pi^2 D_n} + \frac{d}{2S}\right), \tag{7}$$

and their values appear in the relevant box interface.

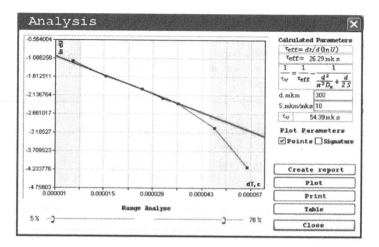

Fig. 6. The program interface window with the results of calculations.

At this step student should analyze obtained experimental curve and choose the maximum number of experimental points that most closely fit to a linear dependence. To can cut off the extreme data student can use the sliders located under the image. As possible consequences of an incorrect choice of parameters of the experiment also can be emergency modes. For example, when excessive voltage or current through the sample applied. Special interactive 3-d model animation module is activated. Figure 7, in this case, the software program of experiment informs the student and offers to repeat the study.

Fig. 7. Interactive 3-d model animation module.

It helps to organize re-study the necessary learning material and testing. The number of research efforts can be fixed by tracking system and affect to the final assessment.

At the last step student receives the printed report. All the required tools are located at the bottom right of the interface (Fig. 6).

The specified courses where these laboratory activities were implemented have a wide range of interdisciplinary connections with other sciences such as chemistry, the theory of quantum computers and microprocessor technologies. Particularly relevant works are available for cloud-based electronic learning environments with the algorithms and methods of information protection between devices using combined communication channels and embedded systems [12].

3   Conclusions

During the course of virtual laboratory activities on natural sciences and IT disciplines, software provided ease of use and improved assessment of learning material in a control group of students. It was discovered that during the use of virtual laboratory work the student feels a subjective sense of presence. The immersion environment provides the ability to interact with virtual objects and tools much more efficiently. The virtual environment can also be used to show the researcher the functioning of automatic methods. For example, iterative methods can be displayed with time sequences of intermediate results. In this virtual laboratory work we can directly interact with data representations and receive new quantitative representations in experiments and simulations. Students can manage virtual simulation models in accordance with the principles of working in real time and interdisciplinary studies of complex systems. The education system is based on a probabilistic student relational model that evaluates the behavior of the researcher. Virtualization of learning experiments can also be done in laboratory work on computer graphics using STEM technologies to improve the visibility and systematic complex processes and phenomena, and to involve the author's computer models in the educational process. The further development of applications for computer graphics, virtual reality, and virtual world technology can significantly extend the use of virtual laboratory works. Tutoring in student groups with the use of remote labs allows reaching an identical level of knowledge compared to students who executed lab activities students in a conventional way.

References

1. Potkonjak, V., et al.: Virtual laboratories for education in science, technology, and engineering. Comput. Educ. **95**(C), 309–327 (2016)
2. Kulesz, B., Sikora, A., Zielonka, A.: The application of ant colony algorithms to improving the operation of traction rectifier transformers. In: The 24th International Conference on Information and Software Technologies (ICIST), 4–6 October 2018, 12 p. Kaunas University of Technology, Lithuania (2018)
3. Tmienova, N., Sus, B.: Interactive demonstrations in information technologies. Bull. Natl. Univ. "Lviv Polytechnic" **732**, 135–141 (2015). Series "Informatization of Higher Educational Institution"
4. Santos, Guetl, Bailey, & Harward (2010). http://web.mit.edu/viz/soft/visualizations/tealsim

5. Sims, J.S., et al.: Accelerating scientific discovery through computation and visualization II. J. Res. Natl. Inst. Stand. Technol. **107**(3), 223–245 (2002)
6. Brady, R., et al.: Crumbs: a virtuality environment tracking tool for biological imaging. In: Proceedings of the IEEE Symposium on Frontiers in Biomedical Visualization (1995)
7. Bethel, E.W., Bastacky, S.J., Schwartz, K.S.: Interactive stereo electron microscopy enhanced with virtual reality. In: Woods, A.J., et al. (eds.) Stereoscopic Displays and Virtual Reality Systems IX (Proceedings of SPIE), vol. 4660, pp. 391–400. SPIE The International Society for Optical Engineering, San Jose (2002)
8. Zimmerman, R.F.: The Universe in a Mirror—The Saga of the Hubble Space Telescope and the Visionaries Who Built It. Princeton University Press, Princeton (2010)
9. Klimová Frydrychová, B.: Teaching and learning enhanced by information and communication technologies. Procedia Soc. Behav. Sci. **186** (2015). ISSN 1877-0428
10. Ozturk, D., Eyikara, E., Baykara, G.Z.: The opinions of nursing students regarding the first implementation of distance education. World J. Educ. Technol. Curr. Issues **9**(2), 51–58 (2016)
11. Larimer, D., Bowman, D.: VEWL: a framework for building a windowing interface in a virtual environment. In: Proceedings of INTERACT: IFIP TC13 International Conference on Human-Computer Interaction, pp. 809–812 (2003)
12. Tmienova, N., Sus, B.: Hardware data encryption complex based on programmable microcontrollers. In: CEUR Workshop Proceedings, pp. 199–208 (2018). http://ceur-ws.org/Vol-2318/paper17.pdf

Software Engineering: Special Session on Intelligent Systems and Software Engineering Advances

Comparison of Rough Mereology Based Path Planning Algorithms for Intelligent Robotics

Lukasz Zmudzinski[(⊠)] [iD]

Faculty of Mathematics and Computer Science, University of Warmia and Mazury in Olsztyn, Słoneczna 54, 10-710 Olsztyn, Poland
lukasz@zmudzinski.me

Abstract. The goal of this paper is to compare rough mereology algorithms for path planning of mobile agents in intelligent robotics. The Square Fill Algorithm and CFill algorithm are considered. Moreover, path planning on the created potential fields is tested in various scenarios. Time and general path planning statistics are given for all used rough mereology algorithms. Potential ideas on improvement are given after analyzing test results.

Keywords: Path planning · Rough mereology · Potential fields · Robot navigation · Mereogeometry · Robotics

1 Introduction

With the rapid development of robotic artificial intelligence [1–6,11–13], such algorithms are created and updated for the field of rough mereology. The main idea is the notion of part carried out in rough mereology, that allows to live down the errors in perception taken from the inaccuracy of sensors readings (highly dependant on types of surface, material fluctuations, poor image resolutions, etc.). Each position for objects (robots, obstacles, etc.) in a given environment is an estimation (probability), rather than an exact value.

The main two algorithms that are currently implemented in rough mereology for path planning are the Square Fill Algorithm [7] and the CFill Algorithm [16]. Both algorithms work with environments of known terrain and object distribution, with the latter offering some form of dynamic interactions after the path has been planned. More on the subject will be explained in Sect. 2 - Rough mereology path planning.

The general scheme of mereology (and in effect rough mereology) is the previously mentioned notion of part, which relates to the idea of containment or partial containment. In practice, an intelligent agent, that enters a previously specified area, can ascertain its connection to it by a degree. Such areas in the provided algorithms are called mereological potential fields. The degree of connection ranges from 0 to 1, where 0 means no inclusion and 1 full inclusion.

© Springer Nature Switzerland AG 2019
R. Damaševičius and G. Vasiljevienė (Eds.): ICIST 2019, CCIS 1078, pp. 397–407, 2019.
https://doi.org/10.1007/978-3-030-30275-7_30

Described by [9], the featured relation can be seen as a rough inclusion $\mu(x, y, r)$, which translates to: x *is a part of* y *to a degree of at least* r. The rough inclusion, when applied to spatial objects can be defined as $\mu(X, Y, r)$ if and only if $\frac{|X \cap Y|}{X} >= r$, X, Y being n-dimensional solids and $|X|$ the n-volume of X. Spatial objects X, Y can be assumed as concept regions and $|x|$ the area of X when the autonomous mobile robot is moving in 3-dimensional environment. Given that, the elements of a mereological potential field created on the base of a rough inclusion $\mu(X, Y, r)$ will have the distance value between them defined as the following calculation:

$$K(X, Y) = min\{max_r \mu(X, Y, r)\}, max_s \mu(Y, X, s)\}. \tag{1}$$

The mereological potential fields work with integrable force fields given by formulas of Coulomb or Newton to describe the force a the given point as inverse-proportional to the squared distance from the target, meaning that the potential field itself is also inversely proportional. The idea behind the Square Fill Algorithm enforces this, assigning the property of density to the potential field, which gets more dense, the closer it gets to the goal point, further modifications to the algorithms (eg. CFill) drop this property to decrease the number of calculations in environments with fewer obstacles (sparse).

2   Rough Mereology Path Planning

The paper focuses on two algorithms: the Square Fill Algorithm, which is the earlier attempt to implement rough mereology path planning, and its modification - the CFill algorithm, which changes the creation methods and path planning to make the process more versatile and adaptive. Moreover, the modifications presented in [14] are taken into consideration.

2.1   Square Fill Algorithm

The algorithm was presented by Osmialowski and Polkowski in [7,9] and described further in [10]. It focuses on creating the mereological potential field using static neighbours for each field present in the queue. After the potential field is created, the algorithm searches for the field with the closest mereological distance to the robot position and adds it as the first path point. Further steps are based on repeating the search for closest path points with decreasing mereological distance, ending at the goal. The pseudocode can be seen in Algorithm 1. The algorithm is described as follows:

1. Define initial algorithm values:
   - Set **current distance** to the goal as zero,
   - Set algorithm **direction** to *clockwise*,
2. Create an empty queue Q,
3. Add to queue Q the first **potential field** $p(x, y, d)$, where x, y describe the location of the field and d represents the **current distance** to the goal.

4. Enumerate through Q until Q is an empty set:
5. If $(\{p_k(x, y, d)\} \cap F) \vee (\{p_k(x, y, d)\} \cap C)$ where $p_k(x, y, d)$ is the current potential field, F is a set of already created potential fields and C is a set of collision objects, then remove the current field $p_k(x, y, d)$ from Q and go over to the next iteration,
6. Add the current potential field to the created potential fields set F,
7. Increase the **current distance** to the goal $d = d(p_k) + 0.01$,
8. Define neighbours depending on the current **direction**:
   - *clockwise* as N:

$$N = \begin{cases} p_0 = p(x - d, y, d), \\ p_1 = p(x - d, y + d, d), \\ p_2 = p(x, y + d, d), \\ p_3 = p(x + d, y + d, d), \\ p_4 = p(x + d, y, d), \\ p_5 = p(x + d, y - d, d), \\ p_6 = p(x, y - d, d), \\ p_8 = p(x - d, y - d, d) \end{cases} \tag{2}$$

   - *anticlockwise* as N':

$$N' = \begin{cases} p_0 = p(x - d, y - d, d), \\ p_1 = p(x, y - d, d), \\ p_2 = p(x + d, y - d, d), \\ p_3 = p(x + d, y, d), \\ p_4 = p(x + d, y + d, d), \\ p_5 = p(x, y + d, d), \\ p_6 = p(x - d, y + d, d), \\ p_8 = p(x - d, y, d) \end{cases} \tag{3}$$

9. Add neighbours to queue Q depending on direction value:
   - If **direction** is *clockwise* then: $Q \cup N$,
   - If **direction** is *anticlockwise* then: $Q \cup N'$,
10. Change the current **direction** to the opposite,
11. Remove the current potential field $p_k(x, y, d)$ from the queue Q.

2.2   CFill Algorithm

The CFill algorithm offers a different approach to the potential field creation. There are two big changes implemented: the creation of potential field neighbours is parametrized (it can be specified how many neighbours should be created around the potential field) and the algorithm takes notice of the obstacle density on the map. This allows the implementation of the *narrowing mode*, where the number and spacing of neighbour creation is either sparse in places without obstacles and dense near obstacles.

The number of neighbours represented by the *neighbours* parameter allows the algorithm to calculate the positions of a number of dynamic positions. The angle between neighbours is calculated in radians as

Algorithm 1. Square Fill Algorithm

1: **procedure** SQUARE FILL
2:      $current\_distance \leftarrow 0$
3:      $direction \leftarrow clockwise$
4:      $potential\_fields \leftarrow$ new empty array
5:      $Q \leftarrow$ new empty array
6:      $potential\_field \leftarrow goal\_x,\ goal\_y,\ current\_distance$
7:      $Q.append(potential\_field)$
8: *For field in Q*:
9:      **if** Q is empty **then end**
10:      **if** *field.out_bounds* **or** *field.created* **or** *field.collision* **then**
11:          $Q.remove(field)$
12:          **continue**
13:      $potential\_fields.append(field)$
14:      $current\_distance \leftarrow current\_distance + 0.01$
15:      $new\_neighbours \leftarrow define\_neighbours(direction)$
16:      $Q.append(new\_neighbours)$
17:      $direction \leftarrow$ **not** $direction$
18:      $Q.remove(field)$

$$\alpha = \frac{350}{neighbours} * \frac{\pi}{180} \tag{4}$$

Then a loop is created that creates neighbours up until 2π increasing each time by the α angle. Each iteration calculates the position of the current neighbour applying the calculations below:

$$x' = sin(\alpha_i) * d \pm x \tag{5}$$

$$y' = -cos(\alpha_i) * d + y \tag{6}$$

The pseudocode can be seen in Algorithm 2. The CFill algorithm can be reproducted in the following steps:

1. Initial algorithm parameters:
   - *neighbours* (how many neighbours should be created),
   - *step* (step distance between potential fields),
   - *radius* (radius of the created potential fields),
   - *goal* (goal position in the environment),
   - *potential_fields* (list to store created potential fields),
   - *narrow_distance* (distance to activate the narrowing mode),
   - *narrow_step* (step distance for narrowing mode),
   - *narrow_neighbours* - (neighbours in narrowing mode).
2. Create an empty queue Q,
3. Set the *is_clockwise* variable to **True**,
4. Add the first potential field at the *goal* location with a *distance* of 0,
5. Enumerate through all potential fields in Q, until Q is empty,

6. Check the conditions, if any is **True**, remove the potential field from Q and go to next iterations:
   - Check, if the potential field is out of bounds of the map,
   - Check, if a potential field at that location is already created,
   - Check, if the potential field isn't overlapping an obstacle.
7. Check, if narrowing mode is set and the potential field is in the distance of *narrow_distance* to obstacle:
   - Create neighbours with number *narrow_neighbours* and *narrow_step* for distance incrementor from the potential field as described above,
   - Add the neighbours to queue Q,
8. Check, if narrowing mode is not set or the potential field isn't in the distance of *narrow_distance* to obstacle:
   - Create neighbours of the potential field with the number *neighbours* and *step* for distance incrementor as described above,
   - Add the neighbours to queue Q
9. Change the *is_clockwise* value to opposite,
10. Remove the potential field from queue Q,
11. Add the potential field to the *potential_fields* list.

Algorithm 2. CFill Algorithm

1: **procedure** CFILL
2:     **set** *neighbours, step, radius, goal, direction*
3:     **set** *n_distance, n_step, n_neighbours*
4:     *potential_fields* ← new empty array
5:     Q ← new empty array
6:     *potential_field* ← *goal_x, goal_y, current_distance*
7:     $Q.append(potential\_field)$
8: *For field in Q:*
9:     **if** Q is empty **then end**
10:    **if** *field.out_bounds* **or** *field.created* **or** *field.collision* **then**
11:        $Q.remove(field)$
12:        **continue**
13:    **if** *narrowing_mode* is *True* **then**
14:        *new_neighbours* ← *define_neighbours(direction, n_neighbours, n_step)*
15:    **else**
16:        *new_neighbours* ← *define_neighbours(direction, neighbours, step)*
17:    $Q.append(new\_neighbours)$
18:    *direction* ← **not** *direction*
19:    $Q.remove(field)$

---

3   Algorithm Comparison

The tests were created to compare two crucial tasks in rough mereology based path planning: the creation of the mereological potential field and the output path. In both cases, time was a considered factor. Moreover, for the potential field the number of created fields were monitored and for the output path - how long the created path was (in pixels) through simulations. The tests were performed several times with various input parameters, which included the generated map size, number of obstacles, random generator seed and algorithm input parameters, that would give near-optimal results for tested algorithms in the given environment (due to the nature of the algorithms, this had to be selected based on personal decision). Parameters used for testing:

- Map size (1000px width, 600px height),
- Start position ($x_s = 50$, $y_s = 50$),
- Goal position ($x_g = 950$, $y_g = 450$),
- Obstacle height and width (ranging from 5 to 60px),
- Radius of the potential field (40px),
- Number of obstacles (ranging from 0 to 20).

The obstacles were placed randomly on the map for each iteration and then the mereological path planning algorithms were run. Due to the nature of the test (randomly placed), measures had to be taken to exclude maps, which didn't allow successful creation of the path. In such cases, the iteration was redone.

All the simulations were run on an Early 2015 Macbook Pro (13 in), with a 2,7 GHz Intel Core i5 processor, 8 GB 1867 MHz DDR3 memory, on the macOS Mojave v.10.14.3 system.

3.1   Potential Field Creation

The first important step for both algorithms is to create the mereological potential field. Both the Square Fill and CFill methods did very well to cover the map for proposed robot navigation. When it comes to the number of created potential fields depending on the number of obstacles (as seen in Fig. 1), the Square Fill algorithm tends to have smaller variance (700–850 as opposed to 150–1000) in the number of generated potential fields. The algorithm doesn't take the distances between obstacles in consideration when calculating the potential field, so the number will generally get smaller with the increase of obstacles by a small slope. To decrease the potential field count, parameters would need to be adjusted in such a way, that the mereological distances aren't too big (the potential fields would still need to overlap, for the proposed path planning algorithm).

In the case of the CFill algorithm, tests revealed that while the number of created potential fields is generally much smaller than the other, the variance in the count of potential fields is higher. Some tests shown that with maps with big clusters of obstacles, the algorithm would create a great number of potential fields, compared to the Square Fill algorithm. This also means that the rest of the map would have a sparse potential field and it is the desired effect. To decrease the number of potential fields for such cases, the parameters would need to be adjusted (eg. decreasing the narrowing mode distance). With randomly generated maps, it was impossible to tell beforehand the best parameters for each situation as the algorithm output greatly depends on the positioning and size of the created obstacles.

An important aspect for comparison is the time of the potential field calculations. Running the algorithms fast is a crucial task for mobile robotics, where reactions should be fast, even on low memory devices. The CFill algorithm was calculating the potential field and the mereological tree much faster than the potential field creation in the Square Fill algorithm. As the author mentioned in [16], decreasing the time and memory usage while implementing the method was the primary goal of the algorithm modification. The method for potential field creation performed extremly well, even when many more potential fields were created. The effects of the tests can be seen in Fig. 2. It is worth noticing that in most situations for the simulation cases, the total time to generate the potential field dropped by around 1 s. As previously, the CFill algorithm can have *peaks* of memory and time usage, although in this case none higher than the Square Fill algorithm were found in multiple tests. This comes from the fact, that the number of calculations needed for neighbour creation in this method are limited.

3.2   Path Creation

The second aspect that was tested, was the output of path generation: the time it took to generate the path and the final path length for the selected potential field. Both paths were smoothed using the same algorithm [15,16] with the same input parameters. This was done to avoid defective results in the test. Both algorithms returned a list of tuple objects containing point positions from the start, to the goal of the path. The total distance for the given path was calculated as in the following equation:

$$total\_distance = \sum_{i=0}^{n-1} \sqrt{(x_{i+1} - x_i)^2 + (y_{i+1} - y_i)^2} \tag{7}$$

The tests have shown that generally the paths are similar, although the paths created by the CFill algorithm tend to be shorter, by a small margin (around 1–5 pixels in this case). This shows that after creating the potential field using the selected method, the proposed algorithms handle the creation of the path at the same level of complexity. Moreover, the paths created by the CFill algorithm produced a smaller variance between the path lengths, than the ones created by the Square Fill algorithm. These results give an interesting overview, especially because two much different methods of calculating next steps are used in both cases - mereological tree and mereological distance based. The results of the test can be seen in Fig. 3.

As for the time needed for creating the path, the tree method has proven more efficient. Going through the reference of parent-child relations is computationally

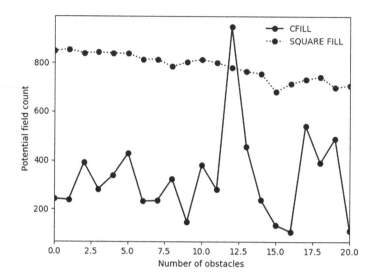

Fig. 1. The comparison between the number of created obstacles and the objects created in the potential field. The CFill data is marked by a solid line and the Square Fill is represented by dotted lines.

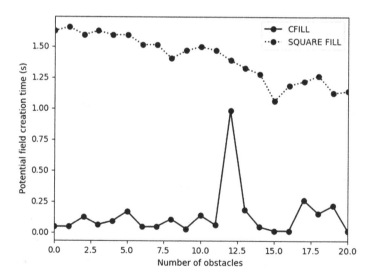

Fig. 2. The comparison between the number of created obstacles and the time needed to create the potential field. The solid line line represents the CFill algorithm, while the dotted one - Square Fill.

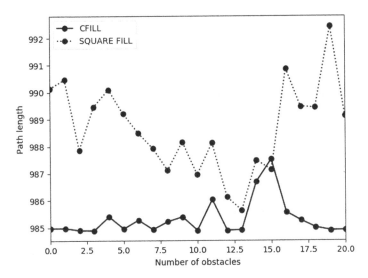

Fig. 3. The comparison between the number of created obstacles and the calculated path length dependant on the created potential field. Path created on the CFill field is marked by a solid line and the path created on the Square Fill field as dotted.

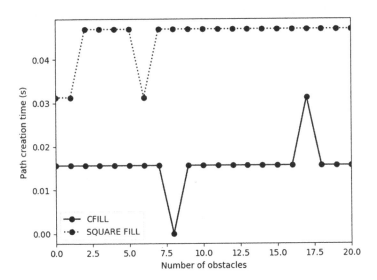

Fig. 4. The comparison between the number of created obstacles and the time needed to calculate a path on the supplied potential field. The solid line represents the path created on the CFill field, dotted line represents the path built on the Square Fill field.

efficient, using almost twice less time to output a path, once the potential field is created. The proposed method for CFill algorithm also gives the possibility of fast recalculations of the path in case that some dynamic changes are made to the environment, meaning it does not need to be recalculated unless the goal changes. This would decrease greatly the time to produce a working solution as compared to the Square Fill algorithm. Additionally, the time for generation of the tree fluctuated more for the CFill algorithm (around ± 0.015 s), than in the Square Fill Algorithm (around ± 0.01 s). Nevertheless, this shows that calculating paths on an already created potential field is fast and can be used for mobile robotics (Fig. 4).

4 Conclusion and Future Work

After testing both algorithms, a clearer picture was given for choosing the best mereology based path planning method. Both algorithms performed admirably in simulation, although generally the new take on the problem by the CFill algorithm has given better results. The author found problems in the CFill algorithm for clustered obstacles and the number of potential fields generated and proposed a way to deal with the problem.

As for path creation, both algorithms have proven that they are capable of creating paths in a fast and precise way. The time needed for creating a path on an already created potential field oscilated between 0.002 and 0.05 s, which is almost unnoticeable during the circle of motion path planning for mobile robotics. The calculation times were smaller for the CFill algorithm. Additionally, the CFill produced shorter paths, but the difference was minimal and can be ommited, when deciding which algorithm to use for specific purposes.

Rough mereology is a great pick for intelligent path planning, but it requires more work to be used in viable situations where many parameters can affect the outcome of robot navigation. The main topics on which future research might be based is path planning in dynamic environments, change of goals, decreasing the memory usage even further or adapting the algorithm for 3-dimensional navigation (eg. drones, autonomous planes).

Moreover, it would be interesting to implement modifications to the CFill algorithm that would decrease the variance of output results or adjusted the algorithm parameters depending on the surrounding environment (eg. decreasing number of neighbours or narrowing mode distance when the robot is nearing to a cluster of obstacles).

References

1. Adamu, P.I., Okagbue, H.I., Oguntunde, P.E.: Fast and optimal path planning algorithm (FAOPPA) for a mobile robot. Wirel. Pers. Commun. (2019). https://doi.org/10.1007/s11277-019-06180-w
2. Li, B., Liu, H., Su, W.: Topology optimization techniques for mobile robot path planning. Appl. Soft Comput. J. **78**, 528–544 (2019). https://doi.org/10.1016/j.asoc.2019.02.044

3. Low, E.S., Ong, P., Cheah, K.C.: Solving the optimal path planning of a mobile robot using improved Q-learning. Robot. Auton. Syst. **115**, 143–161 (2019). https://doi.org/10.1016/j.robot.2019.02.013

4. Moradi, B.: Multi-objective mobile robot path planning problem through learnable evolution model. J. Exp. Theor. Artif. Intell. **31**(2), 325–348 (2019). https://doi.org/10.1080/0952813X.2018.1549107

5. de Oliveira, G.C.R., de Carvalho, K.B., Brandão, A.S.: A hybrid path-planning strategy for mobile robots with limited sensor capabilities. Sensors (Basel, Switzerland) **19**(5) (2019). https://doi.org/10.3390/s19051049

6. Orozco-Rosas, U., Montiel, O., Sepúlveda, R.: Mobile robot path planning using membrane evolutionary artificial potential field. Appl. Soft Comput. J. **77**, 236–251 (2019). https://doi.org/10.1016/j.asoc.2019.01.036

7. Osmialowski, P.: On path planning for mobile robots: introducing the mereological potential field method in the framework of mereological spatial Reasoning. J. Autom. Mobile Robot. Intell. Syst. (JAMRIS) **3**(2), 24–33 (2009)

8. O'smialowski, P., Polkowski, L.: Spatial reasoning based on rough mereology: a notion of a robot formation and path planning problem for formations of mobile autonomous robots. In: Peters, J.F., Skowron, A., Słowiński, R., Lingras, P., Miao, D., Tsumoto, S. (eds.) Transactions on Rough Sets XII. LNCS, vol. 6190, pp. 143–169. Springer, Heidelberg (2010). https://doi.org/10.1007/978-3-642-14467-7_8

9. Polkowski, L.: Rough mereology: a new paradigm for approximate reasoning. Int. J. Approx. Reasoning **15**(4), 333–365 (1996)

10. Polkowski, L., Zmudzinski, L., Artiemjew, P.: Robot navigation and path planning by means of rough mereology. In: Proceedings of IEEE International Conference on Robotic Computing (2018)

11. Wang, L., Kan, J., Guo, J., Wang, C.: 3D path planning for the ground robot with improved ant colony optimization. Sensors (Switzerland) **19**(4) (2019). https://doi.org/10.3390/s19040815

12. Xu, R.: Path planning of mobile robot based on multi-sensor information fusion. Eurasip J. Wirel. Commun. Netw. **2019**(1) (2019). https://doi.org/10.1186/s13638-019-1352-1

13. Yuan, J., Wang, H., Lin, C., Liu, D., Yu, D.: A novel GRU-RNN network model for dynamic path planning of mobile robot. IEEE Access **7**, 15140–15151 (2019). https://doi.org/10.1109/ACCESS.2019.2894626

14. Zmudzinski, L., Artiemjew, P.: Path planning based on potential fields from rough mereology. In: Polkowski, L., et al. (eds.) IJCRS 2017. LNCS (LNAI), vol. 10314, pp. 158–168. Springer, Cham (2017). https://doi.org/10.1007/978-3-319-60840-2_11

15. Zmudzinski, L., Polkowski, L., Artiemjew, P.: Controlling robot formations by means of spatial reasoning based on rough mereology. Adv. Robot. Res. **2**(3), 219–236 (2018)

16. Zmudzinski, L.: Rough Mereology based CFill algorithm for robotic path planning. In: Proceedings of Concurrency Specification and Programming (2019, in review)

Low-Complexity Video Quality Assessment Based on Spatio-Temporal Structure

Yaqi Lu, Mei Yu, and Gangyi Jiang[(✉)]

Ningbo University, Ningbo 315211, China
jianggangyi@126.com

Abstract. Low-complexity is as important as prediction accuracy for video quality assessment (VQA) metrics to be practically deployable. In this paper, we develop an effective and efficient full-reference VQA algorithm, called Spatio-temporal Structural-based Video Quality Metric (SSVQM). To be more specific, spatio-temporal structural information is sensitive to both spatial distortions and temporal distortions. We calculate spatio-temporal structure based local quality according to spatio-temporal gradient characteristics and chrominance information. Then, these local quality scores are integrated to yield an overall video quality via a spatio-temporal pooling strategy simulating three most important global temporal effects of the human visual system, i.e. the smooth effect, the asymmetric tracking effect. Experiments on VQA databases LIVE and CSIQ demonstrate that our SSVQM achieves highly competitive prediction accuracy and delivers very low computational complexity.

Keywords: Video quality · Low-complexity · Spatio-temporal structure

1 Introduction

Video quality assessment (VQA) plays a central role in various video-related applications. It is often employed in quality control of various video services and performance comparison of various video processing algorithms. Objective VQA models [1, 2] have been designed to evaluate video quality in line with the human visual system (HVS). Considering accurate and stable, full-reference VQA (FR-VQA) has been widely used in video processing and coding [2]. FR-VQA intends to estimate video quality quickly and precisely, in which peak signal-to-noise ratio (PSNR) has been the dominant quantitative indicator in image and video processing. However, PSNR does not always correlate well with HVS [3]. The drawback will slow down the development of video processing technology, especially the further promoting of video compression efficiency. In image quality assessment (IQA), based on the assumption that the HVS is highly adapted for extracting structural information from the scene, Structural SIMilarity (SSIM) index [4] was proposed to bring IQA from pixel-based stage to structure-based stage. Then, some state-of-the-art FR-IQA algorithms were developed, such as Feature SIMilarity (FSIM) index [5] and Gradient Magnitude Similarity Deviation [6], etc.

© Springer Nature Switzerland AG 2019
R. Damaševičius and G. Vasiljevienė (Eds.): ICIST 2019, CCIS 1078, pp. 408–415, 2019.
https://doi.org/10.1007/978-3-030-30275-7_31

A straightforward approach to VQA is to use these state-of-the-art IQAs for an independent frame and then average all the frame level scores to obtain a composite score. However, due to the lack of temporal information, this approach did not worked well. Other methods deal with motion information either by incorporating motion characteristics into the frame weighting to account for their effects on the spatial distortion, or by modeling the temporal distortion and spatial distortion independently. Video Quality Metric (VQM) [7], MOtion-based Video Integrity Evaluation (MOVIE) [8], Spatio-Temporal MAD (STMAD) [9], spatial and spatiotemporal slices based ViS3 [10] and [11, 12] are the state-of-the-art FR-VQA metrics. Although these approaches improved performance compared to PSNR, a number of shortcomings, including high implementation and computational complexity, long latency and difficulty to integrate, still need to be resolved.

This paper proposes an efficient FR-VQA algorithm, called Spatio-temporal Structural-based Video Quality Metric (SSVQM). We extend the assumption of SSIM to VQA, i.e. HVS is highly adapted for extracting spatio-temporal structural information from dynamic scene. The whole video sequence is regarded as a pixel volume, and local quality is calculated according to spatio-temporal gradient and chrominance characteristics, which are both sensitive to spatial distortions and temporal distortions. Then, local quality scores are integrated to yield an overall video quality via a spatio-temporal pooling strategy simulating three most important global temporal effect.

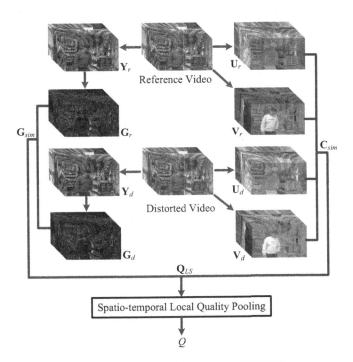

Fig. 1. Framework of the proposed SSVQM.

2 The Proposed SSVQM

In Fig. 1, the framework of the proposed SSVQM mainly consists of two phases: spatio-temporal structure based local quality calculating and spatio-temporal pooling. We use 3D Prewitt operator to calculate spatio-temporal gradients of reference and distorted video sequences.

We compare the video gradients detected by 2D Prewitt operator used in [7] and 3D Prewitt operator used in our SSVQM and the results are shown in Fig. 2. It can be clear that 2D Prewitt operator only detects spatial gradients, whereas 3D Prewitt operator can detect both temporal and spatial gradients. The rough edge represents motion, and the thin edge represents static, which can be used to measure temporal distortion.

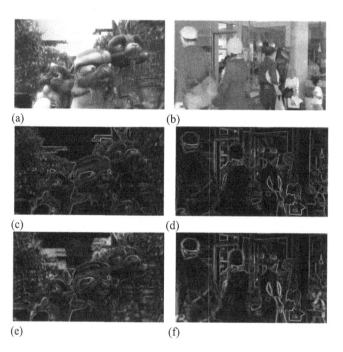

(a)   (b)

(c)   (d)

(e)   (f)

Fig. 2. Comparison of gradient calculated by 2D Prewitt operators and 3D Prewitt operators. (a) and (b) are frames from distorted video, (c) and (d) are gradients detected by 2D Prewitt operators, (e) and (f) are gradients detected by 3D Prewitt operators.

The proposed SSVQM estimates video quality of the reference and distorted videos in the YUV color space. The luminance component of the reference and distorted video are denoted as $\mathbf{Y}_r$ and $\mathbf{Y}_d$, respectively. The spatial resolution of each video is $W \times H$, F is the total frames evaluated. Assume the luminance component of each video as a 3-D matrix with size of $H \times W \times F$. The original video gradient amplitude and distorted video gradient magnitude, denoted as $\mathbf{G}_r$ and $\mathbf{G}_d$, are computed via.

$$G_r = \sqrt{\left(\mathbf{Y}_r \otimes \mathbf{F}_x\right)^2 + \left(\mathbf{Y}_r \otimes \mathbf{F}_y\right)^2 + \left(\mathbf{Y}_r \otimes \mathbf{F}_z\right)^2} \tag{1}$$

$$G_d = \sqrt{\left(\mathbf{Y}_d \otimes \mathbf{F}_x\right)^2 + \left(\mathbf{Y}_d \otimes \mathbf{F}_y\right)^2 + \left(\mathbf{Y}_d \otimes \mathbf{F}_z\right)^2} \tag{2}$$

where the symbol $\otimes$ denotes the convolution operation, and $\mathbf{F}_x$, $\mathbf{F}_y$ and $\mathbf{F}_z$ are three templates of 3D Prewitt operator along direction of x-axis, y-axis and t-axis, respectively. The gradient similarity of reference and distorted video sequence denoted as G_{sim}, is computed via

$$G_{sim} = \frac{2\mathbf{G}_r \cdot \mathbf{G}_d + c_1}{\mathbf{G}_r^2 + \mathbf{G}_d^2 + c_2} \tag{3}$$

where c_1 is a positive constant to increase stability and fine-tune the feature sensitivity to distortions.

Distortions of chrominance information will also seriously affect the video quality. Generally, the spatial size of two chrominance components both are only 1/4 of the luminance component in widely used YUV420 format. In addition, chrominance components adopt the same encoding scheme as luminance component when video is encoded. Both factors make chrominance components an easy source of degeneration, and therefore chrominance information is an important factor to be considered in the VQA algorithm.

We calculate the chrominance similarity using two chrominance components in YUV format video as [5]. Two chrominance components of the original and distorted video are denoted as $\mathbf{U}_r$, $\mathbf{V}_r$ and $\mathbf{U}_d$, $\mathbf{V}_d$ respectively, and the chrominance similarity denoted as $\mathbf{C}_{sim}$, is computed via

$$\mathbf{C}_{sim} = \frac{2\mathbf{U}_r \cdot \mathbf{U}_d + c_2}{\mathbf{U}_r^2 + \mathbf{U}_d^2 + c_2} \cdot \frac{2\mathbf{V}_r \cdot \mathbf{V}_d + c_3}{\mathbf{V}_r^2 + \mathbf{V}_d^2 + c_3} \tag{4}$$

where c_2 and c_3 are positive constants. Here, we set $c_1 = 90$, $c_2 = c_3 = 300$, and fix them for all databases so that SSVQM can be conveniently used. G_{sim} and $\mathbf{C}_{sim}$ can then be combined to get the spatio-temporal structure based local quality, denoted as $\mathbf{Q}_{LS}$.

$$\mathbf{Q}_{LS} = \mathbf{G}_{sim} \cdot \left(\mathbf{C}_{sim}\right)^{\lambda} \tag{5}$$

where $\lambda > 0$ is the parameter for adjusting the importance of two chromatic components. Here, λ is set to 3 in order to emphasize the effect of severely distorted in chrominance components.

In this paper, each video is regarded as a pixel volume at the local quality calculating stage ignoring global temporal effects of HVS. At the spatio-temporal pooling stage, the frame-level quality is obtained via an efficient spatial pooling method, then these frame-level quality scores are integrated to yield an overall video quality via a temporal pooling method simulating three most important global temporal effects.

Spatial pooling: The simplest and widely used pooling strategy is average pooling. Here, we adopt a more efficient standard deviation pooling [7] method to calculate frame-level quality. Each pix-level quality in $\mathbf{Q}_{LS}$ is denoted as $Q_{LS}(x, y, t)$, where $x \in \{1,\ldots, H\}$, $y \in \{1,\ldots, W\}$, $z \in \{1,\ldots, F\}$, and frame-level quality can be computed via.

$$Q_{mean}(t) = \frac{1}{H \times W} \sum_{x=1}^{H} \sum_{y=1}^{W} Q_{LS}(x, y, t) \tag{6}$$

$$Q_{frame}(t) = \sqrt{\frac{1}{H \times W} \sum_{x=1}^{H} \sum_{y=1}^{W} (Q_{LS}(x, y, t) - Q_{mean}(t))^2} \tag{7}$$

Note that a smaller value indicate higher quality, which is opposite to the average pooling method.

Temporal pooling: In this paper, we mainly consider three most important global temporal effects of HVS: (1) the smooth effect [13], *i.e.* the subjective ratings of the whole video sequence typically demonstrate far less variation than the frame-level quality scores. This effect can be simulated by low-pass filtering frame-level quality scores; (2) the asymmetric tracking effect [14], *i.e.* HVS is more sensitive to frame-level quality degradation than improvement. This effect can be simulated using different weights for quality rising and quality declining; (3) the recency effect [15], *i.e.* subjects tend to put a higher weigh on what they have seen most recently. This effect can be simulated using a time-related weight. The implementation in [16] accurately describes the smooth effect and the asymmetric tracking effect. We improved the model by integrating logarithmic function weights to simulate the recency effect. The final video quality denoted as Q, is computed via

$$Q_{LP} = \begin{cases} Q_{LP}(t-1) + \alpha \cdot \Delta Q(t), & if \ \Delta Q(t) \leq 0 \\ Q_{LP}(t-1) + \beta \cdot \Delta Q(t), & if \ \Delta Q(t) > 0 \end{cases} \tag{8}$$

$$Q = \frac{1}{F} \sum_{t=1}^{F} (Q_{LP}(t) \cdot \ln(r \cdot t + 1)) \tag{9}$$

where $\Delta Q = Q_{frame}(t) - Q_{LP}(t-1)$, $Q_{LP}(1) = Q_{frame}(1)$, α and β are asymmetric weighs, and γ is a positive constant for adjusting time-related weighs. Unlike [11], we just rough-tune these parameters and fix them as fallow: $\alpha = 0.03$, $\beta = 0.2$ and $\gamma = 1000$. It is worth noting that the performance can be improved if we independently fine-tune these parameters for each database, but generalization capability of our pooling method will be slightly affected.

3   Experimental Results and Discussion

Two publicly VQA databases are used in experiments:

(1) *LIVE* [17]: LIVE VQA database contains 10 reference videos with four different distortions: MPEG-2 compression, H.264/AVC compression, simulated transmission of H.264-compressed bit-streams through error-prone IP networks and error-prone wireless networks, a total of 150 distorted videos. All videos are in YUV420 format with a resolution of 768 × 432 pixels, two kinds of frame rates: 25 and 50 fps, and about 10 s in duration.

(2) *CSIQ* [18]: CSIQ VQA database contains 12 reference videos with six different distortions: MJPEG compression, H.264/AVC compression, H.265/HEVC compression, wavelet compression, packet-loss simulated transmission of H.264-compressed bit-streams through wireless networks and additive white Gaussian noise, a total of 216 distorted videos. All videos are in YUV420 format with a resolution of 832 × 480 pixels, 10 s in duration and five kinds of frame rates: 24, 25, 30, 50 and 60 fps.

Two performance indicators are used in our experiments: Linear Correlation Coefficient (LCC) and Spearman Rank Order Correlation Coefficient (SROCC). LCC measures the prediction accuracy and SROCC measures the prediction monotonicity. We apply a four-parameter logistic transform before computing LCC as recommended by video quality experts group (VQEG) [19]. It is worth noting that VQA on the appropriate scale will be most effective and efficient. Instead of up-sampling two chrominance components for YUV420 format video, luminance component is filtered by a 2 × 2 average filter in spatial domain first, and then down-sampled by a factor of 2. In this way, not only the size of luminance component and two chrominance components match, but also the complexity of SSVQM is reduced without jeopardizing the prediction accuracy.

The proposed FR-VQA metric, SSVQM, compared with eight well-known quality metrics, including three FR-IQA metrics: PSNR, SSIM, FSIM, four FR-VQA metrics: VQM, MOVIE, STMAD, ViS$_3$, and one RR-VQA metric STRRED [20] on the LIVE and CSIQ VQA databases. Here, three FR-IQA metrics are extended to video. The results are listed in Table 1 and clearly SSVQM is superior to other metrics on the LIVE database. On the CSIQ database, SSVQM and ViS$_3$ provide similar SROCC, and both are superior to the other metrics.

We also compare the complexity of our SSVQM with other eight metrics on a video sequence with 250 frames from LIVE VQA database using a Lenovo desktop (Intel Core i5-4590 CPU @3.30 GHz, 8G RAM, Windows 7 64-bit, MATLAB® R2014b). Except MOVIE implemented using C++, all other metrics are implemented using MATLAB, and all source codes were obtained from the original authors. Our SSVQM is also implemented using MATLAB without any optimization. The results are listed in Table 2. The complexity of SSVQM is very low, only 5 times of PSNR. The complexity of ViS$_3$, STMAD and MOVIE are 28 times, 70 times and 380 times of our SSVQM, respectively.

Table 1. LCC and SROCC on LIVE and CSIQ VQA databases

Metrics	LIVE		CSIQ	
	LCC	SROCC	LCC	SROCC
PSNR	0.5397	0.5231	0.5663	0.5798
SSIM	0.5068	0.5233	0.6389	0.5811
FSIM	0.6823	0.7318	0.7211	0.7503
VQM	0.7708	0.7563	0.7697	0.7893
MOVIE	0.8116	0.7890	0.7884	0.8061
STRRED	0.8038	0.8007	0.7894	0.8129
STMAD	0.8303	**0.8251**	0.7237	0.7355
ViS$_3$	**0.8336**	0.8168	**0.8222**	**0.8325**
SSVQM	**0.8632**	**0.8475**	**0.8099**	**0.8302**

Table 2. Running time of SSVQM and other eight metrics

Metrics	Running time (s)
PSNR	1.3
SSIM	6.3
SSVQM	**6.5**
VQM	26
FSIM	53
STRRED	97
ViS$_3$	182
STMAD	455
MOVIE	2470

4 Conclusions

In this paper, an effective and efficient full-reference video quality assessment algorithm has been proposed, called Spatio-temporal Structural-based Video Quality Metric (SSVQM). Spatio-temporal structure based local quality is calculated according to spatio-temporal gradient characteristics and chrominance information. Then, these local quality scores are integrated to yield an overall video quality via a spatio-temporal pooling strategy simulating three most important global temporal effects of human visual system, i.e. the smooth effect, asymmetric tracking effect. Experiments on LIVE and CSIQ VQA databases demonstrate that the proposed SSVQM can achieve highly competitive prediction accuracy and delivers very low computational complexity. In future work, we will focus on low-complexity video quality assessment of high-definition videos and stereoscopic videos.

Acknowledgments. The work was partly supported by the Natural Science Foundation of China (61671258,61871247).

References

1. Fan, Q., Luo, W., Xia, Y., Li, G., He, D.: Metrics and methods of video quality assessment: a brief review, Multimedia Tools and Applications (2017)
2. He, M., Jiang, G., Yu, M., Song, Y., et al.: Video quality assessment method motivated by human visual perception. J. Electron. Imaging 25(6), 061613 (2016)
3. Huynh-Thu, Q., Ghanbari, M.: Scope of validity of PSNR in image/video quality assessment. Electron. Lett. 44(13), 800–801 (2008)
4. Wang, Z., Bovik, A.C., Sheikh, H.R., et al.: Image quality assessment: from error visibility to structural similarity. IEEE Trans. Image Process. 13(4), 600–612 (2004)
5. Zhang, L., Zhang, L., Mou, X., et al.: FSIM: a feature similarity index for image quality assessment. IEEE Trans. Image Process. 20(8), 2378–2386 (2011)
6. Xue, W., Zhang, L., Mou, X., et al.: Gradient magnitude similarity deviation: a highly efficient perceptual image quality index. IEEE Trans. Image Process. 23(2), 684–695 (2014)
7. Pinson, M.H., Wolf, S.: A new standardized method for objectively measuring video quality. IEEE Trans. Broadcast. 50(3), 312–322 (2004)
8. Seshadrinathan, K., Bovik, A.C.: Motion tuned spatio-temporal quality assessment of natural videos. IEEE Trans. Image Process. 19, 335–350 (2010)
9. Vu, P., Vu, C., Chandler, D.: A spatiotemporal most-apparent-distortion model for video quality assessment, International Conference on Image Processing (ICIP) (2011)
10. Vu, P., Chandler, D.: ViS3: an algorithm for video quality assessment via analysis of spatial and spatiotemporal slices. J. Electron. Imaging 23(1), 013016 (2014)
11. Li, S., Ma, L., Ngan, K.N.: Full-reference video quality assessment by decoupling detail losses and additive impairments. IEEE Trans. Circuits Syst. Video Technol. 22(7), 1100–1112 (2012)
12. Loh, W., Bong, D.B.L.: An error-based video quality assessment method with temporal information. Multimedia Tools Appl. 77(23), 30791–30814 (2018)
13. Tan, K.T., Ghanbari, M., Pearson, D.E.: An objective measurement tool for MPEG video quality. Sig. Process. 70(3), 279–294 (1998)
14. Horita, Y., Miyata, T., Gunawan, I.P., et al.: Evaluation model considering static-temporal quality degradation and human memory for SSCQE video quality, Visual Communications and Image Processing, pp. 1601–1611 (2003)
15. Hands, D.S., Avons, S.E.: Recency and duration neglect in subjective assessment of television picture quality. Appl. Cogn. Psychol. 15(6), 639–657 (2001)
16. Masry, M., Hemami, S.S., Sermadevi, Y.: A scalable wavelet-based video distortion metric and applications. IEEE Trans. Circuits Syst. Video Technol. 16(2), 260–273 (2006)
17. Seshadrinathan, K., Soundararajan, R., Bovik, A.C., et al.: Study of subjective and objective quality assessment of video. IEEE Trans. Image Process. 19(6), 1427–1441 (2010)
18. Laboratory of Computational Perception & Image Quality, Oklahoma State University: CSIQ video database (2013). http://vision.okstate.edu/csiq/
19. VQEG, Final Report from the Video Quality Experts Group on the Validation of Objective Models of Video Quality Assessment, Phase II, August 2003. http://www.vqeg.org
20. Soundararajan, R., Bovik, A.C.: Video quality assessment by reduced reference spatio-temporal entropic differencing. IEEE Trans. Circuits Syst. Video Technol. 23(4), 684–694 (2013)

Fuzzy Predictive Model of Solar Panel for Decision Support System in the Management of Hybrid Grid

Sergii Tymchuk[1], Sergii Shendryk[2], Vira Shendryk[2(✉)],
Oleksii Piskarov[1], and Anastasia Kazlauskayte[2]

[1] Kharkiv Petro Vasilenko National Technical University of Agriculture,
Kharkiv, Ukraine
stym@i.ua, pannerpost@gmail.com
[2] Sumy State University, Sumy, Ukraine
{s.shendryk, v.shendryk}@cs.sumdu.edu.ua

Abstract. This paper describes the features of decision-making process about working modes of hybrid energy grid and indicates tasks, which has to solve the appropriate information system. In order to managing the hybrid electricity grid, it is necessary to have current data and forecast indicators of the functioning of its constituent elements. The fuzzy predictive model of power by solar panel is developed in this research. This model a certain way takes into account the uncertainty associated with both constructive, commutation influences and the impact of predicted insolation and temperature. In the developed model it is possible to use the results of direct measurements of insolation and temperature and the results of their operational forecasting.

Keywords: Fuzzy predictive model · Decision support system · Hybrid grid · Solar panel · Predictive model of insolation and temperature

1 Introduction

Modern world trends are associated with an increase in the cost of traditional fuel resources and are manifested in increasing the share of dispersed electricity production through renewable energy sources (RES). This leads to complicated planning and operational management of hybrid power system.

Insufficient level of research of RES operation issues, their influence on electric networks operation modes, the absence of typical decisions regarding the means of protection and automation of the electricity production process does not allow to make informed decisions during their operation. An important aspect in this direction is the complexity and methodological unity in decision-making regarding the improvement of operational characteristics of RES in their work in power grids.

In order to ensure decision-making in the decision support system when managing the hybrid electricity supply system, it is necessary to have current data and forecast indicators of the functioning of its constituent elements, namely, solar panels (SP), wind turbines, micro-hydro-electric power stations, diesel and gas generators, etc. [1, 2].

© Springer Nature Switzerland AG 2019
R. Damaševičius and G. Vasiljevienė (Eds.): ICIST 2019, CCIS 1078, pp. 416–427, 2019.
https://doi.org/10.1007/978-3-030-30275-7_32

The collection of current data is carried out using a variety of sensors. Forecast indicators can be obtained only on the basis of mathematical models [3].

In this research, attention is focused on the SP. Electrical parameters of the SP depend on external meteorological factors such as temperature and insolation, as well as on constructive factors such as the size, material and amount of photocells, the presence of concentrators and heat transfer, etc. All these parameters are characterized by some uncertainty. For example, the temperature and insolation depend on meteorological conditions that carry uncertainty. In addition, these parameters have some unevenness on the plane of the SP, which is difficult to measure, as well as a certain measurement error [4]. Constructive factors also depend on the quality of the technological process in their manufacture.

Usually, a local charge-level controller supports the maximum power selection from the SP, which is redistributed between the panel and the load, therefore, from the point of view of the decision-making system, the mathematical model of the SP should describe the dependence of the maximum power of the SP from external meteorological and constructive factors. Moreover, it is desirable that this model should take into account the uncertainty of the input information. The disclosure of this type of uncertainty is expedient to implement within the fuzzy approach.

2   Literature Review and Formulation of Problem

The mentioned problem was not investigated comprehensively, but solved only separate tasks.

Among recent developments in control techniques for advanced control strategies, fuzzy logic and multi agent systems have emerged due to its strong control action in an uncertain environment [5].

But traditionally, modeling of SP capacity is based on a deterministic approach. In most cases, the basis of constructing a mathematical model of the power of the SP is the model of the voltage-ampere characteristic of the individual photocell [6–8], obtained theoretically or based on the processing of experimental data. This is explained by the relative simplicity of the research of the characteristics of photocells. However, when calculating the characteristics of a large-scale SP, difficulties arise in the determination of various losses due to the non-identity of the photocells, switching, unevenness of temperature and insolation along the plane of the SP.

The introduction of the appropriate coefficients [9, 10] does not solve these problems, and attempts to improve the deterministic mathematical model of the SP leads to a significant complication [10].

Also, in a number of papers it is proposed to take into account the integrally defined losses due to experimental studies of non-photocells, and small SPs with the subsequent propagation of the result to the SP parameters of any plane [9]. However, this approach justifies itself within certain limits. In addition, errors are added due to the use of regression analysis for constructing a model of volt-ampere characteristics in conditions of small sampling of experimental data. In this case, it seems more expedient to apply a fuzzy regression analysis.

3 Definition of the Goal

The purpose of the article is to construct a fuzzy predictive model of solar cell power for a decision-making support system under the control of a hybrid electricity grid in conditions of uncertainty of external and constructive factors.

4 Basic Research Materials

The efficiency and cost-effectiveness of using renewable energy sources in a hybrid power grid depends on choosing the optimal mode of operation of the hybrid network and matching the capacities in it. The operation of such an electric grid is characterized by a rapid change in operating modes, depending on weather conditions and consumption.

Therefore, the set of tasks Z, which must execute a decision support system for the management of a hybrid power system, can be represented as follows.

$$Z = Z_m \cup Z_{pg} \cup Z_{pu} \cup Z_f, \tag{1}$$

where Z_m is the set of metrology data monitoring tasks, Z_{pg} is the set of predictors for the electricity generation level, Z_{pu} is the set of tasks for predicting electricity consumption, Z_f is the set of tasks for the formation of solutions.

When creating predictive models of energy generation, it is necessary to take into account the uncertainty of the input data.

It is proposed to determine the maximum power of the SP in the form of a triangular fuzzy number, that is, a tuple

$$P = \langle P_{mod}, P_{min}, P_{max} \rangle, \tag{2}$$

where P_{mod} is modal value, P_{min}, P_{max} are left and right boundary interval of uncertainty.

In this case, the representation of fuzzy numbers with a triangular membership function is accepted in the form of:

$$\mu_P = \max \left[0, min \left(\frac{P - P_{min}}{P_{mod} - P_{min}}, \frac{P_{max} - P}{P_{max} - P_{mod}} \right) \right], \tag{3}$$

In the limit of uncertainty, all of the above parameters fall into an integral direction, which can not be directly determined and even those that are unknown.

To take into account the dependence of P_{mod}, P_{min}, P_{max}, P_{opt}, m, the experimental data presented in [11] were processed from external and constitutive factors, since these experiments were performed precisely in order to detect the influence of undetermined factors on the electrical characteristics of the SP. 16 groups of solar cells were investigated with a plane of 0.0403 m^2 in the range of temperature (12–70) °C and insolation (550–1260) W/m^2. As part of the group, photocells of various sizes are loaded to account for this kind of uncertainty. The unevenness of the temperature along the plane of the groups was established at $\pm 1°$ C from the mean, and the insolation – within $\pm 3\%$. Near the point of maximum power, several control points of the volt-ampere characteristics were recorded to account for the error of the controller, which regulates the maximum power selection from the SP.

For processing, a fuzzy regression analysis with two quality criteria was used: the degree of coincidence and the degree of uncertainty.

The procedure of fuzzy regression analysis, in contrast to the traditional one, generally uses two criteria: the degree of coincidence and the degree of uncertainty. Based on these two criteria, one criterion was formed by their superposition. The search for fuzzy regression coefficients is implemented as part of the nonlinear programming problem. The method of spatial grid with variable pitch was applied.

As a result of the processing of experimental data, the dependences included in the fuzzy model (1) (Fig. 1) are obtained in the form:

$$P_{mod} = (0.0901E + 0.0873t - 0.00032Et)S,$$
$$P_{min} = (0.0876E + 0.0499t - 0.00027Et)S, \qquad (4)$$
$$P_{max} = (0.0918E + 0.1055t - 0.00035Et)S.$$

The average degree of coincidence (4) is 0.32, and the average degree of uncertainty does not exceed 0.11.

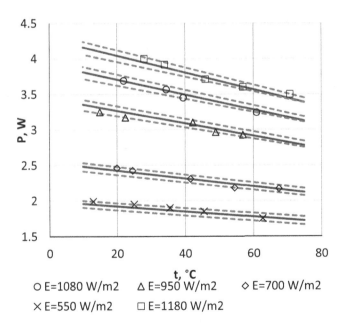

Fig. 1. Results of processing of experimental data by fuzzy regression analysis

It is difficult to establish definitely the correspondence of fuzzy estimates of the effectiveness of regression with traditional estimates. The closest such correspondence was to establish between the degree of coincidence and the mean absolute percentage error (MAPE). These parameters correspond to MAPE = 1.1% when all experimental data arrive at the limit of the interval of fuzziness.

In dependencies (4) S is the total area of solar panels included in the hybrid power supply system. If expressions (4) do not use the results of operational measurements of E – insolation, t – temperature, and predictive data, then the dependencies (4) should be adjusted in accordance with the generalization of Zadeh, taking into account the forecast error.

We offer concrete data on insolation for the relevant period (day, month, season, year) to present in relative terms by dividing them by the magnitude of the corresponding maximum power. For periods of time during which insolation is observed, it is also envisaged the transition to relative values, which will ensure the correctness of the comparison of relative values of insolation for different months.

In order to determine the possible value of energy generated by the year, it is necessary to have statistics on insolation for the chosen location of the solar panels, namely data on the duration of the corresponding solar power during the calculation period.

For the development of a prediction model of insolation, the data are presented in the Tables 1 and 2. The results of the conversion carried out by dividing the hourly values of insolation for each month by the maximum value for 13:00 is given. Despite the fact that for February, April, June and July this maximum was observed at 14:00, in calculations conditionally selected 13:00 [12].

The values of insolation in these tables are averaged over the months of the year, and then they have a certain uncertainty, which can be disclosed with the help of a fuzzy regression apparatus [13].

It is proposed to construct a fuzzy predictive model that allows obtaining the value of insolation in the form of a fuzzy number with a triangular membership function, that is, in the form of a tuple (similar to dependencies (2))

$$E = \langle E_{mod}, E_{max}, E_{min} \rangle. \tag{5}$$

where E_{mod} is modal value of a triangular number, E_{max}, E_{min} are maximum and minimum values limiting the base set of fuzzy numbers.

Obviously, these parameters depend on Earth's motion in orbit around the Sun and from the rotation of the Earth around its own axis.

The construction of regression dependencies is divided into two stages.

The first stage is the construction of dependencies for maximal daily insolation during the year, which correlates with the motion of the Earth around the Sun in orbit. For this purpose from the Tables 1 and 2 selected maximal average insolation values. To obtain a model of regression dependence, a sinusoidal type function is chosen

$$E_i^{ma} = a_i + b_i \sin(d_i m - c_i), \tag{6}$$

Table 1. Average monthly insolation data for Ukraine

Month	January	February	March	April	May	June
Time	1	2	3	4	5	6
0.00	0	0	0	0	0	0
0.04	0	0	0	0	0	0
0.08	0	0	0	0	0	0
0.13	0	0	0	0	0	0
0.17	0	0	0	0	0	0
0.21	0	0	0	0	0	0
0.25	0	0	0.2	0.6	10	20.5
0.29	0	0	7.7	24.2	77.9	101.2
0.33	0.1	0.5	47.8	112.4	188.8	217.7
0.38	3.5	20.6	135.8	231.1	316.3	347.4
0.42	33.5	75.9	239	356.7	435.2	480.3
0.46	82.6	137.2	330.3	466.4	555.9	591.1
0.50	120.6	192.3	403.3	533.8	646.4	677.6
0.54	138.7	227.4	418.7	570.8	679.4	711.5
0.58	137.8	236.1	397.4	581.2	671.5	714.4
0.63	117.7	214.8	361.1	564.9	639.6	627.3
0.67	82.5	171.7	288.2	471.8	565.1	535.3
0.71	35.8	105.3	199.5	346.5	445.3	433.7
0.75	3.7	30.7	86.7	213.1	307.7	317.5
0.38	0	1.6	14.7	92.6	164.5	193.8
0.83	0	0	0.2	14.1	50.3	81.8
0.88	0	0	0	0	2.6	12.5
0.92	0	0	0	0	0	0.1
0.96	0	0	0	0	0	0

where a_i, b_i, d_i, c_i are coefficients of regression, m is month number, index i takes values *mod*, *max*, *min*.

As a result of data processing, the regression coefficients are given, which are listed in Table 3.

The type of dependencies (6) is shown in Fig. 2.

At the second stage, dependencies were developed describing the change in insolation during the day. The basis for developing a kind of regression dependence is the Gauss curve chosen

$$E_i = E_i^{ma} \exp\left(-\frac{(h - n_i)^2}{2r_i^2}\right), \tag{7}$$

where h – time during the day, in units of particles days, n, r – coefficients of regression.

The results of processing are shown in Table 4 and on Fig. 3

Table 2. Average monthly insolation data for Ukraine (continuation of Table 1)

Month	July	August	September	October	November	December
Time	7	8	9	10	11	12
0.00	0	0	0	0	0	0
0.04	0	0	0	0	0	0
0.08	0	0	0	0	0	0
0.13	0	0	0	0	0	0
0.17	0	0	0	0	0	0
0.21	0	0	0	0	0	0
0.25	8.2	1	0.2	0	0	0
0.29	58.5	33.6	7.4	0.1	0	0
0.33	147.3	137.1	71.5	16.6	0.7	0
0.38	246.4	265.4	186.8	84	19.1	2.7
0.42	347.3	385.3	312.3	163.9	62.1	31
0.46	453	495.7	425	247.8	113.4	74
0.50	548.1	597	500.7	306	149.3	108.9
0.54	605.9	636.5	557.2	339.1	166.7	130.9
0.58	644.8	619.6	545.3	335.6	169.2	126.1
0.63	640.7	580.3	508.9	294.2	141.4	102
0.67	592.1	504.1	412.5	216.2	98.2	64.1
0.71	523.2	390.4	292.9	119.1	36.6	18.8
0.75	432.2	259.2	146	24.9	2.5	0.4
0.38	315.4	133.1	37.5	1.5	0	0
0.83	195.6	31	1.5	0	0	0
0.88	113.6	0.7	0	0	0	0
0.92	79.9	0	0	0	0	0
0.96	47.4	0	0	0	0	0

Table 3. Obtained regression coefficients for dependence (5)

a	b	c	d	i
385.2	335.757	1.275	4.969	mod
384.2	355.724	1.151	4.687	max
349.8	333.199	1.206	4.885	min

Substituting (6) in (7), taking into account the data Tables 3 and 4 we obtain a fuzzy predictive model of insolation (Fig. 4). The estimation of the forecast error of the modal component of the fuzzy model on the MAPE indicator was 20.7%. The average degree of uncertainty was 4.15. Average degree of coincidence 0.48.

A similar approach is also applied to the construction of a fuzzy forecasting model of the daytime air temperature, which is included in the expression (4). The change in daytime temperatures during the year depends on Earth's orbiting around the Sun.

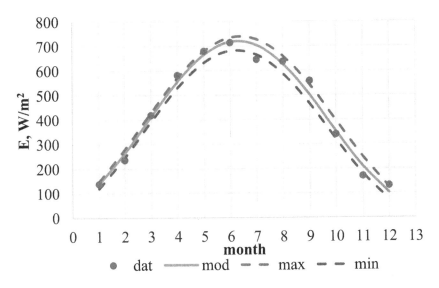

Fig. 2. Changing the maximum average insolation during the year

Table 4. Obtained regression coefficients for dependence (7)

n	r	i
0.562014	0.11798	*mod*
0.562014	0.124167	*max*
0.562014	0.105833	*min*

Therefore, the sinusoidal function of the species is also chosen as the basis for developing a fuzzy forecast model

$$t_i = a_{ti} + b_{ti} \sin(d_{ti}m - c_{ti}), \tag{8}$$

where a_{ti}, b_{ti}, d_{ti}, c_{ti} are coefficients of regression, m is month number, index i takes values *mod, max, min*.

As a result of data processing, regression coefficients are presented, which are given in Table 5.

The type of dependencies (8) is shown in Fig. 5.

For processing, data from researches on the temperature of air from the meteorological site GISMETEO.UA for 2016, 2017, 2018 years are used. The average degree of coincidence of dependencies (8) is 0.17, and the average degree of uncertainty does not exceed 0.8. These parameters correspond to MAPE = 21.1% when all experimental data arrive at the limit of the interval of fuzziness.

Since the variation in the power of a solar cell during a light depending on the temperature, lies within the uncertainty interval (Fig. 1), depending on the effect of the temperature on the power of the solar cell, there is sufficient dependence (8).

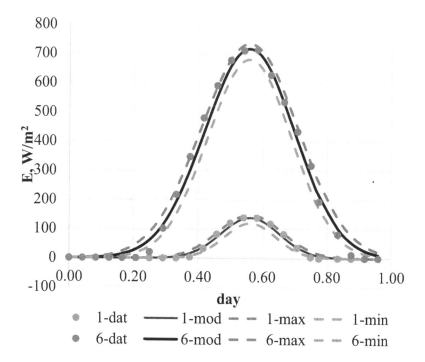

Fig. 3. Change of insolation during the middle of January (1) and June (6)

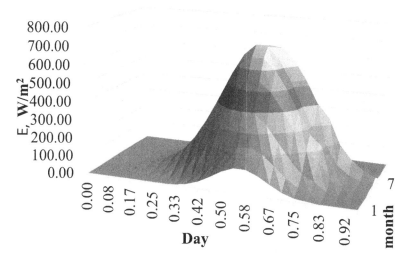

Fig. 4. Changing insolation during the year

Thus, according to the generalized operations Zadeh, the of dependence (3), which make up the forecast model (2), taking into account (7) and (8) will take the form:

Table 5. Obtained regression coefficients for dependence (8)

a_t	b_t	c_t	d_t	i
11.85	16.16	1.942	5.554	*mod*
10.77	15.98	2.187	5.874	*min*
13.61	16.02	1.832	5.369	*max*

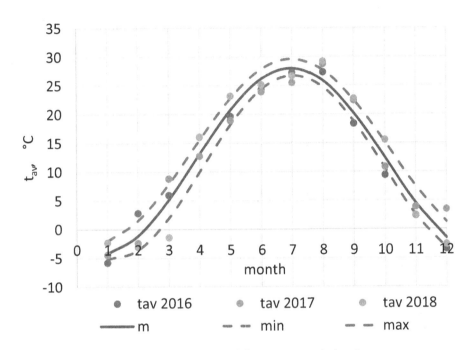

Fig. 5. Changing the average daily temperature during the year

$$P_{mod} = (0.0901E_{mod} + 0.0873t_{mod} - 0.00032E_{mod}t_{mod})S,$$
$$P_{min} = (0.0876E_{min} + 0.0499t_{min} - 0.00027E_{max}t_{max})S, \qquad (9)$$
$$P_{max} = (0.0918E_{max} + 0.1055t_{max} - 0.00035E_{min}t_{min})S.$$

The fuzzy predictive model (2), (9) can be used in the Mamdani fuzzy inference circuit. When forming the membership functions of fuzzy power levels of the SP, the rule of fuzzy conjunction should be used. For example, let us enter 3 power levels of the SP: low, medium, high (P_l, P_m, P_h) with the corresponding membership functions (μ_l, μ_m, μ_h). Then, taking into account the fact that the predicted capacity of the SP is also a fuzzy number, the resulting level membership functions will be in the form:

$$\mu_{P_l} = \min(\mu_l, \mu_P); \mu_{P_m} = min(\mu_m, \mu_P); _{P_h} = min(\mu_h, \mu_P).$$

Using of predictive models in fuzzy logic inference schemes Mamdani expands the capabilities of the decision-making system.

5 Conclusions

The fuzzy predictive model of solar power panel is developed for the decision-support system in the control of a hybrid power system, which in a certain way takes into account the uncertainty associated with both constructive and commutation influences, and the effects of predicted insolation and temperature.

The accuracy of the forecast largely depends on the degree of uncertainty of the forecast insolation and air temperature. Therefore, in the developed model it is possible to use both the results of direct measurements of insolation and temperature, as well as the results of their operational forecasting.

Using of predictive models allows you to anticipate abnormal situations, and also to use management criteria that are not directly related to the operational parameters of the system, for example, the economic efficiency criterion.

References

1. Perekrest, A., Shendryk, V., Shendryk, S.: Complex information and technical solutions for energy management of municipal energetics. In: Proceedings of SPIE - The International Society for Optical Engineering, vol. 10445 (2017)
2. Lazarou, S., Oikonomou, D.S., Ekonomou, L.: A platform for planning and evaluating distributed generation connected to the hellenic electric distribution grid. In: Proceedings of the 11th WSEAS International Conference on Circuits, Systems, Electronics, Control and Signal Processing, pp. 80–86 (2012)
3. Shulyma, O., Shendryk, V., Baranova, I., Marchenko, A.: The features of the smart microgrid as the object of information modeling. In: Dregvaite, G., Damasevicius, R. (eds.) ICIST 2014. CCIS, vol. 465, pp. 12–23. Springer, Cham (2014). https://doi.org/10.1007/978-3-319-11958-8_2
4. Pakštas, A., Shulyma, O., Shendryk, V.: On defining and assessing of the energy balance and operational logic within hybrid renewable energy systems. In: Dregvaite, G., Damasevicius, R. (eds.) ICIST 2016. CCIS, vol. 639, pp. 151–160. Springer, Cham (2016). https://doi.org/10.1007/978-3-319-46254-7_12
5. Hettiarachchi, D., et al.: Review of applications of fuzzy logic in multi-agent-based control system of AC-DC hybrid microgrid. IEEE Access 7, 1284–1299 (2019). https://doi.org/10.1109/access.2018.2884503
6. Nema, R.K., Agnihotri, G.: Computer simulation based study of photovoltaic cells/modules and their experimental verification. Int. J. Recent Trends Eng. 1(3), 151–156 (2009)
7. Znajdek, K.: Review of simulation models suitability for characterization of actual Si PV cells. In: XII International PhD Workshop OWD 2010, pp. 423–425

8. Tsuno, Y., Kurokawa K.: Temperature and irradiance dependence of the I-V curves of various kinds of solar cells. In: 15th International Photovoltaic Science and Engineering Conference, PSEC, pp. 422–423 (2005)
9. Bazilevski, A.B., Lukianenko, M.V.: Simulation of current-voltage characteristics of solar cells. Bulletin of the Siberian State Aerospace University named by Academician M.F. Reshetnyov, no. 4, pp. 63–66 (2005). (in Russian)
10. Gamarko, A.V.: Methods of numerical approximation of volt-ampere curves of a photovoltaic module. Renewable Energy **1**, 33–38 (2016). (in Ukrainian)
11. Tymchuk, S., Shendryk, S.: Mathematical model of solar battery for balance calculations in hybrid electrical grids. In: International Conference on Modern Electrical and Energy Systems (MEES 2017), Kremenchuk, Ukraine, pp. 204–207
12. Dotsenko, S.I., Shulyma, O.V.: Calculation of insolation capacity for predicting the production of electric energy by photovoltaic panels. Bulletin of the KHNTUA "Problems of energy supply and energy conservation in the agroindustrial complex of Ukraine", vol. 176, pp. 8–11 (2016). (in Ukrainian)
13. Kravchenko, E.V., Bondar, I.V.: Instrumental definition of insolation in the Odessa city. Power Eng. Econ. Technol. Ecol. **1**, 20–27 (2016). (in Ukrainian)

Modification of Parallelization of Modified Merge Sort Algorithm

Zbigniew Marszałek[1,2(✉)] and Giacomo Capizzi[1,2]

[1] Institute of Mathematics, Silesian University of Technology,
ul. Kaszubska 23, 44-100 Gliwice, Poland
`Zbigniew.Marszalek@polsl.pl`
[2] Electronics and Informatics Engineering (DIEEI),
University of Catania, 95125 Catania, Italy
`gcapizzi@diees.unict.it`

Abstract. An important issue in sorting large data sets in the NoSQL databases is the ability to sort process parallelism in order to accelerate the application. The work presents the use of the parallelized method for merging strings in a modified merge sort algorithm. The static tests of the proposed sort algorithm verify the stability and the theoretical time complexity of the method.

Keywords: Parallel algorithm · Data sorting · Data mining ·
Analysis of computer algorithms

1 Introduction

The architecture of modern computers enables the use of independently working processors to process information. Applications oriented to concurrent processing of information are designed under the architecture of multicore CPUs with multiple threads. As always, sorting algorithms play an important role in NoSQL databases, and in particular the algorithm for sorting by merging. The problem of parallelizing the sort algorithms was devoted to a number of works [1, 2], which presented different platform to the subject of parallel computation [3, 4]. The main problem in parallel computing is to add as many processors as possible, working independently, so as not to lead to a deadlock. This work shows the use of the merge method, in the parallelized strings to the modified merge sort algorithm [7]. Using a parallel method of merging strings has managed to reduce the complexity of sorting algorithm and confirm the effectiveness of the methods of statistical studies.

1.1 Related Work

The issue of parallel information processing is the subject of many works [11–13]. Specifically, the sort algorithms performed on multiple threads of modern CPUs were discussed in [14–16]. Sorting methods by merging strings are often used as an algorithm for organizing large data sets. Research into theoretical time complexities with static tests confirming the complexity of the method called fast sorting is in [5, 6, 8–10].

© Springer Nature Switzerland AG 2019
R. Damaševičius and G. Vasiljevienė (Eds.): ICIST 2019, CCIS 1078, pp. 428–440, 2019.
https://doi.org/10.1007/978-3-030-30275-7_33

In article [7] describes the parallelized modified sort algorithm by merging with time complexity O (n) with a time constant equal to two. This algorithm is uneven distribution of efficiently running processors. In the final step of sorting methods merge strings makes only one processor. In this paper uses a parallelized algorithm merge strings [12] and managed to reduce the complexity of the proposed time of the algorithm. statistical studies on a computer in a multiprocessor architecture confirm the effectiveness of the use of more processors in the sort method.

A Parallel Random Access Machine (PRAM) machine is used to research the computational complexity of parallel algorithms. The theoretical PRAM machine is composed of n processors $P_i, i = 0, \ldots, n - 1$ and shared memory Fig. 1. The algorithm analysis in this work will be done in the Concurrent Read Exclusive Write PRAM model to read the memory of all the processor and to write in the same cell only by one of the processors.

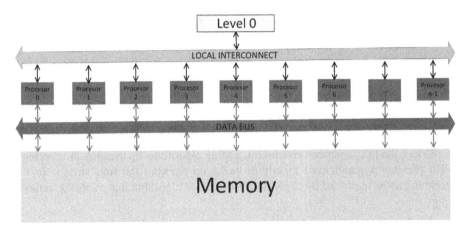

Fig. 1. Parallel Random Access Machine

2 The Use of Parallel Algorithms in Large Databases

NoSQL databases store information in different types of data that are valid for statistical purposes to compile the reports you need or to select information for further processing. Applications running in databases must be designed to be as optimal as possible to operate in real time. An important role here is the ability to use multiprocess architecture of computers and to distribute tasks appropriately. Sorting algorithms must be executed as many threads as possible, so that they provide a fast time to search for information. Immigration for processing is taken in smaller blocks so that parallel computations can be performed Fig. 2.

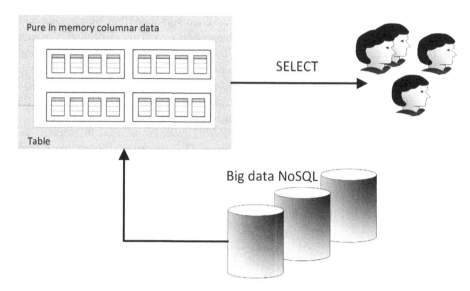

Fig. 2. In memory columnar data is fragmented into smaller units to enable parallelization

3 Parallel Modified Merge Sort Algorithm

To organize information in the databases are often used algorithm is the merge sort. In the work of the [12] describes concurrent, sorting algorithms by merging three strings. In [7] presents a parallelized algorithm based on merging the four strings. In the algorithm can be improved by applying a parallelized algorithm that merges a numeric strings.

3.1 Parallel Algorithm for Merging Two Strings

Method on input receives two sorted in previous step sequences $x_0 \leq x_1 \leq \cdots \leq x_{t-1}$ and $y_0 \leq y_1 \leq \cdots \leq y_{t-1}$. It returns sorted sequence $z_0 \leq z_1 \leq \cdots \leq z_{2t-1}$. We merge two sequences X and Y into one sequence Z with using two processor P_0 and P_1. The first processor begins the comparison elements from the begging of the string X and Y, an element x_0 of y_0 inserting the element z_0 and ends with a comparison after insertion of the element into the sequence Z under the index $\lfloor (2t-1)/2 \rfloor$. The processor P_0 executes the insertion of the element $z_0, \ldots, z_{\lfloor (2t-1)/2 \rfloor}$. The second processor begins the comparison elements from the end of the string X and Y, an element x_{t-1} of y_{t-1} inserting the element z_{2t-1} and ends with a comparison after insertion of the element into the sequence Z under the index $\lfloor (2t-1)/2 \rfloor + 1$. The processor P_1 executes the insertion of the element $z_{2t-1}, \ldots, z_{\lfloor (2t-1)/2 \rfloor + 1}$. For example, a process of merging two strings $x = [5, 9]$ and $y = [1, 7]$ by the P_0 and P_1 processors into an array z. In the first step, the P_0-processor compares the first elements of the x and y string and inserts the smaller element into the z array. In the next step, the consecutive x and y elements are compared and the smaller element is inserted into the array z Fig. 3.

Processor 0

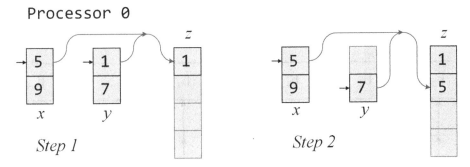

Fig. 3. Process of merging strings by processor P_0.

In the first step, the P_1-processor compares the past x and y elements and inserts the largest element into the z array. In the next step, the consecutive x and y elements are compared and the largest element is inserted into the z array Fig. 4.

Processor 1

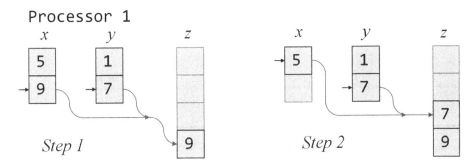

Fig. 4. Process of merging strings by processor P_1.

Note that each of the processors running independently when merging two strings of t elements performs no more comparisons than t. Thus, the time complexity of the parallel merge algorithm of two strings of t elements is $O(t)$.

3.2   Parallel Merge Sort Algorithm

Let's present the modifications to the modified sorting method by merging [7] by presenting the parallelized string merge algorithm. The sorting algorithm at first merges one-element strings into a working array. At this stage, n processors can be used independently, where n is the dimension of the Fig. 5 sort job.

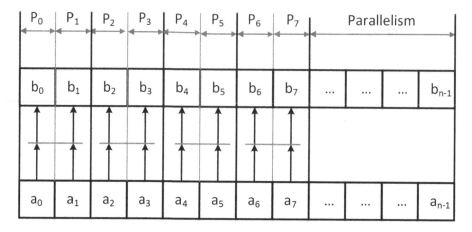

Fig. 5. Parallel merging of strings into the working array

The sorting algorithm then merges the two-element strings stored in the work array into input array Fig. 6. At this stage of the merge can be used up to $n/2$ independently operating processors.

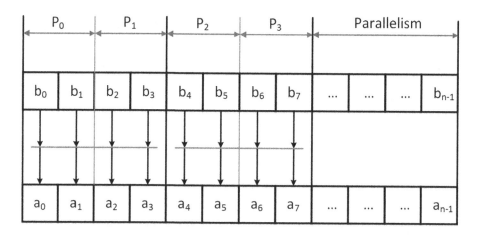

Fig. 6. Parallel merging of strings from the working array

In each step the sort algorithm performs the merge four strings, and the sort result is saved in the input array Fig. 7.

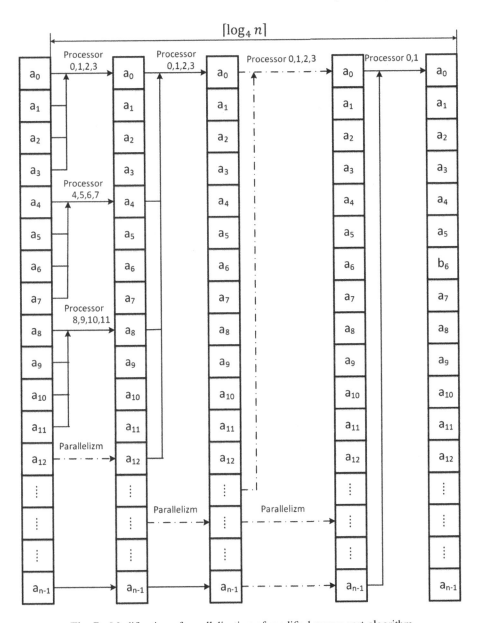

Fig. 7. Modification of parallelization of modified merge sort algorithm

Theorem. The time complexity of the modified parallel sorting algorithm by merging using n independently running processors are as follows:

$$T_{max} = n - \frac{1}{3} \tag{1}$$

Proof. The proof will be limited to $n = 4^k$, $k = 1, 2, \ldots$.

Note that merge two strings t element using a parallelized algorithm that merges sorted strings by use of two independently working threads we can perform using no more than t comparisons of the merged elements strings.

In each step $t = 1, \ldots, k$, the sorting algorithm performs the merging of the four strings. First, it merges each two strings of length 4^{t-1} into a working array by using independently-working thread processors. It then merges all $2 \cdot 4^{t-1}$ length string pairs from the work array into the input array. Summing up the number of simultaneous comparisons made by independently working threads in each step we get:

$$4^{t-1} + 2 \cdot 4^{t-1} \tag{2}$$

Summing up the comparisons made by independently working CPU threads we get:

$$\sum_{t=1}^{k} (4^{t-1} + 2 \cdot 4^{t-1}) = 3 \cdot \sum_{t=1}^{k} 4^{t-1}$$
$$= 3(1 + 4 + \ldots + 4^{k-1}) = 3 \cdot \left(\frac{4^k - 1}{3} \right) \tag{3}$$
$$= n - \frac{1}{3}$$

which was to prove.

Statistical test of stability of the proposed method of sorting have been made in Visual Studio Ultimate 2015 in C#. Programmable algorithm was class to create concurrent programs, in which there is a parallel loop. Iterator parallel loop indexes sequentially allocated threads available on sort algorithm and indexes the threads were further merged numbers of pairs of strings. Synchronization in each step is followed by sorting after merging all the pairs of strings.

3.3   Statistical Study of Modification of Parallel Sorting Methods

Benchmark For the statistical tests on the performance of this parallel method have been used measures similar to other works []. The arithmetic mean of all of the observed measures for CPU clock, and sorting time can help to estimate performance. Statistically, this measure is equal to the mean value:

$$\bar{x} = \frac{1}{n} \sum_{i=1}^{n} x_i, \tag{4}$$

the standard deviation is defined by the formula:

$$\sigma = \sqrt{\frac{\sum_{i=1}^{n} (x_i - \bar{x})^2}{n - 1}}, \tag{5}$$

where n is the number of measurements $x_1, x_1, \ldots, x_n$, $\bar{x}$ is the arithmetic mean of the sample. The analysis for sorting time and CPU clock was carried out in 100 benchmark tests for each of the fixed dimensions on the input. The algorithm's stability in a statistical sense is best described on the basis of the coefficient of variation. The coefficient of variation is a measure that allows the determination of the value of diversity in the research. It is determined by the formula:

$$V = \frac{\sigma}{\bar{x}}, \tag{6}$$

where we use arithmetic mean (3) and standard deviation (4). The coefficient of variation reflects the stability of the method in a statistical sense. The study was performed on a collection of data containing from 100 elements up to 100 million elements, increasing the number of elements ten times each new comparison. The results are presented in tables and figures below (Tables 1, 2 and Figs. 8, 9).

Table 1. The result of the statistical study in [ms].

Elements	Processors			
	One	Two	Four	Eight
100	1	1	1	1
1 000	1	1	1	1
10 000	8	6	4	3
100 000	66	36	25	19
1 000 000	663	342	236	186
10 000 000	7562	3871	2601	2067
100 000 000	85478	42947	28619	22080

Table 2. The result of the statistical study in [ti].

Elements	Processors			
	One	Two	Four	Eight
100	289	263	224	197
1 000	1053	894	732	605
10 000	12468	6628	5278	4233
100 000	103119	50531	40286	31346
1 000 000	1032737	511411	366771	265096
10 000 000	11785832	5800525	3898912	2688487
100 000 000	133229349	65615329	44606736	29208354

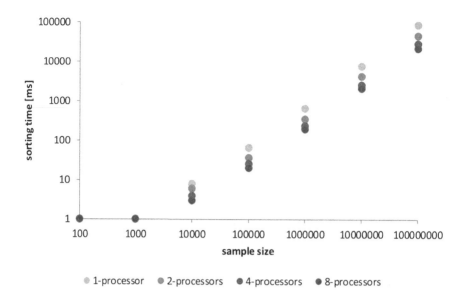

Fig. 8. Graph of statistical study in [ms]

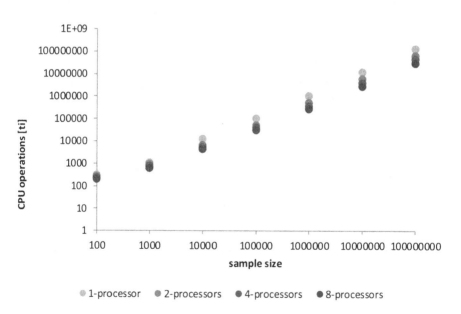

Fig. 9. Graph of statistical study in [ti]

The presented parallel sorting algorithm by merging retains stability for large dimensions of the task, which illustrates the coefficients of variation in Tables 3 and 4. Note that the parallelized string-merging algorithm has a predetermined minimum and maximum number of comparisons of the merged string elements. Hence, a modified parallel sort method by merging does not contain critical string settings that increase or decrease the time that the algorithm is running. Statistical experiments are supposed to demonstrate how the method behaves in medium time. Studies show that the average sorting time is half the maximum and minimum time of the algorithm.

Table 3. The coefficients of variation [ms]

Elements	Processors			
	One	Two	Four	Eight
100	0.506312	0.492301	0.410862	0.477310
1 000	0.415157	0.425820	0.342016	0.373089
10 000	0.419490	0.187261	0.183391	0.351877
100 000	0.183523	0,104972	0.130023	0.379974
1 000 000	0.116204	0.119204	0.148857	0.096052
10 000 000	0.114139	0.127947	0.103173	0.094150
100 000 000	0.118620	0.124269	0.104640	0.072412

Table 4. Coefficients of variation [ti].

Elements	Processors			
	One	Two	Four	Eight
100	0.466004	0.490012	0.381016	0.468140
1 000	0.391603	0.419360	0.323524	0.361945
10 000	0.476100	0.170455	0.171317	0.338931
100 000	0.185090	0.109342	0,123435	0.378947
1 000 000	0.116506	0.118780	0.149649	0.095501
10 000 000	0.114127	0.127914	0.103136	0.096151
100 000 000	0.118619	0.124272	0.104637	0.072415

3.4   Compression and Analyses of Sorting Time

The analysis of the duration of the proposed method was based on a percentage reduction in multi-processor uptime compared to the computation time of a single processor. Figures 10 and 11 make it more efficient to use multiple processors in a sorting method.

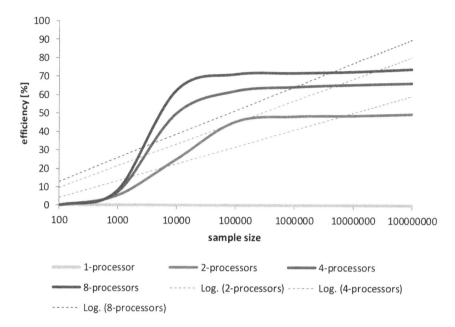

Fig. 10. Efficient use of multiple processors in the sorting algorithm [ms].

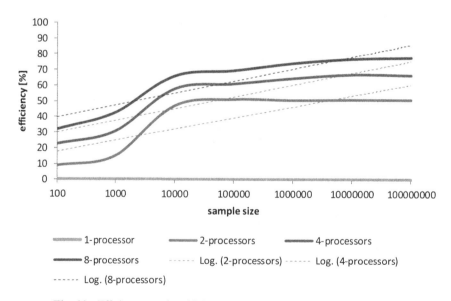

Fig. 11. Efficient use of multiple processors in the sorting algorithm [ti].

Let's leave out comparing the speed of the presented method using multiple processors in relation to other methods. As a baseline comparison in relation to other methods assume that the duration of the trigeminal methods heapsort. Figure 12 shows the efficiency of the use of multiple processors in the process of sorting large data sets presented method.

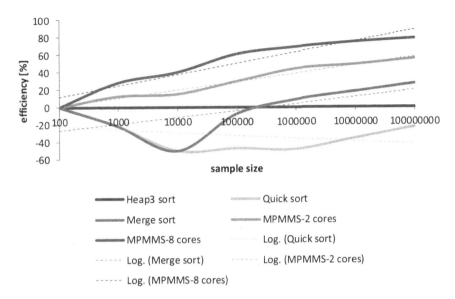

Fig. 12. Comparison of the efficiency of the presented methods in relation to other methods [ms].

The results obtained from sorting times in experimental studies show the high effectiveness of the proposed method of parallelization of the modified sorting algorithm by merging. This is due to the fact that only one processor can participate when using the traditional merge algorithm in the last sorting step. Allowing the second processor to be added shortens the sorting algorithm time.

4   Final Remarks

The work describes a new version of the parallel sort algorithm by merging. This method allows you to use more processors in the sorting process and shorten the time of the algorithm. The method is particularly efficient when you use a small number of processors. Experimental research confirms the theoretical complexity and stability of the method. The proposed version of the parallel sorting method by merging can find practical use in sorting large datasets in NoSQL databases.

Acknowledgement. The project is financed by the Polish National Agency for Academic Exchange no PPI/APM/2018/1/00004/U/001.

References

1. Shi, H., Schaeffer, J.: Parallel sorting by regular sampling. J. Parallel Distrib. Comput. **14**(4), 361–372 (1992)
2. Preparata, F.P.: New parallel-sorting schemes. IEEE Trans. Comput. **7**, 669–673 (1978)
3. Rajasekaran, S., Reif, J.H.: Optimal and sublogarithmic time randomized parallel sorting algorithms. SIAM J. Comput. **18**(3), 594–607 (1989)
4. Hirschberg, D.S.: Fast parallel sorting algorithms. Commun. ACM **21**(8), 657–661 (1978)
5. Włodarczyk-Sielicka, M., Wawrzyniak, N.: Problem of bathymetric big data interpolation for inland mobile navigation system. In: Damaševičius, R., Mikašytė, V. (eds.) ICIST 2017. CCIS, vol. 756, pp. 611–621. Springer, Cham (2017). https://doi.org/10.1007/978-3-319-67642-5_51
6. Wlodarczyk-Sielicka, M., Stateczny, A.: General concept of reduction process for big data obtained by interferometric methods. In: 2017 18th International Radar Symposium (IRS), pp. 1–10. IEEE (2017)
7. Marszałek, Z.: Parallelization of modified merge sort algorithm. Symmetry **9**(9), 176 (2017)
8. Gabryel, M.: A bag-of-features algorithm for applications using a NoSQL database. In: Dregvaite, G., Damasevicius, R. (eds.) ICIST 2016. CCIS, vol. 639, pp. 332–343. Springer, Cham (2016). https://doi.org/10.1007/978-3-319-46254-7_26
9. Marszałek, Z.: Performance tests on merge sort and recursive merge sort for big data processing. Tech. Sci. **21**(1), 19–35 (2018)
10. Marszałek, Z.: Novel recursive fast sort algorithm. In: Dregvaite, G., Damasevicius, R. (eds.) ICIST 2016. CCIS, vol. 639, pp. 344–355. Springer, Cham (2016). https://doi.org/10.1007/978-3-319-46254-7_27
11. Marszałek, Z.: Parallelization of fast sort algorithm. In: Damaševičius, R., Mikašytė, V. (eds.) ICIST 2017. CCIS, vol. 756, pp. 408–421. Springer, Cham (2017). https://doi.org/10.1007/978-3-319-67642-5_34
12. Marszałek, Z.: Modification of parallelization for fast sort algorithm. In: Damaševičius, R., Vasiljevienė, G. (eds.) ICIST 2018. CCIS, vol. 920, pp. 270–278. Springer, Cham (2018). https://doi.org/10.1007/978-3-319-99972-2_21
13. Lucas, K.T., Jana, P.K.: An efficient parallel sorting algorithm on OTIS mesh of trees. In: 2009 IEEE International Advance Computing Conference, pp. 175–180. IEEE, March 2009
14. Satish, N., Harris, M., Garland, M.: Designing efficient sorting algorithms for manycore GPUs. In: 2009 IEEE International Symposium on Parallel & Distributed Processing, pp. 1–10. IEEE, May 2009
15. Durad, M.H., Akhtar, M.N.: Performance analysis of parallel sorting algorithms using MPI. In: 2014 12th International Conference on Frontiers of Information Technology, pp. 202–207. IEEE, December 2014
16. Marszałek, Z., Woźniak, M., Połap, D.: Fully flexible parallel merge sort for multicore architectures. Complexity **2018** (2018)

Missing Values Absorption
Based on Homogenous Granulation

Piotr Artiemjew[(✉)] and Krzysztof Ropiak

Faculty of Mathematics and Computer Science,
University of Warmia and Mazury in Olsztyn, Olsztyn, Poland
{artem,kropiak}@matman.uwm.edu.pl

Abstract. In the recent works we have developed new methods of granulation - homogenous variants - in the family of techniques founded by Lech Polkowski. The level of approximation of decision systems for these methods is not the highest among previously developed algorithms, but the basic advantage is its dynamic behaviour - there is no need to estimate any parameters for this methods. Granulation level is dependent on the indiscernibility ratio of decision classes. Additionally to the fact that our new methods found successful application in the context of data approximation is their utility in ensemble models. We have developed a novel technique - ensemble of random granular reflections. In this paper we continue the series of works and we have carried out experiments to check effectiveness of our new granulation technique in the context of missing values absorption.

Keywords: Homogenous granulation · Rough sets ·
Decision systems · Classification · Missing values

1 Introduction

The basic theoretical works, which are the background for our new method can be found in [6,7] and later in [8]. The paper is continuation of a series of works, which are a consequence of developing a new granulation technique by us - homogenous granulation - see [2]. This is significantly different technique in comparison with our previously developed, because there is no need to estimate the granulation parameters. Granulation radii are set in automatic way depending on the indiscernibility level of decision classes. Following the basic method we have created its epsilon variant [3] for numerical data. Except of using in approximation of decision systems our new method finds application in a novel ensemble model - Ensemble of granular reflections - see [1]. In this particular work we carried out preliminary experiments to check effectiveness of our new technique in the context of possible application to missing values absorption. Four strategies of missing values absorption were considered - A, B, C and D strategy. Initial experiments, in which we use selected strategies (A - D) are available in Polkowski and Artiemjew [5,9] - what was extensively checked on data from UCI Repository in [8]. We begin with a details of strategies chosen by us.

© Springer Nature Switzerland AG 2019
R. Damaševičius and G. Vasiljevienė (Eds.): ICIST 2019, CCIS 1078, pp. 441–450, 2019.
https://doi.org/10.1007/978-3-030-30275-7_34

1.1 A Set of Basic Strategies

We consider missing values in four various cases,

1. *Strategy A: during building granules* $* = $ *don't care, in repairing of not absorbed values* $*, * = $ *don't care.*
2. *Strategy B: during building granules* $* = $ *don't care, in repairing of not absorbed values* $*, * = *.$
3. *Strategy C: during building granules* $* = *$, *in repairing of not absorbed values* $*, * = $ *don't care.*
4. *Strategy D: during building granules* $* = *$, *in repairing of not absorbed values* $*, * = *.$

Considering granulation process - in case of A and B strategy, stars are treated as all possible values. For C and D strategy stars are treated as new values in the system. Granules in the context of our strategies may be defined as follows:

In case of $* = $ ***don't care*** **- granule building phase is as follows:** Considering $i - th$ training data set TRN_i - and the phase of granulation, the granules can be defined as:

$$g_{r_{gran}}^{cd,*=don't\ care}(u) = \{v \in TRN_i : \frac{|IND^{*=don't\ care}(u,v)|}{|A|} \leq r_{gran}\ AND\ d(u) = d(v)\},$$

where

$$IND^{*=don't\ care}(u,v) = \{a \in A : a(u) = a(v)\ OR\ a(u) = *\ OR\ a(v) = *\}.$$

In Case of $* = *$ **- granule building phase is as follows:** Granules used in C and D strategies have the form:

$$g_{r_{gran}}^{cd,*=*}(u) = \{v \in TRN_i : \frac{|IND^{*=*}(u,v)|}{|A|} \leq r_{gran}\ AND\ d(u) = d(v)\},$$

where

$$IND^{*=*}(u,v) = \{a \in A : a(u) = a(v)\}.$$

In case of $* = $ ***don't care*** **in the repairing phase:** In case of A and C strategies, in order to repair objects containing missing values after granulation, we immerse objects with stars on specific positions j into original disturbed training set. We fill the value for the star by means of majority voting on non missing values of the attribute j.

In case of the strategy A, the granule around the disturbed object $MV(g_{r_{gran}}^{cd,*=don't\ care}(u))$ can be defined as follows,

$$if\ a_j(MV(g_{r_{gran}}^{cd,*=don't\ care}(u))) = *,$$

then the missing value could be repaired by the granule,

$$g_{r_{gran},a_j}^{cd,*=don't\ care}(MV(g_{r_{gran}}^{cd,*=don't\ care}(u))) =$$

$$\{v \in TRN_i : \frac{|IND_{a_j}^{*=don't\ care}(MV(g_{r_{gran}}^{cd,*=don't\ care}(u)),v)|}{|A|}$$

$$\leq r_{gran}\ AND\ d(MV(g_{r_{gran}}^{cd,*=don't\ care}(u))) = d(v)\},$$

where

$$IND_{a_j}^{*=don't\ care}(MV(g_{r_{gran}}^{cd,*=don't\ care}(u)),v) =$$

$$\{a \in A : (a(MV(g_{r_{gran}}^{cd,*=don't\ care}(u))) = a(v)$$

$$OR\ a(MV(g_{r_{gran}}^{cd,*=don't\ care}(u))) = *\ OR\ a(v) = *)\ AND\ a_j(v)! = *\}.$$

In case of the strategy C, the granule around the disturbed object $MV(g_{r_{gran}}^{cd,*=*}(u))$ can be defined as follows,

$$if\ a_j(MV(g_{r_{gran}}^{cd,*=*}(u))) = *,$$

then the missing value could be repaired by the granule,

$$g_{r_{gran},a_j}^{cd,*=don't\ care}(MV(g_{r_{gran}}^{cd,*=*}(u))) =$$

$$\{v \in TRN_i : \frac{|IND_{a_j}^{*=don't\ care}(MV(g_{r_{gran}}^{cd,*=*}(u)),v)|}{|A|}$$

$$\leq r_{gran}\ AND\ d(MV(g_{r_{gran}}^{cd,*=*}(u))) = d(v)\},$$

where

$$IND_{a_j}^{*=don't\ care}(MV(g_{r_{gran}}^{cd,*=*}(u)),v) =$$

$$\{a \in A : (a(MV(g_{r_{gran}}^{cd,*=*}(u))) = a(v)$$

$$OR\ a(MV(g_{r_{gran}}^{cd,*=*}(u))) = *\ OR\ a(v) = *)\ AND\ a_j(v)! = *\}.$$

In case of $* = *$ in reparing phase: As above, also in case of B and D strategies, in order to repair objects containing missing values after granulation, we immerse objects with stars on specific positions j into original disturbed training data set. We fill the star based on majority voting from non missing values of attribute number j.

In case of the strategy B, the granule around the disturbed object $MV(g_{r_{gran}}^{cd,*=don't\ care}(u))$ can be defined as follows,

$$g_{r_{gran},a_j}^{cd,*=*}(MV(g_{r_{gran}}^{cd,*=don't\ care}(u))) =$$

$$\{v \in TRN_i : \frac{|IND_{a_j}^{*=*}(MV(g_{r_{gran}}^{cd,*=don't\ care}(u)),v)|}{|A|}$$

$$\leq r_{gran}\ AND\ d(MV(g_{r_{gran}}^{cd,*=don't\ care}(u))) = d(v)\},$$

where

$$IND_{a_j}^{*=*}(MV(g_{r_{gran}}^{cd,*=don't\ care}(u)),v)$$

$$= \{a \in A : a(MV(g_{r_{gran}}^{cd,*=don't\ care}(u))) = a(v)\ AND\ a_j(v)! = *\}.$$

In case of the strategy D, the granule around the disturbed object $MV(g_{r_{gran}}^{cd,*=*}(u))$ can be defined as follows,

$$g_{r_{gran},a_j}^{cd,*=*}(MV(g_{r_{gran}}^{cd,*=*}(u))) =$$

$$\{v \in TRN_i : \frac{|IND_{a_j}^{*=*}(MV(g_{r_{gran}}^{cd,*=*}(u)),v)|}{|A|}$$

$$\leq r_{gran}\ AND\ d(MV(g_{r_{gran}}^{cd,*=*}(u))) = d(v)\},$$

where

$$IND_{a_j}^{*=*}(MV(g_{r_{gran}}^{cd,*=*}(u)),v)$$

$$= \{a \in A : a(MV(g_{r_{gran}}^{cd,*=*}(u))) = a(v)\ AND\ a_j(v)! = *\}.$$

2   Homogenous Granulation in $* = *$ and $* = don't\ Care$ Cases

Considering previously defined $IND^{*=don't\ care}(u,v)$, in case of $* = don't\ care$ the granules are formed as follows,

$$g_{r_u}^{homogenous,*=don't\ care} = \{v \in U : |g_{r_u}^{cd,*=don't\ care}| - |g_{r_u}^{*=don't\ care}| == 0,$$

$$for\ minimal\ r_u\ fulfills\ the\ equation\}$$

where

$$g_{r_u}^{cd,*=don't\ care} = \{v \in U : \frac{IND^{*=don't\ care}(u,v)}{|A|} \leq r_u\ AND\ d(u) == d(v)\}$$

and

$$g_{r_u}^{*=don't\ care} = \{v \in U : \frac{IND^{*=don't\ care}(u,v)}{|A|} \leq r_u\}$$

$$r_u = \{\frac{0}{|A|}, \frac{1}{|A|}, ..., \frac{|A|}{|A|}\}$$

for $* = *$ variant and previously defined $IND^{*=*}(u,v)$ we have:

$$g_{r_u}^{homogenous,*=*} = \{v \in U : |g_{r_u}^{cd,*=*}| - |g_{r_u}^{*=*}| == 0,$$

$$for\ minimal\ r_u\ fulfills\ the\ equation\}$$

where

$$g_{r_u}^{cd,*=*} = \{v \in U : \frac{IND^{*=*}(u,v)}{|A|} \leq r_u\ AND\ d(u) == d(v)\}$$

and

$$g_{r_u}^{*=*} = \{v \in U : \frac{IND^{*=*}(u,v)}{|A|} \leq r_u\}$$

$$r_u = \{\frac{0}{|A|}, \frac{1}{|A|}, ..., \frac{|A|}{|A|}\}$$

3 The Experimental Session - Procedures and Model Settings

In the section we have described the experimental part with results presentation. We have checked the effectiveness of out techniques on artificially damaged (filled with 10% of missing values) selected data from UCI Repository [11].

3.1 Pseudo-code of Experiments Design

(i) We uploaded selected data set,
(ii) Data was split according to Cross Validation 5 model,
(iii) Training decision systems $TRN_i^{complete}$ are granulated with use of the selected method,
(iv) The TST_i are classified using set $TRN_i^{complete}$ by kNN classifier (its the nil result),
(v) $TRN_i^{complete}$ is filled with ten percent of randomly located stars,
(vi) TRN_i is treated by selected missing values handling strategy - A, B, C or D in granulation process.
(vii) The TST_i systems are classified by repaired granular systems using kNN classifier,
(viii) The final result is an average from all five tests.

The above CV5 procedure is repeated 5 times, and our result is the average value from all tests.

3.2 The Results Evaluation

To evaluate our results we have proposed to compute bias of accuracy from $5 \times$ CV-5, based on the formula,

$$AccBias = \frac{\sum_{i=1}^{5}(max(acc_1^{CV5}, acc_2^{CV5}, ..., acc_5^{CV5}) - acc_i^{CV5})}{5}, \quad (1)$$

where

$$Acc = \frac{\sum_{i=1}^{5} acc_i^{CV5}}{5}.$$

As a reference classifier we use kNN in decision classes, where a class is winning if the summary distance of k-nearest objects from the class is the smallest. Parameter k is estimated on the sample of data based on Cross Validation five method.

We use $k = 5$ for Australian Credit data set and $k = 3$ for Pima Indians Diabetes.

3.3 The Results Discussion

The results for classic parameterized concept-dependent granulation are in Tables 1 and 2. For homogenous granulation are in Tables 3 and 4. As we previously checked in [8], granulation is effective in missing values absorbtion. For all examined techniques the quality of classification is preserved on damaged data in comparison with original one - without missing values. In case of granulation techniques we have additional reduction in object numbers, even up to 80 percent of original training data size for concept dependent method. Seeing the results in [8] - the effectiveness of methods and their behavior depends strictly on the type of data set. For instance for typical data sets with high diversity of attribute values, like Australian Credit, Pima Indians Diabetes, the result is predictable. And in case of A and B strategies approximation is faster for lower values of granulation radii, its because for $* = don't\ care$ the granules contain more objects. In case of $* = *$, the approximation is similar to the nil result, but is slightly slower, because the stars could increase diversity of the data, and the granules could contain a smaller number of objects which in consequence gives a larger number of granules in coverings.

The interpretation of missing values absorption for homogenous granulation is significantly different - see Tables 3 and 4. In case of this technique, damage of the data increase the number of granules in coverings, the granules became smaller because the indiscernibility level in decision classes is lowering. It is higher probability to find the objects, which brake homogeneity of granules. In case of A and B strategies, the granules are smaller than for C and D, thus in the first one we have bigger granular decision systems.

The methods work in a stable way and results are fully comparable with nil results. The most advantage of homogenous granulation is its single run behaviour, where granulation radius is fixed individually (automatically) for each granule - depends on the indiscernibility level in each decision class around central objects of granules.

Table 1. Missing values absorption based on **Concept dependent granulation**; 5 × CV-5; A, B, C, D strategies vs complete data classification; **Australian Credit**; **10% of missing values**; r_{gran} = Granulation radius; nil = result for data without missing values; Acc = Accuracy of classification; $AccBias$ = Accuracy bias defined based on equation efAcccBiasEquation; $GranSize$ = The size of data set after granulation in the fixed r

r_{gran}	Acc					AccBias				
	nil	A	B	C	D	nil	A	B	C	D
0	0.772	0.77	0.77	0.77	0.77	0.009	0.006	0.006	0.006	0.006
0.0714286	0.772	0.77	0.77	0.772	0.772	0.01	0.006	0.006	0.008	0.008
0.142857	0.77	0.77	0.771	0.773	0.773	0.006	0.006	0.007	0.011	0.011
0.214286	0.781	0.766	0.767	0.786	0.785	0.008	0.01	0.012	0.02	0.018
0.285714	0.799	0.775	0.777	0.811	0.81	0.014	0.012	0.007	0.015	0.009
0.357143	0.82	0.786	0.786	0.826	0.832	0.01	0.014	0.014	0.015	0.004
0.428571	0.841	0.806	0.8	0.838	0.838	0.007	0.032	0.012	0.009	0.002
0.5	0.838	0.817	0.818	0.84	0.847	0.005	0.012	0.012	0.008	0.004
0.571429	0.839	0.828	0.826	0.847	0.844	0.006	0.019	0.021	0.007	0.01
0.642857	0.848	0.832	0.826	0.847	0.839	0.007	0.007	0.017	0.007	0.008
0.714286	0.853	0.833	0.841	0.844	0.843	0.009	0.019	0.007	0.011	0.012
0.785714	0.857	0.843	0.843	0.847	0.843	0.007	0.01	0.012	0.008	0.014
0.857143	0.86	0.838	0.838	0.845	0.844	0.007	0.01	0.014	0.01	0.008
0.928571	0.862	0.842	0.841	0.844	0.843	0.005	0.005	0.017	0.014	0.013
1	0.861	0.843	0.843	0.843	0.843	0.004	0.014	0.013	0.014	0.014

r_{gran}	GranSize				
	nil	A	B	C	D
0	2	2	2	2	2
0.0714286	2.32	2	2	3	2.96
0.142857	3.24	2.16	2.16	4.64	4.68
0.214286	5.16	2.52	2.52	8.68	8.4
0.285714	8.4	4.04	3.84	16.2	16.32
0.357143	16.08	7.12	6.96	32.44	31.92
0.428571	32	10.08	9.76	72.04	72.24
0.5	70.8	18.28	18	150.04	149.6
0.571429	156.6	34.6	34.72	286.24	284.8
0.642857	318.12	73.44	73.32	438.08	438.28
0.714286	467.6	164.2	164.44	524.64	525.08
0.785714	536.12	325.92	328.04	547	546.96
0.857143	547.16	476.76	476.76	551.28	551.28
0.928571	548.84	537.8	537.36	551.88	551.88
1	552	550.84	550.8	552	552

Table 2. Missing values absorption based on **Concept dependent granulation**; 5 × CV-5; A, B, C, D strategies vs complete data classification; **Pima Indians Diabetes**; Concept dependent granulation; **10% of missing values**; r_{gran} = Granulation radius; nil = result for data without missing values; Acc = Accuracy of classification; $AccBias$ = Accuracy bias defined based on equation efAcccBiasEquation; $GranSize$ = The size of data set after granulation in the fixed r

	Acc					AccBias				
r_{gran}	nil	A	B	C	D	nil	A	B	C	D
0	0.605	0.609	0.609	0.609	0.609	0.009	0.012	0.012	0.012	0.012
0.125	0.608	0.615	0.61	0.609	0.617	0.006	0.009	0.027	0.011	0.019
0.25	0.632	0.624	0.61	0.634	0.62	0.013	0.013	0.015	0.018	0.024
0.375	0.639	0.6	0.602	0.636	0.641	0.009	0.018	0.017	0.02	0.015
0.5	0.649	0.602	0.618	0.647	0.648	0.017	0.02	0.021	0.018	0.02
0.625	0.647	0.614	0.61	0.645	0.646	0.009	0.013	0.026	0.019	0.019
0.75	0.648	0.637	0.639	0.647	0.647	0.009	0.012	0.013	0.029	0.023
0.875	0.648	0.639	0.645	0.65	0.647	0.009	0.015	0.017	0.021	0.023
1	0.648	0.647	0.647	0.647	0.647	0.009	0.023	0.023	0.023	0.023

	GranSize				
r_{gran}	nil	A	B	C	D
0	2	2	2	2	2
0.125	35.2	3.16	3.2	33.16	31.68
0.25	155.88	8.96	8.8	145.96	145.44
0.375	365.52	29.04	26.72	364.84	363.6
0.5	540.28	87	84.24	546.72	546.48
0.625	609.72	282.04	282	609.24	609.16
0.75	614.4	491.2	488.04	614.24	614.24
0.875	614.4	593.64	593.6	614.4	614.4
1	614.4	613.64	613.6	614.4	614.4

Table 3. Missing values absorption based on **Homogenous granulation**; 5 × CV-5; A, B, C, D strategies vs complete data classification; **Australian Credit**; Homogenous granulation; **10% of missing values**; r_{gran} = Granulation radius; nil = result for data without missing values; Acc = Accuracy of classification; $AccBias$ = Accuracy bias defined based on equation efAcccBiasEquation; $GranSize$ = The size of data set after granulation in the fixed r

Acc					AccBias				
nil	A	B	C	D	nil	A	B	C	D
0.843	0.841	0.843	0.838	0.841	0.012	0.008	0.015	0.021	0.014

GranSize				
nil	A	B	C	D
283.64	426.4	424.16	311.48	313.08

Table 4. Missing values absorption based on **Homogenous granulation**; 5 × CV-5; A, B, C, D strategies vs complete data classification; **Pima Indians Diabetes**; Homogenous granulation; **10% of missing values**; r_{gran} = Granulation radius; nil = result for data without missing values; Acc = Accuracy of classification; $AccBias$ = Accuracy bias defined based on equation efAcccBiasEquation; $GranSize$ = The size of data set after granulation in the fixed r

	Acc				AccBias			
nil	A	B	C	D	nil	A	B	C	D
0.646	0.644	0.646	0.636	0.642	0.026	0.015	0.015	0.02	0.021

	GranSize			
nil	A	B	C	D
490.88	578	577.12	490	492.12

4 Conclusions

Homogenous granulation - in the context of missing values absorption - works differently in comparison with classic concept dependent technique. Using $* = don't\ care$ variant - in case of concept-dependent method - the granulation process reduce diversity in data sets, for $* = *$ diversity may be increased. And the granules are smaller for C and D strategies than for A and B. In consequence the size of granular reflections of training decision systems is smaller in case of A and B strategies - approximation level is higher. Additionally the reduction of training decision systems size - in case of granulation of damaged systems - is significant in comparison with granulation of undamage data sets. Missing values increase the approximation level in many cases.

Missing values absorption for homogenous variant, where granulation radius dynamically increases until the objects in granules belong only to central object class, behave in a different way. The number of objects in homogeneous granulation process increase in comparison with nil case - where the granulation process is performed on the undamaged data. In case of A and B strategies the granules are smaller than for C and D - its because the $* = don't\ care$ break homogeneity of decision classes in a higher level than in case of $* = *$. The approximation level decrease in case of damaged data sets, because in all variants homogeneity of classes is affected.

As we expected granulation techniques absorbs missing values in an effective way and the knowledge judge in classification process from completed data seems to be preserved in a high level. The classification accuracy in the CV model is on decent level in comparison with the data without missing values. For each method the most missing values are repaired during granulation process, thus the missing values repairing part has small influence on classification - the results are comparable.

In the next works we plan to extend our technique to check their effectiveness in the context of well-known classifiers to find the most effective ones for specific data sets. Another direction of research is to apply the granular technique in the process of image recognition with use of convolutional deep neural networks (in deep learning approach).

Acknowledgements. The research has been supported by grant 23.610.007-300 from Ministry of Science and Higher Education of the Republic of Poland.

References

1. Artiemjew, P., Ropiak, K.: A novel ensemble model - the random granular reflections. In: Proceedings of the 27th International Workshop on Concurrency, Specification and Programming. CEUR, Berlin (2018)
2. Ropiak, K., Artiemjew, P.: On granular rough computing: epsilon homogenous granulation. In: Nguyen, H.S., Ha, Q.-T., Li, T., Przybyła-Kasperek, M. (eds.) IJCRS 2018. LNCS (LNAI), vol. 11103, pp. 546–558. Springer, Cham (2018). https://doi.org/10.1007/978-3-319-99368-3_43
3. Ropiak, K., Artiemjew, P.: A study in granular computing: homogenous granulation. In: Damaševičius, R., Vasiljevienė, G. (eds.) ICIST 2018. CCIS, vol. 920, pp. 336–346. Springer, Cham (2018). https://doi.org/10.1007/978-3-319-99972-2_27
4. Polap, D., Wozniak, M., Wei, W., Damasevicius, R.: Multi-threaded learning control mechanism for neural networks. Future Gener. Comput. Syst. **87**, 16–34 (2018)
5. Polkowski, L., Artiemjew, P.: On granular rough computing with missing values. In: Kryszkiewicz, M., Peters, J.F., Rybinski, H., Skowron, A. (eds.) RSEISP 2007. LNCS (LNAI), vol. 4585, pp. 271–279. Springer, Heidelberg (2007). https://doi.org/10.1007/978-3-540-73451-2_29
6. Polkowski, L.: Formal granular calculi based on rough inclusions. In: Proceedings of IEEE 2005 Conference on Granular Computing, GrC 2005, Beijing, China, pp. 57–62. IEEE Press (2005)
7. Polkowski, L.: A model of granular computing with applications. In: Proceedings of IEEE 2006 Conference on Granular Computing, GrC 2006, Atlanta, USA, pp. 9–16. IEEE Press (2006)
8. Polkowski, L., Artiemjew, P.: Granular Computing in Decision Approximation - An Application of Rough Mereology. ISRL, vol. 77. Springer, Cham (2015). https://doi.org/10.1007/978-3-319-12880-1
9. Polkowski, L., Artiemjew, P.: Granular computing: granular classifiers and missing values. In: Proceedings of the 6th IEEE International Conference on Cognitive Informatics, ICCI 2007, pp. 186–194 (2007)
10. Ohno-Machado, L.: Cross-validation and bootstrap ensembles, bagging, boosting, Harvard-MIT Division of Health Sciences and Technology, HST.951J: Medical Decision Support, Fall (2005). https://ocw.mit.edu/courses/health-sciences-and-technology/hst-951j-medical-decision-support-fall-2005/lecture-notes/hst951_6.pdf
11. University of California, Irvine Machine Learning Repository. https://archive.ics.uci.edu/ml/index.php

Rule Set Complexity in Mining Incomplete Data Using Global and Saturated Probabilistic Approximations

Patrick G. Clark[1], Jerzy W. Grzymala-Busse[1,2(✉)], Teresa Mroczek[2], and Rafal Niemiec[2]

[1] Department of Electrical Engineering and Computer Science, University of Kansas, Lawrence, KS 66045, USA
patrick.g.clark@gmail.com, jerzy@ku.edu
[2] Department of Artificial Intelligence,
University of Information Technology and Management, 35-225 Rzeszow, Poland
{tmroczek,rniemiec}@wsiz.rzeszow.pl

Abstract. We discuss incomplete data sets with two interpretations of missing attribute values, lost values and "do not care" conditions. For data mining we use two probabilistic approximations, global and saturated. In our previous research, we compared four approaches, combining two interpretations of missing attribute values with two types of probabilistic approximations, using the error rate evaluated by ten-fold cross validation as the criterion of quality. Results of this research showed that though there are significant differences (with a 5% level of significance), however no approach is a winner. So in this paper the main objective is to compare complexity of rule sets induced by our four approaches. We show that there are significant differences between the four approaches; however, the difference between used probabilistic approximations is not significant. The only significant difference is between the two interpretations of missing attribute values. Our main result is that using the "do not care" condition interpretation of missing attribute values significantly reduces the complexity of induced rule sets.

Keywords: Incomplete data mining · Characteristic sets · Rough set theory · Probabilistic approximations

1 Introduction

We discuss incomplete data sets with two interpretations of missing attribute values, lost values and "do not care" conditions. We assume that a missing attribute value is lost if the original value was erased or not inserted. In this case we should use only existing, specified attribute values for data mining. A lost value is denoted by "?". A "do not care" condition means that the missing attribute value is irrelevant, so it may be replaced by any specified attribute value. A "do not care" condition is denoted by "*".

© Springer Nature Switzerland AG 2019
R. Damaševičius and G. Vasiljevienė (Eds.): ICIST 2019, CCIS 1078, pp. 451–462, 2019.
https://doi.org/10.1007/978-3-030-30275-7_35

Probabilistic approximations are a generalization of the idea of lower and upper approximations known in rough set theory. A probabilistic approximation is associated with a probability α, if $\alpha = 1$, a probabilistic approximation is reduced to the lower approximation; if α is a small positive number, e.g., 0.001, the probabilistic approximation is the upper approximation. Usually, probabilistic approximations are applied to completely specified data sets [13–21], such approximations were generalized to incomplete data sets in [9]. Probabilistic approximations used for incomplete data sets are based on characteristic sets [8].

Recently, two new types of approximations were introduced, global probabilistic approximations in [1] and saturated probabilistic approximations in [4]. Our previous research [4] shows that there are significant differences in prediction error rate between the four approaches to rule induction, based on two interpretations of missing attribute values and two types of probabilistic approximations, neither is universally best for all data sets. When the main criterion is the prediction error rate, all approaches should be tried.

The main objective of this paper is to compare the same four approaches using rule complexity, measured by the number of rules and the total number of conditions in the rule set. Complexity of rule sets is important. Processing smaller rule sets is more efficient. Additionally, analysis of smaller rule sets is easier for experts.

The Modified Learning from Examples Module, version 2 (MLEM2) [3,7] was used for rule induction. The MLEM2 algorithm is used in the Learning from Examples using Rough Sets (LERS) data mining system [2,6,7].

Our main result is that the "do not care" condition interpretation of missing attribute values is associated with smaller rule sets and smaller total number of conditions in rule sets. On the other hand, differences between complexity of rule sets induced using either global or saturated probabilistic approximations are not significant.

Usually, the criterion of smaller prediction rate is more important, so in mining incomplete data sets, first we should select the best approach to data mining. If the difference is insignificant, complexity of induced rule sets is essential. In this case we should use a "do not care" condition as an interpretation of the missing attribute values.

2   Incomplete Data

We assume that the input data sets are presented in the form of a decision table. An example of a decision table is shown in Table 1. Rows of the decision table represent cases, while columns are labeled by variables. The set of all cases will be denoted by U. In Table 1, $U = \{1, 2, 3, 4, 5, 6, 7, 8\}$. Independent variables are called attributes and a dependent variable is called a decision and is denoted by d. The set of all attributes will be denoted by A. In Table 1, $A = \{$ *Temperature, Headache, Cough*$\}$. The value for a case x and an attribute a will be denoted by $a(x)$. For example, *Temperature*$(1) = high$.

Table 1. A decision table

Case	Attributes			Decision
	Temperature	Headache	Cough	Flu
1	high	*	no	yes
2	*	?	no	yes
3	high	*	yes	yes
4	very-high	yes	*	yes
5	high	no	?	no
6	*	?	yes	no
7	?	no	no	no
8	normal	no	*	no

The set X of all cases defined by the same value of the decision d is called a *concept*. For example, a concept associated with the value *yes* of the decision *Flu* is the set $\{1, 2, 3, 4\}$.

For a variable a and its value v, (a, v) is called a variable-value pair. A *block* of (a, v), denoted by $[(a, v)]$, is the set $\{x \in U \mid a(x) = v\}$ [5]. For incomplete decision tables, the definition of a block of an attribute-value pair is modified in the following way:

- if for an attribute a and a case x we have $a(x) = ?$, the case x should not be included in any blocks $[(a, v)]$ for all values v of attribute a;
- if for an attribute a and a case x we have $a(x) = *$, the case x should be included in blocks $[(a, v)]$ for all specified values v of attribute a.

For the data set from Table 1, the blocks of attribute-value pairs are:

[(Temperature, normal)] = $\{2, 6, 8\}$,
[(Temperature, high)] = $\{1, 2, 3, 5, 6\}$,
[(Temperature, very-high)] = $\{2, 4, 6\}$,
[(Headache, no)] = $\{1, 3, 5, 7, 8\}$,
[(Headache, yes)] = $\{1, 3, 4\}$,
[(Cough, no)] = $\{1, 2, 4, 7, 8\}$, and
[(Cough, yes)] = $\{3, 4, 6, 8\}$.

For a case $x \in U$ and $B \subseteq A$, the *characteristic set* $K_B(x)$ is defined as the intersection of the sets $K(x, a)$, for all $a \in B$, where the set $K(x, a)$ is defined in the following way:

- if $a(x)$ is specified, then $K(x, a)$ is the block $[(a, a(x))]$ of attribute a and its value $a(x)$;
- if $a(x) = ?$ or $a(x) = *$, then $K(x, a) = U$.

For Table 1 and $B = A$,

$K_A(1) = \{1, 2\}$,
$K_A(2) = \{1, 2, 4, 7, 8\}$,
$K_A(3) = \{3, 6\}$,
$K_A(4) = \{4\}$,
$K_A(5) = \{1, 3, 5\}$,
$K_A(6) = \{3, 4, 6, 8\}$,
$K_A(7) = \{1, 7, 8\}$, and
$K_A(8) = \{8\}$.

3   Probabilistic Approximations

In this section, we will discuss two types of probabilistic approximations: global and saturated.

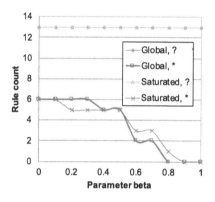

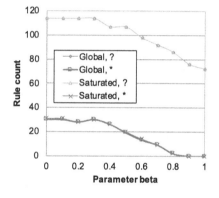

Fig. 1. Number of rules for the *bankruptcy* data set

Fig. 2. Number of rules for the *breast cancer* data set

3.1   Global Probabilistic Approximations

An idea of the global probabilistic approximation, though restricted only to lower and upper approximations, was introduced in [11,12], and presented in a general form in [1]. Let X be a concept, $X \subseteq U$. A B-*global probabilistic approximation* of the concept X, based on characteristic sets, with the parameter α and denoted by $appr_{\alpha,B}^{global}(X)$ is defined as the following set

$$\bigcup \{K_B(x) \mid \exists\, Y \subseteq U\ \forall\, x \in Y,\ Pr(X|K_B(x)) \geq \alpha\}.$$

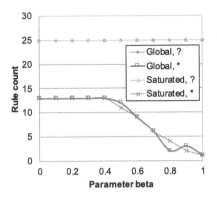

Fig. 3. Number of rules for the *echocardiogram* data set

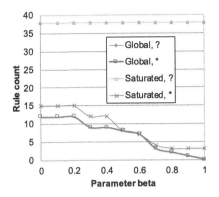

Fig. 4. Number of rules for the *hepatitis* data set

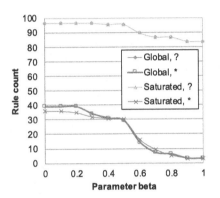

Fig. 5. Number of rules for the *image segmentation* data set

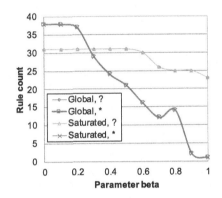

Fig. 6. Number of rules for the *iris* data set

In general, for given sets B and X and the parameter α, there exist many B-global probabilistic approximations of X. Additionally, an algorithm for computing B-global probabilistic approximations is of exponential computational complexity. Therefore, we decided to use a heuristic version of the definition of B-global probabilistic approximation, called a MLEM2 B-global probabilistic approximation of the concept X, associated with a parameter α and denoted by $appr_{\alpha,B}^{mlem2}(X)$ [1]. This definition is based on the rule induction algorithm MLEM2. The approximation $appr_{\alpha,B}^{mlem2}(X)$ is constructed from characteristic sets $K_B(y)$, the most relevant to the concept X, i.e., with $|X \cap K_B(y)|$ as large as possible and $Pr(X|K_B(y)) \geq \alpha$, where $y \in U$. If more than one characteristic set $K_B(y)$ satisfies both conditions, we pick the characteristic set $K_B(y)$ with the largest $Pr(X|K_B(y))$. If this criterion ends up with a tie, a characteristic set is picked up heuristically, as the first on the list [1].

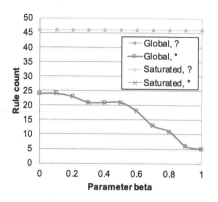

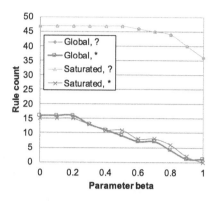

Fig. 7. Number of rules for the *lymphography* data set

Fig. 8. Number of rules for the *wine recognition* data set

In this paper we study MLEM2 B-global probabilistic approximations based on characteristic sets, with $B = A$, and calling them, for simplicity, *global probabilistic approximations* associated with the parameter α, denoted by $appr_\alpha^{mlem2}(X)$. Similarly, for $B = A$, the characteristic set $K_B(X)$ is denoted by $K(x)$.

Let $E_\alpha(X)$ be the set of all eligible characteristic sets defined as follows

$$\{K(x) \mid x \in U, Pr(X|K(x)) \geq \alpha\}.$$

A heuristic version of the MLEM2 global probabilistic approximation is computed using the following algorithm.

MLEM2 global probabilistic approximation algorithm
input: a set X (a concept), a set $E_\alpha(X)$,
output: a set T $(appr_\alpha^{mlem2}(X))$
begin
        $G := X$;
        $T := \emptyset$;
        $Y := E_\alpha(X)$;
        while $G \neq \emptyset$ **and** $Y \neq \emptyset$
            begin
                select a characteristic set $K(x) \in Y$
                such that $|K(x) \cap X|$ is maximum;
                if a tie occurs, select $K(x) \in Y$
                with the smallest cardinality;
                if another tie occurs, select the first $K(x)$;
                $T := T \cup K(x)$;
                $G := G - T$;
                $Y := Y - K(x)$
            end
end

For Table 1, all distinct MLEM2 global probabilistic approximations are

$$appr_1^{mlem2}(\{1,2,3,4\}) = \{1,2,4\},$$

$$appr_{0.667}^{mlem2}(\{1,2,3,4\}) = \{1,2,3,4,5\},$$

$$appr_{0.6}^{mlem2}(\{1,2,3,4\}) = \{1,2,3,4,5,7,8\},$$

$$appr_1^{mlem2}(\{5,6,7,8\}) = \{8\},$$

$$appr_{0.667}^{mlem2}(\{5,6,7,8\}) = \{1,7,8\},$$

$$appr_{0.5}^{mlem2}(\{5,6,7,8\}) = \{1,3,4,6,7,8\},$$

$$appr_{0.4}^{mlem2}(\{5,6,7,8\}) = \{1,2,3,4,6,7,8\} \text{ and}$$

$$appr_{0.333}^{mlem2}(\{5,6,7,8\}) = \{1,2,3,4,5,6,7,8\}.$$

3.2   Saturated Probabilistic Approximations

Another heuristic version of the probabilistic approximation is based on selection of characteristic sets while giving higher priority to characteristic sets with larger conditional probability $Pr(X|K(x))$. Additionally, if the approximation covers all cases from the concept X, we stop adding characteristic sets.

Let X be a concept and let $x \in U$. Let us compute all conditional probabilities $Pr(X|K(x))$. Then we sort the set

$$\{Pr(X|K(x)) \mid x \in U\}.$$

Let us denote the sorted list of such conditional probabilities by $\alpha_1, \alpha_2, ..., \alpha_n$, where α_1 is the largest. For any $i = 1, 2, ..., n$, the set $E_i(x)$ is defined as follows

$$\{K(x) \mid x \in U, Pr(X|K(x)) = \alpha_i\}.$$

If we want to compute a saturated probabilistic approximation, denoted by $appr_\alpha^{saturated}(X)$, for some α, $0 < \alpha \leq 1$, we need to identify the index m such that

$$\alpha_m \geq \alpha > \alpha_{m+1},$$

where $m \in \{1, 2, ..., n\}$ and $\alpha_{n+1} = 0$. Then the saturated probabilistic approximation $appr_{\alpha_m}^{saturated}(X)$ is computed using the following algorithm.

Saturated probabilistic approximation algorithm
input: a set X (a concept), a set $E_i(x)$ for
$i = 1, 2,..., n$ and $x \in U$, index m
output: a set T $(appr_{\alpha_m}^{saturated}(X))$
begin

$\qquad T := \emptyset;$
$\qquad Y_i(x) := E_i(x)$ for all $i = 1, 2,..., m$ and $x \in U;$
$\qquad$ **for** $j = 1, 2,..., m$ **do**
$\qquad\qquad$ **while** $Y_j(x) \neq \emptyset$
$\qquad\qquad\qquad$ **begin**
$\qquad\qquad\qquad\qquad$ select a characteristic set $K(x) \in Y_j(x)$
$\qquad\qquad\qquad\qquad$ such that $|K(x) \cap X|$ is maximum;
$\qquad\qquad\qquad\qquad$ if a tie occurs, select the first $K(x);$
$\qquad\qquad\qquad\qquad Y_j(x) := Y_j(x) - K(x);$
$\qquad\qquad\qquad\qquad$ **if** $(K(x) - T) \cap X \neq \emptyset$
$\qquad\qquad\qquad\qquad\qquad$ **then** $T := T \cup K(x);$
$\qquad\qquad\qquad\qquad$ **if** $X \subseteq T$ **then exit**
$\qquad\qquad\qquad$ **end**

end

For Table 1, all distinct saturated probabilistic approximations are

$appr_1^{saturated}(\{1, 2, 3, 4\}) = \{1, 2, 4\},$

$appr_{0.667}^{saturated}(\{1, 2, 3, 4\}) = \{1, 2, 3, 4, 5\},$

$appr_1^{saturated}(\{5, 6, 7, 8\}) = \{8\},$

$appr_{0.667}^{saturated}(\{5, 6, 7, 8\}) = \{1, 7, 8\},$

$appr_{0.5}^{saturated}(\{5, 6, 7, 8\}) = \{1, 3, 4, 6, 7, 8\},$

$appr_{0.4}^{saturated}(\{5, 6, 7, 8\}) = \{1, 2, 3, 4, 6, 7, 8\}$ and

$appr_{0.333}^{saturated}(\{5, 6, 7, 8\}) = \{1, 2, 3, 4, 5, 6, 7, 8\}.$

Note that $appr_{0.6}^{mlem2}(\{1, 2, 3, 4\})$ covers the cases 7 and 8 in spite of the fact that these cases are not members of the concept $\{1, 2, 3, 4\}$. The set $\{1, 2, 3, 4, 5, 7, 8\}$ is not listed among saturated probabilistic approximations of the concept $\{1, 2, 3, 4\}$.

3.3 Rule Induction

Once the global and saturated probabilistic approximations associated with a parameter α are constructed, rule sets are induced using the rule induction algorithm based on another parameter, also interpreted as a probability, and denoted by β. This algorithm also uses MLEM2 principles [10].

The parameter β is used to control quality of induced rules. If a rule covers a subset Y of U and the rule indicates the concept X, a rule is outputted by the rule induction system if $Pr(X|Y) \geq \beta$.

For example, for Table 1 and $\alpha = \beta = 0.5$, using the global probabilistic approximations, the MLEM2 rule induction algorithm induces the following rules:

(Cough, yes) $\rightarrow$ (Flu, no),
(Cough, no) & (Headache, no) $\rightarrow$ (Flu, no) and
(Cough, no) $\rightarrow$ (Flu, yes).

On the other hand, for Table 1 and $\alpha = \beta = 0.5$, using the saturated probabilistic approximations, the MLEM2 rule induction algorithm induces the following rules:

(Cough, yes) $\rightarrow$ (Flu, no),
(Cough, no) & (Headache, no) $\rightarrow$ (Flu, no),
(Temperature, high) & (Headache, no) $\rightarrow$ (Flu, yes) and
(Temperature, very-high) & (Cough, no) $\rightarrow$ (Flu, yes).

It is difficult to tell what are optimal parameters α and β, even as we restrict our attention to the predicted error rate of induced rule sets.

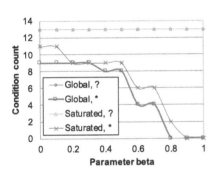

Fig. 9. Total number of conditions for the *bankruptcy* data set

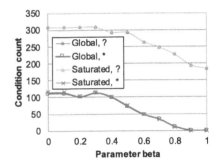

Fig. 10. Total number of conditions for the *breast cancer* data set

4   Experiments

For our experiments, we used eight data sets that are available in the University of California at Irvine *Machine Learning Repository.*

For every data set, a template was created. Such a template was formed by replacing randomly 35% of existing specified attribute values by *lost values.* The same templates were used for constructing data sets with "do not care" conditions, by replacing "?"s with "*"s.

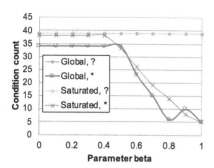

Fig. 11. Total number of conditions for the *echocardiogram* data set

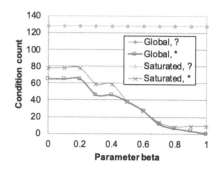

Fig. 12. Total number of conditions for the *hepatitis* data set

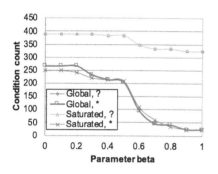

Fig. 13. Total number of conditions for the *image segmentation* data set

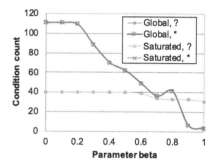

Fig. 14. Total number of conditions for the *iris* data set

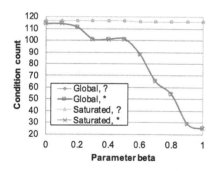

Fig. 15. Total number of conditions for the *lymphography* data set

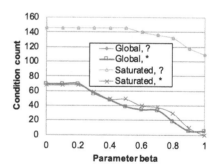

Fig. 16. Total number of conditions for the *wine recognition* data set

In all experiments, the parameter α was equal to 0.5. Results of our experiments are presented in Figs. 1, 2, 3, 4, 5, 6, 7, 8, 9, 10, 11, 12, 13, 14, 15 and 16, where "Global" denotes a MLEM2 global probabilistic approximation, "Saturated" denotes a saturated probabilistic approximation, "?" denotes lost values and "*" denotes "do not care" conditions. In our experiments, four approaches for mining incomplete data sets were used, since we combined two options of probabilistic approximations: global and saturated with two interpretations of missing attribute values: lost and "do not care" conditions.

These four approaches were compared by applying the distribution free Friedman rank sum test and then by the post-hoc test (distribution-free multiple comparisons based on the Friedman rank sums), with a 5% level of significance. The null hypothesis H_0 of the Friedman test, claiming that differences between these approaches are insignificant, was rejected for all data sets. Results of the post-hoc distribution free all-treatments multiple comparisons Friedman, Kendal-Babington and Smith test for the remaining six data sets are that there are insignificant differences between the two probabilistic approximations, global and saturated. On the other hand, difference between two interpretations of missing attribute values is significant. Using the "do not care" condition interpretation of missing attribute values reduces significantly the complexity of induced rule sets.

5   Conclusions

We compared four approaches for mining incomplete data sets, combining two interpretations of missing attribute values with two types of probabilistic approximations. Our criterion of quality was complexity of induced rule sets. As follows from our experiments, there were significant differences between the four approaches. However, the difference between used probabilistic approximations is not significant. The only significant difference is between the two interpretations of missing attribute values. Our main result is that using the "do not care" condition interpretation of missing attribute values significantly reduces the complexity of induced rule sets.

References

1. Clark, P.G., Gao, C., Grzymala-Busse, J.W., Mroczek, T., Niemiec, R.: A comparison of concept and global probabilistic approximations based on mining incomplete data. In: Damaševičius, R., Vasiljevienė, G. (eds.) ICIST 2018. CCIS, vol. 920, pp. 324–335. Springer, Cham (2018). https://doi.org/10.1007/978-3-319-99972-2_26
2. Clark, P.G., Grzymala-Busse, J.W.: Experiments on probabilistic approximations. In: Proceedings of the 2011 IEEE International Conference on Granular Computing, pp. 144–149 (2011)
3. Clark, P.G., Grzymala-Busse, J.W.: Experiments on rule induction from incomplete data using three probabilistic approximations. In: Proceedings of the 2012 IEEE International Conference on Granular Computing, pp. 90–95 (2012)
4. Clark, P.G., Grzymala-Busse, J.W., Mroczek, T., Niemiec, R.: A comparison of global and saturated probabilistic approximations using characteristic sets in mining incomplete data. In: Eighth International Conference on Intelligent Systems and Applications (2019, submitted)

5. Grzymala-Busse, J.W.: LERS—a system for learning from examples based on rough sets. In: Slowinski, R. (ed.) Intelligent Decision Support. Handbook of Applications and Advances of the Rough Set Theory, pp. 3–18. Kluwer Academic Publishers, Dordrecht, Boston, London (1992)

6. Grzymala-Busse, J.W.: A new version of the rule induction system LERS. Fundamenta Informaticae **31**, 27–39 (1997)

7. Grzymala-Busse, J.W.: MLEM2: a new algorithm for rule induction from imperfect data. In: Proceedings of the 9th International Conference on Information Processing and Management of Uncertainty in Knowledge-Based Systems, pp. 243–250 (2002)

8. Grzymala-Busse, J.W.: Rough set strategies to data with missing attribute values. In: Notes of the Workshop on Foundations and New Directions of Data Mining, in Conjunction with the Third International Conference on Data Mining, pp. 56–63 (2003)

9. Grzymała-Busse, J.W.: Generalized parameterized approximations. In: Yao, J.T., Ramanna, S., Wang, G., Suraj, Z. (eds.) RSKT 2011. LNCS (LNAI), vol. 6954, pp. 136–145. Springer, Heidelberg (2011). https://doi.org/10.1007/978-3-642-24425-4_20

10. Grzymala-Busse, J.W., Clark, P.G., Kuehnhausen, M.: Generalized probabilistic approximations of incomplete data. Int. J. Approximate Reasoning **132**, 180–196 (2014)

11. Grzymala-Busse, J.W., Rzasa, W.: Local and global approximations for incomplete data. In: Greco, S., Hata, Y., Hirano, S., Inuiguchi, M., Miyamoto, S., Nguyen, H.S., Słowiński, R. (eds.) RSCTC 2006. LNCS (LNAI), vol. 4259, pp. 244–253. Springer, Heidelberg (2006). https://doi.org/10.1007/11908029_27

12. Grzymala-Busse, J.W., Rzasa, W.: Local and global approximations for incomplete data. Trans. Rough Sets **8**, 21–34 (2008)

13. Grzymala-Busse, J.W., Ziarko, W.: Data mining based on rough sets. In: Wang, J. (ed.) Data Mining: Opportunities and Challenges, pp. 142–173. Idea Group Publ., Hershey (2003)

14. Pawlak, Z., Skowron, A.: Rough sets: some extensions. Inf. Sci. **177**, 28–40 (2007)

15. Pawlak, Z., Wong, S.K.M., Ziarko, W.: Rough sets: probabilistic versus deterministic approach. Int. J. Man Mach. Stud. **29**, 81–95 (1988)

16. Ślęzak, D., Ziarko, W.: The investigation of the Bayesian rough set model. Int. J. Approximate Reasoning **40**, 81–91 (2005)

17. Wong, S.K.M., Ziarko, W.: INFER—an adaptive decision support system based on the probabilistic approximate classification. In: Proceedings of the 6-th International Workshop on Expert Systems and Their Applications, pp. 713–726 (1986)

18. Yao, Y.Y.: Probabilistic rough set approximations. Int. J. Approximate Reasoning **49**, 255–271 (2008)

19. Yao, Y.Y., Wong, S.K.M.: A decision theoretic framework for approximate concepts. Int. J. Man Mach. Stud. **37**, 793–809 (1992)

20. Ziarko, W.: Variable precision rough set model. J. Comput. Syst. Sci. **46**(1), 39–59 (1993)

21. Ziarko, W.: Probabilistic approach to rough sets. Int. J. Approximate Reasoning **49**, 272–284 (2008)

New Attempts in Solving Image Recognition Tasks

Catalina-Lucia Cocianu, Alexandru Stan$^{(\boxtimes)}$,
and Mihai Avramescu

Bucharest University of Economic Studies, Piata Romana 6,
010317 Bucharest, Romania
alexandru.stan1@yahoo.com

Abstract. The paper focuses on the problem of registration in solving image alignment tasks. The proposed techniques are developed using evolutionary algorithms (EA) to align and compare two binary images. We first introduce a hybrid two-stage technique based on the evolution strategy (ES) population-based search scheme (ESP) and a local search ES algorithm, namely Two Membered Evolution Strategy (2M-ES). The main aim is to speed up the computation without decreasing the recognition accuracy. The second proposed technique embeds ESP and 2M-ES to obtain a memetic algorithm. The ultimate goal of the memetic approach is to improve the recognition accuracy keeping the computational complexity growth at a reasonable level. In order to experimentally establish the performances of our methods, we compare them against two most commonly used techniques for image registration in case of rigid type perturbation, namely PAT registration and an evolution strategy (ES) population-based search scheme. The experimental results together with some conclusive remarks regarding the quality of the proposed methods are reported in the final part of the paper.

Keywords: Image recognition · Evolution strategy · Memetic algorithms · Mutual information

1 Introduction

Registration is one of the fundamental tasks in image processing and pattern recognition. Image alignment or registration is a technique used to match two or more pictures acquired at different times, from different sensors or from different viewpoints. The main approaches consider that the variations in the images to be aligned are induced by the acquisition system and are usually modeled in terms of certain spatial transformations. In most of the cases, the registration techniques consider that the perturbation induced by the acquisition system is of rigid, affine, projective, or global polynomial type. The rigid transformation is a mixture of rotation, translation and scale changes. The affine transformation consists of rigid, shear and aspect ratio changes. The projective transformation describes the true imaging geometry, while the polynomial functions model the distortion induced by standard point-mapping techniques [1–3].

© Springer Nature Switzerland AG 2019
R. Damaševičius and G. Vasiljevienė (Eds.): ICIST 2019, CCIS 1078, pp. 463–474, 2019.
https://doi.org/10.1007/978-3-030-30275-7_36

The registration methods usually belong to three major computer vision research areas - pattern recognition, medical image analysis and remotely sensed data processing. In case of computer vision and pattern recognition filed, registration is applied for segmentation purposes, object recognition, shape reconstruction, motion tracking, OCR systems and so on. In medical image analysis, image alignment is applied in disease localization and monitoring. In remotely sensed data processing the registration is used for civilian and military applications [4–10].

So far a series of registration techniques, as for instance landmark-based registration, principal axes transformation (PAT), multiresolution techniques, boundary registration, model-based approaches, adaptive methods and optimization-based registration, have been developed and reported in the literature. The optimization-based registration techniques include, in addition to direct methods, a series of metaheuristics as for instance simulated annealing, genetic algorithms, memetic algorithms and particle swarm optimization [11–16].

The work reported in this paper address the problem of binary image registration for pattern recognition purposes using evolutionary-based methodologies. The methodologies are specially tailored for security systems based on signatures digitally recorded, but they can also be applied on binary images represented by sparse matrices. In most of the cases the signature to be recognized differs from the target (the stored signature) in the sense that it could be a geometrically distorted variant of it. In our work we address the problem of rigid transformation, when only translation, rotation, and scale changes are considered, but the model can be easily extended to affine transformation model. The proposed algorithms use fitness function defined in terms of mutual information computed between the transformed image and the target image.

Regarding the type of processed images, in most cases the registration and recognition tasks can be performed using only the image contours. Consequently, the proposed methods can be applied on grey-scale images after a contour detection pre-processing step.

The starting point of the proposed hybrid algorithms is a method that exclusively uses the ES population-based search scheme (ESP) to optimize the similarity between the analyzed images [17]. The aim is to improve both the accuracy and the efficiency of the technique reported in [17]. The performances of the investigated algorithms are measured in terms of the success rate, the mutual information similarity measure, the Signal-to-Noise Ratio and the run times respectively.

The first introduced technique is a hybrid two-stage approach that involves ESP and a local search algorithm, namely 2M-ES. The main aim is to speed up the computation without significantly decreasing the recognition accuracy. The technique is of batch execution type consisting of two stages. First, an ESP technique is used to compute a candidate solution having the fitness above a specific threshold. Then, the resulted best individual is used as input for the 2M-ES algorithm. The basic idea is to apply a global search technique to compute a sub-optimal solution belonging to a proper search direction then apply a local search algorithm to reach an optimal solution. The resulted hybrid technique is very fast and also proves good accuracy performances.

The second technique embeds ESP and 2M-ES to obtain a memetic algorithm. The aim of the resulted memetic approach is to improve the recognition accuracy, keeping the computational complexity growth at a reasonable level.

The experimental results and concluding remarks regarding the accuracy of the proposed methodologies together with some comparative analysis against the reported ES based methodology [17] and the well-known PAT registration are provided in the final part of the paper.

2 ES-Based Methodologies for Image Alignment and Recognition

Evolution strategies (ES) is a class of evolutionary algorithms (EAs) typically used for continuous parameter optimization problems [18]. The most important characteristic of ES is self-adaptability, a mechanism that adjusts the ES's parameters as the search is progressing [19]. The simplest ES algorithm, 2M-ES, implements a local search mechanism.

The 2M-ES algorithm represents the first and the simplest model of the evolutionary strategies where the aspect of the collective learning is missing. The changes involve one individual which evolves using the mutation operator. Mutations are represented by normal perturbations with defined amplitude, characterized by dispersion σ. The change is uniform for all directions. In order to adapt exploitation and exploration to the space condition, the mutation step is adjustable for each component using the celebrated 1/5-th success rule proposed by Rechenberg [19].

The general ES scheme is a population-based search mechanism that implements the self-adaptation of strategy parameters. The procedure involves the variation of certain ES's parameters during the evolution process in a particular manner [19]. Consequently, the corresponding parameters are included in the chromosome representation and the computation scheme updates their values together with the other alleles.

Typically, ES techniques use the fixed-size population model, the first generation being computed by random draws. The mating pool coincides with the current population. ES algorithms compute an offspring population significantly larger than the parent multiset, usually the ration being 1:7. The children are computed either using local recombination or global schemes. In case of local recombination each child is computed based on a single pair of parents. The global crossover involves more general computation scheme, each allele of a child resulting from a randomly selected pair of parents. Therefore each child has possibly more than two parents. The mutation procedure involves either a single Gaussian distribution for all directions, or multiple distributions, one for each size. The idea behind mutation with multiple step sizes is to treat dimensions differently such that different solution variables are mutated using different Gaussian distributions. The survivor selection mechanism is strictly deterministic.

The ES-based approach of image alignment when the perturbation is of rigid type is briefly described in the following. We denote by T the $M \times N$ stored image and by I the sensed one. The image I is defined by

$$I(x,y) = T\left(x^1, y^1\right) \tag{1}$$

where for each $1 \leq x \leq M$ and $1 \leq y \leq N$.

$$\begin{pmatrix} x^1 \\ y^1 \end{pmatrix} = \begin{pmatrix} a \\ b \end{pmatrix} + s \cdot \begin{pmatrix} cos\theta & -sin\theta \\ sin\theta & cos\theta \end{pmatrix} \cdot \begin{pmatrix} x \\ y \end{pmatrix} \tag{2}$$

where $\begin{pmatrix} a \\ b \end{pmatrix}$ represents the translation, s defines the scale factor and $\begin{pmatrix} cos\theta & -sin\theta \\ sin\theta & cos\theta \end{pmatrix}$ is the rotation matrix.

The aim is to compute a function $f(x,y)$ such that $I\left((f(x,y))^T\right) = T(x,y)$. Obviously,

$$f_{a,b,s,\theta}(x,y) = \frac{1}{s} \cdot R^T \cdot \left[\begin{pmatrix} x \\ y \end{pmatrix} - \begin{pmatrix} a \\ b \end{pmatrix} \right] \tag{3}$$

where R is the rotation matrix.

The solution sequence of an individual is a four size vector $c_{sol} = (a_c, b_c, s_c, \theta_c)$. We define the genotype space taking into account the uncorrelated multistep mutation operator. Each chromosome consists of the following components

$$c = \underbrace{\left(a_c, b_c, s_c, \theta_c,}_{c_{sol}} \underbrace{\sigma_{a_c}, \sigma_{b_c}, \sigma_{s_c}, \sigma_{\theta_c}\right)}_{c_{step size}} \tag{4}$$

where $\sigma_{a_c}, \sigma_{b_c}, \sigma_{s_c}, \sigma_{\theta_c}$ are the step sizes corresponding to the solution alleles.

The fitness function defines the similarity between the target image T and the sensed image $I_c = I\left(f_{a_c,b_c,s_c,\theta_c}\right)$ and it is computed based on the mutual information measure (*MI*) [17].

Local crossover is successfully implemented when the number of children is at most the current population size, for instance in case of genetic algorithms. In standard ES the most commonly used recombination strategy is the global one. However, in case of very complex problems, the global crossover has a major drawback from the computational complexity point of view. This is the reason why we introduced hybrid methods to compute the offspring population [17].

The recombination procedure is developed to enable self-adaptability capabilities. The offspring population is computed using a hybrid crossover mechanism that deals with the relationships between the alleles belonging to solution part of chromosomes. For instance, we can divide the solution part of a chromosome c into two groups, the translation variables (a_c, b_c) and the rotation and scale factors (s_c, θ_c), each group of variables being treated in a local manner. The corresponding crossover procedure that produces λ children is described as follows [17]:

Hybrid Crossover
Offspring ← ∅
for $i = 1 \dots \lambda$
   compute $c = \left(a_c, b_c, s_c, \theta_c, \sigma_{a_c}, \sigma_{b_c}, \sigma_{s_c}, \sigma_{\theta_c} \right)$ as follows:
   randomly select   the parents $p1, q1$ and recombine them to compute
   $\left(a_c, b_c, \sigma_{a_c}, \sigma_{b_c} \right)$
   randomly select the parents $p2, q2$ and recombine them to compute
   $\left(s_c, \theta_c, \sigma_{s_c}, \sigma_{\theta_c} \right)$
   add c to Offspring

The mutated offspring population is obtained using the uncorrelated multistep mutation operator. The survivor selection is then performed in a deterministic manner to obtain the next generation.

3   The Proposed Hybrid Techniques Based on Evolution Strategies

In this section we introduce two techniques that combine ES-based registration method with the basic 2M-ES local search algorithm to obtain improved image recognition algorithms. The chromosome representation together with the variation operators and the fitness function of the ESP method are described in the previous section.

The first technique is a two-stage mechanism that first uses an ESP technique to compute a sub-optimal solution, *best*, then applies a simple 2M-ES algorithm on the input best to reach an optimal solution, *best$_c$*. The main aim of the proposed hybrid technique is to obtain faster recognition algorithms, taking into account that most of the population-based search techniques involve significantly high execution time.

The idea behind this hybridization relies on the following remarks. Despite the fact that EAs are in general very suitable to rapidly identify good areas of the space search, they are less good to finely tune solutions. A more efficient method might be to incorporate a more systematic search of the vicinity of good solutions by adding a local search mechanism [19]. Consequently, the proposed hybrid approach computes a good solution using EAs – a solution having high fitness value, for instance above a specific threshold, and improve it via a local search procedure.

The ESP component of the hybrid technique is characterized by: σ_{ini}, the initial values of σ - parameter; ε_σ, the minimum value of each step size; *NMax*, the maximum number of generations; and the threshold parameter τ controlling the desired sub-optimal fitness value, $\tau < 1$.

The parameters of 2M-ES algorithm are presented in the following. We denote by *Max* the maximum number of generations, $\sigma 1_{ini}$ the initial value of σ - parameter, γ the number of generation to evaluate the success probability, ν the parameter of the Rechenberg updating rule and $\tau 1$ a threshold parameter controlling the best fitness value, $\tau 1 \in (0, 1)$. For each iteration t, we denote by P_t, O_t and MO_t the current population, the offspring and the mutated offspring respectively. The computation scheme of the proposed method is described as follows.

Hybrid ES algorithm

Inputs : $\mu, \lambda, \sigma_{ini}, \varepsilon_\sigma, NMax, \tau, I, T, \sigma1_{ini}, \gamma, v, \tau1, Max$

$t \leftarrow 0$

Step 1. Randomly generate P_t

Step 2. Evaluate each $c \in P_t$ using (3) and compute the best fitted individual, $best$

Step 3. $While\ t < NMax\ and\ fitness(best) < \tau$

   Step 3.1. Compute O_t using a recombination procedure

   Step 3.2. Compute MO_t, the mutated variants of individuals belonging to O_t

   Step 3.3. Evaluate each $c \in MO_t$ using (3)

   Step 3.4. Select the next generation P_{t+1} using either $(\mu + \lambda)$ procedure or (μ, λ) mechanism and determine the chromosome best;

$t \leftarrow t + 1$

Step 4. Compute $best_c$: $2M - ES(best, \sigma1_{ini}, \gamma, v, \tau1, Max)$

Output: I_{best_c}

The next approach is of memetic type. Briefly, memetic algorithms are optimization techniques developed based on principles belonging to various algorithmic solvers, as for instance population based-search and local search. The idea underlying the memetic approaches is that, during the evolution process, information is not only transmitted from one individual to another, but it is enhanced by the communicating parts. The enhancement of the information is accomplished by incorporating heuristics, local search methods, exact methods, etc. [20].

The general scheme of a memetic algorithm is given as follows [19].

Generic memetic algorithm

Step 1. Initialize population

Step 2. Evaluate each candidate

Step 3. $While\ Not\ Termination\ Condition$

   Step 3.1 Select parents

   Step 3.2 Recombine parents to obtain offspring

   Step 3.3 Mutate offspring

   Step 3.4 Evaluate offspring

   Step 3.5 Improve offspring via local search

   Step 3.6 Select the next generation

Note that one can initialize the population using already known good solutions. For instance, the local search procedure can be incorporated in the initialization step too. It means that, instead of using only randomly drawn individuals, the algorithm starts with a mixed population, in which some individuals are solutions computed by a certain local optimization procedure. Other methods include selective initialization, algorithms underlying mass mutation, etc. [19–21].

We developed a memetic approach that uses ES mechanisms taking into account that the offspring population size is about seven times larger than the number of parents. Therefore, if a local search procedure is applied for each child then the computational effort becomes excessively high. Moreover, to preserve diversity and avoid the premature convergence, the local search step should be applied on a small subset of children [19]. In our approach the local search is used only when the best individual of the mutated offspring population is less fitted than the current best candidate solution. In such cases we randomly select λ_s offspring and apply the 2M-ES search procedure, $\lambda_s \ll \lambda$.

The initial population is computed also to avoid the local convergence. In other words, when initializing the population with good individuals only few of them are going to be inserted in the first population, the rest of the individuals being randomly generated.

Using the same notation for the parameters of ESP and 2M-ES respectively, the proposed memetic algorithm is listed below.

Memetic ES-based algorithm
Inputs: $\mu, \lambda, \sigma_{ini}, \varepsilon_\sigma, NMax, \tau, I, T, s, \sigma 1_{ini}, \gamma, \nu, \tau 1, Max$
$t \leftarrow 0$
Step 1. Randomly generate initial population P_t with μ chromosomes
Step 2. For $i = 1 \dots \mu/s$
    Step 2.1 Randomly choose $x \in P_t$
    Step 2.2 Compute x_{new}: $2M - ES(x, \sigma 1_{ini}, \gamma, \nu, \tau 1, Max)$
    Step 2.3 Replace x with x_{new} in P_t
Step 3 Identify the chromosome $best$ with $fitness(best) = \max\limits_{x \in P_t} fitness(x)$

Step 4 $While\ t < NMax\ and\ fitness(best) < \tau$
    Step 4.1 Compute O_t using a recombination procedure
    Step 4.2 Compute MO_t, the mutated variants of individuals belonging to O_t
    Step 4.3 Evaluate each $c \in MO_t$ using (3)
    Step 4.4 Compute $best_c$ with $fitness(best_c) = \max\limits_{x \in P_t} fitness(x)$
    Step 4.5 $If\ fitness(best_c) \leq fitness(best)$
        Step 4.5.1 $For\ i = 1 \dots \mu/s$
            Step 4.5.1.1 Randomly choose $x \in MO_t$
            Step 4.5.1.2 Compute x_{new} : $2M - ES(x, \sigma 1_{ini}, \gamma, \nu, \tau 1, Max)$
            Step 4.5.1.3 Replace x with x_{new} in MO_t
        Step 4.5.2 Compute $best_c$ with $fitness(best_c) = \max\limits_{x \in MO_t} fitness(x)$
    Step 4.6 $If\ fitness(best_c) > fitness(best)$
        Step 4.6.1 $best = best_c$
    Step 4.7 Select the next generation P_{t+1} using either $(\mu + \lambda)$ procedure or (μ, λ) mechanism
$t \leftarrow t + 1$
Output: I_{best}

4 Experimental Results

In order to derive conclusions regarding the accuracy and the computational complexity of the proposed methods, we have conducted a long series of experiments on various images representing signatures. Note that, for each image, each technique has been tested 500 times to come to meaningful results. The reported results correspond to a set of 18 pairs of images representing signatures perturbed by the same degradation model (3).

The accuracy of resulted algorithms has been measured in terms of success rate. Let us denote by *NRun* the number of algorithm executions and let *NSuccess* be the number of successful runs. A successful run corresponds to a solution whose fitness value exceeds 0.89. The success rate of a certain algorithm, *SR*, is given by

$$SR = \frac{NSuccess}{NRun} \cdot 100\% \tag{5}$$

We also computed the SNR (Signal-to-Noise-Ratio) quantitative similarity measure, to derive conclusions on the registration quality. The SNR value computed for a certain sensed image S versus a reference image T of the same size (M, N) is defined by:

$$SNR(T, S) = 10 * log_{10} \left[\frac{\sum_{x=1}^{M} \sum_{y=1}^{N} (S(x, y))^2}{\sum_{x=1}^{M} \sum_{y=1}^{N} (T(x, y) - S(x, y))^2} \right] \tag{6}$$

The computational complexity of each algorithm is evaluated in terms of execution time.

In the following we present the experimentally established results in case of using each class of metaheuristics. The success rate, the mean values of mutual information ratio (MIR), SNR and run time respectively, together with their corresponding minimum values and maximum values are reported below. The reported results were obtained using a computer with the following configuration: Processor – Intel Core I7-7700k 3.6 GHZ, Memory – 8 GB DDR4 2400 MHz, Storage – 1 TB HDD 7200 RPM SATA 3.

The mean value corresponding to each above-mentioned performance measure has been computed by averaging the values of the corresponding measure resulted for each run. The results reported below correspond to two classes of images, denoted by TI1 and TI2. TI1 is the class of images easy to register by the simplest global ES algorithm. TI2 consists of more complex images perturbed in the same manner, but the information lost because of the degradation process is significantly larger than in case of TI1.

Note that the performances of the proposed methods in case of the all tested pairs of images are better than those reported when the input is TI2.

The results of ES-based method reported in [17] are listed below, in Tables 1 and 2.

The proposed hybrid technique implementing the generic ES procedure that uses local recombination followed by the simple 2M-ES local search has been tested using

Table 1. The performances of proposed hybrid approach.

Input	SR	Run time Mean value	Run time Min value	Run time Max value
TI1	100%	3.38	1.10	11.16
TI2	98.6%	12.96	2.03	74.54

Table 2. The accuracy of different ES implementation.

Input	SR	MIR SNR Mean value	MIR SNR Min value	MIR SNR Max value
TI1	100%	0.92	0.9	0.969
		26.44	25.02	31.16
TI2	99%	0.905	0.89	0.926
		26.29	25.32	27.51

the following parameters values. The ES population sizes are $\mu = 30, \lambda = 200$. The values of the threshold used to end the global ES search were set in the interval $[0.5, 0.7]$. The minimum values of step sizes are $[0.0075, 0.0075, 0.004, 0.004]$. Again, the search is over either when the fitness value is above 0.89 or the maximum number of iterations was reached. The parameters used in 2M-ES algorithm are as follows: $v = 0.87$, the initial dispersions values are $[1, 1, 0.01, 0.01]$ while the on-line adjustment of step sizes is performed after every 50 iterations. The values of *NMax* and *Max* were set to 150 and 3000 respectively. This way, the number of fitness function evaluations does not exceed the one corresponding to the first reported approach. The performances of the obtained algorithm are displayed in Tables 3 and 4. Note that the efficiency of the hybrid approach (runtime) is far better than the ES-based method.

Table 3. The performances of proposed hybrid approach.

Input	SR	Run time Mean value	Run time Min value	Run time Max value
TI1	100%	3.38	1.10	11.16
TI2	98.6%	12.96	2.03	74.54

The memetic technique described in Sect. 3 has been tested also based on the same images set. The ES parameters were set as follows: $\mu = 30, \lambda = 200$, $NMax = 200$, $\tau = 0.89$ while the vector of minimum values of step sizes is $[0.0075, 0.0075, 0.004, 0.004]$. The number of individuals considered for local search optimization is $\mu/4$. The parameters used in 2M-ES algorithm are $v = 0.87$, $Max = 200$, the initial dispersions values being $[1.0, 1.0, 0.01, 0.01]$. The online adjustment of step sizes is performed every 40 iterations. The performances of the algorithm are displayed in Tables 5 and 6.

Table 4. The accuracy of proposed hybrid approach.

Input	SR	MIR SNR Mean value	MIR SNR Min value	MIR SNR Max value
TI1	100%	0.919	0.9	0.964
		26.91	25.02	30.71
TI2	98.6%	0.903	0.9	0.927
		26.2	25.71	27.58

Table 5. The performances of proposed memetic approach.

Input	SR	Run time Mean value	Run time Min value	Run time Max value
TI1	100%	13.00	3.57	34.57
TI2	99.8%	29.75	3.85	369.58

Table 6. The accuracy of proposed memetic approach.

Input	SR	MIR SNR Mean value	MIR SNR Min value	MIR SNR Max value
TI1	100%	0.931	0.9	0.970
		27.27	25.03	31.50
TI2	99.8%	0.911	0.9	0.930
		26.52	25.66	27.72

Obviously, the proposed memetic approach outperforms the other two methods.

Also, a series of tests to evaluate the quality of the proposed classes of algorithms against the quality of well-known Principal Axes Transformation (PAT) registration have been performed. PAT is an image registration technique based on features automatically extracted from images mainly developed to address the problem of rigid perturbation. The image features are defined by its principal axes. Thus, the aim is to align the principal axes of sensed images to those corresponding to the reference one. Note that, in most of our tests, the MI ratio in case of PAT registration is below 0.87. Let us denote by I_{PAT} the result of PAT registration. The experiments pointed out that $SNR(T, I_{PAT})$ is around 23 while the minimum $SNR(T, TI2)$ is around 25.

5   Conclusions

The research reported in the paper aims to develop evolutionary-based binary image registration methodologies to accurately recognize binary images. In our work we addressed the problem of rigid transformation. Note that the proposed techniques can be straightforward extended to deal with the more general affine transformation model.

Also, the methods can be applied on grey-scale images after a pre-processing step involving contour detection.

The first technique is a hybrid two-stage approach of batch execution type. First, an ESP technique is used to compute a candidate solution having the fitness above a given threshold. Then, the resulted best individual is used as input for the 2M-ES algorithm. The second proposed method combines ESP and 2M-ES to obtain a memetic algorithm.

We conclude that the results are encouraging and entail future work toward extending this approach to more complex perturbation models as well as more complex hybrid techniques.

References

1. Goshtasby, A.A.: Image Registration: Principles, Tools and Methods. Advances in Computer Vision and Pattern Recognition, 1st edn. Springer, London (2012). https://doi.org/10.1007/978-1-4471-2458-0

2. Modersitzki, J.: Numerical Methods for Image Registration. Oxford University Press, New York (2004). https://doi.org/10.1093/acprof:oso/9780198528418.001.0001

3. Schwabe, M., Rubin-Zuzic., M., Rath., C., Pustylnik, M.: Image registration with particles, examplified with the complex plasma laboratory PK-4 on board the international space station. J. Imaging 5(3), 39 (2019). https://doi.org/10.3390/jimaging5030039

4. Wozniak, M., Polap, D.: Object detection and recognition via clustered features. Neurocomputing **320**, 76–84 (2018). https://doi.org/10.1016/j.neucom.2018.09.003

5. Liu, G., Liu, Z., Liu, S., et al.: Registration of infrared and visible light image based on visual saliency and scale invariant feature transform. EURASIP J. Image Video Process. (2018). https://doi.org/10.1186/s13640-018-0283-9

6. Cocianu, C., State, L., Panayiotis, V.: A new adaptive PCA scheme for noise removal in image processing. In: 50th International Symposium ELMAR-2008, Croatia, pp. 129–132 (2008). ISSN 1334-2630

7. Lijing, T., Yan, Z., Huiqun, Z.: A warped document image mosaicing method based on registration and TRS transform. In: 10th IEEE/ACIS International Conference on Computer and Information Science, ICIS, pp. 179–183. IEEE, China (2011). https://doi.org/10.1109/icis.2011.34

8. Xiang, Y., Wang, F., You, H.: An automatic and novel SAR image registration algorithm: a case study of the Chinese GF-3 satellite. Sensors **18**(2), 672 (2018). https://doi.org/10.3390/s18020672

9. Ke, Q., et al.: A neuro-heuristic approach for recognition of lung diseases from X-ray images. Expert Syst. Appl. **126**, 218–232 (2019). https://doi.org/10.1016/j.eswa.2019.01.060

10. Cocianu, C., Stan, A.: Neural architectures for correlated noise removal in image processing, Math. Probl. Eng. **2016** (2016). https://doi.org/10.1155/2016/6153749

11. Sarvamangala, D.R., Kulkarni, R.V.: A comparative study of bio-inspired algorithms for medical image registration. In: Mandal, J.K., Dutta, P., Mukhopadhyay, S. (eds.) Advances in Intelligent Computing. SCI, vol. 687, pp. 27–44. Springer, Singapore (2019). https://doi.org/10.1007/978-981-10-8974-9_2

12. Abdul Khalid, N.E., Md Ariff, N., Yahya, S., Mohamed Noor, N.: A review of bio-inspired algorithms as image processing techniques. In: Mohamad Zain, J., Wan Mohd, WMb, El-Qawasmeh, E. (eds.) ICSECS 2011. CCIS, vol. 179, pp. 660–673. Springer, Heidelberg (2011). https://doi.org/10.1007/978-3-642-22170-5_57

13. Valsecchi, A., Dubois-Lacoste, J., Stutzle, T., Damas, S., Santamaria, J., Marrakchi-Kacem, L.: Evolutionary medical image registration using automatic parameter tuning. In: IEEE Congress on Evolutionary Computation 2013, pp. 1326–1333. IEEE (2013). https://doi.org/10.1109/cec.2013.6557718

14. Cao, X., Yang, J., Wang, L., Xue, Z., Wang, Q., Shen, D.: Deep learning based inter-modality image registration supervised by intra-modality similarity. In: Shi, Y., Suk, H.-I., Liu, M. (eds.) MLMI 2018. LNCS, vol. 11046, pp. 55–63. Springer, Cham (2018). https://doi.org/10.1007/978-3-030-00919-9_7

15. Zhu, Q., Shi, Q.: Application of improved genetic algorithm in medical image registration. In: Yang, G. (ed.) Proceedings of the 2012 International Conference on Communication, Electronics and Automation Engineering. AISC, vol. 181, pp. 1063–1071. Springer, Heidelberg (2013). https://doi.org/10.1007/978-3-642-31698-2_150

16. Santamaría, J., Damas, S., García-Torres, J., Cordón, O.: Self-adaptive evolutionary image registration using differential evolution and artificial immune systems. Pattern Recognit. Lett. **33**(16), 2065–2070 (2012). https://doi.org/10.1016/j.patrec.2012.07.002

17. Cocianu C., Stan A.: New attempts in binary image registration. In: The Proceedings of 5th International Conference on Control, Decision and Information Technologies, pp. 253–258. IEEE, Thessaloniki (2018). https://doi.org/10.1109/codit.2018.8394806

18. Edelkamp, S., Schrödl, S.: Heuristic Search: Theory and Applications. Morgan Kaufmann, Amsterdam (2012). https://doi.org/10.1016/c2009-0-16511-x

19. Eiben, A.E., Smith, J.E.: Introduction to Evolutionary Computing. NCS. Springer, Heidelberg (2015). https://doi.org/10.1007/978-3-662-44874-8

20. Gendreau, M., Potvin, J.-Y. (eds.): Handbook of Metaheuristics, vol. 146, 2nd edn. Springer, New York (2010)

21. Hart, W.E., Krasnogor, N., Smith, J.E. (eds.): Recent Advances in Memetic Algorithms. Springer, New York (2005). https://doi.org/10.1007/3-540-32363-5

Parameter Identification of the Fractional Order Heat Conduction Model Using a Hybrid Algorithm

Rafał Brociek[1]([⊠]), Damian Słota[1], Giacomo Capizzi[2], and Grazia Lo Sciuto[2]

[1] Institute of Mathematics, Silesian University of Technology, Kaszubska 23, 44-100 Gliwice, Poland
rafal.brociek@polsl.pl
[2] Department of Electrical, Electronics and Informatics Engineering, University of Catania, Viale A. Doria 6, 95125 Catania, Italy

Abstract. In this paper authors present hybrid algorithm to solve heat conduction inverse problem. Considered heat conduction equation with Riemann-Liouville fractional derivative can be used to model heat conduction in porous materials. In order to effectively model the phenomenon of heat flow, all parameters of the model must be known. In considered inverse problem thermal conductivity coefficient, initial condition and heat transfer coefficient are unknown and must be identified having some information about output of the model (measurements of temperatures). In order to do that, function describing the error of approximate solution is constructed and then minimized. The hybrid algorithm, based on the probabilistic Ant Colony Optimization (ACO) algorithm and the deterministic Nelder-Mead method, is responsible for searching minimum of the objective function. Goal of this paper is reconstruction unknown parameters in heat conduction model with fractional derivative and show that hybrid algorithm is effective tool and works well in these type of problems.

Keywords: Fractional heat conduction equation · Identification · Ant colony algorithm · Inverse problem

1 Introduction

Nowadays, the possibility of modeling and optimizing various types of technological process is an extremely important issue in science, technology or industry. For correct modeling a given process, one should know its model and all parameters related it (so-called input data). Then, in the output, we get the assumed state.

This article deals with the issue of heat conduction modeling and the related to it inverse problem. To model heat conduction in porous materials fractional differential equation was used. These types of derivatives are applicable in the modeling of anomalous diffusion phenomena, an example of such phenomenon is the flow of heat in porous media [1–4]. Definitions of fractional derivatives are several, the most common in the literature are derivatives of Caputo, Riemann-Liouville and Riesz [5, 6]. Examples of applications of fractional derivatives are: a supercapacitor model [7],

© Springer Nature Switzerland AG 2019
R. Damaševičius and G. Vasiljevienė (Eds.): ICIST 2019, CCIS 1078, pp. 475–484, 2019.
https://doi.org/10.1007/978-3-030-30275-7_37

in the automation tuning of PID controllers [8], in image processing [9], model of wave propagation in human cancellous bone based on the fractional differential calculus [10] and heat conduction modeling in porous media [11].

In this article authors present hybrid algorithm based on Nelder-Mead method and Ant Colony Optimization (ACO) algorithm to solve inverse heat conduction problem with fractional derivative. In order to solve this problem, functional defining error of approximate solution is created. Then it is required to find a point, in the search space, for which the value of the objective function is the smallest. Considered function does not have the form of an analytical formula, hence the classical methods of calculating the smallest value of a function are not applicable. In this case, the authors have combined two algorithms: probabilistic (Ant Colony Optimization algorithm) [12], deterministic (Nelder-Mead method) [13]. The aim of the ACO algorithm is to narrow down the search area (exploration), and the Neldera-Mead method is responsible for finding the best point in the solution space (exploitation). Artificial intelligence algorithms such as the ant algorithm are widely used in various fields of science [14–18]. More about application of intelligent algorithms to solve inverse problems can be found in [19–23]. The problems discussed in the paper were also considered by another authors. For example the identification of the fractional order models of one dimensional heat transfer process is presented in papers [24–27].

This paper is organized as follows. In Sect. 2 authors present model – space fractional heat conduction equation with Neumann, Robin boundary conditions and Riemann-Liouville fractional derivative. Inverse problem consist on identifying heat transfer coefficient and thermal conductivity coefficient based on temperature measurements. The problem is reduced to the optimization problem. Short description of solution of direct problem is presented in Sect. 3. In Sect. 4 we present description of presented algorithm. Section 5 presents numerical example with conclusions.

2   Mathematical Model

In this section we present a mathematical model which describes process of heat conduction in porous media - space fractional heat conduction equation:

$$c\varrho \frac{\partial u(x,t)}{\partial t} = \lambda \frac{\partial^\beta u(x,t)}{\partial x^\beta}, \tag{1}$$

where $x \in [0, L_x]$, $t \in [0, T)$, β is an order of fractional derivative and c, ϱ, λ denotes specific heat, density and thermal conductivity coefficient. Function u describes temperature. To the Eq. (1) an initial-boundary conditions are posted:

$$u(x, 0) = f, \quad x \in [0, L_x], \tag{2}$$

$$-\lambda \frac{\partial u(0, t)}{\partial x} = q(t), \quad t \in (0, T), \tag{3}$$

$$-\lambda\frac{\partial u(L_x,t)}{\partial x} = h(t)(u(L_x,T) - u^\infty), \quad t \in (0,T), \tag{4}$$

where q is a heat flux, h is heat transfer coefficient, function f describes initial condition and u^∞ is ambient temperature. Fractional derivative occurring in right side of Eq. (1) is Riemann-Liouville derivative defined by formula ($\beta \in (1,2)$):

$$\frac{\partial u(x,t)}{\partial t} = \frac{1}{\Gamma(2-\beta)}\frac{\partial^2}{\partial x^2}\int_0^x u(s,t)(x-s)^{1-\beta}ds, \tag{5}$$

where Γ is the Gamma function.

In considered inverse problem heat transfer coefficient h, initial condition f and thermal conductivity λ are unknown parameters, which must be reconstructed. Heat transfer coefficient h has a form:

$$h(t) = a_1 t, \tag{6}$$

while $\lambda = a_2$ and $f = a_3$ are constants. Considered inverse problem consist of identifying the parameters a_i ($i = 1,2,3$) (and therefore heat transfer coefficient, thermal conductivity coefficient and initial condition). Information for inverse problem are temperature measurements from boundary, called input data and denoted by:

$$u(x_p, t_k) = \widehat{U}_k, \quad k = 1,2,\dots,N, \tag{7}$$

where x_p is a point from boundary and N denotes number of measurements. Solving the direct problem for fixed values of h, λ, gives an approximate temperatures in point x_p. These values is denoted by $U_k(h, \lambda, f)$. Therefore, based on computed temperature from model and input data, we create functional describing the error of approximate solution:

$$F(h,\lambda,f) = \sqrt{\sum_{k=1}^N \left(U_k(h,\lambda,f) - \widehat{U}_k\right)^2}. \tag{8}$$

Using hybrid algorithm to minimize objective function (4), we can restore parameters h, λ, f.

3   Direct Problem

Direct problem is solved using finite difference method. Riemann-Liouville fractional derivative is approximate using Grünwald formula [28]:

$$\frac{\partial^\beta u(x_i, t_k)}{\partial x^\beta} \approx \sum_{j=0}^{i+1} \omega(\beta, j) U_{i-j+1}^k \tag{9}$$

where

$$\omega(\beta, j) = \frac{\Gamma(j - \beta)}{\Gamma(-\beta)\Gamma(j+1)}.$$ (10)

To find direct problem solution we used mesh:

$$S = \{(x_i, t_k) : x_i = i\Delta x, \quad t_k = k\Delta t, \quad i = 0, 1, \ldots, N, \quad k = 0, 1, \ldots, M\}.$$

$N \times M$ is size of the mesh, while $\Delta x = L_x/N$, $\Delta t = T/M$ are steps. U_i^k means temperature in point (x_i, t_k). By discretizing the Eq. (1), approximating the boundary conditions and the fractional derivative, we get a differential scheme from which we obtain the temperature values in mesh points. More about numerical scheme and solution of direct problem can be found in [29].

4   Hybrid Algorithm

In order to find unknown parameters of the model, we need to minimize functional (8). In this section, we present hybrid algorithm which is combination of Ant Colony Optimization algorithm and Nelder-Mead method. First, we used ACO algorithm to locate area, in solution space, where solution could be. The advantages of this algorithm are: simple description, easy implementation, the ability to run the algorithm on many threads. An important feature of this algorithm is also the avoidance of falling into local minima, so it is ideal for exploring the space of solutions. Second algorithm - Nelder-Mead method, which is used after ACO algorithm, is deterministic. Results obtained from ACO algorithm is used as an input data (input simplex) for NM method. Thus, the ACO algorithm is good for the exploration part, and the NM method is well suited to the exploitation part.

Now, we describe only ACO algorithm, Nelder-Mead method (downhill simplex method) is described very well in literature [13].

4.1   Ant Colony Optimization Algorithm

To describe ACO algorithm we assume following symbols:

F – minimized function (objective function),
nT – number of threads,
$M = nT \cdot k$ – number of ants ($k \in \mathbb{Z}$),
L – number of pheromone spots,
I – number of iterations,
$\xi = 1.0, q = 0.9$ – parameters of algorithm.

ACO algorithm
Initialization of the algorithm

1. Setting parameters of the algorithm L, M, I, nT.
2. Generating L pheromone spots (solutions) in random way and creating the initial archive solutions T_0.

3. Computing values of minimized function for every pheromone spot (solution) and assigning rank to the solutions referring to the value of the minimized function. Sort elements in T_0, according to their qualities (descending).

Iterative process

4. Assigning the probabilities to the pheromone spots (solutions) according to the formula:

$$p_l = \frac{\omega_l}{\sum_{l=1}^{L} \omega_l} \quad l = 1, 2, \ldots, L, \tag{11}$$

where ω_l is the weight associated to the l-th solution (solution which rank is l) and expressed by the formula

$$\omega_l = \frac{1}{qL\sqrt{2\pi}} e^{\frac{-(l-1)^2}{2q^2L^2}}. \tag{12}$$

5. The ant chooses the l-th solution according to probabilities p_l.
6. The ant transforms the j-th ($j = 1, 2, \ldots, n$) coordinate of the l-th solution s_j^l by sampling the neighborhood using the probability density function (Gaussian function):

$$g(x, \mu, \sigma) = \frac{1}{\sigma\sqrt{2\pi}} e^{\frac{-(x-\mu)^2}{2\sigma^2}}, \tag{13}$$

where $\mu = s_j^l, \sigma = \frac{\xi}{L-1} \sum_{p=1}^{L} |s_j^p - s_j^l|$.
7. Steps 5–6 are repeated for each ant. Hence, we obtain M new solutions (pheromone spots).
8. Dividing the population on nT groups (groups will be calculated in parallel way).
9. Determination the value of minimized function for each new solution in population (parallel calculation).
10. Assign rank to the elements from T_i and sort them.
11. Repeating steps 4–10 I times.
12. Return best solution from last archive T_i.

For fixed values of parameters L, M, I number of calculation of minimized function F is equal to $L + M \cdot I$.

5 Results

The following data has been adopted in the numerical example:

$$t \in [0, 71.82][\text{s}], \; x \in [0, 3.825][\text{mm}], \; c = 900\left[\frac{\text{J}}{\text{kg} \cdot \text{K}}\right], \; \varrho = 2106\left[\frac{\text{kg}}{\text{m}^3}\right],$$

$$u^\infty = 298[\text{K}], \; q(t) = 0[\frac{\text{kg}}{\text{s}^3 \cdot \text{m}^{2-\beta}}].$$

Unknown parameters are sought in the forms:

$$h(t) = a_1 t\left[\frac{\text{kg}}{\text{s}^3 \cdot \text{m}^{3-\beta} \cdot \text{K}}\right], \quad \lambda = a_2\left[\frac{\text{W}}{\text{m}^{3-\beta} \cdot \text{K}}\right], \quad f = a_3[\text{K}].$$

Exact values of sought parameters are equal to: $a_1 = 170$, $a_2 = 184$, $a_3 = 573.15$. Mesh used in calculations was size 100×1995 ($\Delta x = 0.03825, \Delta t = 0.036$) and mesh used to generate input data was 200×3990 ($\Delta x = 0.019125, \Delta t = 0.018$). First, in order to explore the solution space, we execute ACO algorithm. Following parameters were used in the ACO algorithm:

$$a_1 \in [100, 250], \; a_2 \in [100, 250], \; a_3 \in [400, 800],$$
$$L = 12, \quad M = 16, \quad I = 2, \quad nT = 4$$

Starting simplex for Nelder-Mead method is created from result obtained from ACO algorithm. Table 1 presents values of identified parameters $a_i (i = 1, 2, 3)$ obtained from hybrid algorithm. Errors of this reconstruction do not exceed 0.1%. Value of minimized function is equal to 0.001135, which is good result. During the execution of the algorithm, the objective function was calculated 180 times (44 in ACO algorithm and 136 in NM method). Table 2 presents errors of reconstruction temperature in measurement point.

Table 1. Results of identification parameters a_i, (e_{a_i}- errors of reconstruction $i = 1, 2, 3$) for hybrid algorithm

a_1	170.13
$e_{a_1}[\%]$	0.08
a_2	183.90
$e_{a_2}[\%]$	0.06
a_3	573.14
$e_{a_3}[\%]$	$1.7 \cdot 10^{-3}$
Value of function F	0.01135
Number of evaluation objective function	180

Table 2. Errors of temperature reconstruction (Δ_{avg}—average absolute error, Δ_{max}—maximal absolute error, δ_{avg}—average relative error, δ_{max}—maximal relative error)

$\Delta_{avg}[K]$	$1.4 \cdot 10^{-3}$
$\Delta_{max}[K]$	$8.1 \cdot 10^{-3}$
$\delta_{avg}[\%]$	$2.6 \cdot 10^{-4}$
$\delta_{max}[\%]$	$1.4 \cdot 10^{-3}$

Figure 1 presents measured data and reconstructed values of temperature in measurement point. As we can see reconstructed values of temperature fit well to the measurement data (input data).

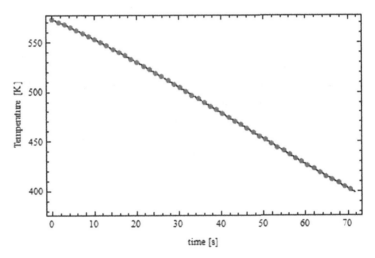

Fig. 1. Measured data (black line) and reconstructed temperature (red points). (Color figure online)

For comparison, the use of only the ACO algorithm, where $L = 12$, $M = 16$, $I = 55$, $nT = 4$ gave results presented in Table 3. The obtained results are worse than in the case of the hybrid algorithm. The value of the objective function was 7.33, and the number of evaluation of the objective function was 892 (approximately five times more than in hybrid algorithm).

Table 3. Results of identification parameters a_i, (e_{a_i}- errors of reconstruction $i = 1, 2, 3$) for only ACO algorithm

a_1	170.66
$e_{a_1} [\%]$	0.39
a_2	183.39
$e_{a_2} [\%]$	0.33
a_3	572.99
$e_{a_3} [\%]$	0.03
Value of function F	7.33
Number of evaluation objective function	892

6 Conclusions

The paper presents heat conduction model with fractional derivative and algorithm to solve inverse problem. In numerical experiment heat transfer coefficient, thermal conductivity and initial condition are identified using hybrid algorithm. This algorithm consist in ACO algorithm (exploration) and Nelder-Mead method (exploitation). Obtained results are acceptable and good, errors of reconstruction temperature in measurement point are small (for example absolute average error is approximately $1.4 \cdot 10^{-3} [\text{K}]$. Algorithm needed 180 evaluations of objective function. In case of using only ACO algorithm, 892 evaluations gave worse result.

Acknowledgements. The project is financed by the Polish National Agency for Academic Exchange no PPI/APM/2018/1/00004/U/001.

References

1. Voller, V.R.: Computations of anomalous phase change. Int. J. Numer. Methods Heat Fluid Flow **26**, 624–638 (2016)
2. Voller, V.R.: Anomalous heat transfer: examples, fundamentals, and fractional calculus models. Adv. Heat Transf. **50**, 333–380 (2018)
3. Szymanek, E., Błaszczyk, T., Hall, M.R., Keikhaei, D.P., Leszczyński, J.S.: Modelling and analysis of heat transfer through 1D complex granular system. Granular Matter **16**, 687–694 (2014)
4. Fabrizio, M., Giorgi, C., Morro, A.: Modeling of heat conduction via fractional derivatives. Heat Mass Transfer **53**, 2785–2797 (2017)
5. Podlubny, I.: Fractional Differential Equations. Academic Press, San Diego (1999)
6. Klafter, J., Lim, S., Metzler, R.: Fractional Dynamics: Resent Advances. World Scientific, Hackensack (2012)
7. Mitkowski, W., Skruch, P.: Fractional-order models of the supercapacitors in the form of RC ladder networks. Bull. Pol. Acad. Sci. Tech. Sci. **61**, 581–587 (2013)
8. Tenreiro Machado, J.A., et al.: Some applications of fractional calculus in engineering. Math. Probl. Eng. 34 pages, (2010). Article ID 639801

9. Mathieu, B., Melchior, B., Oustaloup, A., Ceyral, Ch.: Fractional differentiation for edge detection. Sig. Process. **83**, 2421–2432 (2003)
10. Sebaa, N., Fellah, Z.E.A., Lauriks, W., Depollier, C.: Application of fractional calculus to ultrasonic wave propagation in human cancellous bone. Sig. Process. Fractional Calc. Appl. Signals Syst. **86**, 2668–2677 (2006)
11. Obrączka, A., Kowalski, J.: Modeling the distribution of heat in the ceramic materials using fractional differential equations. In: Szczygieł, M. (ed.) Materiały XV Jubileuszowego Sympozjum "Podstawowe Problemy Energoelektroniki, Elektromechaniki i Mechatroniki", PPEEm 2012, vol. 32 of Archiwum Konferencji PTETiS, Komitet Organizacyjny Sympozjum PPEE i Seminarium BSE, pp. 132–133 (2012). (in Polish)
12. Socha, K., Dorigo, M.: Ant colony optimization in continuous domains. Eur. J. Oper. Res. **185**, 1155–1173 (2008)
13. Nelder, J.A., Mead, R.: A simplex method for function minimization. Comput. J. **7**, 308–313 (1965)
14. Woźniak, M., Połap, D.: Bio-inspired methods modeled for respiratory disease detection from medical images. Swarm Evol. Comput. **41**, 69–96 (2018)
15. Woźniak, M., Połap, D.: Hybrid neuro-heuristic methodology for simulation and control of dynamic systems over time interval. Neural Networks **93**, 45–56 (2017)
16. Połap, D., Woźniak, M., Damaševičius, R., Maskeliūnas, R.: Bio-inspired voice evaluation mechanism. Appl. Soft Comput. **80**, 342–357 (2019)
17. Tuccitto, N., Capizzi, G., Torrisi, A., Licciardello, A.: Unsupervised analysis of big ToF-SIMS data sets: a statistical pattern recognition approach. Anal. Chem. **90**, 286–2866 (2018)
18. Słowik, A., Kwaśnicka, H.: Nature inspired methods and their industry applications—swarm intelligence algorithms. IEEE Trans. Ind. Inf. **14**, 1004–1015 (2017)
19. Brociek, R., Słota, D.: Reconstruction of the Robin boundary condition and order of derivative in time fractional heat conduction equation. Math. Model. Nat. Phenom. **13** (2018). Article number 5
20. Chen, S., Liu, F., Jiang, X., Turner, I., Burrage, K.: Fast finite difference approximation for identifying parameters in a two-dimensional space-fractional nonlocal model with variable diffusivity coefficients. SIAM J. Numer. Anal. **56**, 606–624 (2016)
21. Ismailov, M.I., Cicek, M.: Inverse source problem for a time-fractional diffusion equation with nonlocal boundary conditions. Appl. Math. Model. **40**, 4891–4899 (2016)
22. Hetmaniok, E.: Inverse problem for the solidification of binary alloy in the casting mould solved by using the bee optimization algorithm. Heat Mass Transf. **52**, 1369–1379 (2016)
23. Brociek, R., Słota, D., Król, M., Matula, G., Kwaśny, W.: Modeling of heat distribution in porous aluminum using fractional differential equation. Fract. Fractional **1**, 1–9 (2017)
24. Oprzedkiewicz, K., Gawin, E., Mitkowski, W.: Modeling heat distribution with the use of a non-integer order, state space model. Int. J. Appl. Math. Comput. Sci. **26**, 749–756 (2016)
25. Oprzedkiewicz, K., Mitkowski, W., Gawin, E.: Parameter identification for non integer order, state space models of heat plant. In: 21st International conference on Methods and Models in Automation and Robotics, MMAR 2016, Miedzyzdroje, Poland, 29 August–01 September 2016, pp. 184–188. ISBN: 978-1-5090-1866-6, ISBN: 978-83-7518-791-5
26. Oprzędkiewicz, K., Dziedzic, K.: New parameter identification method for the fractional order, state space model of heat transfer process. In: Szewczyk, R., Zieliński, C., Kaliczyńska, M. (eds.) AUTOMATION 2018. AISC, vol. 743, pp. 401–417. Springer, Cham (2018). https://doi.org/10.1007/978-3-319-77179-3_38. ISBN: 978-3-319-77178-6; e-ISBN: 978-3-319-77179-3

27. Dziedzic, K.: Identification of fractional order transfer function model using biologically inspired algorithms. In: Szewczyk, R., Zieliński, C., Kaliczyńska, M. (eds.) AUTOMATION 2019, vol. 920, pp. 47–57. Springer, Cham (2020). https://doi.org/10.1007/978-3-030-13273-6_5. ISBN: 978-3-030-13272-9; e-ISBN: 978-3-030-13273-6
28. Miller, K., Ross, B.: An Introduction to the Fractional Calculus and Fractional Differential. Wiley, New York (1993)
29. Brociek, R., Słota, D.: Implicit finite difference method for space fractional heat conduction equation with mixed boundary conditions. Silesian J. Pure Appl. Math. **6**, 125–136 (2016)

Data Reduction via Stratified Sampling for Chance Constrained Optimization with Application to Flood Control Planning

Kiyoharu Tagawa[✉]

Kindai University, Higashi-Osaka 577-8502, Japan
tagawa@info.kindai.ac.jp

Abstract. Due to advanced information technologies, huge data are available to cope with Chance Constrained Problems (CCPs). In this paper, a relaxation problem of CCP is formulated by using such a huge data set. Then a new data reduction method based on stratified sampling is proposed to deal with the huge data set practically. A sample saving technique is also proposed to solve the relaxation problem efficiently by using an adaptive differential evolution algorithm. Finally, the proposed method is applied to the flood control planning formulated as CCP.

Keywords: Data reduction · Big data · Chance Constrained Problem

1 Introduction

In real-world optimization problems, a wide range of uncertainties have to be taken into account. Chance Constrained Problem (CCP), which is also referred to as probabilistic constrained problem, is one of the major approaches to solve optimization problems under various uncertainties. Specifically, CCP ensures that the probability of meeting constraints is above a certain level. Actually, many real-world applications have been formulated as CCPs [12,22,23].

CCP has been studied in the field of stochastic programming [18] for many years. Recently, evolutionary algorithms have been also reported for solving CCPs [11,17,21]. In the conventional formulations of CCP, the uncertainties have been modeled by a theoretical probability distribution such as the normal distribution. Otherwise, very few data (or scenarios) observed actually have been used to represent uncertainties. Consequently, as a drawback of the conventional formulations of CCP, the modeling error of uncertainties is unavoidable.

In recent years, due to advanced information technologies such as Wireless Sensor Networks (WSN) and Internet of Things (IoT) [24], huge data sets called big data can be easily obtained in various fields including culture, science, and industry. Since some huge data sets come from the uncertainties in real-world applications, it may be possible to describe CCP accurately with them.

In this paper, a relaxation problem of CCP is formulated based on a huge data set called the full data set. However, we suppose that the full data set is

© Springer Nature Switzerland AG 2019
R. Damaševičius and G. Vasiljevienė (Eds.): ICIST 2019, CCIS 1078, pp. 485–497, 2019.
https://doi.org/10.1007/978-3-030-30275-7_38

too large to evaluate the empirical probability for the relaxation problem. Thus, we propose a new data reduction method based on stratified sampling [8] and compare the method with well-known random sampling. Incidentally, the data reduction is neither dimensionally reduction nor data compression [1].

Clustering is one of the popular data reduction techniques [7,10]. Clustering divides a data set into some subsets so as to meet two requirements: (1) Internal cohesion; (2) External isolation. Consequently, the result of clustering depends on the structure of data. Sampling is another technique of data reduction [9]. Especially, the random sampling is widely used due to its simplicity and easy execution. As a drawback of sampling, since most of data are discarded without consideration, the key information in many data is likely to be lost.

As well as clustering, the proposed data reduction method based on stratified sampling also divides the full data set into some subsets (or strata), but the stratification does not require "External isolation". Therefore, the full data set can be reduced to an arbitrary size without losing information in data.

In order to solve the relaxation problem of CCP efficiently by using the latest adaptive Differential Evolution (DE) algorithm [25], a sample saving technique is also proposed. The sample saving technique is a pruning method that can detect and discard fruitless solutions without evaluating them. Finally, the proposed method is applied to the flood control planning formulated as CCP [22].

2   Problem Formulation

2.1   Chance Constrained Problem (CCP)

Let $\boldsymbol{x} = (x_1, \cdots, x_D) \in \boldsymbol{X} \subseteq \Re^D$ be a vector of decision variables or a solution. Uncertainties are shown by a vector of random variables $\boldsymbol{\xi} = (\xi_1, \cdots, \xi_K) \in \boldsymbol{\Omega}$. We suppose that both the sample space $\boldsymbol{\Omega} \subseteq \Re^K$ and the distribution of $\boldsymbol{\xi} \in \boldsymbol{\Omega}$ are unknown. CCP has $M \geq 1$ constraints $g_m(\boldsymbol{x}, \boldsymbol{\xi}) \leq 0$ including $\boldsymbol{\xi} \in \boldsymbol{\Omega}$. The joint probability $p(\boldsymbol{x}, \boldsymbol{\Omega}) \in [0, 1]$ that all constraints are satisfied is

$$p(\boldsymbol{x}, \boldsymbol{\Omega}) = \Pr(\forall \boldsymbol{\xi} \in \boldsymbol{\Omega} : g_m(\boldsymbol{x}, \boldsymbol{\xi}) \leq 0, \ m = 1, \cdots, M) \tag{1}$$

where $g_m : \boldsymbol{X} \times \boldsymbol{\Omega} \to \Re$, $m = 1, \cdots, M$ are measurable functions.

By using a sufficiency level $\alpha \in (0, 1)$, CCP is formulated as

$$\min_{\boldsymbol{x} \in \boldsymbol{X}} \ f(\boldsymbol{x}) \quad \text{s.t.} \quad p(\boldsymbol{x}, \boldsymbol{\Omega}) \geq \alpha \tag{2}$$

where $f : \boldsymbol{X} \to \Re$ is the objective function to be minimized.

Since $\boldsymbol{\Omega} \subseteq \Re^K$ is unknown, it is impossible to solve CCP in (2).

2.2   Relaxation Problem of CCP Using Full Data Set

As stated above, we assume that a huge data set $\boldsymbol{B} = \{\boldsymbol{\xi}^\ell\} \subseteq \boldsymbol{\Omega}$ is available for evaluating the probability in (1) empirically. Let $\boldsymbol{\xi}^\ell \in \boldsymbol{B}$ be a sample of $\boldsymbol{\xi} \in \boldsymbol{\Omega}$. For each constraint in (1), the indicator function is defined as

$$\mathbb{1}(g_m(\boldsymbol{x}, \boldsymbol{\xi}^\ell) \leq 0) = \begin{cases} 1 & \text{if } g_m(\boldsymbol{x}, \boldsymbol{\xi}^\ell) \leq 0 \\ 0 & \text{otherwise.} \end{cases} \tag{3}$$

From the full data set $\boldsymbol{B} = \{\boldsymbol{\xi}^\ell\}$ and the indicator function, the empirical probability that a solution $\boldsymbol{x} \in \boldsymbol{X}$ satisfies all constraints is evaluated as

$$\hat{p}(\boldsymbol{x}, \boldsymbol{B}) = \frac{1}{|\boldsymbol{B}|} \sum_{\boldsymbol{\xi}^\ell \in B} \left(\prod_{m=1}^{M} \mathbb{1}(g_m(\boldsymbol{x}, \boldsymbol{\xi}^\ell) \leq 0) \right) \tag{4}$$

where $|\boldsymbol{B}|$ denotes the size of the data set $\boldsymbol{B}$ or the total number of $\boldsymbol{\xi}^\ell \in \boldsymbol{B}$.

From (4), the relaxation problem of CCP in (2) is formulated as

$$\min_{\boldsymbol{x} \in \boldsymbol{X}} \ f(\boldsymbol{x}) \quad \text{s.t.} \quad \hat{p}(\boldsymbol{x}, \boldsymbol{B}) \geq \alpha. \tag{5}$$

The size of the data set $\boldsymbol{B} \subseteq \boldsymbol{\Omega}$ is so huge. Therefore, from the law of large number [2], we can expect that $\hat{p}(\boldsymbol{x}, \boldsymbol{B}) \approx p(\boldsymbol{x}, \boldsymbol{\Omega})$ holds, and we can adopt the solution of the relaxation problem in (5) as the solution of CCP in (2).

3   Data Reduction via Sampling

In practical CCP, each of the function value $g_m(\boldsymbol{x}, \boldsymbol{\xi}^\ell)$ is usually evaluated through time-consuming computer simulation. Therefore, we assume that the full data set $\boldsymbol{B} = \{\boldsymbol{\xi}^\ell\}$ is too large to evaluate the empirical probability in (4). In order to reduce the size of $\boldsymbol{B}$, we compare the following two methods.

3.1   Simple Random Sampling (SRS)

Simple Random Sampling (SRS) is the most popular technique used to reduce the number of data. We select N samples $\boldsymbol{\xi}^n \in \boldsymbol{\Xi}$, $n = 1, \cdots, N$ randomly from the full data set $\boldsymbol{B} = \{\boldsymbol{\xi}^\ell\}$. The sample size N is usually far smaller than the data size $|\boldsymbol{B}|$. By using the subset $\boldsymbol{\Xi} = \{\boldsymbol{\xi}^1, \cdots, \boldsymbol{\xi}^N\} \subseteq \boldsymbol{B}$, the following empirical probability $\hat{p}(\boldsymbol{x}, \boldsymbol{\Xi})$ can be used in (5) instead of $\hat{p}(\boldsymbol{x}, \boldsymbol{B})$.

$$\hat{p}(\boldsymbol{x}, \boldsymbol{\Xi}) = \frac{1}{N} \sum_{n=1}^{N} \left(\prod_{m=1}^{M} \mathbb{1}(g_m(\boldsymbol{x}, \boldsymbol{\xi}^n) \leq 0) \right) \tag{6}$$

3.2   Weighted Stratified Sampling (WSS)

We propose a new data reduction method called Weighted Stratified Sampling (WSS). As a stratification technique that divides the full data set into some subsets exclusively, we employ K-dimensional equi-width histogram [16]. By using the histogram, the full data set $\boldsymbol{B}$ is divided into N bins $\boldsymbol{B}_n$ as

$$\boldsymbol{B} = \boldsymbol{B}_1 \cup \cdots \cup \boldsymbol{B}_n \cup \cdots \cup \boldsymbol{B}_N. \tag{7}$$

We decide an exemplar sample $\boldsymbol{\theta}^n \in \Re^K$ for each bin $\boldsymbol{B}_n$, which represents all data $\boldsymbol{\xi}^\ell \in \boldsymbol{B}_n$. Let $\boldsymbol{\Theta} = \{\boldsymbol{\theta}^1, \cdots, \boldsymbol{\theta}^N\}$ be the set of the exemplar samples. The best $\boldsymbol{\Theta} \subseteq \Re^K$ minimizes the error metric of histogram [4] defined as

$$e_H(\boldsymbol{\Theta}, \boldsymbol{B}) = \sum_{n=1}^{N} e_H(\boldsymbol{\theta}^n, \boldsymbol{B}_n) = \sum_{n=1}^{N} \sum_{\boldsymbol{\xi}^\ell \in B_n} (\boldsymbol{\theta}^n - \boldsymbol{\xi}^\ell)^2. \tag{8}$$

Since $e_H(\boldsymbol{\theta}^n, \boldsymbol{B}_n)$ is convex, we solve the following differential equation.

$$\frac{\partial e_H(\boldsymbol{\theta}^n, \boldsymbol{B}_n)}{\partial \boldsymbol{\theta}^n} = 2 \left(|\boldsymbol{B}_n| \boldsymbol{\theta}^n - \sum_{\boldsymbol{\xi}^\ell \in \boldsymbol{B}_n} \boldsymbol{\xi}^\ell \right) = 0 \tag{9}$$

From (9), we can obtain the optimal $\boldsymbol{\theta}^n \in \Re^K$ for $\boldsymbol{B}_n \subseteq \boldsymbol{B}$ as

$$\boldsymbol{\theta}^n = \frac{1}{|\boldsymbol{B}_n|} \sum_{\boldsymbol{\xi}^\ell \in \boldsymbol{B}_n} \boldsymbol{\xi}^\ell. \tag{10}$$

From (10), $\boldsymbol{\Theta} = \{\boldsymbol{\theta}^1, \cdots, \boldsymbol{\theta}^N\}$ is not a subset of the full data set $\boldsymbol{B}$.

The weight $w_n \in \Re$ of each $\boldsymbol{\theta}^n \in \boldsymbol{\Theta}$ is given by the size of $\boldsymbol{B}_n$ as $w_n = |\boldsymbol{B}_n|$. Then, by using the set of weighted exemplar samples $\boldsymbol{\Theta} \subseteq \Re^K$, the empirical probability that a solution $\boldsymbol{x} \in \boldsymbol{X}$ satisfies all constraints is evaluated as

$$\hat{p}(\boldsymbol{x}, \boldsymbol{\Theta}) = \frac{1}{W} \sum_{n=1}^{N} w_n \left(\prod_{m=1}^{M} \mathbb{1}(g_m(\boldsymbol{x}, \boldsymbol{\theta}^n) \leq 0) \right) \tag{11}$$

where $W = w_1 + \cdots + w_n + \cdots + w_N$ and $w_n > 0$, $n = 1, \cdots, N$.

3.3   Relaxation Problem of CCP Using Reduced Data Set

From (11), the relaxation problem of CCP in (5) is revised as

$$\min_{\boldsymbol{x} \in \boldsymbol{X}} f(\boldsymbol{x}) \quad \text{s.t.} \quad \hat{p}(\boldsymbol{x}, \boldsymbol{\Theta}) \geq \beta \tag{12}$$

where a level $\beta \geq \alpha$ is chosen to compensate the estimation error of $\hat{p}(\boldsymbol{x}, \boldsymbol{\Theta})$.

4   Adaptive Differential Evolution

Differential Evolution (DE) has been proven to be one of the most powerful global optimization algorithms [5, 20]. Especially, JADE [25] is the most effective Adaptive DE (ADE), which adjusts the control parameters of DE adaptively. However, JADE is applicable only to unconstrained optimization problems. For solving the relaxation problem in (12), we develop a new ADE by introducing an elaborate Constraint Handling Technique (CHT) into the original JADE.

4.1   Constraint Handling and Pruning Method

Among a number of CHTs reported recently [15], the feasibility rule [6] is one of the most widely used CHTs because of its simplicity and efficiency. Thus, we employ a feasibility rule with the constraint violation defined from (12) as

$$h(\boldsymbol{x}) = \max\{\beta - \hat{p}(\boldsymbol{x}, \boldsymbol{\Theta}), 0\} \tag{13}$$

where the solution $\boldsymbol{x} \in \boldsymbol{X}$ is infeasible if $h(\boldsymbol{x}) > 0$ holds.

The proposed ADE has a set of solutions $x_i \in P_t \subseteq X$, $i = 1, \cdots, N_P$ called population in each generation t. Every $x_i \in P_t$ is assigned to a target vector in turn. By using the strategy of JADE, namely DE/current-to-$p$best/1/bin [25], a trial vector $z_i \in X$ is generated from the current target vector $x_i \in P_t$.

Each trial vector $z_i \in X$, $i = 1, \cdots, N_P$ is compared with the corresponding target vector $x_i \in P_t$. Then, if the following condition is satisfied, $z_i \in X$ is discarded immediately and $x_i \in P_t$ is chosen for a successor $x_i \in P_{t+1}$.

$$(h(x_i) = 0) \wedge (f(x_i) < f(z_i)) \tag{14}$$

Since the pruning method based on the condition in (14) doesn't require the value of $h(z_i)$, it is very effective to save the run time of ADE. Only when the condition in (14) is not satisfied, the empirical probability $\hat{p}(z_i, \Theta)$ is evaluated by using exemplar samples $\theta^n \in \Theta$, $n = 1, \cdots, N$ to get the value of $h(z_i)$. Thereafter, if either of the following conditions is satisfied, $z_i \in X$ is chosen for a successor $x_i \in P_{t+1}$. Otherwise, $x_i \in P_t$ is chosen for $x_i \in P_{t+1}$.

$$\begin{bmatrix} h(z_i) < h(x_i) \\ (h(z_i) = h(x_i)) \wedge (f(z_i) < f(x_i)) \end{bmatrix} \tag{15}$$

4.2 Algorithm of Proposed ADE

The maximum number of generations N_T is used as the termination condition. Thereby, the algorithm of the proposed ADE is described as follows.

Step 1: Generate $x_i \in P_0 \subseteq X$, $i = 1, \cdots, N_P$ randomly. $t := 0$.
Step 2: If $t = N_T$ holds, output the best solution $x_b \in P_t$.
Step 3: Generate the trial vectors $z_i \in X$ from $x_i \in P_t$, $i = 1, \cdots, N_P$.
Step 4: Choose $z_i \in X$ or $x_i \in P_t$ for $x_i \in P_{t+1}$, $i = 1, \cdots, N_P$.
Step 5: Adjust the control parameters of DE as shown in [25].
Step 6: $t := t + 1$. Go back to Step 2.   □

In the above ADE, the values of $h(z_i)$ are evaluated $N_P \times N_T$ times at the most. Therefore, from (11), the time complexity of ADE becomes $\mathcal{O}(N \times M)$.

5 Flood Control Planning: Case Study 1

5.1 Formulation of CCP

In the flood control planning [22], we minimize the cost to protect an urban area from the flood damage caused by torrential rain. The flood control reservoir system design has been formulated as CCP [19]. In addition to the reservoir, the water-retaining capacity of forest is counted in the flood control planning.

Figure 1 shows a topological river model. Symbol $\triangledown$ denotes a forest. There are two forests in watersheds. The area of each forest a_j, $j = 1, 2$ is a constant.

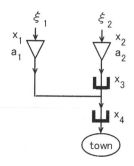

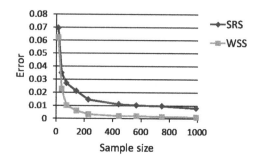

Fig. 1. River model (Case 1)   **Fig. 2.** Error for sample size ($K = 2$)

It rains in the two forests. The amount of rainfall $\xi_j \in \Re$ per unit area is a random variable. The water-retaining capacity of forest $x_j \in \Re$ per unit area is regarded as a decision variable because it can be controlled through the forest maintenance such as afforestation. From the model of forest mechanism [13], the inflow of water $Q_j \in \Re$ from the forest to river can be described as

$$Q_j = a_j \left(\xi_j - x_j \left(1 - \exp(-\xi_j / x_j) \right) \right) \tag{16}$$

where the effect of past rainfall is not considered in the model [13].

Symbol ⊔ denotes a reservoir in Fig. 1. There are two reservoirs and the capacities of them (x_3 and x_4) are decision variables. From (16), the inflow of water from the river to the town located at the lower part of the river is

$$g(\boldsymbol{x}, \boldsymbol{\xi}) = \max\{\max\{Q_2 - x_3,\ 0\} + Q_1 - x_4,\ 0\}. \tag{17}$$

The inflow of water described in (17) can be rewritten as

$$g(\boldsymbol{x}, \boldsymbol{\xi}) = \begin{cases} g_1(\boldsymbol{x}, \boldsymbol{\xi}) & \text{if } (Q_2 > x_3) \wedge (Q_1 + Q_2 > x_3 + x_4) \\ g_2(\boldsymbol{x}, \boldsymbol{\xi}) & \text{if } (Q_2 \leq x_3) \wedge (Q_1 > x_4) \\ 0 & \text{otherwise} \end{cases} \tag{18}$$

where $g_1(\boldsymbol{x}, \boldsymbol{\xi}) = Q_1 + Q_2 - x_3 - x_4$ and $g_2(\boldsymbol{x}, \boldsymbol{\xi}) = Q_1 - x_4$.

The probability that $g(\boldsymbol{x}, \boldsymbol{\xi}) \leq 0$ holds has to be greater than $\alpha \in (0, 1)$. The maintenance cost of a forest is proportional to its capacity. The construction cost of a reservoir is proportional to the square of its capacity. From (18), the flood control planning to minimize the total cost is formulated as CCP:

$$\begin{bmatrix} \min_{\boldsymbol{x} \in X} & f(\boldsymbol{x}) = a_1 x_1 + a_2 x_2 + c_3 x_3^2 + c_4 x_4^2 \\ \text{s.t.} & \Pr\left(\forall \boldsymbol{\xi} \in \boldsymbol{\Omega} :\ g_m(\boldsymbol{x}, \boldsymbol{\xi}) \leq 0,\ m = 1,\ 2 \right) \geq \alpha \\ & 0.5 \leq x_1 \leq 1.5,\ 0.5 \leq x_2 \leq 1.5,\ 0 \leq x_3 \leq 2,\ 0 \leq x_4 \leq 3 \end{bmatrix} \tag{19}$$

where $a_1 = 2$, $a_2 = 2$, $c_3 = 3$, $c_4 = 1$, and $\alpha = 0.9$.

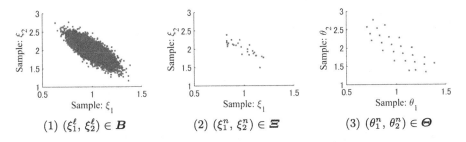

$(1)\ (\xi_1^\ell,\ \xi_2^\ell) \in B$ $(2)\ (\xi_1^n,\ \xi_2^n) \in \Xi$ $(3)\ (\theta_1^n,\ \theta_2^n) \in \Theta$

Fig. 3. Patterns of (1) Full data; (2) SRS with $N = 26$; (3) WSS with $N = 26$

Table 1. Experimental result of case study 1

α	β	N	$f(x_b)$	$\hat{p}(x_b, \Theta)$	$\hat{p}(x_b, B)$	Rate
0.90	0.95	95.4	11.230	0.955	0.943	0.397

5.2   Comparison of SRS and WSS

The amount of rainfall $\xi_j \in \Re$ in (19) is defined by a normal distribution as

$$\xi_j \sim \mathcal{N}(\mu_j\ \sigma_j^2), \quad j = 1,\ 2 \tag{20}$$

where $\boldsymbol{\mu} = (\mu_1, \mu_2) = (1,\ 2)$ and $\boldsymbol{\sigma}^2 = (\sigma_1^2, \sigma_2^2) = (0.1^2,\ 0.2^2)$. The correlation matrix of the amounts of rainfall $\boldsymbol{\xi} = (\xi_1, \xi_2) \in \Omega$ is given as

$$\boldsymbol{R} = \begin{pmatrix} 1.0 & \rho_{12} \\ \rho_{21} & 1.0 \end{pmatrix} = \begin{pmatrix} 1.0 & -0.8 \\ -0.8 & 1.0 \end{pmatrix}. \tag{21}$$

From (20), we generate the full data set $\boldsymbol{B} \subseteq \Omega$, $|\boldsymbol{B}| = 10^4$ randomly.

For a solution $\boldsymbol{x} \in \boldsymbol{X}$ of CCP in (19), we evaluate the empirical probability $\hat{p}(\boldsymbol{x}, \boldsymbol{B})$ as shown in (4). Then, by using SRS and WSS, we estimate the value of $\hat{p}(\boldsymbol{x}, \boldsymbol{B})$. Figure 2 shows the estimation errors of them defined as

$$\begin{bmatrix} e_P(\boldsymbol{\Xi}, \boldsymbol{B}) = |\hat{p}(\boldsymbol{x}, \boldsymbol{\Xi}) - \hat{p}(\boldsymbol{x}, \boldsymbol{B})| \\ e_P(\boldsymbol{\Theta}, \boldsymbol{B}) = |\hat{p}(\boldsymbol{x}, \boldsymbol{\Theta}) - \hat{p}(\boldsymbol{x}, \boldsymbol{B})|. \end{bmatrix} \tag{22}$$

The above estimation errors are evaluated 100 times by using different full data sets $\boldsymbol{B} \subseteq \Omega$ and averaged in Fig. 2. From Fig. 2, the value of $e_P(\boldsymbol{\Theta}, \boldsymbol{B})$ is smaller than $e_P(\boldsymbol{\Xi}, \boldsymbol{B})$ for any sample sizes. Furthermore, $e_P(\boldsymbol{\Theta}, \boldsymbol{B})$ converges to almost zero faster than $e_P(\boldsymbol{\Xi}, \boldsymbol{B})$. Therefore, we can say that the proposed WSS outperforms the popular SRS in the accuracy of estimation.

Figure 3 shows the spatial patterns of $\boldsymbol{\xi}^\ell \in \boldsymbol{B}$, $\boldsymbol{\xi}^n \in \boldsymbol{\Xi}$, and $\theta^n \in \boldsymbol{\Theta}$. From Fig. 3, we can see that the exemplar samples $\theta^n \in \boldsymbol{\Theta}$, $n = 1, \cdots, N$ by WSS are scattered more widely as compared to the random samples $\boldsymbol{\xi}^n \in \boldsymbol{\Xi}$ by SRS. Especially, SRS can't take any samples from the sparse tail of $\boldsymbol{B}$.

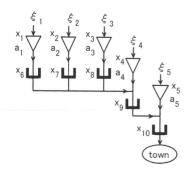

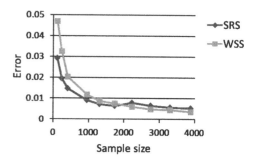

Fig. 4. River model (Case 2)   **Fig. 5.** Error for sample size ($K = 5$)

5.3 Numerical Experiment

The proposed ADE is coded in MATLAB [14]. The parameters of ADE are chosen as $N_T = 60$ and $N_P = 20$. According to the proposed method, the CCP in (19) is transformed into the relaxation problem in (12) with $\beta = 0.95$. By using different $B \subseteq \Omega$ and $P_0 \subseteq X$, ADE is applied to the relaxation problem 20 times. Therefore, a new set $\Theta \subseteq \Re^2$ is generated from B in each time. Besides, the best solution $x_b \in X$ obtained by ADE is checked whether it satisfies the constraint of the relaxation problem of CCP in (5) such as $\hat{p}(x_b, B) \geq \alpha$.

Table 1 shows the result of experiment averaged over 20 runs. In Table 1, N is the sample size of $\theta^n \in \Theta$. $f(x_b)$ is the objective function value achieved by $x_b \in X$, or the best solution obtained by ADE. $\hat{p}(x_b, \Theta)$ and $\hat{p}(x_b, B)$ are the empirical probabilities achieved by $x_b \in X$. The rate denotes the percentage of the trial vectors $z_i \in X$ discarded by the pruning method shown in (14).

From the result of Table 1, we can confirm the availability of the proposed method. Even though the sample size N is small, $\hat{p}(x_b, \Theta)$ is close to $\hat{p}(x_b, B)$. The best solution $x_b \in X$ satisfies the constraint $\hat{p}(x_b, B) \geq \alpha$. Therefore, if we suppose that $\hat{p}(x_b, B) \approx p(x_b, \Omega)$ holds, we can regard $x_b \in X$ as a feasible solution of CCP in (19). From the high rate in Table 1, we can also confirm that the pruning method works effectively for saving the number of samples.

6   Flood Control Planning: Case Study 2

6.1   Formulation of CCP

Figure 4 shows another topological river model in the same way with Fig. 1. There are five forests and five reservoirs in Fig. 4. The water-retaining capacities of forests x_j, $j = 1, \cdots, 5$ and the capacities of reservoirs x_j, $j = 6, \cdots, 10$ are decision variables. The amounts of rainfall ξ_j, $j = 1, \cdots, 5$ are random variables. Thereby, the flood control planning in Fig. 4 is formulated as CCP:

$$
\begin{bmatrix}
\min_{x \in X} \ f(x) = \sum_{j=1}^{5} a_j x_j + \sum_{j=6}^{10} c_j x_j^2 \\
\text{s.t.} \quad \Pr\left(\forall \xi \in \Omega : g_m(x, \xi) \leq 0, \ m = 1, \cdots, 9\right) \geq \alpha \\
0.5 \leq x_j \leq 1.5, \ j = 1, \cdots, 5, \ 0 \leq x_j \leq 3, \ j = 6, 7, 8 \\
0 \leq x_9 \leq 4, \ 0 \leq x_{10} \leq 4
\end{bmatrix}
\tag{23}
$$

where $a_j = 2$, $j = 1, \cdots, 5$, $c_j = 3$, $j = 6, 7, 8$, $c_9 = 2$, $c_{10} = 1$, and $\alpha = 0.9$.

In the same way as we have shown in (17) and (18), by using $Q_j \in \Re$ in (16), we can derive the function $g_m(x, \xi)$, $m = 1, \cdots, 9$ for CCP in (23) as

$$
\begin{bmatrix}
g_1(x, \xi) = Q_1 + Q_2 + Q_3 + Q_4 + Q_5 - x_6 - x_7 - x_8 - x_9 - x_{10} \\
g_2(x, \xi) = Q_1 + Q_2 + Q_4 + Q_5 - x_6 - x_7 - x_9 - x_{10} \\
g_3(x, \xi) = Q_1 + Q_3 + Q_4 + Q_5 - x_6 - x_8 - x_9 - x_{10} \\
g_4(x, \xi) = Q_2 + Q_3 + Q_4 + Q_5 - x_7 - x_8 - x_9 - x_{10} \\
g_5(x, \xi) = Q_1 + Q_4 + Q_5 - x_6 - x_9 - x_{10} \\
g_6(x, \xi) = Q_2 + Q_4 + Q_5 - x_7 - x_9 - x_{10} \\
g_7(x, \xi) = Q_3 + Q_4 + Q_5 - x_8 - x_9 - x_{10} \\
g_8(x, \xi) = Q_4 + Q_5 - x_9 - x_{10} \\
g_9(x, \xi) = Q_5 - x_{10}.
\end{bmatrix}
\tag{24}
$$

6.2 Comparison of SRS and WSS

For convenience, the amount of rainfall $\xi_j \in \Re$ in (23) is also defined by a normal distribution as shown in (20). The mean $\mu \in \Re^5$, variance $\sigma^2 \in \Re^5$, and correlation matrix of $\xi = (\xi_1, \xi_2, \xi_3, \xi_4, \xi_5) \in \Omega$ are given as

$$
\begin{bmatrix}
\mu = (\mu_1, \mu_2, \mu_3, \mu_4, \mu_5) & = & (2.0, \ 1.5, \ 2.5, \ 0.8, \ 1.0) \\
\sigma^2 = (\sigma_1^2, \sigma_2^2, \sigma_3^2, \sigma_4^2, \sigma_5^2) & = & (0.2^2, \ 0.1^2, \ 0.2^2, \ 0.1^2, \ 0.1^2) \\
R = \begin{pmatrix}
1.0 & \rho_{12} & \rho_{13} & \rho_{14} & \rho_{15} \\
\rho_{21} & 1.0 & \rho_{23} & \rho_{24} & \rho_{25} \\
\rho_{31} & \rho_{32} & 1.0 & \rho_{34} & \rho_{35} \\
\rho_{41} & \rho_{42} & \rho_{43} & 1.0 & \rho_{45} \\
\rho_{51} & \rho_{52} & \rho_{53} & \rho_{54} & 1.0
\end{pmatrix} & = & \begin{pmatrix}
1.0 & -0.5 & 0.0 & 0.3 & -0.5 \\
-0.5 & 1.0 & -0.8 & 0.0 & 0.2 \\
0.0 & -0.8 & 1.0 & 0.0 & 0.3 \\
0.3 & 0.0 & 0.0 & 1.0 & 0.0 \\
-0.5 & 0.2 & 0.3 & 0.0 & 1.0
\end{pmatrix}.
\end{bmatrix}
\tag{25}
$$

We generate the full data set $B \subseteq \Omega$, $|\Omega| = 10^4$ randomly. For a solution $x \in X$ of CCP in (23), we evaluate the empirical probability $\hat{p}(x, B)$ as shown in (4). Then, by using SRS and WSS, we estimate the value of $\hat{p}(x, B)$. Figure 5 shows the estimation errors of them in the same way with Fig. 2. Contrary to Fig. 2, we can't see the advantage of WSS in Fig. 5. The effect of WSS seems to be reduced when the dimensionality of $B \subseteq \Omega \subseteq \Re^K$ gets higher.

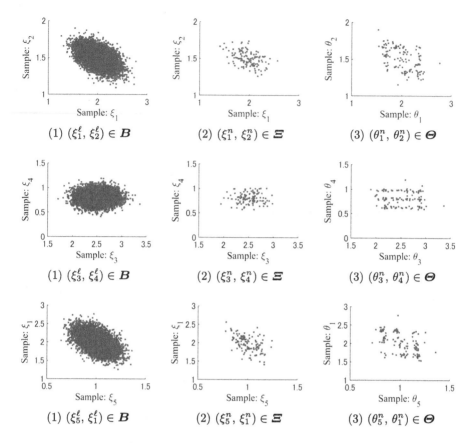

Fig. 6. Patterns of (1) Full data; (2) SRS with $N = 121$; (3) WSS with $N = 121$

Figure 6 shows the patterns of $\boldsymbol{\xi}^\ell \in \boldsymbol{B}$, $\boldsymbol{\xi}^n \in \boldsymbol{\Xi}$, and $\boldsymbol{\theta}^n \in \boldsymbol{\Theta}$. We can see that the exemplar samples $\boldsymbol{\theta}^n \in \boldsymbol{\Theta}$, $n = 1, \cdots, N$ are scattered more widely as compared to random samples $\boldsymbol{\xi}^n \in \boldsymbol{\Xi}$. However, we can't confirm the uniformity in the pattern of $\boldsymbol{\theta}^n \in \boldsymbol{\Theta}$ due to the high dimensionality $K = 5$ of them.

Table 2. Experimental result of case study 2

α	β	N	$f(\boldsymbol{x}_b)$	$\hat{p}(\boldsymbol{x}_b, \boldsymbol{\Theta})$	$\hat{p}(\boldsymbol{x}_b, \boldsymbol{B})$	Rate
0.90	0.95	407.3	34.157	0.952	0.934	0.396

6.3 Numerical Experiment

The CCP in (23) is transformed into a relaxation problem in (12) with $\beta = 0.95$. The parameters of ADE are chosen as $N_T = 200$ and $N_P = 50$. By using different $B \subseteq \Omega$ and $P_0 \subseteq X$, ADE is applied to the relaxation problem 20 times.

Table 2 shows the result of experiment in the same way with Table 1. The best solution $x_b \in X$ satisfies the constraint $\hat{p}(x_b, B) \geq \alpha$. Therefore, if we suppose that $\hat{p}(x_b, B) \approx p(x_b, \Omega)$ holds, we can regard $x_b \in X$ as a feasible solution of CCP in (23). From the high rate in Table 2, we can confirm that the pruning method works effectively for saving the number of samples.

7 Discussion and Conclusion

In this paper, we have proposed and investigated a practical method to solve CCP by using a huge data set. Specifically, the relaxation problem of CCP is formulated by using the full date set. Since the full date set is too large to evaluate the empirical probability that all constraints of CCP are satisfied, a new data reduction method based on stratified sampling is proposed. Furthermore, a new sample saving technique is also proposed to solve the relaxation problem of CCP efficiently by using a new ADE. Finally, the proposed method is applied to two problem instances of the flood control planning formulated as CCP.

Since huge data sets are available in various fields due to novel information technologies nowadays, the proposed method to solve CCP by using a huge data set seems to be promising. However, there are the following open problems in the proposed data reduction method based on stratified sampling.

- How to decide the bins of K-dimensional histogram. The number and the accuracy of the samples $\theta^n \in \Theta$ depend on the selection of bins.
- How to cope with high-dimensional data sets. Since the similarity of data $\xi^\ell \in B_n$ which are assigned in the same bin is reduced in the high-dimensional data set, all data $\xi^\ell \in B_n$ can't be represented by one sample $\theta^n \in \Theta$.

In our future work, we will develop a technique to decide the bins of histogram adaptively. Thereby, we can execute a kind of importance sampling by using the exemplar samples $\theta^n \in \Theta$. Furthermore, in order to cope with high-dimensional data sets, we will develop a clustering technique of the full data set $B = \{\xi^\ell\}$ based on the correlation between those elements. Thereby, we can divide the full data set into several low-dimensional and mutually independent subsets. As a result, we may apply the proposed data reduction method to each of the subsets effectively. In addition, we also need to compare the proposed ADE with other evolutionary algorithms such as Ant Colony Optimization algorithm [3].

Acknowledgment. This work was supported by JSPS (17K06508).

References

1. Aggarwal, C.C.: An efficient subspace sampling framework for high-dimensional data reduction, selectivity estimation, and nearest-neighbor search. IEEE Trans. Knowl. Data Eng. **16**(10), 1247–1262 (2004)
2. Ash, R.B.: Basic Probability Theory. Dover, New York (2008)
3. Brociek, R., Słota, D.: Application of real ant colony optimization algorithm to solve space and time fractional heat conduction inverse problem. In: 22nd International Conference on Information and Software Technologies, ICIST 2016, vol. 639, pp. 369–379. Communications in Computer and Information Science (2016)
4. Cormode, G., Garofalakis, M.: Histograms and wavelets on probabilistic data. IEEE Trans. Knowl. Data Eng. **22**(8), 1142–1157 (2010)
5. Das, S., Suganthan, P.N.: Differential evolution: a survey of the state-of-the-art. IEEE Trans. Evol. Comput. **15**(1), 4–31 (2011)
6. Deb, K.: An efficient constraint handling method for genetic algorithms. Comput. Methods Appl. Mech. Eng. **186**, 311–338 (2000)
7. Fahad, A., et al.: A survey of clustering algorithms for big data: taxonomy and empirical analysis. IEEE Trans. Emerg. Top. Comput. **2**(3), 267–279 (2014)
8. Han, J., Kamber, M., Pei, J.: Data Mining - Concepts and Techniques. Morgan Kaufmann (2012)
9. Jayaram, N., Baker, J.W.: Efficient sampling and data reduction techniques for probabilistic seismic lifeline risk assessment. Earthquake Eng. Struct. Dynam. **39**, 1109–1131 (2010)
10. Kile, H., Uhlen, K.: Data reduction via clustering and averaging for contingency and reliability analysis. Electr. Power Energy Syst. **43**, 1435–1442 (2012)
11. Liu, B., Zhang, Q., Fernández, F.V., Gielen, G.G.E.: An efficient evolutionary algorithm for chance-constrained bi-objective stochastic optimization. IEEE Trans. Evol. Comput. **17**(6), 786–796 (2013)
12. Lubin, M., Dvorkin, Y., Backhaus, S.: A robust approach to chance constrained optimal power flow with renewable generation. IEEE Trans. Power Syst. **31**(5), 3840–3849 (2016)
13. Maita, E., Suzuki, M.: Quantitative analysis of direct runoff in a forested mountainous, small watershed. J. Jpn. Soc. Hydrol. Water Resour. **22**(5), 342–355 (2009)
14. Martinez, A.R., Martinez, W.L.: Computational Statistics Handbook with MATLAB ®, 2nd edn. Chapman & Hall/CRC, Boca Raton (2008)
15. Montes, E.E., Coello Coello, C.A.: Constraint-handling in nature inspired numerical optimization: past, present and future. Swarm Evol. Comput. **1**, 173–194 (2011)
16. Muralikrishna, M., DeWitt, D.J.: Equi-depth histograms for estimating selectivity factors for multi-dimensional queries. In: Proceedings of ACM SIGMOD International Conference on Management of Data, pp. 28–36 (1988)
17. Poojari, C.A., Varghese, B.: Genetic algorithm based technique for solving chance constrained problems. Eur. J. Oper. Res. **185**, 1128–1154 (2008)
18. Prékopa, A.: Stochastic Programming. Kluwer Academic Publishers, London (1995)
19. Prékopa, A., Szántai, T.: Flood control reservoir system design using stochastic programming. Math. Program. Study **9**, 138–151 (1978)
20. Price, K.V., Storn, R.M., Lampinen, J.A.: Differential Evolution - A Practical Approach to Global Optimization. Springer, Heidelberg (2005). https://doi.org/10.1007/3-540-31306-0

21. Tagawa, K., Miyanaga, S.: Weighted empirical distribution based approach to chance constrained optimization problems using differential evolution. In: Proceedings of IEEE Congress on Evolutionary Computation, pp. 97–104 (2017)
22. Tagawa, K., Miyanaga, S.: An approach to chance constrained problems using weighted empirical distribution and differential evolution with application to flood control planning. Electron. Commun. Jpn. **102**(3), 45–55 (2019). https://doi.org/10.1002/ecj.12148
23. Uryasev, S.P.: Probabilistic Constrained Optimization: Methodology and Applications. Kluwer Academic Publishers, Dordrecht (2001)
24. Xu, L.D., He, W., Li, S.: Internet of things in industries: a survey. IEEE Trans. Ind. Inform. **10**(4), 2233–2243 (2014)
25. Zhang, J., Sanderson, A.C.: JADE: adaptive differential evolution with optional external archive. IEEE Trans. Evol. Comput. **13**(5), 945–958 (2009)

Extending an Anomaly Detection Benchmark with Auto-encoders, Isolation Forests, and RBMs

Mark Pijnenburg[1,2]([✉]) and Wojtek Kowalczyk[1]

[1] Leiden Institute of Advanced Computer Science, Leiden University,
Niels Bohrweg 1, Leiden, The Netherlands
{m.g.f.pijnenburg,w.j.kowalczyk}@liacs.leidenuniv.nl
[2] Netherlands Tax and Customs Administration, Utrecht, The Netherlands

Abstract. In this paper, the recently published benchmark of Goldstein and Uchida [3] for unsupervised anomaly detection is extended with three anomaly detection techniques: Sparse Auto-Encoders, Isolation Forests, and Restricted Boltzmann Machines. The underlying mechanisms of these algorithms differ substantially from the more traditional anomaly detection algorithms, currently present in the benchmark. Results show that in three of the ten data sets, the new algorithms surpass the present collection of 19 algorithms. Moreover, a relation is noted between the nature of the outliers in a data set and the performance of specific (clusters of) anomaly detection algorithms.

Keywords: Anomaly detection · Sparse auto-encoder ·
Isolation forest · Restricted Boltzmann machine · Benchmark · U-index

1 Introduction

The expanding number of anomaly detection algorithms creates the need to compare algorithms objectively. Goldstein and Uchida [3] made a start by providing a benchmark for unsupervised anomaly detection, consisting of 10 data sets and 19 algorithms. In this paper, we extend the number of algorithms by adding three anomaly detection algorithms: Sparse Auto-encoders, Isolation Forests, and Restricted Boltzmann Machines (RBMs).

The three algorithms are interesting since they have a different underlying mechanism compared to the current algorithms in the benchmark: two of the new algorithms, Sparse Auto-encoders and RBMs, originate from the popular field of (deep) neural networks. Within this field, they are among the simplest and best-known algorithms for detecting anomalies [7]. The third algorithm is based on random trees. The underlying mechanisms differ substantially from the more traditional algorithms in the benchmark that are mostly distance-based, like the k-Nearest Neighbors algorithm and the Local Outlier Factor. Moreover, when auto-encoders and RBMs are applied to anomaly detection this

© Springer Nature Switzerland AG 2019
R. Damaševičius and G. Vasiljevienė (Eds.): ICIST 2019, CCIS 1078, pp. 498–515, 2019.
https://doi.org/10.1007/978-3-030-30275-7_39

paper, the recently published benchmark of Goldstein and Uchida [3] for unsupervised anomaly detection is extended with three anomaly detection techniques: Sparse Auto-Encoders, Isolation Forests, and Restricted Boltzmann Machines. The underlying mechanisms of these algorithms differ substantially from the more traditional anomaly detection algorithms, currently present in the benchmark. Results show that in three of the ten data sets, the new algorithms surpass the present collection of 19 algorithms. Moreover, a relation is noted between the nature of the outliers in a data set and the performance of specific (clusters of) anomaly detection algorithms. On, it is usually on image data [14,15] or sequential data [10,16]. Hence it is of interest to see their performance on the (small) classical tabular data used in the benchmark [3].

The paper is organized as follows. In Sect. 2, the three anomaly detection algorithms are described. Then, in Sect. 3, the actual experiments performed are described as well as the data sets of the benchmark. In Sect. 4 we present the results of the experiments and compare these with results mentioned in [3]. The paper ends with Conclusions and Discussion in Sect. 5. The code used in the experiments is published at [12].

2 Theoretical Background

2.1 Sparse Auto-encoder

Standard auto-encoders are neural networks with architecture as depicted in Fig. 1. Sometimes it is required that $W_1 = W_2^t$, for regularization purposes. We will not impose this restriction in this paper. In its most basic form, as shown in the figure, the network consists of one input layer, a hidden layer, and an output layer with the same number of nodes as the input layer. The network is

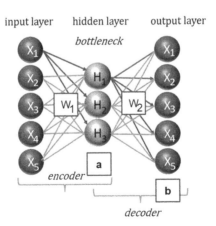

Fig. 1. Architecture of the simplest form of a standard auto-encoder with one hidden layer. In general, the encoder and the decoder part may consist of more complex neural networks.

trained by providing the same observation $\mathbf{v}$ as input *and* output, and requiring to minimize the reconstruction error $\|\text{auto}(\mathbf{v}) - \mathbf{v}\|^2$. Essentially, the network must learn the identity function ('auto' means 'self' in Greek).

The number of nodes in the hidden layer is intentionally limited, such that the encoder has to extract the essential information from the input features in order for the decoder to reconstruct the original input as closely as possible. The encoder part of an auto-encoder can thus be seen as a dimensionality-reducing algorithm, reducing the original dimensionality of the input space to the dimensionality of the space formed by the hidden nodes.

Training an auto-encoder is usually done by gradient descent, in particular *stochastic* gradient descent. The latter algorithm speeds up convergence in comparison with standard gradient descent and also introduces some noise that helps to avoid local minima. Backpropagation is generally used to compute the gradient by going backward from the output layer to the input layer.

In the experiments, see Algorithm 1, we used the BFGS (Broyden Fletcher Goldfarb Shanno) algorithm, a quasi-Newton optimization algorithm for minimizing the target function. The BFGS algorithm works well for data sets with a small number of features as are most data sets in the benchmark. The target function in the experiments consists of the reconstruction error – Eq. (1) in Algorithm 1–, a standard L_2 regularization term (2) that is added more routinely in training neural networks nowadays, and a sparsity constraint term (3) that is typical for *sparse* auto-encoders.

Sparse auto-encoders are a variant on classical auto-encoders where the 'bottleneck' is not created by limiting the number of hidden nodes, but by requiring that only a limited number of hidden nodes have a high activation value for each observation.

When applying auto-encoders to anomaly detection, at least two approaches may be taken. The first approach uses the dimensionality-reduction characteristic of the auto-encoder part. Once trained, the auto-encoder will transform the original features into a new low-dimensional feature space (i.e., the hidden layer). In the new feature space, traditional distance-based anomaly detection techniques may be applied that would not work properly in the original, high-dimensional space due to the 'curse of dimensionality'. This first approach works in particular well for standard auto-encoders. The second approach will work for standard auto-encoders as well as sparse auto-encoders. The idea underlying this approach is that the network will only achieve a low reconstruction error if it focuses on frequently occurring patterns. As a result, observations belonging to infrequent patterns will receive a high reconstruction error. Hence the reconstruction error can serve as an anomaly score. This approach is adopted in this paper.

2.2   Isolation Forest

Isolation forest [9], see Algorithm 2, is an algorithm specifically developed to find anomalies. It resembles the random forest algorithm. As such it is a collection of many trees. However these trees are no decision trees, but 'random trees'.

Algorithm 1: Training and Scoring of an auto-encoder with one hidden layer.

Input : A data set $\mathbf{V}$ with p (numeric) features and n observations. We assume each column to be scaled into the range [0,1] using min-max scaling.

$h = \{5, 10, \lfloor p/2 \rfloor, p\}$ the number of hidden nodes,

$\lambda = 0.001$ the learning rate,

$\rho = 0.1$ sparsity hyper-parameter,

$\beta = 0.05$ factor influencing the relative importance of the sparsity term

in the cost function,

Output: Reconstruction error of all observations $\mathbf{v} \in \mathbf{V}$.

1 Initialize weight matrix W with random number from a $\mathcal{N}(0, 0.01)$ distribution

2 Call a standard BFGS optimizer for minimizing the target function that consists of the reconstruction error, a regularization term and the sparsity constraint:

3

$$J(W_1, W_2, \mathbf{a}, \mathbf{b}) = \frac{1}{n} \sum_{i=1}^{n} \frac{1}{2} \|\mathrm{auto}(\mathbf{v}_i) - \mathbf{v}_i\|^2 \tag{1}$$

$$+ \frac{\lambda}{2}(\|W_1\|^2 + \|W_2\|^2) \tag{2}$$

$$+ \beta \sum_{i=1}^{n} [\rho \log \frac{\rho}{\widehat{\rho}(\mathbf{v}_i)} + (1 - \rho) \log \frac{1 - \rho}{1 - \widehat{\rho}(\mathbf{v}_i)}], \tag{3}$$

where $\mathrm{auto}(\mathbf{v})$ is the output of the feedforward pass through the network:

$$\mathrm{auto}(\mathbf{v}) = 1/(1 + \exp(-W_2 A(\mathbf{v}) - \mathbf{b})), \tag{4}$$

$$A(\mathbf{v}) = 1/(1 + \exp(-W_1 \mathbf{v} - \mathbf{a})), \tag{5}$$

and $\widehat{\rho}(\mathbf{v}))$ is the average activation of the nodes in the hidden layer:

$$\widehat{\rho}(\mathbf{v})) = \frac{1}{h} \sum_{i=1}^{h} A_i(\mathbf{v}). \tag{6}$$

4 After convergence, pass all observations $\mathbf{v} \in \mathbf{V}$ through the trained auto-encoder and compute the reconstruction error $e(\mathbf{v}) = \|\mathrm{auto}(\mathbf{v}_i) - \mathbf{v}_i\|^2$.

5 **return** the vector of reconstruction errors: $e(\mathbf{v}_1), \dots, e(\mathbf{v}_n)$.

A 'random tree' is a tree where each split involves a randomly selected feature, which is split based on a random value. The underlying assumption of an isolation forest is that anomalies are few and have different values from most observations. As a result, anomalies will often be isolated from the other observations in very few splits. Therefore, by observing the leaf of an observation in many trees, and computing the average distance of these leaves to the root of the trees, anomalies will have a small distance, while normal observations will have a large distance. Hence, the average distance to the root can be used as an anomaly score.

Algorithm 2: Training and Scoring of Isolation Forest

Input : A data set $\mathbf{V}$ with p (numeric) features. We assume each column to be scaled into the range $[0,1]$ using min-max scaling.

$n\_tree = 100$ the number of trees,

$hlim = 8$ the maximum depth of a single tree,

$n\_samp = 256$ number of observations used in the training sample,

$min\_leaf = 1$ minimum number of observations in a leaf.

Output: Scaled Version of the average path length of each observation $\mathbf{v} \in \mathbf{V}$.

1 Create n_tree random trees:

2 **for** i in $1 \dots n\_tree$ **do**

3 | Take a random sample $X \subset \mathbf{V}$ of size n_samp

4 | Initialize first node of tree

5 | **while** *there is a node N with depth $< hlim$ and $\#$ observations $> min\_leaf$* **do**

6 | | randomly select an attribute q

7 | | randomly select a split point $s \in [0,1]$

8 | | Split node N in 2: $q <= p, q > p$

9 | **end**

10 **end**

11 Compute (scaled version of) Average Path Length, $APL(\mathbf{v})$, for all observations $\mathbf{v} \in \mathbf{V}$

12 **return** the vector of average path lengths: $(APL(\mathbf{v_1}), \dots, APL(\mathbf{v_n}))$.

2.3   Restricted Boltzmann Machine

A Restricted Boltzmann Machine (RBM) is a stochastic neural network with two layers: a *visible layer*, and a *hidden* layer, see Fig. 2. The network has no output layer like auto-encoders, and signals in the network travel back and forth between the two layers, starting at the visible layer. Both layers are fully connected, i.e., each input node is connected to each hidden node, and vice versa. Moreover the weights of the connections are symmetric $W_{ij} = W_{ji}$. No connections between nodes of the same layer are allowed. All nodes in a *classical* RBM are binary, i.e. can take two values: 0 and 1. This in contrast to auto-encoders. Consequently, numerical inputs have to be discretized and transformed to binary dummy variables. In our experiments, the 'thermometer encoding' is used for the latter, as it preserves the ordering present in numerical features. The difference between thermometer encoding and standard dummy encode can best be illustrated by the example of representing the value 0.45 of continuous feature with a range $[0,1]$ that is discretized in ten equal width bins $[0,0.1), [0.1,0.2), \dots$. With standard encoding 0.45 falls in the bin $[0.4, 0.5)]$ and will be representated by the vector $(0,0,0,0,1,0,0,0,0,0)$. With thermometer encoding 0.45 would be represented by the vector $(1,1,1,1,1,0,0,0,0,0)$.

visible layer   hidden layer

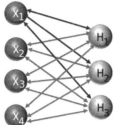

Fig. 2. Architecture of a Restricted Boltzmann Machine.

An RBM can be interpreted as a graphical model, or a 'Markov Random Field', see [2]. Consequently, there is a model for the probability distribution over the feature space:

$$p(\mathbf{v}) = \frac{1}{Z} \sum_{\text{all feasible } \mathbf{h}} e^{-E(\mathbf{v},\mathbf{h})}, \tag{7}$$

where Z is a normalization constant (also known as the *partition function*) ensuring that $\sum p(\mathbf{v}) = 1$,

$$Z = \sum_{\substack{\text{all feasible} \\ \mathbf{v},\mathbf{h}}} e^{-E(\mathbf{v},\mathbf{h})}, \tag{8}$$

and E is the so-called *energy function*,

$$E(\mathbf{v},\mathbf{h}) = - \sum_{i \in \text{visible}} a_i v_i - \sum_{j \in \text{hidden}} b_j h_j - \sum_{i,j} w_{ij} v_i h_j. \tag{9}$$

This family of probability distributions is known as 'Boltzmann distributions' and has been subject of study in statistical physics.

Training an RBM amounts to adjusting the parameters of the energy function (9) such that the distribution fits the observations of the training data set, see Algorithm 3. Fitting the distribution to observations is done by maximizing the likelihood over the the training set V,

$$\underset{a_i,b_i,w_{ij}}{\arg \max} \prod_{\mathbf{v} \in V} p(\mathbf{v}). \tag{10}$$

The maximization is usually done by with the help of Contrastive Divergence, see [2], a 'stochastic gradient descent'-like algorithm, showing fast convergence at the cost of approximating the gradient.

Algorithm 3: Training and Scoring of an RBM using Contrastive Divergence (CD-1)

Input : A data set $\mathbf{V}$ with p (numeric) features. We assume each column to be scaled into the range [0,1] using min-max scaling.
$h = \{5, 10, \lfloor p/2 \rfloor, p\}$ the number of hidden nodes,
$b = \{3, 5, 7, 10\}$ the number of bins for each feature,
$k = 10$ batch size,
$\lambda = 0.01$ initial learning rate,
$m = 0.95$ momentum term (only used for bias vectors)

Output: for each $\mathbf{v} \in \mathbf{V}$: $\exp(-F(\mathbf{v}))$. This expression is proportional to $p(\mathbf{v})$. The negative of this expression can be used as an outlier score.

1 Discretize columns of $\mathbf{V}$ into b bins each, using equal width binning followed by thermometer encoding. Denote the new data set with $p \cdot b$ binary columns $\mathbf{V}'$.
2 Initialize values of matrix W and vectors $\mathbf{a}$ and $\mathbf{b}$ with small uniform random numbers
3 **while** *convergence = FALSE* **do**
4   randomize order of rows and put rows in batches of size k
5   **for** *each batch V_0* **do**
6   sample binary values H_0 based on values V_0:
         $H_0 = \text{random}_{\{0,1\}}(1/(1 + \exp(-WV_0^t - \mathbf{b})))$
7   compute new values V_1 based on H_0: $V_1 = 1/(1 + \exp(-(H_0W)^t - \mathbf{a}))$
8   Compute probabilities of hidden nodes H_1 based on V_1 (without sampling): $H_1 = 1/(1 + \exp(-WV_1^t - \mathbf{b}))$
9   Adjust weights:
10        $W = W + \lambda \cdot (H_0^t V_0 - H_1^t V_1)/k$
11        $d\mathbf{a} = d\mathbf{a}_{-1} \cdot m + \lambda \cdot \text{column\_means}(V_0 - V_1)$
12        $\mathbf{a} = \mathbf{a} + d\mathbf{a}$
13        $d\mathbf{b} = d\mathbf{b}_{-1} \cdot m + \lambda \cdot \text{column\_means}(H_0 - H_1)$
14        $\mathbf{b} = \mathbf{b} + d\mathbf{b}$
15   **end**
16   compute the total free energy $F(\mathbf{V}') = \sum_{\mathbf{v} \in \mathbf{V}'} F(\mathbf{v})$, see equation (12)
17   Check on convergence:
18   **if** $|(F(\mathbf{V}') - F_{previous}(\mathbf{V}'))/F_{previous}(\mathbf{V}')| < 0.001$ **then**
19   convergence = TRUE
20   **end**
21   Check on adjustment of λ:
22   **if** $(F(\mathbf{V}') - F_{previous}(\mathbf{V}'))/F_{previous}(\mathbf{V}') > 0.01$ **then**
23        $\lambda = 0.1 \cdot \lambda$
24   **end**
25 **end**
26 **return** for each $\mathbf{v} \in \mathbf{V}'$: $\exp(-F(\mathbf{v}))$, see equation (12).

After training, the probability of each observation $p(\mathbf{v})$ may be computed by Eq. (7). In practice, however, applying Eq. (7) requires computing the partition function (8), which is computationally intractable. Instead, one may notice that $p(\mathbf{v})$ is proportional to,

$$p(\mathbf{v}) \propto e^{-F(\mathbf{v})} = \sum_{\mathbf{h}} e^{-E(\mathbf{v},\mathbf{h})}. \tag{11}$$

Here $F(\mathbf{v})$ is the *free energy of an observation* $\mathbf{v}$: the energy that a single configuration would need to have in order to have the same probability as all of the configurations that contain $\mathbf{v}$ [5].

The free energy of an observation can be calculated in linear time, due to the special architecture of a *Restricted* Boltzmann Machine, which does not allow links between hidden nodes, leading to an energy function (9) that involves no cross terms like $h_j h_k$. Hence the sum over all possible values of $\mathbf{h}$ in Eq. (11), comes down to summing over each element of $\mathbf{h}$ separately, essentially reducing the time to compute the free energy of an observation from exponential to linear. The free energy of an observation can be expressed most conveniently as,

$$F(\mathbf{v}) = - \sum_{i \in \text{visible}} v_i a_i - \sum_{j \in \text{hidden}} \log(1 + e^{x_j}), \tag{12}$$

where $x_j = b_j + \sum_i v_i w_{ij}$ is the input for the hidden node j, see equation (22) of [2] for a derivation.

Applying the procedure above, we obtain for each observation the expression $\exp(-F(\mathbf{v}))$, which is proportional to $p(\mathbf{v})$. Now one may proceed along two lines: (1) if interest lies only in obtaining the k most anomalous cases in a data set, one may order the observations according to $F(\mathbf{v})$ and report the k observations with largest free energy. (2) otherwise, one may obtain a set of outliers by computing the median m and interquartile range IQR of $\exp(-F(\mathbf{v}))$ for all $\mathbf{v} \in V$ and set a threshold $\theta = m - c \cdot IQR$ below which observations are considered outliers.

2.4   Type of Outliers

A distinction between type of outliers, that will prove fruitful in explaining differences among algorithms in Sect. 4, is that some outliers are multivariate in nature while others are univariate, compare Fig. 3. In the left subplot a uniovariate outlier is shown. This outlier can be detected by only looking at one feature (x), while the multivariate outlier of the right subplot requires knowledge about both features.

In practice we do not know a priori the nature of the outliers, as we do not know what observations are outliers. However, in a benchmark situation, we *know* what observations are outliers. The outliers are indicated by a binary feature y taking the value 1 for an outlier and 0 otherwise. In a benchmark situation we can thus quantify the univariate nature of the outliers by defining a new concept, called the Univariate-index, or *U-index*, as

$$\text{U-index} = \max_{i \in \{1...p\}} (|\text{corr}(x_i, y)|), \tag{13}$$

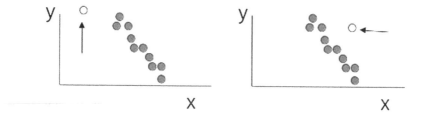

Fig. 3. 'Univariate' outlier (left, U-index = 0.74) and 'multivariate' outlier (right, U-index = 0.43).

where corr is the correlation function, p is the number of features of the data set (without the outlier label y). In words, Eq. (13) says to take the maximum of the absolute value of the correlation coefficient of any feature with the binary label indicating the outliers. The index is added to Table 1 and will prove useful in Sect. 4.

3   Experimental Setup

3.1   General

To test the effectiveness of the algorithms mentioned in the previous section, the algorithms are applied to the benchmark data sets of Goldstein and Uchida [3]. The complete code of the experiments can be at [12]. In the experiments we used implementations of the algorithms as can be found in the R-packages: 'autoencoder' (version 1.0) [1], 'IsolationForest' (version 0.0-26) [8], and 'deepnet' (version 0.2) [13]. The latter package is used for the RBM and is adjusted slightly in order to implement a dynamic stopping criterion and the automatic adjustment of the learning rate, see Sect. 3.2.

The set of hyper-parameters that are tested for each algorithm will be explained in Sect. 3.2. For each set of hyper-parameters we will run ten experiments, each time with a different random seed. This will reduce the noise introduced by the random component that is present in all three algorithms. Reported results are averages over all runs. For instance, for an RBM we will test 16 different hyper-parameter settings (4 different number of hidden nodes times 4 different settings for the number of bins). A reported auc in Tables 2 and 3 is thus an average over $4 \cdot 4 \cdot 10 = 160$ experiments.

Results are measured using the 'area under the curve' statistic, in line with the approach of Goldstein and Uchida [3].

3.2   Setting Hyper-parameters

Sparse Auto-encoder. In the experiments the most basic architecture of a sparse auto-encoder is tested, i.e., with one hidden layer. Since this simple architecture already achieved good results, see Sect. 4, we have not experimented with more complex variants of auto-encoders.

The main architectural hyper-parameter is the number of hidden nodes h. We choose $h \in \{5, 10, p/2, p\}$, where p is the number of features in the data set, excluding the label indicating the outliers. If $p/2$ is not an integer, we rounded downwards. An exception is made for the 'speech' data set that contains 400 features, requiring an exceptional long run time. For 'speech' we take $h \in \{5, 10, 25, 50\}$. The numbers 5 and 10 hidden nodes have been chosen since some initial experiments indicated that a reasonably low reconstruction error could be obtained with these numbers. The numbers $p/2$ and p are added to ensure that data sets with more features (more possible patterns) have a network with larger expressive power.

The learning rate λ is set to a value of 0.001 for all data sets, since this value ensured a smooth decreasing target function for all data sets. The sparsity parameter ρ is fixed to 0.1 as recommended by Ng in his lecture notes on auto-encoders [11].

Isolation Forest. The isolation forest algorithm is robust concerning the values of its hyper-parameters. For all hyper-parameters we choose the values as recommended by Liu et al. [9].

Restricted Boltzmann Machine. The number of hidden nodes for the RBM is set equal to the values chosen for the sparse auto-encoder, i.e. $h \in \{5, 10, \lfloor p/2 \rfloor, p\}$ and $h \in \{5, 10, 25, 50\}$ for the 'speech' data set.

A classical RBM needs binary input. For this reason we pre-processed the data for RBM's by discretizing each feature into b bins, using equal width binning. Subsequently, a dummy variable is constructed for each bin, using thermometer encoding as mentioned in Sect. 2.3. In the experiments we set $b \in \{3, 5, 7, 10\}$.

The learning rate λ and the stopping criterion of the RBM is set dynamically. Initially $\lambda = 0.01$, subsequently λ is decreased by a factor 10 as soon as free energy of all observations between two epochs rises with more than 1%. The algorithm is stopped as soon as the free energy of the data set changes less than 1 promille. The *free energy* serves as a proxy for the (log-) likelihood (10). The log-likelihood can be separated in two terms like,

$$\log \prod_{\mathbf{v} \in V} p(\mathbf{v}) = -\log Z(W, \mathbf{a}, \mathbf{b}) - \sum_{\mathbf{v} \in V} F(\mathbf{v}). \tag{14}$$

The last term is the free energy of the data set.

3.3 Data Sets

Table 1 provides a summary of the data sets of the benchmark of Goldstein and Uchida [3]. All features in the data sets are numeric. Most data sets are originally posted for classification tasks. To make the data sets suitable for anomaly detection, typically observations from one specific class are labeled anomalies, while all other observations are considered normal cases.

As a data pre-processing step, a min-max scaling is applied to all features x of all data sets, resulting in a range of $[0, 1]$ for each feature.

$$x_{sc} = \frac{x - x_{min}}{x_{max} - x_{min}}. \qquad (15)$$

Below we will give a short description of each data set.

Table 1. Summary of the data sets used to compare the various anomaly detection algorithms. See Eq. (13) for the definition of the U-index.

	Data set name	Number of rows	Number of columns	Outliers	Percentage outliers	U-index
1	breast cancer	367	30	10	2.72	0.570
2	pen global	809	16	90	11.1	0.600
3	letter	1.600	32	100	6.25	0.193
4	speech	3.686	400	61	1.65	0.079
5	satellite	5.100	36	75	1.49	0.308
6	pen local	6.724	16	10	0.15	0.047
7	annthyroid	6.916	21	250	3.61	0.419
8	shuttle	46.464	9	878	1.89	0.675
9	aloi	50.000	27	1.508	3.02	0.029
10	kdd 1999	620.098	29	1.052	0.17	0.678

Breast Cancer. This data set is derived from the Wisconsin Breast Cancer data set that contains medical data of 569 patients. The data consists of features derived from digitized images of breast mass, obtained via a Fine Needle Aspirate. In the original data set there are 357 patients with benign breast cancer and 212 patients with malignant breast cancer. In the data set prepared for anomaly detection, all benign patients are kept, while the first 10 patients with malignant breast cancer are labeled as anomalies.

Pen Global. The observations in this data set are feature vectors derived from images of the digit '8', handwritten several times by 44 different writers. The feature vectors have a length of 16 and contain eight (x, y) pairs. These pairs are positions that are recorded after fixed intervals when the digit is written. The anomalies are 10 observations from the digits '0', '1', '2', '3', '4', '5', '6', '7', '9' each, leading to 90 anomalies.

Letter. This data set consists of features extracted from 3 letters from the English alphabet. The outliers consist of the same features but extracted from the other letters of the alphabet. To make the anomaly detection task more challenging, the contributors added randomly some features to each observation, coming from all letters of the English alphabet.

Speech. This data set comes from the domain of speech recognition. Each observation is a so-called 'i-vector representation' of a speech segment. The normal cases come from persons with an American accent, while outliers consist of persons with other accents.

Satellite. This data set consists of features extracted from satellite images. These images are used to determine the soil type. In this data set the soil types: 'red soil', 'gray soil', 'damp gray soil' and 'very damp gray soil' are normal instances. Anomalies were sampled from the classes: 'cotton crop' and 'soil with vegetation stubble'.

Pen Local. This data set has the same underlying data set as 'Pen Global'. However, instead of focusing on the digit '8', all digits are kept with the exception of the digit '4'. From the latter digit only the first ten observations are included and these form the anomalies.

Annthyroid. This data set is derived from the annthyriod data set, also known as the Thyroid disease data set, and comes from the medical domain. It contains features from patients; normal cases represent healthy patients, the outliers are sampled from the patients that suffer from hypothyroid cancer. The first fifteen features are binary features, the next six features are continuous.

Shuttle. This data set is used in the Statlog project and contains features that are connected to the normal and abnormal functioning of radiators in a NASA space shuttle. The original data set is designed for supervised anomaly detection. The version used in this paper is adjusted by Goldstein and Uchida [3] mainly by reducing the number of outliers.

ALOI. The aloi data set originates from a data set provided by the Amsterdam Library of Object Images (ALOI). This library contains images of objects. This particular data set contains a feature vector of length 27 for each image, derived by apply a HSB color histogram. Such a histogram gives the distribution of colors in an image. Each object is photographed many times under different angles and lighting conditions. The 1.508 observations labeled as anomalies correspond to a few objects selected as anomalies.

KDD Challenge 1999. This data set comes from a challenge presented at the Knowledge Discovery and Data Mining conference of 1999. The data set contains artificially created observations that represent HTTP traffic in a computer network. The data set is enriched with observations representing observations typically seen in attacks. The current data set has undergone some data preparations to make it more suitable for testing various anomaly detection algorithms, see [3] for details.

4   Results

Table 2 summarizes the findings of the experiments. The isolation forest algorithm realizes the highest area under the curve on the 'shuttle' data. The RBM reaches first place for 'breast cancer' and 'kdd 1999', although the first position is shared with HBOS (Histogram-Based Outlier Score) for the latter data set. The auc-values for all algorithms in the benchmark can be found in Table 3.

Table 2. Mean Area Under the Curve (AUC) and standard deviation when applying the anomaly detection algorithms with various settings on the benchmark data sets.

	data set	auto-encoder	isolation forest	RBM	mean benchmark	best benchmark	best alg. benchmark
1	breast cancer	0.9091 ± 0.0040	0.9810 ± 0.0014	**0.9858** ± 0.00005	0.9067	0.9827 ± 0.0016	HBOS
2	pen global	0.9420 ± 0.0008	0.9304 ± 0.0016	0.8282 ± 0.0014	0.7836	0.9872 ± 0.0055	k-NN
3	letter	0.7667 ± 0.0042	0.6337 ± 0.0052	0.5794 ± 0.0026	0.7850	0.9068 ± 0.0078	LoOP
4	speech	0.4716 ± 0.0002	0.4699 ± 0.0052	0.4715 ± 0.0002	0.4936	0.5347 ± 0.0343	LoOP
5	satellite	0.9057 ± 0.0017	0.9479 ± 0.0018	0.9060 ± 0.0018	0.8734	0.9701 ± 0.0007	k-NN
6	pen local	0.8346 ± 0.0039	0.7828 ± 0.0064	0.8220 ± 0.0036	0.9129	0.9816 ± 0.0024	LOF
7	annthyroid	0.5657 ± 0.0010	0.6456 ± 0.0058	0.5089 ± 0.0026	0.6312	0.9150 ± 0.0123	HBOS
8	shuttle	0.9881 ± 0.0000	**0.9973** ± 0.0002	0.9832 ± 0.0004	0.7684	0.9925 ± 0.0039	rPCA
9	aloi	0.5415 ± 0.0004	0.5408 ± 0.0003	0.5311 ± 0.0006	0.6229	0.7899 ± 0.0093	LoOP
10	kdd 1999	0.9718 ± 0.0001	0.9656 ± 0.0017	**0.9990** ± 0.00004	0.7926	0.9990 ± 0.0007	HBOS

Figure 4 displays the overall performance of the algorithms on all data sets.

The k-NN and kth-NN algorithms perform the best in general. Only on the 'annthyroid' data, these algorithms perform below average. The main characteristic of the 'annthyroid' data are its binary features. These binary features have almost no relation with the outlierness of an observation, but do have a large influence on the distance-based k-NN and kth-NN algorithms. Hence we may say that for distance based methods, scaling is important and may give problems when combining binary (or categorical) features with continuous ones.

The Cluster-Based Local Outlier Factor (CBLOF) is clearly the worst algorithm, although variants of this algorithm (uCBLOF and LDCOF) clearly improve performance considerably. The uCBLOF algorithm even reaches the

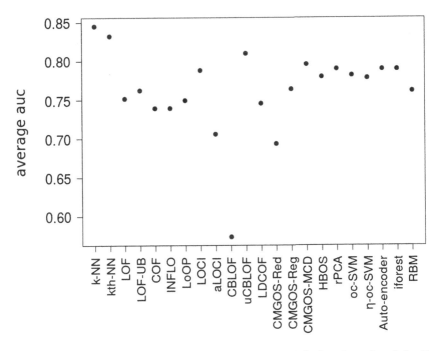

Fig. 4. Average Area Under the Curve of all algorithms of the benchmark and the three newly added algorithms. The average is taken over all data sets in the benchmark.

third place in the ranking of algorithms in Fig. 4. However it performs always worse than the simpler k-NN and kth-NN algorithms, except for data sets with a large U-index (shuttle, kdd 1999). Here the underlying clustering approach may have its advantages.

The Histogram-Based Outlier Score (HBOS) algorithm and the Local Outlier Probability (LoOP) algorithm deserve attention as well, since they are the top performers for 6 of the 10 data sets among the original 19 algorithms of the benchmark. The simple HBOS algorithm is clearly strong on data sets with a large U-index (an indication for univariate outliers) like breast cancer, shuttle and kdd 1999, while weak on data sets with a small U-index (aloi, letter). It performs also well on annthyroid, where it does not get distracted by the binary features that have almost no correlation with the outliers. In contrast to HBOS, the LoOP algorithm performs well for data sets with a small U-index (letter, pen local, speech, aloi), but badly on data sets with a large U-index (shuttle, kdd 1999).

If we now turn our attention to the newly added algorithms, then we see that all three algorithms are good in finding outliers in data sets with a large U-index (shuttle, kdd 1999, breast cancer, pen global and satellite), often surpassing the currently best algorithm. However the new algorithms perform badly on data sets with a small U-index (letter, speech, aloi). The isolation forest algorithm can best handle the binary features that are present in annthyroid. Because of this property and the fact that isolation forest has the shortest run times and requires almost no tuning of hyper-parameters, this algorithm could be labeled as the preferred choice between the three new algorithms.

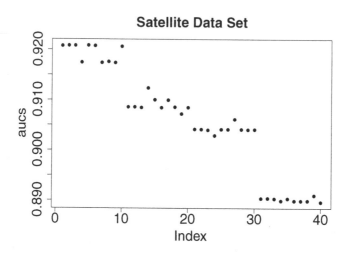

Fig. 5. Value of the Area Under the Curve for the auto-encoder on the 'Satellite' data.

The time complexity for training one epoch and scoring the data is linear in the number of observations n, the number of features p and the number of hidden nodes h ($\mathcal{O}(nph)$) for standard sparse auto-encoders and RBMs. The time to train and score an isolation forest is linear in the number of observations and independent of the number of features ($\mathcal{O}(n)$). In practice, the run time of the algorithms is to a large extent dependent on the number of epochs needed before reaching convergence during training. With respect to this, isolation forest is the fastest algorithm. From the remaining two, RBMs reached convergence sooner than auto-encoders in our experiments. However this may be caused to a large extent by the use of the BGFS algorithm to optimize the target function for auto-encoders instead of the generally faster stochastic gradient descent method.

After running the experiments for auto-encoders, we have plotted the number of hidden nodes against the auc in order to get more insight in the number of hidden nodes needed in the context of anomaly detection. One of these plots is displayed in Fig. 5. Observations with index 1 to 10 in this plot are coming from auto-encoders with 5 hidden nodes, index 11 to 20 with 10 hidden nodes, index 21 to 30 with 18 hidden nodes, and finally, index 31 to 40 with 36 hidden nodes. All other hyper-parameters are fixed (except for the random seed that changes for each run). It is clear from the graph that auto-encoders with a small number of hidden nodes are better able to find the outliers (larger auc value). Also for the plots of the other data sets, it is clear that for most data sets 5 or 10 hidden nodes are sufficient.

Table 3. Mean Area Under the Curve for all data sets and algorithms in the benchmark. *Red* stands for CMGOS-Red, *Reg* stands for CMGOS-Reg, *MCD* stands for CMGOS-MCD

Algorithm Alg.	breast cancer	pen-global	pen-local	letter	speech	satellite	thyroid	shuttle	aloi	kdd 1999
k-NN	0.9791	**0.9872**	0.9837	0.8719	0.4966	**0.9701**	0.5956	0.9424	0.6502	0.9747
kth-NN	0.9807	0.9778	0.9757	0.8268	0.4784	0.9681	0.5748	0.9434	0.6177	0.9796
LOF	0.9816	0.8495	**0.9877**	0.8673	0.5038	0.8147	0.647	0.5127	0.7563	0.5964
LOF-UB	0.9805	0.8541	0.9876	0.9019	0.5233	0.8425	0.6663	0.5182	0.7713	0.5774
COF	0.9518	0.8695	0.9513	0.8336	0.5218	0.7491	0.6505	0.5257	0.7857	0.5548
INFLO	0.9642	0.7887	0.9817	0.8632	0.5017	0.8272	0.6542	0.493	0.7684	0.5524
LoOP	0.9725	0.7684	0.9851	**0.9068**	**0.5347**	0.7681	0.6893	0.5049	**0.7899**	0.5749
LOCI	0.9787	0.8877		0.788	0.4979					
aLOCI	0.8105	0.6889	0.8011	0.6208	0.4992	0.8324	0.6174	0.9474	0.5855	0.6552
CBLOF	0.2983	0.319	0.6995	0.6792	0.5021	0.5539	0.5825	0.9037	0.5393	0.6589
uCBLOF	0.9496	0.8721	0.9555	0.8192	0.4692	0.9627	0.5469	0.9716	0.5575	0.9964
LDCOF	0.7645	0.5948	0.9593	0.8107	0.4366	0.9522	0.5703	0.8076	0.5726	0.9873
Red	0.914	0.5693	0.9727	0.7711	0.5077	0.9054	0.4395	0.5425	0.5852	0.7265
Reg	0.8992	0.6994	0.9449	0.8902	0.5081	0.9056	0.6587	0.5679	0.5855	0.9797
MCD	0.9196	0.6265	0.9038	0.7848		0.912	0.8014	0.6903	0.5547	0.9696
HBOS	0.9827	0.7477	0.6798	0.6216	0.4708	0.9135	**0.915**	0.9925	0.4757	**0.999**
rPCA	0.9664	0.9375	0.7841	0.8095	0.5024	0.9461	0.6574	0.9963	0.5621	0.7371
oc-SVM	0.9721	0.9512	0.9543	0.5195	0.465	0.9549	0.5316	0.9862	0.5319	0.9518
η-oc-SVM	0.9581	0.8993	0.9236	0.7298	0.4649	0.943	0.5625	0.9848	0.5221	0.7945
Auto-enc.	0.9091	0.942	0.8346	0.7667	0.4716	0.9057	0.5657	0.9881	0.5415	0.9718
iforest	0.981	0.9304	0.7828	0.6337	0.4699	0.9479	0.6456	**0.9973**	0.5408	0.9656
RBM	**0.9858**	0.8282	0.822	0.5794	0.4715	0.906	0.5089	0.9832	0.5311	**0.999**

5   Conclusions and Discussion

Table 3 shows the performance of all algorithms on the benchmark of Goldstein and Uchide [3], including the three newly added algorithms. A main observation is that the three algorithms are able to meet or beat the current best algorithm in the benchmark several times: isolation forest is superior on the 'shuttle' data set, while the RBM outperforms all current algorithms on 'breast cancer' and matches the best performance on the 'kdd 1999' data set, see Table 2.

Isolation Forest seems to be the preferred choice of the three algorithms that are newly added to the benchmark; the area under the curve on the benchmark is rather similar to the other two algorithms, but it has shorter run times and its hyper-parameters are easy to set. Moreover it handles the binary features in the 'annthyroid' data set well.

Another observation is that there are (at least) two types of data sets with outliers: in the first type of data sets there is at least one feature that has a correlation with the label indicating an outlier. Anomaly detection algorithms that perform well on these data sets are: HBOS, rPCA, oc-SVM, η-oc-SVM, auto-encoder, isolation forest, RBM, and uCBLOF. We see that all three new algorithms fall in this category. The second type of data sets lack such a univariate feature. On these data sets LOF-like (Local Outlier Factor) algorithms perform well: LOF, LOF-UB, COF, INFLO, and LoOP. The U-index, as introduced by Eq. (13), helps to classify the data sets in the benchmark in these two groups, see Table 1.

Further, it is noteworthy that simplicity seems to go hand in hand with power at several places. This is evident in Fig. 4, where it becomes clear that the simple algorithms of k-NN and kth-NN perform the best when considering the average performance on all data sets. Also, Table 2 shows that the relatively simple HBOS algorithm belongs to the top performers for data sets with a large U-index. Finally, we note that simplicity in the number of nodes (i.e. a small number) for auto-encoders and RBMs does not decrease performance, see for instance Fig. 5.

When reflecting on the results, then some reservations are in order. First, the benchmark contains a limited number of data sets (ten), and a disproportional large number of these data sets are features extracted from images ('breast cancer', 'pen global', 'pen local', 'letter', 'satellite', 'aloi'). Moreover all data sets are tabular data and contain no categorical features. Second, in this paper only the most common implementations of the three newly added algorithms are tested. Each algorithm knows extensions that are worth further investigation in the future: the isolation forest algorithm has recently been extended by allowing splits in the feature space that are not parallel to coordinate axes, see the paper of Hariri et al. [4]. Auto-encoders can be extended by allowing more hidden layers, while also interesting variants exist that are mainly developed for large data sets (variational auto-encoders, GAN-networks [15]). RBMs can be stacked, leading to deep belief networks. Also a combination of auto-encoders and RBMs exists, see the paper of Hinton and Salakhutdinov [6]. Here RBMs initialize the weights in deep auto-encoders, making it feasible to train these networks with gradient descent.

For further research we also want to mention the 'speech' data set. None of the current algorithms performs well on this data set due to the combination of many features (400) and a low U-index.

References

1. Dubossarsky, E., Tyshetskiy, Y.: R package autoencoder, May 2014. https://CRAN.R-project.org/package=autoencoder
2. Fischer, A., Igel, C.: An introduction to restricted Boltzmann machines. In: Alvarez, L., Mejail, M., Gomez, L., Jacobo, J. (eds.) CIARP 2012. LNCS, vol. 7441, pp. 14–36. Springer, Heidelberg (2012). https://doi.org/10.1007/978-3-642-33275-3_2
3. Goldstein, M., Uchida, S.: A comparative evaluation of unsupervised anomaly detection algorithms for multivariate data. PloS One **11**(4), e0152173 (2016)
4. Hariri, S., Kind, M.C., Brunner, R.J.: Extended isolation forest. arXiv preprint arXiv:1811.02141 (2018)
5. Hinton, G.E.: A practical guide to training restricted Boltzmann Machines. In: Montavon, G., Orr, G.B., Müller, K.-R. (eds.) Neural Networks: Tricks of the Trade. LNCS, vol. 7700, pp. 599–619. Springer, Heidelberg (2012). https://doi.org/10.1007/978-3-642-35289-8_32

6. Hinton, G.E., Salakhutdinov, R.R.: Reducing the dimensionality of data with neural networks. Science **313**(5786), 504–507 (2006)
7. Kwon, D., Kim, H., Kim, J., Suh, S.C., Kim, I., Kim, K.J.: A survey of deep learning-based network anomaly detection. Cluster Comput. **9**(5), 1–13 (2017)
8. Liu, F.T.: R package isolationforestd, August 2009. https://rdrr.io/rforge/IsolationForest/
9. Liu, F.T., Ting, K.M., Zhou, Z.H.: Isolation forest. In: 2008 Eighth IEEE International Conference on Data Mining, pp. 413–422. IEEE (2008)
10. Malhotra, P., Vig, L., Shroff, G., Agarwal, P.: Long short term memory networks for anomaly detection in time series. In: Proceedings, p. 89. Presses universitaires de Louvain (2015)
11. Ng, A.: Lecture notes on sparse autoencoders (2011). https://web.stanford.edu/class/cs294a/sparseAutoencoder-2011.pdf
12. Pijnenburg, M.: Code used in experiments. https://github.com/PijnenburgMark/anomaly_detection_benchmark (2019). Accessed 01 June 2019
13. Rong, X.: R package deepnet, March 2014. https://CRAN.R-project.org/package=deepnet
14. Sabokrou, M., Fayyaz, M., Fathy, M., Moayed, Z., Klette, R.: Deep-anomaly: fully convolutional neural network for fast anomaly detection in crowded scenes. Comput. Vis. Image Underst. **172**, 88–97 (2018)
15. Schlegl, T., Seeböck, P., Waldstein, S.M., Schmidt-Erfurth, U., Langs, G.: Unsupervised anomaly detection with generative adversarial networks to guide marker discovery. In: Niethammer, M., Styner, M., Aylward, S., Zhu, H., Oguz, I., Yap, P.-T., Shen, D. (eds.) IPMI 2017. LNCS, vol. 10265, pp. 146–157. Springer, Cham (2017). https://doi.org/10.1007/978-3-319-59050-9_12
16. Xu, J., Saebi, M., Ribeiro, B., Kaplan, L.M., Chawla, N.V.: Detecting anomalies in sequential data with higher-order networks. arXiv preprint arXiv:1712.09658 (2017)

Prediction of Poker Moves Using Sequential Model and TensorFlow

Raulis Radziukas[1], Rytis Maskeliūnas[2],
and Robertas Damaševičius[1(✉)]

[1] Software Engineering Department,
Kaunas University of Technology, Kaunas, Lithuania
robertas.damasevicius@ktu.lt
[2] Multimedia Engineering Department, Kaunas University of Technology,
Kaunas, Lithuania

Abstract. We analyze neural network algorithms that can play poker game. Poker is attributed to the group of games with incomplete information, i.e. all game-related information is unknown until the end of the game. Therefore, poker is an interesting case used to check the abilities of machine learning models to make optimal decisions. We created a sequential model of poker move prediction using TensorFlow.js machine learning library and its sequential model. The model was trained on UCI Poker Hand dataset. We tested various combinations of model parameters: number of model layers, activation, loss function, optimization function, and number of epochs. The best model configuration for predicting the moves of the poker game with three layers with Mean Squared Error (MSE) loss function, Adam (0.001) optimizer, relu activation in the first layer had, relu6 activation in the second layer and selu activation in the third layer has achieved an accuracy of 99%.

Keywords: Collaborative intelligence · Game modelling · Poker prediction · Artificial neural network · TensorFlow

1 Introduction

Poker is a complex game that involves dealing with incomplex and hidden information, which is similar to many real world situations. As such, the game is an interesting object of research for the artificial intelligence (AI) community and can be considered as one of benchmarks to judge on the progress of AI methods [1, 2]. Analyzing poker game is also interesting in terms of gamification, as the game is very popular and its rules could be adopted for implementing serious games [3].

The number of new poker agents (poker playing programs) has seen strong growth in recent years. Most of them are used for research, usually for academic purposes. Loki [4] poker agent uses a probabilistic, formula-based methodology, combined with the GNU poker library. The game is controlled in two main stages: hand evaluation and game strategy creation. Poki [5] is a simulation-based system that plays the most likely scenario of a game and tracks every expected value and action of the opponent's bet. It uses a neural network with miximax and miximin algorithms to improve the

© Springer Nature Switzerland AG 2019
R. Damaševičius and G. Vasiljevienė (Eds.): ICIST 2019, CCIS 1078, pp. 516–525, 2019.
https://doi.org/10.1007/978-3-030-30275-7_40

opponent's modeling and decision making. Bluffbot [6] is a combination of pseudo-optimal gaming theory-based strategies and unique systems designed to determine game course. GS1 [7] used various abstractions to create the approximation of GameShrink algorithm. GS3 [8], introduced a new game abstraction algorithm for sequential imperfect information games [9]. The algorithm did not split the poker game into stages, thus evaluating all stages immediately. Smallbot [10] use ε-Nash equilibria strategies. The main idea is that every generation must be able to beat the previous one in a game and the value of overcoming must be at least ε. Finally, an optimal strategy is found that is called ε-Nash equilibria. Vexbot [11] creates the opponent's model by playing with him, and calculates the appropriate strategies to use the opponent's weaknesses effectively. However, it was slow to learn and needed to play many games to firstly understand the game and then develop appropriate strategies.

Neural networks were applied in several works. Carneiro et al. [12] use Multi-Layer Perceptron (MLP) and Support Vector Machine (SVM) to learn player strategy in Zoom Texas Hold'em poker variant of the game. Yakovenko et al. [13] propose Poker-CNN, a Convolutional Neural Network (CNN) model specifically adapted for learning from an input representation of a poker game, and producing poker drawing and betting models. Li and Miikkulainen [14] used Long Short-Term Memory (LSTM) recurrent neural networks (RNN) and Pattern Recognition Trees (PTR) to discover opponent models. Moravčik [15] introduce DeepStack, a decision-tree based algorithm for modelling imperfect-information settings that combines recursive reasoning with decomposition and a form of intuition that is learned automatically using deep learning.

Summarizing the poker agent usually are rule based [6], strategy-based [16–18], and opponent modelling based [19, 20].

In this study, we apply a sequential model from the TensorFlow.js library and analyze its space of parameters to find the best performing solution for the poker game.

2 Materials and Methods

2.1 Model

To model the poker game, the model was created using JavaScript programming language and Node.js library, and TensorFlow.js library. The model creates random but significant and logical situations. For example, if an opponent raises a bet, the possible solutions are only to raise the bet, fold the cards or call opponent's bet. All game data was created by looking at the 5-card poker game flow. In this variant of a game, all players have maximum 2 moves. Figure 1 shows data flow diagram. The algorithm considers the sequence of moves in the game.

To test the model, we developed an algorithm (Fig. 2), which changes the parameters of a neural network, which includes activation functions, the layer number and optimizer with loss function. The algorithm automatically creates layers and sets needed activation function for each layer, and initializes network for every activation item.

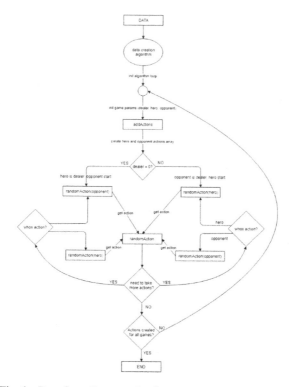

Fig. 1. Data flow diagram of poker game generator algorithm

3   Experiments and Results

3.1   Research Plan

We divided the experiments into three stages:

1. First phase of the test - many tests are performed with different combinations of model parameters and one layer.
2. The second stage of the test - testing with the best models found in Stage 1, testing with 2 and 3 layers.
3. Stage Three - Repeat steps 1 and 2, but with optimized data sets.

3.2   Research Data

The data needed for the study were obtained from UCI Machine Learning Repository [21]. The data file contains 25010 different cases, containing the color of the card in hand, the value of the card and the overall strength of the cards in hand. Each value is given in the array. The specific value is given by marking the required array element 1. Card values can be from A (Ace - the first element in the array is marked with 1 all the other 0) to K (King last array element is marked with 1 all other 0). For example, the value of the array C1 is J (Jack, because 10 element in array is marked) and its color is

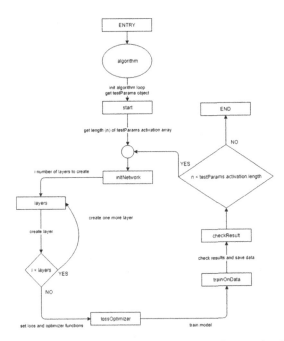

Fig. 2. Data flow diagram of model parameter changer algorithm

found by looking at the value of S1, in this case it is a red drum. Below are all possible values presented:

- S1 – S5: [Heart, Spade, Drum, Club];
- C1 – C5: [A, 2, 3, 4, 5, 6, 7, 8, 9, 10, J, Q, K];
- CLASS: [Nothing in hand, One pair, Two pairs, Three of a kind, Straight, Flush, Full house, Four of a kind, Straight flush, Royal flush].

Since attempts are made to find the optimum moves, this data array has been complemented by five additional lines describing the simple course of a five-card poker game: DEALER (shows who is dealer), HA1 (hero first action), HA2 (hero second action), OA1 (opponent first action), OA2 (opponent second action).

3.3   Settings

All calculations were made using Intel(R) Core(TM) i7-4770k CPU @ 3.50 GHz, 16 GB RAM. Models are trained on 85% of data set. Leftover 15% of data is used for model validation and accuracy testing.

The value of the loss function was followed during the tests. In order to find the right number of epochs, it is necessary to observe when the value of the loss function no longer decreases or begins to increase. After calculating the values obtained during the tests and averaging the mean, we found that on average 5 epochs were enough, since the values of loss function either increase or become very similar after that. Once the average number of epochs was found, we checked all other possible configurations.

The tests were initially performed using a single layer and all other possible combinations of settings until the best-performing models were found. The parameters of the neural network model is given in Table 1.

Table 1. Combinations of parameter values for stage 1

Activation	Loss function	Optimizer	Optimizer value			
elu, hardSigmoid, linear, relu, relu6, selu, sigmoid, softmax, softplus, softsign, tanh	MSE (Mean Squared Error)	Adam	0.001	0.01	0.06	0.1
		RMSProp	0.001	0.01	0.06	0.1
	CE (Categorical Crossentropy)	Adam	0.001	0.01	0.06	0.1
		RMSProp	0.001	0.01	0.06	0.1

For evaluation, we used accuracy, which is calculated by giving model the leftover data to predict optimal game moves and comparing expected results with predictions.

3.4   Results

In Table 2, we can see an experiment with sigmoid activation function, Mean square error (MSE) and Cross-Entropy (CE) loss functions, Adam and RMSProp optimizers with different optimizer values.

Table 2. Results for sigmoid activation

		Loss function			
		MSE		CE	
Optimizer	Value	Time (s)	Accuracy (%)	Time (s)	Accuracy (%)
Adam	0.001	19.053	46	35.25	65
	0.01	23.935	59	35.852	62
	0.06	24.071	51	35.999	63
	0.1	24.812	59	34.907	63
RMSProp	0.001	23.755	62	**34.348**	**65**
	0.01	20.421	63	35.662	57
	0.06	22.139	64	37.385	56
	0.1	**22.118**	**64**	37.282	55

The fastest calculation time was achieved when Adam (value 0.001) optimizer and MSE loss function was used, but the most accurate calculations are obtained using CE loss function and Adam (value 0.001) optimizer, also we get the same result with CE and RMSProp (value 0.001) optimizer. A closer look at the time of the calculations leads to the conclusion that the best model is CE and RMSProp (value 0.001). A 95% confidence interval for RMSProp is from 53.92% to 63.08%. A 95% the confidence interval for CE is from 57.91% to 63.59%. The results are summarized in Table 3.

Table 3. Summary of the first stage testing results

Activation	Loss function	Optimizer	Optimizer val.	Time (s)	Accuracy (%)
elu	MSE	Adam	0.1	19.268	62
hardSigmoid	MSE	Adam	0.06	25.687	65
linear	MSE	Adam	0.001	16.715	59
relu	MSE	Adam	0.06	20.333	65
relu6	MSE	RMSProp	0.1	21.99	65
selu	MSE	Adam	0.06	23.458	63
sigmoid	CE	RMSProp	0.001	34.348	65
softmax	CE	RMSProp	0.01	52.005	62
softplus	MSE	RMSProp	0.001	26.311	65
softsign	MSE	Adam	0.01	55.723	61
tanh	MSE	RMSProp	0.06	22.483	62

From Table 3 we can see that the minimum accuracy is 59% and the highest is 65%. With 95% confidence interval from 61.80% to 64.38%. Such results are rather inaccurate, as the models predict 65% of all predictions correctly. However, this inaccuracy can be seen as a lack or complexity of data for model training. It is for these reasons that it is possible to obtain fewer good results than expected. However, we empirically selected the best performing model settings are: activation – relu; optimizer – Adam (0.06); loss function – MSE.

Continuing the study with the above-mentioned best features, the calculations were made with 2 (11 different combinations) and 3 (121 different combinations) layers. The second and third layers are used with the same activation or other (see Table 1). In Table 4, the results with 2-layer activations are presented. 11 possible 2-layer combinations were tested when the first layer uses relu activation. We can see that the obtained accuracy results range from 34% to 66% with a 95% confidence interval from 48.92% to 64.9% (Table 4). The first layer is with relu activation, the second is with elu activation.

Table 4. Test results when first layer is with relu activation

Activation	Time (s)	Accuracy (%)
relu + elu	**29.032**	**66**
relu + hardSigmoid	32.519	66
relu + linear	33.621	66
relu + relu	31.991	66
relu + relu6	31.103	66
relu + selu	30.242	66
relu + sigmoid	30.317	40
relu + softmax	42.764	34
relu + softplus	31.805	53
relu + softsign	33.022	37
relu + tanh	38.229	66

Comparing the data with the previously obtained data, when the tests were performed using one layer, a slight improvement of 1% is seen. However, the 66% accuracy is quite bad, but still higher than the best previously found. It also shows that calculations using two layers take longer. Figure 3 shows loss function and validation values for each epoch of best-found model with relu + elu activations. Table 5 below shows results of calculations made with 2 layers, when first layer has activation of softplus.

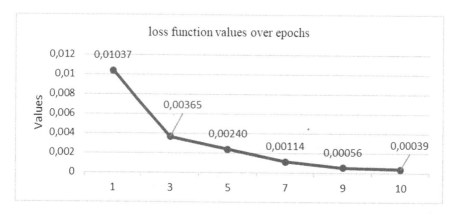

Fig. 3. MSE loss function changes in each epoch with relu + relu6 + selu and Adam (0.001)

11 possible 2-layer combinations were tested when the first layer uses softplus activation. We can see that the obtained accuracy results range from 28% to 66% with a 95% confidence interval from 47.21% to 63.7% (Table 5). The best value is when the first layer is with softplus activation, the second is with sigmoid activation.

Comparing the data with the previously obtained data, when the tests were performed using one layer, a slight improvement of 1% is seen. Comparison of data with data from Table 4 shows that the accuracy is the same, but the counting time is longer by 1 s when using softplus + sigmoid. That is why the better-performing combination is relu + elu. Accuracy results that we see in Table 5 and indicate that the model is lacking in accuracy. Also well-established val_loss value shows that 2 epochs are enough to train this model. Since there are many possible testing combinations with 3 layers, in Table 6 the best 2 models and values are shown.

The experiment shows that the results are not changing (comparing with results from Tables 4 and 5). The accuracy of the models does not exceed 66%. However, increasing the number of layers increases model training time. The 95% confidence interval for the first value is from 56.22% to 59.94%, and for second, - from 57.87% to 58.5%.

Comparing the results of Tables 3, 4, 5 and 6, it can be concluded that it is best to use 2 layers for calculation with data as in Fig. 2. If the timing of the calculations is more important than the accuracy obtained, one layer can be used, as this results in only 1% worse results, but the model can be trained faster.

Table 5. Test results when first layer is with softplus activation

Activation	Time (s)	Accuracy (%)
softplus + elu	31.168	60
softplus + hardSigmoid	34.851	66
softplus + linear	33.611	28
softplus + relu	33.876	58
softplus + relu6	33.321	42
softplus + selu	32.956	45
softplus + sigmoid	30.197	66
softplus + softmax	43.06	65
softplus + softplus	34.756	66
softplus + softsign	36.145	66
softplus + tanh	37.904	48

Table 6. Best results for 3-layer models

Activation	Time (s)	Accuracy (%)
relu + relu6 + selu	40.247	66
softplus + relu6 + relu	43.183	66

In order to get better accuracy results the experiments were repeated with simpler data as in Fig. 3. The data was simplified using a simple strategy: (1) count the number of available options; (2) check what the value of current data; (3) the value of the current data is divided by the total number of possible values.

In Table 7, the results are shown using a simpler data format, one layer, and all activation features, with all values of loss functions and optimizers. Selected best options in each case and presented in the same form as Table 3. Note that in this case we decided to use 10 epochs instead of 5. The resulting values are much more accurate than those obtained in Table 3. Therefore, smaller data helps to achieve better results.

This time it was possible to get as much as 94% accuracy with one layer, the loss function of MSE and Adam (value 0.001) optimizer. Hence, this model predicts 94 correct moves from 100. The accuracy of other models also improved when compared to Table 3. Using 2 layers (see Table 8), the accuracy was worse, but with the help of third layer we have improved accuracy up to 99% with a 95% confidence interval from 89.09% to 99.31%.

In Fig. 3, we can see that the constant decline of loss and val_loss values. This shows that the model's predictions are improving in every epoch. The follow-up study failed to improve the accuracy of this model any more. If more epochs are executed, the value of loss function decreases, but the value of validation increases or decreases disproportionately to loss. Hence, we conclude that over-fitting is occurring in later epochs.

Comparing with results achieved by other authors, our results are better than those achieved by Ambekar et al. [22], who used statistical analysis and modified Naive Bayes method to achieve an accuracy of 92.13%.

Table 7. Summarized results using simpler data format

Activation	Loss function	Optimizer	Optimizer val.	Time (s)	Accuracy (%)
elu	CE	RMSProp	0.001	9.44	87
hardSigmoid	MSE	Adam	0.01	8.293	81
linear	MSE	Adam	0.01	7.969	76
relu	MSE	Adam	0.001	8.58	94
relu6	MSE	Adam	0.001	8.264	81
selu	MSE	Adam	0.01	9.41	71
sigmoid	MSE	Adam	0.01	9.135	81
softmax	MSE	Adam	0.01	13.527	76
softplus	CE	RMSProp	0.01	13.617	82
softsign	MSE	Adam	0.01	12.308	78
tanh	MSE	Adam	0.001	9.947	75

Table 8. Simpler data and 2, 3 layers.

Activation	Time (s)	Accuracy (%)
relu + elu	10,456	88
relu + relu6 + selu	**15,489**	**99**

4 Conclusion

Neural models for predicting poker game moves can have many different configurations. In order to find the most accurate result model, there were lot of possible configurations to explore. In order to test the configurations of such a model, we created an algorithm that allows the model parameters to be changed automatically. We also developed an algorithm to complement and simplify the data sets needed for the investigation, thus solving the problem of limited and poorly described data. The best solution found was using simplified data for neural network model training (3 layers, where the first layer activation was "relu", second "relu6" and third "selu"). The model loss function was the CPS and the optimizer - Adam (value 0.001). The model predictions were 99% accurate (95% confidence interval is from 89.09% to 99.31%).

References

1. Rubin, J., Watson, I.: Computer poker: a review. Artif. Intell. **175**(5–6), 958–987 (2011)
2. Knight, W.: Why poker is a big deal for artificial intelligence. Technol. Rev. **120**(2), 16 (2017)
3. Ašeriškis, D., Damaševičius, R.: Gamification patterns for gamification applications. Procedia Comput. Sci. **39**(C), 83–90 (2014)
4. Billings, D., Peña, L., Schaeffer, J., Szafron, D.: Using probabilistic knowledge and simulation to play poker. In: 16th National Conference on Artificial Intelligence and 11th Innovative Applications of Artificial Intelligence Conference (AAAI 1999/IAAI 1999), pp. 697–703 (1999)

5. Billings, D., Davidson, A., Schaeffer, J., Szafron, D.: The challenge of poker. Artif. Intell. **134**(1–2), 201–240 (2002)
6. Billings, D.: Algorithms and assessment in computer poker. Ph.D. thesis. University of Alberta (2006)
7. Gilpin, A., Sandholm, T.: Better automated abstraction techniques for imperfect games, with application to Texas Hold'em. In: 6th International Joint Conference on Autonomous Agents and Multi-Agent Systems (AAMAS 2007), pp. 1168–1175 (2007)
8. Gilpin, A., Sandholm, T., Sørensen, T.: Potential-aware automated abstraction of sequential games, and holistic equilibrium analysis of Texas Hold'em poker. In: 22nd National Conference on Artificial Intelligence, vol. 1, pp. 50–57 (2007)
9. Gilpin, A., Hoda, S., Peña, J., Sandholm, T.: Gradient-based algorithms for finding nash equilibria in extensive form games. In: Deng, X., Graham, F.C. (eds.) WINE 2007. LNCS, vol. 4858, pp. 57–69. Springer, Heidelberg (2007). https://doi.org/10.1007/978-3-540-77105-0_9
10. Johanson, M.: Robust strategies and counter-strategies: building a champion level computer poker player. M.Sc. thesis. University of Alberta (2007)
11. Billings, D., et al.: Game-tree search with adaptation in stochastic imperfect-information games. In: van den Herik, H.J., Björnsson, Y., Netanyahu, N.S. (eds.) CG 2004. LNCS, vol. 3846, pp. 21–34. Springer, Heidelberg (2006). https://doi.org/10.1007/11674399_2
12. Carneiro, M.G., De Lisboa, G.A.: What's the next move? Learning player strategies in zoom poker games. In: IEEE Congress on Evolutionary Computation, CEC 2018 (2018)
13. Yakovenko, N., Cao, L., Raffel, C., Fan, J.: Poker-CNN: a pattern learning strategy for making draws and bets in poker games using convolutional networks. In: 30th AAAI Conference on Artificial Intelligence, AAAI 2016, pp. 360–367 (2016)
14. Li, X., Miikkulainen, R.: Opponent modeling and exploitation in poker using evolved recurrent neural networks. In: 2018 Genetic and Evolutionary Computation Conference, GECCO 2018, pp. 189–196 (2018)
15. Moravčík, M., et al.: DeepStack: expert-level artificial intelligence in heads-up no-limit poker. Science **356**(6337), 508–513 (2017)
16. Frank, I., Basin, D., Matsubara, H.: Finding optimal strategies for imperfect information games. In: 15th National/10th Conference on Artificial Intelligence/Innovative Applications of Artificial Intelligence, AAAI 1998/IAAI 1998, pp. 500–507 (1998)
17. Billings, D., et al.: Approximating game-theoretic optimal strategies for full-scale poker. In: International Joint Conference on Artificial Intelligence (IJCAI 2003), pp. 4–8 (2003)
18. Ganzfried, S., Yusuf, F.: Computing human-understandable strategies: deducing fundamental rules of poker strategy. Games **8**(4), 49 (2017)
19. Davidson, A.: Opponent modeling in poker: learning and acting in a hostile and uncertain environment. M.Sc. thesis. University of Alberta (2002)
20. Fedczyszyn, G., Koszalka, L., Pozniak-Koszalka, I.: Opponent modeling in Texas Hold'em poker. In: Nguyen, N.-T., Hoang, K., Jędrzejowicz, P. (eds.) ICCCI 2012. LNCS (LNAI), vol. 7654, pp. 182–191. Springer, Heidelberg (2012). https://doi.org/10.1007/978-3-642-34707-8_19
21. UCI Machine Learning Repository. Poker Hand Data Set (2007)
22. Ambekar, G., Chikane, T., Sheth, S., Sable, A., Ghag, K.: Anticipation of winning probability in poker using data mining. In: IEEE International Conference on Computer Communication and Control, IC4 2015 (2016)

Information Systems: Special Session on e-Health Information Systems

Investigation on the Dependencies Between HRV, Physical Training, and Focus of Attention in Virtual Environment

Edgaras Ščiglinskas[1,2], Aurimas Mačiukas[3], Aušra Vidugirienė[2(✉)], and Tomas Krilavičius[1,2]

[1] Baltic Institute of Advanced Technology,
J. Lelevelio g. 4, 01102 Vilnius, Lithuania
[2] Vytautas Magnus University, K. Donelaičio g. 58, 44248 Kaunas, Lithuania
{edgaras.sciglinskas,ausra.vidugiriene}@vdu.lt
[3] Lithuanian Sports University, Sporto g. 6, 44221 Kaunas, Lithuania

Abstract. In this study we investigate the dependencies between human focus of attention and heart rate variability while performing concentration task in virtual environment, using attention improvement device, and taking into account daily physical activity of the participants. For this purpose, a virtual testing environment – football arena – was developed. A volunteer had to "kick" a ball to the gate. He scores a goal if he has reached high attention focus level. The experiments were performed using NeuroSky device for attention level recording, Polar V800 device for heart rate (RR intervals) recording and ElfEmmit device as a better focus stimulator. At the same time, some virtual environment parameters and human action in it were recorded as well. We have used RMSSD parameter as heart rate variability measure. The results showed some unexpected tendencies. RMSSD parameter was in normal range and outside it for both: volunteers who have regular trainings and who do not have any training at all. A tendency was noticed that ElfEmmit device might increase focus of attention during virtual reality game.

Keywords: Heart rate variability · Attention focus · Virtual reality

1 Introduction

Various sports activities of appropriate individual intensity are important for good human health. Individual sport intensities nowadays are regulated with the help of portable heart rate measuring devices both: in daily life and training of athletes.

Heart balance is controlled by two autonomous nervous system branches: sympathetic and parasympathetic. Sympathetic nervous system mobilizes human resources in both psychological and physical stress cases, and parasympathetic nervous system helps to recover after a stress. Heart rate variability (HRV) shows the interaction between those two nervous systems and allows to identify when a human is resting and when he is in stress [1–3].

© Springer Nature Switzerland AG 2019
R. Damaševičius and G. Vasiljevienė (Eds.): ICIST 2019, CCIS 1078, pp. 529–540, 2019.
https://doi.org/10.1007/978-3-030-30275-7_41

There are plenty of HRV parameters [1, 4–9] used to identify different heart diseases or to analyze heart health when one wants to set appropriate individual regime of physical activities and recovery after them. All heart rate variability parameters are calculated using RR intervals – intervals between heart beats. HRV parameters are classified to the following groups: time domain parameters (statistical and geometrical), frequency domain parameters, nonlinear methods, and long-term correlations. Time domain statistical methods include mainly RR, NN, SDNN, SDANN, SDANN-i, RMSSD, SI, NN50, pNN50, SDSD [10–14]. Time domain geometrical methods usually include HRV triangular index, TINN, Differential index, and Logarithmic index [1, 9, 13]. Frequency domain parameters are calculated after performing Fast Fourier Transformation (FFT) for a rhythmogram signal and include ULF power, VLF power, LF, HF, LF/HF Ratio, VHF, etc. [1, 13]. Nonlinear methods include DFA α1 and α2, S, SD1, SD2, SD1/SD2, Poincare plot [15].

In this study we are investigating how sports activities influence human heart health, and focus of attention in interactive virtual computer game. Measuring heart rate variability and EEG-based parameters during the experiments, and knowing if the participant has regular physical activities, we search for correlations with focus of attention as various studies identify links between physical health and mental tasks [16, 17].

The experiments were planned so, that besides our main goal we can test if attention improvement device is effective and makes influence on the participants.

2 Virtual Environment and Experimental Setup

To investigate the connection between focus of attention and heart rate variability an experiment using virtual reality application was planned. In some cases, we have used a non-medical device which might increase focus and analyzed if it is able to perform this task.

A virtual football field and stadium was developed using Unity software (Fig. 1).

Fig. 1. Football arena virtual environment

The scene is viewed from the first-person position (Fig. 2). The participant had to "kick" a ball to the gate by clicking "space" button on a keyboard. If the focus of attention of a volunteer is higher than 60%, then the ball goes to the gates (Fig. 3) and if it is less, then the ball goes outside the gates (Fig. 4). In case of the largest focus level (100%), the ball goes to the very center of the gate.

The planned duration of the experiment for one participant was 180 s. It did not include preparation for the experiment, as putting on/off measuring devices, explanations of the process, answering questions of a participant if there are any. It was allowed to make as many kicks and as often as a volunteer wants. The volunteers were not informed about a threshold for the focus of attention (60%) and they didn't see their focus level in real time. They knew, that the focus was high enough if the ball went to the gate.

Fig. 2. Virtual environment scene from the first-person perspective before a "kick".

Fig. 3. Virtual environment scene from the first-person perspective after a successful kick.

Fig. 4. Virtual environment scene from the first-person perspective after unsuccessful kick.

Figure 5 presents the experiment scheme. Participant was playing the game on a desktop computer and his/her bio signals were recorded synchronously.

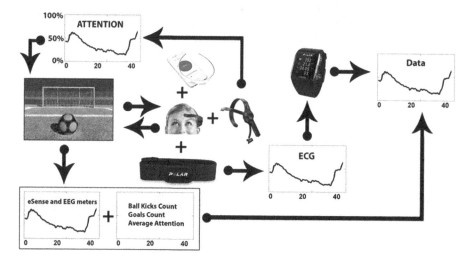

Fig. 5. Experiment scheme

We have used the following bio-signal measuring equipment:

- POLAR V800 heart rate measuring device, which measure RR intervals with resolution of 1000 Hz. We have chosen this device because of the validity in the scientific research [18, 19].
- NeuroSky Mindwave device was used to measure a level of human attention. This device was chosen because of its user-friendliness (as it is a headset with one dry electrode on the forehead and one clip on the ear) [20] and acceptable accuracy in non-medical applications [21]. This device is capable to record eye blinks and meditation level as well as EEG power spectra (alpha, gamma, theta, beta, and delta waves).

- ElfEmmit device among other functionalities have focus improvement regime that we used for some of the volunteers. This device was chosen and an experimental one to investigate its efficiency when reaching higher attention focus level.

3 Data

The experiment was performed with 21 university students (19–20-year-old) – 6 females and 15 males. In random order 9 of them were wearing ElfEmmit device with focus improvement regime and 10 of them were performing the tests without ElfEmmit device. The data of 2 females were not included, as the records were corrupted and signal quality was too low for the investigation. In total the data of 19 volunteers were included to the research (4 female and 15 male). The volunteers were asked if they have regular trainings of any sport at the moment and 13 of then agreed to answer the questions. One of them was a professional athlete, 6 – having regular trainings, and 6 – not having regular trainings at the moment.

During the experiment RR intervals were recorded using Polar V800 device and the following data were recorded every 0.5 s using NeuroSky device (it is the smallest duration possible between measures in NeuroSky when using pre-processed signals):

- Blinking (as stronger the blink was, the higher parameter value was recorded),
- Meditation (from 0% to 100%),
- Average focus (concentration) value (from 0% to 100%). The average was taken between the kicks, and it was recalculated every 0.25 s,
- Number of kicks,
- Number of goals.

A questionnaire with following questions was presented to every volunteer (they were free to answer or not):

- What kind of sport are you doing?
- Do you have regular trainings? How many times and hours a week?
- Are you an athlete?

4 Methods

After analysis of the scientific papers describing HRV parameters and methods, we concluded that one of the best parameter to assess human heart health in real time is RMSSD parameter.

RMSSD is the square root of the root mean square of the sum of all differences between successive NN intervals. Higher values indicate increased parasympathetic activity) [7]. This parameter is calculated as follows:

$$RMSSD = \sqrt{\frac{1}{N-1}\left(\sum_{i=1}^{N-1}(RR_{i+1}-RR_i)^2\right)}, \tag{1}$$

where RR is intervals between heart beats, and N – a number of heart beats.

The RMSSD norms for people with different physical activities differs. Figure 6 demonstrates different parameter results for people who are not physically active, for people, who have regular trainings and for athletes [11]. Physically inactive people has the lowest values of RMSSD parameter with the density peak around 45 ms. Physically active people has higher values of RMSSD with density peak around 55–75 ms. At the same time RMSSD range for athletes are very wide and the density peak is around 95 ms. It is worth to mention that average value of this parameter of nonathletes is 42 ms, and the normal range is between 19 and 75 ms [10].

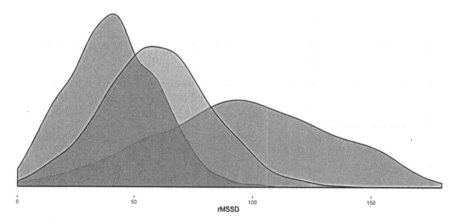

Fig. 6. RMSSD dependency from human physical activity in daily life [11]. Left peak – RMSSD of physically passive people, middle peak – RMSSD of physically active people, right peak – RMSSD of athletes.

5 Results

As a result of this research we analyzed lots of comparing diagrams of various parameter pairs. Figure 7 demonstrates RMSSD and training duration dependency.

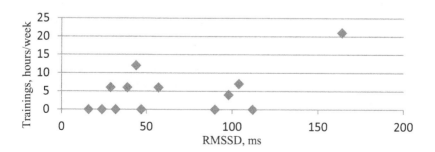

Fig. 7. RMSSD dependency from training duration (hours/week).

In respect to RMSSD normal range between 19 and 75 ms, we can see that both groups – those who have regular trainings and those who have no trainings – are in normal range as well as out of normal range of this parameter. However, there is a big difference between athlete RMSSD value and other participants. More detailed information on volunteers' health and training intensity would be needed to find more tendencies.

When analyzing dependencies between training duration and focus of attention (Fig. 8), there are no strict classification, but the experiment showed that in our group of 13 participants who answered questions about their physical activity there is a tendency that the highest focus (60–80%) was reached by the participants who do not have weekly trainings.

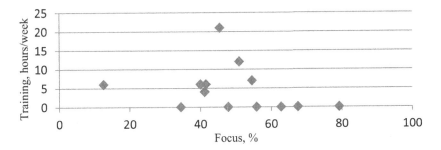

Fig. 8. Dependencies between training duration and focus of attention.

The analysis of the three following diagrams is dedicated for the evaluation of efficiency of ElfEmmit device and focus stimulator.

We have compared the percentage of goals (from all the kicks) for every participant (Fig. 9) in respect to two groups: those who were wearing ElfEmmit device (triangles) and those who were not wearing it (diamonds). Although there are various situations, but the tendency can be noticed that most of the highest results were reached in the group where participants were wearing ElfEmmit device.

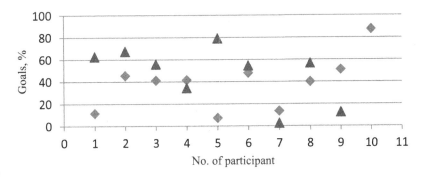

Fig. 9. Goals in percentage from all the kicks with ElfEmmit (triangles) and without ElfEmmit (diamond)

We were also comparing the focus level in percentage before every goal (Fig. 10) in the same two groups: those who were wearing ElfEmmit device (squares) and those who were not wearing it (diamonds). A tendency was found that using ElfEmmit device there were more higher focus cases before a goal than without this device.

When analyzing focus levels of every participant before every kick, participants wearing ElfEmmit device (squares) in more cases had higher focus levels than participants not wearing it (diamonds) (Fig. 11).

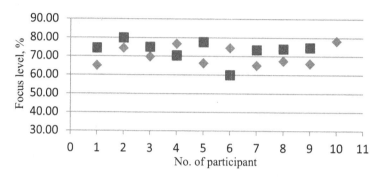

Fig. 10. Average focus of attention in percentage before goals with ElfEmmit (square) and without ElfEmmit (diamond)

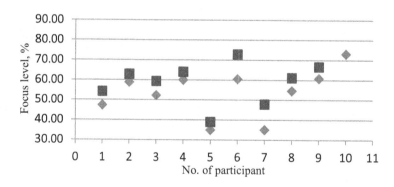

Fig. 11. Average focus in percentage before kicks with ElfEmmit (square) and without ElfEmmit (diamond)

The following table (Table 1) summarizes average values of some parameters when participants were using ElfEmmit device and when it was not used. It is seen that average values are higher when using ElfEmmit device: 9% more goals, 3% higher focus before a goal, 5% higher focus before a kick, 4 goals more and 1 kick less. The results cannot be considered as confident difference, but the tendencies that ElfEmmit might positively influence human focus are visible.

Table 2 gives a summary of various measured and calculated parameter results for every participant including average focus before a goal, percentage of goals, RMSSD values, and training hours per week. Average focus before a goal is marked in bold when the value exceeds 70%. It appears in 4 of 10 cases when ElfEmmit is not used and in 8 of 9 cases when it is used. Percentage of goals is marked in bold when it exceeds 50%. It appears in 2 of 10 cases when ElfEmmit is not used and in 6 of 9 cases when it is used. RMSSD value is marked in bold when it is out of normal range. There are no significant links seen between RMSSD and average focus between goals or number of goals.

Table 1. Average parameter values, when using ElfEmmit device and when not using it.

	ElfEmmit off	ElfEmmit on
No. of participants	10	9
Goals, %	38.7	**47.39**
Average focus before a goal, %	70.30	**73.25**
Average focus before a kick, %	53.75	**58.70**
Average no. of goals	15.20	**19.22**
Average no. of kicks	39.10	38.33

Table 2. Summary of measured and calculated parameters.

Male/Female	ElfEmmit	Average focus before goal, %	Goals, %	RMSSD, ms	Trainings, h/week
F	off	65,00	11,5	28	–
M	off	**74,29**	45,45	**164**	21
M	off	69,75	41,18	**98**	4
M	off	**76,72**	41,51	29	6
M	off	66,25	7,41	63	–
M	off	**74,42**	47,83	32	0
M	off	65,00	13,64	**100**	–
M	off	67,40	40	57	6
M	off	66,04	**50,94**	44	12
M	off	**78,17**	**87,5**	44	–
F	on	**74,35**	**62,79**	**16**	0
M	on	**74,99**	**67,5**	24	0
F	on	**79,87**	**55,88**	**112**	0
F	on	**70,38**	34,48	**90**	0
M	on	**77,63**	**79,25**	47	0
M	on	**73,43**	**54,55**	**104**	7
M	on	60	2,7	**132**	–
M	on	**73,95**	**56,82**	34	–
M	on	**74,67**	12,5	39	6

6 Conclusions

The research showed that RMSSD parameter does not depend on participant physical activities, except the case of professional sports (and intensive training program). RMSSD parameter was in normal range and outside it in both cases: when a participant has regular (not too intensive) trainings and when he does not have regular trainings at all. More detailed information is needed on volunteers health and intensity of physical activities to make more precise conclusions.

No significant dependencies between focus of attention and weekly training time were found, but it is visible that the participants who are not having regular trainings, reached the highest focus values (60–80%).

When investigating the influence of ElfEmmit device on the focus of attention of participants, we have found that participants kicked 10% more goals on average when wearing the device (they concentrated more often to the needed level). Average focus level was 3–5% higher before kicks and before goals for the participants using the device. Although we cannot claim that the device helps to increase focus, but such tendency is visible.

7 Discussion

A larger set of participants would be needed to check dependencies between focus of attention and weekly training time as other studies show dependencies between physical and mental health [16, 17].

There is a need for a larger scale experiments, to confirm or reject the positive impact of ElfEmmit device to the focus of attention.

After processing the data and getting the results, there were also some suggestions for the future experiments made. It would be useful to make the experiment longer and give a possibility to the same participant to perform the task with ElfEmmit device and without it as well as to ask the participants to provide more data about their health. It would be also interesting to compare the results to the psychological type of the participant.

Although some studies [22] criticize NeuroSky device to measure brainwave signals against Emotiv EPOC, but here are several advantages of using it: simple to put on, does not use dry electrodes, more devices on the head can be easily used at the same time, etc. There were also different type of experiments performed in [22] than in our study. Our experiment was designed so, that we would be sure which part of signal appears before and after every goal or missing it. Still it would be interesting to use other non-medical devices for our experiments, to compare the results with present research.

Acknowledgements. We thank UAB "De Futuro" and Ph.D. Gintaras Rimša for cooperation. Research was partially funded by Lithuanian Agency for Science, Innovation and Technology (01.2.1-MITA-K-824-01-0067-S).

References

1. Ablonskytė-Dūdonienė, R.: Širdies ritmo variabilumo ir hemodinamikos žymenų vertė prognozuojant ūminio miokardo infarkto eigą ir baigtis sergantiesiems cukriniu diabetu. Ph.D. dissertation, Biomedicine sciences (2014). https://publications.lsmuni.lt/object/elaba:2199280/2199280.pdf
2. The science and application of heart rate variability. https://hrvcourse.com/heart-rate-variability-vs-heart-rate. Accessed 05 Apr 2018
3. Techo.lt homepage. http://techo.lt/sirdies-ritmo-variabilumas-budas-kasdieniam-stresui-sekti. Accessed 05 Apr 2018
4. Shaffer, F., Ginsberg, J.P.: An overview of heart rate variability metrics and norms. Front. Public Health **5**, 258 (2017)
5. Esco, M.R., Williford, H.N., Flatt, A.A., Freeborn, T.J., Nakamura, F.Y.: Ultra-shortened time-domain HRV parameters at rest and following exercise in athletes: an alternative to frequency computation of sympathovagal balance. Eur. J. Appl. Physiol. **118**, 175–184 (2018)
6. Rad, A.M., Ryoo, H.C., Akin, A., Sun, H.H.: Classification of Heart Rate Variability (HRV) parameters by Receiver Operating Characteristics (ROC). In: Proceedings of the IEEE 28th Annual Northeast Bioengineering Conference (2002)
7. Heart rate variability and hear rate comparison. http://www.ans-analysis.com/hrv/hrv-measuring-parameter.html. Accessed 05 Apr 2019
8. Vollmer, M.: A robust, simple and reliable measure of Heart Rate Variability using relative RR intervals. In: Computing in Cardiology Conference (CinC) (2015)
9. Malik, M., et al.: Guidelines. Heart rate variability, Standards of measurement, physiological interpretation, and clinical use. Eur. Heart J. **17**, 354–381 (1996)
10. Norms of HRV parameter. https://www.hrv4training.com/blog/heart-rate-variability-normal-values. Accessed 05 Apr 2019
11. RMSSD parameter description. https://www.biopac.com/application/ecg-cardiology/advanced-feature/rmssd-for-hrv-analysis. Accessed 05 Apr 2019
12. DeGiorgio, C.M., et al.: RMSSD, a measure of heart rate variability, is associated with risk factors for SUDEP: the SUDEP-7 inventory. Epilepsy Behav. **19**(1), 78–81 (2010)
13. Wang, H.-M., Huang, S.-C.: SDNN/RMSSD as a surrogate for LF/HF: a revised investigation. Model. Simul. Eng. **2012**, 8 p. (2012). Article ID 931943
14. Trimmel, M.: Relationship of Heart Rate Variability (HRV) parameters including pNNxx with the subjective experience of stress, depression, well-being, and every-day trait moods (TRIM-T): a pilot study. Ergon. Open J. **8**, 32–37 (2015)
15. www.gtec.at research presentation: Heart Rate Variability (2004). http://www0.cs.ucl.ac.uk/research/vr/Projects/Presencia/ConsortiumPublications/graz_papers/HRVanalysis.pdf. Accessed 05 Apr 2019
16. Coxa, E.P., et al.: Relationship between physical activity and cognitive function in apparently healthy young to middle-aged adults: a systematic review. J. Sci. Med. Sport **19**, 616–628 (2016)

17. Ohrnberger, J., Ficher, E., Sutton, M.: The relationship between physical and mental health: a mediation analysis. Soc. Sci. Med. **195**, 42–49 (2017)
18. Giles, D., Draper, N., Neil, W.: Validity of the Polar V800 heart rate monitor to measure RR intervals at rest. Eur. J. Appl. Physiol. **116**, 563–571 (2016)
19. Polar V800 specification. www.polar.com. Accessed 05 Apr 2019
20. Neurosky Mindwave specification. https://store.neurosky.com/pages/mindwave. Accessed 05 Apr 2019
21. Brain Wave Signal (EEG) of NeuroSky, Inc. (2009). http://www.frontiernerds.com/files/neurosky-vs-medical-eeg.pdf. Accessed 05 Apr 2019
22. Maskeliunas, R., et al.: Consumer-grade EEG devices: are they usable for control tasks? PeerJ (3) (2016). https://doi.org/10.7717/peerj.1746

Mobile Platform for Fatigue Evaluation: HRV Analysis

Eglė Butkevičiūtė[1]([⊠]), Matīss Eriņš[2], and Liepa Bikulčienė[1]

[1] Kaunas University of Technology, K. Donelaičio str. 73, 44249 Kaunas,
Lithuania
egle.butkeviciute@ktu.lt
[2] Riga Technical University, 1 Kalku Street, Riga 1658, Latvia

Abstract. Recent studies report that heart rate variability (HRV) is related to increased self-control abilities, greater social skills, and fatigue where the decision support systems often use RR interval signal data directly. The RR interval data filtering is compared by using different data sets and artefact removal methods when data were recorded during various training intensity. The results of artefact analysis indicate the intensity of the exercise which increases as the amount of artefact RR interval data increase. Furthermore, for artefact evaluation and fatigue estimation the Poincare plots were selected. The SD1 and SD2 indexes (standard deviation in two orthogonal directions of the Poincare plot) carry similar information to the spectral analysis and simple statistical means (like average pulse and standard error) but are easier calculated and lesser stationarity dependence. In this article Poincare diagram parameters were used to analyze HRV parameters during five stage training sessions for stages with less signal artefacts and evaluate the training impact on human fatigue. The process of HRV signal analysis described in this article is a basis for RR data processing which is important in parameter expertise and method repeatability. Systematic comparison of multiple signal sources enables different RR interval sensor evaluation based on their signal artefacts by using current findings. This research contains different methods of HRV analysis that will be used to support development of a mobile fatigue evaluation system.

Keywords: HRV analysis · HRV artefacts · Poincare plot · Fatigue

1 Introduction

Mobile systems for health monitoring are popular in health and fitness centres, clinics and become popular in working and living places. These systems are used by elderly people, patients, sportsmen etc. The electronic remote health monitoring systems sometimes can replace the conventional health care methods. The Internet of Things (IoT) based systems in smart health monitoring systems can connect and share the information with each other through the Internet automatically. Every year low cost consumer-grade electrocardiographic (ECG) and heart rate (HR) recording devices are even more used in consumer market, a large amount of data can be collected through IoT, smart wearables and Body Area Networks (BAN) and used for numerous e-health and well-being applications such as workplace ergonomics [1], epileptic seizure

© Springer Nature Switzerland AG 2019
R. Damaševičius and G. Vasiljevienė (Eds.): ICIST 2019, CCIS 1078, pp. 541–552, 2019.
https://doi.org/10.1007/978-3-030-30275-7_42

detection [2], tele-monitoring of chronic diseases [3], activity recognition [4], depression monitoring [5], as well as for fatigue detection [6].

The collected data can be very useful in the assessment of human condition but still requires effective computational intelligence algorithms to derive useful information in near real time. Usually consumers want instant feedback on his state and trends of wellbeing. Also, the development of automated expert systems to assist both professional experts and nonprofessional users to analyse of physiological data is very important for real-world e-health applications. The integration of smart multimodal interfaces, modelling and data mining techniques should guarantee that the developed system is comfortable and effective. Also, the dynamics and individual daily-life activities are important to the human health status. Unfortunately, analysis of human vital signals during daily life activities in almost real time still is quite complicated task. Of course, the vital human signals can be recorded during regular daily life activities, but then before decision makings it is important to have reliable signals.

Electrocardiogram (ECG) and HRV analysis is commonly used and is known to be useful tool for screening a variety of heart diseases due to its simple application [7] although there is a high cost and long waiting required to meet the specialist for screening [8]. Reliable monitoring systems cost from 3000 to 5000 EUR (CardioScout, Heart rhythm analysis system etc.), whereas good smart watches as Polar can cost only from 50 EUR, but then an advanced analysis of signals must be made.

Due to the complex nature of fatigue, its measures are generally multidimensional approaches instead of single question (e.g. "Are you tired?") [9]. These multidimensional measures assess the level of fatigue based on daily activities, mental and physical performance, and other related characteristics. One of these characteristics is heart rate variability (HRV), which is widely used in different types fatigue estimation [10].

2   Materials and Methods

2.1   HRV Parameters and Fatigue

The HRV could be analysed in both time domain and frequency domain. In the time domain, global descriptive statistics such as standard deviation of the heart rate could be used. In the frequency domain, the HR needs to be modelled into periodic patterns to extract specific frequency by the power spectrum density. The spectral power on certain frequency bands such as the low and high frequency regions could then be quantified by calculating the area under the spectral density function. Data processing procedures may include preliminary processing such as artefact cancelling, peak-to-peak interval fetching and periodic heart rate justification [11].

Except for the traditional time- and frequency-domain analysis assessment of HRV the non-linear Poincare plot analysis can be used. Poincare plot parameters are easy to compute and associated with the 'width' of the scattergram. It can be suggested that they could be used to indicate fatigue and/or prevent overtraining. Information about HRV has been commonly obtained by using linear methods such as power spectral analysis. However, a number of studies dealing about HRV have shown that RR intervals fluctuate in a very complex manner exhibiting patterns suggestive of non-linear processes [12]. Because of these non-linear components, the RR interval time series signal cannot be properly assessed using linear techniques such as spectral analysis. A Poincare plot of HRV, where each RR interval is plotted as a function of the previous interval, is a non-linear method that allows calculation of changes in heart dynamics with trends.

The Poincare plot gives useful visual contact to the RR data by representing qualitatively with graphical mean the kind of RR variations included in the recording, [13]. For athletes also, assessment by the Poincare plot analysis as a method is quite popular [14]. For big data the machine learning methods also can be used [15]. This approach was applied to the data gathered by the wearable devices for various types and levels of physical activities, and for people with various physical conditions.

The major drawback is that a stationary signal is required and the HRV signal cannot be properly assessed using linear techniques [15], especially during short-term recording. Poincare plot method is a non-linear technique and the single shape of the plot can be used to classify the signal into various classes of disease or to indicate fatigue after prolonged exercise [12], what is also important in current research. Furthermore, a recent study has shown that the LF components decrease over the course of the fatigue-inducing tasks, while HF components increase. In paper [16] was suggested that even in the absence of noticeable changes in the subjective symptoms, postpartum fatigue status can be objectively identified by evaluating the autonomic nervous activity via heart rate variability analysis.

Among the tools proposed to assess the athlete's fatigue, the analysis of heart rate variability (HRV) provides an indirect evaluation of the settings of autonomic control of heart activity [17]. Prolonged, disabling fatigue is the hallmark of chronic fatigue syndrome (CFS). The results of this study suggest that HRV is a potentially important measure of adaptive capacity in chronic illnesses [18]. While methods such as HRV analysis show promise in detecting both cognitive and physical fatigue, identifying different physical activities seem necessary to improve the accuracy and robustness of this detection. Such robustness is necessary particularly in diagnosing chronic fatigue [19].

The review [20] provides a brief overview of heart rate variability and its effect on fatigue. The linkage between recognizing an individual's unique physical activities, and its possible feedback to manage fatigue levels were explored. Overall, triangulations of heart rate variability show promise in identify chronic cognitive and physical fatigue levels. There was indicates on different physical activities studied and classified by the researchers, as well as methodologies used for activity classification. The most popular category was walking, second - different types of exercising [21]. Based on this, physical activities for experimental data in the current research were chosen.

HRV calculation in this research was organised as presented in Fig. 1. In this case RR data were found from ECG, but in future data from smart watches can be used in order to avoid big expenses of the final product.

2.2   R Peaks Finding Algorithm

Analysis of ECG signals is an important task in diagnosis and detection of many cardiac disorders. ECG signal consists of both linear and nonlinear components, and

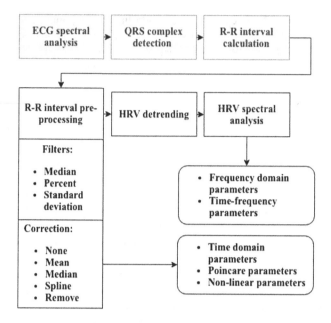

Fig. 1. HRV calculation scheme

nonlinear components have significant changes between normal and abnormal beats [22]. A good performance of an ECG analysis depends mainly on the accurate and reliable detection of the R wave, QRS complex as well as the T and P wave. The first step in ECG signal analysis is R wave detection, RR interval estimation and beat segmentation into beat-to-beat intervals [23]. Series of beat-to-beat intervals is the main criteria used in analysing heart rate variability (HRV).

Electromyogram (EMG) is a high frequency noise due to random muscles contractions and baseline wander as a low frequency noise that appears due to sudden movement of body and respiration [24]. Higher order spectral cumulants are found to be an effective tool with its ability to suppress the Gaussian noise with unknown spectral characteristics in the analysis of nonlinear data [22]. Several algorithms have been proposed for the EMG decomposition task. Some algorithms are fast (like Sparse derivatives [25], K-Nearest Neighbour algorithm [26] or method that uses dynamic plosion index [27]), but they suffer from low accuracy and are unable to reduce superpositions and interferences. Other algorithms such as redundant discrete wavelet transform, algorithms with fire pulse train automaton integration in the thresholding or any other morphological filter, are computationally heavy and hence slow and not suitable for long time recordings like ECG signal for fatigue recognition [29]. To achieve an acceptable trade-off between speed and accuracy in analysis of noisy EMG measurements a multiresolution Teager energy operator algorithm (MTEO) [30] was selected as R peak detection algorithm.

Teager Energy operator (TEO) mainly reflects the instantaneous frequency and signal amplitude changes that are very sensitive for the small signal changes. Nonlinear energy in the time domain for the discrete time signal $x(n)$ is given as

$$x(n) = A\cos(\Omega n + \varphi), \tag{1}$$

where $\Omega = 2\pi f/f_s$, and φ is the initial phase angle, f_s – sampling frequency, f – frequency, A – amplitude of recordings [22]. If T is defined as a sampling rate and k as an arbitrary integer called lag parameter than TEO general form could be expressed as:

$$Y_n(nT) = x^2(nT) - x(nT - kT)x(nT + kT), \tag{2}$$

where the choice of k is based on the period of the spike that is being searched for [30]. If $Y_i(nT)$ after it is smoothed with Hamming window of size $4k+1$ is defined as $\widehat{Y}_i(nT)$, the final output of MTEO $t(nT)$ could be expressed as:

$$t(nT) = \max_{i=1:k}\left(\widehat{Y}_i(nT)\right) \tag{3}$$

The final expression detects the R wave peaks in the ECG signal. This algorithm achieves a fast processing speed by using a fiducial point detection method instead of processing the whole signal. It is very important in real time signal analysis and fatigue estimation. MTEO algorithm could also work with signals that contain huge baseline wanders that are caused by registering ECG during physical activity.

2.3 Poincare Diagram and Parameters

One of the first things to know to understand heart rate is that the most informative metrics rely not just on heat rate, but how much the heart rate varies (HRV). Higher heart variability is associated with good health because the more heart jumps around, the readier the person is for action. While a low HRV is associated with illness. Heart rate variability could be expressed in different ways. One of the most popular metrics is Root Mean Square Standard Deviation (RMSSD) that could be expressed as:

$$RMSSD = \sqrt{\frac{1}{n-1}\sum_{i=1}^{n}\left(RR_{i+1} - RR_i\right)^2} \tag{4}$$

where $RR_1, RR_2, \ldots, RR_n$ are RR sequentially listed RR intervals [31]. Even though fairly good results have been obtained using such technique, it seems to provide only a limited amount of information about ECG signal, because it ignores the underlying nonlinear signal dynamics [28].

The Poincare mapping is a technique, rooted in non-linear dynamics theory, that is particularly useful for inspecting stability of systems displaying periodic behaviour. The Poincare plot is a technique that makes it possible to analyse short as well as long recordings. It can be expressed in two different ways: a visual technique where the human eyes could recognize patterns, and a quantitative one, that introduces various parameters that quantify the information contained in a Poincare plot [31]. A typical Poincare plot is constructed as a relationship between RR intervals RR_i on the x-axis and RR_{i+1} intervals on the y-axis, which means that each point in the plot corresponds to two consecutive RR intervals [21]. Typically, the shape of a Poincare plot is an elongated cloud of points around the line of identity (LoI) that usually has the form of an ellipse. The ellipse minor axis perpendicular to LoI is identical with the standard deviation $SD1$ and represents short-term variability (which means fast changes in HRV). The major axis, that could be defined as $SD2$, represents long-term variability. $SD1$ and $SD2$ could be estimated as follows, where $Var(x)$ is the variance of x:

$$SD1 = \sqrt{Var(x_1)}; \quad SD2 = \sqrt{Var(x_2)}, \tag{5}$$

$$x_1 = \frac{RR_{i+1} - RR_i}{\sqrt{2}}; \quad x_1 = \frac{RR_{i+1} + RR_i}{\sqrt{2}}; \tag{6}$$

However, the ellipse rotation is needed by the angle of $\varphi = \frac{\pi}{4}$ and the final expression is written below:

$$\begin{bmatrix} x_1 \\ x_2 \end{bmatrix} = \begin{bmatrix} \cos\varphi & -\sin\varphi \\ \sin\varphi & \cos\varphi \end{bmatrix} \begin{bmatrix} RR_i \\ RR_{i+1} \end{bmatrix}. \tag{7}$$

It is common procedure to draw an ellipse with axes $(SD1, SD2)$ centered on $\overline{RR_i}, \overline{RR_{i+1}}$ – the overbar denotes of the mean vector. Additionally, the parameter $SDRR$ is defined which reflects to the total variability as measured by the Poincare plot:

$$SDRR = \frac{SD1}{SD2}. \tag{8}$$

2.4   Artefacts Detection and Outliers

There are mainly two artefact types present in RR intervals that are visible in the examples. The artefacts from either ectopic beats or missing/misread QRS complexes that only produce upward or downward spike in the signal. Three artefact detection methods are observed which form the corrected signal data point with spline interpolation of detected artefact. Each of the three functions is effective for specific artefact. Figure 2 shows different effect for each artefact function. The functions are more impact in short examples during the active exercise state. Overall the *Percentage* filter function shows most detected artefacts, it locates any sudden or abrupt RR intervals. Filter *StdDev* is used to detect ectopic intervals defined by standard deviation distance from mean RR interval. Method *Median* acts as an impulse rejection filter with threshold to delineate ectopic intervals and correct high side and low side artefacts of exercise specific HRV recordings. The *Median* filter of a random variable x of length N using a threshold of τ is given by

$$D(n) = \frac{|x(n) - med(x)|}{1.483 \cdot med\{|x(n) - med(x)|\}}. \tag{9}$$

If $D(n) \geq \tau$, then not ectopic; else ectopic.

Artefact detection	Examples with motion artefacts corrected on one sample using spline interpolation method
None	
StdDev functon with treshold of SD= 3	
Percentage function with treshold of 20%	
Median function with threshold 4	
All functions together	

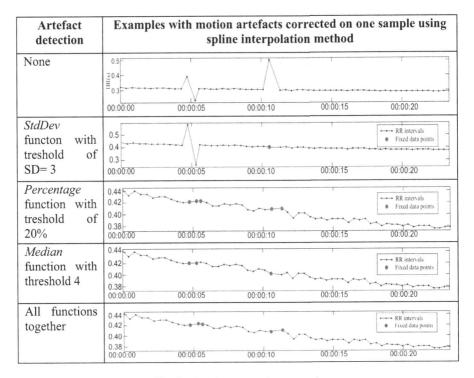

Fig. 2. Artefact correction example

3   Experimental Results and Discussion

3.1   Artefacts Removal

In research two types of experiment were used: long training session for several athletes with rest and recovery (protocol and example of artefact removal is presented in Fig. 3 and repeatable block of some special exercises).

Table 1 represents results of artefact removal during same experiment for different persons (from A to F). Multiple exercises are performed by the same subject in successive order and only the active stage ECG is recorded. Further the RR interval pre-processing filters were compared against 4 different exercises performed. Usage of all three RR interval pre-processing filters leads to the best result – maximum outlier detection. However, the percentage filter shows the same behavior as all together (except for A and E people). Further analysis was made with only percentage RR filter because using all of them can be time consuming.

The example data is split into 5 stages: preparation, low intensity, rest, high intensity and recovery. In Fig. 3(a) part represents sample after artefact removal and detrended RR intervals using Wavelet (b) part - ECG spectrogram. The higher intensity exercise is, the lower RR interval values are reached. This means that heart works faster and harder. The spectrogram shows how noisy the ECG data is in all stages. It can be noticed that stage S4 contains a lot of noise (compared with other stages). This is

Stages	S1 Before training	S2 Lo. load	S3 Resting	S4 Hi. load	S5 Recovery
(a)					
(b)					

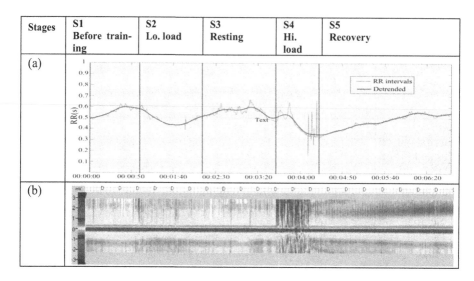

Fig. 3. Example of artefacts removal functions during training session with rest and recovery

Table 1. Count of RR peaks and outliers during training session

Subject	Total RR (count)	*StdDev* function outliers (count)	*Percentage* function outliers (count)	*Median* function outliers (count)	All functions together outliers (count)
A	697	10	61	17	63
B	735	4	34	4	34
C	812	2	44	0	44
D	879	11	36	14	36
E	756	14	59	15	60
F	877	1	10	0	10

because high intensity exercises usually lead more muscle movements and then the electrode contact instability.

3.2 Poincare Analysis

The previous section was shown that all three observed artefact filtering algorithms have an impact on non-linear and frequency domain analysis results. In further analysis the filtered RR data will be used to avoid interpretation failures.

Figure 4 shows the heart rate variability in training session (this example was taken while participant was in resting stage). The exercise intensity could be seen from the ellipse position in the pictures, how scattered are the dots and ellipse form. Furthermore, the more flattened the ellipse is, the worse heart condition it represents. Parameters *SD*1 and *SD*2 represent ellipse form and how RR intervals are scattered.

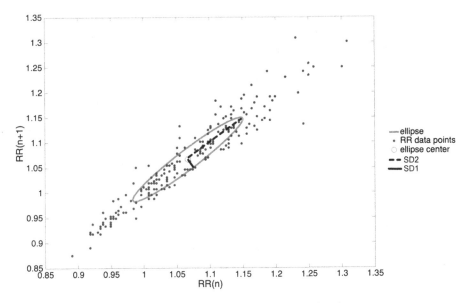

Fig. 4. Poincare plot example during resting time

Table 2 demonstrates the heart rate variability changes in different training stages. The estimated parameters are expressed in seconds. In this example a participant performed squats as a low intensity exercise and squats with jump – as high intensity exercise. S1 illustrates a good heart condition with scattered dots. This means, that heart variability is high. The same tendency could be noticed in S3 and S5. While S2 and S4 stages show limited heart rate variability. In resting time heart recovered and *SDRR* increased and reached even better than it had before training session ($SDRR_1 = 0.086 < 0.142 = SDRR_3$). This means that after low intensity exercises HRV back to normal condition. However, after training session (recovery time) *SDRR* parameter decreased and heart hardly back to normal condition. This could be described as a fatigue.

Table 2. Poincare parameters in different training stage

Stage	Training intensity	SD1	SD2	SDRR	RMSSD
S1	Before training	0.010	0.111	0.086	0.015
S2	Low intensity exercise	0.006	0.064	0.087	0.008
S3	Resting time	0.017	0.116	0.142	0.024
S4	High intensity exercise	0.007	0.088	0.078	0.011
S5	Recovery time	0.009	0.131	0.065	0.011

To see how fatigue effects the *SDRR* parameter, long time ECG signals should be recorded and after RR extraction the comparison should be made. All RR interval data is filtered while participant was doing exercises at the same day one after another (different rounds). There were 13 rounds for each exercise. How *SDRR* parameter fluctuates can be seen in Table 3. The less intensive exercise is, the bigger *SDRR* parameter value can be found. Furthermore, for the high intense exercises this parameter is less scattered. In Table 3 the Friedman test is applied and *p*-value is found. Friedman tests the null hypothesis that the column effects distributions are all the same against the alternative that they are not all the same. In this example the different exercises were as different columns and estimated $p < 0.001$ value leads to null hypothesis rejection. This result shows that there is a statistically significant difference in *SDRR* parameter between exercises. This statistic approach together with data sampling methods can be used for the machine learning analysis [32, 33] to create exercise classifier. However, this require more data samples and additional ECG parameters estimation.

Table 3. Poincare and fatigue parameters with statistical significance

Statistic	SDRR in different exercises			
	Dead-bug	Skater-jump	Squat	Walk
Mean	0.129	0.051	0.062	0.170
Standard deviation	0.029	0.010	0.025	0.039
p-value	<0.001 (Friedman test)			
First round	0.127	0.040	0.138	0.239
Last round	0.109	0.043	0.052	0.141

Usually fatigue appears in the end of the training session. The higher intense the exercise is the higher fatigue can be found and lower *SDRR* parameter value is estimated. For example, walking took some time to reduce *SDRR* value and feel fatigue. However, it did not reach the "dead-bug" or "skater-jump" values. As it can be seen from Table 3 the higher intense the exercise leads to the faster fatigue appearance. In "Skater-jump" exercise *SDRR* parameter value was low from the beginning. It had some variations, but never reached the value like "walk" exercise has.

4   Conclusions

Signal artefact correction for the recordings of physiological signals during the dynamic activities of human behaviour is important for analysing and understanding the way a human body works. The paper presents a novel approach for analysis of signal artefacts from the RR interval data and usage with physical fatigue estimation from HRV during daily activities.

The different algorithms with adaptive parameters to identify and extract artefacts in order to achieve better HRV estimation were applied. The results were calculated using different athletes exercising techniques, in order to find fatigue symptoms and evaluate HRV parameter sensitivity to the signal processing. After the artefact removal, Poincare plot parameters SD1 and SD2 indicated informative change towards increased physical fatigue.

Comparison of data recorded during exercises shows that for more intense exercises the *SDRR* parameter is lower, and fatigue appears faster. Even in the first round of walking exercise $SDRR_{walk} = 0.239$ while $SDRR_{skater-jump} = 0.040$.

In future work, these algorithms of HRV calculation will be implemented to the mobile human fatigue evaluation system to experimentally evaluate the parameter relation with cognitive, physical and psychological components of human fatigue.

Acknowledgment. This research was funded by a grant (No. 1.2.2-MITA-K-702) from the Agency for Science, Innovation and Technology (MITA) regarding Eureka project "Non-intrusive human fatigue assessment" (Eureka 11169 Fatigue).

References

1. Raudonis, V., Maskeliunas, R., Stankevicius, K., Damasevicius, R.: Gender, age, colour, position and stress: how they influence attention at workplace? ICCSA **5**, 248–264 (2017)
2. Vandecasteele, K., et al.: Automated epileptic seizure detection based on wearable ECG and PPG in a hospital environment. Sensors (Basel, Switzerland) **17**(10), 2338 (2017)
3. Wen, C., Yeh, M.-F., Chang, K.-C., Lee, R.-G.: Real-time ECG telemonitoring system design with mobile phone platform. Measurement **41**(4), 463–470 (2008)
4. Damasevicius, R., Vasiljevas, M., Salkevicius, J., Wozniak, M.: Human activity recognition in AAL environments using random projections. Comput. Math. Methods Med. 4073584:1–4073584:17 (2016)
5. Maskeliunas, R., Blazauskas, T., Damasevicius, R.: Depression behavior detection model based on participation in serious games. IJCRS **2**, 423–434 (2017)
6. Ulinskas, M., Wozniak, M., Damasevicius, R.: Analysis of keystroke dynamics for fatigue recognition. ICCSA **5**, 235–247 (2017)
7. Elgendi, M., Mohamed, E., Ward, R.: Efficient ECG compression and QRS detection for E-health applications. Sci. Rep. **7**, 1–16 (2017)
8. Peritz, D.C., Howard, A., Ciocca, M., Chung, E.H.: Smartphone ECG aids real time diagnosis of palpitations in the competitive college athlete. J. Electrocardiol. **48**, 896–899 (2015)
9. Susan Torres-Harding, L.: What is fatigue? History and epidemiology. In: Susan Torres-Harding, L.A. (ed.) Fatigue as a Window to the Brain. The MIT Press, Cambridge (2005)
10. Sherwood, L.: Human Physiology From Cells to Systems, 5th edn. Thomson Learning, Belmont (2005)
11. Berntson, G.G., Bigger, J.T.: Heart rate variability: origins, methods, and interpretive caveats. Psychophysiology **34**, 623–648 (1997)
12. Braun, C., Kowallik, P., Freking, A., Hadeler, D., Kniffki, K.D., Meesmann, M.: Demonstration of nonlinear components in heart rate variability of healthy persons. Am. J. Physiol. **275**, H1577–H1584 (1998)
13. Hautala, A., Tulppo, M.P., Makikallio, T.H., Laukkanen, R., Nissila, S., Huikuri, H.V.: Changes in cardiac autonomic regulation after prolonged maximal exercise. Clin. Physiol. **21**, 238–245 (2001)
14. Mourot, L., et al.: Decrease in heart rate variability with overtraining: assessment by the Poincare plot analysis. Clin. Physiol. Funct. Imaging **24**, 10–18 (2004)
15. Stirenko, S., et al.: Parallel statistical and machine learning methods for estimation of physical load. In: Vaidya, J., Li, J. (eds.) ICA3PP 2018. LNCS, vol. 11334, pp. 483–497. Springer, Cham (2018). https://doi.org/10.1007/978-3-030-05051-1_33

16. Tokoro, K., Ito, Y., Emori, Y., et al.: Relationship between fatigue and heart rate variability in mothers up to three months postpartum. MOJ Womens Health **6**(3), 391–395 (2017)

17. Schmitt, L., Regnard, J., Millet, G.P.: Monitoring fatigue status with HRV measures in elite athletes: an avenue beyond RMSSD? Front. Physiol. **6**, 343 (2015)

18. Boissoneault, J., Letzen, J., Robinson, M., Staud, R.: Cerebral blood flow and heart rate variability predict fatigue severity in patients with chronic fatigue syndrome. Brain Imaging Behav. **13**, 789–797 (2018)

19. Tanaka, M., Mizuno, K., Tajima, S., Sasabe, T., Watanabe, Y.: Central nervous system fatigue alters autonomic nerve activity. Life Sci. **84**(7–8), 235–239 (2009)

20. Gonzalez, K., Sasangohar, F., Ranjana, K.M.: Measuring fatigue through heart rate variability and activity recognition: a scoping literature review of machine learning techniques **61**(1), 1748–1752

21. Kubickova, A., Kozumplik, J., et al.: Heart rate variability analyzed by Poincare plot in patients with metabolic syndrome. J. Electrocardiol. **49**, 23–28 (2016)

22. Sharmila, V., Krishna, E.H., Reddy, K.A.: Cumulant based Teager energy operator for ECG signal modeling. In: IEEE Proceedings of 2013 International Conference on Advances in Computing, pp. 1959–1963 (2013)

23. Phukpattaranont, P.: QRS detection algorithm based on the quadratic filter. J. Expert Syst. Appl. **42**, 4867–4877 (2015)

24. Rangayan, R.M.: Biomedical Signal Analysis: A Case Study Approach. IEEE Press/Wiley, New York (2002)

25. Ning, X., Selesnick, I.W.: ECG enhancement and QRS detection based on sparse derivatives. J. Biomed. Signal Process. Control **8**, 713–723 (2013)

26. Saini, I., Singh, D., Khosla, A.: QRS detection using K-Nearest Neighbor algorithm and evaluation on standard ECG databases. J. Adv. Res. **4**, 331–344 (2013)

27. Ramakrishnan, A.G., Prathosh, A.P.: Threshold-independent QRS detection using the dynamic plosion index. IEEE Signal Process. Lett. **21**, 554–558 (2014)

28. Karimui, R.Y., Azadi, S.: Cardiac arrhythmia classification using the phase space sorted by Poincare sections. J. Biocybern. Biomed. Eng. **37**, 690–700 (2017)

29. Nallathambi, G., Principe, J.C.: Integrate and fire pulse train automaton for QRS detection. IEEE Trans. Biomed. Eng. **61**(2), 317–326 (2013)

30. Sedghamiz, H., Santonocito, D.: Unsupervised detection and classification of motor unit action potentials in intramuscular electromyography signals. In: Proceedings of the 5th IEEE International Conference on EHB (2015)

31. Vollmer, M.: A robust, simple and reliable measure of Heart Rate Variability using relative RR intervals. In: IEEE 2015 Computing in Cardiology Conference (2015)

32. Beritelli, F., Capizzi, G., Sciuto, L.G., Napoli, C., Wozniak, M.: A novel training method to preserve generalization of RBPNN classifiers applied to ECG signals diagnosis. Neural Networks **108**, 331–338 (2018)

33. Borys, M., Plechawska-Wójcik, M., Wawrzyk, M., Wesołowska, K.: Classifying cognitive workload using eye activity and EEG features in arithmetic tasks. In: Damaševičius, R., Mikašytė, V. (eds.) ICIST 2017. CCIS, vol. 756, pp. 90–105. Springer, Cham (2017). https://doi.org/10.1007/978-3-319-67642-5_8

The Stress Level Assessment Based on Socio-demographic and Gender Factors Among Polish and Taiwanese Female and Male Junior Dental Students

Katarzyna Mocny-Pachońska[1], Rafał Doniec[2], Agata Trzcionka[1],
Marta Lang[2], Marek Pachoński[3], Natalia Piaseczna[2],
Szymon Sieciński[2], Henryk Twardawa[1], and Marta Tanasiewicz[1](✉)

[1] Department of Conservative Dentistry with Endodontics,
School of Medicine with the Division of Dentistry,
Medical University of Silesia in Katowice,
Pl. Akademicki 17, 41-902 Bytom, Poland
{kpachonska, atrzcionka, martatanasiewicz}@sum.edu.pl
[2] Department of Biosensors and Biomedical Signal Processing,
Faculty of Biomedical Engineering, Silesian University of Technology,
Roosevelta 40, 41-800 Zabrze, Poland
{rafal.doniec, marta.wadas, natalia.piaseczna,
szymon.siecinski}@polsl.pl
[3] Pachonscy Dental Clinic, Lubliniecka 38, 42-288 Strzebiń, Poland
marek@pachonski.net

Abstract. The aim of this study was to assess the perceived levels and sources of stress for Polish Female and Male Dental Junior Students, who study in Polish and compare the results of those students with Taiwanese Female and Male Junior Students, who study in English which is not their native language. The procedure was done by the usage of the JINS MEME ES_R (eye sensing for researchers) device. That device is equipped with three-point electrooculography (EOG) and six axis IMU (a 3-axis accelerometer and a 3-axis gyroscope). GPS Smartwatch Garmin Vivoactive 3 was used in order to measure the heart rate. All the participants of the experiment received, precise information about the task to be performed (filling in a close test on dental knowledge composed of 5 questions with five descriptors, analysis of the 3D model; range, shape and depth of the cavity; explanation about the time limit of preparation) and the recommendations to fully concentrate on the precise shape modeling.

Keywords: Dental students · Gender · Socio-demographic factors · Stress level

1 Introduction

Dentists are prone to professional burnout, anxiety disorders and clinical depression, owing to the nature of clinical practice and the personality traits common among those who decide to pursue careers in dentistry. The professional stress is beginning in dental

© Springer Nature Switzerland AG 2019
R. Damaševičius and G. Vasiljevienė (Eds.): ICIST 2019, CCIS 1078, pp. 553–564, 2019.
https://doi.org/10.1007/978-3-030-30275-7_43

school. This stress can have a negative impact on their personal and professional lives - in particular with regard to the quality of their subsequent clinical work [1–5]. The results reported by Boran *et al.*, shows that the specialized dentists had a lower level of stress, compared to the students and general dentists, who are in line with the [6]. Dyrye et al. in their systematic review reported that medical students experience the highest levels of anxiety and depression [7]. The dental environmental stress can be greatly influenced during the undergraduate study program (program for Junior Students). Clinical training, in particular, can affect dental students' performance due to their exposure to different patient-related stressors which are similar to the ones faced by dental practitioners [8, 9]. Unless necessary steps are taken, the dental environment-induced stress can negatively affect the students' well-being. If stress persists, students may be unable to continue working, may find difficulty to interact with their patients. Ultimately, elevated levels of stress can deteriorate academic achievement and reduce career options and life style choices [10, 11]. It can also be expected that students from other countries who have had to deal with a foreign environment and who are additionally exposed to stress from socio-cultural confrontation may be less resistant to stress in contact with the patient, for example due to language barriers. The females showed a higher level of stress as compared to the males. These findings are in alignment with those obtained by *Gambetta-Tessini et al.* reported that women are more responsive, sympathetic, and supportive toward the patients, which causes them to show higher level of the stress [12]. *Myers* and *Myers* revealed that the patient's stress is significantly correlated with physician's stress and that increased stress in the patients lead to elevate stress in the dentists [13].

The aim of this study were to assess the perceived levels and sources of stress for Polish Female and Male Dental Junior Students, who study in Polish and compare the results of those students with Taiwanese Female and Male Junior Students, who study in English which is not their native language.

2 Materials and Methods

During the experiments blink occurrence (its speed and strength), vertical and horizontal eye movement and head movement (rotation roll, pitch and yaw) were assessed. The procedure was done by the usage of the JINS MEME (eye sensing for researchers) device. That device is equipped with three-point electrooculography (EOG) and six axis (an accelerometer and a gyroscope) [14].

JINS MEME ES_R (produced by JIN Co. Ltd.) acquires electrooculographic (EOG) data and acceleration/angular rate. In order to acquire data, the subject needs only to wear the device [15]. GPS Smartwatch Garmin Vivoactive 3 was used to measure the heart rate. That device has the heart rate sensor located on its back, which enables to measure current heart rate in beats per minute (bpm) which is displayed on the watch in a form of a graph.

2.1 Research Group

The study was conducted on 20 Polish and Taiwanese students of a third year of Dental Division of Silesian Medical University in Katowice who were divided into four equal groups: Polish Female Junior Students (PFJS), Polish Male Junior Students (PMJS), Taiwanese Female Junior Students (TFJS) and Taiwanese Male Junior Students (TMJS). The Taiwanese students were included to examine the influence of communicating in English as an additional stressor.

All the participants of the experiment received, precise information about the task to be performed (filling in a close test on dental knowledge composed of 5 questions with five descriptors, analysis of the 3D model; range, shape and depth of the cavity; explanation about the time limit of preparation) and the recommendations to fully concentrate on the precise shape modeling. Polish students from PFJS and PMJS groups were given all the information regarding the test in their native language, the test itself was also in Polish, while the test prepared for the Taiwanese students (groups: TFJS and TMJS) was in English that is their second language. All the participants of the experiment during both filling in the test and the cavity preparation procedure were equipped with a set of monitoring appliances (the smart glasses and the smartwatch) in order to control the vital parameters defining stress intensity.

2.2 Experiments

In the first stage of the research students were asked to fill in a test composed of 5 questions regarding the knowledge required from the third year dentistry students in 5 min. Then students from all groups were asked to perform a task of preparing a cavity in a standard phantom tooth in type of molar tooth 36 in 1:1 scale (Frasaco GmbH Germany) in limited or non-limited time. The matrix with the outline of the cavity has been prepared (See Fig. 1). Each student used the same type of the burr (Round End Taper NTI Rotary Dental Instruments, head length 4 mm, diameter 009, medium dirt), turbine with water cooling (350,000 revolution per minute). A model tooth with prepared cavity was prepared (shown in Figs. 2 and 3) by the usage of 3D printer (Formlabs 2).

The characteristics of the model are as follows:

– magnification ×10,
– material: Photopolymer Resin Black FLPBK04,
– volume: 389.82 ml,
– layer thickness: 0.025 mm,
– number of layers: 3312,
– print time: 57 h 13 min.

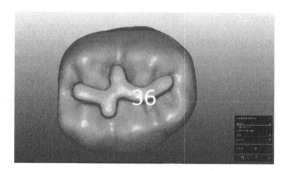

Fig. 1. Matrix with outline of cavity.

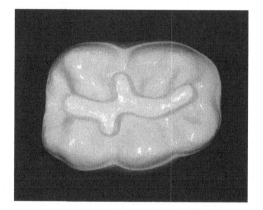

Fig. 2. Printed tooth 36 with matrix.

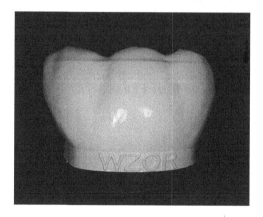

Fig. 3. Printed tooth 36 with matrix.

3   Results

The average time of filling the test in PFJS group was 2 min and 11 s. Due to the decision that 60% of proper answers results in satisfactory mark, the results obtained in that group were: two good marks, one satisfactory and two students failed. In the PMJS group the obtained results were: two failed tests, one satisfactory mark, two good marks. The average time of filling the test was 2 min and 13 s. In case of TFJS group the average time of writing was 2 min, students obtained: two good marks, two satisfactory marks and one student failed. In TMJS group there were four good marks and one satisfactory, the average time of filling the test was 2 min and 25 s.

The central trend is pointed by a single value that defines the data set. In our case we used the arithmetic mean as the most probable measure of central tendency. The analysis of the heart rate has shown no statistically significant differences between the groups. However, higher heart rate was observed in women in comparison to men when performing the same tasks (Tables 1 and 2). The heart rate was measured before the procedure started (shaping tooth or writing a test) and after they were finished.

Table 1. Mean heart rate in women.

	PFJS Heart rate [BPM]		TFJS Heart rate [BPM]
	Before	After	Before
Shaping a tooth	106.2	107.8	103.4
Writing a test	105.0	105.8	90.8

Table 2. Mean heart rate in men.

	PMJS Heart rate [BPM]		TMJS Heart rate [BPM]
	Before	After	Before
Shaping a tooth	92.4	85.6	92.2
Writing a test	86.8	81.8	87.8

Data received from electrooculography (EOG), gyroscope (GYRO) and accelerometer (ACC) are presented in Tables 3 and 4. Then, we performed the normality test on acquired data.

Data from electrooculography marked as H describe the movement of eyeballs in horizontal axis (right-left), while marked as V describes the movement of eyeballs in vertical axis (up-down). In Tables 1, 2, 3, and 4 the mean values of signal amplitude are shown. We can observe higher amplitudes of the signals in women both Polish and Taiwanese in comparison to men.

Table 3. Mean values of EOG, angular velocity and acceleration amplitudes in women.

	Shaping a tooth		Writing a test	
	PFJS	TFJS	PFJS	TFJS
EOG H	50.64	32.68	111.38	91.39
EOG V	54.23	21.81	97.86	37.34
GYRO X	37.57	21.55	44,15	41.1
GYRO Y	31.79	21.25	40.17	29.40
GYRO Z	62.95	26.14	53.09	30.49
ACC X	89.88	75.42	126.02	106.70
ACC Y	114.85	70.78	145.26	122.55
ACC Z	67.02	74.60	158.72	171.58

The arithmetic mean is in normal distribution the most common value, although it may not be observed in the data set. However, one of its important properties is minimizing the value prediction error in the data set. An important feature of the mean is including each value in the data set as part of the calculation and is the only measure of the central tendency in which the sum of deviations of each value from the mean is always zero. Thanks to this property, we can instantly identify in the single experimental data set the fundamental differences in the mean of men and women.

Table 4. Mean values of EOG, angular velocity and acceleration amplitudes in men.

	Shaping a tooth		Writing a test	
	PMJS	TMJS	PMJS	TMJS
EOG H	13.10	36.80	41.66	42.36
EOG V	24.58	24.55	52.18	40.37
GYRO X	21.47	16.51	29.84	36.58
GYRO Y	19.09	11.05	37.02	27.32
GYRO Z	13.42	8.95	23.78	27.33
ACC X	108.76	41.58	97.46	92.14
ACC Y	70.17	41.32	87.50	117.30
ACC Z	66.69	41.00	118.20	147.44

The mean for subsequent signals from JINS spectacles for women who deal only with tooth shaping generally does not exceed 100. Signal from the accelerometer the signal amplitude for women given to the test is 30% greater than the group of women who were not given a stressful stress in form of the test. However, raw data control suggests that this average value may not be the best way to accurately reflect differences in the range 60 to 171. The average is skewed by an amplitude of 114.85 for a "comfortable" situation. In the case of the same signal, in a "stress" situation is even worse. Therefore, in this second situation, we would like to have a better measure of the central tendency. It seems that taking a median would be a better measure of the central tendency in this situation.

For comparison, consider the same signal from the accelerometer for men after the test is up to 50% greater than the group of men who were not given a stressful stimulus. Which, in turn, suggests that this average value may not be the best way to accurately reflect differences in the range and is expressed by the amplitudes of 108.76 and 147.44 for both situations in which the test was conducted. Therefore, we should look at an average standard error. Statistics provide factual information including numbers in our case, these are data in the form of a sequence of signal amplitude values for time points.

The confidence interval for the difference between the two measures determines the range of values in which there can be a difference between the means of two populations, in our case two genders, two different circumstances of conducting the test. To examine the statistical significance of the differences in the mean response in the analyzed groups we performed for the two means with known standard deviations. The results are shown in Table 5.

Assuming that the level of significance $\alpha = 0.1$ (for which the expected value is 1.65) it can be told that the means marked with underlining present statistically significant differences in groups. When the level of significance is 0.2, the values of means marked in italics are statistically important differences.

Table 5. The results of statistical analysis with the test for the two averages with known standard deviations.

	The results of statistical analysis with the test for the two averages with known standard deviations			
	PFJS/PMJS tooth	PFJS/PMJS test	TFJS/TMJS tooth	THJS/TMJS test
EOG H	2.49	1.93	−0.22	*1.31*
EOG V	*1.53*	*1.39*	−0.24	−0.18
GYRO X	0.68	1.16	0.61	0.35
GYRO Y	0.69	0.16	*1.44*	0.32
GYRO Z	0.99	1.75	*1.33*	0.36
ACC X	−0.36	0.70	0.93	0.39
ACC Y	0.69	*1.25*	0.96	0.11
ACC Z	0.008	1.19	0.95	0.49

Some examples of the electrooculograms in particular groups are presented in Figs. 4, 5, 6, 7, 8, 9, 10 and 11. Figure 4 presents the EOG signal acquired during shaping a tooth and Fig. 5 shows the EOG signal registered while writing a test in subject A (PFJS). Electrooculograms acquired on subject B (PMJS) are shown in Fig. 6 (shaping a tooth) and in Fig. 7 (writing a test). In Fig. 8 the EOG signal acquired while shaping a tooth is shown and in Fig. 9 the EOG signal registered while writing a test in subject C (TFJS). EOG signals registered on subject D (TMJS) are shown in Fig. 10 (shaping a tooth) and in Fig. 11 (writing a test). The higher amplitudes of the signals can be seen in case of writing the test which was more stressful than shaping a cavity.

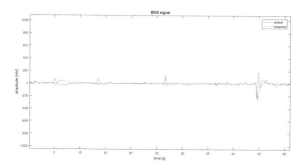

Fig. 4. Data from EOG-PFJS-shaping a tooth in subject A.

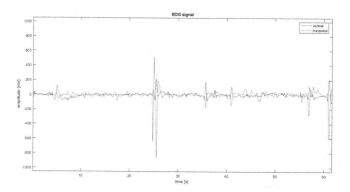

Fig. 5. Data from EOG-PFJS-writing a test in subject A.

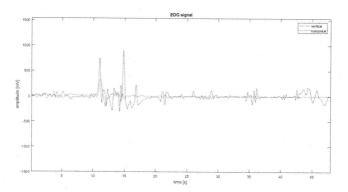

Fig. 6. Data from EOG-PMJS-shaping a tooth in subject B.

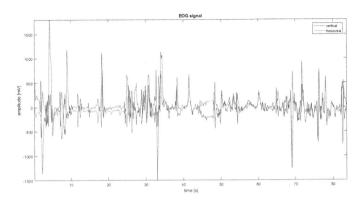

Fig. 7. Data from EOG-PMJS-writing a test in subject B.

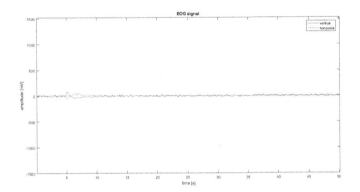

Fig. 8. Data from EOG- TFJS-shaping a tooth in subject C.

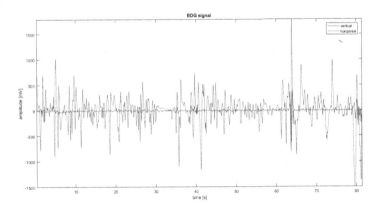

Fig. 9. Data from EOG- TFJS-writing a test in subject C.

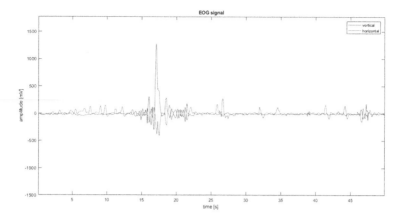

Fig. 10. Data from EOG -TMJS-shaping a tooth in subject D.

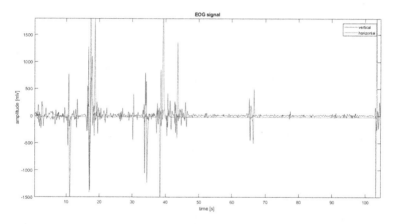

Fig. 11. Data from EOG- TMJS-writing a test in subject D.

The higher amplitudes of the signals can be seen in case of the procedure of filling the test. That procedure was much more stressful than shaping a cavity.

4   Discussion and Conclusions

The main aim of this experiment was to assess the level of stress among dental students – with regard to gender and socio-demographic environment, the country of origin and place of study. Dental students need to obtain training in both theoretical and surgical aspects of dental care, including performing treatments on patients to qualify as competent dental professionals. In the preclinical years, dental students need to manage laboratory requirements that require a significant amount of time and manual skills. These factors contribute to significant amounts of stress for dental students that put them at additional risk for psychological problems like anxiety, depression, and burnout [14]. Sometimes the support provided by medical faculties for foreign students vary greatly in type and extent. Support offered is seen to be insufficient in coping with the needs of the international students in many cases [16].

The number of women applying to dental schools and entering the profession of dentistry increases globally. Women dentists aim to advance their careers; however, differences exist between men and women dentists regarding for resistance to stress [17]. Such literature reports confirm the results of our research. Results of *te Brake* et al. showed male dentists to report a higher score on the depersonalization dimension of the *Maslach Burnout Inventory* than female dentists did [18]. Pool research carried out in the United States on a group of 300 men and 300 women (the selection of respondents) provides some interesting observations. The most common reason for stress was the interaction between doctor and patient (90%), for both women and men. Conflict situations were more accurately and sooner noticed, felt and resolved by women. They were the ones who better dealt with their patient's "pain" (empathy at a higher level of sensitivity) therefore it wasn't a source of as intensive stress as it was in the case of men, who often became aware that the result of their actions was a physical discomfort to their patients when it was too late [19].

From the static point of view, the method of comparing averages or standard deviations is checked when we want to compare and separate two groups of data, it is fast and in its simple way is not unreliable, giving results immediately. The method of average comparisons in the case of statistical inference for one population parameter, zero hypothesis, confidence intervals and significance tests for two unknown data sets and known standard deviations seems to be an adequate tool. However, in this process we lose a lot of important information, such as the reasons for the creation of limit values, which may be the result of measurement error as well as real measurement in special circumstances. Therefore, further research on other classifiers based on artificial intelligence, such as fuzzy sets, expert systems, or gaining popularity as a machine learning tool based on advanced, statistical data mining would be beneficial.

The future research needs to consider more precise measures of stress level to aid in better understanding dental students' experience and accordingly improving their learning environment. Hence, a better coverage of international students as well as further research efforts to the specific needs and the effectiveness of applied interventions seem to be essential. Both Polish and Taiwanese female students were more prone to stressful situations than male students. For students filling in the test was more stressful than the practical part of the research.

References

1. Rada, R.E., Johnson-Leong, C.: Stress, burnout, anxiety and depression among dentist. J. Am. Dent. Assoc. **135**(6), 788–794 (2004)
2. Piazza-Waggoner, C.A., Cohen, L.L., Kohli, K., Taylor, B.K.: Stress management for dental students performing their first pediatric restorative procedure. J. Dent. Educ. **67**(5), 542–548 (2003)

3. Hawazin, W.E., Allison, P.J., Kumar, A.R., Mancini, L., Lambrou, A., Bedos, C.: A systematic review of stress in dental students. J. Dent. Educ. **78**(2), 226–242 (2014)
4. Farokh-Gisour, E., Hatamvand, M.: Investigation of stress level among dentistry students, general dentists, and pediatric dental specialists during performing pediatric dentistry in Kerman, Iran, in 2017. Open Dent. **12**, 631–637 (2018)
5. Chandrasekaran, B., Cugati, N., Kumaresan, R.: Dental students' perception and anxiety levels during their first local anesthetic injection. Malays. J. Med. Sci. **21**(6), 45–51 (2014)
6. Boran, A., Shawaheen, M., Khader, Y., Amarin, Z., Hill Rice, V.: Work-related stress among health professionals in northern Jordan. Occup. Med. **62**(2), 145–147 (2012)
7. Dyrye, L.N., Thomas, M.R., Shanafelt, T.D.: Systematic review of depression, anxiety, and other indicators of psychological distress among U.S. and Canadian medical students. Acad. Med. **81**(4), 354–373 (2006)
8. Fredericks, M.A., Mundy, P.: Dental students: relationship between social class, stress, achievement, and attitudes. J. Am. Coll. Dent. **34**(4), 218–228 (1967)
9. Davis, E.L., Tedesco, L.A., Meier, S.T.: Dental student stress, burnout, and memory. J. Dent. Educ. **53**(3), 193–195 (1989)
10. Schmitter, M., Liedl, M., Beck, J., Rammelsberg, P.: Chronic stress in medical and dental education. Med. Teach. **30**(1), 97–99 (2008)
11. Uraz, A., Tocak, Y.S., Yozgatligil, C., Cetiner, S., Bal, B.: Psychological well-being, health, and stress sources in Turkish dental students. J. Dent. Educ. **77**(10), 1345–1355 (2013)
12. Gambetta-Tessini, K., Mariño, R., Morgan, M., Evans, W., Anderson, V.: Stress and health-promoting attributes in Australian, New Zealand, and Chilean dental students. J. Dent. Educ. **77**(6), 801–809 (2013)
13. Myers, H.L., Myers, L.B.: 'It's difficult being a dentist': stress and health in the general dental practitioner. Br. Dent. J. **197**(2), 89–93 (2004)
14. Lloyd, C., Musser, L.A.: Psychiatric symptoms in dental students. J. Nerv. Ment. Dis. **177**(2), 61–69 (1989)
15. Ishimaru, S., Kunze, K., Uema, Y., Kise, K., Inami, M., Tanaka, K.: Smarter eyewear using commercial EOG glasses for activity recognition. In: Proceedings of the 2014 AMC International Joint Conference on Pervasive and Ubiquitous Computing, pp. 239–242 (2014)
16. Huhn, D., et al.: International medical students–a survey of perceived challenges and established support services at medical faculties. GMS Z Med Ausbild **32**(1), 9 (2015). https://doi.org/10.3205/zma000951.eCollection
17. Rajeh, M., Nicolau, B., Pluye, P., Qutob, A., Esfandiari, S.: Are there barriers for professional development of women dentists? A qualitative study in Saudi Arabia. JDR Clin. Trans. Res. **2**(2), 119–131 (2017)
18. te Brake, H., Blemendal, E., Hoogestraten, J.: Gender differences in burnout among Dutch dentists. Community Dent. Oral Epidemiol. **31**(5), 119–131 (2017)
19. Rankin, J.A., Harris, M.B.: A comparison of stress and coping in male and female dentists. J. Dent. Prac. Admin. **11**(12), 166–172 (1990)

Information Systems: Special Session on Digital Transformation

Constrained Software Distribution
for Automotive Systems

Robert Höttger[1][✉], Burkhard Igel[1][✉], and Olaf Spinczyk[2][✉]

[1] IDiAL Institute, Dortmund University of Applied Sciences and Arts,
Dortmund, Germany
{robert.hoettger,igel}@fh-dortmund.de
[2] Computer Science Institute, Osnabrück University, Osnabrück, Germany
olaf.spinczyk@uos.de

Abstract. A variety of algorithms and technologies exist to cope with design space exploration for software distribution in terms of real-time, embedded, multiprocessor, and mixed-critical systems. The automotive domain not only combines those domains but even introduces further constraints and requirements due to several design decisions, standards, or evolved methodologies. In addition, solutions are predominantly proprietary, often lack in perspicuity, and sophisticated approaches towards the comprehensive concern of constraints are rather rare.

This paper presents typical constraints along with distributing automotive applications across the processing units of vehicles, outlines three software distribution methodologies based on the constraint programming paradigm, and evaluates those in comparison to related design space exploration approaches. Benchmarks upon hypothetical and industrial models show that the constraint-based approaches outperform other forms in many cases regarding quality and effectiveness. Additionally, the presented approach benefits from a holistic consideration of constraints such as processing unit affinities, safety level aggregations, communication costs as well as processing unit utilization optimization among others whilst being applicable to heterogeneous, networked, hierarchical, embedded, multi and many core architectures.

Keywords: AMALTHEA · AUTOSAR · APP4MC ·
Embedded real-time systems · Constraint programming

1 Introduction

Software distribution for embedded multi and many core systems gained significant importance in the recent years especially in the automotive domain due to the increasing demands of advanced driver assistance systems, autonomous driving, as well as architectural changes towards the centralization and consolidation of functional domains and Electronic Control Units (ECUs). Additionally, standardization (e.g. AUTOSAR[1], automotive SPICE[2]), collaboration across Tier

---

[1] Automotive Open System Architecture www.autosar.org, accessed 01.2019.
[2] Automotive SPICE http://www.automotivespice.com, accessed 12.2018.

© Springer Nature Switzerland AG 2019
R. Damaševičius and G. Vasiljevienė (Eds.): ICIST 2019, CCIS 1078, pp. 567–590, 2019.
https://doi.org/10.1007/978-3-030-30275-7_44

suppliers, Original Equipment Manufacturer (OEMs), and various tool vendors, and requirements from legacy applications necessitate sophisticated approaches when applying software distribution methodologies to the already highly constrained domain of heterogeneous, embedded, real-time, and mixed-critical environments. In order to reach reliability, safety, modularity, scalability, real time, or other goals, OEMs and suppliers introduced AUTOSAR in 2002 to overcome the tremendous amount of common challenges in the automotive industry and build up a basis to exchange, simulate, integrate, and even develop respective software. AUTOSAR undergoes regular releases since then, defining certain requirements and constraints such software has to address in order to be AUTOSAR compliant.

The basic concern of software distribution in the AUTOSAR context is the **partitioning** of runnables, i.e., atomic functions to tasks and the **mapping** of such tasks to processing units across micro controllers and ECUs. More precisely, given a set of runnables and a set of processing units, the goal is to find (a) a runnable to task assignment that is calculated by the partitioning process and forms the task set, and (b) a task to processing unit assignment denoted as mapping. This two phase approach yields a multitude of advantages such as distribution flexibility, level-based pairings or separations, as well as the consideration of various constraints described in Sect. 3. While this rather generic perceiving challenge has been studied for decades and is NP-complete [13], the holistic concern of the mandatory domain-specific constraints has been either omitted or only partially investigated. By making use of the open source AMALTHEA[3] model that is AUTOSAR compliant, this paper's work applies to a widely established superset of automotive constraints on the one hand, and can further cover industry driven requirements on the other hand. AMALTHEA features the typical combinatorial patterns to which constraint programming is preferably applicable. It comes with the APP4MC[4] platform and has, similar to AUTOSAR, regular maintenance and update releases. The APP4MC version used for this paper's investigations is 0.8.3 and implementations have been migrated to 0.9.1.

A promising and flexible paradigm applicable to partitioning and mapping is Constraint Programming (CP). CP allows natural problem modeling by making use of a huge variety of constraints that need to be satisfied for a valid solution. Typical features are logical, arithmetical, set, graph, or real-value expressions and coherencies among others. CP solver can be configured in various ways to investigate the solution space, optimize given objectives, and consequently solve the modeled Constraint Satisfaction Problem (CSP). Therefore, an algorithm is chosen to investigate the problem space of partitioning and mapping, e.g., incremental assignment combined with backtracking search or complete assignment combined with stochastic search. In order to remove invalid values from a variable's domain, propagation identifies inconsistent value combinations regarding the defined constraints and assigned values.

---

[3] AMALTHEA model http://eclip.se/eV, accessed 01.2019.

[4] Eclipse APP4MC, https://www.eclipse.org/app4mc/, accessed 01.2019.

Alternatively to using CP, local search approaches often follow a greedy-based structure and therefore may miss optimal values and valuable parts of the solution space. Furthermore, local search often has a dedicated model or application to work with and its applicability to different problems is very limited. In contrast to mathematical programming such as (Mixed) Integer Linear Programming (M)ILP, quadratic programming, or evolutionary (genetic) algorithms (GA), CP not only covers most of the mathematical operations of such, but also comes with powerful paradigms to further constrain combinatorial problem spaces and consequently increase exploration efficiency.

The **contribution** of this paper is the **formal outline of various constraints in the automotive industry** and their application to constraint programming used as a paradigm to **solve partitioning and mapping problems** of industry driven AMALTHEA models. Partitioning here concerns the distribution of runnables, which are atomic functions, to tasks, which can run both in parallel on the same processor, or concurrently across a multi core platform. The mapping problem defines the distribution of tasks to processing units which has to fulfill the amount of constraints outlined in the following sections and can be optimized towards various goals such as minimizing response times, balancing resource consumption, and others. The contribution includes considering a broad set of automotive constraints such as pairings, separations, affinities, timings (deadlines), sequences (precedence), ASIL- (Automotive Safety Integrity Level), partitioning-, and mapping-properties, balancing, hardware capacities, and communication costs when distributing software across tasks and processing units of vehicles. Presented (near) optimal solutions that consider this broad range of industry driven constraints has, to the best of the authors' knowledge, not been covered by related work. Along with the second contribution, the CP technique is compared with other design space exploration (DSE) approaches such as MILP, GA, and a heuristic whereas strengths and pitfalls of each are outlined along with hypothetical and industrial models. The comparison reveals new insights and assessments for applying DSE approaches to the highly constrained automotive software distribution problem. Results show that using the CP methodology significantly mitigates error prone and ineffective manual processes, partially outperforms other DSEs, and potentially eases software development and maintenance in the respective application field.

This paper is organized as follows. The subsequent section outlines related work as well as preliminaries this paper makes use of. Afterwards, Sect. 3 describes model entities required for the constraint descriptions in Sect. 4 and the optimization in Sect. 5. Finally, Sect. 6 provides benchmarks of the presented constraint solving approach, whereas Sect. 7 compares the results with some available related work. Finally, the conclusion in Sect. 8 summarizes this paper's contributions and results.

2 Related and Prior Work

Related work stretches across a huge variety of application domains when targeting DSE via heuristics, (M)ILP, Genetic Algorithms (GA), or CP. Since this work focuses on the automotive domain, various requirements of embedded, real-time, mixed-critical, and highly interconnected systems define specifics such DSE approaches have to address. In fact, avionics, robotics, or logistic domains have certain similarities with this paper's automotive constraints. Furthermore, model-based programming techniques are used to utilize model checking, validation, and generation on the one hand and to specify data the DSE approaches are applied to on the other hand.

Typical optimization goals reach from execution time, energy consumption, resource utilization to reliability or solution quality as stated in a mapping survey in [30]. With the CP-based approach of this paper, multi-objective optimization is applied to different models and a variety of requirements and constraints is considered at the same time. Any typical optimization approaches can be configured whereas the remainder especially targets communication costs and resource utilization.

(M)ILP is one of the most used paradigms to cope with challenges such as partitioning and mapping, e.g., presented in [4]. MILP has though shown scalability issues for large-scale problems as stated in [29] and [17]. Laurent Perron also stated in [26] that the usage of CP is beyond MILP for optimizing applications in industrial operations research projects.

There is also a variety of papers stating that processing unit affinities are beneficial regarding application performance, fault tolerance, or security such as [7] or [20]. Such affinities are also considered within this paper via *arithmetical* constraints ensuring that a solution must contain given task to processing unit pairing.

Xiao et al. have shown in [33] that satisfying reliability goals and reducing resource consumption is challenging for precedence-constraints, mixed-critical, parallel, and embedded systems. However, the AMALTHEA model used in this work is based on AUTOSAR and highly differs from the presented reliability goal in [33] that is based on the *constant failure rate per time unit* combined with ensuring that tasks are mapped to processors that maximize a certain reliability value. In contrast, approaches presented in this paper ensure reliability via considering the various constraints such as affinities, pairings, separations, activations, safety levels, etc.

Thiruvady et al. studied the component deployment problem for vehicles in [32] that is similar to the partitioning and mapping problems of this work via CP. However, due to the consideration of only three major constraints (memory, colocation, and communication), their approach covers just a subset of this paper's constraints.

Oliveira et al. [10] provide one of the few publications that compares (M)ILP with CP for the JSSP (job shop scheduling problem). Their results show that CP outperforms MILP in many cases and that CP is assessed as being the prior choice to MILP in generic cases. The GA approach, however, has neither been applied to the JSSP problems in [10] nor compared with CP or ILP. Also, the according JSSP does not cover the specific constraints presented in this work.

Limtanyakul et al. apply CP to test scheduling for the automotive industry in [23]. Although the problem is different from this work's partitioning and mapping approaches, results have shown that the automotive domain comprises typical requirements and constraints that CP can fully utilize such that CP-based DSE can potentially be more effective and efficient.

Along with the FMTV benchmark that is used in Sect. 6, several research was presented in the recent years regarding solutions towards event chain latency calculation [14], contention analysis [4] under different communication paradigms [15,24], worst case execution/response time (WCET/WCRT) analyses [8], label mapping [6] and more. However, none of those publications covers the broad constraints described in this paper.

Hilbrich et al. present the most similar constraint programming approach towards safety, time, and mixed critical systems in [16]. The ASSIST Toolsuite is publicly available[5] and addresses typical concerns of the avionics industry. However, there are certain differences to the AMALTHEA model that is used for this paper's work. For instance, label (memory) accesses, label sizes, access rates, runnable sequencing, stimuli diversity, or event chains of AMALTHEA result in an increased amount of constraints as well as a deviation from respective propagation approaches and variable domains.

Krawczyk et al. [22] present mapping algorithms in order to map tasks to processing units via ILP and GA that have been extended by Cuadra et al. in [9] towards the incorporation of the simulated annealing paradigm. These implementations are taken as a reference to compare this work's results in Sect. 7. GA-based applications to automotive systems have been also investigated in [25]. Those results show, similar to generic multi-objective genetic algorithms in [11], that evolutionary algorithms scale well especially for large-scale problems.

Finally, some commercial tools exist from companies such as Inchron GmbH, Symtavision GmbH, Vector Informatik GmbH, and others that were not accessible to the authors that probably address constrained software distribution. Apart from the scope, efficiency, and quality assessment of such commercial products, it is expected that certain model transformations and integration activities consume additional efforts when using a multitude of tools during the development process.

Along with the investigation of related work, no publication could be found that considers both a broader set of automotive constraints and an analysis of different DSE methodologies for the partitioning and mapping problems.

3   System Model

This section defines model entities the subsequent sections make use of in order to scope the problem space when distributing

(a) a set of runnables $\mathcal{R} = \{r_1, ..., r_o\}, |\mathcal{R}| = o$ to tasks (**partitioning**) and

---

[5] ASSIST   Toolsuite   https://github.com/roberthilbrich/assist-public,   accessed 10.2018.

(b) a set of tasks $\mathcal{T} = \{\tau_1, ..., \tau_m\}, |\mathcal{T}| = m$ to a set of processing units $\mathcal{PU} = \{pu_1, ..., pu_n\}, |\mathcal{PU}| = n$ (**mapping**)

while considering a vast amount of constraints. The partitioning result is denoted by $\mathcal{RA} = (ra_{i,j}) \in \{0,1\}^{o \times m}$, i.e., a distinctive runnable assignment, and the mapping result is denoted as $\mathcal{TA} = (ta_{j,k}) \in \{0,1\}^{m \times n}$, i.e., a distinctive task assignment. We assume that each runnable and each task must be assigned statically to exactly one target, i.e., task and processing unit respectively. After the partitioning, a task τ_j consists of an ordered sequence of p_j runnables $\tau_j = \{r_{j,1}, ...r_{j,p}\}$. Processing units $\mathcal{PU}$ can be obtained from higher abstraction levels such as micro controllers, cores, or ECUs, whereas communication costs are considered according to the modeled architecture properties such as labels, label sizes, label accesses, and access rates. Each processing unit pu_k is associated with a capacity $puc_k = f_k \cdot ipc_k$, i.e., the multiplication of the processing unit's frequency with its static instruction per cycle value. Consequently, puc_k is normalized towards 1 s. We assume fixed priority scheduling as well as distinct preemptive and cooperative task sets. Consequently, preemptive tasks can preempt any lower priority tasks and cooperative tasks can preempt lower priority cooperative tasks at runnable bounds only. Each runnable is associated with an activation T_i and a worst case execution time c_i that represents the instruction costs the runnable requires for execution. Runnables inherit their activation to the tasks they are assigned to: $\forall\, i$ with $ra_{i,j} = 1 : T_j = T_i$. Since c_i often varies and is described via Weibull distributions in AMALTHEA, upper bounds are chosen as the worst case execution times in this paper. Despite Weibull estimations, AMALTHEA provides different forms of instruction representations that are omitted in this paper. Such properties are especially useful for simulation frameworks such as [31] or others. The instruction cost IC_j value of a task τ_j is defined by the sum of its contained runnable instruction costs:

$$IC_j = \sum_{r_i : ra_{i,j}=1} c_i \tag{1}$$

A task's worst case execution time $C_{j,k}$ is derived from IC_j and depends on the processing unit's capacity puc_k the task is mapped to ($ta_{j,k} = 1$). For calculations in this paper, task's activation patterns T_j are considered via one second normalization as shown in the following Eq. 2.

$$C_{j,k} = \frac{IC_j \cdot \frac{10^{24}}{T_j}}{puc_k} \tag{2}$$

with T_j in pico seconds that has been chosen as an appropriate time scale but can also be changed to a different accuracy. 10^{24} is derived from 10^{12} for the 1 s normalization in pico seconds multiplied with another 10^{12} to compensate the denominator that is given in Hz, i.e., $\frac{1}{second}$. We assume that task's deadlines are implicit to their activation. Activations can be periodic, sporadic, event-driven, variable rate, relative periodic, and more[6] whereas the former two are considered

---

[6] See APP4MC documentation at http://eclip.se/fA, accessed 04.2019.

in this paper. For sporadic activation, the lower bound recurrence value (see Footnote 6) is used to consider worst case arrival rates of the corresponding tasks. Other activations go beyond the scope of this paper.

Data propagation between tasks is assumed to be achieved via the asynchronous use of shared labels. Labels correspond to parameters saved to memory. To determine the communication costs, a communication model like explicit, implicit, or logical execution time (LET) is preferred to be used in terms of AUTOSAR. The worst case response times (WCRT) of runnables and tasks depend on scheduling and corresponding preemptions. The response time analysis from Baruah et al. in [3] that has been extended by Balsini et al. in [2], can be used to calculate WCRT as well as event chain latency properties via recurrence relations. In addition, recent response time analysis solutions for adaptive variable rate tasks presented by Biondi et al. in [5] can be further incorporated to achieve more accurate WCRT analysis with a precise estimation of worst-case interference. However, the communication cost cc_k calculation presented in Sect. 5 uses $C_{j,k}$ only and can be configured to consider latencies, WCRT, and a corresponding communication paradigm. This configuration is omitted here in order to achieve comparable results in regard to the existing evolutionary algorithms, ILP solutions, and heuristics in Sect. 7. If configured differently, the solution space would be more constrained and results could be worse. Minor additions to this system model are made in the next sections along with specific concerns that are correspondingly described.

The above mentioned model entities, that are just a subset of AMALTHEA, excellently apply to the CP paradigm when addressing highly combinatorial problems. The huge amount of sets, relations, and properties constitute all data that a constraint model requires to potentially utilize CP benefits. For example, aggregations such as activations, tags, or ASIL properties can be directly converted to .allEqual($x[]$) constraints that ensure that a valid solution must have equal values for all variables in x.

4 Constraint Modeling

This section describes a subset of constraints applied to the previously outlined model in order to calculate (a) the runnable to task partitioning and (b) the task to processing unit mapping. Constraints are modeled using the open source choco-library and its solver from Prud'homme et al. [27].

4.1 Runnable Partitioning Constraints

The first constraint shown in Eq. 3 outlines the activation aggregation (i.e. grouping) that applies consecutively to *ASIL properties, tags,* and *runnable pairings*. For ASIL level and Tag references, T_i of Eq. 3 is replaced with $Asil_i$ or Tag_i respectively, whereas $Asil_i$ denotes the ASIL level reference of runnable r_i and Tag_i its tag reference. Runnable pairings are modeled via $\forall i \in rp :$

.allEqual $(j|ra_{i,j} = 1)$. Equation 3 defines that a partition, i.e., task, must not contain runnables that commonly reference more than one activation.

$$\forall \ j \ \text{with} \ ra_{i,j} \in \mathcal{RA} : \ \texttt{.allEqual} \left(\{T_i | ra_{i,j} = 1\} \right) \tag{3}$$

Or in other words, a task must not contain runnables of different activations. However, the amount of tasks per activation is not restricted by this constraint.

A combination of the Eq. 3 constraint and a dedicated existing heuristic from [19] that is available at the APP4MC platform is chosen in order to quickly partition models consisting of large runnable sets. In fact, a directed acyclic graph is built from runnables and their label accesses and graph branches are cut into tasks in order to ensure cause-effect-chains, i.e., read/write dependencies that represent causal relationships. The heuristic forms the parameter initialization of the constraint-based partitioning that incorporates the various constraints of this section.

As mentioned above, the same constraint of Eq. 3 is implemented for

- ASIL properties that classify automotive safety integrity levels into *A, B, C, D,* and *undefined* according to ISO 26262 safety requirements and corresponding identification of the software's relation to potential hazards and risks (A = lowest to D = highest)
- runnable pairings to pair e.g. functionally close runnables
- and tags in order to group, e.g., software components.

Since runnables inherit their properties to tasks, such constraints also hold for the mapping process. Consequently, the constraint of Eq. 3 is also applied to the task mapping for *activations, pairings,* and *ASIL* properties.

After ensuring the correct aggregations, Eq. 4 defines the constraint to ensure runnable sequencing. Runnable sequencing constraints can have multiple groups that can each reference an arbitrary amount of runnables. The constraint application is straight forward. For each subsequent group pairs $(rscg_x, rscg_y)$ across all runnable sequencing constraints, the following rule holds:

$$\forall \ r_a \in rscg_x, r_b \in rscg_y : a < b \ \text{with} \ \tau_j = \{r_{j,1}, ..., r_{j,a}, ..., r_{j,b}, ...\} \tag{4}$$

The constraint of Eq. 4 is implemented as an arithmetical constraint using the smaller expression. Strictly defining runnable sequencing constraints ensures causal orders and significantly eases system determinism.

Finally, the actual runnable to task partitioning constraint can be defined. For this purpose, the $\mathcal{RA}$ boolean matrix is applied to a .sum constraint as shown in Eq. 5.

$$\forall \ r_i \in \mathcal{R} : \sum_{j \leq m} ra_{i,j} = 1 \tag{5}$$

I.e., a runnable is assigned to exactly one task.

In order to balance runnable loads to tasks, Eq. 6 sets the minimal task weight (i.e. execution time) to a lower bound value (lb_{τ_i}). Each scalar length equals the number of runnables (scalar constraint) so that the dot product of both scalars has to be less or equal to the task's lower bound value:

$$\forall \ \tau_j \in \mathcal{T} : \sum_i \langle ra_{i,j}, c_i \rangle \leq lb_{\tau_j} \tag{6}$$

The lower bound definition in Eq. 6 has been found useful for larger models in order to decrease resolution time for load balancing.

Presented constraints are derived from the AUTOSAR standard [1]. They are mandatory for real and valid scenarios and have been evolved since 2004. New constraints can easily be added to the existing model in form of CP typical constraints or even new variables and corresponding modeling.

4.2 Task Mapping Constraints

When mapping tasks to processing units, several assumptions must be made. First of all, tasks must be mapped to exactly one processing unit, i.e., when having a boolean matrix $|\mathcal{T}| \times |\mathcal{PU}|$, i.e., $n \times m$, the sum of booleans ($\mathtt{true} = 1$) across all processing units must be 1 for each task as stated in the following Eq. 7:

$$\forall \ \tau_j \in \mathcal{T} : \sum_k ta_{j,k} = 1 \tag{7}$$

Equation 7 for task mapping corresponds to Eq. 5 for the runnable partitioning.

Of course, additional constraints have to follow to consider the various model properties such as safety levels and avoid arbitrary results. Equation 8 begins with defining the processing unit capacity constraint and ensures that no processing unit is assigned with a set of tasks that would exceed the processing unit's execution capacity puc_k. Therefore, the task assignment scalar ta_k for all tasks at processing unit pu_k is multiplied with the execution time scalar for all tasks at the processing unit C_k (note here that $C_{i,j}$ is the execution time of τ_i at pu_j, and C_k is a scalar denoting all task execution times at pu_k). Hence, given $\langle ta_k, C_k \rangle = \sum_j (C_{j,k} \cdot ta_{j,k})$, and the task cost equation from Eq. 2 that contains the task's activation, the processing unit capacity constraint is defined by:

$$\forall \ pu_k \in \mathcal{PU} : \langle ta_k, C_k \rangle + cc_k(\mathcal{TA}) \leq puc_k \tag{8}$$

This capacity constraint incorporates inter processing unit, inter micro controller, and inter ECU communication costs denoted as cc_k. Additionally, timing constraints are added such that every task τ_j meets its deadline D_j via Eq. 9:

$$WCRT_j \leq D_j \tag{9}$$

with D_j denoting the deadline of task τ_j. In order to calculate $WCRT$, the classical recurrence relation method for preemptive tasks $WCRT_{j,k} = C_{j,k} + \sum_{h \in hp(j)} \left\lceil \frac{WCRT_{h,k}}{T_h} \right\rceil C_{h,k}$ is used. Memory access and contention costs go beyond the scope of this paper and are assumed to be accounted within $C_{j,k}$ values.

The communication costs cc_k for each processing unit depend on the mapping result $\mathcal{TA}$ as well as label to memory mapping. This specific label mapping is omitted in this paper due to lack of space. The cc_k values are defined by the label access rate derived from T_j, the label bit width bw_l, and the available hardware (e.g. crossbar) bit width bw_{hw}, i.e., $bm_l = \left\lceil \frac{bw_l}{bw_{hw}} \right\rceil$, and the label access cycles ac_l that is 9 cycles for accessing global memory or local memory of different processing units and 1 cycle for local pu_k memory:

$$cc_k = \sum_{j \,:ta_{j,k}=1} T_j \left(\sum_{l \text{ accessed by } \tau_j} bm_l \cdot ac_l \right) \text{ with } ac_l = \begin{cases} 1 & \text{if } l \text{ is at } pu_k's \text{ LRAM} \\ 9 & \text{otherwise} \end{cases}$$

(10)

Here, ac_l values are derived from the FMTV challenge description in [21]. More (formal) information about label accesses and dependency derivation can be found at [18]. By replacing 9 with $9 + n - 1$, further maximal FIFO arbitration at the crossbar can be considered as described in [28]. For calculating communication costs for a single task, the notation cc_j is used that uses the same calculation as in Eq. 10 but without the first sum over all tasks j.

After applying *tag* and *pairing* constraints to tasks as in Eq. 3, activation aggregations, i.e. grouping runnables referencing the same activation, can be further extended with a validation of a hyper period existence as shown in Eq. 11:

$$\forall \tau_j \text{ with } ta_{j,k} = 1 : T_j \in hyp \in P_{hyp}$$

(11)

Equation 11 states that each task τ_j of a task set mapped to a processing unit pu_k must reference an activation within a hyperperiod set $hyp \in P_{hyp}$. Each hyperperiod set hyp is defined by $hyp \subset T : \forall T_u \in hyp \,\exists\, v \cdot \text{lcm}_{hyp}, v \in \mathbb{Z}$. A hyperperiod set is a set of periodic activations, that has a single integer least common multiple, i.e., the hyper period of the hyperperiod set. Hyperperiod sets do not necessarily have to be distinct, such that periodic activations may occur in several hyperperiod sets. Such validation can be used to lessen the pessimism of response time analysis approaches such as [3] and examine WCRT values for scheduling approaches regarding a given task to processing unit mapping set. This paper's investigations cover fixed-priority WCRT analysis for rate monotonic scheduling (RMS) as referred to in Eq. 9. Work on considering more sophisticated scheduling approaches, dynamic scheduling such as earliest deadline first (EDF), and event-chain latencies go beyond the scope of this paper.

Equation 12 defines the separation constraints in order to ensure that tasks are not mapped to the same processing unit. Each task separation constraint contains at least 1 group, i.e., a task subset, and optionally a target processing unit or target scheduler. $ts_{f,g}$ denotes the f-th task separation constraint and the g-th group within the separation constraint.

$$TS = \{ts_0, ...\} : \quad ts = \{g_0, ..., tpu\} : g \subset T, tpu \in [1, k]$$
$$(a) \; \forall \, \tau_j \in ts_{f,0} : \quad \texttt{.allDifferent}\,(k : ta_{j,k} = 1)$$
$$(b) \; \forall \, g, \tau_j \in ts_f : \quad \texttt{.notMember}\,(k : ta_{j,k} = 1, k_{og})$$
$$(c) \; \forall \, \tau_j \in ts_f : \quad \texttt{.arithm}\,(k : ta_{j,k} = 1, "! = ", tpu)$$

(12)

If no target and a single group is defined, case (a) shows that all tasks must be mapped to different processing units via using the `.allDifferent` constraint. If no target and multiple groups are defined, case (b) of Eq. 12 shows that each group must be mapped to different processing units via applying the `.notMember` constraint. Here, k_{og} is the set of processing unit indexes the other groups of the same separation constraint are mapped to. If a specific target is defined in a separation constraint, case (c) of Eq. 12 shows that all tasks across all groups must not be mapped to the specified processing unit via using the arithmetical constraint with an not equal operator.

Affinity constraints correspond to the task separation model whereas the constraints (a)–(c) of Eq. 12 are replaced by (a) `.allEqual`, (b) `.Member`, and (c) "=" instead of "!=".

Typical use cases for separation and affinity constraints are separations from interfering tasks or affiliations to specific hardware, e.g., floating point units, I/O interfaces, memory intensive tasks, or similar.

5   Optimization

Within this paper, the focus is on two optimization parameters: minimizing the maximal processing unit utilization across all processing units in percent $(\max_{k}(puu_k))$, i.e., load balancing, and minimizing the overall communication costs (occ). Both optimization criteria are important to maximize resource utilization and correspondingly the throughput, i.e., the amount of jobs finished in a given time frame. In fact, both bad load balancing and high communication costs lower the job throughput (amount of finished tasks to a given time) and result in higher hardware costs as well as aggravated determinism and timing analysis. Apart from the optimization, it is important to note that this work's DSE approaches are accompanied with the validation of previously described constraints. A multitude of additional optimization criteria can be added but are omitted here for comprehension reasons.

Beginning with the processing unit utilization optimization, Eq. 13 presents the respective calculation using the dot product along the C_k and ta_k scalars:

$$puu_k = \frac{\langle ta_k, C_k \rangle}{puc_k} \tag{13}$$

As described in Eq. 2 and Sect. 3, this calculation uses normalization towards one second and considers task activation rates. The processing unit utilization metric has been chosen over, e.g., remaining processing unit capacity because of its simplicity and its applicability to heterogeneous architectures.

There are multiple ways to minimize the overall processing unit utilization value. The most obvious one is defining a variable that is applied as a maximum constraint across all processing unit utilization values, i.e., $puu_{max} = $ `.max`(puu). This value is then applied to the solver with the minimization objective.

Instead of minimizing the maximal processing unit utilization, maximizing the minimal processing unit utilization is also possible. However, the latter approach usually results in a larger solution space so that optimization time is increased significantly because the amount of variable combinations is much higher. Consequently, getting good or optimal results for large industrial models takes significantly longer when targeting to maximize puu_{min}. In other words, if the upper bound on processing unit utilization is found, the $min(puu_{max})$ approach would stop the resolution process whereas the $max(puu_{min})$ process would continue aligning (maximizing) the remaining utilization values. In all of the cases studied in this paper, minimizing the maximal processing unit utilization provided sufficient results since the load balancing across lower utilized processing units is not accounted within the measurements.

In addition to single parameter optimization, optimizing multiple parameters can also be addressed with CP. Therefore, a pareto front is calculated that optimizes multiple values towards the same objective, i.e., min or max. From a value set of a pareto front, optimization parameters can also be weighted in order to identify a single solution from a pareto front as being the final solution. For example, having a pareto front with three solutions and two optimization parameters to be minimized such as $op_0 = [2, 3, 8]; op_1 = [4, 3, 1]$, the third solution would be omitted when equally weighting op_0 and op_1 since its cumulated optimization parameter is higher than the results from solutions 1 and 2 $(2 + 4 = 6; 3 + 3 = 6; 8 + 1 = 9; \rightarrow opt_3 > (opt_1, opt_2))$. However, when weighting op_1 with 3, the results are $2 + 3 \cdot 4 = 14, 3 + 3 \cdot 3 = 12, 8 + 3 \cdot 1 = 11$ and consequently solution three would be the best one. For the measurements presented in this work, optimization parameters from the pareto front are equally weighted as shown in Eq. 15.

Inter task communication (for the partitioning) and inter processing unit communication (for the mapping) costs are combined with load balancing so that both criteria are optimized towards their minimum value within the CPMO approach (constraint programming using multi objective optimization).

Communication costs are derived from Eq. 10 with the addition that they are 0 if a task pair is mapped to the same processing unit as stated in Eq. 14.

$$cc(\mathcal{TA}) = (td_{j,h})^{m \times m} \; : \; td_{j,h} \;\; = \begin{cases} 0, & \text{if } (j = h) \vee (ta_{j,k} = ta_{h,k}) \\ cc_j, & \text{if } ta_{j,k} \neq ta_{h,k} \end{cases} \qquad (14)$$

This approach can be advanced in order to consider hardware ports that connect arbitrary hardware instances using interfaces like CAN, Flexray, LIN, MOST, Ethernet, SPI, I2C, AXI, AHB, APB, SWR, or custom ones[7]. While this advancement is already in development, it is omitted here in order to compare results with the existing DFG, ILP, and GA approaches.

By using the choco_solver [27], one can make use of the powerful reification paradigm in order to set constraints for certain situations only. Without reification, calculating communication costs (i.e. $occ(\mathcal{TA})$) would be significantly more complex. The approach of calculating overall communication costs based on a

---

[7] http://eclip.se/f0 gives more information on hardware ports, accessed 01.2019.

Algorithm 1. OCC calculation

Data: task communication costs td, task assignments ta

Result: overall communication costs $occ(\mathcal{TA})$

1 **forall the** processing units $pu \in \mathcal{PU}$ **do**

2   **forall the** task combinations $\tau_j, \tau_h \in td$ **do**

3   only consider cases where at least one task is mapped to the current processing unit pu:

4   **if** $(ta_{j,k} \vee ta_{h,k}) \Rightarrow \tau_j$ or τ_h is mapped to pu_k **then**

5   **if** $(ta_{j,k} \underline{\vee} ta_{h,k})$ **then**

6   set task dependency of pu_k for tasks at different processing units to the task dependency value $cc_{j,h} = td_{j,h}$

7   **else**

8   set task dependency for tasks mapped to the same pu_k to 0: $cc_{j,h} = 0$

9   **end**

10   **end**

11   **end**

12 **end**

13 $occ(\mathcal{TA}) = \sum_{j,h} cc_{j,h}$ = the sum of all task's communication costs

---

static dependency matrix td and reification (cf. Algorithm 1 line 3) is shown in Algorithm 1. It uses the pseudo code notation for a better understanding.

Line 8 ensures that the task dependency matrix is set to 0 for every task pair that is mapped to the same processing unit. Instead of using a simple `.ifThenElse` constraint at line 4, lines 4–8 are important to only keep a task dependency, i.e., setting $cc_{j,h}$ to $td_{j,h}$, if and only if a task pair is mapped to different processing units in line 6. If tasks are mapped to the same processing unit, $cc_{j,h}$ is set to 0 in line 8. Such situation is implemented using the `exclusive_or` statement in line 5 that is used as a reification for the arithmetic constraint setting cc, i.e., the communication cost matrix, to the task dependency value in line 8. Consequently, if no task of a task pair is mapped to a processing unit (line 4 is *false*), $cc_{j,h}$ is not changed in any way since it may still be either 0 or $td_{j,h}$.

As mentioned in Sect. 4, the method of calculating overall communication costs shown in Algorithm 1 is independent of the underlying communication paradigm such as explicit, implicit, or LET. Those paradigms are necessary when calculating latencies and contention effects along with WCRT that is not in scope of this paper.

Table 1 summarizes briefly the AMALTHEA constraints, requirements, or methodologies as well as the correspondingly implemented constraints. Some constraints were used in combination with additional variables or reification such as the `.ifThen` constraint combined with the `.addClausesXorEqVar` boolean variable (shown in Algorithm 1, line 5). Additionally, different approaches are implemented, e.g., for the partitioning, considering either integer or boolean variables resulting in different constraint types. This was done in order to

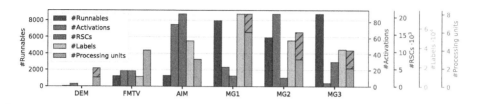

Fig. 1. Properties of DEM, FMTV, AIM, MG1, MG2, and MG3 models

overcome some scalability challenges and comparing the .binpacking constraint with a combination of arithmetical constraints. Measurements showed that the .binpacking constraint introduced overheads compared with the combination of arithmetical expressions and boolean variables.

Nevertheless, Table 1 also shows the benefits of using constraint definitions in contrast to, e.g., MILP, since the number of constraints remains relatively small and their usage is more natural compared with a combination of multiple inequality definitions.

6   Benchmarks

With the previously described constraint model, solution and optimization processes have been applied to three industrial models as well as three hypothetical models generated from a model generator as listed in Table 2.

Figure 1 presents the model properties of the respective models with the number of runnables, activations, runnable sequencing constraints (*RSCs*), labels, and processing units. The slash pattern above some processing unit bars indicate the amount of heterogeneous processing units that differ in frequency, instructions per cycle, or clock ratio from the basis processing units. In general, the

Table 1. Applied constraint types

AMALTHEA constraint	Choco [27] constraint
Runnable-, process-, ASIL-, or tag-pairing	.allEqual; .arithm(=);
Runnable-, or process-separation	.allDifferent; .arithm($\neq$); .notMember;
Runnable sequencing	.arithm($<,=$); .allDifferentEx0; .max;
Processing unit utilization	.scalar; .count; .min / .max;
Partitioning	.binpacking; .min; .sum; .scalar;
Activations	.allEqual; .arithm($\leq$); .and; .or;
Inter task communication	.addClausesXorEqVar; .ifThen;.arithm(=); .count; .and;

Table 2. Examined models

DEM	Democar, an academic engine management system available at [12]
FMTV	An industry driven anonymized model available at [21]
AIM	An anonymized industrial model the authors have been granted access to
MG1, MG2, MG3	Generated models

number of processing units shown in Fig. 1 has been used to calculate quality values for the evaluation shown in Fig. 2, but more processing units can be modeled to calculate wider software mapping as exemplarily shown in Fig. 3.

Compared with other models, the Democar model contains fewest properties due to the fact that it represents a single engine control unit only and it has been manually modeled with academic content only in [12].

Each model is partitioned and mapped via six DSE approaches outlined in Table 3.

Additionally, the above outlined benchmarks have been extended to feature a varying number of (a) tasks and (b) processing units. Therefore, the measurements were performed upon several benchmark clusters. Results are presented and discussed in the following Sect. 7.

Results are saved within the model and utilized by compiler and linker scripts in order to be executed as binaries on a target hardware. After the compilation process, the static software distribution is not changed in accordance with AUTOSAR.

7   Evaluation

This section discusses obtained results along with quality, runtime, as well as scalability measurements. The partitioning process is not in scope of this evaluation but forms a requirement for the different task numbers along with measurements such as Fig. 4. Quality results are shown as scatter plots $puu_{max}(occ)$ in Fig. 2 as well as line charts that form speedup plots $su_{max}(\#processingunits)$ in Fig. 3, and the $occ(\#processing\ units)$ plot in Fig. 5(b). Runtimes are presented in line charts along Figs. 4 and 5(a). All line charts also provide information about the DSE's scalabiliy, due to their x axis representing either the number of tasks or the number of processing units as indicated.

7.1   Quality

Figure 2 presents the qualities of the six different DSE approaches measured as $puu_{max}(occ)$, i.e., the maximal processing unit utilization of the results depending on the number of overall communication costs. Each scatter plot (a)–(f) in

Table 3. DSE approaches applied to the models

DFG	Data flow graph heuristic [22]
ILP	Integer linear programming using oj!algo[8] [22]
GA	Genetic algorithm using jenetics[9] [22]
CP	Constraint programming without any optimization using the library from [27]
CPLB	CP + optimization for load balancing, i.e., minimizing the maximal processing unit utilization using the library from [27]
CPMO	CPLB + optimization for overall communication costs (occ) → multi objective optimization using the library from [27]

[8] ojAlgo library http://ojalgo.org, accessed 10.2018
[9] Jenetics library http://jenetics.io, accessed 10.2018

Fig. 2 concerns a distinct model (each model's properties are shown in Fig. 1) and features measurements of 3 different task amount configurations for each solution. The respective model and task configurations are indicated along with each subplot's title. For comprehension purposes, the concrete results are in light gray color whereas the mean values across the three tasks configurations are added as colored symbols.

With (a), the Democar model, the optimal puu_{max} value was achieved for CPLB and GA whereas CPLB features a lower occ value. DFG and ILP results are close to the optimum and GA has slightly higher occ values for 10 and 20 tasks. Interestingly, CPMO found solutions with significantly less communication costs across all task configurations. Whilst weighting the optimization objectives equally, this difference in communication costs even compensates the worse puu_{max} values > 0.9. This pareto front evaluation is shown in Eq. 15.

$$\forall s_q \in pf \; : 0 \geq \frac{puu_{s_f} - puu_{s_q}}{puu_{s_f}} + \frac{occ_{s_f} - occ_{s_q}}{occ_{s_f}} \tag{15}$$

Here, pf denotes the pareto front, s_q is any solution from the pareto front, and s_f is the final (chosen) solution. Consequently, for the two example solutions $s_1 : puu_{s_1} = 0.7; \; occ_{s_1} = 15$ and $s_f : puu_{s_f} = 0.8; \; occ_{s_f} = 5$, Eq. 15 ensures that $0 \geq \frac{0.8-0.7}{0.7} + \frac{5-15}{5} \Rightarrow \frac{1}{7} - 2 = -\frac{13}{7} \leq 0$ holds for all solutions of the pareto front.

The CP approach only identifies valid solutions, has no optimization at all, and consequently creates the worst solution quality across almost all models and configurations. However, CP features the lowest execution time compared with any other approach, even with DFG. Given the fact that all constraints can be easily covered with CP in contrast to DFG, CP may still be an appropriate choice for quickly identifying valid solutions whilst considering a variety of necessary constraints that all need to be fulfilled in a given solution.

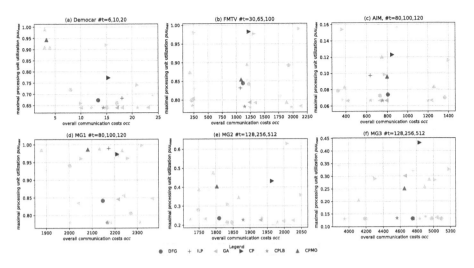

Fig. 2. Quality of six DSE approaches (DFG, ILP, GA, CP, CPLB, CPMO) along with the six models DEM, FMTV, AIM, MG1, MG2, and MG3

As soon as larger models are addressed, i.e., subplots (b)–(f) in Fig. 2, CPLB creates the best (lower puu_{max}, lower occ values) results for most measurements. Even setting the runtime to a single minute created better results compared with other DSE approaches. For instance, at the generated model (d) MG1, CPLB has lowest puu_{max} across all results. Here, the runtime was set to one minute whereas the ILP solver did not create any feasible results. The shown ILP values feature a runtime of 5 min and still do not reach comparable results to CPLB. For (e) MG2 and (f) MG3, ILP was not able to provide any results for 256 and 512 tasks, such that no ILP mean values are shown in the diagrams. This is due to the fact that the ILP solver does not scale well with the number of processing units and tasks as shown in the next Subsect. 7.2 and it does not reliably address heterogeneous processing units at all.

Interestingly, the DFG approach quickly found the optimal solution for 256 and 512 tasks in Fig. 2(e) i.e., the MG2 model. This is due to the fact that there is a relatively large task that contains a long sequence of runnables, i.e., a task that can not be further subdivided, and the DFG simply sorts tasks by their instruction costs and assigns those beginning with the largest chronologically to an ordered list of processing units beginning with the fastest (most instructions per second). However this greedy heuristic rarely results in good solutions as the other subplots, e.g., (b), (c), or (d) show.

Figure 3 presents the **speedup** of (a), the MG1 model, and (b), the FMTV model, along with an increasing number of homogeneous **processing units** (speedup (#processing units)). The used speedup calculation is based on [13] and provided in Eq. 16. Measurements from here on were repeated five times and shown values are mean values across those five benchmarks in order to mitigate measurement jitter caused by the operating system.

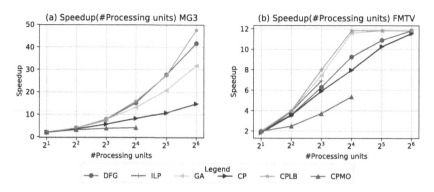

Fig. 3. Speedup (#processing units) of different DSE results for (a) MG3 and (b) FMTV

$$\text{speedup} = \frac{\sum_j \left(\min_k (C_{j,k}) \right)}{\max_k \left(\sum_j C_{j,k} \mid ta_{j,k} = 1 \right)} \tag{16}$$

Here, the nominator defines the minimal **sequential runtime** of all tasks $(\sum_j)$ being mapped to the fastest processing unit. The denominator depends on the task mapping ta and identifies the maximal runtime across all processing units, i.e., **parallel runtime**. This speedup calculation is applicable to a heterogeneous processing unit structure and can be seen as the fraction of the time before the parallelization and the time after the parallelization as introduced in [13].

Due to limited dependencies between the tasks and runnables as well as a relatively homogeneous instruction distribution, almost optimal speedup factors can be reached whereas CPLB found the best values correspondingly to Figs. 2(f) and 3. Surprisingly, the DFG approach creates better results for the MG3 model compared to GA. However, this is not the case for the FMTV model as shown in Fig. 3(b) due to its more heterogeneous nature. While ILP was not able to scale beyond 8 processing units, CPLB required significantly more runtime after the amount of 16 processing units. The optimal, model independent, speedup value equals the number of processing units, but is barely achievable due to communication costs and varying task sizes.

With the FMTV model (cf. Fig. 3(b)), the speedup is saturated at 16 processing units due to the fact that there is a single task that can not be subdivided further and consequently forms the lower bound on schedule length. In order to avoid saturation, the model would have to provide less dependencies and more homogeneous tasks regarding their sum of instruction costs. While the difference between GA and CPLB is smaller in (b) compared with (a), CPLB still provides the best results along all number of processing units. As mentioned before, the DFG approach produces worse results in (b) whereas CP was able to achieve

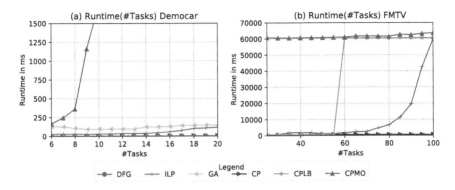

Fig. 4. Runtime(#tasks) of different DSEs for (a) Democar and (b) FMTV

better results than in (a). Other than that, results are similar to the MG3 model in (a).

7.2   Runtime and Scalability

Figure 4 presents the **runtime**, i.e., the efficiency, of different DSE approaches along with an increasing number of **tasks** ($rt(\#Tasks)$) for (a) the Democar and (b) the FMTV model. Measurements were taken with an Intel i7 quad core computer running at 2,2 GHz with 16 GB Ram.

Results show that the multi-objective constraint programming approach (CPMO) scales worst with the number of tasks as it is the only approach with multi-objective optimization. The way the CPLB approach scales highly depends on the model structure. As soon as there is a single task defining the lower bound on the maximal processing unit utilization, i.e., a comparably large task that contains a high instruction cost and is consequently mapped to the fastest processing unit, CPLB will run quicker than ILP, DFG, or GA. If tasks' instruction costs are balanced, CPLB scales worse than ILP with the number of tasks, but better with the number of processing units. It is important to note though, that CPLB was always able to find at least a valid solution, while the ILP solver failed, e.g., regarding MG2 and MG3 (cf. Fig. 2(e), (f)), even with 12 h of resolution time. Furthermore, even if the constraint solver did not investigate the complete solution space, solutions feature better results, i.e., lower inter task communication and lower processing unit utilization, compared with DFG, ILP, or GA results (cf. CPLB marks at Fig. 2(a)). Concerning larger models, the single objective constraint approach (CPLB) outperforms almost every DFG, ILP, and GA result (except Fig. 2(e) and (f) for $|T| = 512$) whereas the CPMO tends to create worse results beyond a task number of 65.

Figure 4(a) also shows that all approaches except CPMO stay almost linear below 200 ms in runtime whereas the CP, DFG, and CPLB approaches are yet the quickest with insignificant deviations. When applying the various DSEs to bigger models, the situation is similar: CPLB meets its limits to investigate the complete solution space at about 60 tasks, whereas ILP does the same at around 100 tasks. CPLB however finds valid solutions already at the same time the CP approach does (< 5ms), while ILP may not provide solutions before its resolution time at all.

Figure 5 presents the **runtime** (a) and the *occ* values (b) of different DSE approaches along with an increasing number of **processing units** (*rt(#processing units)*) for the FMTV model.

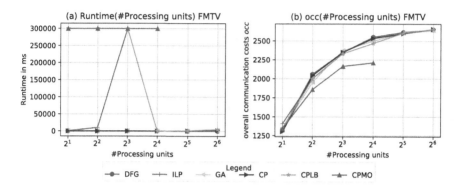

Fig. 5. (a) Runtime (#processing units); (b) occ (#processing units) of different DSEs for FMTV

Once again, CPMO performs with its maximal runtime definition (here set to 15 min) and CP finds valid solutions most quickly. The GA approach performs well but still takes longer than CP for each result. The worst scaling behavior shows the ILP approach. Above 8 processing units, the ILP solver did not find a valid solution at all. CPMO does also not scale well with the number of processing units and fails beyond 16 processing units for the same execution time restriction. Interestingly, the CPLB approach starts with requiring the full defined runtime but drops to the minimal runtime with 16 processing units and above. This is due to the fact that below 16 processing units, the solution space covers a huge variety of task to processing unit mapping combinations resulting in different maximal processing unit utilizations. As soon as 16 or more processing units are available, one relatively huge task defines the upper bound of processing unit utilization and mapping the other tasks to other processing units will not reduce this maximal processing unit utilization. Consequently, since the optimization targets only at minimizing the upper processing unit utilization bound but not maximizing the lower bound (this would in contrast keep the CPLB resolution time high), its optimization is done and solutions are available quickly. Figure 5(b) also shows a linear increase of communication costs with the increasing number of processing units as well as the CPMO approach with lowest *occ* values.

As soon as a heterogeneous structure of processing units is present, the puu_k metric shows its benefits since no additional calculations must be performed and the utilization values consider processing unit specific properties. Additionally, the CP solver can be configured to a specific initialization in order to overcome the arbitrary initial assignment values that often creates an undesired homogeneous mapping along with the heterogeneous system. For example, instead of the processing unit capacity constraint only, the initial assignment could feature another lower bound comparable to Eq. 6, i.e., $\forall\, pu_k : \sum_j ta_{j,k} \geq 1$ with $m \geq n$. Assuming that the task number is higher than the number of processing units, this equation ensures that at least one task is mapped to each processing unit. This could also be extended in order to map the largest tasks to the fastest processing units following the DFG strategy. Therefore, tasks and processing units are arranged in a descending order (regarding IC_j and puc_k) and the ta matrix is initialized with corresponding values such that the largest task is mapped to the fastest processing unit and following tasks are mapped respectively to mitigate initial mapping efforts and reduce resolution time.

With applying the 6 DSE approaches to more generated models, results did not show significant deviation from results presented above. It was observed that the threshold for speedup limitation and the CPLB runtime always depends on whether there exists a task that defines the lower bound on execution time when increasing the number of processing units (cf. Figs. 3(b) and 5(a)).

8   Conclusion

The proposed CP-based DSEs provide a wide flexibility for engineers facing the highly constrained problem of distributing real-time and mixed-critical software to heterogeneous hardware with varying architectural structures and patterns. The lightweight CP approach without any optimization has shown to provide valid solutions faster than any other comparable approach such as DFG, ILP, or GA. The single objective optimization approach CPLB provides optimal or nearly optimal solutions for most of the measurements. In only 11% of all measurements, CPLB did not provide the best processing unit utilization values. For 73% of all measurements, CPLB defines the best overall result quality regarding occ and puu_{max} values. The CPMO approach covers multi objective optimization with assessable pareto fronts in an appropriate amount of time. For optimal results however, the multi object constraint programming solution requires significantly more time.

A great benefit of using the CP paradigm is also an automatic constraint validation that will inform programmers about any contradicting or erroneous model entities, variable bounds, or constraints. Such validation requires additional efforts when using different DSEs.

Additionally, this paper's work has shown that CP applies very well to highly constrained domains consisting of combinatorial design spaces such as automotive systems. It preserves the natural modeling and programming activities while providing optimal, pareto optimal, or nearly optimal solutions in an appropriate amount of resolution time. Typical automotive constraints, consecutive constraint modeling, and solving partitioning and mapping problems with a constraint solver are presented. The CP solver's perception is very natural since its constraints often directly correspond to AMALTHEA entities and the CP SAT solver uses mainly clauses and backtracking search rather than linear inequalities only as in ILP. This also takes effect when adapting optimization goals which CP tackles on a more natural level. In addition to the efficiency and quality assessments of the described approaches, their benefits of effort mitigation when investigating highly constrained solution spaces are presented. We can conclude that if optimization is less important rather than getting valid solutions as quick as possible, CP is the prior choice. If constraints are of non integer nature or if the model is subject to a high amount of interleaving constraints of different types, CP, CPMO, and CPLB are the prior choice. If implementation simplicity is in focus, local search heuristics (such as DFG) can be useful for simple problems without any optimality demands. Genetic algorithms scale well for single objective optimization if the problem can be represented via few and simple mutation characteristics. Further work is intended to advance the utilization and response time analysis for various scheduling methods and to adjust optimization goals to consider further parameters such as memory contention or task chain latency.

To the best of the authors' knowledge, this paper is the first approach that considers AUTOSAR compliant constraints on a broader level and compares different DSE methodologies for the software distribution problem in the automotive domain.

References

1. AUTOSAR Consortium. Automotive Open System Architecture - Classic Platform 4.4.0 : Requirements on Timing Extensions (2019). https://bit.ly/32gVClq. Accessed 7 2019
2. Balsini, A., Melani, A., Buonocunto, P., Di Natale, M.: FMTV 2016 : where is the actual challenge? In: International Workshop on Analysis Tools and Methodologies for Embedded and Real-time Systems (WATERS) (2016)
3. Baruah, S.K., Burns, A., Davis, R.I.: Response-time analysis for mixed criticality systems. In: Proceedings of the IEEE 32nd Real-Time Systems Symposium, RTSS 2011, pp. 34–43. IEEE Computer Society (2011)
4. Becker, M., Dasari, D., Nicolic, B., Åkesson, B., Nélis, V., Nolte, T.: Contention-free execution of automotive applications on a clustered many-core platform. In: 28th Euromicro Conference on Real-Time Systems, July 2016
5. Biondi, A., Di Natale, M., Buttazzo, G.: Response-time analysis of engine control applications under fixed-priority scheduling. IEEE Trans. Comput. **67**(5), 687–703 (2018)
6. Biondi, A., Pazzaglia, P., Balsini, A., Di Natale, M.: Logical execution time implementation and memory optimization issues in autosar applications for multicores. In: International Workshop on Analysis Tools and Methodologies for Embedded and Real-Time Systems (WATERS) (2017)
7. Bonifaci, V., Brandenburg, B., D'Angelo, G., Marchetti-Spaccamela, A.: Multiprocessor real-time scheduling with hierarchical processor affinities. In: 28th Euromicro Conference on Real-Time Systems, ECRTS 2016, Toulouse, France, 5–8 July 2016, pp. 237–247 (2016)

8. Choi, J., Kang, D., Ha, S.: A novel analytical technique for timing analysis of FMTV 2016 verification challenge benchmark. In: International Workshop on Analysis Tools and Methodologies for Embedded and Real-time Systems (WATERS) (2016)

9. Cuadra, P., Krawczyk, L., Höttger, R., Heisig, P., Wolff, C.: Automated scheduling for tightly-coupled embedded multi-core systems using hybrid genetic algorithms. In: Damaševičius, R., Mikašytė, V. (eds.) ICIST 2017. CCIS, vol. 756, pp. 362–373. Springer, Cham (2017). https://doi.org/10.1007/978-3-319-67642-5_30

10. Melo e Silva de Oliveira, R., Oliveira de Castro Ribeiro, M.S.F.: Comparing mixed & integer programming vs. constraint programming by solving job-shop scheduling problems. Indep. J. Manag. Prod. 6(1), 211–238 (2015)

11. Fonseca, C.M., Fleming, P.J.: Genetic algorithms for multiobjective optimization: formulation, discussion and generalization. In: Proceedings of the Fifth International Conference on Genetic Algorithms, pp. 416–423, July 1993

12. Frey, P.: A timing model for real-time control-systems and its application on simulation and monitoring of AUTOSAR systems dissertation. Ph.D. Thesis, Ulm University (2010)

13. Garey, M.R., Johnson, D.S.: Computers and Intractability; A Guide to the Theory of NP-Completeness. W. H. Freeman & Co., New York (1990)

14. Hamann, A., Dasari, D., Kramer, S., Pressler, M., Wurst, F.: Communication centric design in complex automotive embedded systems. In: 29th Euromicro Conference on Real-Time Systems (ECRTS 2017), volume 76 of Leibniz International Proceedings in Informatics (LIPIcs), pp. 10–20 (2017)

15. Hannig, F., Cardoso, J.M.P., Pionteck, T., Fey, D., Schröder-Preikschat, W., Teich, J. (eds.): ARCS 2016. LNCS, vol. 9637. Springer, Cham (2016). https://doi.org/10.1007/978-3-319-30695-7

16. Hilbrich, R., Behrisch, M.: Improving the efficiency of dislocality constraints for an automated software deployment in safety-critical systems. In: Combined Proceedings of the Workshops of the German Software Engineering Conference 2018 (SE 2018), Workshop on Software Engineering for Applied Embedded Real-Time Systems, SEERTS 2018, pp. 90–95. ceur-ws.org, March 2018

17. Hooker, J.N.: A hybrid method for the planning and scheduling. Constraints J. 10(4), 385–401 (2005)

18. Höttger, R., Igel, B., Spinczyk, O.: On reducing busy waiting in AUTOSAR via task-release-delta-based runnable reordering. In: Proceedings of the 2017 Design, Automation & Test in Europe Conference & Exhibition, DATE 2017, pp. 1510–1515. IEEE, March 2017

19. Höttger, R., Krawczyk, L., Igel, B.: Model-based automotive partitioning and mapping for embedded multicore systems. In: International Conference on Parallel, Distributed Systems and Software Engineering, volume 2 of ICPDSSE 2015, pp. 2643–2649 (2015)

20. Jang, H.C., Jin, H.W.: MiAMI: multi-core aware processor affinity for TCP/IP over multiple network interfaces, pp. 73–82. In: Proceedings - Symposium on the High Performance Interconnects, Hot Interconnects (2009)

21. Kramer, S., Ziegenbein, D., Hamann, A.: Real world automotive benchmarks for free. In: 6th International Workshop an Analysis Tools and Methodologies for Embedded and Real-time Systems (WATERS) (2015)

22. Krawczyk, L., Wolff, C., Fruhner, D.: Automated distribution of software to multi-core hardware in model based embedded systems development. In: Dregvaite, G., Damasevicius, R. (eds.) ICIST 2015. CCIS, vol. 538, pp. 320–329. Springer, Cham (2015). https://doi.org/10.1007/978-3-319-24770-0_28

23. Limtanyakul, K.: Scheduling of tests on vehicle prototypes using constraint and integer programming. In: Kalcsics, J., Nickel, S. (eds.) Operations Research, pp. 421–426. Springer, Heidelberg (2008). https://doi.org/10.1007/978-3-540-77903-2_65

24. Martinez, J., Sa, I., Burgio, P., Bertogna, M.: End-To-end latency characterization of implicit and LET communication models. In: Workshop on Analysis Tools and Methodologies for Embedded and Real-time Systems (WATERS) (2017)

25. Papadopoulos, Y., Grante, C.: Evolving car designs using model-based automated safety analysis and optimisation techniques. J. Syst. Softw. **76**(1), 77–89 (2005)

26. Perron, L.: Operations research and constraint programming at google. In: Lee, J. (ed.) CP 2011. LNCS, vol. 6876, p. 2. Springer, Heidelberg (2011). https://doi.org/10.1007/978-3-642-23786-7_2

27. Prud'homme, C., Fages, J.-G., Lorca, X.: Choco solver documentation. TASC, INRIA Rennes, LINA CNRS UMR 6241, COSLING S.A.S. (2016). http://www.choco-solver.org. Accessed November 2018

28. Rivas, J.M., Javier Gutiérrez, J., Medina, J.L., Harbour, M.G.: Comparison of memory access strategies in multi-core platforms using MAST. In: International Workshop on Analysis Tools and Methodologies for Embedded and Real-time Systems (WATERS) (2017)

29. Sadykov, R., Wolsey, L.A.: Integer programming and constraint programming in solving a multimachine assignment scheduling problem with deadlines and release dates. INFORMS J. Comput. **18**, 209–217 (2006)

30. Singh, A.K., Dziurzanski, P., Mendis, H.R., Indrusiak, L.S.: A survey and comparative study of hard and soft real-time dynamic resource allocation strategies for multi-/many-core systems. ACM Comput. Surv. **50**(2), 24:1–24:40 (2017)

31. Stattelmann, S., Ottlik, S., Viehl, A., Bringmann, O., Rosenstiel, W.: Combining instruction set simulation and WCET analysis for embedded software performance estimation. In: 7th IEEE International Symposium on Industrial Embedded Systems (SIES), pp. 295–298 (2012)

32. Thiruvady, D.R., Moser, I., Aleti, A., Nazari, A.: Constraint programming and ant colony system for the component deployment problem. In: Proceedings of the International Conference on Computational Science, ICCS 2014, Cairns, Australia, 10–12 June 2014, pp. 1937–1947 (2014)

33. Xie, G., Chen, Y., Liu, Y., Wei, Y., Li, R., Li, K.: Resource consumption cost minimization of reliable parallel applications on heterogeneous embedded systems. IEEE Trans. Industr. Inf. **13**(4), 1629–1640 (2016)

Mobile River Navigation for Smart Cities

Witold Kazimierski[1], Natalia Wawrzyniak[2],
Marta Wlodarczyk-Sielicka[2(✉)], Tomasz Hyla[3],
Izabela Bodus-Olkowska[2], and Grzegorz Zaniewicz[2]

[1] Marine Technology Ltd., Klonowica 37/5, 71-248 Szczecin, Poland
w.kazimierski@marinetechnology.pl
[2] Faculty of Navigation, Institute of Geoinformatics,
Maritime University of Szczecin, Żołnierska 46, 71-250 Szczecin, Poland
{n.wawrzyniak, m.wlodarczyk, i.olkowska, g.zaniewicz}
@am.szczecin.pl
[3] Faculty of Computer Science and Information Technology, West Pomeranian
University of Technology, Żołnierska 52, 71-210 Szczecin, Poland
thyla@zut.edu.pl

Abstract. One of the main aspects of smart city is smart mobility, covering mainly smart transport solutions for users. On the other hand smart living includes also touristic attractiveness of the city and its information systems. The paper presents a mobile solution, which integrate both – supporting of smart transportation and touristic needs of the users. It is a system of mobile navigation for inland waters. The concept of the system is presented, followed by the methodological aspects of its designing and implementation. The mobility of system is presented in various aspects (spatial data integration, cartographic model and spatial analysis and implementation issues). Although the system may be independent technology, it is shown from the point of view of possible integration in wider smart city concept. In such approach the functional possibilities of the system are increased and smart city implementation may be also enhanced.

Keywords: Mobile GIS · Mobile navigation · Smart rivers · Smart cities

1 Introduction

Smart City concept has been emerging for last times rapidly and has resulted in many applications all over the world. The idea itself however is not unified and has been variously understood in many cities, areas, fields and papers. The most general definition seems to be the one given in ISO report, where the "smartness" of a city describes its ability to bring all its resources together, to effectively and seamlessly achieve the goals and fulfil the purposes it has set itself [1]. Similar approach can be seen in [2], where smart cities are examples of adoption of scalable solutions that take advantage of information and communications technology (ICT) to increase efficiencies, reduce costs, and enhance quality of life. In [3] it is suggested that due to large variety of cities and the complexity of the urbanization processes, it is impossible to find one definition suitable to all cases. Authors suggested even that strict definition

© Springer Nature Switzerland AG 2019
R. Damaševičius and G. Vasiljevienė (Eds.): ICIST 2019, CCIS 1078, pp. 591–604, 2019.
https://doi.org/10.1007/978-3-030-30275-7_45

would result in unnecessary restrictions in vision of cities development. Thus for more practical purposes the more narrow and precise definitions are being made. Common framework of all approaches seems to be that from an infrastructural point of view, the concept integrates central ICT system connected to network of wired or wireless sensors and advanced analytic modules for developing intelligent applications and services for citizens [4].

Smart City may be also defined from user's point of view as a set of solutions influencing directly or indirectly user's life. In [5], six dimensions of smart city are given – smart economy, smart people, smart environment, smart mobility, smart governance and smart living. This paper addresses directly two of them - smart mobility and smart living, presenting mobile navigation system for inland navigation.

It can be noticed that majority of large cities all over the world are settled at the river bank or has direct access to open waters (lake, sea, ocean). Many examples can be given here, like Amsterdam, New York, Szczecin or Hamburg. These cities are at the same usually important touristic hubs with many attractions distributed in their area. Therefore smart transportation solutions should be proposed for touristic purposes for inland waters within smart urban agglomerations. The problem of sustainable tourism application has been undertaken for example in [4], providing IoT architecture for this. In this paper we propose to look at the problem from water point of view and we describe a framework of mobile river navigation. We assume that proper handling of spatial data can provide for user both – reliable navigation application, as well as tourist guide. Simultaneously we do believe that such a system may become a part of smart mobility and smart living modules within smart cities concept. The framework presented here has been tested in system demonstrator called MobiNav. It was shown in [3], that the basis for many aspects of smartness in city is proper handling of spatial data.

During the research, the existing solutions were analyzed in detail. The main conclusions that were drawn from the analysis can be included:

- none of the applications fully exploits the opportunities offered by the use of a mobile cartographic presentation;
- applications use their own closed data model, which results in limited possibilities of data interoperability;
- applications usually allow to work in off-line mode;
- the technological advancement of the application is at a similar level;
- inland applications do not involve building communities for mutual information on useful places;
- the use of advanced spatial analyzes in applications is small.

MobiNav - Mobile Inland Navigation was a scientific project in which a navigation mobile application for inland navigation was designed and created. The main purpose of the application is planning and executing travel and exchanging data among friends on social networks. The system is dedicated for users of pleasure crafts in inland waters and is equipped with data, tools and information presentation model dedicated for them. The idea was to use available data for providing the information in a readable way to the user, facilitating broad navigation. Functionality is not limited to navigational aspects. It is intended to provide additional functions needed by tourists on the sailing route. MobiNav has the visualization of data adapted to the needs of the user, with the purpose of using modern mobile cartography. The main user of MobiNav system is a skipper of floating recreational vessel on inland waters: motor yacht, sailboat, kayak and any other. The functionalities of such kind of mobile application must meet the potential users' requirements. Main user's activities in handling with mobile maps were pointed out in [6, 7] locating, navigating, searching, identifying and checking the status of the objects. Those are the base of MobiNav functionalities. In order to refine the usability level of the application, the authors have developed a questionnaire and distributed it in the environment of inland water concerned people and such like companies. The analysis of the results has been fully described in [8].

Summarizing, the most important research achievements in the process of building the system include:

- development of a mobile map implementation technology in an application, in which the data and cartographic presentation layer is independent of the application itself;
- development and implementation of the navigation assistant as the most advanced set of spatial analyzes together with a dynamic presentation model;
- development and implementation of the method of using geofencing technology for navigational needs;
- development of technologies for integration of internal and external sensors;
- development of a complete model of a mobile cartographic presentation, including generalization and cartographic editing;
- development of a new data model dedicated for inland navigation and development of a method for importing data from various external sources;
- development and implementation of a comprehensive tool for the design of mobile cartographic presentations;

Thanks to the above, the designed system is an innovative solution.

2 Method of Creating the Mobile River Navigation System

Designing and test implementation of mobile river navigation system was corresponding with consecutive tasks in the project and was following in fact methodologically classical process of GIS project development with additional focus on mobile cartographic presentation and mobile technologies.

2.1 System Architecture

The MobiNav system has a modular architecture (Fig. 1). It consists of a mobile application, server-side systems and can easily incorporate information provided by some external systems, including smart city services. The mobile application is designed to work in online and offline modes. It stores charts in local storage and uses chart management module to synchronize or update charts from MobiNav servers. Apart from visualisation module, which is responsible for displaying charts stored in vector and raster formats overlaid with navigation data, the application has two major components. One is responsible for conducting different types of spatial analyses while the other gathers and processes data from both internal and external sensors, which is accessible from a ships wireless network.

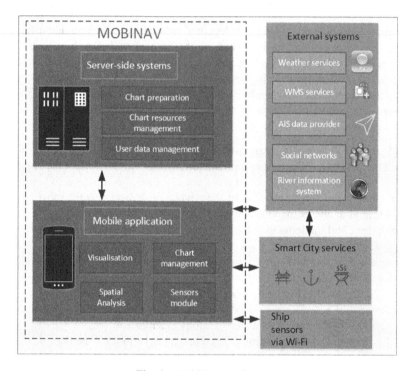

Fig. 1. MobiNav architecture

The server-side part of the system has three basics modules. Two modules are related to charts. First one allows creating lightweight vector charts in a custom format. Second one is responsible for storage and synchronizing new data with mobile applications. Also, on the server-side, the user management module allow users to store personal data (e.g., settings, waypoints, tracks) that can be shared with other users. The connection between servers and mobile users is encrypted. All basic functions are available in the offline mode. Additionally, when application is in online mode (internet connection is available), which is usually the case in all urban areas - especially in cities, the mobile application can use several external systems and services. The most common are: Web Map Services (as additional configurable raster chart layers), weather services, AIS (Automatic Identification System) which provides information about nearby ships when AIS is not available on the ship, RIS (River Information System) and a variety of social networks. This solution heads towards reducing of own sensors on-board, incorporating interoperability of any information exchange within smart city services.

When a user navigates on a waterway across a city, the mobile application can also communicate with several possible smart city services. It can support smart traffic monitoring with automatic bridge and lock opening, providing information about queues.

2.2   Methodology of Map Data Management

The basis of the system are geodata from publicly available sources. In case of inland waterway shipping, the best source of navigation data is Inland Electronic Navigational Chart, which are more and more common products in river cities. In order to ensure functionality of the system in other areas, use of other data sources is necessary and thus data integration is also indispensable. Test implementation of system was created for two test sides in Poland, thus it was decided to use topographic data base BDOT10k, database of Vmap level 2, publically available data covered by open source project Open Street Map and data entered manually by the operator. The final effect is multiresolution and multirepresentation database, from which a numerical map is generated. The maps are prepared on the server and then send to mobile devices. It is very important to remember about control of geometrical properties of features based on the geodetic control points [9].

Implementation of integrated spatial data model means precise description of required spatial data format MODEF (MO-binav Data Exchange Format). The data model is defined as a UML class diagram according to the commonly used methodology. It consists of 27 feature classes and one abstract class, called the MobiNav class, from which the others inherit the basic attributes (e.g. name, minimum scale, maximum scale). To implement a new spatial data model, the rules for importing objects from all source data are also defined. The rules are set in the form of algorithms which cover spatial and attributes aspects, describing which object form specified layers is imported. Furthermore attribute mapping is provided and resulting data validation. Preparing data in MODEF format covers four steps:

- importing source data to PostgreSQL/PostGIS database,
- processing and validation of geodata,
- projection od source tables to MODEF standard,
- export of final data to GML format.

It can be concluded that due to significant differences between the source databases, the integration of geodata with selection have been made. During creation the output database, the algorithm checks in turn which sources exist for the specified water area and then selects the data for presentation, starting with the most reliable [10].

2.3   Methodology of Dynamic Sensor Data Integration

In the MobiNav application, the GNSS system is primarily used to determine the position of the user, but also as a course source (relative to the land) and the speed of the boat that moves. For this purpose, a position sensor built into the user's mobile device was used. With a designated location, it is possible to perform a series of analyzes, such as routing, distance from selected objects, and determination of a safety buffer for navigational obstacles.

The application, depending on the conditions, uses the positioning system that is optimal for the situation. The selection is not limited to the use of a GNSS sensor only, where the accuracy of the resulting position may be insufficient, but also for the use of the combined method with AGPS support.

The use of GNSS sensors in mobile devices seems to be appropriate for users of the inland mobile navigation system. Full mobility of the GNSS sensor, no cable between the device and the antenna, is the primary advantage of such a solution. The GNSS receivers analyzed during the project, receive sub-meter accuracy, which seems good enough for safe navigation on inland waterways [11].

In the second case, with more data received from the sensors, MobiNav proposed the distribution of data by the WIFI module installed on the boat. All data should be sent in the NMEA protocol through the aforementioned wireless network. The most important data include: AIS – traffic information (VDO), depth below the transducer (DBT) and wind information (MWV) [12]. These data can be shared between users via shore server, creating smart city community in river waters.

2.4   Mobile Cartographic Presentation Model

Mobile cartographic presentation model of the MobiNav system has been developed as a result of three theoretical foundations: traditional cartography, GIS presentation principles and cartographic presentation methodology for land mobile location systems.

Mobile cartographic presentation model has been defined as a discrete set of absolute number of elementary cartographic presentation, generated by application based on trigger conditions. The concept of model is presented as follows [13]:

$$CP = \left\{ GC_{p1}, \ldots, GC_{pm} \right\}, p_1, \ldots, p_m \subseteq \{1, \ldots, n\} \tag{1}$$

$$GC_p = \; <GCP_{i1}, \ldots, GCP_{ik}>, P = \{i_1, \ldots, i_k\} \subseteq \{1, \ldots, n\} \tag{2}$$

$$GCP_i \subseteq CITU, i = \{1, \ldots, n\} \tag{3}$$

where:

CP – cartographic presentation which is a family of geocomposition sets,
GC – geocomposition is an indexed and sorted family of sets of Partial Geocompositions - *GCP* under the condition that $i_m \neq i_l$, while $m \neq l$.

The mobile cartographic presentation model of MobiNav is understood as a set of specified number of geocompositions and their components, generated by the application under the influence of trigger conditions: manually or automatically. MobiNav cartographic model has been described in detail in [8, 14, 15].

It is worth noting that the development of an original tool for the design of a mobile cartographic presentation (Fig. 2) allows for a fuller use of the possibilities of mobile cartography.

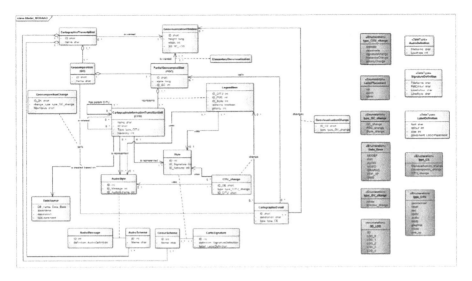

Fig. 2. Mobile cartographic presentation model of MobiNav

2.5 Mobile Technologies in River Navigation Systems

There is a variety of possibilities for supporting inland navigation with a use of newest achievements in mobile technology, sensors miniaturization and accessibility or social networking. All of them uses advanced techniques of data management and information flow between on-board sensors network, mobile device embedded sensors, mobile systems software solutions and also external services, including smart services. Thanks to wildly accessible internet connection via cellular network, information can be shared and be re-used by other users of smart technology.

Mass Collaboration for Navigational Safety

During MobiNav development we proposed a model of inter-user data exchange to support systems with information acquired by individual participants of inland waterways.

Our approach was based on using mass collaboration technique to provide system with up to date information, which might be missing from other sources of data (charts) or services [16]. Users' input in co-creating, developing, and maintaining modern systems is an interesting solution worth consideration in designing any support decision systems, also for navigation. However, allowing users to share and update information crucial for navigational safety needs developing a dedicated data model and data flow before taking such an approach. To achieve this goal a dedicated model of collaborative data exchange had to be designed. User data types and their significances differ greatly and the distinction has to be made to ensure validity and preservation of information strictly concerning users immediate safety. The most flexible way to ensure data control and transfer to other systems (if needed) is through XML technology and Simple Object Access Protocol (SOAP). Its application allows to use push and pop services and to transfer data to other systems by SOAP interfaces.

This technology is applied in existing RIS systems, which provides many services that MobiNav application could already use. The full model was implemented in a MobiNav system and can be found in [16] described in detail. Figure 3 presents a high level data flow diagram, that show data flows inside the MobiNav system from the perspective of the "live data" (collaborative data). It shows how systems manages receiving different kinds users data, saves it in repository and how systems processes monitor changes in this repository react accordingly.

The developed solution allows to reduce costs of developing such systems by using simpler architecture, needing less maintenance and limiting data acquisition costs. The fact of users mass collaboration can also provide more interesting additional functionality for other smart services related for navigational and recreational purposes that are supported by MobiNav system.

Geofencing

Several complex spatial analyses can be implemented using a geofencing technology that is available in all modern mobile operating systems. Geofencing allows monitoring objects' location in a specified area [17]. When some areas are monitored using geofencing, the operating system tracks user's location and triggers events when entering or leaving any of given areas. Generally the geofences can be of any shape. However, standard libraries in mobile operating systems have only circular geofences implemented. It is possible to write libraries or use external ones that support geofencing of any shape, but in most of use cases circular geofences are enough. The geofencing accuracy depends mostly on a position accuracy of GPS receivers built into mobile devices. Nowadays, the accuracy is in the order of several meters in an open air [18].

The geofencing is a simplified solution to proximity and buffer analyses that are used in MobiNav in systems alarms and warnings regarding approaching defined by navigational hazard, shallow waters etc. These analyses can be implemented on mobile devices without using geofences, but the result will not be as efficient and some problems such as monitoring positions when application is suspended or works in background mode must be solved. The major advantage of geofencing is that a developer can implement it without having the knowledge about certain mathematics of spatial analysis [19].

The basic application of this technology is marketing, e.g. sending messages to potentials clients who are near the shop, and fleet or asset management, e.g. sending notification if a car position change outside designated area. In MobiNav, the geofencing is used, among others, for smart navigation purposes. In the context of smart city, the most important feature is automatic lock and bridge opening support. The MobiNav application tracks all locks and bridges which are on route. The event is triggered when a pleasure craft is approaching a bridge and information with request to open a bridge can be automatically send to a bridge operator, if some information system for the management of the bridges and locks exists.

Sensors in Mobile Devices

Nowadays, mobile devices have high quality sets of sensors. Many sensors can be used for inland navigation purposes. MobiNav uses two categories of sensors: sensors embedded in a mobile device where the application is installed and sensors on-board of

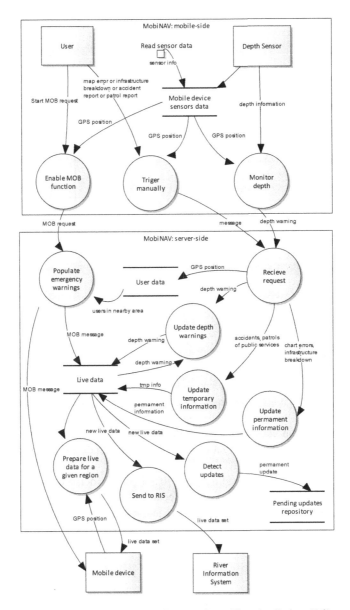

Fig. 3. MobiNav data flow diagram from "live data" view [16]

a pleasure craft available through Wi-Fi connection (Fig. 4). Embedded sensors can be divided further into two subcategories [20]: raw sensors and derived sensors. Raw sensors (e.g., 3D Accelerometer, 3D Magnetometer, 3D Gyroscope, Ambient Light, Short Range Proximity, GPS) allow reading data directly from hardware sensors embedded into the device. Derived sensors (e.g., Simplified Device Orientation, Device Orientation, Inclinometer, Compass, Shake, Geolocation) offer processed and fused data coming from few raw sensors at once forming different information for the system user.

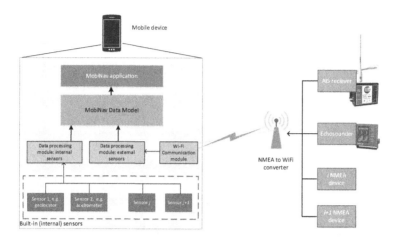

Fig. 4. MobiNav sensors data flow

Some sensors, such as an echosounder, AIS, a radar or a weather station obviously cannot be integrated with mobile devices. But ff a boat is equipped with such devices together with a standardized Wi-Fi network that broadcast that data, MobiNav application can use it for navigation purposes as any sensor that provides data in a form of NMEA 0183 string. For inland navigation purposes, the most important external sensors are a radar, an echosounder and Inland AIS. The data strings can be easily decoded and used to enhance navigation, e.g., display depth or display ships navigating nearby based on AIS data.

The access to the sensors readings and to the fused, derived information varies depending on a mobile operating system. Because the philosophy behind each of the mobile operating systems is different, the type and availability of information from the sensors differs too.

3 Results

The requirements of system are set to fulfill the needs of touristic/non-professional users. The system, thanks to its functionality, has to support user in easy and relaxing navigation on rivers and canals in cities. The basis for providing proper functionality is to integrate spatial data required. It is a good idea to use for this purpose spatial databases already existing in cities for cadastral and other purposes. In test implementation polish local databases were used, however implementation of the other requires only providing other attribute mapping rules and the data can be easily provided in developed data exchange.

In the last stage, the MobiNav and commercial Periscal Inland ECDIS (Electronic Chart Display and Information System) were compared. On the IECDIS system used, standardized electronic navigational charts were downloaded from the distributor's website to the RIS (River Information System). Comparing the display of the IECDIS system and the MobiNav application, two routes were proposed for the ship (Fig. 5). The studied area is included in the port of Szczecin.

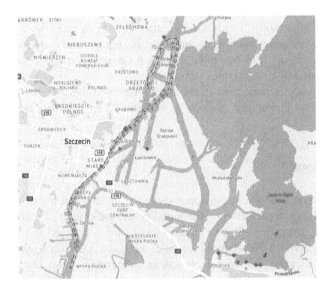

Fig. 5. MobiNav sensors data flow

The proposed routes allowed to test the function and display in the MobiNav application and compare this information with the IECDIS system. As part of the tests, the navigation assistant was checked, message display, geofencing, data visualization and correctness of the data model.

When comparing two applications, you can indicate many common features. Both applications cooperate with external sensors necessary for navigation, i.e. a GNSS antenna, AIS system, weather station and echosounder. Another feature is the display of maps in various orientation modes and the ability to change colors, due to external lighting conditions. The display and colors used in ENC are another feature combining two applications.

However, it should be clearly stated that the MobiNav application has been extended compared to IECDIS with many new map layers, mainly related to tourist elements. It is mainly about points of interest POI and extended attribute information for points with harbor ports. An interesting solution, implemented in the new application is the navigation assistant. The well-known audio information module, known from car navigation, also works well on water bodies. The information provided by him supports the user without taking his eyes off the direction of travel.

The smartness of the solution is also supported by processing of user data and allowing of their exchange between users. Thus much additional information, not included in original dataset may flow in the system according to users' needs. Further improvement of the smartness of system can be done by providing servers for processing dynamic information about ships. Thus user can have information about other targets even without having own observation sensors.

Using of mobile appliances as a target device seems to be necessity nowadays, especially in any smart transport solution. It put however some restrains on cartographic presentation model. Firstly the data model has to be generalized to from basic scale to others, providing multiresolution and multi-representation database. Secondly the cartographic model itself has to be suitable for mobile solution relying of various geovisualizations and cartographic events.

Tests and analysis performed in the research proved the usability of system for mobile inland navigation and as such to become a part of smart city information infrastructure.

4   Conclusions

The paper describes mobile navigational system for inland waters as an example of mobile GIS solution for smart city. The mobility and integration of spatial data seems to be crucial for providing effective smart solutions nowadays and in future.

Taking into account that many of the cities are laid at the river banks or sea coast, water tourism may be one of the attractions influencing smart living quality for inhabitants and for tourists. There is a need for mobile transport solution supporting navigation and tourism. An example of such system is presented in the paper.

MobiNav was developed in the project and the main idea was to create technology of building of such systems, taking into account all aspects – user needs, technological restrictions of mobile solution, spatial data and sensor data integration as well as information visualization. In general the technology of mobile navigation dedicated for water users was created. The solution consists of mobile application supported by shore server site and as such can be integrated with smart city spatial data infrastructure. The system is a modern solution that is not on the market today.

The future works are planned to prepare system for other test sites and to enhance the technology focused on more possibilities for data exchange between users.

Acknowledgment. This research outcome has been achieved under the grant No. 1/S/IG/16 and 17/MN/IG/18 financed from a subsidy of the Ministry of Science and Higher Education for statutory activities.

This scientific research work was supported by National Centre for Research and Development (NCBiR) of Poland (grant No. LIDER/039/693/L-4/12/NCBR/2013) in 2013–2016.

References

1. ISO/IEC JTC 1: Smart cities. Preliminary Report 2014, ISO Copyright Office (2015)
2. Falconer, G., Mitchell, S.: Smart City Framework - A Systematic Process for Enabling Smart + Connected Communities. Cisco Internet Business Solutions Group (2012)
3. Gotlib, D., Olszewski, R. (eds.): Smart City – Spatial Information in Smart City Management. PWN, Warsaw (2016). (in Polish)
4. Nitti, M., Pilloni, V., Giusto, D., Popescu, V.: IoT architecture for a sustainable tourism application in a smart city environment. Mob. Inf. Syst. **2017** (2017). https://doi.org/10.1155/2017/9201640
5. Giffinger, R., Haindl, G.: Smart cities ranking: an effective instrument for the positioning of cities? In: 5th International Conference Virtual City and Territory, Centre dePolitica de Soli Valoracions, Barcelona (2009)
6. Meng, I., Zipf, A., Reichenbacher, T. (eds.): Map-Based Mobile Services. Springer, Heidelberg (2005). https://doi.org/10.1007/b138407
7. Ling, W.: Adaptive concepts for mobile cartography. In: 2011 International Conference on Multimedia Technology (ICMT), Hangzhou, pp. 2907–2910 (2011). https://doi.org/10.1109/icmt.2011.6002036
8. Bodus-Olkowska, I., Kazimierski, W., Zaniewicz, G.: Selection of geocomposition components for the mobile inland water navigation system based on users' needs. In: 2016 Baltic Geodetic Congress (BGC Geomatics), pp. 205–210 (2016). https://doi.org/10.1109/bgc.geomatics.2016.44
9. Pokonieczny, K., Bielecka, E., Kaminski, P.: Analysis of spatial distribution of geodetic control points and land cover. In: 14th International Multidisciplinary Scientific Geoconference (SGEM) Geoconference on Informatics, Geoinformatics and Remote Sensing, Albena, Bulgaria, vol. II, pp. 49–56 (2014)
10. Włodarczyk-Sielicka, M., Kazimierski, W., Marek, M.: Proposal of algorithms of integration of various spatial data in mobile navigation system for inland waters. Ann. Geomatics **XII**(4 (66)), 445–457 (2014). (in Polish)
11. Zaniewicz, G., Sawczak, A.: Quality and using of GNSS sensors in mobile navigation system for inland waters. Ann. Geomatics **XIV**(2(72)) (2016). (in Polish)
12. Zaniewicz, G., Kazimierski, W., Bodus-Olkowska, I.: Integration of spatial data from external sensors in the mobile navigation system for inland shipping. In: Proceedings of Baltic Geodetic Congress (2016). https://doi.org/10.1109/bgc.geomatics.2016.37
13. Gotlib, D.: A cartographic presentation model for navigation and location-based applications. In: Joint Symposium of ISPRS Commission IV/AutoCarto Annual Conference. Book Series: International Archives of the Photogrammetry Remote Sensing and Spatial Information Sciences, Orlando, vol. 38, part 4 (2010)
14. Kazimierski, W., Zaniewicz, G., Olkowska, I.: Integrated presentation of navigational data in a mobile navigation system for inland waters with the use of HUD. Sci. J. Marit. Univ. Szczecin **49**(121), 84–92 (2017). https://doi.org/10.17402/203
15. Bodus-Olkowska, I., Zaniewicz, G., Wlodarczyk-Sielicka, M.: Evaluation of cartographic presentation of MOBINAV, the inland mobile navigation system. Ann. Geomatics **15**(1(79)) (2017). (in Polish)
16. Hyla, T., Wawrzyniak, N., Kazimierski, W.: An innovative model of user-aquired data exchange for inland mobile navigation. In: Wilinski, A., et al. (eds.) Soft Computing in Computer and Information Science. Advances in Intelligent Systems and Computing, Springer, Cham (2015)

17. Wawrzyniak, N., Hyla, T.: Application of geofencing technology for the purpose of spatial analyses in inland mobile navigation. In: Proceedings of Baltic Geodetic Congress (2016). https://doi.org/10.1109/bgc.geomatics.2016.15
18. Namiot, D.: GeoFence services. Int. J. Open Inf. Technol. (2013)
19. Zimbelman, E., Keefe, R., Strand, E., Colden, C., Wempe, A.: Hazards in motion: development of mobile geofences for use in logging safety. Sensors **17**(4), 822 (2017)
20. Hyla, T., Kazimierski, W., Wawrzyniak, N.: Analysis of radar integration possibilities in inland mobile navigation. In: Rohling, H. (ed.) 16th International Radar Symposium (IRS), International Radar Symposium Proceedings, Dresden, Germany, pp. 864–869 (2015)

New Paradigm of Model-Oriented Control in IoT

Kazymyr Volodymyr, Prila Olga, Usik Anna[✉], and Sysa Dmytro

Chernihiv National University of Technology,
95 Shevchenka Str., Chernihiv 14035, Ukraine
vvkazymyr@gmail.com, olga.prila1986@gmail.com,
usik18@gmail.com, dmitriy.sysa@gmail.com

Abstract. The Internet of Things (IoT) is a growing network infrastructure that links Cyber-Physical Systems (CPS) for solving of Industry 4.0 tasks. Such systems can be considered as an extension of embedded systems that can be used to create applications of various levels of complexity. On the other hand, the cyber-physical system is a holonic system, which consists of a "physical object" and its "cyber twin", connected together. This "cyber-twin" is a "computational relationship model" of a physical object, which means that it can virtually copy the behavior of a physical machine and give an idea of how the machine will react when different actions appear. The article describes a new paradigm of Model-Oriented Control (MOC) by entities of the CPS based on the principles of High-Level Architecture (HLA). Traditionally, HLA is used for organization of distributed simulation with providing the execution of different type models in common model time. New control paradigm considers control programs as "cyber-twin" models realized and interconnected as federates of HLA in real time instead of model time. For a description of control programs executed by controllers the embedded models of algorithms in the form of Control E-networks (CEN) are proposed. CEN is an extension of Petri nets with support of needed calculations and interconnection with the environment. High-speed data exchange between CEN-models of control programs is organized through a Real-Time Infrastructure (RTI) that includes specially developed communication module realized with the use of CEN and acts as an IoT cloud network service.

Keywords: Internet of Things · Cyber-physical systems · Model-oriented control · High Level Architecture · Control E-networks

1 Target Settings

The Internet of Things (IoT) is a growing networking infrastructure which is increasingly connecting computer-augmented physical systems worldwide, singularly known as Embedded Systems. Embedded Systems are traditionally aimed at the control of a single phenomenon by sensors and actuators and are often committed to a small number of related physical objects, usually performing a simple task or application by a single controller. Cyber-physical systems (CPS) can be seen as an extension of Embedded Systems by the availability of ubiquitous connectivity which can be used to

© Springer Nature Switzerland AG 2019
R. Damaševičius and G. Vasiljevienė (Eds.): ICIST 2019, CCIS 1078, pp. 605–614, 2019.
https://doi.org/10.1007/978-3-030-30275-7_46

build applications at the macro level (towns, villages, rural areas) as well as at the micro level (single houses or factories, the latter with emphasis on smart manufacturing and robotics), possibly integrating them. Useful applications at both levels include, but are not limited to, monitoring complex real-world phenomena and smart manufacturing. Cyber-physical systems are moreover required to exhibit a high degree of autonomy and adaptation ideal for industry 4.0 applications [1].

Cyber-Physical System is a holonic system which consists of a 'physical entity' and its 'cyber-twin' connected together. This 'cyber-twin' is basically a 'computational-relation-model' of the physical entity which means that it can virtually replicate the behavior of the physical machine, and give an insight on how will the machine react when prompted with various actions. The connection can be done using sensors and actuators [2].

Main conceptions of IoT architecture is described in AIOTI WG03 – IoT Standardisation [3] and include requirements as for architectural models, in particular:

- the Domain Model, that describes entities in the IoT domain and the relationships between them;
- the Functional Model, that describes functions and interfaces (interactions) within the IoT domain.

The purpose of the article is to describe the methodology of control the cyber-physical system entities based on principals of High Level Architecture. In fact, the proposed approach is the implementation of the model-oriented control in the environment IoT.

2   Actual Scientific Researches and Issues Analysis

2.1   High Level Architecture

The most promising technology of distributed modeling is a High Level Architecture (HLA), which is actively used to build models of the external environment. HLA is a set of methodologies and standards for building distributed systems, including ensuring the interaction of geographically distributed participants of different types of modeling.

HLA for distributed modeling was developed in the late 90s by the US Department of Defense to ensure interoperability of all types of models and support their reusable use, and since 2000 it is defined by standards IEEE 1516, 1516.1 и 1516.2 [4].

HLA is a set of methods and standards for building distributed modeling systems that allow you to use existing simulation models and modeling systems that already exist and differ in their essence, thereby reducing the time to develop a new modeling system, as well as provide interaction of geographically distributed participants of modeling of various types [5]. Although HLA comes from a military simulation community, where one of its main tasks is the creation of networks of military simulators, due to its openness and general character, it also has a great influence on the application for non-military simulation [6]. In addition, it is possible to use simulation components in various distributed environments including grids and clouds [7].

There are three main components of the HLA architecture:

- Object Model Template (OMT), which defines the format of information that is of general interest for several participants in the modeling process;
- HLA rules, which include ten basic rules that define the basic principles for the development of simulation software in the HLA environment;
- interface specification.

The key concepts in the HLA architecture are federates and federation. A federate is a component of simulation. Federates can be heterogeneous and represent simulation models, simulators, as well as real ("live") participants. A federation is an association of federates that interact in order to solve a specific task.

HLA technology supports high-speed communications and real-time data exchange, using the real-time infrastructure (Run-Time Infrastructure - RTI), which contains common services for coordinating the interaction and exchange of data between the participants of the simulation - the federates. It supports various ways of synchronization within the federation, including real-time control, event management and "fast as possible" control (ASAP). That is, like a distributed operating system, RTI provides the functionality necessary for the interaction of objects within a distributed model. All data exchanges between federates occur through RTI (Fig. 1).

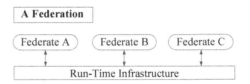

Fig. 1. HLA component interaction scheme

Thus, HLA can be defined as the main functional elements, interfaces, design rules that are valid for use in all applications in the field of simulation, and allowing you to create a basis for creating new simulation systems with a specific architecture.

HLA is designed to provide support for distributed modeling of user applications that have experience with DIS protocols. However, the main difference between HLA and DIS is the use of models of arbitrary objects that can describe any modeled entity, including those that do not have such physical characteristics as position and orientation in space. For this reason, this architecture has several advantages over DIS. HLA allows for various time management schemes during the simulation process, while DIS focuses only on the real-time mechanism with an unregulated discrete increment.

HLA selectively distributes information between interacting models, while DIS uses an approach to data distribution based on the broadcast principle (broadcast), which does not allow for effective scaling of systems.

The listed advantages are provided by the architectural solutions incorporated in the HLA and fixed by a system of international open standards, which allows independent developers to modify the mechanisms of distributed modeling to ensure their compliance with the specific tasks to be solved.

However, in spite of these advantages, the HLA technology is characterized by a significant drawback - the lack of methods for the formalization of models represented by federations. This disadvantage significantly complicates the process of verification of models and requires further study.

2.2   Control E-Net

We propose to consider the federation as a conceptual model of IoT system, which is the basis for further formalization. To construct a formalized model of federate, it is proposed to use control E-networks (CEN) [8], which are the extension of E-Networks [9] for purpose of control. Formally, CEN is given by the set:

$$CEN = (P, T, F, V, U, M_0), \tag{1}$$

where $P = \{P_S, P_R\}$ – finite nonempty set of positions consisting of disjoint subsets P_S – simple positions and P_R – crucial positions, $P_S \cap P_R = \varnothing$; a set of simple positions may contain a subset of the input positions $P_{in} \subseteq P_S$ and a subset of output positions, which are called boundary, is allowed $P_{in} = \varnothing$ и $P_{out} = \varnothing$, $P_{in} \cap P_{out} = \varnothing$;

T – finite nonempty set of transitions, which may consist of five types of transitions $\{\text{"}T_T\text{"}, \text{"}T_F\text{"}, \text{"}T_j\text{"}, \text{"}T_X\text{"}, \text{"}T_Y\text{"}\}$, so-called ordinary E-networks and two types of additional transitions-queues "T_{QL}" и "T_{QF}", $T \cap P = \varnothing$;

$F : P \times T \cup T \times P \to \{0, 1\}$ – incidence function;

$V = V_I \cup V_O$ – finite set of network variables consisting of disjoint subsets V_I – input and V_O – output signals, $V_I \cap V_O = \varnothing$;

$U = \{r, \sigma, \alpha, \tau, z\}$ – a set of control mappings that define the rules for triggering transitions.

$M_0 : P \to \{0, 1\}$ – initial marking function that specifies the presence or absence of marks in positions.

The structure of CEN is equivalent to an oriented bipartite graph, in which one set of vertices is P, another T, and the arcs between the vertices of two named sets are defined by the incidence function F. From the definition of the incidence function, it follows that CEN is an ordinary network—there are no multiple arcs between positions and transitions in it. The dynamic properties of the network are determined by the change in the network marking and depend on the values of the components of the control mapping.

The marking of the control E-network is the vector $M = (M(p_1), M(p_2), \ldots, M(p_n))$, where $n = |P_S|$. The position $p_i \in P_S$ is free (doesn't contain a label) if $M(p_i) = 0$, otherwise $M(p_i) = 1$ the position is considered to be occupied. For a given marking M the set of marked positions is defined as $P_M = \{p \in P_S \mid M(p) > 0\}$.

For all CEN positions it is performed $M(p_i) \le 1$, that transfers CEN into the class of secure networks, which are now commonly called "condition-event" Petri nets – Condition/Event-Net (C/E-Net). As in ordinary E-networks, each label in the CEN position is assigned a descriptor, or a tuple of numeric attributes, defining the information content of the label $d_i = (d_{i1}, d_{i2}, \ldots, d_{ij}, \ldots, d_{iN})$, where d_{ij} – value j - attribute i - label. While tags are moving around the network, their attribute values may change.

When performing a network, labels can move from input positions to transitions, changing the label of the network. Since the number of CEN positions is of course, then the number of possible markings of it is also of course equal to $2^{|P_s|}$, including the initial marking $M_0 = (M_0(p_1), M_0(p_2), \ldots, M_0(p_n))$.

The structural component of the control E-network, which determines its dynamics, is the set of control mappings $U = (r, \sigma, \alpha, \tau, z)$, including five functions associated with network transitions:

r – crucial transition function;
σ – function of readiness of transition to operation;
α – transition activation function;
τ – transition delay function;
z – transform conversion function

Decisive function

$$r : P_R \rightarrow \{1, 2, 3, \ldots\}, \tag{2}$$

It is associated with decision positions that do not contain labels and control the operation of the associated transitions of types T_x and T_y by calculating the values of the so-called decision functions $r : P_R \rightarrow \{1, 2, 3, \ldots\}$. The decision function can be calculated, including, taking into account the attribute values of tags and network variables, i.e. $r(q) = f(d_p, V_I), q \in P_S, p \in P_R$. The value of the decision function determines the direction of movement of the label when the transition is triggered. The boundaries of the possible values of the decision functions depend on the number of positions incident to the transition, by default $r_0(q) = 1$.

Readiness function is a predicate

$$\sigma : T \rightarrow \{0, 1\}, \tag{3}$$

which determines the readiness of the transition to trigger: if $\sigma(t) = 0$, then the transition $t \in T$ to triggering is not ready, otherwise, if $\sigma(t) = 1$, then the transition t to triggering is ready.

Each type of transition has its own definition of the readiness function. The predicate value (4) depends on the marking of simple positions incident to the transition, as well as the value of the crucial transition position, if any, and is calculated each time the network marking changes. In this way, $\sigma(t) = f[M(p), r]$, if $r \in \{\bullet t, t \bullet\}$ for transitions where $p \in \{\bullet t, t \bullet\}$. Markings of input and output positions at which the transitions occur will be called valid.

The activation function is missing in the definition of transitions of an ordinary E-network. Its use in CEN is caused by the need to take into account the state of the OS when determining the conditions for triggering a transition in addition to the analysis of permissible marking. The activation function is a predicate

$$\alpha : T \rightarrow \{0, 1\}, \tag{4}$$

which is calculated for each transition and determines the possibility of its activation: if $\alpha(t) = 0$, then the transition $t \in T$ remains inactive, otherwise, if $\alpha(t) = 1$, then the transition is activated. When calculating the activation function takes into account the values of the input signals of the network V_I, i.e. $\alpha(t) = f(DI, AI)$. By default, the activation function is 1, and the transition is activated at any values of the input signals.

The delay function calculates the delay time on transition τ based on the values of label attributes in the network positions, as well as the values of network variables, i.e. $\tau(t) = f(d_p, V_I), p \in P_S$. As a special case, the default delay time can be set to zero. In general, the delay function can be represented as a display

$$\tau : T \rightarrow \Re^+, \tag{5}$$

where T – a quantity of network hops;
$\Re^+$ – a quantity of positive real numbers, including zero.
Conversion function

$$z : T \rightarrow \delta \tag{6}$$

sets the sequence of operations $\delta : \{d_p \cup V\} \rightarrow \{d_p \cup V\}, p \in P_M \cap P_t$,

which are performed on network variables and label attributes when moving them from input positions to output transition positions. When defining the standard conversion function z_0, which is the default, the attribute values of the labels do not change.

3 Definition Methodology

We confine ourselves to considering two levels of system interpretation: a macromodel is a structure consisting of separate elements, and a micromodel is a process of functioning of these elements.

Let us choose the theory of aggregates as the formal system that provides the description of the CPS structure, and the control E-networks (CEN) to determine the dynamics of the aggregates. Then, formal model of CPS can be defined as a triple:

$$CPS = (\Sigma, E, \gamma), \tag{7}$$

where Σ – control programs structure, which is a graph with a set of aggregates A and a set of arcs $\Gamma \subseteq A \times A$;
E – finite set of management control processes implemented by entities A;
$\gamma : \Sigma \rightarrow E$ – aggregative mapping, which combines formal definitions Σ and E, thereby determining the distribution of functioning processes into the structure of system entities.

Then the HLA construction scheme, presented in Fig. 1, will have the following interpretation:

– as federations, we will consider controlled physical entities of the cyber-physical (holonic) system, which we will call aggregates (A);

– control processes implemented by aggregates are determined by CEN-models, which we call implementation models (E);
– RTI is an aggregation mapping (γ) that implements the interaction of units through the IoT network.

Examples of the formalized representation of the CPS structure and a separate element of this structure are shown in Figs. 2 and 3, respectively.

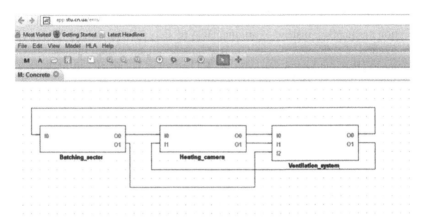

Fig. 2. Aggregative representation of CPS consisting of three elements

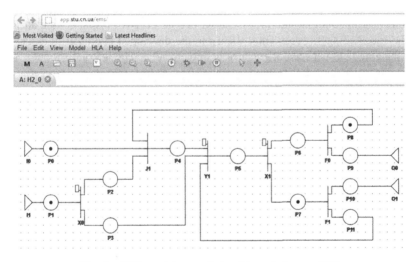

Fig. 3. CEN-model control algorithm of element CPS

To ensure the interaction between entities of CPS within the framework of the HLA architecture, have been developed that perform the connecting function between entities through RTI during the execution of control algorithms. Using the CM module, data transfer is carried out by transfer of marks with attributers in XML format over the WEB-protocol.

The exchange mechanism is implemented as a "subscription": an aggregate that is interested in obtaining certain attributes must subscribe to them using the RTI services. Note that in order to reduce the load on the channels, RTI only monitors data changes and, as a result, events (transmitted via network variables) are always transmitted instantly, and attributes only when their values change and at a certain point in time.

The developed CM accepts attributes and variables that come from other aggregates (hierarchical E-network models), transfers attributes to aggregates according to the subscription mechanism. Instead of original HLA model environment in IoT network the synchronization of entities is executed in real time for all aggregates included in CPS.

Similar to HLA the interaction with the RTI services is carried out on the basis of the developed interfaces (RTIInput, RTIOutput, respectively) CM (Fig. 4).

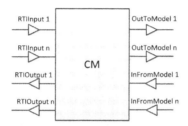

Fig. 4. Interface CM

Each such input/output interface is subscribed to receive/transmit certain attributes from the specified aggregates. Thus, thanks to the developed interfaces, a mechanism for exchanging data between aggregates is implemented. The internal structure of the CM is represented by the E-network model. Thus, in fact, CM is an aggregate.

Since in the exchange process only the values of attributes are transmitted, a label is permanently functioning in the structure of the connecting module, into which attributes from other federates are entered (Fig. 5). When an attribute arrives at the RTInput, the method is triggered, which sets a new attribute in the attribute list of the label that is received from another aggregate or updates the value of the old one. Then the label with the attribute enters the priority queue, where it is ordered according to the received value of the mark in the attribute and transferred to the model. Also, if necessary, the values of the input variables (parameters) of the network can be changed.

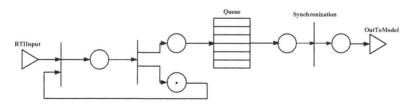

Fig. 5. CEN model of the CM module

CM has the ability to form queues (lists) of messages. This feature is dictated by the need to synchronize the work of the aggregates. Since each aggregate can work in its local time, which, as a rule, does not coincide with the local time of another aggregate, it becomes necessary to form lists of messages. In these lists, the time of receiving the message and the start time of the execution are saved to avoid losing the message with a timestamp greater than the model time of the message skipping aggregate, in which the timestamp is less than real time, when sending messages according to HLA standards. Thus, during the transmission of a message, in addition to the attribute values of the label and network variables, a timestamp is transmitted (as a label attribute), which indicates the update time of the attributes and synchronizes the operation of the aggregates. Accordingly, when a tag hits the output of the RTIOutput, the method is overridden to send messages to RTI.

Thus, in the proposed approach, all interaction between aggregates and RTI is carried out through the developed connecting modules with the help of the RTI services (Fig. 6).

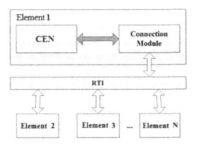

Fig. 6. HLA architecture

4   Conclusions

In our new model-oriented control paradigm we use embedded models in form CEN as control algorithms to manage entities in CPS which in terms of HLA represent the federates. A formal description of the federation is based on the aggregate approach by combining the federates. To provide interconnection between CPS entities it is proposed to use the RTI of HLA but with changed time interpretation: instead of model time we consider real time of CPS execution. For this purpose developed connecting module is used which realizes the functions of integration and synchronization of control CEN models in the distributed IoT architecture. RTI synchronizes the work of distributed models so that they are performed in real time. This circumstance suggests the exchange of data between CPS entities in real time. As result, CPS entities, which in our case are entities of IoT (sensors, control objects), exchange signals among themselves. Proposed paradigm corresponds to the AIOTI WG03 - IoT standardization in that federation level (aggregated models) correspondents to domain model and federate level (CEN models) correspondents to function model.

References

1. Pazzi, L., Pellicciari, M.: From the Internet of Things to cyber-physical systems: the holonic perspective. In: 27th International Conference on Flexible Automation and Intelligent Manufacturing, FAIM 2017, Modena, Italy (2017)
2. Esterline, A., BouSaba, C., Pioro, B., Homaifar, A.: Hierarchies, holons, and agent coordination. In: Hinchey, M.G., Rago, P., Rash, J.L., Rouff, C.A., Sterritt, R., Truszkowski, W. (eds.) WRAC 2005. LNCS (LNAI), vol. 3825, pp. 210–221. Springer, Heidelberg (2006). https://doi.org/10.1007/11964995_19
3. High Level Architecture (HLA), Release 3.0, AIOTI WG03 – IoT Standardisation. European Communities (2017)
4. IEEE Std. 1516 - 2010. IEEE Standard for Modeling and Simulation (M&S) High Level Architecture (HLA). IEEE Computer Society, New York (2010)
5. Fujimoto, R.M.: Parallel and Distributed Simulation Systems. Wiley, New York (2000)
6. Straßburger, S.: Overview about the high level architecture for modelling and simulation and recent developments. Simul. News Europe **16**, 5–14 (2006)
7. Awais, M.U., Palensky, P., Elsheikh, A., Widl, E.: The high level architecture RTI as a master to the functional mock-up interface components. In: International Conference on Computing, Networking and Communications, ICNC 2013, San Diego, USA (2013)
8. Kazymyr, V.V., Sira, G.A.: Distributed modeling in EMS based on HLA architecture. Mathematical Machines and Systems, Kyiv, no. 4, pp. 125–135 (2011)
9. Nutt G.J.: Evaluation nets for computer systems performance analysis. In: FJCC, vol. 41, pp. 279–286. AFIPS Press (1972)

Author Index